Vocabulary   Chapter 2

Vocabulary in Context: *"Are there clues within the sentence or surrounding sentences that can help me deduce the meaning of an unfamiliar word?"*

Word-Structure Clues: *"Are there roots, prefixes, or suffixes that give me clues to the meaning of an unfamiliar word?"*

Connotative Meaning: *"Is there a positive or negative association in addition to the literal meaning of a word?"*

Figurative Language: *"Should these words or this expression be interpreted figuratively?"*

Studying   Chapters 3, 10, and 11

Previewing: *"What topics does the author seem to be emphasizing? How are the topics organized?"*

Assessing Your Prior Knowledge: *"What do I already know about this topic? How familiar am I with this topic?"*

Planning Your Study Time: *"How can I best allot my time for this assignment? Do I need to divide the assignment into smaller units?"*

Asking and Answering Questions as You Read: *"Am I understanding the important information the author and my instructor expect me to know?"*

Reviewing by Rehearsing Your Answers: *"Can I recite answers to questions about the material and write the answers from memory?"*

Evaluating an Author's Argument   Chapter 9

Identifying the Issue: *"What controversial topic is this passage about?"*

Determining the Author's Argument: *"What is the author's position on the issue?"*

Determining the Author's Bias: *"Which side of the issue does the author support?"*

Identifying the Author's Assumptions: *"What does the author take for granted?"*

Identifying Support: *"What types of support does the author present?"*

Deciding Whether an Author's Support Is Relevant: *"Does the support pertain directly to the argument?"*

Evaluating Whether an Author's Argument Is Objective and Complete: *"Is the argument based on facts and other appropriate evidence? Did the author leave out information that might weaken or disprove the argument?"*

Evaluating Whether an Author's Argument Is Valid and Credible: *"Is the author's argument logical and believable?"*

Identifying Propaganda Devices: *"Has the author tried to unfairly influence me to accept his or her point of view?"*

"After using *Opening Doors* this summer, I really pushed my colleagues to use the text by describing the excellent readings, presentation of skills, and of course, the excellent reputation of Cortina and Elder."

Bob Rogers, San Antonio College

"I would describe this as a great book, one which would fit a lot of teachers' and students' learning styles."

Linda S. Edwards, Chattanooga State Technical Community College

"The design of *Opening Doors* is one of its best features. My students enjoy the marginal annotations and the boxes which encourage them to review the most important information."

Barbara Levy, Nassau Community College

"I am very pleased to see the standardized test-taking skills included here. This is a real bonus. I also very much like the "Respond in Writing" items. They are excellent conversation stimulators and ask students to look critically to see what the text said as well as to respond on a more cosmic level. Collaborative workshops are an effective tool in the reading class and I applaud this feature as one of *Opening Doors's* greatest strengths."

Gertrude Coleman, Middlesex County College

"I have enjoyed reading *Opening Doors*. The use of vocabulary in context is excellent. The authors have also responded to a national need for better writers by including the "Respond in Writing" section. Some of these sections can be done as a group and others can become class assignments."

Dianne Cates, Central Piedmont Community College

Praise for *New Worlds*, also by Cortina and Elder

"I am exhilarated by *New Worlds*."

Ellen McMurdie, Montgomery College

"*New Worlds* is a well organized and well written text that presents the material wonderfully for developmental students. It not only tells the student what the skill is, but it also tells why the student is learning it and how to apply it step-by-step in his or her reading."

Lori Partlow, Chesapeake College

THIRD EDITION

Opening Doors

Understanding College Reading

Joe Cortina and Janet Elder

Richland College
Dallas County Community College District

Boston   Burr Ridge, IL   Dubuque, IA   Madison, WI   New York   San Francisco   St. Louis
Bangkok   Bogotá   Caracas   Kuala Lumpur   Lisbon   London   Madrid   Mexico City
Milan   Montreal   New Delhi   Santiago   Seoul   Singapore   Sydney   Taipei   Toronto

McGraw-Hill Higher Education

*A Division of The **McGraw-Hill** Companies*

OPENING DOORS: UNDERSTANDING COLLEGE READING

Published by McGraw-Hill, an imprint of The McGraw-Hill Companies, Inc. 1221 Avenue of the Americas, New York, NY, 10020. Copyright © 2002, 1998, 1995, by The McGraw-Hill Companies, Inc. All rights reserved. No part of this publication may be reproduced or distributed in any form or by any means, or stored in a database or retrieval system, without the prior written consent of The McGraw-Hill Companies, Inc., including, but not limited to, in any network or other electronic storage or transmission, or broadcast for distance learning.

Some ancillaries, including electronic and print components, may not be available to customers outside the United States.

This book is printed on acid-free paper.

2 3 4 5 6 0 DOC/DOC 0 9 8 7 6 5 4 3 2 1

ISBN 0-07-231496-6 (student edition)
ISBN 0-07-245628-0 (annotated instructor's edition)

Editorial director: *Phillip A. Butcher*
Senior sponsoring editor: *Sarah Touborg*
Developmental editor: *Chris Narozny*
Marketing manager: *David S. Patterson*
Project manager: *Rebecca Nordbrock*
Production supervisor: *Debra Sylvester*
Senior designer: *Jennifer McQueen*
Photo research coordinator: *Judy Kausal*
Supplement coordinator: *Carol Loreth*
Media technology producer: *Gregg Di Lorenzo*
Cover and interior design: *Michael Warrell*
Cover image: *©BoZaunders/The Stock Market*
Compositor: *Shepherd Incorporated*
Typeface: *10.5/12 Times Roman*
Printer: *R.R. Donnelley & Sons Company*

Library of Congress Card Number: 2001086108

www.mhhe.com

About the Authors

Joe Cortina

(John Pollack)

Janet Elder

(John Pollack)

Joe Cortina and Janet Elder are professors of reading in the Human and Academic Development Division at Richland College, a member of the Dallas County Community College District. Both are trained reading specialists, and both teach courses in basic and advanced reading improvement and study skills. Their combined teaching experience spans elementary, secondary, and under-graduate levels, as well as clinical remediation.

Dr. Cortina and Dr. Elder began collaborating in 1985. Their first book, *Comprehending College Textbooks: Steps to Understanding and Remembering What You Read,* is now in its third edition. Their newest book, *New Worlds: An Introduction to College Reading,* is designed for introductory-level developmental reading courses.

Dr. Elder is also a coauthor of the reading section of *How to Prepare for the TASP,* a study guide for students entering public colleges and universities who must take the Texas Academic Skills Program Test.

Joe Cortina earned his bachelor of arts degree in English from San Diego State University and his master's degree and doctoral degree in curriculum and instruction in reading from the University of North Texas. He has taught under-graduate teacher education courses in reading at the University of North Texas and Texas Woman's University. In 1981 he was selected to represent the Dallas County Community College District as a nominee for the Piper Award for

Teaching Excellence. In addition, Dr. Cortina was selected as his division's nominee for Richland's Excellence in Teaching Award in 1987, 1988 and 1993. In 1992 he was selected as an honored alumnus by the Department of Elementary, Early Childhood, and Reading Education, of the University of North Texas. And in 1994 he was a recipient of an Excellence Award given by the National Institute for Staff and Organizational Development. In addition to teaching reading courses at Richland College, he has served on interdisciplinary teaching teams for honors English courses and has served as a faculty leader of Richland's writing-across-the-curriculum program. Dr. Cortina has served as a member of the editorial advisory board of *The Journal of Adolescent and Adult Literacy.* He is a frequent speaker at professional meetings and in-service workshops.

Janet Elder graduated summa cum laude from the University of Texas in Austin with a B.A. in English and Latin. She is a member of Phi Beta Kappa. She was the recipient of a government fellowship for Southern Methodist University's Reading Research Program, which resulted in a master's degree. Her Ph.D. in curriculum and instruction in reading is from Texas Woman's University, where the College of Education presented her the Outstanding Dissertation Award. She established the first comprehensive secondary reading program in the Dallas Independent School District and has conducted extensive staff development training for Dallas area teachers. After teaching reading and study skills courses at Richland for several years, she was asked to develop and implement an honors program for the college. After coordinating the honors program during its first six years, she resumed teaching full time. In addition to teaching reading courses, Dr. Elder periodically serves on interdisciplinary teaching teams for honors English and humanities courses. She has served on a task force that reevaluated Richland's program in writing across the curriculum program. She used a sabbatical to create multimedia instructional materials in reading. She has received the Extra Mile Award from special services students, has twice been her division's Piper Award nominee for excellence in teaching, and in 1993 received an Excellence Award from the National Institute for Staff and Organizational Development. In 1999 she was one of three nominees for Richland's Excellence in Teaching Award. Dr. Elder often conducts in service workshops and makes presentations at professional conferences.

Brief Contents

Contents

CHAPTER 3

Approaching College Assignments: Reading Textbooks and Following Directions   133

PART TWO

Comprehension: *Understanding College Textbooks by Reading for Ideas* 187

CHAPTER 4

Determining the Topic and the Stated Main Idea   189

Skills   191

CHAPTER 5

Formulating Implied Main Ideas   245

Skills   247

CHAPTER 6

Identifying Supporting Details   295

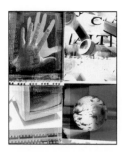

CHAPTER 7

Recognizing Authors' Writing Patterns   345

CHAPTER 8

Reading Critically   409

Skills 411

What Is Critical Reading?   411

Critical Reading Skills   411

> *Determining an Author's Purpose and Intended Audience • Determining an Author's Point of View, Tone, and Intended Meaning*

A Word about Standardized Reading Tests: Critical Reading   427

Creating Your Summary: Developing Chapter Review Cards 429

CHAPTER 9

Thinking Critically   469

Skills 471

What Is Critical Thinking, and Why Is It Important?   471

Critical Thinking Skills   471

> *Why Readers Fail to Think Critically • Distinguishing Facts from Opinions and Determining Whether Opinions Are Well-Supported • Making Inferences and Drawing Logical Conclusions • Distinguishing between Deductive and Inductive Reasoning • Evaluating an Author's Argument • Identifying Propaganda Devices*

A Word about Standardized Reading Tests: Critical Thinking   504

PART THREE

SYSTEMS FOR STUDYING TEXTBOOKS: *Developing a
System that Works for You*   547

CHAPTER 10

Selecting and Organizing Textbook Information   549

To The Instructor

Opening Doors is designed to help college students move from a pre-college reading level to a college reading level. It also presents a systematic way of approaching college textbook material that can make students more efficient in the study skills integral to their college success.

While the scope of this book is broad, the focus is ultimately on comprehension. Comprehension skills are introduced early in the text and are integrated throughout subsequent chapters so that students learn how to apply them. Though the emphasis is on main ideas and essential supporting details, (Part Two, Comprehension), the book gives thorough attention to skills that range from predicting and questioning actively as you read (Part One, Orientation), to selecting, organizing and rehearsing texbook material to be learned for a test (Part Three, Systems for Studying Textbooks). In Part Three, students learn how to use textbook features to full advantage, how to underline and annotate textbook material, and how to organize material in writing so that it can be mastered for a test.

Although *Opening Doors* is designed for developmental readers, we have chosen to use only college textbook excerpts and other materials students would be likely to encounter in college. The selections are the result of field-testing with hundreds of our students over several semesters to identify material that is interesting, informative, and appropriate. We believe that this extensive field-testing provides a much more useful indicator of appropriateness than a readability formula. Field-testing revealed that, with coaching and guidance from the instructor, students can comprehend these selections. Equally important is that students like dealing with "the real thing"—actual college textbook material—since that is what they will encounter in subsequent college courses. This type of practice enables them to transfer skills to other courses and to avoid the frustration and disappointment of discovering that their reading improvement course did not prepare them for "real" college reading. Finally, these passages help students acquire and expand their background knowledge in a variety of subjects.

Extensive and varied exercises accompany the reading selections in *Opening Doors*. (These are described in "To the Student," page xxii.) The exercises prepare students to read the selection and give them an opportunity to apply comprehension and study skills during and after reading. Comprehension Quiz questions are the same type that content-area teachers ask on tests (rather than "The main idea of the selection is . . . ," etc.). All vocabulary words in each Vocabulary Quiz are from the reading selections and are presented in context. There are also Respond in Writing activities that include short-answer and essay-type questions with options for students to work collaboratively.

PROVEN FEATURES

- An extensive "comprehension core" as the heart of the text (Part Two).
- Clear explanations and understandable examples of each essential comprehension skill.
- Numerous textbook passages for application of reading and study skills.
- Three full-length reading selections in each of the first nine chapters. Chapters 10 and 11 each present an *actual textbook chapter* as the reading selection.
- Exercises that integrate writing and reading and call for both objective and essay responses.
- Cumulative review and continued application of skills taught in the comprehension core.
- Presentation of vocabulary and study skills as they relate to learning from college textbooks and other college-level materials.
- Flexibility, allowing instructors to adapt assignments to the specific needs of their own students.
- Skills typically included on state-mandated reading competency tests are addressed, as well as tips for scoring well on standardized reading tests.
- Consistency in philosophy and approach with *New Worlds: An Introduction to College Reading* and *Comprehending College Textbooks,* our other reading comprehension textbooks.
- An extensive *Instructor's Manual and Test Bank* that contains supplemental materials, answer keys, teaching strategies, and pages that can be used to make transparency masters.

ENHANCEMENTS AND NEW FEATURES IN THE THIRD EDITION

- Eleven new reading selections with accompanying activities and exercises:
  1-1 "Why Go to College?" (Study Skills)
  1-2 "Walter Anderson: Hero on Parade" (Nonfiction)
  2-1 "What Is on the Web?" (Information Technology)
  4-1 "The New Workforce" (Magazine Article)
  4-2 "Latinos" (Sociology)
  5-3 "Demography" (Sociology)
  6-1 "Benjamin Franklin" (Newspaper Article)
  7-1 "Career Choice" (Personal Finance)
  8-3 Excerpt from *The Joy Luck Club* (Literature)
  9-1 "Sport Utility Vehicles: How Do I Hate Thee? Let Me Count the Ways" (Editorial)
  9-3 "Take Out the Trash, and Put It . . . Where?" (Magazine Article)

- Completely revised chapter on critical reading (Chapter 8)

  Author's purpose

  Author's intended audience

  Author's point of view (including a new discussion on author's bias)

  Author's tone and intended meaning (including expanded discussion of satire and irony and the definition of words commonly used to describe tone)

- A completely new chapter on critical thinking (Chapter 9)

  Distinguishing facts from opinions (including an enhanced chart)

  Making inferences and drawing logical conclusions

  Evaluating an author's argument

  Identifying propaganda devices (including exercises)

  Distinguishing between inductive and deductive reasoning (with diagrams)

- Enhanced chapter on selecting and organizing textbook information (Chapter 10)

  Additional charts, graphs and diagrams (with exercises on interpreting these visual aids)

  Instructions and an example of a concept map (learning map) as alternative to outlining

  Brief introduction to the Cornell note-taking format

- Comprehension monitoring questions (for reading comprehension, critical reading and thinking, vocabulary, studying, and evaluating an author's argument) are now featured throughout the book in the margins and are summarized inside the front cover of the book.

- Dozens of new full-color photographs, cartoons, graphic materials, and other visual aids

- Use of color to designate important headings, subheadings, and key terms

- Informal learning-style inventory in Chapter 1

- Web links for each reading selection so that students can read more about the topic or the author of the selection

- New section on major versus minor supporting details (accompanied by diagrams) in Chapter 6

While many instructors will choose to use the eleven chapters in *Opening Doors* in the order in which they are presented, others may choose an alternative sequence (three possible sequences are included in the *Instructor's Manual and Test Bank*) that suits their specific course. For this reason, the previewing prompts and the instructions for completing chapter review cards are deliberately repeated in each chapter. Similarly, the previewing prompts and instructions for the practice exercises that accompany each reading selection are included with each selection so that instructors may assign the reading selections in any order.

We hope that you, along with your students, will learn new and interesting things in the selections in this book. Your enthusiasm for acquiring new information, your willingness to become engaged with the material, and your pleasure in learning will serve as a model for your students.

We wish you success in using *Opening Doors* to prepare your students to read textbooks effectively and to be successful in college. We hope the endeavor will be enjoyable and rewarding for both you and your students.

SUPPLEMENTS TO OPENING DOORS

Print Resources

- *Annotated Instructor's Edition* (AIE) (0-07-245628-0)

  The *AIE* contains the full text of the student edition of the book with answers as well as marginal notes that provide a rich variety of teaching tips, related resources, and relevant quotations.

- *Instructor's Manual and Test Bank* (0-07-245627-2)

  This manual provides specific suggestions for teaching each course topic in the text, for transparency masters, audiovisual resources, sample syllabi, tips on incorporating the Web into your course, and a bank of quizzes. In this edition of the *IMTB* we have added reading selections (with accompanying quizzes) from previous editions of *Opening Doors* that can be used in a variety of ways.

Digital Resources

- *Opening Doors* Website

  Look to us for online teaching and learning tools at www.mhhe.com/cortina. Instructors and students will find downloadable resources, demonstrations of all our software programs, opportunities for online discussion, e-mail access to the authors, Web exercises, and a bank of links related to college success.

- *Opening Doors* Interactive CD-ROM (0-07-245630-2)

  This CD-ROM provides students with a rich multimedia extension of the text's content. Each module of the CD-ROM is tied to a chapter of the text, featuring interactive quizzes with feedback for both right and wrong answers, video and audio clips, crossword puzzles, Web links, journal activities, and an Internet primer. Available free in both Windows and Mac when packaged with the text.

- PageOut: The Course Website Development Center

  Let us help you build your own course website. PageOut lets you offer students instant access to your syllabus and lecture notes, original material, recommended website addresses, and related material from the *P.O.W.E.R. Learning* website. Students can even check their grades online. PageOut also provides a discussion board where you and your students can exchange questions and post announcements, as well as an area for students to build personal Web pages.

To find out more about PageOut: The Course Website Development Center, ask your McGraw-Hill representative for details, or fill out the form at www.mhhe.com/pageout.

- *Study Smart* (0-07-552888-6)

This innovative study skills tutorial for students is an excellent resource for the learning lab. Teaching students note-taking methods, test-taking strategies, and time management secrets, Study Smart operates with a sophisticated answer analysis that students will find motivational. Available on CD-ROM or online free when packaged with the text.

Additional Value-Added Packaging Options

- *Random House Webster's College Dictionary* (0-07-366069-8) and *Student Notebook* (0-07-243099-0)

Updated for the twenty-first century, the dictionary is available for a nominal cost when packaged with the text.

- The Paperback Deal

A number of Random House and HarperCollins paperbacks are available at minimal cost when shrink-wrapped with *Opening Doors.* Titles include: Cisneros's *The House on Mango Street* (0-07-243517-8), Hurston's *Their Eyes Were Watching God* (0-07-243420-1), Marquez's *One Hundred Years of Solitude* (0-07-243422-8), Achebe's *Things Fall Apart* (0-07-243518-6) Tan's *The Joy Luck Club* (0-07-243509-7), and many more. For a complete list of titles please contact your local McGraw-Hill sales representative, or visit www.mhhe.com/english.

ACKNOWLEDGMENTS

We are deeply grateful to Sarah Touborg, Senior Sponsoring Editor of Developmental English/Literature at McGraw-Hill, for her astute guidance and unwavering support. Special thanks also to Becky Nordbrock, Chris Narozny, Alexis Walker, and Kristen Silver for lending their extensive talents and expertise. Our talented assistant, typist, and Web researcher, Jamie Hardy, was invaluable to us in this project. Despite challenging deadlines, she was always equal to the task.

Our students at Richland College offered wonderful suggestions and insightful comments during the field-testing of this edition. They continue to be among our best and most helpful critics. We also extend our thanks to Richland's outstanding adjunct reading faculty for their ongoing encouragement and support: Annamarie Alberts, Deborah Atchley, Patricia Bowman, Lajuana Buescher, Jane Buxton, Erlann Clark, Sara Dosch, Ann Fielder, Doris Piwonka, and Mae Spicer-Hudson. We dedicate this book to our students and these adjunct professors.

Our reviewers also served us well with their constructive criticism, suggestions, and supportive comments. We are grateful to:

Barbara Levy	Nassau Community College, NY
Amy Kurata	Kapiolani Community College, HI
Bob Rogers	San Antonio College, TX
Cathy Jeanne Smith	Austin Community College, TX
Dorothy Booher	Florida Community College, Jacksonville, FL
Linda S. Edwards	Chattanooga State Technical College, TN
Gertrude Coleman	Middlesex County College, NJ
Susan Phillips	Rogue Community College, OR
Dianne Cates	Central Piedmont Community College, NC
Deborah De La Rosa	Evergreen Valley College, CA
Lori Pangborn	Saddleback College, CA
Phyllis Sisson	Central Texas College, TX
Sharon Mosher	University of Akron, OH
Arlene Jellineck	Palm Beach Community College, FL
Patricia Hale	Kilgore College, TX
Merle Meyers	Santa Rosa Junior College, CA
Chris Anderson	Black Hawk College, IL

Additionally, we would like to thank the following people who consulted with us at CRLA on the cover selection for the new edition:

Chris Anderson, Black Hawk College; Sherrie Browning, Wayland Baptist University; Maureen Connolly, Elmhurst College; Marty Connolly and Marcia Oppenheim, Pima Community College; Margaret Cunningham, Rogue Community College; Nancy Gates, Xavier University; Sharon Green, Niagara University; Marc Oehlman, California State University at Monterey Bay.

Joe Cortina
Janet Elder

To the Student

"Didn't I realize that reading would open up whole new worlds? A book could open doors for me. It could introduce me to people and show me places I never imagined existed."

Richard Rodriguez, *Hunger of Memory*

Welcome to *Opening Doors*. We hope that this reading improvement textbook will, in fact, "open doors" for you, doors to success in college.

Opening Doors is designed to help you acquire and polish the reading and study skills that will make you a success in college. Described below are the special features that will help you learn efficiently from this book.

SPECIAL FEATURES OF OPENING DOORS

Opening Doors is organized into three parts. Each part focuses on skills that are essential to your success.

Part I: Orientation—Preparing and Organizing Yourself for Success in College (Chapters 1–3)

This section includes chapters on goal-setting, motivation, time management, learning styles, making sense of college reading, and approaching textbook assignments effectively.

Part II: Comprehension— Understanding Your College Textbooks by Reading for Ideas (Chapters 4–9)

Comprehending what you read is vital to your success as a college student. This section will help you:

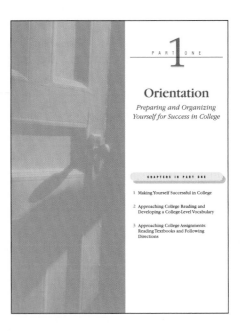

PART ONE

1

Orientation

Preparing and Organizing Yourself for Success in College

CHAPTERS IN PART ONE

1 Making Yourself Successful in College

2 Approaching College Reading and Developing a College-Level Vocabulary

3 Approaching College Assignments: Reading Textbooks and Following Directions

- Identify the topic and stated main idea
- Formulate implied main idea sentences
- Identify supporting details
- Understand the organization of the details (the authors' writing patterns)

- Read critically
- Think critically

Part III: Study Systems—Developing a Textbook Study System that Works for You (Chapters 10–11)

This part teaches you how to select and organize essential textbook information in order to prepare for a test. Each chapter includes a chapter-length reading selection. We think you will enjoy applying the study skills to actual textbook chapters.

BUILT-IN LEARNING AIDS

Chapter Introduction

These pages contain questions to focus your learning. You should be able to answer these questions after reading and studying the chapter.

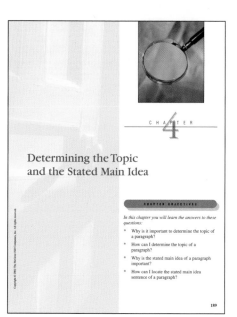

CHAPTER

4

Determining the Topic and the Stated Main Idea

CHAPTER OBJECTIVES

In this chapter you will learn the answers to these questions:

- Why is it important to determine the topic of a paragraph?
- How can I determine the topic of a paragraph?
- Why is the stated main idea of a paragraph important?
- How can I locate the stated main idea sentence of a paragraph?

189

CHAPTER CONTENTS

SKILLS

The Topic of a Paragraph

- What Is the Topic of a Paragraph, and Why Is It Important?
- Determining and Expressing the Topic

The Stated Main Idea of a Paragraph

- What Is a Stated Main Idea, and Why Is It Important?
- Locating the Stated Main Idea Sentence
- How to Tell if You Have Identified the Stated Main Idea Sentence
- Stated Overall Main Ideas in Longer Passages

A Word about Standardized Reading Tests: Topics and Stated Main Ideas

CREATING YOUR SUMMARY

Developing Chapter Review Cards

READINGS

Selection 4-1 (*Magazine Article*)
"The New Workforce" from *Business Week*
by Michelle Conlin

Selection 4-2 (*Sociology*)
"Latinos" from *Sociology: An Introduction*
by Richard J. Gelles and Ann Levine

Selection 4-3 (*History*)
"Muhammad" from *The 100: A Ranking of the Most Influential Persons in History*
by Michael Hart

190

Chapter Table of Contents

These pages list the skills presented in the chapter. They show the material in the chapter and how it is organized. They also list the chapter reading selections.

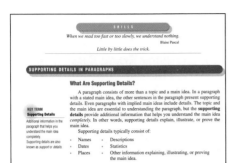

Chapter Opening Page

Each chapter has major headings and subheadings that make the chapter's organization clear. Pertinent quotations begin each chapter.

Key Term Boxes

Important terms appear in Key Term Boxes in the margins so that the terms and their definitions are easy to locate.

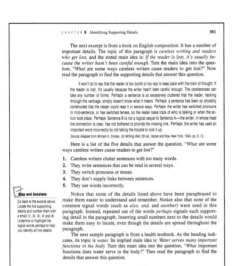

Stop and Annotate Exercises

These exercises give you the opportunity to "stop and annotate" actual college textbook excerpts. You will learn actively by underlining or highlighting stated main idea sentences, writing formulated main ideas in the margin, or numbering the important supporting details in a passage, for example.

Tips for Standardized Reading Tests

Each chapter in Part Two includes special tips for scoring well on standardized reading tests. These tips illustrate various reading skills as well as specific strategies for handling different types of questions.

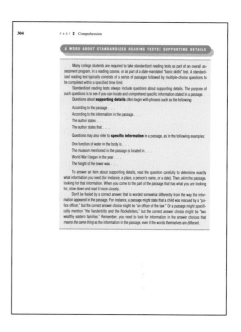

Chapter Review Cards

These simulated index cards allow you to create your own summary of the important points in the chapter. Each card includes questions and prompts with page numbers to direct you to the significant information.

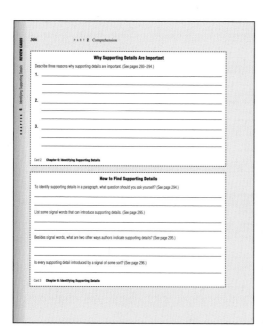

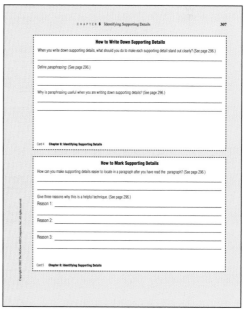

CHAPTER READING SELECTIONS FOR CHAPTERS 1 TO 9

All the reading selections in Chapters 1 through 9 (three selections per chapter) are excerpts taken from widely used introductory-level college textbooks, news magazines, and literary selections of the type you are likely to encounter in college. These selections provide important practice, and they will increase your background knowledge in a variety of interesting subjects. They were chosen to give you the practice, skill, and confidence you need to handle subsequent college courses successfully.

Each reading selection is accompanied by preliminary and follow-up exercises. In order, the exercises are:

Prepare Yourself to Read

This exercise allows you to use techniques (such as previewing and making predictions) that will help you read the selection more actively and effectively.

READING

SELECTION 2-1   **WHAT IS ON THE WEB?**
Information   From *A Guidebook to the Web*
Technology   By Robert Harris

Prepare Yourself to Read

Directions: Do these exercises *before* you read Selection 2-1.

1. First, read and think about the title. What do you already know about what is on the World Wide Web?

2. In general, do you feel positive about what the Web offers, or are you alarmed about its content?

3. Next, complete your preview by reading the following:

   Introduction (in *italics*)
   First paragraph (paragraph 1)
   First sentence of each of the other paragraphs
   Diagram

   On the basis of your preview, what three aspects of the Web does the selection seem to be about?

Apply Comprehension Skills

Directions: Do these exercises as you read Selection 2-1. Apply three skills from this chapter:

Adjust your reading rate. On the basis of your preview and your prior knowledge of what is on the World Wide Web, do you think you should read Selection 2-1 slowly or rapidly?

95

Introduction to the Selection and Annotation Practice Exercises

Each selection begins with an introduction that provides helpful background information about the selection's topic. The Annotation Practice Exercises give you the opportunity to apply to the selection the reading skills you are learning.

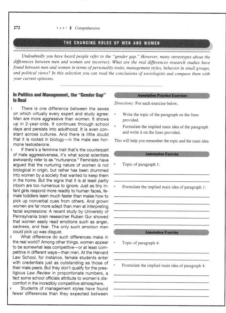

Comprehension Quiz

This exercise offers the kind of objective test (true-false and multiple-choice) that a college instructor might ask on a test about information, concepts, and facts in the selection.

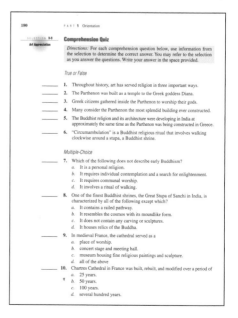

Extend Your Vocabulary by Using Context Clues

This exercise asks you to deduce the definition of ten important words that appear in the selection. Pronunciations are given for all of the words.

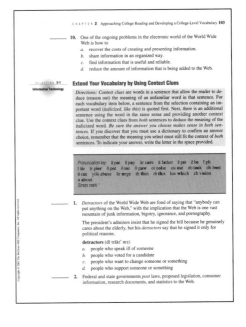

_____ 10. One of the ongoing problems in the electronic world of the World Wide Web is how to
   a. recover the costs of creating and presenting information.
   b. share information in an organized way.
   c. find information that is useful and reliable.
   d. reduce the amount of information that is being added to the Web.

SELECTION 2-1
Information Technology

Extend Your Vocabulary by Using Context Clues

Directions: Context clues are words in a sentence that allow the reader to deduce (reason out) the meaning of an unfamiliar word in that sentence. For each vocabulary item below, a sentence from the selection containing an important word (_italicized, like this_) is quoted first. Next, there is an additional sentence using the word in the same sense and providing another context clue. Use the context clues from _both_ sentences to deduce the meaning of the italicized word. _Be sure the answer you choose makes sense in both sentences._ If you discover that you must use a dictionary to confirm an answer choice, remember that the meaning you select must still fit the context of _both_ sentences. To indicate your answer, write the letter in the space provided.

Pronunciation key: ă pat   ā pay   âr care   ä father   ĕ pet   ē be   ĭ pit
ī tie   îr pier   ŏ pot   ō toe   ô paw   oi noise   ou out   ŏŏ took   ōō boot
ŏ cut   yōō abuse   ûr urge   th thin   _th_ this   hw which   zh vision
ə about
Stress mark '

_____ 1. _Detractors_ of the World Wide Web are fond of saying that "anybody can put anything on the Web," with the implication that the Web is one vast mountain of junk information, bigotry, ignorance, and pornography.

The president's admirers insist that he signed the bill because he genuinely cares about the elderly, but his _detractors_ say that he signed it only for political reasons.

detractors (dĭ trăkt' ərz)
   a. people who speak ill of someone
   b. people who voted for a candidate
   c. people who want to change someone or something
   d. people who support someone or something

_____ 2. Federal and state governments _post_ laws, proposed legislation, consumer information, research documents, and statistics to the Web.

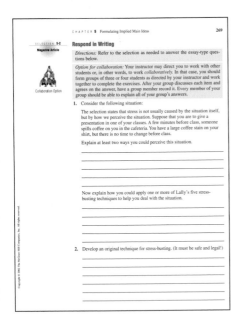

SELECTION 5-2
Magazine Article

Collaboration Option

Respond in Writing

Directions: Refer to the selection as needed to answer the essay-type questions below.

Option for collaboration: Your instructor may direct you to work with other students or, in other words, to work _collaboratively._ In that case, you should form groups of three or four students as directed by your instructor and work together to complete the exercises. After your group discusses each item and agrees on the answer, have a group member record it. Every member of your group should be able to explain all of your group's answers.

1. Consider the following situation:

   The selection states that stress is not usually caused by the situation itself, but by how we perceive the situation. Suppose that you are to give a presentation in one of your classes. A few minutes before class, someone spills coffee on you in the cafeteria. You have a large coffee stain on your shirt, but there is no time to change before class.

   Explain at least two ways you could perceive this situation.

   _____
   _____
   _____

   Now explain how you could apply one or more of Lally's five stress-busting techniques to help you deal with the situation.

   _____
   _____
   _____

2. Develop an original technique for stress-busting. (It must be safe and legal!)

   _____
   _____
   _____
   _____

Respond in Writing

These short-answer and essay-type exercises ask you to write about the selection. They will help you relate the material to your own experiences. They will also give you practice in determining the overall main idea of the selection.

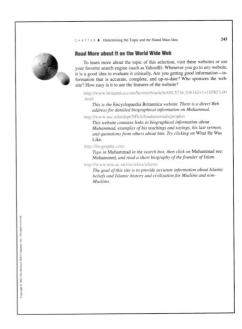

Read More about It on the World Wide Web

To learn more about the topic of this selection, visit these websites or use your favorite search engine (such as Yahoo®). Whenever you go to _any_ website, it is a good idea to evaluate it critically. Are you getting good information—information that is accurate, complete, and up-to-date? Who sponsors the website? How easy is it to use the features of the website?

http://www.britannica.com/bcom/eb/article/00,5716,108142+1+105853,00.html
   This is the Encyclopaedia Britannica website. There is a direct Web address for detailed biographical information on Muhammad.

http://www.usc.edu/dept/MSA/fundamentals/prophet
   This website contains links to biographical information about Muhammad, examples of his teachings and sayings, his last sermon, and quotations from others about him. Try clicking on What He Was Like.

http://biography.com
   Type in Muhammad _in the search box, then click on_ Muhammad _see: Mohammed, and read a short biography of the founder of Islam._

http://www.uem.ac.uk/societies/islam/
   The goal of this site is to provide accurate information about Islamic beliefs and Islamic history and civilization for Muslims and non-Muslims.

Read More about It on the World Wide Web

This consists of a list of websites related to the topic or author of the selection. This gives you an opportunity to explore the topic further.

SPECIAL STUDY SKILLS FEATURES IN CHAPTERS 10 AND 11

Chapter Review Cards

Chapters 10 and 11 give you specific strategies to enable you to help you understand and remember important information in your college textbooks. The Chapter Review Cards for Chapters 10 and 11 do not contain any prompts or page numbers, in order to give you a "real life" simulation of studying textbook material.

Full-Length Reading Selections

Chapters 10 and 11 each contain a chapter-length selection rather than three shorter reading selections. Instead of taking a Comprehension Quiz and Vocabulary Quiz, you are asked to highlight and annotate the selection as you read. You are then asked to prepare an outline, study map, or test review cards for a subsection of the reading selection.

SPECIAL LEARNING AIDS

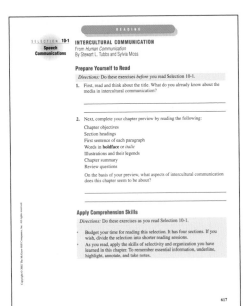

SELECTION 10-1
**Speech
Communications**

READING

INTERCULTURAL COMMUNICATION
From *Human Communication*
By Stewart L. Tubbs and Sylvia Moss

Prepare Yourself to Read

Directions: Do these exercises *before* you read Selection 10-1.

1. First, read and think about the title. What do you already know about the media in intercultural communication?

2. Next, complete your chapter preview by reading the following:

   Chapter objectives
   Section headings
   First sentence of each paragraph
   Words in **boldface** or *italic*
   Illustrations and their legends
   Chapter summary
   Review questions

   On the basis of your preview, what aspects of intercultural communication does this chapter seem to be about?

Apply Comprehension Skills

Directions: Do these exercises as you read Selection 10-1.

• Budget your time for reading this selection. It has four sections. If you wish, divide the selection into shorter reading sessions.

• As you read, apply the skills of selectivity and organization you have learned in this chapter. To remember essential information, underline, highlight, annotate, and take notes.

617

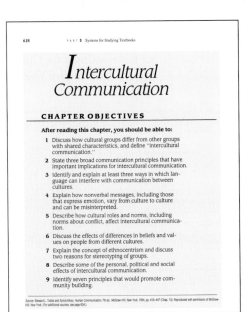

Intercultural Communication

CHAPTER OBJECTIVES

After reading this chapter, you should be able to:

1 Discuss how cultural groups differ from other groups with shared characteristics, and define "intercultural communication."

2 State three broad communication principles that have important implications for intercultural communication.

3 Identify and explain at least three ways in which language can interfere with communication between cultures.

4 Explain how nonverbal messages, including those that express emotion, vary from culture to culture and can be misinterpreted.

5 Describe how cultural roles and norms, including norms about conflict, affect intercultural communication.

6 Discuss the effects of differences in beliefs and values on people from different cultures.

7 Explain the concept of ethnocentrism and discuss two reasons for stereotyping of groups.

8 Describe some of the personal, political and social effects of intercultural communication.

9 Identify seven principles that would promote community building.

Source: Steward L. Tubbs and Sylvia Moss, *Human Communication*, 7th ed. McGraw-Hill, New York, 1994, pp. 419–447 (Chap. 13). Reproduced with permission of McGraw-Hill, New York. (For additional sources, see page 634.)

New technology is creating many opportunities for intercultural communication.

OBSTACLES TO INTERCULTURAL COMMUNICATION

Although modern means of travel and communication have brought us into contact with virtually the whole world, the technical capacity to transmit and receive messages is not, in itself, enough to allow people who have vastly different cultures to communicate with one another. Dramatic improvements in the technological means of communication have in many instances outstripped our abilities to communicate effectively with people who have different languages, different beliefs and values, and different expectations of relationships. Repeatedly, interaction between people of different cultures has created far more misunderstanding than understanding.

Of the many principles used by theorists to describe the communication process, several clearly apply to intercultural exchanges. The first is *a shared code system*, which of course will have *two aspects—verbal and nonverbal*. Sarbaugh (1979) argues that without such a shared system, communication will be impossible. There will be degrees of difference, but the *less* a code system is shared, the *less* communication is possible.

In his work anthropologist Edward Hall makes the distinction between high- and low-context cultures (1976). We can think of them along a continuum as, for example, in Figure 13.1. High- and low-context cultures have several important differences in the way information is coded. Members of **high-context cultures** are more skilled in reading nonverbal behaviors "and in reading the environment"; and they assume that other people will also be able to do so. Thus they speak less than members of low-context cultures; and in general their communication tends to be indirect and less explicit. **Low-context cultures** on the other hand, stress direct and explicit communication: "verbal messages are extremely important . . . and the information to be shared is coded in the verbal message" (Samovar and Porter, 1991b, pp. 234–235; Gudykunst and Kim, 1992, pp. 44–45).

Among members of high-context cultures are the Chinese, Korean, and Japanese. Notice our own position in Figure 13.1—within the low-context end of the spectrum, yet not at the *very* bottom. In comparing Americans with

As you work through this book, we hope that you will take advantage of all of its features and that you will discover that you are becoming a better reader. Not only will you have a clearer understanding of reading comprehension skills; you also will have had a great deal of practice with them. You will also discover that you are able to use these skills in your other college courses.

In addition to the built-in learning aids that occur in each chapter, *Opening Doors* offers you summary charts, diagrams, photos, cartoons, study maps, and outlines.

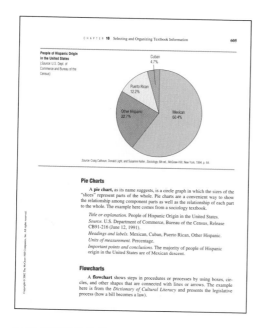

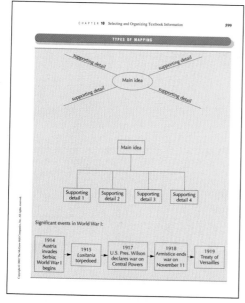

We welcome you to *Opening Doors*. We hope your journey through this textbook is an enjoyable and rewarding experience.

Joe Cortina   **Janet Elder**

1

Orientation

*Preparing and Organizing
Yourself for Success in College*

© PhotoDisc

CHAPTER

1

Making Yourself Successful in College

CHAPTER OBJECTIVES

In this chapter you will learn the answers to these questions:

- What do successful college students do?

- How can I set goals for myself?

- How can I motivate myself to do well in college?

- How can I manage my time more effectively?

- What are learning styles?

SKILLS

Doing What Successful Students Do

Setting Your Goals

Motivating Yourself

Managing Your Time

- Setting Up a Weekly Study Schedule

- Making the Most of Your Study Time

- Planning Further Ahead: Creating a Monthly Assignment Calendar and Using a Daily To Do List

Understanding Learning Styles

CREATING YOUR SUMMARY

Developing Chapter Review Cards

READINGS

Selection 1-1 *(Study Skills)*
"Why Go to College?" from *P.O.W.E.R. Learning: Strategies for Success in College and Life*
by Robert S. Feldman

Selection 1-2 *(Nonfiction)*
"Walter Anderson: Hero on Parade" from
The Big Picture
by Ben Carson with Gregg Lewis

Selection 1-3 *(Literature)*
"Saved" from *The Autobiography of Malcolm X,*
as told to Alex Haley

The way you spend your days is the way you spend your life.

Annie Dillard

Lost time is never found again.

Benjamin Franklin

Poor Richard's Almanack

DOING WHAT SUCCESSFUL STUDENTS DO

Some students are more successful than others. Why? One answer is that successful students know how to set goals for themselves, motivate themselves, and manage their time. In this chapter, you will learn how to do these things. If you start now and consistently apply the techniques and strategies in the chapter, you will become a more successful college student. Getting off to a good start is important because, as the proverb says, "Well begun is half done." This is just a way of saying that a good beginning goes a long way toward your ultimate success.

Moreover, the Greek philosopher Aristotle observed, "We are what we repeatedly do. Excellence then is not an act, but a habit." This is valuable advice. If you make good study techniques a habit, each semester you can become a better, more effective student.

It is helpful to look more closely at exactly what successful students do. One especially interesting research study involved college students who were highly effective *despite the fact that they did not have high entrance scores.* In other words, anyone looking at these students' test scores would not have predicted that they would do well in college. The researchers asked the students themselves what it was that enabled them to be so successful. They learned from these effective students that they all shared five important characteristics:

1. **Effective students are highly motivated.** Successful students have an inner drive to do well. They are goal-oriented; they have specific careers in mind. They believe that they are responsible for their own success or failure; they attribute nothing to "good luck" or "bad luck."

2. **Effective students plan ahead.** Successful students are organized. They develop good study habits. They establish a study schedule and stick to it. They study at the same time each day, and in the same place.

3. **Effective students focus on understanding.** Successful students use instructors' oral and written feedback to monitor their progress and make changes if necessary. They assess their own strengths and weaknesses on the basis of instructors' comments in class, evaluations of homework assignments, and grades on tests. If they start to do poorly or fall behind in a subject, they adjust their schedule to spend more time on it, and they immediately seek help from an instructor, a tutor, or a friend.

5

4. **Effective students are highly selective.**   Successful students concentrate on main ideas and important supporting details when they read assignments. They do not try to memorize everything. To identify important information, they pay attention to signals in their textbooks and class notes. They use instructors' suggestions, course outlines, and textbook features to guide their efforts.

5. **Effective students are involved and attentive.**   Successful students focus on their academic work in class and outside of class. In class, they pay attention, take notes, and participate in discussions. They make a point of arriving early, and they help themselves concentrate by sitting near the front. Outside of class, they study in quiet places to avoid distractions. They put academic work ahead of social life, and they limit television watching. They study with others who are serious about school. They concentrate on the present rather than worrying about the past or daydreaming too much about the future.

Source: Adapted from John Q. Easton, Don Barshis, and Rick Ginsberg, "Chicago Colleges Identify Effective Teachers, Students," *Community and Junior College Journal,* December–January 1983–1984, pp. 27–31.

Perhaps the most interesting aspect of these characteristics of successful college students is that there is nothing that is especially complicated or difficult about them. With planning and determination, any student can make these behaviors part of his or her own life in college.

Another, more recent study also looked at students who had low high school grades and low college entrance scores. Although these students were not expected to do well in college, half of them achieved a relatively high college grade point average (GPA). The rest were on scholastic probation after several semesters. Researchers wanted to know, What was the difference between those who succeeded and those who did not?

Careful interviews with all the students revealed these characteristics of the successful students:

1. They attend and participate in class.
2. They are prepared for class.
3. They perceive instructors as experts.
4. They adhere to an organized study routine.
5. They develop a repertoire of study skills and strategies.
6. They take responsibility for their own learning.

Sounds familiar, doesn't it? The findings were strikingly similar to those of the earlier study conducted by different researchers at a different college. The unsuccessful students in this study "readily admitted that they did not engage in these behaviors and explained that their social lives held higher priority." Clearly, knowing about and practicing these obvious "success behaviors" and making school a priority can make you more successful too.

Source: JoAnn Yaworski, Rose-Marie Weber, and Nabil Ibrahim. "What Makes Students Succeed or Fail? The Voices of Developmental College Students," *Journal of College Reading and Learning,* Vol. 30, No. 2, Spring 2000, 195–221.

SETTING YOUR GOALS

Most successful students (in fact, most successful people) have this in common: they establish goals, and they put their goals *in writing*. They write down *what they want to accomplish* and the *length of time* in which they plan to accomplish it. Putting your goals in writing is a very simple technique that can help you turn wishes into reality.

Why should you bother to write out your goals? There are several reasons. First, goals that are not written down are not much better than wishes. ("I wish I had a college degree." "I wish I had a career I enjoyed.") In fact, they will probably remain just that: wishes. Second, writing your goals helps you make a commitment to them. If a goal is not even important enough to write down, how likely do you think you are to accomplish it? Third, writing out your goals gives you a yardstick, a written record, that you can use to measure your progress. Finally, no one wants to look back and feel regret about things he or she might have done or accomplished but haven't. When your life is over, what do you want to be remembered for? Surely that is important enough to write down. Another way to think about this is to ask yourself what you *don't* want to be doing a year from now, several years from now, or several decades from now.

You may find it helpful to put your goals into categories, such as educational, financial, spiritual, personal (including family matters), physical (health and fitness), and career-related. An example of an educational goal might be, "To complete all my courses this semester and earn at least a B in each." An example of a financial goal might be, "To save enough money during the next year to make a down payment on a new car."

Sometimes it becomes necessary to choose between two or more competing goals. For example, suppose that you wanted to attend college full time and work full time. You would have to give one goal or the other priority in order to allow for studying. Or you would have to modify both goals, deciding to attend college part time and work part time. Competing goals do not always make it necessary to give up a goal, but they do make it necessary to be realistic, to set priorities, and to adjust your time and efforts.

One expert in time management, Alan Lakein, gives these recommendations for setting goals:

- **Be specific.** An example of a specific goal is, "I will exercise 30 minutes a day for the next month." A vague goal such as "I will get more exercise" is not very helpful.
- **Be realistic.** "I will exercise 30 minutes a day" is also an example of a realistic goal. An unrealistic goal would be "I will exercise 2 hours a day for the next six months." Unrealistic goals are not helpful, and they can be very frustrating as well.
- **Revise your goals at regular intervals.** People change, and so do their situations and priorities. Therefore, it is important to review your goals regularly and revise them whenever necessary.

Source: Alan Lakein, *How to Get Control of Your Time and Your Life,* Signet, New York, 1973, pp. 30–37, 64–65.

KEY TERMS
Long-term Goal

Goal you want to accomplish
during your lifetime.
Intermediate Goal

Goal you want to accomplish
in the next 3 to 5 years.
Short-term Goal

Goal you want to accomplish
in the next 3 to 6 months.

Lakein also recommends setting three types of goals based on how impor-tant the goals are and the amount of time required to accomplish or achieve them. The three types are long-term, intermediate, and short-term. **Long-term goals** are ones you want to accomplish during your lifetime; **intermediate goals** are ones you want to achieve in the next 3 to 5 years; **short-term goals** are ones you want to accomplish in the next 3 to 6 months. (As a student, you may find it helpful to think of short-term goals as ones you would like to ac-complish during the semester.) Your short-term goals should help you achieve your intermediate goals, which in turn should help you achieve your long-term, lifetime goals. For instance, improving your reading skills is a short-term goal that will contribute to the intermediate goal of earning a college degree, and ul-timately to the long-term goal of an interesting, satisfying career. Of course, some goals will fall between half a year and three years. Regardless of the pre-cise length of time, it's still helpful to think in terms of long-term, intermediate, and short-term goals.

The box on pages 8 and 9 will give you an opportunity to formulate and record your long-term, intermediate, and short-term goals. When you have put your goals in writing, identify one or two from each category that are especially important to you now. Whenever you must decide how to use your time, choose activities that help you reach those goals.

Keep a copy of your goals where you can see and read them often. You might keep them at the front of a notebook, for instance, or on your desk. Some of your goals will be achieved quickly and removed from your list, but you may find that others will remain on your list for a long time, perhaps a lifetime.

PUTTING YOUR GOALS IN WRITING

Take a few minutes to write down your goals. Write at least three goals for each category. (These are personal and private, and they do not have to be shared with anyone.)

What are my long-term goals?

On the lines below, write three things you want to accomplish and achieve during your lifetime.

1. _____

2. _____

3. _____

What are my intermediate goals?

On the lines below, write three things you want to accomplish during the next 3 to 5 years.

1. _____

2. _____

3. _____

What are my short-term goals?

On the lines below, write three things you want to accomplish this semester.

1. _____

2. _____

3. _____

MOTIVATING YOURSELF

In college, you are responsible for motivating yourself. Developing an interest in and a commitment to your courses is not your instructors' responsibility; it is your responsibility. Developing the discipline and commitment to make yourself successful is not your parents' responsibility; it is your responsibility. If you assume the responsibility, then you can feel justifiably proud when you succeed because the credit goes to you. The truly valuable and worthwhile things in life are seldom easy, but that is precisely what gives them their value.

Fortunately, motivating yourself is easier than you may think. For one thing, college is a stimulating place to be! As you progress through college, you will find that learning becomes increasingly pleasurable and satisfying. Also, there are specific, effective self-motivation techniques you can use. Here are a dozen strategies that you can use to get yourself motivated and to stay motivated throughout the semester.

1. **Write down your educational goals for the semester.** As noted earlier, the act of writing down goals for the semester can be motivating in and of itself. Clear goals can also motivate you to use your time well. Specific goals (for class attendance and participation, homework, and grades) help you select activities that will move you toward your goals. In addition, achieving any worthwhile goal is a deeply satisfying experience that will motivate you to achieve more goals.

2. **Visualize your success.** Visualize successful situations that you want to make happen in the near future, such as earning a high grade on an assignment or completing the semester successfully. Then visualize the future further ahead: imagine yourself in a cap and gown being handed your college diploma; imagine an employer offering you the job you've dreamed of. Make your mental images as sharp and vivid as possible; imagine the feelings as well, such as the happiness and pride you will feel in your accomplishment.

3. **Think of classes as your easiest learning sessions.** If you spend 3 hours a week in class for a course, look on those hours as your *easiest* 3 hours of learning and studying for the course. Remind yourself of this whenever you feel annoyed or frustrated by a difficult college course. Your instructor, who

Doing the things that successful students do will enable you to succeed in college.
(Peter Hvizdak/The Image Works)

is an expert, is there to explain and to answer questions. Adopting this perspective can make a big difference.

4. **View your courses as opportunities.**   Especially if a course is difficult, consider it a challenge rather than a problem or an obstacle. Accept the fact that you are required to take a variety of courses to broaden your educational background. Later in life, you will most likely come to appreciate these courses more than you can now. Taking the "long view" can be motivating.

5. **Develop emotional strategies for dealing with difficult courses.**   For example, to keep from feeling overwhelmed, a good strategy is to focus on the material you are studying at the time rather than worrying about what is coming next or whether it will be difficult. Another strategy is to consider the feeling of accomplishment that will come from mastering a difficult subject, and the pride you can take in succeeding at a challenging subject. Realize, too, that you can enjoy a subject even if you may never become an expert in it.

6. **Seek advice and study tips from good students in your courses.**   Ask them what they are doing to be successful. If they like a course that seems difficult or boring to you, ask them why they enjoy the subject.

7. **Choose the right friends.**   By "right" friends, we mean friends who support and encourage your studying. Find a "study buddy" or form a small

study group with others who are serious about school. It is also helpful to find a mentor (a wise and trusted counselor or instructor) who can give you advice, support, and encouragement.

8. **Divide big projects into smaller parts.** To motivate yourself, break large projects into smaller, more manageable tasks. (For instance, a 20-page reading assignment can be divided into four shorter readings of 5 pages each, and you may even want to read these during short study sessions on different days.) Sometimes you will find it necessary to set priorities or to sequence the smaller tasks. (For example, to write a paper, you might have to get information from library books or the Internet, take notes, write a rough outline of your paper, and so forth.)

9. **Give yourself rewards.** Reward yourself for successfully completing an activity such as a homework assignment or studying for a test. For example, have a snack or take a short walk.

10. **Make positive "self-talk" a habit.** Say encouraging things to yourself: "I think I can do this assignment, even though it might take a while." "If other students in my class can do this, I can too." Also, use a technique called *thought stopping* to shut off negative self-talk: when you find that you are giving yourself negative feedback, just say "Stop!" and substitute some *positive* self-talk. Don't let frustration overcome you and destroy your productivity. Recognizing that frustration is a normal part of learning (and of life) will help you develop tolerance for it.

11. **Think in terms of being satisfied if you do your best.** Reassure yourself that if you truly do your best, you can feel satisfied with your effort, regardless of the outcome. You will never have to wonder whether you could have done better if only you had tried harder.

12. **Remind yourself that motivation and success reinforce each other.** Motivation leads to success; success increases motivation; increased motivation leads to more success; and so on! In other words, motivation and success go hand in hand. Celebrate each small success and use it as a springboard to even greater success.

From the list above, pick at least two strategies that are new to you and that you think would work for you. Then use them throughout the semester to increase your motivation.

Sometimes students who are having a difficult time in a subject mistakenly believe that the subject is easy for those who are doing well in it. They do not realize that the most successful students are usually working very hard to make themselves successful. Sometimes students who are having difficulty in a course tell themselves that they just don't have the ability to do well, and therefore, there is no reason for them to try. Thinking that a subject is easy for everyone else or that you just don't have the ability are really just excuses for not trying very hard or for not trying at all. Don't fall into that trap.

MANAGING YOUR TIME

Managing your time means making decisions about how you choose to spend time. When you look at the numbers in the following box, you will realize how much decision making is necessary in order to gain control of your time. Fortunately, there are several reliable strategies that you can use to control your time. In this section, you'll learn how to set up a weekly study schedule and make the most of your study sessions; you'll also look at two important planning tools: a monthly calendar and a daily list of things to do.

MAKING DECISIONS ABOUT HOW TO SCHEDULE YOUR TIME

There are 168 hours in a week.

If you sleep 8 hours a night, you spend 56 hours a week sleeping.

If you spend 1 hour at each meal, you spend 21 hours a week eating.

If you have a full college schedule, you spend about 12 to 20 hours a week attending classes and labs.

This leaves you about 70 hours a week, or 10 hours a day, for everything else: studying, recreation, personal chores, and so on.

For 10 out of every 24 hours, you must make decisions about how you will spend your time.

Setting Up a Weekly Study Schedule

KEY TERM
Study Schedule

Weekly schedule with specific times set aside for studying.

If you tell yourself that you will study "whenever you find time," you may never "find time." To be a truly effective student, you must set aside time specifically for studying. In other words, it is essential to have a study schedule. A weekly **study schedule** is just what it sounds like: a weekly schedule with specific times set aside for studying. A realistic, well-thought-out weekly schedule will assure you of ample study time.

College students often say that they have too much to do in too little time. In fact, they cite this as their number one source of stress. Scheduling your time can work like a charm to lower this kind of stress, and to reduce tension, worry, and inefficiency. A realistic schedule does not turn you into a robot; rather, it frees you from constant decision making (and indecision!) and lets you make the best use of your time.

It's important to balance study time and relaxation time. Study first; then relax or have fun. That's the rule successful students go by. If you stick to this rule, you will have more free time. Also, you will genuinely enjoy that free time because you won't feel guilty about unfinished work. These become your rewards for completing your studying first.

To develop your weekly study schedule, use the planning form on page 15, and follow these steps:

- **Step 1.** Identify times that are already committed to other activities (such as classes, meals, work, organizations, commuting, sleeping, etc.) and are therefore definitely not available for study. Write these activities on your weekly planner.

- **Step 2.** Identify other times when you probably would not be able to study (for example, times devoted to household and personal chores, family, rest, and leisure activities). Write these on your weekly planner. These are somewhat more flexible parts of your schedule because you have more control over when you do many of them.

- **Step 3.** Identify the best general times for you to study. On the list below circle the time periods when you are most alert and energetic:

  Early morning (6–9 A.M.)

  Midmorning (9 A.M. to noon)

  Early afternoon (12–3 P.M.)

  Late afternoon (3–6 P.M.)

  Early evening (6–9 P.M.)

  Late evening (9 P.M. to midnight)

  Late night (after midnight)

  Studying when you are alert and rested allows you to accomplish more in less time. Try to schedule as much studying as possible during the hours you identified as your "best times."

- **Step 4.** Determine how much study time you need. Allow a *minimum* of 1 hour of study time for each hour you spend in class. (For a typical three-credit course, that means a minimum of 3 hours of study time per week; difficult courses may require more time. You will also need to schedule more study time if you are a slow reader or if you have not yet developed effective study habits.) Set aside an appropriate number of study hours for each course. Be sure to plan enough study time for each subject: it is better to overestimate than to underestimate. College students are expected to be much more independent in their learning than high school students, and many new college students are surprised at how much time studying takes. To meet the challenge of college courses, plan as much study time as you think you will possibly need.

- **Step 5.** From the times that are still available, select your study times and mark them on your schedule. Be specific about what you intend to study at each time (such as "Study psychology," "Accounting homework," "Study history"). A sample weekly study schedule on page 14 has been filled in to show you how a typical study schedule might look.

Once you have set up your study schedule, keep it where you can see it—*then follow it.* You will probably need about 3 weeks to become accustomed to

Here is a sample of a weekly study schedule that has been completed according to the directions on page 13. Notice that *specific study times have been identified for each course.* Use the blank form on page 15 to create your own weekly study schedule.

SAMPLE WEEKLY STUDY SCHEDULE

Time	Sunday	Monday	Tuesday	Wednesday	Thursday	Friday	Saturday
6:00 A.M.		←		Get ready for school	→	→	
7:00				Travel to school			
8:00		Accounting	*Read English*	Accounting	*Review English*	Accounting	
9:00		History	English	History	English	History	Tennis →
10:00	Family time →	Psychology		Psychology		Psychology	
11:00		Lunch	Biology	Lunch	Biology	Lunch	
12:00 noon		*Accounting homework*		*Accounting homework*		*Accounting homework*	Work
1:00 P.M.	*English assignments* →	*English assignments*	Lunch	*English assignments*	Lunch	*English assignments*	
2:00		*Study biology*	Biology lab →	*Study biology*	*Biology*		
3:00	Tennis →				*study group*	Snack	
4:00	→	Dinner		Dinner		Work →	
5:00		Work →	*Read history text*	Work →	*Read history text*		
6:00	*Read Biology assignments*						Spend time with friends
7:00			Dinner		Dinner		
8:00	*English assignments*		*Read psychology text*		*Read psychology text*		
9:00		→	*psychology text* →	→	*psychology text*	→	→
10:00		Relax/watch news	Relax/watch news	Relax/watch news	Relax/watch news	Relax/watch news	
11:00	Sleep	Sleep	Sleep	Sleep	Sleep	Sleep	Sleep
12:00 midnight	→	→	→	→	→	→	→
1:00 A.M.	→						

WEEKLY STUDY SCHEDULE

Time	Sunday	Monday	Tuesday	Wednesday	Thursday	Friday	Saturday
6:00 A.M							
7:00							
8:00							
9:00							
10:00							
11:00							
12:00 noon							
1:00 P.M.							
2:00							
3:00							
4:00							
5:00							
6:00							
7:00							
8:00							
9:00							
10:00							
11:00							
12:00 midnight							
1:00 A.M.							

a new schedule. It takes approximately 3 weeks to establish a new habit or to break an old one. Don't get discouraged if using a schedule feels awkward at first. That's normal.

Adjust your schedule if you need to, but make a every effort to stick to it. Each time you deviate from your schedule, returning to it becomes harder. Sticking with it will get you past one big obstacle to studying: simply getting started. Having a regular study routine makes it easier to become a more effective, successful student.

Making the Most of Your Study Time

Once you have set up a weekly study schedule, it is important to make your study time as productive as possible. There are various strategies you can use to get the most out of your study sessions. Here are some proven techniques:

1. **Find or create a suitable place to study.**   Your study place can be at home or elsewhere. A library or any other quiet place on campus can serve as well. Don't use your study place for any purpose except studying. Buy whatever materials and supplies you will need, and have them at hand in a drawer or book bag. Decide that when you are in your study place, you are there to study!

2. **Study in the same place at the same time every day.**   This will help you "get into" studying immediately because it makes studying automatic, a habit. Knowing when, where, and what you are going to study will keep you from indecision and procrastination.

3. **Make your study time more productive, not longer.**   Strive for, say, 1 or 2 productive study hours rather than 3 or 4 unproductive hours. To keep your study time productive, you must stay focused. Remember that just sitting at a desk is not studying, and just looking at a book is not reading. If you find yourself daydreaming, stop and refocus your thinking. After 1 or 2 hours of study, you may begin to tire, and your ability to concentrate may decrease. If so, take a break or switch to another subject to maintain your efficiency. Be sure, however, to take your break at a logical stopping point—not in the middle of a task that is going well.

4. **Study as soon as possible after lecture classes.**   One hour spent studying immediately or soon after a lecture class will do as much to develop your understanding and recall of the material as several hours of studying would a few days later. Review and improve your lecture notes while they are still fresh in your mind. Start assignments while your understanding of the directions and the material is still accurate. If there are points you do not understand, take steps immediately to clear them up: look up an unknown word, make a note to ask the instructor about something that confused you, etc.

5. **Take advantage of short periods of free time for studying.**   Brief, scattered periods of time (for instance, periods of 15 to 45 minutes before, be-

tween, and after classes) are often wasted. Use these brief times for study or review. Before a lecture class, for example, it's wise to spend a few minutes reviewing your notes from the previous lecture or going over the reading assignment. When you look for short periods of free time to use, keep in mind that (in general) daytime study is more efficient than nighttime study: what you can accomplish in 1 hour during the day might take 2 hours at night. Also, look for usable time on Saturdays and Sundays.

6. **Don't try to study your most difficult subject last.**   You may have favorite subjects that you enjoy studying. It is tempting to focus on these subjects first and leave the harder subjects until last. But if you do this, you will often find that you have run out of time for a difficult subject or are too tired to work on it. Study your most difficult subjects when you still have the time and energy to do a good job on them.

7. **If you can't study at a scheduled time, take some time from another, nonstudy activity.**   When unexpected events arise that take up time you had planned to use for studying, decide immediately where in your schedule you can make up the study session you missed, and make a temporary adjustment in your schedule. Don't overlook weekends, including Saturday and Sunday evening. Successful students often take advantage of weekends by using part of them for productive, unhurried study times.

8. **Experiment to develop study strategies and techniques that work for you.** Try out techniques that allow you to capitalize on your learning style or make learning easier. (Learning styles are explained later in this chapter.) Be creative. If you get sleepy when you read your textbook assignments, try standing up and walking back and forth in your room as you read. Try reading out loud or taking notes. Try reviewing your week's class notes and textbook markings to help you learn and remember the material. Study hard for 45 minutes, then take a 15-minute break. The key is to discover the particular strategies that work best for you.

9. **Don't let friends, the telephone, or television interfere with your study time.**   Students say over and over again that, along with trying to working too many hours, these are the main reasons they do not get all of their studying done. Every time you interrupt your study session to visit with friends, talk on the telephone, or watch a TV program, you make your study session longer and less effective. If you honor your commitment to your study time, so will your friends.

10. **Improve your concentration.**   You can do this by dealing immediately with any external and internal distractions. To deal with external distractors in your environment, you may need to find a place that is quieter or has better light, adjust the room temperature, etc. To deal with internal (emotional) distractors, you will need to develop strategies to reduce worrying and daydreaming. The last section of the box on page 74 in Chapter 2 describes some techniques that work. Your instructor or a counselor can give you additional suggestions.

Planning Further Ahead: Creating a Monthly Assignment Calendar and Using a Daily To Do List

Two useful tools for planning ahead are a monthly assignment calendar and a daily To Do list. In this section you'll learn about each of these.

Students sometimes discover too late that they have three tests, a paper, and a project all due in the same week. To alert themselves to upcoming weeks that will be especially busy and to give themselves an overview of the semester, effective students use a monthly assignment calendar. A **monthly assignment calendar** is a calendar that shows the test dates and due dates in *all* your courses for each month of the semester. A monthly assignment calendar helps you plan ahead so that you can meet each deadline and produce better work. As a result, you will feel more in control, experience less stress, and enjoy the semester more.

Setting up a monthly calendar is simple. As soon as you receive the syllabi for your courses, transfer all the test dates and due dates (for projects, papers, oral reports, etc.) to *one* calendar. If you see that several due dates coincide in one week, plan to finish some of the projects ahead of time. (To complete a project comfortably in advance of its deadline, remember the motivational strategy of breaking big projects into smaller parts.) Or, if several tests coincide, begin reviewing for each of them well ahead of time.

Pages 19–20 show monthly assignment calendars. The sample has been filled in to give you an idea of how a typical student's calendar might look. Make photocopies of the blank calendar and create your own monthly calendar.

Another effective tool for time management is a daily **To Do list,** a prioritized list of things to be done in a single day. To Do lists are a proven way to get more accomplished. Make your list every morning or, if you prefer, make it up each evening for the coming day. Regardless of when you make it, be sure to make a list for each day. An index card, which is both small and sturdy, works well for a To Do list. Keep your list with you so that you can refer to it throughout the day and check off items as you complete them. The steps for creating a To Do list are described below.

The most valuable feature of a To Do list is that you identify which items you consider high priorities and which ones you consider less important. This is what makes the To Do list so useful: it helps you resist the temptation to do easy, unimportant tasks first rather than the important, often more challenging ones. If you use a To Do list daily, you will be more productive and have more free time.

Here are the steps to follow when making a daily To Do list:

- **Step 1. Write down everything you would like to accomplish today**   (or tomorrow, if you are making the list the night before). Some of the activities will be school-related (such as "buy graph paper at bookstore"). Others will not be related to school (such as "make appointment for haircut"). You can include activities related to long-term goals ("practice the piano" or "exercise for 45 minutes") as well as activities related to short-term goals. Do not include routine activities ("eat lunch" or "go to work").

- **Step 2. On the basis of how important it is to accomplish an item that day, rank each item on your list into one of three categories: A, B, or C.**

SAMPLE MONTHLY ASSIGNMENT CALENDAR

Month of September

Sunday	Monday	Tuesday	Wednesday	Thursday	Friday	Saturday
			1	2	3	4
5	6 History group report	7	8	9	10	11
12	13	14	15 Accounting Project due	16	17 English paper due	18
19	20	21	22	23	24	25
26	27					

Month of October

Sunday	Monday	Tuesday	Wednesday	Thursday	Friday	Saturday
					1 Psychology midterm	2
3	4 History test	5 Math test	6	7	8	9
10	11	12	13 English paper due	14	15	16
17	18	19	20	21	22	23
24 / 31	25					

Month of November

Sunday	Monday	Tuesday	Wednesday	Thursday	Friday	Saturday
		1	2	3 English oral report due	4	5	6
7	8	9	10	11	12 Psychology project due	13
14	15	16 Math test	17	18	19	20
21	22	23	24	25	26	27
28	29					

Month of December

Sunday	Monday	Tuesday	Wednesday	Thursday	Friday	Saturday
			1	2	3	4
5	6 History Test	7	8	9	10 English Paper due	11
12 Finals Begin	13 History Exam	14	15 Psy & English Exams	16 Math Exam	17 Acct Exam	18
19	20	21	22	23	24	25
26	27	28	29	30	31	

MONTHLY ASSIGNMENT CALENDAR

Sunday	Monday	Tuesday	Wednesday	Thursday	Friday	Saturday

Mark an item A if accomplishing it that day is *very* important. Mark an item B if it is *moderately* important. Mark it C if it is *less* important. In other words, set priorities. Step 2 is crucial: if you do not set priorities, you will more than likely spend your time on easy but unimportant items while the important items are left undone.

- **Step 3. Now you must set final priorities by ranking all your A's, then all your B's, and then your C's.** Consider the A's and label them A-1, A-2, A-3, etc., according to the importance of each. Do the same for the B's and C's. This gives you the *overall* order in which you should do the items on the list. (You may want to rewrite the list at this point, putting the items in their final order.) Try to do all of your A items first, starting with item A-1. When you complete it, tackle item A-2. When you have completed all your A items, start on the B items, beginning with B-1, and so forth.

The box below shows a sample of a finished To Do list which will give you an idea of how your own lists might look.

When you make the To Do list for the following day, look at the items on the previous day's list that you did not complete. If some of them still need to be done, carry them over to the new list. Priorities may change from day to day, of course. An item that was priority C, on Thursday ("pick up suit at cleaners") may become an A item on Friday (if you plan to wear the suit that night).

SAMPLE TO DO LIST

A-1 Study for history test
A-2 Write draft of English paper
A-3 Schedule dental appointment
A-4 Pay bills

B-1 Return library books
B-2 Cleaners
B-3 Birthday present for Pat

C-1 Buy stamps
C-2 Call Lynn
C-3 Wash car

UNDERSTANDING LEARNING STYLES

In addition to managing your study time, you need to think about your learning style, or how you prefer to learn. To gain insight into your learning style, complete this short survey. Do this now before reading the rest of this section. After you have completed the survey and totaled your responses, read the rest of the section.

IDENTIFYING YOUR LEARNING STYLE

To gain insight into your learning style, answer the following questions. For each item, circle all the answers that describe you.

1. When I go someplace I have not been before, I usually
   A. trust my intuition about the right direction or route to take.
   B. ask someone for directions.
   C. look at a map.

2. I like to go to places where
   A. there is lots of space to move around.
   B. people are talking or there is music that matches my mood.
   C. there is good "people watching" or there is something else interesting to watch.

3. If I have lots of things to do, I generally
   A. feel nervous until I get most of them done.
   B. repeat things to myself so I won't forget to do them.
   C. jot them down on a list or write them on a calendar or organizer.

4. When I have free time, I like to
   A. work on a handicraft or hobby, or do an activity such as play a sport or exercise.
   B. listen to a tape, a CD, or the radio, or talk on the phone.
   C. watch television, play a video game, or see a movie.

5. When I am talking with other people, I typically
   A. move close to them so I can get a feel for what they are telling me.
   B. listen carefully so I can hear what they are saying.
   C. watch them closely so that I can see what they are saying.

6. When I meet someone new, I usually pay most attention to
   A. the way the person walks or moves, or the gestures the person makes.
   B. the way the person speaks and how his or her voice sounds.
   C. the person's appearance or clothes.

7. When I select books or articles to read, I generally choose ones that
   A. deal with sports or fitness, hobbies and crafts, or other activities.
   B. tell me about something that happened or that tells a story.
   C. include lots of photos, pictures, or illustrations.

8. Learning something is easier for me when I can
   A. use a hands-on approach.
   B. have someone explain it to me.
   C. watch someone show me how to do it.

Total up your A's, then total up your B's, and your C's.

_____ A's   _____ B's   _____ C's

If your highest total is A's, you are a *tactile* or *kinesthetic* learner.
If your highest total is B's, you are an *auditory* learner.
If your highest total is C's, you are a *visual* learner.

KEY TERM
Learning Style

The modality through which an individual learns best.

Learning style refers to the modality through which an individual learns best. Everyone has a *modality,* or sensory channel, through which he or she prefers to learn because learning is easier and more efficient that way. Your learning style, of course, is the way you learn best.

The three primary modalities for learning are seeing (visual modality), hearing (auditory modality), and physical involvement or touch (tactile modality) or movement (kinesthetic modality). People who are *visual learners* prefer to see or read the material to be learned and will benefit from books, class notes, "concept maps", review cards, test review sheets, and the like. Others are *auditory learners,* preferring to hear the material in the form of lectures and discussions. Auditory learners often benefit from reciting material or reading aloud to themselves, making or using audiotapes, and participating in study groups. Still others are *tactile learners* who benefit from touching and manipulating materials, or *kinesthetic learners* who benefit from physical movement. Tactile learners prefer laboratory work and other hands-on projects. Kinesthetic learners like to "go through the motions" of doing something; they also benefit from writing things down. (The three basic styles are summarized in the box on page 24.) Of course, most people can, and do, learn in more than one way, and most people use some combination of modalities simultaneously. And even though most people prefer to use one modality over the others, a person's learning style can change as he or she acquires more practice and skill in using the other modalities.

Did your results on the learning style survey surprise you, or did they simply confirm what you already knew about how you prefer to learn? If you know your learning style, you can put yourself in situations in which you learn best; you can utilize study techniques and strategies that take advantage of your strengths. Moreover, when material is presented in a way that does not match your learning style, you can take steps to compensate and "work around" the problem.

There is one other aspect of learning that you might also want to think about: whether you prefer to work by yourself or with others. If you prefer working alone, make it a priority to find a quiet place where you will not be disturbed. You may also find that self-paced courses, computer-assisted instruction, telecourses, or other distance-learning options work well for you. On the other hand, if you are a person who finds it advantageous to study with others, you will probably like being part of a study group or having a study partner. Remember that it's important to select other students who are motivated. Also, keep in mind that participating in a study group does not guarantee success. To prepare yourself to work with a group, you must still read and study on your own first.

THREE LEARNING STYLES

If this is your learning style . . .	Then these activities are the most helpful to your learning
Visual learner (prefers to read or see information)	Reading textbooks and seeing information in print Reviewing class notes and concept maps Reading your chapter review cards Studying test review sheets
Auditory learner (prefers to hear information)	Listening to class lectures and discussions Reciting material (saying it out loud) Reading aloud to yourself Listening to audiotapes Participating in study groups
Tactile or kinesthetic learner (prefers to manipulate materials physically or incorporate movement)	Doing laboratory work (science labs, computer labs, etc.) Taking hands-on classes (science, engineering, computer, and other technical or vocational subjects) Taking notes from lectures and from textbooks or making concept maps Actually going through steps or procedures in a process

DEVELOPING CHAPTER REVIEW CARDS

Review cards, or *summary cards,* are an excellent study tool. They are a way to select, organize, and review the most important information in a textbook chapter. The process of creating review cards helps you organize information in a meaningful way and, at the same time, transfer it into long-term memory. The cards can also be used to prepare for tests (see Part Three). The review card activities in this book give you structured practice in creating these valuable study tools. Once you have learned how to make review cards, you can create them for textbook material in your other courses.

Now, complete the seven review cards for Chapter 1 by answering the questions or following the directions on each card. When you have completed them, you will have summarized: (1) what successful college students do, (2) important information about setting goals, (3) ways to motivate yourself, (4) ways to make the most of study time, (5) how to develop a monthly assignment calendar, (6) steps in making a To Do list, and (7) three learning styles.

Doing What Successful Students Do

What are five things successful college students do? (See pages 5–6)

1. _____

2. _____

3. _____

   _____

4. _____

5. _____

Card 1   Chapter 1: Making Yourself Successful in College

Setting Goals

1. Why should goals be written down? (See page 7.)

_____

_____

2. What are Lakein's three recommendations for setting goals? (See page 7.)

_____

_____

_____

3. List and define the three types of goals. (See page 8.)

_____

_____

_____

Card 2   Chapter 1: Making Yourself Successful in College

Motivating Yourself

What are twelve ways to motivate yourself? (See pages 9–11.)

1. _____

2. _____

3. _____

4. _____

5. _____

6. _____

7. _____

8. _____

9. _____

10. _____

11. _____

12. _____

Card 3   Chapter 1: Making Yourself Successful in College

Making the Most of Your Study Time

What are ten ways to make the most of your study time? (See pages 16–17.)

1. _____
2. _____
3. _____
4. _____
5. _____
6. _____
7. _____
8. _____
9. _____
10. _____

Card 4   Chapter 1: Making Yourself Successful in College

Developing a Monthly Assignment Calendar

How can you prepare a monthly assignment calendar? (See page 18.)

1. What should you do as soon as you receive the syllabi for your courses?

_____

_____

_____

2. What should you do if several project or test dates coincide? (See page 18.)

_____

_____

_____

Card 5   Chapter 1: Making Yourself Successful in College

Making a To Do List

Describe briefly the three steps to follow in making a daily To Do list. (See pages 18–21.)

Step 1: _____

_____

_____

Step 2: _____

_____

_____

_____

Step 3: _____

_____

_____

Card 6   Chapter 1: Making Yourself Successful in College

Learning Styles

Briefly describe these three learning styles. (See pages 23–24.)

Visual learners:

_____

_____

_____

Auditory learners:

_____

_____

_____

Tactile or kinesthetic learners:

_____

Card 7   Chapter 1: Making Yourself Successful in College

SELECTION 1-1
Study Skills

WHY GO TO COLLEGE?

From *P.O.W.E.R. Learning: Strategies for Success in College and Life*
By Robert S. Feldman

Prepare Yourself to Read

Directions: Do these exercises *before* you read Selection 1-1.

1. Read and think about the title of this selection. Why are *you* going to college? Write 1, 2, and 3 next to the three most important reasons that you have for attending college:

    _____ I want to get a good job when I graduate.

    _____ My parents want me to go.

    _____ I couldn't find a job.

    _____ I want to get away from home.

    _____ I want to get a better job as soon as possible.

    _____ I want to gain a general education and appreciation of ideas.

    _____ I want to improve my reading and study skills.

    _____ I want to become a more cultured person.

    _____ I want to make more money.

    _____ I want to learn more about things that interest me.

    _____ A mentor or role model encouraged me to go.

    _____ I want to prove to others that I can succeed.

    How do you think your reasons compare with those of other first-year students?

    _____

    _____

2. Next, complete your preview by reading the following:

    Introduction (in *italics*)
    Chart
    First sentence of each paragraph

    On the basis of your preview, what does the selection seem to be about?

    _____

    _____

Apply Comprehension Skills

Directions: Do these exercises as you read Selection 1-1. Apply two skills from this chapter:

Set your goal for reading.   What do you expect to discover about the reasons for pursuing a college education?

_____

_____

Plan your time.   Estimate how long it will take you to read Selection 1-1.

_____

_____

WHY GO TO COLLEGE?

This selection comes from the study skills textbook P.O.W.E.R. Learning: Strategies for Success in College and Life *by Robert S. Feldman, professor of psychology at the University of Massachusetts at Amherst. At the beginning of this selection Professor Feldman presents the reasons that first-year college students cited most frequently when they are asked, "Why are you going to college?" Then, to support his belief that "the value of college extends far beyond dollars and cents," Professor Feldman presents five other important reasons for going to college that first-year students may be unaware of.*

1   Congratulations. You're in college.

2   Why?

3   Although it seems as if it should be easy to say why you're continuing your education, for most students it's not that simple. The reasons that people go to college vary. Some people want to go to college for practical reasons ("I want to get a good job"). Some reasons for going to college are lofty ("I want to learn about people and the world"). And some reasons are unreflective ("Why not?—I don't have anything better to do"). Think about your own reasons for attending college.

4   Surveys of first-year college students show that almost three-quarters say they want to get a better job and make money (see Figure 1). But most students also have additional goals in mind: They want to learn about things that interest them (74 percent) and gain a general education and appreciation of ideas (61 percent).

5   And, in fact, it's not wrong to expect that a college education helps people find better jobs. The average person with a college degree earns about 50 percent more each year than the average person with only a high school education. Furthermore, as jobs become increasingly complex and technologically sophisticated, college will become more and more of a necessity.

6   But the value of college extends far beyond dollars and cents. Consider these added reasons for pursuing a college education:

7   **You'll learn to think and communicate better.** Here's what one student said about his college experience after he graduated: "It's not about what you major in or which classes you take. . . . It's really about learning to *think* and to *communicate*. Wherever you end up, you'll need to be able to analyze and solve problems— to figure out what needs to be done and do it."

College can be the starting point for a more successful and satisfying journey through life.
(Stone/Brian Bailey)

Figure 1
Choosing College
These are the most
frequently-cited reasons that
first-year college students
gave for why they enrolled in
college when asked in a
national survey.

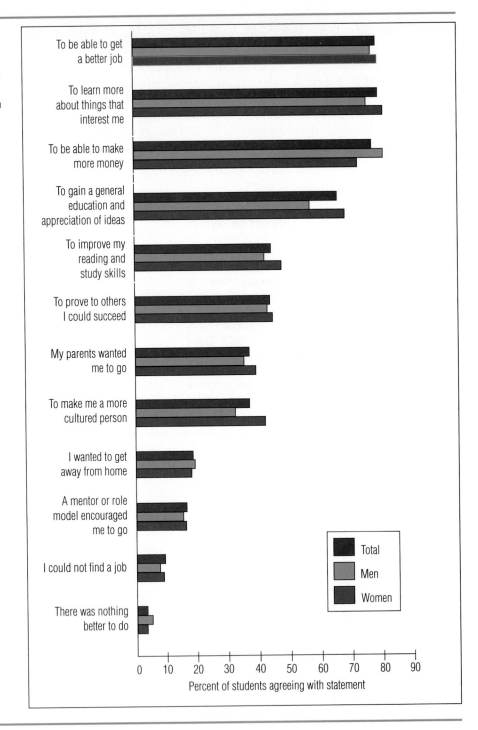

8   Education improves your ability to understand the world—understand it as it now is, and prepare to understand it as it will be. By showing you how to develop your capacity for critical and creative thinking, education will increase your abilities to think clearly and to communicate more effectively with others.

9   **You'll be able to better deal with advances in knowledge and technology that are changing the world.**   Genetic engineering . . . drugs to reduce forgetfulness . . . computers that respond to our voices. Innovations such as these—and the ones that haven't even been thought of yet—illustrate how rapidly the world is changing.

10   No one knows what the future will hold. But education can provide you with the intellectual tools that you can apply regardless of the specific situation in which you find yourself. You can't anticipate what the future holds, but you can prepare for it through a college education.

11   **You'll be better prepared to live in a world of diversity.**   The United States is changing rapidly. In fact, by the middle of the twenty-first century, non-Hispanic whites will become a minority group. You'll be working and living with people whose backgrounds, lifestyles, and ways of thinking may be entirely different from your own.

12   The greater diversity of the United States, along with the fact that we live in a global society, necessitates a deeper understanding of other cultures. Culture provides a lens through which people view the world. You won't be prepared for the future unless you understand others and their cultural backgrounds—as well as how your own cultural background affects you.

13   **You'll make learning a lifelong habit.**   Higher education isn't the end of your education. If you make the most of college, you will develop a thirst for more knowledge, a lifelong quest that can never be fully satisfied. Education will build upon your natural curiosity about the world, and it will make you aware that learning is a rewarding and never-ending journey.

14   **You'll understand the meaning of your own contributions to the world.**   No matter who you are, you are poised to make your own contributions to society and the world. Higher education provides you with a window to the past, present, and future, and it allows you to understand the significance of your own contributions. Your college education provides you with a compass to discover who you are, where you've been, and where you're going.

Source: Adapted from Robert S. Feldman, *P.O.W.E.R. Learning: Strategies for Success and Life,* McGraw-Hill, New York, 2000, pp. 3–5.

SELECTION **1-1**

Study Skills

Comprehension Quiz

Directions: For each comprehension question below, use information from the selection to determine the correct answer. You may refer to the selection as you answer the questions. Write your answer in the space provided.

The answer to the first item and an explanation are given below.

True or False

_____F_____ **1.** Professor Feldman believes that the value of a college education should be measured mainly in terms of dollars and cents.

Explanation

In paragraph 6 Professor Feldman states, "But the value of college extends far beyond dollars and cents." He then goes on to present five other important reasons for pursuing a college education. Consequently, this statement is false because Professor Feldman does *not* believe that "the value of a college education should be measured mainly in terms of dollars and cents."

_____T_____ **2.** The average person with only a high school education earns about 50 percent less each year than the average person with a college degree.

_____F_____ **3.** According to the national survey results presented in Figure 1, first-year college students most frequently cited being able to make more money as their reason for enrolling in college.

_____T_____ **4.** Surveys show that 61 percent of first-year college students cite gaining a general education and appreciation of ideas as their reason for enrolling in college.

_____T_____ **5.** Professor Feldman believes that college can help you develop your capacity for creative and critical thinking.

Multiple-Choice

_____c_____ **6.** Of the following, which is cited more often by women than men as a reason for enrolling in college?
  a. the ability to make money
  b. there was nothing better to do
  c. to improve my reading and study skills
  d. to get away from home

_____D_____ **7.** Of the following, which is cited more often by men than women as a reason for attending college?
  a. to make me a more cultured person
  b. to prove to others I could succeed
  c. my parents wanted me to go
  d. to be able to make more money

_____β_____   **8.** The author states that college will become more and more of a necessity because

    a. higher incomes will be required in the future.

    b. jobs are becoming increasingly complex and technologically sophisticated.

    c. the economy of the United States is becoming global.

    d. there will be fewer jobs in the future.

_____D_____   **9.** Which of the following is *not* listed as a beneficial reason for pursuing a college education?

    a. to understand the meaning of your own contributions to the world

    b. to make learning a lifelong habit

    c. to be better prepared to live in a world of diversity

    d. to anticipate what will be required in the future

_____D_____   **10.** The author states that college can provide students with

    a. skills that will help them find a better job.

    b. a deeper understanding of other cultures.

    c. intellectual tools.

    d. all of the above.

S E L E C T I O N **1-1**

Study Skills

Extend Your Vocabulary by Using Context Clues

Directions: Context clues are words in a sentence that allow the reader to deduce (reason out) the meaning of an unfamiliar word in that sentence. For each vocabulary item below, a sentence from the selection containing an important word (*italicized, like this*) is quoted first. Next, there is an additional sentence using the word in the same sense and providing another context clue. Use the context clues from *both* sentences to deduce the meaning of the italicized word. *Be sure the answer you choose makes sense in both sentences.* If you discover that you must use a dictionary to confirm an answer choice, remember that the meaning you select must still fit the context of *both* sentences. To indicate your answer, write the letter in the space provided.

Since the skill of using context clues is not introduced until the next chapter, the answer to the first vocabulary item and an explanation are given below. (Chapter 2 presents the skill of using context clues. It includes examples and practice exercises to teach you this skill.)

Pronunciation Key: ă pat   ā pay   âr care   ä father   ĕ pet   ē be   ĭ pit
ī tie   îr pier   ŏ pot   ō toe   ô paw   oi noise   ou out   oͦo took   ōo boot
ŭ cut   yōo abuse   ûr urge   th thin   *th* this   hw which   zh vision   ə about
Stress mark: ′

_____d_____   **1.** The reasons that people go to college *vary*.

Prices of new homes *vary* depending on their size and location.

vary   (vār′ ē)
a.   disappear
b.   decrease
c.   remain the same
d.   differ

Explanation

- Answer choice **a**, *disappear* (meaning *to vanish* or *to cease to exist*), does not make sense in either sentence.
- Answer choice **b**, *decrease* (meaning *to grow smaller*), also does not make sense in either sentence.
- Answer choice **c**, *remain the same* (meaning *does not change*), does not make sense in the second sentence.
- Answer choice **d**, *differ* (meaning *to be different*), is the only choice that makes sense in *both* sentences: "The reasons that people go to college *differ*" and "Prices of new homes *differ* depending on their size and location."

_____B_____   **2.** Some people want to go to college for *practical* reasons ("I want to get a good job").

Patricia's *practical* knowledge of Spanish helped her have a successful business trip to Mexico City.

practical   (prak′ tĭ kəl)
a.   private
b.   useful
c.   enjoyable
d.   limited

_____D_____   **3.** Consider these added reasons for *pursuing* a college education.

In *pursuing* his goal to become a commercial airline pilot, Ted spent many years training.

pursuing   (pər sōō ′ ĭng)
a.   chasing or running after
b.   attending
c.   studying
d.   striving to gain or accomplish

_____ *A*   **4.** By showing you how to develop your *capacity* for critical and creative thinking, education will increase your abilities to think clearly and to communicate more effectively with others.

Mr. Nichols has an amazing *capacity* for remembering the first and last names of everyone he meets.

capacity   (kə pǎs ′ ĭ tē)
a. ability to do something
b. creativity
c. maximum amount
d. ability to communicate

_____ *C*   **5.** But education can provide you with the *intellectual* tools that you can apply regardless of the specific situation in which you find yourself.

Cassandra preferred *intellectual* activities such as playing chess and bridge, reading, working crossword puzzles, and writing poetry.

intellectual   (ĭn tl ĕk ′ chōo əl)
a. helpful
b. interesting
c. pertaining to the ability to learn
d. challenging; difficult to grasp

_____ *B*   **6.** You can't *anticipate* what the future holds, but you can prepare for it through a college education.

Studying for an exam is easier if you can *anticipate* some of the questions that you may be asked.

anticipate   (ăn tǐs ′ ə pāt)
a. prevent; avoid
b. foresee; predict
c. change; alter
d. study; remember

_____ *B*   **7.** You'll be better prepared to live in a world of *diversity.*

New York City is famous for the *diversity* of its ethnic restaurants—Italian, Chinese, French, Indian, Russian, Vietnamese—you name it!

diversity   (dǐ vûr ′ sǐ tē)
a. opportunity
b. variety
c. difficulty
d. quantity

_____ C **8.** The greater diversity of the United States, along with the fact that we live in a global society, *necessitates* a deeper understanding of other cultures.

Being successful as a full-time student often *necessitates* reducing the number of hours that you work and spending less time socializing.

necessitates (nə sĕs ′ ī tāts)

a. creates

b. provides

c. requires

d. reduces

_____ A **9.** If you make the most of college, you will develop a thirst for more knowledge, a lifelong *quest* that can never be fully satisfied.

Michael's *quest* for an exciting and challenging sport ended when he discovered the thrills of motorcycle racing.

quest (kwĕst)

a. search

b. problem

c. question

d. habit

_____ B **10.** No matter who you are, you are *poised* to make your own contributions to society and the world.

After graduating from college, Kim was *poised* for the challenges and responsibilities of her first full-time job.

poised (poizd)

a. afraid; fearful

b. positioned; balanced

c. required

d. allowed; permitted

SELECTION **1-1**

Study Skills

Respond in Writing

Directions: As Oliver Wendell Holmes observed, "Writing is good for us because it brings our thoughts out into the open." These are essay-type exercises that will help you bring your thoughts into the open. Refer to this selection as needed to answer them.

Collaboration Option

Option for collaboration: It has been said that "None of us is as smart as all of us." Adults, in particular, learn well from each other. For this reason, your instructor may direct you to work with other students, or, in other words, to work *collaboratively.* In that case, you should form groups of three or four students as directed by your instructor and work together to complete the exercises. After your group discusses each item and agrees on the answer, have a group member record it. Every member of your group should be able to explain all of your group's answers.

1. In paragraph 6 Professor Feldman states, "But the value of college extends far beyond dollars and cents." He then goes on to present five other important reasons for pursuing a college education. In the space below, summarize these five reasons.

_____

_____

_____

_____

_____

_____

_____

2. Why does Professor Feldman believe that it is valuable to make learning a lifelong habit? List the three reasons he cites.

_____

_____

_____

_____

3. In some cases, men and women's reasons for attending college are quite different. What are these differences?

Men more often say that they enrolled in college:

_____

_____

_____

_____

Women more often say that they enrolled in college:

_____

_____

_____

_____

4. Overall main idea. What is the overall main idea the author wants you to understand about reasons for pursuing a college education? Answer this question in one sentence.

   Because this is the first time you are asked to write an overall main idea, the answer and an explanation are given below. (Chapters 4 and 5 present the skills of identifying and expressing main ideas. These chapters include examples and practice exercises.)

There are several valuable reasons for pursuing a college education beyond

getting a better job, making more money, and learning interesting things.

_____

Explanation

Notice that this sentence expresses the one most important point the author wants readers to understand after reading the *entire* selection.

Read More about It on the World Wide Web

To learn more about the topic of this selection, visit these websites or use your favorite search engine (such as Yahoo®). Whenever you go to *any* website, it is a good idea to evaluate it critically. Are you getting good information—information that is accurate, complete, and up-to-date? Who sponsors the website? How easy is it to use the features of the website?

   http://www.aboutcollege.com
      This site is devoted to student success and contains information for students interested in adjustment to college life.

   http://collegeprep.okstate.edu/
      This site has a variety of information aimed at helping students prepare for success in college.

   http:www.ee.calpoly.edu/~jbreiten/htbas.html
      This site contains advice from a college professor about how to be a successful student.

   http:www.mhhe.com/power
      This site presents information about Dr. Feldman's textbook, P.O.W.E.R. Learning: Strategies for Success in College and Life.

WALTER ANDERSON: HERO ON PARADE
From *The Big Picture*
By Ben Carson with Gregg Lewis

Prepare Yourself to Read

Directions: Do these exercises *before* you read Selection 1-2.

1. Read and think about the title. On the basis of the title, what do you think this selection might be about?

_____

_____

2. Next, complete your preview by reading the following:

Introduction (in *italics*)
First paragraph (paragraph 1)
First sentence of each of the other paragraphs
All of the last paragraph (paragraph 13)

On the basis of your preview, what does the selection now seem to be about?

_____

_____

Apply Comprehension Skills

Directions: Do these exercises as you read Selection 1-2. Apply two skills from this chapter:

Set your goal for reading.   What do you hope to discover about who the "hero" is and why he is "on parade"?

_____

_____

Plan your time.   Estimate how long it will take you to read Selection 1-2.

_____

_____

WALTER ANDERSON: HERO ON PARADE

This selection comes from a book entitled The Big Picture *by Ben Carson. Carson came from a background of extreme poverty. He was failing fifth grade when his mother, in desperation, began requiring him to read and write reports on two books a week. Ultimately this helped him turn his academic work and his life around: he is now a highly respected and internationally known pediatric neurosurgeon.*

Because Carson overcame remarkable odds, he was chosen for membership in the Horatio Alger Association of Distinguished Americans. Founded in 1947 and named for an early twentieth century author who wrote tales about dedicated, honest boys who rose from humble beginnings, this organization annually recognizes men and women who personify success through hard work and courage, who have accomplished great things despite personal adversity, and who have made extraordinary civic contributions. They are people who have given above and beyond what is expected of them. Other well-known members of the Horatio Alger Society include Oprah Winfrey, General Colin Powell, the actress Carol Burnett, and the poet Maya Angelou. In the selection below, Ben Carson tells about another member of the Horatio Alger Society, Walter Anderson, the editor of Parade *magazine. (*Parade *magazine is featured as a supplement in many Sunday newspapers across the nation.)*

1   Walter Anderson joined the ranks of the Horatio Alger Society the same year I did. I felt a special kinship to him as I heard his story—for reasons that will be obvious as I relate it here.

2   Walter grew up in a four-room railroad flat on the wrong side of the tracks in Mt. Vernon, New York, in an atmosphere made volatile and violent by an illiterate, abusive, alcoholic father. "I lived with fear every day, nearly every minute of my childhood," Walter remembers. "Often my father would beat me for things I might do, not for things I had done. I felt safer on the street corner than in my own home."

3   Like me, my friend Walter credits his mother and reading as key influences in his life. His mom always tried to shield him from his father's abuse. "I never doubted my mother's love," Walter says. "She encouraged me to read despite the fact that my father would beat me if he found me reading. Years later, after my father's death, I asked her why she would do so when she knew my father would beat me, and she said, 'I believed that if you could learn to read, somehow you would find your way out. And you did.'"

4   The Mt. Vernon Public Library became a secret sanctuary where Walter regularly escaped the abuse of his father and the cruel ridicule of classmates who laughed at the holes in his ragged clothes. "I read myself out of poverty long before I worked myself out of poverty," he says.

"By reading I could go anywhere, I could be anybody. I could imagine myself out of a slum."

5   Six days after his seventeenth birthday, he found another way out. He joined the Marines. That decision altered his perspective, his values, and his life forever. "I was able to develop self-respect, self-esteem, and a belief in noble motives and noble purposes. I learned about honor and dignity." In 1965, just months before he was to complete his active duty, Walter volunteered for Vietnam.

6   When he returned home from overseas and was discharged, Walter first took a job as a laboratory assistant, then as a sales trainee. But what he really wanted to do more than anything else was to write. "Ever since I was fourteen or fifteen years old, I had a tremendous need to express myself."

7   Carrying the only thing he had ever had published, an emotional and articulate "letter to the editor" he had written from the front lines in Vietnam, Walter walked into a newspaper office to plead with the editor for a job. After reading Walter's one-clipping portfolio (his home-town paper, the *Mt. Vernon Daily Argus,* had printed his letter on page one under the title "Just What Is Vietnam?"), the editor of the *Reporter Dispatch* in White Plains, New York, hired him for $90 a week.

8   While working as a reporter in White Plains, Walter enrolled in a local community college and graduated two years later—first in his class of six hundred students. By that time he was "night editor" of his paper and had started his own action-line column, which was syndicated in seven other newspapers. Nearby Mercy College awarded him a full scholarship to continue his education. He graduated from there summa cum laude, once again class valedictorian.

9   After serving as editor and general manager of two daily newspapers, first in New Rochelle and then back in White Plains where he began his career, he moved to *Parade* magazine. He served as managing editor there, before being promoted to editor of the largest-circulation Sunday magazine in the world at the age of thirty-five.

10   From the time he took over the editorial reins of *Parade* in 1980, until he was inducted into the Alger Society with me, circulation of his

Walter Anderson, editor of *Parade* magazine and member of the Horatio Alger Association of Distinguished Americans.
(Photo, Aaron Rapoport/Courtesy Parade Publications)

magazine had risen from 21 million copies in 129 Sunday newspapers to more than 37 million copies in 353 papers.

11   During the course of his journalistic success, Walter met and interviewed a lot of famous people from whom he learned some valuable lessons. "I thought for the longest time that I was the only human being who worried that others would find out that I was inferior, that I was vulnerable, that I deserved to be rejected. I now know that all sane human beings worry that others will find out that they are not quite good enough, that they can be hurt, that maybe they don't belong."

12   So, from his own life and from what he has learned from talking to some of the most successful people in our society, Walter has compiled his Seven Rules to Live By. I think they make a pretty good prescription for curing the victim mentality.

13   Here are Walter's seven rules:

- *Know who is responsible.* "I am responsible." When you begin with these three words, you can build a new life, even a new world.
- *Believe in something big.* When we commit to high ideals, we succeed before the outcome is known. Your life is worth a noble motive.
- *Practice tolerance.* You'll like yourself a lot more and so will others.
- *Be brave.* Remember, courage is acting with fear, not without it. If the challenge is important to you, you're supposed to be nervous; we worry only about things we care about.
- *Love someone.* Because you should know joy.
- *Be ambitious.* No single effort will solve all of your problems, achieve all of your dreams, or even be enough—and that's okay. To want to be more than we are is real and normal and healthy.
- *Smile.* Because no one else can do this for you.

Source: Ben Carson with Gregg Lewis, *The Big Picture,* Zondervan Publishing House, Grand Rapids, Michigan, 1999, pp. 202–204.

SELECTION **1-2**

Nonfiction

Comprehension Quiz

Directions: For each comprehension question below, use information from the selection to determine the correct answer. You may refer to the selection as you answer the questions. Write your answer in the space provided.

True or False

___F___ **1.** As a boy Walter Anderson went to a four-room railroad flat to escape his abusive father and cruel classmates.

___F___ **2.** Walter Anderson's mother encouraged him to join the Marines.

___T___ **3.** One of the jobs Walter Anderson had after leaving the military was working as a laboratory assistant.

___F___ **4.** Walter Anderson obtained his position with the *Reporter Dispatch* by offering to work for only $90 a week.

Multiple-Choice

___B___ **5.** The first publication for which Walter Anderson worked was
  a. the *Reporter Dispatch.*
  b. the *Mt. Vernon Daily Argus.*
  c. the student newspaper at the community college he attended.
  d. *Parade* magazine.

___D___ **6.** Walter Anderson joined the Marines
  a. in 1965.
  b. as soon as he graduated from community college.
  c. when he completed Mercy College.
  d. when he was barely 17 years old.

___A___ **7.** It is Walter Anderson's belief that we all
  a. have doubts about whether others perceive us as being good enough.
  b. can learn to write well.
  c. should develop a set of rules to live by.
  d. ought to read the newspaper daily.

___B___ **8.** Mercy College is located in which city in New York?
  a. Mt. Vernon
  b. White Plains
  c. New Rochelle
  d. Alger

_____C_____   **9.** As a college student, Walter Anderson made
          a.   low grades.
          b.   average grades.
          c.   high grades.
          d.   high grades only in reading and writing.

_____D_____   **10.** Since Walter Anderson became editor of *Parade,* the magazine's circulation has
          a.   decreased only slightly.
          b.   increased slightly.
          c.   nearly doubled.
          d.   tripled.

S E L E C T I O N **1-2**

Nonfiction

Extend Your Vocabulary by Using Context Clues

Directions: Context clues are words in a sentence that allow the reader to deduce (reason out) the meaning of an unfamiliar word in that sentence. For each vocabulary item below, a sentence from the selection containing an important word (*italicized, like this*) is quoted first. Next, there is an additional sentence using the word in the same sense and providing another context clue. Use the context clues from *both* sentences to deduce the meaning of the italicized word. *Be sure the answer you choose makes sense in both sentences.* If you discover that you must use a dictionary to confirm an answer choice, remember that the meaning you select must still fit the context of *both* sentences. To indicate your answer, write the letter in the space provided.

Pronunciation key: ă **pat**   ā **pay**   âr **care**   ä **father**   ĕ **pet**   ē **be**   ĭ **pit**
ī **tie**   îr **pier**   ŏ **pot**   ō **toe**   ô **paw**   oi **noise**   ou **out**   ŏŏ **took**   ōō **boot**
ŭ **cut**   yōō **abuse**   ûr **urge**   th **thin**   *th* **this**   hw **which**   zh **vision**
ə **about**
Stress mark: ′

1. Walter grew up in a four-room railroad flat on the wrong side of the tracks in Mt. Vernon, New York, in an atmosphere made *volatile* and violent by an illiterate, abusive, alcoholic father.

The secretary tried not to upset her boss when a deadline was near: his temper became *volatile* when he was under stress, and the smallest thing could send him into a rage.

volatile (vŏl ′ ə tĭl)
    a.   disgusting
    b.   stable
    c.   stressed
    d.   explosive

2. His mom always tried to *shield* him from his father's abuse.

As the movie star made her way from the courthouse to her limousine, her attorney tried to *shield* her from the throng of photographers and reporters.

shield (shēld)
   a. to keep safe from
   b. to distract
   c. to disguise
   d. to scold

3. The Mt. Vernon Public Library became a secret *sanctuary* where Walter regularly escaped the abuse of his father and the cruel ridicule of classmates who laughed at the holes in his ragged clothes.

To escape the hailstorm, the hikers sought *sanctuary* in a cave.

sanctuary (săngk ′ chōō ĕr ē)
   a. a sacred place
   b. a place that provides protection
   c. a place that provides quiet and solitude
   d. a comfortable place

4. I was able to develop self-respect, self-esteem, and a belief in *noble* motives and *noble* purposes.

Mother Teresa will be forever remembered for her lifetime of compassionate and *noble* service to the poorest people of India.

noble (nō′ bəl)
   a. belonging to a high social class
   b. eternal
   c. imitated by many people
   d. reflecting a high moral level

5. After reading Walter's one-clipping *portfolio* (his hometown paper, the *Mt. Vernon Daily Argus,* had printed his letter on page one under the title "Just What Is Vietnam?"), the editor of the *Reporter Dispatch* in White Plains, New York, hired him for $90 a week.

When Kim applied to the Art Institute, she had to submit an extensive *portfolio* of her drawings to the admissions committee.

portfolio (pôrt fō ′ lē ō)
   a. a folder designed to hold loose papers
   b. a collection of materials that are representative of a person's work
   c. a leather briefcase
   d. a person's award-winning work

_____A_____   **6.** By that time he was "night editor" of his paper and had started his own action-line column, which was *syndicated* in seven other newspapers.

For decades the highly popular cartoon strip "Peanuts" has been *syndicated* in thousands of newspapers around the world.

syndicated   (sĭn ′ dĭ kā təd)

a.   sold for publication in a number of newspapers simultaneously

b.   divided equally among

c.   published weekly in the newspaper

d.   sold to the highest bidder

_____D_____   **7.** He served as managing editor there before being promoted to editor of the largest-*circulation* Sunday magazine in the world at the age of thirty-five.

The newspaper offered one-month trial subscriptions at special rates in order to increase its *circulation.*

circulation (sûr kyə lā ′ shən)

a.   having a large number of pages

b.   distribution free of charge

c.   the number of copies of a publication sold or distributed

d.   movement in a circle or circuit

_____A_____   **8.** From the time he took over the editorial reins of *Parade* in 1980, until he was *inducted* into the Alger Society with me, circulation of his magazine had risen from 21 million copies in 129 Sunday newspapers to more than 37 million copies in 353 papers.

At a special ceremony last spring, 47 outstanding students were *inducted* into the college's Honor Society.

inducted   (ĭn dŭkt ′ əd)

a.   formally admitted as a member

b.   honored with a certificate

c.   cheered by observers

d.   administered an oath of office

_____C_____   **9.** I thought for the longest time that I was the only human being who worried that others would find out that I was inferior, that I was *vulnerable,* that I deserved to be rejected.

Small sailboats are more *vulnerable* to large ocean waves than heavier boats are.

vulnerable   (vŭl ′ nər ə bəl)

a.   likely to give in to temptation

b.   resistant

c.   open to attack

d.   well-suited for a task

_____D_____ **10.** So, from his own life and from what he has learned from talking to some of the most successful people in our society, Walter has *compiled* his Seven Rules to Live By.

After my aunt gathered hundreds of documents and photographs, she *compiled* a family history for us.

compiled (kəm pīld ′)
a. collected in a single book
b. edited carefully
c. wrote a complete history of
d. put together material gathered from several sources

SELECTION **1-2**

Nonfiction

Collaboration Option

Respond in Writing

Directions: Refer to the selection as needed to answer the essay-type questions below.

Option for collaboration: Your instructor may direct you to work with other students—in other words, to work *collaboratively*. In that case, you should form groups of three or four students as directed by your instructor and work together to complete the exercises. After your group discusses each item and agrees on the answer, have a group member record it. Every member of your group should be able to explain all of your group's answers.

1. What experiences in his childhood and young adult life does Walter Anderson view as influences that shaped his life?

_____

_____

_____

_____

2. Walter Anderson's gives Seven Rules to Live By. Choose two that you are not following now. Think about how they could be helpful to you if you followed them consistently. Explain which two you chose and how you think they could benefit you.

_____

_____

_____

_____

3. Although we might not be consciously aware of it, all of us have values (good and bad) that guide our decisions and our behavior. In effect, we have "rules" that we live by. What are at least two of your own rules that

you try to live by? (Choose rules that are different from those Walter Anderson gives.)

_____

_____

_____

_____

4. The title of this selection is "Hero on Parade." (Did you notice that this title is especially clever, since Walter Anderson is the editor of *Parade Magazine?*) In what way is Walter Anderson a "hero"?

_____

_____

_____

_____

5. Overall main idea. What is the overall main idea the author wants you to understand about Walter Anderson and his story? Answer this question in one sentence.

_____

_____

_____

_____

Read More about It on the World Wide Web

To learn more about the topic of this selection, visit these websites or use your favorite search engine (such as Yahoo ®) to discover more about this topic on your own. Whenever you go to *any* website, it is a good idea to evaluate it critically. Are you getting good information—information that is accurate, complete, and up-to-date? Who sponsors the website? How easy is it to use the features of the website?

http://www.ihot.com/~has/
> *This is the Horatio Alger Society website. It contains links for all kinds of information about the HAS.*

http://www.parade.com/
> *This is* Parade Magazine's *Reader Response Center. While you're here, you can respond to a* Parade *article or test yourself with the e-Marilyn Brain Teaser.*

http://carsonscholars.org
This website contains information about Ben Carson and the Carson Scholar Fund.

http://amazon.com
(Type in the book title, The Big Picture, *and then click on the word "Go.") This on-line bookstore website sells* The Big Picture *and other books by Ben Carson. Also included are editorial and customer reviews, and recommendations of books on related subjects.*

SAVED

From *The Autobiography of Malcolm X*
As Told to Alex Haley

Prepare Yourself to Read

Directions: Do these exercises *before* you read Selection 1-3

1. First, read and think about the title. What do you already know about Malcolm X?

   _____

   _____

2. Next, complete your preview by reading the following:

   Introduction (in *italics*)
   First paragraph (paragraph 1)
   All of the last paragraph (paragraph 19)

   On the basis of your preview, what aspect of Malcolm X's life do you think will be discussed?

   _____

   _____

Apply Comprehension Skills

Directions: Do these exercises as you read Selection 1-3. Apply two skills from this chapter:

Set your goal for reading. What do you hope to learn about Malcolm X?

_____

_____

Plan your time. Estimate how long it will take you to read Selection 1-3.

_____

_____

SAVED

Born Malcolm Little in 1925, Malcolm X was a member of the American Black Muslims (1952–1963), an organization that advocated separatism and black pride. Before Malcolm X became a prominent Black Muslim and political leader, he served time in prison.

In this selection, Malcolm X describes a life-changing experience he had while he was in prison. His desire to write letters to Elijah Muhammad during this time motivated Malcolm X to make this profound change in his life. (Elijah Muhammad was an activist and leader of the Black Muslims in this country from 1934 to 1975; he favored political and social equality, as well as economic independence for black Americans.)

Malcolm X eventually separated from the Black Muslims and converted to orthodox Islam, a religion which believes in the unity of the human race. He founded the Organization of Afro-American Unity in 1964. In 1965, Malcolm X was assassinated in Harlem as he was about to give a speech.

In 1992 Warner Studios produced the film Malcolm X, *directed by Spike Lee and starring Denzel Washington. And in 1995 A&E Network produced a documentary on Malcolm X for its "Biography" series. In 1999 the United States Postal Service issued a stamp in honor of Malcolm X (El-Hajj Malik El-Shabazz).*

---

1 It was because of my letters that I happened to stumble upon starting to acquire some kind of a homemade education.

2 I became increasingly frustrated at not being able to express what I wanted to convey in letters that I wrote, especially those to Mr. Elijah Muhammad. In the street, I had been the most articulate hustler out there—I had commanded attention when I said something. But now, trying to write simple English, I not only wasn't articulate, I wasn't even functional. How would I sound writing in slang, the way I would say it, something such as, "Look, daddy, let me pull your coat about a cat, Elijah Muhammad—"

3 Many who today hear me somewhere in person, or on television, or those who read something I've said, will think I went to school far beyond the eighth grade. This impression is due entirely to my prison studies.

4 It had really begun back in the Charlestown Prison, when Bimbi first made me feel envy of his stock of knowledge. Bimbi had always taken charge of any conversation he was in, and I had tried to emulate him. But every book I picked up had few sentences which didn't contain anywhere from one to nearly all of the words that might as well have been in Chinese. When I just skipped those words, of course, I really ended up with little idea of what the book said. So I had come to the Norfolk Prison Colony still going

through only book-reading motions. Pretty soon, I would have quit even these motions, unless I had received the motivation that I did.

5   I saw that the best thing I could do was get hold of a dictionary—to study, to learn some words. I was lucky enough to reason also that I should try to improve my penmanship. It was sad. I couldn't even write in a straight line. It was both ideas together that moved me to request a dictionary along with some tablets and pencils from the Norfolk Prison Colony school.

6   I spent two days just riffling uncertainly through the dictionary's pages. I'd never realized so many words existed! I didn't know which words I needed to learn. Finally, just to start some kind of action, I began copying.

7   In my slow, painstaking, ragged handwriting, I copied into my tablet everything printed on that first page, down to the punctuation marks.

8   I believe it took me a day. Then, aloud, I read back, to myself, everything I'd written on the tablet. Over and over, aloud, to myself, I read my own handwriting.

9   I woke up the next morning, thinking about those words—immensely proud to realize that not only had I written so much at one time, but I'd written words that I never knew were in the world. Moreover, with a little effort, I also could remember what many of these words meant. I reviewed the words whose meanings I didn't remember. Funny thing, from the dictionary first page right now, that "aardvark" springs to my mind. The dictionary had a picture of it, a long-tailed, long-eared, burrowing African mammal, which lives off termites caught by sticking out its tongue as an anteater does for ants.

10   I was so fascinated that I went on—I copied the dictionary's next page. And the same experience came when I studied that. With every succeeding page, I also learned of people and places and events from history. Actually the dictionary is like a miniature encyclopedia. Finally the dictionary's A section had filled a whole tablet—and I went on into the B's. That was the way I started copying what eventually became the entire dictionary. It went a lot faster after so much practice helped me to pick up handwriting speed. Between what I wrote in my tablet, and writing letters, during the rest of my time in prison I would guess I wrote a million words.

Malcolm X. 1925–1965
(Hulton Getty/Liaison Agency)

11   I suppose it was inevitable that as my word-base broadened, I could for the first time pick up a book and read and now begin to understand what the book was saying. Anyone who has read a great deal can imagine the new world that opened. Let me tell you something: from then until I left that prison, in every free moment I had, if I was not reading in the library, I was reading on my bunk. You couldn't have gotten me out of books with a wedge. Between Mr. Muhammad's teachings, my correspondence, my visitors—usually Ella and Reginald—and my reading of books, months passed without my even thinking about being imprisoned. In fact, up to then, I never had been so truly free in my life.

12   The Norfolk Prison Colony's library was in the school building. A variety of classes was taught there by instructors who came from such places as Harvard and Boston universities. The weekly debates between inmate teams were also held in the school building. You would be astonished to know how worked up convict debaters and audiences would get over subjects like "Should Babies Be Fed Milk?"

13   Available on the prison library's shelves were books on just about every general subject. Much of the big private collection that Parkhurst had willed to the prison was still in crates and boxes in the back of the library—thousands of old books. Some of them looked ancient: covers faded, old-time parchment-looking binding. Parkhurst, I've mentioned, seemed to have been principally interested in history and religion. He had the money and the special interest to have a lot of books that you wouldn't have in general circulation. Any college library would have been lucky to get that collection.

14   As you can imagine, especially in a prison where there was heavy emphasis on rehabilitation, an inmate was smiled upon if he demonstrated an unusually intense interest in books. There was a sizable number of well-read inmates, especially the popular debaters. Some were said by many to be practically walking encyclopedias. They were almost celebrities. No university would ask any student to devour literature as I did when this new world opened to me, of being able to read and *understand*.

15   I read more in my room than in the library it-self. An inmate who was known to read a lot could check out more than the permitted maximum number of books. I preferred reading in the total isolation of my own room.

16   When I had progressed to really serious reading, every night at about ten P.M. I would be outraged with the "lights out." It always seemed to catch me right in the middle of something engrossing.

17   Fortunately, right outside my door was a cor-ridor light that cast a glow into my room. The glow was enough to read by, once my eyes ad-justed to it. So when "lights out" came, I would sit on the floor where I could continue reading in that glow.

18   At one-hour intervals the night guards paced past every room. Each time I heard the ap-proaching footsteps, I jumped into bed and feigned sleep. And as soon as the guard passed, I got back out of bed onto the floor area of that light-glow, where I would read for another fifty-eight minutes—until the guard approached again. That went on until three or four every morning. Three or four hours of sleep a night was enough for me. Often in the years in the streets I had slept less than that. . . .

19   I have often reflected upon the new vistas that reading opened to me. I knew right there in prison that reading had changed forever the course of my life. As I see it today, the ability to read awoke inside me some long dormant crav-ing to be mentally alive. I certainly wasn't seeking any degree, the way a college confers a status symbol upon its students. My homemade educa-tion gave me, with every additional book that I read, a little bit more sensitivity to the deafness, dumbness, and blindness that was afflicting the black race in America. Not long ago, an English writer telephoned me from London, asking ques-tions. One was, "What's your alma mater?" I told him, "Books." You will never catch me with a free fifteen minutes in which I'm not studying some-thing I feel might be able to help the black man.

Source: "Saved," from *The Autobiography of Malcolm X* with the assistance of Alex Haley, Ballantine, New York, 1992, pp. 171–174, 179. Copyright © 1964 by Alex Haley and Malcolm X and © 1965 by Alex Haley and Betty Shabazz. Reprinted by per-mission of Random House, Inc.

SELECTION **1-3**

Literature

Comprehension Quiz

Directions: For each comprehension question below, use information from the selection to determine the correct answer. You may refer to the selection as you answer the questions. Write your answer in the space provided.

True or False

_____ 1. There were a small number of well-read inmates at the prison in which Malcolm X served time.

_____ 2. Despite Malcolm's initially limited ability to read and write, he was a person capable of learning.

_____ 3. Norfolk Prison Colony liked prisoners to exhibit an interest in rehabilitating themselves.

_____ 4. Malcolm's prison experience provided him with no opportunity to improve his reading or writing skills.

Multiple-Choice

_____ 5. What did Malcolm X mean when he said, "In fact, up to then, I had never been so truly free in my life"?
  a. He had been freed from prison.
  b. He was able to explore a "new world" of books and ideas even though he was in prison.
  c. He could devote as much time as he wanted to learning.
  d. He felt carefree.

_____ 6. According to Malcolm X, he felt a need to begin to acquire more education because of
  a. his inability to express himself well in conversation.
  b. his desire to write letters and his envy of Bimbi.
  c. the influence of Parkhurst.
  d. the encouragement of a certain prison guard.

_____ 7. Prison inmates who were outstanding debaters were
  a. looked down on by other inmates.
  b. regarded almost as celebrities by other inmates.
  c. ignored by other inmates.
  d. disliked.

_____ **8.** The Norfolk Prison Colony was exemplary because of

   a. its strong emphasis on rehabilitation.

   b. its unusually large library.

   c. the quality of instructors in the prison school.

   d. all of the above.

_____ **9.** Parkhurst was

   a. the prison warden.

   b. a teacher who taught at the prison.

   c. the donor of the library books.

   d. Malcolm's cellmate.

_____ **10.** The dictionary was the book that opened the door of learning for Malcolm X; he used it

   a. as a miniature encyclopedia, which provided background knowledge about a variety of subjects.

   b. to improve his penmanship by copying its pages.

   c. to improve and expand his vocabulary.

   d. all of the above.

SELECTION **1-3**
Literature

Extend Your Vocabulary by Using Context Clues

Directions: Context clues are words in a sentence that allow the reader to deduce (reason out) the meaning of an unfamiliar word in that sentence. For each vocabulary item below, a sentence from the selection containing an important word (*italicized, like this*) is quoted first. Next, there is an additional sentence using the word in the same sense and providing another context clue. Use the context clues from *both sentences* to deduce the meaning of the italicized word. *Be sure the answer you choose makes sense in both sentences.* If you discover that you must use a dictionary to confirm an answer choice, remember that the meaning you select must still fit the context of both sentences. To indicate your answer, write the letter in the space provided.

Pronunciation key: ă pat ā pay âr care ä father ě pet ē be ĭ pit
ī tie îr pier ŏ pot ō toe ô paw oi noise ou out ŏŏ took ōō boot
ŭ cut yōō abuse ûr urge th thin *th* this hw which zh vision
ə about
Stress mark: ′

——————— **1.** I had become increasingly frustrated at not being able to express what I wanted to *convey* in letters that I wrote, especially those to Mr. Elijah Muhammad.

I am sorry that I was unable to attend your uncle's funeral; please *convey* my sympathy to your aunt.

convey   (kən vā′) means:
a.   remember
b.   achieve
c.   write
d.   communicate

——————— **2.** In the street, I had been the most *articulate* hustler out there—I had commanded attention when I said something.

Because former Prime Minister Winston Churchill was so *articulate,* his speeches are considered some of the finest ever given.

articulate   (är tĭk′ yə lət) means:
a.   using clear, expressive language
b.   liking to talk
c.   talking extensively
d.   talking rapidly

——————— **3.** Bimbi had always taken charge of any conversation he was in, and I had tried to *emulate* him.

Parents should be good role models, since children often *emulate* them.

emulate   (ĕm′ yə lāt) means:
a.   surpass by diligent effort
b.   try to equal or excel, especially through imitation
c.   reject
d.   ridicule or make fun of

——————— **4.** In my slow, *painstaking,* ragged handwriting, I copied into my tablet everything printed on that first page, down to the punctuation marks.

Rebuilding and restoring antique furniture is a *painstaking* process.

painstaking (pānz′ tā kĭng) means:
a.   involving great speed and dexterity
b.   involving significant physical pain
c.   involving considerable boredom
d.   involving great effort or care

_____ **5.** With every *succeeding* page, I also learned of people and places and events from history.

In the years *succeeding* his presidency, Jimmy Carter worked on his memoirs.

succeeding   (sək sēd′ ĭng) means:
a.   coming next or after
b.   coming before
c.   inserted or inserted in
d.   preceding

_____ **6.** I suppose it was *inevitable* that as my word-base broadened, I could for the first time pick up a book and read and now begin to understand what the book was saying.

It is *inevitable* that summer follows spring.

inevitable   (ĭn ĕv′ ĭ tə bəl) means:
a.   likely to happen
b.   uncertain
c.   incapable of being prevented or avoided
d.   unreasonable

_____ **7.** Much of the big private collection that Parkhurst had *willed* to the prison was still in crates and boxes in the back of the library—thousands of old books.

Since my grandmother is no longer alive, I treasure the piano she *willed* to me, and I play it often.

willed   (wĭld) means:
a.   kept in storage
b.   taken back
c.   received as a gift
d.   granted in a legal will; bequeathed

_____ **8.** As you can imagine, especially in a prison where there was heavy emphasis on *rehabilitation,* an inmate was smiled upon if he demonstrated an unusually intense interest in books.

It took three months of *rehabilitation* for the actor to recover fully from his drug and alcohol addiction.

rehabilitation (rē hĭ bĭl ĭ tā′ shən) means:
a.   regaining useful life through education or therapy
b.   hard physical labor
c.   rest and relaxation
d.   cooperation

_____ **9.** Fortunately, right outside my door was the *corridor* light that cast a glow in the room.

When the fire alarm sounded, students quickly left their classrooms and walked down the *corridor* to the exit.

corridor (kôr′ ĭ dər) means:

a. door that leads to an exit

b. large room

c. passageway with rooms opening into it

d. an open area outside a building

_____ **10.** Each time I heard the approaching footsteps, I jumped into bed and *feigned* sleep.

Have you ever *feigned* illness so that you wouldn't have to go to work?

feigned (fānd) means:

a. endured

b. experienced

c. pretended; gave a false appearance of

d. suffered or felt pain

SELECTION **1-3**

Literature

Respond in Writing

Collaboration Option

Directions: Refer to the selection as needed to answer the essay-type questions below.

Option for collaboration: Your instructor may direct you to work with other students—in other words, to work *collaboratively.* In that case, you should form groups of three or four students as directed by your instructor and work together to complete the exercises. After your group discusses each item and agrees on the answer, have a group member record it. Every member of your group should be able to explain all of your group's answers.

1. List at least three surprising or interesting facts you learned about Malcolm X.

_____

_____

_____

_____

_____

_____

_____

_____

_____

_____

2. Although Malcolm X may not have realized it, he used many of the same study and learning techniques that effective college students use. What were some of them?

_____

_____

_____

_____

_____

_____

_____

_____

3. Today there are nearly 2 million people in prison in the U.S.—one out of every 147 people. Malcolm X used his time in prison to change his life. What, in your opinion, can be done to help those in prison benefit from it?

_____

_____

_____

_____

_____

_____

_____

_____

_____

_____

4. What are at least three ways in which Malcolm X's prison experience may have "saved" him while he was in prison and after he was released?

_____

_____

_____

_____

_____

_____

_____

_____

5. Overall main idea. What is the overall main idea the author wants the reader to understand about Malcolm X's experience in prison? Answer this question in one sentence.

_____

_____

_____

_____

_____

Read More about It on the World Wide Web

To learn more about the topic of this selection, visit these websites or use your favorite search engine (such as Yahoo ®) to discover more about this topic on your own. Whenever you go to *any* website, it is a good idea to evaluate it critically. Are you getting good information—information that is accurate, complete, and up-to-date? Who sponsors the website? How easy is it to use the features of the website?

http://www.wabash.edu/orgs/mxi/el-links.htm
> *This site contains numerous links containing information about Malcolm X. The site is sponsored by the Malcolm X Institute of Black Studies at Wabash College.*

http://www.brothermalcolm.net/
> *This site contains general information about Malcolm X and is sponsored by the Africana Studies Program of the University of Toledo.*

http://www.unn.ac.uk/societies/islamic
> *The goals of this site are to provide accurate information about Islamic beliefs and Islamic history and civilization for Muslims and non-Muslims.*

http://www.refdesk.com
> *Click on site map, then choose World Religions under the Facts Subject Index.*

© PhotoDisc

C H A P T E R

Approaching College Reading and Developing a College-Level Vocabulary

In this chapter you will learn the answers to these questions:

- What do I need to know about the reading process?

- How can I improve my reading?

- Why should I make predictions as I read?

- How can I monitor my comprehension while I read?

- What do I need to know about adjusting my reading rate?

- How can I develop a college-level vocabulary?

- What are denotations and connotations?

- What is figurative language?

SKILLS

Understanding the Reading Process

Improving Your Reading

- Predicting as You Read

- Monitoring Your Comprehension

- Adjusting Your Reading Rate

Developing a College-Level Vocabulary

- Using Context Clues

- Using Word-Structure Clues

- Using a Dictionary Pronunciation Key

- Understanding Denotations and Connotations of Words

- Understanding Figurative Language

CREATING YOUR SUMMARY

Developing Chapter Review Cards

READINGS

To read without reflecting is like eating without digesting.

Edmund Burke

We read books to find out who we are. What other people, real or imaginary, do and think and feel is an essential guide to our understanding of what we ourselves are and may become.

Ursula K. LeGuin

UNDERSTANDING THE READING PROCESS

Understanding the reading process can make you a better reader and help you study more effectively. You should be aware of several important points about reading.

1. **Reading is a form of thinking.**   It is your brain that does the reading, not your eyes. Your eyes merely transmit images to the brain for it to interpret. (To understand this, consider a blind person reading Braille: in this case, it is the fingertips that transmit images to the brain.) Therefore, improving your reading means improving your thinking. Remember that meaning resides in the reader's mind, not in symbols printed on a page. It is the readers who construct meaning by associating their knowledge and experience with what is on the printed page.

2. **Reading requires no unique mental or physical abilities.**   The processes you typically use when you read are the same processes of vision, reasoning, and memory that you use in other areas of your daily life.

3. **The reading process includes three stages.**   The three stages of reading are *preparing yourself to read, processing information,* and *reacting to what you read.* These stages overlap, but all three are needed for the reading process to be complete. In Chapter 3, this process will be explained as it applies to college reading.

4. **Effective reading is active and interactive.**   Effective reading requires that you interact with the material you are reading. One way to interact with an author's ideas is to mentally ask yourself questions as you read and then seek answers to these questions. Another way to interact with material you are reading is by relating your own experience and knowledge to the author's ideas. Reading actively also means being aware of how the material is organized. Finally, active reading means that you *monitor your comprehension* as you read, and that you take steps to correct the situation when you are not comprehending. (Monitoring your comprehension will be discussed later in this chapter.)

Developing strong reading
and vocabulary skills will
make you more successful in
college.
(Philip Gould/Corbis)

5. **Comprehension problems often result from a reader's lack of back-ground knowledge.**   Many comprehension problems are not strictly read-ing comprehension problems but instead are more general comprehension problems that occur when the reader lacks sufficient background knowl-edge. To put it another way, comprehension problems occur when a reader does not possess enough information about a subject to understand what an author is saying about it. This means that if you are having difficulty under-standing new or unfamiliar material, you may need to increase your back-ground knowledge. (For example, you could read a simplified explanation in an encyclopedia first.) Finding out more about an unfamiliar topic can often clear up this kind of problem.

6. **Your reading rate and your comprehension are related.**   The more you know about a topic and the better you understand the material, the faster you can read it. Conversely, if you know very little about a topic, you should reduce your reading rate.

7. **Your reading strategies should fit your purpose for reading.**   You read for many different purposes, and your reason for reading any particular ma-terial affects the way you approach it. (For example, your approach to read-ing a newspaper article or a letter from a friend will be different from your approach to reading and studying a college textbook.) You should choose reading strategies that fit your purpose.

   With these things in mind, let's look at general ways you can improve your reading and your reading rate.

IMPROVING YOUR READING

Predicting as You Read

KEY TERM
Predicting

Anticipating what is coming
next as you read.

Predicting means making educated guesses about what is coming next as you read. Predicting is often a natural part of reading, but you may not always do it when you are reading college textbooks. As you read an assignment, you should make a conscious effort to anticipate not only what is coming next, but also the author's writing pattern. (Chapter 7 examines authors' writing patterns.)

Of course, when you preview a chapter or reading selection you are predicting in a general way what it will be about and how the material is organized. However, when you actually read and study it carefully, you should continue to make predictions as you read. For example, if an author presents one side of an issue, you might predict that he or she is going to discuss the other side as well. If a paragraph in a psychology textbook begins with the question "Why do people have nightmares?" you would expect the author to explain the reason or reasons.

Predicting helps you concentrate and comprehend; it focuses your attention because it makes you want to keep reading to see if your prediction is correct. In other words, predicting helps you stay involved with the material you are reading.

Instead of passively waiting to see what comes up next when you are reading, try to anticipate what the author will say or present. You will discover that making predictions helps you become a more active, effective reader.

Monitoring Your Comprehension

KEY TERM
Monitoring Your
Comprehension

Evaluating your
understanding as you read
and correcting the problem
whenever you realize that you
are not comprehending.

Monitoring your comprehension means evaluating your understanding as you read and correcting the problem whenever you realize that you are not comprehending. You should monitor your comprehension whenever you read and study college textbooks.

To monitor your comprehension, follow this procedure:

- First, ask yourself, "*Am I understanding what I am reading?*"
- If you do not understand what you are reading, ask yourself, "*Why* don't I understand?"
- Once you determine why you are not comprehending, do whatever is necessary to correct the situation.

Specific types of comprehension problems and strategies for correcting them are listed in the box on page 74. Make monitoring your comprehension a habit. After all, unless you comprehend what you are reading, you are not really reading.

STRATEGIES FOR CORRECTING CERTAIN COMPREHENSION PROBLEMS

Problems	Solutions
I am not understanding because the subject is completely new to me. College reading frequently introduces you to subjects you have not learned about before. Textbooks contain a great deal of new information, sometimes even within a single paragraph.	• Keep reading to see if the material becomes clearer. • Ask for a brief explanation from someone who is knowledgeable about the topic. • Read supplemental material or simpler material on the same topic (perhaps an encyclopedia, another textbook, or a book from the library).
I am not understanding because there are words I do not know. College material often contains new words and specialized or technical vocabulary that you must learn.	• Try to use the context (the rest of the sentence or paragraph) to figure out the meaning of an unfamiliar word. • Look up unfamiliar words in a dictionary or in the glossary at the back of the textbook. • Ask someone the meaning of unfamiliar words.
I am not understanding because I am not concentrating as I read. Distractors are interfering with my concentration. Your mind may sometimes wander while you are reading long or difficult passages.	• Identify what is bothering you. Is it a *physical distraction* (such as a noisy room or being tired), or is it a *psychological distraction* (such as being worried or daydreaming)? • Take some action that will help you eliminate the distraction. For example, close the door or move to a quiet room. • Turn off the television. Turn off the music. Don't answer the telephone. • If you are worrying about a personal problem or worrying about finding time for important errands, write it down (for example, jot the items down on a To Do list). Then, after studying, tackle your To Do list. The point is to take some action toward solving problems that are distracting you. • Make a deliberate decision to concentrate on what you are reading. Concentration does not happen automatically.

Adjusting Your Reading Rate

Have you ever been asked, "What's your reading rate?" The fact is that each reader has, or should have, *several* reading rates. Reading everything at the same rate is a sign of poor reading. (Reading at any rate without comprehending is a sign of poor reading, even if the rate is a fast one.)

Having flexible reading rates is an important skill. You will find it helpful to begin developing flexibility in your reading rates right away. To become a more flexible reader, you may find it useful to think of developing a "collection" of reading speeds. The information below provides a brief introduction to adjusting your reading rate. A range of reading rates and when to use each are presented in the box below.

Factors Influencing Reading Rate: Purpose and Difficulty

In order to be a flexible, efficient reader you should adjust your reading rate according to two factors: their *purpose* for reading, and *how difficult* the material is for you.

Obviously, you read for many different purposes. For instance, your purpose in reading a textbook may be to understand and learn the material thoroughly for a test. Or there may be some specific bit of information you are searching for, such as the definition of a term in a textbook, a name in an index, or the starting time of a movie in a newspaper listing. Sometimes, of course, you read a magazine or a book just for pleasure.

What determines how difficult certain material will be for you to read? Actually, there are several factors, such as its vocabulary level, writing style, and "idea density." However, the most important factor is *how much you already know about the subject*. If you are reading about computers, for instance, and you already know a great deal about them, then you will easily understand the terms and concepts you encounter. The information will make more sense to you than it would to someone who knows nothing about computers.

FLEXIBLE READING: INFORMATION-GATHERING TECHNIQUES AND READING RATES

	Approximate rate (wpm)	Uses
Information-gathering techniques:		
Scanning	1,500 words per minute (wpm) or more	To find a particular piece of information (such as a name, date, or phone number)
Skimming	800–1,000 wpm	To get an overview of the highlights of the material
Reading rates:		
Rapid reading	300–500 wpm	For fairly easy material; when you want only important facts or ideas; for leisure reading

(Continued on next page)

(Continued from previous page)

	Approximate rate (wpm)	Uses
Reading rates:		
Average reading	200-300 wpm	For textbooks, complex magazines and journals, and literature
Study reading	50-200 wpm	For new vocabulary, complex concepts, technical material, and retaining details (such as legal documents, material to be memorized and material of great interest or importance)

When you are assigned to read a textbook chapter, you should look through it first. Ask yourself why you are reading it and how much you already know about the subject. If the material is new to you, then you will need to read more slowly. If you are very familiar with the subject, you can probably read at a faster rate. The point is to read flexibly, adjusting your rate as needed.

Often, you must continue to adjust your rate as you are reading. How can you tell when you should slow down and when you should speed up? The following lists describe situations in which you should do each.

When to Slow Down

Here are some situations in which you should slow down your reading:

- You know very little about the topic, or it is entirely new to you.
- A passage consists of complicated or technical material that you need to learn.
- A passage has details you need to remember.
- A passage contains new or difficult vocabulary.
- There are directions that you must follow.
- The material is accompanied by charts or graphs to which you must shift your attention as you read.
- The material requires you to visualize something in your mind (a section on the digestive system in a biology text would be an example).
- The writing is beautiful, artistic, descriptive, or poetic and invites you to linger and enjoy each word. (You may want to read such material aloud to yourself.)
- The material contains ideas you want to consider carefully (such as two sides of an argument) or "words to live by" (such as philosophical, religious, or inspirational writing).

When to Speed Up

Here are some situations in which you can speed up your reading:

- The whole passage is easy; there are no complicated sentences, no complex ideas, and no difficult terms.
- There is an easy passage within a longer, more difficult section.
- A passage gives an example of something you already understand, or explains it in different words.
- You are already knowledgeable about the topic.
- You want only main ideas and are not concerned about details.
- The material is not related to your purpose for reading (for example, a section of a magazine article that does not pertain to the topic you are researching).

Here is a simple technique for increasing your reading rate on material:

1. Practice regularly with easy, interesting material, such as a newspaper, a magazine (like *Reader's Digest*), or a short, easy novel.
2. Read for 15 minutes each day, pushing yourself to read at a rate that is slightly too fast for you—in other words, a rate that is slightly uncomfortable. Once it becomes comfortable, push yourself a little more.
3. Monitor your concentration. If you are momentarily distracted, return immediately to your reading.
4. Keep track of the number of pages you read each day.

As you continue to practice, you will find that you are able to read more pages in the same amount of time. You will also find that you can usually understand the important points in a passage even though you are reading it at a faster rate. There is another bonus: as you read each day, you will be adding to your background knowledge. This will enable you to read related material more effectively in the future.

DEVELOPING A COLLEGE-LEVEL VOCABULARY

Developing a powerful vocabulary is a process that takes time; but every time you read, you have an opportunity to expand your vocabulary. The more you read, the better your vocabulary can become—*if* you develop a real interest in words and their meanings. Remember that writers take special care to select words that convey precisely what they want to say.

Developing a large vocabulary will make your college work easier, and your speech and your writing will become more interesting and more precise. If all that is not enough, your increased vocabulary may ultimately lead to an increased salary. Research tells us that the size of a person's vocabulary correlates with his or her income. Thinking of each word you learn as "money in the bank" may be an incentive for you to pay attention to new words and add them to your vocabulary!

There are three techniques that you can use to develop and expand your vocabulary as you read:

1. **Use context clues.**   This means that you figure out the meaning of an unfamiliar word from clues provided by the surrounding words and sentences.
2. **Use word-structure clues.**   That is, determine a word's meaning on the basis of its parts, (prefix, root, and suffix).
3. **Use a dictionary.**   Use a dictionary to determine a word's pronunciation and meaning as it is used in the passage you are reading.

The vocabulary exercises that follow each of the reading selections in *Opening Doors* will give you ongoing opportunities to use context clues and practice pronouncing words correctly.

Using Context Clues

Writers want you to understand what they have written. When they use words that they think might be unfamiliar to their readers, they often help the reader by offering various clues in the rest of the sentence so that the reader can deduce (reason out) the meaning of the word. Such clues are called **context clues.** (The word *context* refers to the sentence and the paragraph in which the unknown word appears.) Since context clues can help you figure out the meaning of an unfamiliar word, think of them as gifts the writer is giving you to make your job easier.

How can you take advantage of these "gifts"? You can do so by reading the sentence carefully and by paying attention to the words and other sentences surrounding the unfamiliar word. Some of the most common types of context clues are summarized in the box below.

KEY TERM
Context Clues

Words in a sentence or paragraph which help the reader deduce (reason out) the meaning of an unfamiliar word.

Comprehension Monitoring Question for Vocabulary in Context

Are there clues within the sentence or surrounding sentences that can help me deduce the meaning of an unfamiliar word?

USING CONTEXT CLUES TO DETERMINE THE MEANING OF UNFAMILIAR WORDS

Type of Clue	What to Ask Yourself	What to Look For	Example
Definition clue	Are there *definition clues* and a definition?	Phrases that introduce a definition, such as: *is defined as, is called, is, is known as, that is, refers to, means, the term;* a term that is in bold print, italics, or color; or certain punctuation marks that set off a definition or a term. (See page 353.)	*Interiority* is defined as a tendency toward looking within during middle age.

Type of Clue	What to Ask Yourself	What to Look For	Example
Synonym clue	Is there a *synonym* for the unfamiliar word? That is, is the meaning explained by a word or phrase that has a *similar meaning?* The synonym may be set off by commas, parentheses, a colon, dashes or brackets. (See page 353.)	Phrases that introduce synonyms, such as: *in other words, or, that is to say, also known as, by this we mean, that is.*	The garden was **redolent,** or *fragrant,* with the scent of roses.
Contrast clue	Is there an *antonym* for the unfamiliar word? That is, is the unfamiliar word explained by a contrasting word or phrase with the *opposite meaning?*	Words and phrases that indicate opposites: *instead of, but, in contrast, on the other hand, however, unlike, although, even though.*	I did the physical therapy exercises incorrectly and, *instead of* helping my back, they were actually **deleterious.**
Experience clue	Can you draw on your *experience and background knowledge* to help you deduce (reason out) the meaning of the unfamiliar word?	A sentence that includes *a familiar experience* (or information you already know) can help you figure out the meaning of the new word.	The campers *were warned that hiking up that steep mountain trail* would **enervate** even the fittest members of their group.
Example clue	Are there *examples* that illustrate the meaning of the unfamiliar word?	Words that introduce examples of the meaning of the unfamiliar word: *for example, such as, to illustrate, like.*	He enjoys **aquatic** sports *such as swimming, scuba diving,* and *water skiing.*
Clue from another sentence	Is there *another sentence* in the paragraph that explains the meaning of the unfamiliar word?	*Additional information in another sentence* that may help explain the unfamiliar word.	When studying for his final exams, the student was told to **eschew** television. *"Just give TV up!"* was his roommate's advice.

Using Word-Structure Clues

Although context clues will be your greatest aid in determining the meaning of unknown words, **word-structure clues** or *word-part clues* can also help you determine meanings. A list of important and useful word parts appears in Appendix 3.

To use word-structure clues, examine an unfamiliar word to see if it has any of the following word parts:

- **Root:** Base word that has a meaning of its own.
- **Prefix:** Word part attached to the beginning of a root that adds its meaning to the meaning of the root.
- **Suffix:** Word part attached to the end of a root word.

KEY TERM
Word-Structure Clue

Roots, prefixes, and suffixes that help you determine a word's meaning. Word structure clues are also known as *word part clues.*

Prefixes and suffixes are also called *affixes,* since they are "fixed" (attached or joined) to a root or base word. A word may consist of a:

Root only (such as *graph*)

Prefix and root (*tele* • *graph*)

Root and suffix (*graph* • *ic*)

Prefix, root, and suffix (*tele* • *graph* • *ic*)

Learning about prefixes and suffixes not only increases your vocabulary but can help you improve your spelling as well. For instance, if you know the meaning of the prefix *mis* ("bad" or "wrong"), then you will understand why the word *misspell* has two *s*'s: one is in the prefix *(mis)* and one in the root word *(spell).*

Roots are powerful vocabulary-building tools, since whole "families" of words in English often come from the same root. For example, if you know that the root *aud* means "to hear," then you will understand the connection between *audience* (people who come to *hear* something or someone), *auditorium* (a place where people come to *hear* something), *audit* (enrolling in a course just to *hear* about a subject, rather than taking it for credit), *auditory* (pertaining to *hearing,* as in auditory nerve), and *audiologist* (a person trained to evaluate *hearing*). Knowing the meaning of a word's root makes it easier to remember the meaning of the word.

Prefixes change the meaning of a root by adding their meaning to the meaning of the root. For example, adding the prefix *tele* ("distant" or "far") to the root word *scope* ("to see") creates the word *telescope,* a device that lets you *see* things which are *far* away. Try adding the prefixes *pre* ("before") and *re* ("back") to the root *cede* ("to go" or "to move"). *Precede* means "go before" something or someone else; *recede* means "move back."

Think of roots and prefixes as parts of a puzzle that can often help you figure out the meaning of an unfamiliar word. Remember, however, that although a word may begin with the same letters as a prefix, it does not necessarily contain that prefix. The words *malt, mall, male,* and *mallard* (a type of duck), for example, have no connection with the prefix *mal* ("wrong" or "bad").

Suffixes are word parts that are attached to the end of a root word. Some add their meaning to a root. Other suffixes change a word's part of speech or inflection. For example, consider these forms of the word *predict:* predic*tion,* predic*tability,* predic*tor* (nouns); predic*table* (adjective); predic*tably* (adverb). Examples of suffixes that serve as inflectional endings include adding *s* to make a word plural or *ed* to make a verb past tense.

Suffixes are not as helpful as roots or prefixes in determining the meaning of unfamiliar words because many suffixes have similar or even the same mean-

KEY TERM
Root

Base word that has a meaning of its own.

KEY TERM
Prefix

Word part attached to the beginning of a root word that adds its meaning to that of the base word.

KEY TERM
Suffix

Word part attached to the end of a root word.

Comprehension Monitoring Question for Word-Structure Clues

Are there roots, prefixes, or suffixes that give me clues to the meaning of an unfamiliar word?

ings. Also, some root words change their spelling before a suffix is added. For instance, when certain suffixes are added to *happy* the *y* becomes an *i: happier, happiness, happily.*

The most common and helpful roots, prefixes, and suffixes in English come from Latin and ancient Greek. These Latin and Greek word parts not only help you figure out the meaning of a word, but also serve as built-in memory aids that make it easy to recall the meaning.

Spanish, French, Italian, Portuguese, and Romanian are called *romance languages* because they draw so heavily on Latin. (Latin was the "Roman" language because it was spoken in ancient Rome.) Although English is not one of the romance languages (it is a Germanic language), English still has many words derived from Latin and ancient Greek. In particular, a considerable number of terms in science, medicine, and technology are derived from Latin and Greek, so learning word parts from these two older languages can be useful to you if you are considering a career in those fields.

KEY TERM
Etymology

The origin and history of a word.

A word's **etymology** (origin and history) will indicate whether it contains Latin or Greek word parts. Because a word's etymology can help you understand and remember a word's meaning, dictionaries often give the etymology of a word in brackets [ ] before or after the definition. When you look up a word in the dictionary, take an extra minute to check its etymology for word-structure clues that you might recognize. This technique of checking a word's etymology will also help you learn and remember the meaning of many roots and affixes.

You may want to familiarize yourself with the common roots, prefixes, and suffixes in Appendix 3. Then watch for them in new words you encounter. Use these word-structure clues whenever possible to help you confirm your "educated guess" about a word's meaning.

Using a Dictionary Pronunciation Key

Most college students already know how to locate a word in the dictionary efficiently and accurately, and how to determine which definition is appropriate for their needs. But like many students, you may still not be proficient at or feel confident using a dictionary pronunciation key. Being able to use a pronunciation key is important, because when you need to remember words, one of the most helpful things you can do is learn their correct pronunciation and say them aloud. Checking and then practicing a word's pronunciation takes only a moment or two.

A complete pronunciation key appears at the beginning of a dictionary. Typically, it looks similar to the example shown in the box on page 82.

DICTIONARY PRONUNCIATION KEY

Examples	Symbols	Examples	Symbols
pat	ă	pop	p
pay	ā	roar	r
care	âr	sauce	s
father	ä	ship, dish	sh
bib	b	tight, stopped	t
church	ch	thin	th
deed, milled	d	this	*th*
pet	ĕ	cut	ŭ
bee	ē	urge, term, firm,	ûr
fife, phase, rough	f	word, heard	
gag	g	valve	v
hat	h	with	w
which	hw	yes	y
pit	ĭ	abuse, use	yo͞o
pie, by	ī	zebra, xylem	z
pier	îr	vision, pleasure,	zh
judge	j	garage	
kick, cat, pique	k	*a*bout, it*e*m, ed*i*ble,	ə
lid, needle	l (nēd'l)	gall*o*p, circ*u*s	
mum	m	butter	ər
no, sudden	n (sŭd'n)		
thing	ng	FOREIGN	
pot	ŏ	*French* feu,	œ
toe, hose	ō	*German* schōn	
caught, paw	ô	*French* tu,	ü
noise	oi	*German* über	
took	o͝o	*German* ich,	KH
boot	o͞o	*Scottish* loch	
out	ou	*French* bon	N

STRESS

Primary stress ′ bi ol′ o gy (bī ŏl′ ə jē)
Secondary stress ′ bi′ o log′ ical (bī ə lŏj′ ĭ kəl)

In most dictionaries an *abridged pronunciation key,* showing only vowel sounds and the more unusual consonant sounds, appears at or near the bottom of each page. It usually looks something like this:

Pronunciation key: ă **pat** ā **pay** âr **care** ä **father** ĕ **pet** ē **be** ĭ **pit**
ī **tie** îr **pier** ŏ **pot** ō **toe** ô **paw** oi **noise** ou **out** o͝o **took** o͞o **boot**
ŭ **cut** yo͞o **abuse** ûr **urge** th **thin** *th* **this** hw **which** zh **vision**
ə **about**
Stress mark: ´

Your instructor can give you guidance in using a dictionary pronunciation key. In *Opening Doors,* you will have numerous opportunities to practice this skill, since the pronunciation is given for each term in the vocabulary quizzes that accompany the reading selections. To help you interpret the symbols, an abridged (shortened) pronunciation key is repeated in each vocabulary section.

Understanding Denotations and Connotations of Words

KEY TERMS
Denotation

Literal, explicit meaning of a word—its dictionary definition.

Connotation

Additional, nonliteral meaning associated with a word.

The literal, explicit meaning of a word—its dictionary definition—is called its **denotation.** But many words also have connotations. A **connotation** is an additional, nonliteral meaning associated with a word. For example, the two words *weird* and *distinctive* have similar denotations (both of them describe something that is out of the ordinary). It is their connotations that cause us to choose one of these words instead of the other when describing someone or something. You might describe the traits of someone you admire as *distinctive* but those of someone you dislike as *weird,* because *distinctive* has a positive connotation and *weird* has a negative one. Most people, for example, would rather be thought of as having *distinctive* clothes than *weird* clothes. *Distinctive* and *weird* have opposite connotations. *Distinctive* is associated with positive qualities; *weird* is associated with negative ones.

As suggested above, there are many words that have positive or negative connotations. For instance, consider your responses to the following pairs of adjectives, nouns, and verbs. They have similar denotations, but different connotations. The word in the left column has a positive connotation while its counterpart in the right column has a more negative one.

Positive connotation:	*Negative connotation:*
distinctive	weird
slender	skinny
assertive	pushy
preowned	used
computer whiz	computer nerd
correctional facility	prison

Positive connotation:	Negative connotation:
political activist	demagogue
study	cram
exaggerate	lie
borrow	plagiarize

Comprehension Monitoring Question for Connotative Meaning:

Is there a positive or negative association in addition to the literal meaning of a word?

Careful readers ask themselves, "Does this word have a connotation as well as a denotation?" That is, "Is there a positive or negative association in addition to the word's literal meaning?"

Here is an excerpt from an essay on gambling by the political analyst, commentator, and columnist George Will. Notice the effect of the author's use of the word *lust*. The author, who opposes gambling, chose this word because of its negative connotation:

> Gambling is debased speculation, a lust for sudden wealth that is not connected with the process of making society more productive of goods and services.
>
> *Source:* George F. Will, "Lotteries Cheat, Corrupt the People," Washington Post Writers' Group, 1994. Reprinted with permission.

According to the dictionary, one denotation (definition) of *lust* is "overwhelming craving"; another definition is "excessive or unrestrained sexual desire." In this passage, the author uses *lust* because of its negative connotations: pursuit of something that is evil or bad for us, a lack of self-control, impurity. The author could have said simply "a *desire* for sudden wealth," but he has used a stronger word to convey that gamblers have an excessive desire for sudden wealth: they crave it.

Understanding Figurative Language

**KEY TERM
Figurative Language**

Words that create unusual comparisons or vivid pictures in the reader's mind. Figurative expressions are also called *figures of speech.*

Figurative language is language that uses imagery—unusual comparisons or vivid words that create certain effects—to paint a picture in the reader's or listener's mind. Figurative expressions are also called *figures of speech.* You use figurative language every day, although you may not know it by that name. Whenever you say something such as "That chemistry test was a monster" or "My mother is a saint," you are using figurative language.

Because figures of speech do not literally mean what the words say, the reader or listener must *interpret* their meaning. If you say, "My landlord is a prince," you do not actually or literally mean that he is a member of a royal family. You expect your listener to interpret your words to mean that you appreciate your landlord, perhaps because he is cooperative and pleasant. If you say, "My landlord is a rat," you do not literally mean that he is a rodent. You expect your listener to interpret your words to mean that you dislike your landlord, perhaps because he has proved to be untrustworthy or unfair.

Comprehension Monitoring Question for Figurative Language

Should these words or this expression be interpreted figuratively?

Four especially common figures of speech are *metaphor, simile, hyperbole,* and *personification.* Let's look at each of these.

KEY TERM
Metaphor

Figure of speech suggesting a comparison between two essentially dissimilar things, usually by saying that one of them *is* the other.

Metaphors and similes both make unusual comparisons. A **metaphor** is an implied comparison between two things that seem very different from each other on the surface yet are alike in some significant way. A metaphor usually states that one thing is something else. The author assumes that readers will not take his or her words literally, but will understand that it is figurative language. (That is, the sentence is to be taken figuratively, not literally.) For example, in the sentence "Jamie's *garden is a rainbow*," the writer is making a comparison between a garden and a rainbow to help the reader envision the colorful array of flowers in the garden. To interpret this metaphor correctly, the reader must compare a garden and a rainbow and determine what they might have in common: a multitude of colors. (The author does not mean that the garden was literally a rainbow.) Another example of a metaphor would be "Joe's *desk was a mountain of paper.*" It creates a vivid image of how high ("a mountain") the paper was stacked on the desk. As noted, metaphor usually states that one thing is something else (in these cases, that a garden *is* a rainbow or that a stack of papers *was* a mountain).

KEY TERM
Simile

Figure of speech presenting a comparison between two essentially dissimilar things by saying that one of them is *like* the other.

A **simile** is also a comparison between two essentially dissimilar things, but instead of saying that one thing *is* something else, the author says that one thing is *like* something else. In fact, a simile is usually introduced by the words *like* or *as*. "Lisa felt *like a lottery winner* when she received the scholarship" and "The marine stood at attention *as rigid as an oak tree*" are examples of similes. In the first sentence, receiving a scholarship is compared to winning a lottery. The author wants us to understand that receiving the scholarship made Lisa feel as excited as if she has won a great deal of money in the lottery. In the second example, a marine, because of his stiff posture, is compared to an oak tree. To repeat: a simile says that one thing is *like* another. To understand a simile, you must determine which things are being compared and the important way in which the author considers them to be similar.

KEY TERM
Hyperbole

Figure of speech using obvious exaggeration for emphasis and effect.

Another type of figurative language is **hyperbole** (pronounced hī *pĕr′* bə lē), in which obvious exaggeration is used for emphasis. "My parents will explode if I get one more speeding ticket!" is an example of hyperbole. The parents would not literally "explode," but the exaggeration conveys how angry they would be.

KEY TERM
Personification

Figure of speech in which nonhuman or nonliving things are given human traits or attributes.

In **personification**, nonliving or nonhuman things are given human characteristics or qualities. "My car groaned, coughed, and wheezed, then crawled to a stop" gives human attributes to an automobile to suggest that the car made strange noises and then quit running. Cars, of course, cannot groan, cough, wheeze, and crawl in the same sense that a person would do these things.

Careful readers ask themselves, "Is the author using figurative language?" "What things are being compared, and how are they alike?" "What exaggeration is being made and why? What human traits are being given to a nonliving thing?"

The box on page 86 summarizes metaphor, simile, hyperbole, and personification.

FIGURATIVE LANGUAGE

Figures of speech	Examples
Metaphor: Implied comparison between two dissimilar things	Television is a junkyard of violence and stupidity.
Simile: Stated comparison between two dissimilar things, usually introduced by the word *like* or *as*	After the party, Ted's apartment looked as if it had been hit by a tornado.
Hyperbole: Obvious exaggeration for emphasis	I'm so excited about graduation that I won't be able to sleep for a month.
Personification: Attribution of human characteristics or qualities to nonhuman or nonliving things	The drab, dilapidated building looked tired and unhappy until it received a face-lift.

Understanding figurative language can help you grasp an author's message exactly, and it also makes material more interesting and enjoyable to read.

Here are some examples of figurative language by famous authors or well-known people. There are also some proverbs. On the lines beside each one, write the meaning of the figure of speech.

What is the meaning of the figurative language?

Metaphor

"A good laugh is sunshine in the house."
William Makepeace Thackeray

_____

_____

"Time is money."
Edward Bulwer-Lytton

_____

_____

"Money is a good servant but a bad master."
Sir Francis Bacon

_____

_____

_____

"Grief is itself a medicine."
William Cowper

_____

_____

"Debt is a bottomless sea."
Thomas Carlyle

_____

_____

"Hope is a good breakfast, but it is a bad supper."

Francis Bacon

_____
_____
_____

"This is what is left of China's army! Only rags to mop up China's blood."

Amy Tan
The Kitchen God's Wife

_____
_____
_____

"Because the Internet originated as a computer-science project rather than a communications utility, it has always been a magnet for hackers—programmers who turn their talents toward mischief or malice by breaking into the computer systems of others."

Bill Gates
The Road Ahead

_____
_____
_____
_____
_____
_____

Simile

"Much of the Internet culture will seem as quaint to future users of the information highway as stories of wagon trains and pioneers on the Oregon Trail do to us today."

Bill Gates
The Road Ahead

_____
_____
_____
_____
_____

"The water from the spring," she said, "is heavy as gold, sweet as honey, but clear as glass. If you look into the pool you can see your face, just like in a mirror."

Amy Tan
The Kitchen God's Wife

_____
_____
_____
_____
_____

Hyperbole

"Here once the embattled farmers stood, And fired the shot heard round the world."

Ralph Waldo Emerson
"Concord Hymn"

_____
_____
_____

"Everybody had made a 'ton of money' in the last few years and expected to make a ton more."

Richard Ford
Independence Day

_____
_____
_____

"He had a big mustache yellowed by eight million Pall Malls."

Richard Ford
Independence Day

Personification

"Those were the kinds of thoughts that crawled into my head."

Amy Tan
Joy Luck Club

"Chance makes our parents, but choice makes our friends."

Delille

"Misery loves company."

English proverb

"Misfortunes always come in by a door that has been left open for them."

Czech proverb

"When money speaks, the truth is silent."

Russian proverb

DEVELOPING CHAPTER REVIEW CARDS

Review cards, or *summary cards,* are an excellent study tool. They are a way to select, organize, and review the most important information in a text-book chapter. The process of creating review cards helps you organize information in a meaningful way and, at the same time, transfer it into long-term memory. The cards can also be used to prepare for tests (see Part Three). The review card activities in this book give you structured practice in creating these valuable study tools. Once you have learned how to make review cards, you can create them for textbook material in your other courses.

Now, complete the eight review cards for Chapter 2 by answering the questions or following the directions on each card. When you have completed them, you will have summarized important information about: (1) the reading process, (2) predicting as you read, (3) monitoring your comprehension, (4) adjusting your reading rate, (5) using context clues to determine the meaning of unfamiliar words, (6) using word-structure clues, (7) interpreting figurative language, and (8) monitoring your understanding of vocabulary.

Understanding the Reading Process

List seven important points about the reading process. (See pages 71–72.)

1. _____

2. _____

3. _____

   _____

4. _____

5. _____

6. _____

7. _____

Card 1   **Chapter 2: Approaching College Reading and Developing a College-Level Vocabulary**

Predicting As You Read

1. What is predicting? (See page 73.)

_____

_____

2. Why is predicting helpful? (See page 73.)

_____

_____

_____

Card 2   **Chapter 2: Approaching College Reading and Developing a College-Level Vocabulary**

Monitoring Your Comprehension

1. What does monitoring your comprehension mean? (see page 73.)

_____

_____

2. Describe the three-part procedure for monitoring your comprehension as you read. (See page 73.)

First: _____

_____

Second: _____

_____

Third: _____

_____

_____

Card 3   **Chapter 2: Approaching College Reading and Developing a College-Level Vocabulary**

Adjusting Your Reading Rate

Efficient readers adjust their rate according to two factors. List them. (See page 75.)

Factor 1: _____

Factor 2: _____

List several situations in which it is appropriate to *slow down* your reading rate. (See page 76.)

_____

_____

_____

List several situations in which it is appropriate to *speed up* your reading rate. (See page 77.)

_____

_____

_____

Card 4   **Chapter 2: Approaching College Reading and Developing a College-Level Vocabulary**

Using Context Clues to Determine Meanings of Words

What are *context clues?* (See page 78.)

_____

_____

Describe six types of context clues. (See the box on pages 78–79.)

1. _____

2. _____

3. _____

4. _____

5. _____

6. _____

Card 5   **Chapter 2: Approaching College Reading and Developing a College-Level Vocabulary.**

Using Word-Structure Clues

Define the following terms. (See pages 79–81.)

Word-structure clues: _____

Root: _____

Prefix: _____

_____

Suffix: _____

Etymology: _____

Card 6   **Chapter 2: Approaching College Reading and Developing a College-Level Vocabulary**

Interpreting Figurative Language

Define the following terms. (See pages 84–85.)

Figurative language: _____

_____

Metaphor: _____

_____

Simile: _____

_____

Hyperbole: _____

_____

Personification: _____

_____

Card 7   **Chapter 2: Approaching College Reading and Developing a College-Level Vocabulary**

CHAPTER 2 Approaching College Reading and Developing a College-Level Vocabulary 93

Monitoring Your Understanding of Vocabulary

1. What question should you ask yourself in order to take advantage of context clues? (See page 78.)

_____

_____

2. What question should you ask yourself in order to take advantage of word-structure clues? (See page 81.)

_____

_____

3. What question should you ask yourself in order to understand the connotation of a word? (See page 84.)

_____

_____

4. What question should you ask yourself in order to understand figurative language? (See page 84.)

_____

Card 8   **Chapter 2: Approaching College Reading and Developing a College-Level Vocabulary**

SELECTION **2-1**

Information Technology

WHAT IS ON THE WEB?

From *A Guidebook to the Web*

By Robert Harris

Prepare Yourself to Read

Directions: Do these exercises *before* you read Selection 2-1.

1. First, read and think about the title. What do you already know about what is on the World Wide Web?

_____

_____

2. In general, do you feel positive about what the Web offers, or are you alarmed about its content?

_____

_____

3. Next, complete your preview by reading the following:

> Introduction (in *italics*)
> First paragraph (paragraph 1)
> First sentence of each of the other paragraphs
> Diagram

On the basis of your preview, what three aspects of the Web does the selection seem to be about?

_____

_____

_____

Apply Comprehension Skills

Directions: Do these exercises as you read Selection 2-1. Apply three skills from this chapter:

Adjust your reading rate.   On the basis of your preview and your prior knowledge of what is on the World Wide Web, do you think you should read Selection 2-1 slowly or rapidly?

_____

_____

Develop a college-level vocabulary.   Did you notice any unfamiliar words while you were previewing Selection 2-1? If so, list them here.

_____

_____

Predict as you read.   As you read Selection 2-1, make predictions about what the author will discuss next. Write your predictions in the blanks provided.

_____

_____

WHAT IS ON THE WEB?

Everyone has heard of the Internet and the World Wide Web (WWW). In fact, in less than five years' time, 25 percent of the world's population has already received information on the Web. However, not everyone knows the types of things the Web makes available to users either free or for a fee. This selection describes those things along with several sample websites. (Be sure that you visit some of them.) It also explains the types of things that are not available on the Web. (Note: See Appendix 1 for "An Introduction to Using Computers, the Internet, and the World Wide Web.")

What Is on the Web—for Free?

1   Detractors of the World Wide Web are fond of saying that "anybody can put anything on the Web," with the implication that the Web is one vast mountain of junk information, bigotry, ignorance, and pornography. While it is true that the items just mentioned are out there on the Web, the important thing to remember is that "anybody" includes a lot more than kooks and perverts. Tens of thousands of smart, caring, knowledgeable individuals, countless corporations, nonprofit organizations like consumer groups, government agencies, and so on, all have websites. The Web is a library that never closes, a reference source of books, articles (including news, sports, weather), photographs, maps, music, video clips, and names and addresses. There is information on the Web for almost anything you can think of. Much of the material on the Web is available free, because of personal generosity or corporate public relations, or through the advertising model (the same method that makes network television free—advertising pays for the cost of the content).

2   What can you find? If you want to learn how to grow and care for orchids, there are several sites created by experienced growers ready to give you advice. If you have ever wondered what those weird chemicals listed on your shampoo or mousse containers do, some of the manufacturers who produce those chemicals host several sites that explain in detail what those ingredients do. If a friend has a strange and rare disease, there are dozens of medical information sites to look at.

3   Here are just some of the kinds of information available on the Web:

4   **Art**   If you are looking for a particular old master painting, a tour of a famous museum, or

---

Practice Exercises

Directions: At each of the points indicated below, answer the question, "What do you predict will happen next?" Write your answer in the lines provided.

Practice Exercise

What do you predict will be discussed in paragraph 2?

_____

_____

some examples of contemporary art, you can find them all. For a sample site, try the National Gallery of London, at www.nationalgallery.org.uk/

5   **Music**   With the advent of MIDI (musical instrument digital interface) keyboards, many pieces of classical and modern music have been recorded for the Web. You can even find instrumental versions of contemporary pop songs, though many are poorly performed and most, if not all, are in probable violation of copyright. For a sample site, try The Classical Music MIDI Page at www.sciortino.net/music.html

6   **Government documents**   Federal and state governments post laws, proposed legislation, consumer information, research documents, and statistics to the Web. Since government sources are generally viewed as reliable, you can find a lot of useful research material on these sites. For a sample site, try the Consumer Information Center at www.pueblo.gsa.gov

7   **Literature**   Novels, poetry, short stories, satire and other literary expressions (including criticism and theory) are offered. Because of copyright restrictions, most of the literature (especially novels) available dates to 1912 and earlier. However, you will be able to find some works that have been posted, either into the public domain or as part of a promotion. For a sample site, try Project Gutenberg at www.promo.net/pg

Accessing information on the World Wide Web is an essential skill for college students. Some students even carry laptop computers with them on campus.
(Jerry Koontz/Index Stock)

WEB TIP

When you are searching for a noncomputer item that may sound like a computer-related item, be sure to specify in your search string that you do not want computers. If, for example, you are looking for information about dehydrated apple chips, recall that Apple is a computer maker and chip can refer to an integrated circuit chip.

8   **News, sports, weather**   What you have enjoyed on television or in the newspaper is also, for the most part, available on the Web. Many commercial news organizations have a Web presence, offering the same information as on their traditional outlets, because the Web eliminates the restrictions of time and space. Articles

can be as long as needed to tell the whole story, and the number of photos that can be mounted is not restricted by the number of magazine pages. All of the information can be updated as often as desired (some sites update every few minutes, some every few hours). For a sample site, try the *New York Times* at www.news.com and *Sports Illustrated* at www.cnnsi.com

9　**Computers**　The inventors of the Web, and the first few million people who began to use it, were very interested in computers and computer technology, so the Web has always had a disproportionate amount of computer information on it. For a sample site, try News.com at www.news.com

10　**Library card catalogs**　Hundreds of libraries have online card catalogs available through the Web. You can connect to the catalog and see what books and journals the library has. For a sample site, try MELVYL, the University of California Online Catalog at www.melvyl.ucop.edu

11　**Corporate information**　Some corporations have what amounts to little more than advertisements on the Web, to puff their products the same way a television commercial might. Others have product catalogs, corporate financial information, and lists of contacts. And many companies have additional resources, ranging from consumer tips and information for the public to detailed information about products and manufacturing processes. For a sample site, try the Gerber website (which includes parenting information and frequently asked questions about baby care) at www.gerber.com

WEB TIP

Be careful about shopping online with a company you have never heard of. Most of the businesses are legitimate, but there are a few scam artists who are ready to take your money (and credit card number) and disappear. Many credit card companies guarantee your card against fraud, limiting your loss either to nothing or to $50. Check with your card issuer to learn about its policy. (Your card issuer probably has a website.)

12 **Addresses and phone numbers** The Web is not always your final destination. It can be a source where you can find telephone numbers and addresses for individuals and businesses and even maps that show you how to get from your location to a destination you choose. For a sample site, try the GTE SuperPages at super-pages.gte.net

13 **Shopping** One of the driving forces that have caused many companies to rush to the Web is the prospect of making money directly through it. Thus, there are many opportunities to shop online, for everything from books to chocolate to medical oxygen to stereo equipment. For a sample site, try shopping for books and CDs at Amazon.com at www.amazon.com

What Is on the Web—for a Price?

14 Now we come to a critical distinction about what you can get on the Web. Information is a product that requires time, effort, and money to produce. While some corporations are willing to give information away because it serves their interest or image to do so, and while others have learned how to support information availability through online advertising, other corporations have not yet done so, and offer to sell their information to the end user. How to recover the costs of creating and presenting information is one of the ongoing problems in the electronic world. A good example would be online newspapers. Some newspapers have their entire paper online, while others have only a few stories. Some papers have freely available archives of past issues, while others want to sell past articles at prices substantially higher than a copy of the entire original paper. As publishers experiment, what was once free may begin to cost and vice versa. For the foreseeable future, however, at least some resources on the Web will be available only for a fee. Here are some examples of commercial databases that charge a fee.

15 **Commercial databases** There are several proprietary databases of periodical articles, which allow you to read and print copyrighted materials for a fee. Lexis/Nexis, Infotrac, Encyclopedia Britannica, and Electric Library are some examples of companies that, in addition to

| Practice Exercise |

What do you predict will be discussed in paragraph 14?

_____

_____

the costs of maintaining a website, as outlined in the paragraph above, must pay license fees to the copyright holders of the information. Northern Light is a hybrid service, providing searching on the Web at large as well as on a commercial database. Users can choose to search for only free websites or for the fee-based articles.

What Is Not on the Web?

16   There are billions of dollars' worth of copyrighted intellectual property in the world, in the form of books, movies, music, articles in periodicals, photographs, and the like. Those who make a living by creating and marketing these works must be able to receive income from them in some way. While an increasing number of magazine and journal articles are available on the Web, either free, for a per use fee, or for a subscription fee, few book publishers have discovered how to charge for reading books online, so most of the books in a typical bookstore or library are not available free on the Web, nor are many other items like commercial releases of popular music. Further, millions of copyrighted but out-of-print books exist which would need to be put into digital form in order to be made available on the Web even for a fee. (And millions of books out of copyright still wait to be put into digital form as well.) Photographs and artworks would need to be scanned, and privately owned databases would have to be converted to Web-friendly format. Magazines and journals with only a small circulation may not have a Web presence, and to read an article in one of them you would have to go to the printed version.

Source: Robert Harris, *A Guidebook to the Web,* Dushkin McGraw-Hill, Guilford, Conn., pp. 11–15.

> **Practice Exercise**
>
> What do you predict will be discussed in paragraph 16?
>
> _____
>
> _____

Comprehension Quiz

Directions: For each comprehension question below, use information from the selection to determine the correct answer. You may refer to the selection as you answer the questions. Write your answer in the space provided.

True or False

_____ **1.** Much of the material on the Web is available free because of the personal generosity of authors and because of the public relations efforts of corporations.

_____ **2.** Government sources on the Web are generally viewed as reliable.

_____ **3.** The Web has a disproportionate amount of computer information on it because the creators of the Web constructed it that way.

_____ **4.** The Web is becoming a vast mountain of junk information, bigotry, violence, and pornography.

_____ **5.** In the foreseeable future, no fee will be charged for information on the Web.

_____ **6.** Articles posted on the Web cannot exceed a certain length.

Multiple-Choice

_____ **7.** One of the most popular reasons that so many companies have started using the Web is that
a. it is the fastest way to share free information.
b. it is an inexpensive way to carry out public relations.
c. there is a prospect of making money directly through it.
d. it contains a wide variety of information.

_____ **8.** Which of the following is *not* an example of something currently available free on the Web?
a. product catalogs and consumer information
b. information from news organizations
c. online library card catalogs
d. new books, such as those found in a typical bookstore or library

_____ **9.** Which of the following sites would be useful if you wanted to learn more about new safety features on sport utility vehicles?
a. www.promo.net/pg
b. www.pueblo.gsa.gov
c. www.news.com
d. superpages.gte.net

_____ **10.** One of the ongoing problems in the electronic world of the World Wide Web is how to

    a. recover the costs of creating and presenting information.

    b. share information in an organized way.

    c. find information that is useful and reliable.

    d. reduce the amount of information that is being added to the Web.

SELECTION **2-1**

Information Technology

Extend Your Vocabulary by Using Context Clues

Directions: Context clues are words in a sentence that allow the reader to deduce (reason out) the meaning of an unfamiliar word in that sentence. For each vocabulary item below, a sentence from the selection containing an important word (*italicized, like this*) is quoted first. Next, there is an additional sentence using the word in the same sense and providing another context clue. Use the context clues from *both* sentences to deduce the meaning of the italicized word. *Be sure the answer you choose makes sense in both sentences.* If you discover that you must use a dictionary to confirm an answer choice, remember that the meaning you select must still fit the context of *both* sentences. To indicate your answer, write the letter in the space provided.

Pronunciation key: ă pat ā pay âr care ä father ĕ pet ē be ĭ pit
ī tie îr pier ŏ pot ō toe ô paw oi noise ou out oŏ took ōō boot
ŭ cut yōō abuse ûr urge th thin *th* this hw which zh vision
ə about
Stress mark: ′

_____ **1.** *Detractors* of the World Wide Web are fond of saying that "anybody can put anything on the Web," with the implication that the Web is one vast mountain of junk information, bigotry, ignorance, and pornography.

The president's admirers insist that he signed the bill because he genuinely cares about the elderly, but his *detractors* say that he signed it only for political reasons.

detractors (dĭ trăkt′ ərz)

    a. people who speak ill of someone

    b. people who voted for a candidate

    c. people who want to change someone or something

    d. people who support someone or something

_____ **2.** Federal and state governments *post* laws, proposed legislation, consumer information, research documents, and statistics to the Web.

Our college placement office has decided to *post* job openings on bulletin boards in the Student Center.

post (pōst)

a. to send through the mail

b. to keep a record of

c. to display in a place of public view

d. to record on paper

_____ **3.** However, you will be able to find some works that have been posted, either into the *public domain* or as part of a promotion.

Because the works of Shakespeare were first published in the late 1500s and early 1600s, they are in the *public domain,* and anyone can republish them today.

public domain (pŭb′ lĭk dō mān′)

a. an open area

b. publications that are not protected under copyright

c. something controlled by the public

d. an area that is highly visible

_____ **4.** The inventors of the Web, and the first few million people who began to use it, were very interested in computers and computer technology, so the Web has always had a *disproportionate* amount of computer information on it.

My roommate is always beautifully dressed, but it is because she spends a *disproportionate* amount of her salary on clothes.

disproportionate (dĭs prə pôr′ shən nĭt)

a. unusually small

b. not quantifiable; cannot be calculated

c. undetectable

d. out of proportion in amount

_____ **5.** One of the driving forces that have caused many companies to rush to the Web is the *prospect* of making money directly through it.

Terry accepted the lower-paying job because she felt it offered a much better *prospect* for advancement in the long run.

prospect (prŏs′ pĕkt)

a. reason

b. unexpected outcome

c. possibility

d. undesirable result

        6. How to *recover* the costs of creating and presenting information is one of the ongoing problems in the electronic world.

Because they won their lawsuit against the swimming pool company, the Smiths were able to *recover* all of the money they paid for the poorly constructed pool.

recover (rĭ kŭv′ ər)

a. repay; pay back

b. reinvest

c. regain; get back

d. return; give back

        7. Some papers have freely available *archives* of past issues, while others want to sell past articles at prices substantially higher than a copy of the entire original paper.

While doing genealogical research, I studied old newspapers, books of deeds, birth certificates, marriage records, and other *archives* that pertained to my ancestors.

archives (är′ kīvs)

a. copies of documents no longer in existence

b. altered versions of old documents

c. collections of records, documents, and other materials of historical interest

d. stories handed down orally

        8. For the *foreseeable* future, however, at least some resources on the Web will be available only for a fee.

It is puzzling why people choose to drink too much alcohol when they know they will be driving; the results are *foreseeable* to anyone.

foreseeable (fôr sē′ ə bəl)

a. fortunate or positive

b. unable to be explained

c. unlikely

d. able to be known beforehand

        9. There are several *proprietary* databases of periodical articles, which allow you to read and print copyrighted materials for a fee.

Pharmaceutical companies have *proprietary* rights for drugs they develop; however, after a certain number of years, other companies are free to manufacture generic versions of the drug.

proprietary (prə prī′ ĭ tĕr ē)
a.   freely available
b.   owned by a private individual or corporation under a trademark or patent
c.   issued by a local government
d.   granted to the public

_____ **10.**   There are billions of dollars' worth of copyrighted *intellectual property* in the world, in the form of books, movies, music, articles in periodicals, photographs, and the like.

Because people sometimes steal other people's ideas and artistic creations, such as a melody, there are now attorneys who specialize in *intellectual property* rights.

intellectual property (ĭn tl ĕk′ cho͞o əl prŏp′ ər tē)
a.   pertaining to land on which an educational institution is situated
b.   pertaining to an original or innovative idea
c.   pertaining to inventors
d.   pertaining to something produced by the mind

S E L E C T I O N **2-1**

Information Technology

Collaboration Option

Respond in Writing

Directions: Refer to the selection as needed to answer the essay-type questions below.

Option for collaboration: Your instructor may direct you to work with other students or, in other words, to work *collaboratively*. In that case, you should form groups of three or four students as directed by your instructor and work together to complete the exercises. After your group discusses each item and agrees on the answer, have a group member record it. Every member of your group should be able to explain all of your group's answers.

1.   Access to the information and material on the World Wide Web offers vast benefits. However, anyone can post almost anything on the World Wide Web. What are some of the negative aspects of having an unregulated World Wide Web?

_____

_____

_____

Are there things that you think should *never* be allowed on the World Wide Web?

_____

_____

_____

2. Do you think the time will come when most people do nearly all of their shopping on the World Wide Web? Why or why not?

_____

_____

_____

3. Books, newspapers, magazines, maps, and all sorts of other printed material appear on the World Wide Web. Do you think that the Web will ever replace libraries, bookstores, and newsstands? Explain why or why not.

_____

_____

_____

_____

4. Overall main idea. What is the overall main idea the author wants the reader to understand about what is available on the World Wide Web? Answer this question in one sentence.

_____

_____

_____

Read More about It on the World Wide Web

To learn more about the topic of this selection, visit these websites or use your favorite search engine (such as Yahoo®). Whenever you go to *any* website, it is a good idea to evaluate it critically. Are you getting good information—information that is accurate, complete, and up-to-date? Who sponsors the website? How easy is it to use the features of the website?

Here are descriptions of some of the websites mentioned in the selection:

http://www.nationalgallery.org.uk/
> *This is The National Gallery of London website. It contains approximately 2,300 paintings, including many instantly recognizable masterpieces, and covers every European school of painting from 1260 to 1900.*

http://www.news.com
> *This is the CNET News website, the source of information for computer users.*

http://www.melvyl.ucop.edu
> *This site is The California Digital Library (CDL), which is responsible for the design, creation, and implementation of systems that support the shared collections of the University of California.*

http://www.pueblo.gsa.gov/
> *This page presents everything you ever wanted to know about the Federal Consumer Information Center.*

http://www.promo.net/pg/history.html
> *Project Gutenberg is the brainchild of historian and writer Michael Hart, who believes that famous and important texts should be made freely available to everyone.*

http://www.gerber.com
> *The Gerber Parents Resource Center website is a site that answers parenting questions.*

http://www.amazon.com
> *Amazon.com is a retail website specializing in books and carries other products.*

THE YELLOW RIBBON
By Pete Hamill

Prepare Yourself to Read

Directions: Do these exercises *before* you read Selection 2-2.

1. This short story is more exciting without a complete preview. For that reason, read *only* the title, the introduction (in *italics*), and the first paragraph.

What comes to your mind when you think of a yellow ribbon?

_____

Who are the characters in the story?

_____

What is taking place?

_____

2. As you read the rest of the selection, try to answer these questions:

Who is Vingo?
Why is he on the bus?

Apply Comprehension Skills

Directions: Do the practice exercises as you read Selection 2-2.

Adjust your reading rate.   On the basis of your preview and your prior knowledge about computers, do you think you should read Selection 2-2 slowly or rapidly?

_____

Develop a college-level vocabulary.   Did you notice any unfamiliar words while you were previewing Selection 2-2? If so, list them here.

_____

Predict as you read.   As you read Selection 2-2, make predictions about what the author will discuss next. Write your predictions in the blanks provided.

_____

_____

THE YELLOW RIBBON

Perhaps you have heard the old Tony Orlando and Dawn song "Tie a Yellow Ribbon 'Round the Old Oak Tree." The inspiration for it undoubtedly came from this wonderful short story. Today, ribbons of different colors are often worn to show support for various causes. For Vingo, the main character in this story, yellow ribbons have a very special significance.

1   They were going to Fort Lauderdale, the girl remembered later. There were six of them, three boys and three girls, and they picked up the bus at the old terminal on 34th Street, carrying sandwiches and wine in paper bags, dreaming of golden beaches and the tides of the sea as the gray cold spring of New York vanished behind them. Vingo was on board from the beginning.

2   As the bus passed through Jersey and into Philly, they began to notice that Vingo never moved. He sat in front of the young people, his dusty face masking his age, dressed in a plain brown ill-fitting suit. His fingers were stained from cigarettes and he chewed the inside of his lip a lot, frozen into some personal cocoon of silence.

3   Somewhere outside of Washington, deep into the night, the bus pulled into a Howard Johnson's, and everybody got off except Vingo. He sat rooted in his seat, and the young people began to wonder about him, trying to imagine his life: Perhaps he was a sea captain, maybe he had run away from his wife, he could be an old soldier going home. When they went back to the bus, the girl sat beside him and introduced herself.

4   "We're going to Florida," the girl said brightly. "You going that far?"

5   "I don't know," Vingo said.

6   "I've never been there," she said. "I hear it's beautiful."

7   "It is," he said quietly, as if remembering something he had tried to forget.

8   "You live there?"

9   "I did some time there in the Navy. Jacksonville."

10   "Want some wine?" she said. He smiled and took the bottle of Chianti and took a swig. He thanked her and retreated again into his silence. After a while, she went back to the others, as Vingo nodded in sleep.

Practice Exercises

Directions: At each of the points indicated below, answer the question, "What do you predict will happen next?"

Practice Exercise

What do you predict will happen next?

_____

_____

11   In the morning they awoke outside another Howard Johnson's, and this time Vingo went in. The girl insisted that he join them. He seemed very shy and ordered black coffee and smoked nervously, as the young people chattered about sleeping on the beaches. When they went back on the bus, the girl sat with Vingo again, and after a while, slowly and painfully and with great hesitation, he began to tell his story. He had been in jail in New York for the last four years, and now he was going home.

12   "Four years!" the girl said. "What did you do?"

13   "It doesn't matter," he said with quiet bluntness. "I did it and I went to jail. If you can't do the time, don't do the crime. That's what they say and they're right."

14   "Are you married?"

15   "I don't know."

16   "You don't know?" she said.

17   "Well, when I was in the can I wrote to my wife," he said. "I told her, I said, Martha, I understand if you can't stay married to me. I told her that. I said I was gonna be away a long time, and that if she couldn't stand it, if the kids kept askin' questions, if it hurt her too much, well, she could just forget me. Get a new guy—she's a wonderful woman, really something—and forget about me. I told her she didn't have to write me or nothing. And she didn't. Not for three-and-a-half years."

18   "And are you going home now, not knowing?"

19   "Yeah," he said shyly. "Well, last week, when I was sure the parole was coming through I wrote her. I told her that if she had a new guy, I understood. But if she didn't, if she would take me back she should let me know. We used to live in this town, Brunswick, just before Jacksonville, and there's a great big oak tree just as you come into town, a very famous tree, huge. I told her if she would take me back, she should put a yellow handkerchief on the tree, and I would get off and come home. If she didn't want me, forget it, no handkerchief, and I'd keep going on through."

20   "Wow," the girl said. "Wow."

21   She told the others, and soon all of them were in it, caught up in the approach of Brunswick, looking at the pictures Vingo showed them of his wife and three children, the woman handsome in a plain way, the children still unformed in a cracked, much-handled snapshot.

What special meaning did the yellow ribbons hold for the main character in this story?
(Eric Kamp/Index Stock)

Practice Exercise

What do you predict will happen next?

_____

_____

Now they were 20 miles from Brunswick and the young people took over window seats on the right side, waiting for the approach of the great oak tree. Vingo stopped looking, tightening his face into the ex-con's mask, as if fortifying himself against still another disappointment. Then it was 10 miles, and then five and the bus acquired a dark hushed mood, full of silence, of absence, of lost years, of the woman's plain face, of the sudden letter on the breakfast table, of the wonder of children, of the iron bars of solitude.

22   Then suddenly all of the young people were up out of their seats, screaming and shouting and crying, doing small dances, shaking clenched fists in triumph and exaltation. All except Vingo.

23   Vingo sat there stunned, looking at the oak tree. It was covered with yellow handkerchiefs, 20 of them, 30 of them, maybe hundreds, a tree that stood like a banner of welcome blowing and billowing in the wind, turned into a gorgeous yellow blur by the passing bus. As the young people shouted, the old con slowly rose from his seat, holding himself tightly, and made his way to the front of the bus to go home.

Practice Exercise

What do you predict will happen next?

_____

_____

Source: Pete Hamill, "The Yellow Ribbon," *New York Post,* 1972. Copyright 1972 by Pete Hamill. Reprinted by permission of International Creative Management, Inc.

Comprehension Quiz

Directions: For each comprehension question below, use information from the selection to determine the correct answer. You may refer to the selection as you answer the questions. Write your answer in the space provided.

True or False

_____ **1.** Six young people boarded a bus for a summer vacation in Florida.

_____ **2.** Vingo told his story to a young woman on the train.

_____ **3.** The author states that Vingo's wife was foolish.

_____ **4.** Vingo was traveling to his home in Jacksonville, Florida.

Multiple-Choice

_____ **5.** Vingo's prison experience had left him
    a. unfeeling and uncaring.
    b. feeling that he had paid his debt to society by serving his jail sentence.
    c. feeling suicidal.
    d. feeling that he had been imprisoned unjustly.

_____ **6.** According to the author, when Vingo saw the yellow handkerchiefs, he felt
    a. relieved.
    b. sad
    c. stunned.
    d. disappointed.

_____ **7.** To Vingo, the yellow handkerchiefs tied to the oak tree meant
    a. an approaching holiday.
    b. welcome home for returning soldiers.
    c. nothing.
    d. forgiveness and a new start.

_____ **8.** At the end of the story, we can conclude that Vingo's wife was
    a. forgiving.
    b. bitter.
    c. unforgiving.
    d. revengeful.

_____ **9.** The six young people were traveling to Florida from
    a. New Jersey.
    b. Philadelphia.
    c. New York.
    d. Washington.

_____ **10.** Perhaps the lesson the young people learned from Vingo's story is that

     a.   despite the hardships of life, there is an opportunity for happiness if one is willing to try again.

     b.   Vingo's wife was justified in not allowing him to return.

     c.   for an ex-con, there is not much chance for happiness.

     d.   there are some things that no marriage can survive.

S E L E C T I O N **2-2**

Literature

Extend Your Vocabulary by Using Context Clues

Directions: Context clues are words in a sentence that allow the reader to deduce (reason out) the meaning of an unfamiliar word in that sentence. For each vocabulary item below, a sentence from the selection containing an important word (*italicized, like this*) is quoted first. Next, there is an additional sentence using the word in the same sense and providing another context clue. Use the context clues from *both* sentences to deduce the meaning of the italicized word. *Be sure the answer you choose makes sense in both sentences.* If you discover that you must use a dictionary to confirm an answer choice, remember that the meaning you select must still fit the context of both sentences. To indicate your answer, write the letter in the space provided.

Pronunciation key: ă pat ā pay âr care ä father ĕ pet ē be ĭ pit
ī tie îr pier ŏ pot ō toe ô paw oi noise ou out o͝o took o͞o boot
ŭ cut yo͞o abuse ûr urge th thin *th* this hw which zh vision
ə about
Stress mark: ′

_____ **1.** There were six of them, three boys and three girls, and they picked up the bus at the old *terminal* on 34th Street.

Before the days of airplanes, every small and large town had a train *terminal*.

terminal (tûr′ mə nal) means:

     a.   fatal illness

     b.   dock or pier

     c.   bus stop

     d.   station, especially one that is the final stop at either end of a railway or bus line

_____ **2.** They were dreaming of golden beaches and the tides of the sea as the gray cold spring of New York *vanished* behind them.

No one knew what happened to Mrs. Martin's diamond necklace; it simply *vanished* from her jewelry box during the dinner party.

vanished (văn′ ĭsht) means:

a. disappeared

b. intensified

c. grew smaller

d. exploded

_____ **3.** His fingers were stained from cigarettes and he chewed the inside of his lip a lot, frozen into some personal *cocoon* of silence.

The fluffy sleeping bag provided a cozy *cocoon* for the drowsy child.

cocoon (kə koōn′) means:

a. wool blanket

b. pupal case spun by the larvae of moths and other insects

c. protective covering

d. coat

_____ **4.** He sat *rooted* in his seat, and the young people began to wonder about him, trying to imagine his life.

Connie wanted to run from the barking dog, but she was so terrified that her feet seemed *rooted* in the ground.

rooted (roōt′ əd) means:

a. buried

b. bored or uninterested

c. frightened

d. firmly established or anchored

_____ **5.** He smiled and took the bottle of Chianti and took a *swig.*

The hot, thirsty tennis player finished his sports drink in a single *swig.*

swig (swĭg) means:

a. glance

b. insult or offense

c. large swallow or gulp

d. taste

_____ **6.** Well, when I was in the *can,* I wrote to my wife.

Mike said that John was sentenced to 30 days in the *can* for reckless driving.

can (kăn) means:

a. rehabilitation center

b. jail or prison

c. food container

d. small town

———— **7.** Vingo stopped looking, tightening his face into an ex-con's mask, as if *fortifying* himself against still another disappointment.

The coach spent half-time *fortifying* his team's sagging morale.

fortifying (fôr′ tə fī ĭng) means:

a. improving

b. strengthening

c. fooling by means of a clever trick

d. making happy or cheerful

———— **8.** Then it was 10 miles, and then five and the bus acquired a dark hushed mood, full of silence, of absence, of lost years, of the woman's plain face, of the sudden letter on the breakfast table, of the wonder of children, of the iron bars of *solitude.*

Because he liked *solitude,* the artist often took long walks in the early morning hours when the beach was deserted.

solitude (sŏl′ ĭ tōōd) means:

a. isolation or being alone

b. quietude or silence

c. loneliness

d. beauty

———— **9.** Then suddenly all of the young people were up out of their seats, screaming and shouting and crying, doing small dances, shaking clenched fists in triumph and *exaltation.*

Nothing could top the *exaltation* I felt when I received my college diploma at the graduation ceremony.

exaltation (ĭgs əl tā′ shən) means:

a. calm, reflective mood

b. disappointment

c. delight or elation

d. memory or recollection

———— **10.** The tree was covered with yellow handkerchiefs, 20 of them, 30 of them, maybe hundreds, a tree that stood like a banner of welcome blowing and *billowing* in the wind.

When the wind came up, the sails of the boat began *billowing* like open parachutes.

billowing (bĭl′ ō ing) means:

a. folding and unfolding

b. disintegrating

c. swelling or surging

d. flapping

SELECTION **2-2**

Literature

Collaboration Option

Respond in Writing

Directions: Refer to the selection as needed to answer the essay-type questions below.

Option for collaboration: Your instructor may direct you to work with other students or, in other words, to work *collaboratively.* In that case, you should form groups of three or four students as directed by your instructor and work together to complete the exercises. After your group discusses each item and agrees on the answer, have a group member record it. Every member of your group should be able to explain all of your group's answers.

1. Yellow ribbons are still used to welcome someone home. Can you think of some examples of whom they might be used to welcome?

    _____

    _____

    _____

2. Ribbons of different colors are often worn to show support for various causes. Give one or more examples. Describe the color of the ribbon and the cause.

    _____

    _____

    _____

    _____

    _____

    _____

3. How did you feel when you read about the "gorgeous yellow blur" that awaited Vingo?

    _____

    _____

    _____

    _____

    _____

    _____

    _____

4. On the basis of what you learned about Vingo in this selection, do you feel he deserved to be forgiven? Explain your answer.

_____

_____

_____

_____

_____

_____

_____

_____

5. This story seems to illustrate several truths about life. What are some of the truths that the story reveals?

_____

_____

_____

_____

_____

_____

6. Overall main idea. What is the overall main idea the author wants the reader to understand? Answer this question in one sentence.

_____

_____

_____

_____

_____

_____

Read More about It on the World Wide Web

To learn more about the topic of this selection, visit these websites or use your favorite search engine (such as Yahoo®). Whenever you go to any website, it is a good idea to evaluate it critically. Are you getting good information—information that is accurate, complete, and up-to-date? Who sponsors the website? How easy is it to use the features of the website?

http://cjr.org/year/97/3/hamill.asp

This is the Columbia Journalism Review *website, which presents an article on Pete Hamill, the author of the short story used for this selection.*

http://www.yellowribbon.org/

This is the Yellow Ribbon Suicide Prevention Program site. Because of the internal nature of depression and loneliness, thousands of young people who appear to be happy are suffering silently in emotional pain. YRSPP offers a way for teens to reach out and seek help.

SELECTION **2-3**

Biology

A WHALE OF A SURVIVAL PROBLEM

From *The Nature of Life*

By John Postlethwait and Janet Hopson

Prepare Yourself to Read

Directions: Do these exercises *before* you read Selection 2-3.

1. First, read and think about the title. What kinds of things do you think threaten the survival of whales?

_____

_____

2. Next, complete your preview by reading the following:

> Introduction (in *italics*)
> First paragraph (paragraph 1)
> First sentence of each paragraph
> Words in *italics*
> Diagram
> All of the last paragraph (paragraph 4)

On the basis of your preview, what specific problem of whale survival do you think will be discussed?

_____

_____

Apply Comprehension Skills

Directions: Do these exercises as you read Selection 2-3.

Adjust your reading rate.   On the basis of your preview and your prior knowledge of how whales survive, do you think you should read Selection 2-3 slowly or rapidly?

_____

Develop a college-level vocabulary.   Did you notice any unfamiliar words while you were previewing Selection 2-3? If so, list them here.

_____

Predict as you read.   As you read Selection 2-3, make predictions about what the authors will discuss next. Write your predictions in the blanks provided.

121

A WHALE OF A SURVIVAL PROBLEM

Blue whales are the largest animals on earth. Unfortunately, they have been hunted almost to extinction and are now on the endangered species list. Human predators have not been their only problem, however. Their size alone presents unique challenges for survival. This textbook selection explores the biological adaptations this immense creature has had to make in order to survive.

1   An intrepid visitor to the perpetually frozen Antarctic could stand at the coastline, raise binoculars, and witness a dramatic sight just a few hundred meters offshore: a spout as tall and straight as a telephone pole fountaining upward from the blowhole of a blue whale *(Balaenoptera musculus),* then condensing into a massive cloud of water vapor in the frigid air. The gigantic animal beneath the water jet would be expelling stale air from its 1-ton lungs after a dive in search of food. Then, resting at the surface only long enough to take four deep breaths of fresh air, the streamlined animal would raise its broad tail, thrust mightily, and plunge into the ocean again. The observer on shore might see such a sequence only twice per hour, since the the blue whale can hold its breath for 30 minutes as it glides along like a submarine, swallowing trillions of tiny shrimplike animals called krill.

2   It is difficult to comprehend the immense proportions of the blue whale, the largest animal ever to inhabit our planet. At 25 to 30 m (80 to 100 ft) in length, this marine mammal is longer than three railroad boxcars and bigger than any dinosaur that ever lumbered on land. It weighs more than 25 elephants or 1600 fans at a basketball game. Its heart is the size of a beetle—a Volkswagen beetle. And that organ pumps 7200 kg (8 tons) of blood through nearly 2 million kilometers (1.25 million miles) of blood vessels, the largest of which could accommodate an adult person crawling on hands and knees. The animal has a tongue the size of a grown elephant. It has 45,500 kg (50 tons) of muscles to move its 54,500 kg (60 tons) of skin, bones, and organs. And this living mountain can still swim at speeds up to 48 km (30 mi) per hour!

Practice Exercises

Directions: At each of the points indicated below, answer the question, "What do you predict will happen next?"

The blue whale is the largest creature on earth.
(Tom Walker/Stock Boston)

3   Leviathan proportions aside, it is difficult to grasp the enormous problems that so large an organism must overcome simply to stay alive. For starters, a blue whale is a warm-blooded animal with a relatively high metabolic rate; to stay warm and active in an icy ocean environment, it must consume and burn 1 million kilocalories a day. This it does by straining 3600 kg (8000 lb) of krill from the ocean water each day on special food-gathering sieve plates. In addition, each of the trillions of cells in the whale's organs must exchange oxygen and carbon dioxide, take in nutrients, and rid itself of organic wastes, just as a single-celled protozoan living freely in seawater must do. Yet a given whale cell—a liver cell, let's

> **Practice Exercise**
>
> What do you predict will be discussed in paragraph 3?
>
> _____
>
> _____

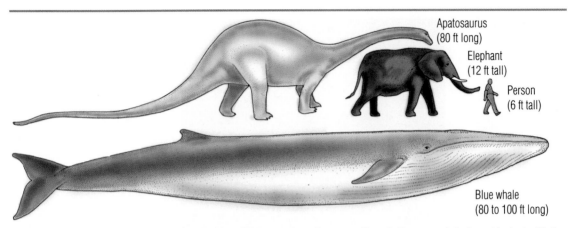

Apatosaurus
(80 ft long)

Elephant
(12 ft tall)

Person
(6 ft tall)

Blue whale
(80 to 100 ft long)

A whale to scale. A blue whale is longer and far heavier than an elephant or even an *Apatosaurus* (formerly *Brontosaurus*), the longest land animal that ever lived.

say—can lie deep in the body, separated from the environment by nearly 2 m (6 ft) of blubber, muscle, bone, and other tissues. For this reason, the whale needs elaborate transport systems to deliver oxygen and nutrients and to carry away carbon dioxide and other wastes. Finally, the galaxy of living cells inside a whale must be coordinated and controlled by a brain, a nervous system, and chemical regulators (hormones) so that the organism can function as a single unit.

4   Although blue whales are the largest animals that have ever lived, they share with all other animals the same fundamental physical problems of day-to-day survival: how to extract energy from the environment; how to exchange nutrients, wastes, and gases; how to distribute materials to all the cells in the body; how to maintain a constant internal environment despite fluctuations in the external environment; how to support the body; and how to protect it from attackers or from damaging environmental conditions. Blue whales have evolved with unique adaptations of form and function that meet such challenges and leave the animals suited to their way of life.

Practice Exercise

What do you predict will be discussed in paragraph 4?

_____

_____

Source: John Postlethwait and Janet Hopson, "A Whale of a Survival Problem," in *The Nature of Life,* McGraw-Hill, New York, 1992, pp. 430–431. Reproduced with permission of McGraw-Hill.

SELECTION **2-3**

Biology

Comprehension Quiz

Directions: For each comprehension question below, use information from the selection to determine the correct answer. You may refer to the selection as you answer the questions. Write your answer in the space provided.

True or False

1. The blue whale expels water through its blowhole.

2. The blue whale can hold its breath for more than 1 hour as it glides under water.

3. The blue whale feeds daily on trillions of tiny shrimplike animals called krill.

4. Although large, the blue whale is not the largest animal that inhabits our earth.

5. A human adult could crawl on hands and knees through the largest blood vessels of a blue whale.

Multiple-Choice

6. In paragraph 1, "a spout as tall and straight as a telephone pole fountaining upward from the blowhole of a blue whale," refers to
   a. ice.
   b. saltwater.
   c. fresh air.
   d. stale air that has condensed into water vapor.

7. The "living mountain" mentioned in paragraph 2 refers to
   a. the dinosaur.
   b. 8000 pounds of krill.
   c. the blue whale.
   d. a grown elephant.

8. After diving for food, the blue whale surfaces and
   a. expels stale air through its blowhole, then dives quickly again.
   b. expels stale air, rests long enough to take four breaths of fresh air, then dives again.
   c. expels stale air, rests on the surface for 30 minutes, then dives again.
   d. none of the above.

————— **9.** Which of the following problems of day-to-day survival does the blue whale share with all other animals?

  a. how to extract energy (food) from the environment

  b. how to distribute materials to all the cells in the body

  c. how to balance the internal environment with the changes in the external environment

  d. all of the above

————— **10.** Because the blue whale is a warm-blooded animal and has a relatively high metabolic rate, it must

  a. rid itself of organic wastes.

  b. expel stale air through its blowhole.

  c. consume and burn 1 million kilocalories a day in order to stay warm and active in the icy ocean.

  d. take four deep breaths of fresh air before diving again for food.

S E L E C T I O N **2-3**

Biology

Extend Your Vocabulary by Using Context Clues

Directions: Context clues are words in a sentence that allow the reader to deduce (reason out) the meaning of an unfamiliar word in that sentence. For each vocabulary item below, a sentence from the selection containing an important word (*italicized, like this*) is quoted first. Next, there is an additional sentence using the word in the same sense and providing another context clue. Use the context clues from *both* sentences to deduce the meaning of the italicized word. *Be sure the answer you choose makes sense in both sentences.* If you discover that you must use a dictionary to confirm an answer choice, remember that the meaning you select must still fit the context of both sentences. To indicate your answer, write the letter in the space provided.

Pronunciation key: ă **pat** ā **pay** âr **care** ä **father** ĕ **pet** ē **be** ĭ **pit**
ī **tie** îr **pier** ŏ **pot** ō **toe** ô **paw** oi **noise** ou **out** o͝o **took** o͞o **boot**
ŭ **cut** yo͞o **abuse** ûr **urge** th **thin** *th* **this** hw **which** zh **vision**
ə **about**
Stress mark:'

————— **1.** An *intrepid* visitor to the perpetually frozen Antarctic could stand at the coastline, raise binoculars, and witness a dramatic sight just a few hundred meters off shore.

Columbus was an *intrepid* explorer who set sail for the unknown New World.

intrepid (ĭn trĕp′ ĭd) means:

a. extremely cold
b. fun-loving
c. fearless; bold
d. weary; fatigued

———— **2.** An intrepid visitor to the *perpetually* frozen Antarctic could stand at the coastline, raise binoculars, and witness a dramatic sight just a few hundred meters off shore.

The Earth moves *perpetually* around the sun.

perpetually (pər pĕch′ o͞o əl lē) means:

a. forever
b. partially
c. erratically
d. once a month

———— **3.** An intrepid visitor to the perpetually frozen Antarctic could stand at the coastline, raise binoculars, and witness a dramatic sight just a few hundred meters off shore: a spout as tall and as straight as a telephone pole fountaining upward from the blow hole of a blue whale, then *condensing* into a massive cloud of water vapor in the frigid air.

When you turn on your car heater in the winter, water vapor may start *condensing* and running down the inside of the windows.

condensing (kən dĕns′ ĭng) means:

a. turning into steam
b. changing from a gas into a liquid
c. becoming colder
d. changing from a liquid into a solid

———— **4.** An intrepid visitor to the perpetually frozen Antarctic could stand at the coastline, raise binoculars, and witness a dramatic sight just a few hundred meters off shore: a spout as tall and as straight as a telephone pole fountaining upward from the blow hole of a blue whale, then condensing into a massive cloud of water vapor in the *frigid* air.

Snowflakes began to fall from the gray, *frigid* sky.

frigid (frĭj′ ĭd) means:

a. smoky
b. dry
c. starry
d. extremely cold

————— **5.** The gigantic animal beneath the water jet would be *expelling* stale air from its 1-ton lungs after a dive in search of food.

Our college is *expelling* five students for cheating on an exam.

expelling (ĭk spĕl′ ĭng) means:

a. maintaining

b. breathing out

c. forcing out or ejecting

d. preventing

————— **6.** *Leviathan* proportions aside, it is difficult to grasp the enormous problems that so large an organism must overcome simply to stay alive.

The deep-sea fishermen swore they had seen a *leviathan*—a shark so huge that it was larger than their boat.

leviathan (lə vī′ ə thən) means:

a. something unusually large of its kind

b. measuring device

c. large shark

d. huge ship

————— **7.** For starters, a blue whale is a warm-blooded animal with a *relatively* high metabolic rate; to stay warm in an icy ocean environment, it must consume and burn 1 million kilocalories a day.

Our boss is usually very talkative, but he was *relatively* quiet at the staff meeting today.

relatively (rĕl′ ə tĭv lē) means:

a. pertaining to family relationships

b. pertaining to reality

c. pertaining to a member of the family

d. in comparison with something else

————— **8.** For starters, a blue whale is a warm-blooded animal with a relatively high *metabolic* rate; to stay warm in an icy ocean environment, it must consume and burn 1 million kilocalories a day.

Exercise and stress increase a person's *metabolic* rate.

metabolic (mĕt ə bŏl′ ĭk) means:

a. pertaining to the speed at which an organism moves

b. pertaining to bodily physical and chemical processes that maintain life

c. pertaining to breathing and respiration

d. pertaining to survival

——— 9. For this reason, the whale needs *elaborate* transport systems to deliver oxygen and nutrients and to carry away carbon dioxide and wastes.

The plans for the queen's coronation ceremony were so *elaborate* that it took a staff of 500 people to carry out the arrangements.

elaborate (ĭ lăb′ ər ĭt) means:
a. time-consuming
b. very complex
c. difficult to understand
d. simple

——— 10. Finally, the *galaxy* of living cells inside a whale must be coordinated and controlled by a brain, a nervous system, and chemical regulators (hormones) so that the organism can function as a single unit.

From the dazzling *galaxy* of toys in the toy department, my young nephew finally selected a remote-controlled car.

galaxy (găl′ ək sē) means:
a. stars in the universe
b. collection of numerous things
c. system
d. display

SELECTION **2-3**

Biology

Collaboration Option

Respond in Writing

Directions: Refer to the selection as needed to answer the essay-type questions below.

Option for collaboration: Your instructor may direct you to work with other students or, in other words, to work *collaboratively.* In that case, you should form groups of three or four students as directed by your instructor and work together to complete the exercises. After your group discusses each item and agrees on the answer, have a group member record it. Every member of your group should be able to explain all of your group's answers.

1. Describe any three comparisons the author uses to illustrate the enormous size of the blue whale.
First comparison:

_____

_____

_____

Second comparison:

_____

_____

_____

Third comparison:

_____

_____

_____

2. Because of its size, what are three special problems that blue whales must overcome to survive?

One problem:

_____

_____

_____

Another problem:

_____

_____

_____

A third problem:

_____

_____

_____

3. Explain why the title of this selection is clever.

_____

_____

_____

_____

4. Overall main idea. What is the overall main idea the author wants the reader to understand about the survival of the blue whale? Answer this question in one sentence.

_____

_____

_____

_____

_____

Read More about It on the World Wide Web

To learn more about the topic of this selection, visit these websites or use your favorite search engine (such as Yahoo ®). Whenever you go to *any* website, it is a good idea to evaluate it critically. Are you getting good information—information that is accurate, complete, and up-to-date? Who sponsors the website? How easy is it to use the features of the website?

http://www.physics.helsinki.fi/whale/
This website is part of the World Wide Web Virtual Library. It contains many interesting links related to whale watching. Click on links for research, view pictures, slide shows, videos, and even interspecies communication.

http://unisci.com/aboutunisci.shtml
Unisci was the first science daily news site on the Web and remains the only one that selects stories on the basis of their scientific importance. For more information on whale survival, type "whale" into archive search box.

http://www.encarta.msn.com/find/Concise.asp?ti=035E4000
This part of an encyclopedia website features an overview of whales: types, anatomy, feeding habits, reproduction, intelligence, behavior, origins, etc. Blue whales are rorquals and are included in the section on baleen whales (the category of whale which obtains food by filtering out small fish and crustaceans through the giant, flexible comb-like baleen in their mouths).

http://www.pacificwhale.org/
This is the website of the nonprofit Pacific Whale Foundation in Maui, Hawaii. It is dedicated to saving the oceans and the life they contain, especially the species of whales that are threatened with extinction. (The organization does not focus on blue whales alone.) The Foundation stresses marine research, education, and conservation.

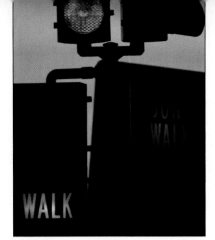

© *PhotoDisc*

C H A P T E R

3

Approaching College Assignments: Reading Textbooks and Following Directions

In this chapter you will learn the answers to these questions:

- What is an effective way to read and study a college textbook?

- How can I prepare to read an assignment?

- How can I guide my reading by asking questions?

- How can I review material by rehearsing?

- What are the keys to following directions on college assignments and tests?

SKILLS

College Textbooks: A Process for Reading and Studying Effectively

- Step 1: Prepare to Read

- Step 2: Ask and Answer Questions to Guide Your Reading

- Step 3: Review by Rehearsing Your Answers

Following Directions in Textbooks and on Tests

- Guidelines for Following Directions

- Example: Directions from a Textbook

- Example: Directions on a Test

CREATING YOUR SUMMARY

Developing Chapter Review Cards

READINGS

Selection 3-1   *(Essay)*
"How to Find the Time to Read"
by Louis Shores

Selection 3-2   *(Human Development)*
"Parenthood" from *Human Development*
by Diane E. Papalia and Sally Wendkos Olds

Selection 3-3   *(Art Appreciation)*
"Art in the Service of Religion"
from *Living with Art*
by Rita Gilbert

If you need a helping hand, look at the end of your sleeve.

If you are not successful, notice how you make yourself unsuccessful.

COLLEGE TEXTBOOKS: A PROCESS FOR READING AND STUDYING EFFECTIVELY

Students often ask, "When should I start studying for final exams?" The answer is, "At the beginning of the semester." From the first day of classes, you should read and study your textbook assignments as if you were preparing for the final exam. If you read and study your assignments effectively the first time, you won't have to start over again and reread them when it is time for a unit test, a major exam, or even a final exam.

Reading your textbooks requires more than casually looking at the pages. Reading and studying take time and effort. Moreover, you must make reading and studying textbook material an active process, not a passive one.

How can you understand and remember what you read in your textbooks? This chapter presents an effective approach for reading a college textbook assignment that will ultimately save you time. This approach is based on doing it right the first time, so that when you prepare for a test, you will not have to spend additional hours rereading textbook chapters. This approach helps you learn more the first time you read your textbook assignments.

The basic steps of this study-reading process are:

- Prepare to read.
- Ask and answer questions as you read.
- Review by rehearsing the answers to your questions.

The following box shows all three steps of this study-reading process. Each of these steps is explained in detail below.

SUMMARY OF THE THREE-STEP PROCESS FOR READING AND STUDYING COLLEGE TEXTBOOKS

Step 1: Prepare to Read

Preview the selection to see what it contains and how it is organized.

- Read the title.
- Read the introduction.
- Read headings and subheadings in each section.
- Read words in italics or bold print.
- Look over illustrations, charts, and diagrams.
- Read any questions that are included in the chapter or a study guide.
- Read the summary.

Ask yourself: "What topics does the author seem to be emphasizing?" and "How are the topics organized?"

(Continued on next page)

(Continued from previous page)

Assess your prior knowledge. Ask yourself: "What do I already know about the topic?" and "How familiar am I with this topic?"
Plan your reading and study time. Ask yourself: "How can I best allot my time for this assignment?" and "Do I need to divide the assignment into smaller units?"

Step 2: Ask and Answer Questions as You Read

Guide your reading by asking and answering questions:

- Turn chapter headings into questions.
- Create questions based on what the paragraphs or sections appear to be about.
- If the author has included questions, answer them.
- Use questions in a study guide, if there is one.
- Use questions given out by the instructor.

Read actively:
- Look for answers to your questions.

Record the answers to your questions:
- Write the answers on notebook paper or in the margins of the textbook.
- Create notes for the material.
- Emphasize the answers by highlighting or underlining them.

Step 3: Review by Rehearsing the Answers to Your Questions

Review the material and transfer it into long-term memory by rehearsing:

- Recite (say aloud) the answers to your questions.
- Try to write the important points from memory.

KEY TERM
Preparing to Read

Previewing the material, assessing your prior knowledge, and planning your reading and studying time.

KEY TERM
Previewing

Examining material to determine its topic and organization before actually reading it.

Step 1: Prepare to Read

Before you begin to read a textbook assignment, you should spend a few minutes preparing to read. **Preparing to read** involves previewing the chapter, assessing your prior knowledge, and planning your reading and study time.

Preview the Selection

Previewing means examining material to determine its topic and organization before actually reading it. This gives you a general idea of what an entire assignment will be about and allows you to see how the material is organized. This not only helps you comprehend what you read but also helps improve your concentration, your motivation, and your interest in what you are about to read. (That is why each of the reading selections in *Opening Doors* is preceded by an activity called "Prepare Yourself to Read.")

It is important to have a process for reading and studying college textbooks effectively.
(Rick Kooker/Index Stock)

To preview a chapter assignment:

- **First, read the chapter title.** This should tell you the overall topic of the chapter.
- **Next, read the chapter introduction.** A chapter introduction (if there is one) usually presents some of the important points to be made in the chapter, or it may give some background information that you will need.
- **Read the heading and subheadings of each section.** Turn through the chapter to read the headings and subheadings. These will tell you what topics the author has included and can provide an outline of how information in the chapter is organized.
- **Read words in *italics*, bold print, or color.** Notice any words that appear in special print (italics or bold print) or in color; these are usually important terms you will be expected to understand and remember.
- **Look over illustrations, charts, and diagrams.** Be sure to look at any pictures, charts, diagrams, and graphs you find in the chapter. These give you visual representations of the material.
- **Read any questions that are included in the chapter or a study guide.** They will alert you to important information you should watch for as you read.
- **Finally, read the chapter summary.** If there is a chapter summary, it will contain in brief form many of the important ideas of the chapter. A chapter summary (like a chapter introduction) is especially useful. Take advantage of it.

Comprehension Monitoring Questions for Previewing

What topics does the author seem to be emphasizing? How are the topics organized?

As you preview, you should ask yourself some questions about the chapter you are about to read. Ask yourself, "What topics does the author seem to be emphasizing?" and "How are the topics organized?"

Assess Your Prior Knowledge

As you learned in Chapter 2, when you lack background knowledge in a subject—and this is often the case when you are reading college textbooks—

KEY TERM

Assessing Your Prior Knowledge

Determining what you already know about a topic.

Comprehension Monitoring Questions for Assessing Your Prior Knowledge

What do I already know about this topic? How familiar am I with this topic?

you may have difficulty comprehending the material. **Assessing your prior knowledge,** determining what you already know about the topic, will enable you to decide whether you need help with the assignment and whether you need to allow additional time. To assess your prior knowledge, simply ask yourself, "What do I already know about this topic?" and "How familiar am I with this topic?" Previewing the chapter can help you determine this. By introducing you to the chapter topics, previewing allows you to predict whether or not you will be dealing with familiar material.

If the material is new to you, you may need to take extra steps to deal with an assignment successfully. While you are previewing, while you are reading, or after you finish reading, you may discover that you do not understand the material adequately, and you may decide that you need more background knowledge. If so, it is your responsibility to take some or all of these steps to fill in missing background information:

- Reading other, perhaps easier, textbooks on the same subject (these might be other college textbooks or more general study aids, such as an outline of American history or a text with a title such as *Accounting Made Easy*).
- Consulting an encyclopedia, a good dictionary, or some other reference book.
- Talking with someone who is knowledgeable about the subject.

These steps require effort, and obviously there are no shortcuts. But going the extra mile to get necessary background information is part of being a responsible, mature learner and student. As a bonus, you may discover that it is exciting and satisfying to understand new or difficult material through your own efforts. You may also find that when you take responsibility for your own learning, you will feel good about yourself as a student. (Remember that a *student* is someone who *studies.*)

Plan Your Reading and Study Time

Comprehension Monitoring Questions for Planning Your Study Time

How can I best allot my time for this assignment? Do I need to divide the assignment into smaller units?

By previewing an assignment, you will be able to decide whether you can read the entire assignment in just one study session or whether you need to divide it into smaller parts.

If you decide that you need more than one study session, you should divide the assignment into several shorter segments and read them at times when you know you can concentrate best. For example, a 15-page chapter may be too much for you to read and study effectively all at once. You could divide the assignment in half and read it over two days. Or you could divide this long assignment into three 5-page segments and read them during three 1-hour study sessions on the same day, perhaps at 1, 5, and 8 P.M. In any case, plan your study-reading session and follow your plan. (Then reward yourself after you complete your studying!)

Step 2: Ask and Answer Questions to Guide Your Reading

The second step in reading and studying a college textbook assignment is guiding your reading by asking and answering questions. To read and study effectively, you need to read and understand each paragraph or section. This means that you must determine what is important to learn and remember in each section. To put it another way, you need to read for a specific purpose. Reading for a specific purpose will increase your interest and concentration, and it will enable you to monitor (evaluate) your comprehension while you are reading. One of the best ways to learn the material in a reading assignment is to ask and answer questions about the material as you read.

Ask Questions as You Read

Creating one or more questions for each section of a reading assignment will guide you to the pertinent, important information and help you remember that information. When you read to seek answers to questions, you will be reading with a specific purpose; in other words, you will be reading selectively and purposefully.

Turning chapter headings and subheadings into questions is the easiest way to accomplish this step. For example, if a section in a history textbook has a heading "The American Revolutionary War Begins," you might want to ask, "Why did the war begin?" You may also want to ask, "When did it begin?" (In Chapters 10 and 11 you will be working with actual college textbook chapters which have headings that can be turned into useful questions.)

When a section or paragraph has no heading, it is a good idea to create a question based on what that section or paragraph appears to be about. If you see a term or phrase in bold print, italics, or color you might create a question about that term or phrase. You can also create questions about names of people, places, events, and so on. Of course, you will be able to refine your questions later, when you read the material more carefully.

In addition to creating your own questions as you read each section of a textbook, you may find that the author has included questions for you. These may appear at the end of a chapter, at the beginning of a chapter, throughout a chapter (perhaps in the margins), or in an accompanying study guide. If a textbook chapter contains such questions, read them before you read the chapter. Then keep them in mind as you read. When you have finished reading the chapter, you should be able to answer these questions. In fact, you will very probably be asked some of these same questions on a test.

Finally, your instructor may give you questions to guide you as you read a chapter. Of course, you should be able to answer these questions by the time you finish reading and studying the chapter. Chapter questions, regardless of the source, enable you monitor your comprehension: Are you understanding the important information the author and your instructor expect you to know? Identifying important information lets you begin preparing for tests from the day you first read the assignment.

Answer Questions When You Come to the End of Each Section

As you read each paragraph or section, look for answers to your questions. Then, after you have finished reading that section, record the answers by writing them down. A word of warning: Do not try to record answers *while* you are

Comprehension Monitoring Question for Asking and Answering Questions as You Read

Am I understanding the important information the author and my instructor expect me to know?

reading a section. Constantly switching between reading and writing disrupts your comprehension and will greatly slow you down. The time to write your answers is immediately after you *finish* reading a section, not while you are reading it for the first time.

There are several effective ways to record your answers. One of the most effective is to write answers on notebook paper or in the margins of your textbook. Another effective way of recording answers is to make review cards for the material. With either of these techniques, be sure your answer makes it clear which question you are answering. In addition to writing out your answers, you may want to mark information in the textbook that answers your questions.

What if you cannot locate or formulate an answer to one of your questions? In that case, there are several things you can do:

- Read ahead to see if the answer becomes apparent.
- If the question involves an important term you need to know, look the term up in the glossary or in a dictionary.
- Go back and reread a paragraph or a section.
- Do some extra reading, ask a classmate, or ask your instructor about it.
- If you still cannot answer all of your questions after you have read an assignment, note which questions remain unanswered. Put a question mark in the margin, or make a list of the unanswered questions. One way or another, be sure to find the answers.

As you can see, actively seeking answers to questions encourages you to concentrate and focus on *understanding* as you read. Reading for a purpose—to answer specific questions—can help you remember more and ultimately score higher on tests. Often, you will discover that questions on tests are identical to the questions you asked yourself as you studied. When this happens, you will be glad that you took the time to use this technique while you were studying.

Step 3: Review by Rehearsing Your Answers

Experienced college students know that if they want to remember what they read in their textbooks and the answers they wrote to questions, they need to take certain steps to make it happen. They also know that it is essential to take these steps immediately after they finish reading a section or a chapter, while the material is still in short-term memory—that is, while the material is still fresh in their minds. Good readers know that forgetting occurs very rapidly and that they need to rehearse material immediately in order to remember it; or in other words, to transfer it into long-term (permanent) memory. The shocking fact is that unless you take some special action beyond simply reading a textbook assignment, you will forget half of what you read by the time you finish the chapter!

One highly effective way to rehearse important points in a chapter is to read your questions and *recite* answers from the material. Simply rereading your answers is not good enough; you should say them *aloud*. Remember, "If you can't say it, you don't know it."

Another highly effective way to rehearse important points in a chapter is to *rewrite them from memory*. When you give yourself a "practice test" in this way, you transfer the material into long-term memory. (A second benefit of this method is that it allows you to pinpoint any weak areas.) When you check your answers, make corrections and add any information needed to make your answers complete.

Taking the time to review and rehearse immediately after you finish reading a chapter will not only help you remember what you learned. It will also give you a feeling of accomplishment, which in turn will encourage you to continue learning. One success will build on another.

To recapitulate, here is the three-step process: (1) Prepare to read by previewing, assessing your prior knowledge, and planning your study time. (2) Ask and answer questions to guide your reading. (3) Review by rehearsing your answers. This process will enable you to learn more as you complete your textbook reading assignments, and it will also be a foundation for effective test preparation.

Remember that preparing for a test *begins* with reading textbook assignments effectively. Specific techniques for preparing for tests are discussed in Chapters 10 and 11. They include annotating textbooks by writing marginal study notes, outlining, "mapping," writing summaries, creating review cards, and developing test review sheets. Part of doing well on any test, of course, is following the directions. The next section focuses on following directions.

Comprehension Monitoring Question for Reviewing by Rehearsing Your Answers

Can I recite answers to questions about the material and write the answers from memory?

FOLLOWING DIRECTIONS IN TEXTBOOKS AND ON TESTS

An important part of success in college is following written directions. In particular, it is important for you to understand directions in order to do your assignments correctly, carry out procedures in classes and labs (such as computer labs and science labs), and earn high grades on tests.

You have probably learned from experience that problems can arise from misunderstanding or failing to follow directions. Perhaps you have answered an entire set of test questions instead of some specific number stated in the directions ("Answer any *five* of the following seven essay questions"). Or you may have had points deducted from your grade on a research paper because you did not follow the correct format ("Double-space your paper and number the pages"). When you do not follow directions, you can waste time and lower your grade.

Guidelines for Following Directions

There are a few simple things to remember about following written directions:

- **Read the entire set of directions carefully before doing any of the steps.** This is one time when you must slow down and pay attention to every word.

- **Make sure you understand all the words in the directions.**   Although directions may use words you see very often, you may still not know precisely what each of the words means. For example, on an essay test you might be asked to compare two poems or contrast two pieces of music. Do you know the difference between *compare* and *contrast?* Unless you do, you cannot answer the question correctly. Other typical words in test questions include *enumerate, justify, explain,* and *illustrate.* Each has a specific meaning. General direction words include *above, below, consecutive, preceding, succeeding, former,* and *latter.* In addition, directions in college textbooks and assignments often include many specialized terms that you must understand. For example, in a set of directions for a biology lab experiment, you might be instructed to "stain a tissue sample on a slide." The words *stain, tissue,* and *slide* have very specific meanings in biology.

- **Circle signals that announce steps in directions and underline key words.**   Not every step in a set of directions will have a signal word, of course, but steps in sets of directions frequently are introduced by letters or numbers (*a, b, c,* or 1, 2, 3, etc.) or words such as *first, second, third, next, then, finally,* and *last* to indicate the sequence or order of the steps.

You should mark directions *before* you begin following them, since you must understand what you are to do *before* you try to do it. This means finding and numbering steps if they are not already numbered. Be aware that a single sentence sometimes contains more than one step. (For example, "Type your name, enter your I.D. number, and press the Enter key.") When you are busy working on a test or an assignment, it is easy to become distracted and do the steps in the wrong order or leave a step out. Another reason it is important to number steps in a set of directions is that even though the steps may not include signal words, you are still responsible for finding each step. Especially on tests, then, you should number each step and mark key words in directions.

Example: Directions from a Textbook

Look at the following box, which shows a set of directions from a textbook entitled *Getting Started with the Internet.* The directions explain how to "log on" in order to establish a connection with a network. (It is necessary to log on so that you can use e-mail, visit Internet websites, and access certain software programs.)

Notice that the steps in the directions are numbered. If you were actually following these directions, you would want to read the entire set first, then mark key words. Notice also that before you can carry out these directions, you must understand certain terms (such as *system, host name, alpha,* and *numeric*) and know certain information (such as your assigned username and the last four digits of your Social Security Number). Notice also that step 5 is written as a single paragraph. This makes it easy to overlook the fact that there are two im-

---

LOGGING ON

The method for logging on may vary by site. The following steps are very general. Check with your instructor for specific steps at your site.

1. Turn on system.

2. Choose Host Name: _____

3. Username: Enter your assigned username.

4. Password: (Enter the last four digits of Soc. Sec. #)

5. The first time you may have to change the password to something of your choice. It should be at least 6 characters (alpha, numeric, or a combination of both. Enter your selection and then verify it by entering the same value again. Remember it or you will not be able to log in again.

6. A $, ¢, or % prompt will appear. You are now on the network. (We will be using the $ as the prompt in our examples.)

7. When you are finished with all your exercises for the day, you exit the system with

$logout   or   *$lo*

Source: Joan Lumpkin and Susan Durnbaugh, *Getting Started with the Internet,* Wiley, New York, 1995, pp. 12–13.

---

portant parts in this step: after typing your password the first time, you must verify it by typing it again.

Example: Directions for a Test

The first box on page 144 shows a set of directions for a unit test in a psychology course. Read these directions carefully.

Notice that this unit has two distinct parts: Part I—Content Questions, and Part II—Discussion Questions. Part I of the test consists of multiple-choice questions, whereas Part II requires the student to write essay answers.

Notice that each multiple-choice question in Part I is worth 2 points (for a total of 50 points), and that the student must use a machine-scorable answer sheet and a number two pencil. Also, notice that Part I is to be completed before beginning Part II.

In Part II, notice that each question is worth a possible 25 points (for a total of 50 points). Next, notice a key point in the directions: only two of the four discussion questions are to be answered. Notice that notebook paper is required for these two essay answers, but either pen or pencil may be used. Finally, notice that the answer to each discussion question must be at least 3 paragraphs long, but not longer than 5 paragraphs.

Marking the test directions as shown in the second box on page 144 would help you follow them accurately.

UNIT TEST: PSYCHOLOGICAL DISORDERS

Directions:

   Part I—Content Questions. (2 points each.) Answer the 25 multiple-choice questions using the machine-scorable answer sheet provided. (You must use a number two pencil on this answer sheet.) Complete this part of the test before you begin Part II.

   Part II—Discussion Questions. (25 points each.) Answer two of the four discussion questions, using notebook paper. (You may use pen or pencil for this portion of the test.) The answer to each discussion question should be 3–5 paragraphs in length.

SAMPLE OF MARKED DIRECTIONS FOR UNIT TEST: PSYCHOLOGICAL DISORDERS

Directions:

(50 points)   ①.

   Part I—Content Questions. (2 points *each*.) *Answer the 25 multiple-choice questions* using the *machine-scorable answer sheet* provided. (*You must use a number two pencil* on this answer sheet) Complete this part of the test *before you begin Part II*. (50 points)   ②.

   Part II—Discussion Questions. (25 points *each*.). *Answer two of the four discussion questions*, using *notebook paper*. (You may use *pen or pencil* for this portion of the test.) The answer to each discussion question should be *3–5 paragraphs in length*.

DEVELOPING CHAPTER REVIEW CARDS

Review cards, or *summary cards,* are an excellent study tool. They are a way to select, organize, and review the most important information in a textbook chapter. The process of creating review cards helps you organize information in a meaningful way and, at the same time, transfer it into long-term memory. The cards can also be used to prepare for tests (see Part Three). The review card activities in this book give you structured practice in creating these valuable study tools. Once you have learned how to make review cards, you can create them for textbook material in your other courses.

Now, complete the eight review cards for Chapter 3 by answering the questions or following the directions on each card. When you have completed them, you will have summarized important information about: (1) preparing to read, (2) previewing a textbook chapter, (3) assessing your prior knowledge, (4) guiding your reading, (5) answering questions as you read, (6) reviewing by rehearsing, (7) following directions in textbooks and on tests, and (8) monitoring your comprehension as you read.

The Three-Step Process for Reading and Studying: Step 1

What is the first step of the three-step study-reading process? (See page 136.)

Step 1: _____

Step 1 involves these three parts: (See pages 136–138.)

_____

_____

_____

Card 1   **Chapter 3: Approaching College Assignments**

Previewing a Textbook Chapter

One part of step 1 in the study-reading process is previewing a chapter. List seven things to do when previewing. (See page 137.)

1. _____

2. _____

3. _____

4. _____

5. _____

6. _____

7. _____

Card 2   **Chapter 3: Approaching College Assignments**

Assessing Your Prior Knowledge

Assessing your prior knowledge is part of step 1 in the study-reading process. Define *prior knowledge.* (See page 138.)

_____

_____

List three things you can do if you need to increase your prior knowledge about a topic. (See page 138.).

1. _____

_____

2. _____

_____

3. _____

Card 3   **Chapter 3: Approaching College Assignments**

The Three-Step Process for Reading and Studying: Step 2

What is the second step of the three-step study-reading process? (See page 138.)

Step 2: _____

List at least four chapter features or other sources on which you can base your own questions to ask as you read. (See page 139.)

_____

_____

_____

_____

Card 4   **Chapter 3: Approaching College Assignments**

Answering Questions as You Read

When should you record the answers to your questions about a passage? (See pages 139–140.)

_____

List three ways to record your answers. (See page 140.)

_____

_____

_____

Describe some things you can do if any of your questions remain unanswered when you have finished a passage. (See page 140.)

_____

_____

_____

Card 5   **Chapter 3: Approaching College Assignments**

The Three-Step Process for Reading and Studying: Step 3

What is the third step of the three-step study-reading process? (See page 140.)

Step 3: _____

When should you rehearse the answers to your questions about material in a reading assignment? (See page 140.)

_____

List two effective way to rehearse. (See pages 140–141.)

1. _____

2. _____

Card 6   **Chapter 3: Approaching College Assignments**

Following Directions

List three things to remember about following written directions. (See pages 141–142.)

1. _____

_____

2. _____

_____

3. _____

_____

Card 7   **Chapter 3: Approaching College Assignments**

Monitoring Your Comprehension as You Read and Study College Textbooks

1. What questions should you ask yourself while you are previewing a chapter? (See page 137.)

   _____

2. What questions should you ask yourself while you are assessing your prior knowledge? (See page 138.)

   _____

3. What questions should you ask yourself while you are planning your study time? (See page 138.)

   _____

   _____

4. What question should you ask yourself as you are asking and answering questions as you read? (See page 139.)

   _____

5. What question should you ask yourself as you review a chapter by rehearsing your answers? (See page 141.)

   _____

Card 8   **Chapter 3: Approaching College Assignments**

HOW TO FIND TIME TO READ

By Louis Shores

Prepare Yourself to Read

Directions: Do these exercises *before* you read Selection 3-1.

1. First, read and think about the title. What does this essay seem to be about?

_____

_____

2. Next, complete your preview by reading the following:

Introduction (in *italics*)
First paragraph (paragraph 1)
First sentence of each paragraph
Last paragraph (paragraph 10)

On the basis of your preview, what do you think will be discussed?

_____

_____

3. How much leisure reading do you currently do? What types of things do you like to read?

_____

_____

Apply Comprehension Skills

Directions: Do these exercises as you read Selection 3-2.

Ask and answer questions as you read. Complete the practice exercises by creating questions based on what each paragraph seems to be about.

Read actively to find answers to your questions. Record the answers to your questions. Write the answer in the margin or highlight the answer in the text.

Review by rehearsing the answers to your questions. Recite your answers or write them down from memory.

HOW TO FIND TIME TO READ

Being able to read well and finding enough time to read have become even more important in today's information age. The majority of information on the Internet must be read. People who lack strong reading skills will have more difficulty accessing information and acquiring new skills.

This classic essay about finding time for leisure reading was written for a general audience. However, finding time for this kind of reading is an even greater problem for busy college students. If you spend considerable time on your required academic reading, you may feel that you have no time to read magazines, newspapers, or books for pleasure. The author of this selection gives a simple, effective solution to the problem of "how to find time to read."

1   If you are an average reader, you can read an average book at the rate of 300 words per minute. You cannot maintain that average, however, unless you read regularly every day. Nor can you attain that speed with hard books in science, mathematics, agriculture, business, or any subject that is new or unfamiliar to you. The chances are you will never attempt that speed with poetry or want to race through some passages in fiction over which you wish to linger. But for most novels, biographies, and books about travel, hobbies, or personal interests, if you are an average reader you should have no trouble at all absorbing meaning and pleasure out of 300 printed words every 60 seconds.

2   Statistics are not always practicable, but consider these: If the average reader can read 300 words a minute of average reading, then in 15 minutes he or she can read 4,500 words. Multiplied by 7, the days of the week, the product is 31,500. Another multiplication by 4, the weeks of the month, makes 126,000. And final multiplication by 12, the months of the year, results in a grand total of 1,512,000 words. That is the total number of words of average reading an average reader can do in just 15 minutes a day for one year.

3   Books vary in length from 60,000 to 100,000 words. The average is about 75,000 words. In one year of average reading by an average reader for 15 minutes a day, 20 books will be read. That's a lot of books. It is 4 times the number of books read by public-library borrowers in America. And yet it is easily possible.

Practice Exercises

Directions: For each paragraph,

- Create a question based on what the paragraph seems to be about. Ask *who, what, when, where, why,* or *how.*
- Write your question in the spaces provided.
- Write the answer to your question in the margin or highlight it in the text.

Doing this will help you understand and remember the material.

Practice Exercise

Question about paragraph 1:

_____

_____

Practice Exercise

Question about paragraph 2:

_____

_____

Practice Exercise

Question about paragraph 3:

_____

_____

4   One of the greatest of all modern physicians was Sir William Osler. He taught at the Johns Hopkins Medical School. He finished his teaching days at Oxford University. Many outstanding physicians today were his students. At some point, nearly all of the practicing doctors had been brought up on his medical textbooks. Among his many remarkable contributions to medicine were his unpublished notes on how people die.

5   His greatness is attributed by his biographers and critics not alone to his profound medical knowledge and insight but to his broad general education, for he was a very cultured man. He was interested in what men have done and thought throughout the ages. And he knew that the only way to find out what the best experiences of the race had been was to read what people had written. But Osler's problem was the same as everyone else's, only more so. He was a busy physician, a teacher of physicians, and a medical-research specialist. There was no time in a 24-hour day that did not rightly belong to one of these three occupations, except the few hours for sleep, meals, and bodily functions.

6   Osler arrived at his solution early. He would read the last 15 minutes before he went to sleep. If bedtime was set for 11:00 P.M., he read from 11:00 to 11:15. If research kept him up to 2:00 A.M., he read from 2:00 to 2:15. Over a very long lifetime, Osler never broke the rule once he had established it. We have evidence that after a while he simply could not fall asleep until he had done his 15 minutes of reading.

7   In his lifetime, Osler read a significant library of books. Just do a mental calculation for half a century of 15-minute reading periods daily and see how many books you get. Consider what a range of interests and variety of subjects are possible in one lifetime. Osler read widely outside of his medical specialty. Indeed, he developed from the 15-minute reading habit an avocational specialty to balance his vocational specialization. Among scholars in English literature, Osler is known as an authority on Sir Thomas Browne, a seventeenth-century English prose master, and Osler's library on Sir Thomas is considered one of the best anywhere. A great many more things could be said about Osler's contribution to medical research, to the reform of medical teaching, to the introduction of modern clinical methods. But the important point for us here is that he an-

It is always possible to find time to read.
(Frank Siteman/Stock Boston)

Practice Exercise

Question about paragraph 4:

_____

_____

Practice Exercise

Question about paragraph 5:

_____

_____

Practice Exercise

Question about paragraph 6:

_____

_____

Practice Exercise

Question about paragraph 7:

_____

_____

swered supremely well for himself the question all of us who live a busy life must answer: How can I find time to read?

8   No universal formula can be prescribed. Each of us must find our own 15-minute period each day. It is better if it is regular. Then all additional spare minutes are so many bonuses. And, believe me, the opportunity for reading-bonuses are many and unexpected. Last night an univited guest turned up to make five for bridge. I had the kind of paperback book at hand to make being the fifth at bridge a joy.

9   The only requirement is the will to read. With it you can find the 15 minutes no matter how busy the day. And you must have the book at hand. Not even seconds of your 15 minutes must be wasted starting to read. Set that book out in advance. Put it into your pocket when you dress. Put another book beside your bed. Place one in your bathroom. Keep one near your dining table.

10   You can't escape reading 15 minutes a day, and that means you will read half a book a week, 2 books a month, 20 a year, and 1,000 or more in a reading lifetime. It's an easy way to become well read.

Practice Exercise

Question about paragraph 8:

_____

_____

Practice Exercise

Question about paragraph 9:

_____

_____

Practice Exercise

Question about paragraph 10:

_____

_____

Source: Adapted from Louis Shores, "How to Find Time to Read," in Frank Christ, ed., *SR/SE Resource Book,* Chicago, Ill., SRA, 1969, pp. 105–107, abridged.

SELECTION **3-1**

Essay

Comprehension Quiz

Directions: For each comprehension question below, use information from the selection to determine the correct answer. You may refer to the selection as you answer the questions. Write your answer in the space provided.

True or False

_____ **1.** The author states that the average reader reads 400 words per minute.

_____ **2.** According to the author, it is possible to read books in science and math at the same rate of speed as novels and biographies.

_____ **3.** The author stresses that readers should never read for more than 15 minutes a day.

_____ **4.** By reading for 15 minutes a day, the average reader can read 20 books a year.

_____ **5.** William Osler maintained a schedule of wide reading by reading 15 minutes each day at bedtime.

_____ **6.** William Osler had time to read only medical books.

Multiple-Choice

_____ **7.** Which of the following statements about William Osler is false?
- *a.* He was an outstanding teacher at Johns Hopkins Medical School and Oxford University.
- *b.* He wrote widely-used medical textbooks.
- *c.* He was noted for his profound medical knowledge and his broad general knowledge.
- *d.* He rarely broke his habit of daily reading once he had established it.

_____ **8.** A lifetime habit of reading enabled William Osler to
- *a.* read widely outside his medical specialty.
- *b.* become an authority on a famous English writer, Sir Thomas Browne.
- *c.* become cultured and highly regarded as a man of broad general knowledge.
- *d.* all of the above.

_____ **9.** It is the writer's opinion that an average reader
- *a.* can become well-read by reading for 15 minutes a day.
- *b.* should build a collection of books he or she has read.
- *c.* should read at least four different types of books.
- *d.* should become an expert in a particular area.

_____ **10.** In the United States, users of public libraries typically read

 a.   5 books a year.

 b.   10 books a year.

 c.   20 books a year.

 d.   40 books a year.

Extend Your Vocabulary by Using Context Clues

Directions: Context clues are words in a sentence that allow the reader to deduce (reason out) the meaning of an unfamiliar word in that sentence. For each vocabulary item below, a sentence from the selection containing an important word (*italicized, like this*) is quoted first. Next, there is an additional sentence using the word in the same sense and providing another context clue. Use the context clues from *both* sentences to deduce the meaning of the italicized word. *Be sure the answer you choose makes sense in both sentences.* If you discover that you must use a dictionary to confirm an answer choice, remember that the meaning you select must still fit the context of both sentences. To indicate your answer, write the letter in the space provided.

Pronunciation key: ă pat ā pay âr care ä father ĕ pet ē be ĭ pit
ī tie îr pier ŏ pot ō toe ô paw oi noise ou out ŏŏ took
ŏŏ boot ŭ cut yŏŏ abuse ûr urge *th* thin *th* this hw which
zh vision ə about
Stress Mark: ′

_____ **1.** The chances are you will never attempt a fast speed with poetry or race through some passages in fiction over which you wish to *linger.*

 After the final football game of a winning season, some students always *linger* at the victory party long after it is scheduled to end.

 linger (lĭng′ gər) means:

 a.   finish quickly

 b.   read slowly

 c.   stay as though reluctant to leave

 d.   be with friends

_____ **2.** Statistics are not always *practicable,* but consider these: If the average reader can read 300 words a minute of average reading, then in 15 minutes he can read 4,500 words.

 The engineer's first plan for stabilizing the bridge was too difficult and expensive to be *practicable.*

practicable (prăk′ tĭ kə bəl) means:

a. feasible or suitable

b. requiring practice

c. reliable; dependable

d. accomplished without practice

_____ **3.** At one point, nearly all of the practicing doctors had been brought up on his medical textbooks.

Judge Carver continued to be a *practicing* judge until the day he died at age 76.

practicing (prăk tĭs ĭng) means:

a. gaining experience

b. not held in high regard

c. working a limited number of hours per week

d. actively engaged in a profession

_____ **4.** His greatness is attributed by his biographers and critics not alone to his *profound* medical knowledge and insight but to his broad general education, for he was a very cultured man.

The Greek philosopher Plato had a *profound* respect for the power of reason.

profound (prə found′) means:

a. limited; partial

b. lifelong

c. absolute; complete

d. incorrect

_____ **5.** His greatness is attributed by his biographers and critics not alone to his profound medical knowledge and insight but to his broad general education, for he was a very *cultured* man.

Knowledge of music, art, and literature is considered a characteristic of a *cultured* person.

cultured (kŭl′ chərd) means:

a. pretentious; snobbish

b. having a college degree

c. elderly

d. having refined intellectual and artistic taste

_____ **6.** Indeed, he developed from this 15-minute reading habit an *avocational* specialty to balance his vocational specialization.

Marty is a pilot, so it is not surprising that his *avocational* interests include making and flying radio-controlled model airplanes.

avocational (ăv ə kā′ shən l) means:

a.   pertaining to food or cuisine

b.   pertaining to a hobby

c.   pertaining to a profession or career

d.   pertaining to the voice

7.   Indeed, he developed from this 15-minute reading habit an avocational specialty to balance his *vocational* specialization.

Vocational courses at our college include data processing, bookkeeping, automotive technology, and robotics.

vocational (vō kā′ shən l) means:

a.   pertaining to an occupation

b.   pertaining to a college or university

c.   pertaining to a vacation or leisure time

d.   pertaining to salary or income

8.   Among scholars in English literature, Osler is known as an authority on Sir Thomas Browne, a seventeenth-century English *prose* master.

Most students feel that *prose* is easier to understand than poetry.

prose (prōz) means:

a.   ordinary speech and writing instead of verse

b.   sonnets and love songs

c.   plays written by Shakespeare

d.   literature by British writers

9.   A great many more things could be said about Osler's contribution to medical research, to the *reform* of medical teaching, to the introduction of modern clinical methods.

Congress wants a *reform* of the federal tax code, which is too complex and confusing for the average person to understand.

reform (rĭ fôrm′) means:

a.   creation; development

b.   abuse or malpractice

c.   improvement by correction of errors or removal of defects

d.   a return to the beginning

10.   But the important point for us is that he answered *supremely* well for himself the question all of us who live a busy life must answer: How can I find time to read?

The Smiths were *supremely* happy after they retired and moved to Hawaii.

supremely (sə prēm′ lē) means:

a. finally

b. temporarily

c. slightly

d. to the best or greatest extent

S E L E C T I O N **3-1**

Essay

Collaboration Option

Respond in Writing

Directions: Refer to the selection as needed to answer the essay-type questions below.

Option for collaboration: Your instructor may direct you to work with other students or, in other words, to work *collaboratively.* In that case, you should form groups of three or four students as directed by your instructor and work together to complete the exercises. After your group discusses each item and agrees on the answer, have a group member record it. Every member of your group should be able to explain all of your group's answers.

1. How much leisure reading (reading other than your assigned reading) do you do each day?

   _____

   _____

   _____

2. If you do not already spend at least 15 minutes a day on leisure reading, when during your day could you perhaps fit in 15 minutes?

   _____

   _____

   _____

3. Most Americans are not regular users of public libraries. According to the author, those who do borrow library books read only five books a year. How often do you check out books from a public library or a college library? How often do you go to bookstores?

   _____

   _____

   _____

4. In what areas would you like to do more reading? Do you do more non-school reading on the Internet or in books, magazines, and newspapers? Would you read more books if they were readily available on the Internet? Why or why not?

_____

_____

_____

5. Overall main idea. What is the overall main idea the author wants the reader to understand about finding time to read? Answer this question in one sentence.

_____

_____

_____

_____

_____

_____

Read More about It on the World Wide Web

To learn more about the topic of this selection, visit these websites or use your favorite search engine (such as Yahoo ®). Whenever you go to any website, it is a good idea to evaluate it critically. Are you getting good information—information that is accurate, complete, and up-to-date? Who sponsors the website? How easy is it to use the features of the website?

http://www.demon.co.uk/mindtool/rdstratg.html
   This is a mindtools.com link, which provides strategies for improving reading skills.

http://www.quitwhining.com
   The goal of the "Quit Whining and Read" Literacy Program is to increase awareness of the need for literacy programs.

SELECTION **3-2**

Human Development

PARENTHOOD

From *Human Development*

By Diane E. Papalia and Sally Wendkos Olds

Prepare Yourself to Read

Directions: Do these exercises *before* you read Selection 3-2.

1. It has been said that "parenthood is the hardest job in the world if you do it right." Do you agree? Why or why not?

    _____

    _____

    _____

2. Next, complete your preview by reading the following:

    Introduction (in *italics*)
    First paragraph (paragraph 1)
    Headings for each section
    Bar graph and explanation beside it
    All of the last paragraph (paragraph 17)

    On the basis of your preview, what aspects of parenthood do you think will be discussed?

    _____

Apply Comprehension Skills

Directions: Do these exercises as you read Selection 3-2.

Ask and answer questions as you read.   Complete the practice exercises by creating questions based on what each paragraph seems to be about.

Read actively to find answers to your questions.   Record the answers to your questions. Write the answer in the margin or highlight the answer in the text.

Review by rehearsing the answers to your questions.   Recite your answers or write them down from memory.

PARENTHOOD

"Just wait until you have children of your own!" At one time or another in our lives, we have all heard these words from our parents. Becoming a parent and being a parent affect every area of a person's life. In this selection, the authors present some of the new, interesting, and sometimes surprising research findings about parenthood.

1   The birth of a baby marks a major transition in the parents' lives. Moving from an intimate relationship between two people to one involving a totally dependent third person changes individuals and changes marriages. Parenthood is a developmental experience, whether the children are biological offspring, are adopted, or are the children of only one spouse.

Why People Have Children

2   At one time, the blessing offered newlyweds in the Asian country of Nepal was, "May you have enough sons to cover the hillsides!" (B. P. Arjyal, personal communication, Feb. 12, 1993). Having children has traditionally been regarded as not only the primary reason for marriage, but its ultimate fulfillment. In preindustrial societies, large families were a necessity: children helped with the family's work and eventually cared for their aging parents. And because the death rate in childhood was high, fewer children reached maturity. Because economic and social reasons for having children were so powerful, parenthood—especially motherhood—had a unique aura.

3   Today, Nepali couples are wished, "May you have a very bright son." Although sons are still preferred over daughters there, even boys are not wished for in such numbers as in the past, in the face of the lessening or even reversal of previous reasons for having children. Because of technological progress, fewer workers are needed; because of modern medical care, most children survive; and because of government programs, some care of the aged is being provided. Overpopulation is a major problem in many parts of the world, and children are an expense rather than an economic asset. Furthermore, children can have negative, as well as positive, effects on a marriage.

4   Still, the desire for children is almost universal. Why? Psychoanalytic theorists like Freud

Practice Exercises

Directions: For each paragraph,

- Create a question based on what the paragraph seems to be about. Ask *who, what, when, where, why,* or *how.*

- Write your question in the spaces provided.

- Write the answer to your question in the margin or highlight it in the text.

Doing this will help you understand and remember the material.

Practice Exercise

Question about paragraph 1:

_____

_____

Practice Exercise

Question about paragraph 2:

_____

_____

Practice Exercise

Question about paragraph 3:

_____

_____

Practice Exercise

Question about paragraph 4:

_____

maintain that women have a deep instinctual wish to bear and nurture infants. Ego psychologists like Erikson see generativity—a concern with establishing and guiding the next generation—as a basic developmental need. Functionalist sociologists attribute reproduction to people's need for immortality, achieved by replacing themselves with their children. Other theorists consider parenthood a part of nature, universal in the animal world. There is also continuing cultural pressure to have children, on the assumption that all normal people want them. For the subjects in one study of 199 married couples—nonparents to parents of four—the chief motivations for parenthood were the wish for a close relationship with another human being and the desire to educate and train a child (F. L. Campbell, Townes, & Beach, 1982).

The birth of a baby marks a major transition in the parents' lives.
(David J. Sams/Stock Boston)

When People Have Children

5   The authors of this book exemplify changing trends in parenthood over the past 30 years. Sally [Wendkos Olds] was 23 years old in 1957, when she had her first child; not until after her third child was born, 5 years later, did she actively pursue her writing career. Diane [Papalia], who is younger, established her academic career first and was 39 when she and Jonathan adopted Anna in 1986.

6   By and large today's couples have fewer children and have them later in life than the previous generation did; now many people spend the early years of their marriage finishing an education and starting a career. More contemporary women—16 percent in 1987 versus 4 percent in 1970—have a first child after age 30 (National Center for Health Statistics, 1990).

7   This pattern is not an accident: today's women see a later "ideal age" for first birth. The most recently married women, the best educated, and the most strongly feminist choose the latest ideal ages (Pebley, 1981). And more educated women actually do have their children later; educational level is the most important predictor of the age when a woman will first give birth (Rindfuss, Morgan, & Swicegood, 1988; Rindfuss & St. John, 1983).

8   The trend toward later motherhood seems to be a blessing for babies. Although mothers over 35 have a higher risk of birth-related complica-

Practice Exercise
Question about paragraph 5:
_____
_____

Practice Exercise
Question about paragraph 6:
_____
_____

Practice Exercise
Question about paragraph 7:
_____
_____

Practice Exercise
Question about paragraph 8:
_____
_____

Today, women tend to have fewer children and have them later in life than their mothers' generation did. More women now have a first child after age 30.

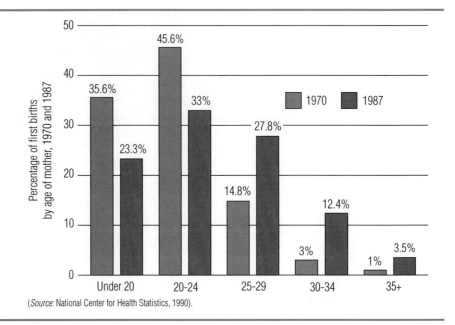

(*Source:* National Center for Health Statistics, 1990).

tions, the risk to the baby's health is only slightly higher than for infants of younger women (Berkowitz, Skovoron, Lapinski, & Berkowitz, 1990). On the positive side, babies of older mothers seem to benefit from their mothers' greater ease with parenthood. When 105 new mothers aged 16 to 38 were interviewed and observed with their infants, the older mothers reported more satisfaction with parenting and spent more time at it. They were more affectionate and sensitive to their babies and more effective in encouraging desired behavior (Ragozin, Basham, Crinic, Greenberg, & Robinson, 1982).

The Transition to Parenthood

9 Both women and men often feel ambivalent about becoming parents. Along with excitement, they usually feel some anxiety about the responsibility of caring for a child and about the permanence that a pregnancy seems to impose on a marriage. Pregnancy also affects a couple's sexual relationship, sometimes making it more intimate, but sometimes creating barriers.

10 What happens in a marriage from the time of the first pregnancy until the child's third birthday? That varies considerably. One research team followed 128 middle- and working-

Practice Exercise

Question about paragraph 9:

_____

_____

Practice Exercise

Question about paragraph 10:

_____

_____

class couples during this time; at the beginning of the study the husbands' ages averaged 29 years and wives' 27 years. Although some marriages improved, many suffered overall, especially for the wives. Many spouses loved each other less, became more ambivalent about their relationship, argued more, and communicated less. This was true no matter what the sex of the child was and whether or not the couple had the second child by the time the first was 3 years old. But when the researchers looked, not at the *overall* quality of the marriage, but at such *individual* measures as love, conflict, ambivalence, and effort put into the relationship, at least half of the sample showed either no change on a particular measure or a small positive change (Belsky & Rovine, 1990).

11 What distinguishes marriages that deteriorate after parenthood from those that improve? This study found no single determining factor. Rather, a number of different factors related to both parents and child seemed influential. In deteriorating marriages, the partners were more likely to be younger and less well educated, to earn less money, and to have been married for fewer years. One or both partners tended to have low self-esteem, and husbands were likely to be less sensitive (Belsky & Rovine, 1990). The mothers who had the hardest time were those with babies who had irregular temperaments and were therefore harder to take care of. . . .

12 Two surprising findings emerged from Belsky and Rovine's study. First, couples who were most romantic "pre-baby" had more problems "post-baby," perhaps because they had unrealistic expectations. Second, women who had planned their pregnancies were unhappier, possibly because they had expected life with a baby to be better than it turned out to be. Another finding of unmet expectations emerged from a study of married, middle-class white women. These mothers too expected things to be better 1 year after their first babies were born—in terms of their relationships with their husbands, their own physical well-being, and their maternal competence and satisfaction—than they turned out to be, and had trouble adjusting (Kalmuss, Davidson, & Cushman, 1992).

13 One often violated expectation involves the division of chores. When a couple has shared them fairly equally before the baby is born, and then, post-baby, the burden shifts to the wife, marital

Practice Exercise

Question about paragraph 11:

_____

_____

Practice Exercise

Question about paragraph 12:

_____

_____

Practice Exercise

Question about paragraph 13:

_____

_____

happiness tends to decline, especially for nontraditional wives (Belsky, Land, & Huston, 1986).

Parenthood as a Developmental Experience

14   As hard as it may be to take on the role of parent, keeping it up is even more demanding. Parenting has rich rewards, but anyone with children will testify that those rewards are earned. Caring for small children can be unsettling, irritating, frustrating, and overwhelming, as well as fulfilling and amusing.

15   About one-third of mothers find mothering both enjoyable and meaningful, a third find it neither, and another third have mixed feelings (L. Thompson & Walker, 1989). Among couples who do not have children, husbands consider having children more important and are more apt to want them than their wives do (Seccombe, 1991). However, once the children come, although fathers treasure and are emotionally committed to them, they enjoy looking after them less than mothers do. Although fathers generally believe they should be involved in their children's lives, most are not nearly as involved as mothers are (Backett, 1987; Boulton, 1983; LaRossa, 1988). Still, men's families are very important to them.

16   In resolving conflicts about their personal roles (parent versus spouse versus worker), most successful parents define their situation positively. They believe that in any conflict, parental responsibilities clearly come first. They concentrate on one set of responsibilities at a time. And they compromise some standards when necessary, letting the furniture go undusted or becoming less active in community affairs to spend more time with their children (B.C. Miller & Myers-Walls, 1983; Myers-Walls, 1984; Paloma, 1972). As children develop, parents do too.

17   Unfortunately, some people cannot meet the physical, psychological, and financial demands and challenges of parenthood. They may abuse, neglect, maltreat, or abandon their children; or they may become physically or emotionally ill themselves. Most parents, however, do cope, sometimes with the help of their family, friends, and neighbors; books and articles about child rearing; and professional advice.

Practice Exercise

Question about paragraph 14:

_____

_____

Practice Exercise

Question about paragraph 15:

_____

_____

Practice Exercise

Question about paragraph 16:

_____

_____

Practice Exercise

Question about paragraph 17:

_____

_____

Source: *Human Development,* 6th ed., by Diane E. Papalia and Sally Wendkos Olds, McGraw-Hill, New York, 1995, pp. 455–456 and 459–461.

SELECTION **3-2**

Human Development

Comprehension Quiz

Directions: For each comprehension question below, use information from the selection to determine the correct answer. You may refer to the selection as you answer the questions. Write your answer in the space provided.

True or False

_____ **1.** Psychoanalytic theorists like Freud believe that women have a deep instinctual wish to bear and nurture children.

_____ **2.** One study found that a chief motivation for parenthood is the wish for a close relationship with another human being.

_____ **3.** In general, today's couples have fewer children and have them earlier in life than the previous generation did.

_____ **4.** Women with less education tend to have their children later in life.

_____ **5.** Both men and women often feel excited about becoming parents, yet anxious about the responsibility of caring for a child.

_____ **6.** Eventually, all mothers find mothering both enjoyable and meaningful.

Multiple-Choice

_____ **7.** Although the desire to have children is almost universal,
  a. people seem to want fewer children today.
  b. people seem to want bigger and bigger families.
  c. fewer children reach maturity in preindustrial societies.
  d. people in industrialized societies need more children.

_____ **8.** There is ongoing cultural pressure to have children because
  a. motherhood seems to have a unique aura.
  b. today children are economic assets.
  c. it is generally assumed that all normal people want them.
  d. all of the above

_____ **9.** One study that interviewed and observed new mothers aged 16 to 38 found that the older mothers
  a. spent more time parenting.
  b. were more affectionate to their babies.
  c. reported more satisfaction with parenting.
  d. all of the above

_____   **10.**   Once a couple become parents, their marital happiness can decline if

    a.   the pregnancy was unplanned.

    b.   the couple have a second child by the time their first child is 3 years old.

    c.   the burden of most of the previously shared chores shifts to the wife.

    d.   the couple have been married for more than 15 years.

S E L E C T I O N **3-2**

Human Development

Extend Your Vocabulary by Using Context Clues

Directions: Context clues are words in a sentence that allow the reader to deduce (reason out) the meaning of an unfamiliar word in that sentence. For each vocabulary item below, a sentence from the selection containing an important word (*italicized, like this*) is quoted first. Next, there is an additional sentence using the word in the same sense and providing another context clue. Use the context clues from both sentences to deduce the meaning of the italicized word. *Be sure the answer you choose makes sense in both sentences.* If you discover that you must use a dictionary to confirm an answer choice, remember that the meaning you select must still fit the context of both sentences. To indicate your answer, write the letter in the space provided.

Pronunciation key: ă pat ā pay âr care ä father ĕ pet ē be ĭ pit
ī tie îr pier ŏ pot ō toe ô paw oi noise ou out oŏ took
ōō boot ŭ cut yōō abuse ûr urge *th* thin *th* this hw which
zh vision ə about
Stress mark: ′

_____   **1.**   The birth of a baby marks a major *transition* in the parents' lives.

Although it represents a milestone in a person's life, the *transition* from college student to full-time employee is often a stressful one.

transition (trăn zĭsh′ ən) means:

    a.   unexpected or unanticipated change

    b.   passage from one state to another

    c.   slow, gradual change

    d.   unwanted event or occurrence

_____   **2.**   Parenthood is a *developmental* experience, whether the children are biological offspring, are adopted, or are the children of only one spouse.

Many new or underprepared college students find that *developmental* reading, writing, and math courses provide the necessary background for subsequent college courses.

developmental (dĭ věl əp mənt′ əl) means:

a. progressing from a simpler stage to a stage that is more advanced, mature, or complex

b. noncredit

c. frustrating

d. decreasing over time in complexity or sophistication

_____ **3.** In *preindustrial* societies, large families were a necessity: children helped with the family's work and eventually cared for their aging parents.

In *preindustrial* times, many items that are now mass-produced by machines were produced singly, by hand.

preindustrial (prē ĭn dŭs′ trē əl) means:

a. relating to a society whose industries do not yet produce manufactured goods on a large scale

b. relating to a society in which all individuals are engaged in industry

c. relating to a society in which all industry exists for profit

d. relating to a society whose economic well-being rests only on the production of manufactured goods

_____ **4.** Because economic and social reasons for having children were so powerful, parenthood—especially motherhood—had a unique *aura*.

Even though final election returns were not yet in, an *aura* of defeat pervaded the candidate's headquarters.

aura (ôr′ ə) means:

a. distinctive but intangible quality of gloom

b. distinctive but intangible quality of joy that seems to disappear and reappear

c. distinctive but intangible quality associated with famous persons

d. distinctive but intangible quality that seems to surround a person or thing

_____ **5.** Still, the desire for children is almost *universal*.

Love is a *universal* emotion.

universal (yōō nə vûr′ səl) means:

a. knowledgeable about many subjects

b. existing all over the world

c. pertaining to the universe

d. cosmic

——————— **6.** Psychoanalytic theorists like Freud maintain that women have a deep *instinctual* wish to bear and nurture infants.

Because most birds have an *instinctual* fear of snakes, many gardeners place rubber snakes in their gardens to scare them away.

instinctual (ĭn stĭngk′ chōō əl) means:
- *a.* learned from repeated experience
- *b.* discovered by chance
- *c.* modified by subsequent experience or learning
- *d.* derived from a natural tendency or impulse

——————— **7.** Both men and women often feel *ambivalent* about becoming parents.

Many citizens and physicists have *ambivalent* feelings about nuclear energy, since it can be used for both constructive and destructive purposes.

ambivalent (ăm bĭv′ ə lənt) means:
- *a.* able to use both the right and the left hand equally skillfully
- *b.* positive
- *c.* clear and distinct; unequivocal
- *d.* having opposing attitudes or feelings at the same time

——————— **8.** Along with the excitement, they usually feel some anxiety about the responsibility of caring for a child and about the permanence that a pregnancy seems to *impose* on a marriage.

Because dictators have total control, they can *impose* their will and their decisions on all who live in their country.

impose (ĭm pōz′) means:
- *a.* to become inconvenient
- *b.* to make available
- *c.* to force something on someone
- *d.* to remove

——————— **9.** Another finding of *unmet* expectations emerged from a study of married, middle-class white women.

The bank robber refused to free his hostages unless the police agreed to his *unmet* demands.

unmet (ŭn mĕt) means:
- *a.* not formally introduced
- *b.* not familiar
- *c.* not known by the general public
- *d.* not satisfied; unfulfilled

_____ **10.** They may abuse, neglect, *maltreat,* or abandon their children; or they may become physically or emotionally ill themselves.

The SPCA (Society for the Prevention of Cruelty to Animals) is an organization that works to prevent and stop those who *maltreat* pets or other animals.

maltreat (măl trēt′) means:

a. abuse; treat in a rough or cruel way

b. ignore; pay no attention to

c. send away to a distant place

d. refuse to interact with

SELECTION **3-2**

Human Development

Collaboration Option

Respond in Writing

Directions: Refer to the selection as needed to answer the essay-type questions below.

Option for collaboration: Your instructor may direct you to work with other students, or in other words, to work *collaboratively.* In that case, you should form groups of three or four students as directed by your instructor and work together to complete the exercises. After your group discusses each item and agrees on the answer, have a group member record it. Every member of your group should be able to explain all of your group's answers.

1. According to the authors, what factors seem to be associated with making parenthood a successful and satisfying experience?

_____

_____

_____

_____

_____

_____

_____

_____

_____

2. If couples wait until they are older, more mature, and better educated before becoming parents, what effects do you think this might have on their children? List at least three effects.

_____

_____

_____

_____

_____

_____

3. If couples are older, more mature, and better educated when they became parents, what effects do you think this might have on society? List at least three effects.

_____

_____

_____

_____

_____

_____

4. Overall main idea. What is the overall main idea the authors want the reader to understand about parenthood? Answer this question in one sentence.

_____

_____

_____

_____

_____

_____

Read More about It on the World Wide Web

To learn more about the topic of this selection, visit these websites or use your favorite search engine (such as Yahoo ®). Whenever you go to any website, it is a good idea to evaluate it critically. Are you getting good information—information that is accurate, complete, and up-to-date? Who sponsors the website? How easy is it to use the features of the website?

http://family.com

This website has hundreds of links for family activities, health, parenting, crafts for kids, family vacations, etc.

http://www.familyeducation.com

This is the Family Education Network Home Page. *The mission of FEN is to help children succeed in school and in life.* FEN *is an interactive community that links parents, teachers, students, and schools to timely resources, to educational activities, and to each other.*

http://www.aak.com/

All About Kids *website. Click on* Disney.com *for fun.*

http://disney.com

Disney.com *website is great fun. Check it out with any young family members or relatives.*

SELECTION **3-3**
Art Appreciation

ART IN THE SERVICE OF RELIGION

From *Living with Art*

By Rita Gilbert

Prepare Yourself to Read

Directions: Do these exercises *before* you read Selection 3-3.

1. First, read and think about the title.

_____

_____

2. Next, complete your preview by reading the following:

Introduction (in *italics*)
First paragraph (paragraph 1)
First sentence of each paragraph
Words in italics
Picture and caption
All of the last paragraph (paragraph 12)

On the basis of your preview, how do you think architecture is used to serve religion?

_____

Apply Comprehension Skills

Directions: Do these exercises as you read Selection 3-3.

Ask and answer questions as you read. Complete the practice exercises by creating questions based on what each paragraph seems to be about.

Read actively to find answers to your questions. Record the answers to your questions. Write the answer in the margin or highlight the answer in the text.

Review by rehearsing the answers to your questions. Recite your answers or write them down from memory.

ART IN THE SERVICE OF RELIGION

Think about various churches, synagogues, mosques, temples, shrines, and other religious structures you have seen, attended, or visited. Have you ever considered how the architecture of a place of worship is related to the activities that occur there? In this selection from an art appreciation textbook, the author explains the relationship between three different religions and the architecture of some of their well known places of worship.

1   Since earliest times art has served religion in two important ways. First, artists have erected the sacred temples where believers join to profess their faith and follow the observances faith requires. Second, art attempts to make specific and visible something that is, by its very nature, spiritual, providing images of the religious figures and events that make up the fabric of faith. In this section we shall explore how the theme of religious art has been adapted for different purposes, for different faiths, in different parts of the world.

2   A very large portion of the magnificent architecture we have was built in the service of religion. Naturally the architectural style of any religious structure reflects the culture in which it was built, but it is also dependent on the particular needs of a given religion. Three examples will show this.

3   On a high hill, the Acropolis, overlooking the city of Athens stands the shell of what many consider the most splendid building ever conceived: the Parthenon. The Parthenon was erected in the 5th century B.C. as a temple to the goddess Athena, patroness of the city, and at one time its core held a colossal statue of the goddess. However, the religion associated with the Parthenon was not confined to worship of a diety. In ancient Greece, veneration of the gods was closely allied to the political and social ideals of a city-state that celebrated its own greatness.

4   Rising proudly on its hill, visible from almost every corner of the city, and for miles around, the Parthenon functioned as a symbol of the citizens' aspirations. Its structure as a religious shrine seems unusual for us in that it turns outward, toward the city, rather than in upon itself. Worshipers were not meant to gather inside the building; actually, only priests could enter the inner

Practice Exercises

Directions: For each paragraph,

- Create a question based on what the paragraph seems to be about. Ask *who, what, when, where, why,* or *how.*
- Write your question in the spaces provided.
- Write the answer to your question in the margin or highlight it in the text.

Doing this will help you understand and remember the material.

Practice Exercise

Question about paragraph 1:

_____

Practice Exercise

Question about paragraph 2:

_____

_____

Practice Exercise

Question about paragraph 3:

_____

_____

Practice Exercise

Question about paragraph 4:

_____

_____

chamber, or *cella,* where the statue of Athena stood. Religious ceremonies on festal occasions focused on processions, which began down in the city, wound their way up the steep path on the west side of the Acropolis, and circled the Parthenon and other sacred buildings at the top.

5   Most of the Parthenon's architectural embellishment was intended for the appreciation of the worshipers outside. All four walls of the exterior were decorated with sculptures high up under the roof, and originally portions of the marble facade were painted a vivid blue and red. In a later chapter we shall consider details of the Parthenon's structure; here we concentrate on the theme of religion and on the Parthenon's purpose, which is both religious *and* political exaltation.

6   At about the same time the Parthenon was being constructed in Athens, but half a continent away, one of the world's great religions was developing and beginning to form its own architecture. Buddhism derives its principles from the teachings of Gautama Siddhartha, later known as the Buddha, who was born in India about 563 B.C. Although of noble birth, the Buddha renounced his princely status and life of ease. When he was about twenty-nine, he began a long period of wandering and meditation, seeking enlightenment. He began with the supposition that humans are predisposed to live out lives of suffering, to die, then to be reborn and repeat the pattern. Ultimately, he worked out a doctrine of moral behavior that he believed could break the painful cycle of life and death, and he attracted many followers.

7   Buddhism is predominantly a personal religion, and its observances depend less on communal worship than on individual contemplation. It places great emphasis on symbolism, much of it referring to episodes in the Buddha's life. Both of these aspects—the personal and the symbolic—are evident in one of Buddhism's finest early shrines, the Great Stupa at Sanchi, in India. Like the Parthenon, the Great Stupa turns more outward than inward, but its moundlike form is more sculptural, intended as a representation of the cosmos. At the very top is a three-part "umbrella," symbolizing the three major aspects of Buddhism—the Buddha, the Buddha's law, and the Monastic Order.

8   Buddhist shrines—the word *stupa* means "shrine"—often housed relics of the Buddha, and worship rituals called for circumambulation

The Parthenon on the Acropolis. Athens, Greece. 447–432 B.C. *(Stone/George Grigoriou)*

Practice Exercise

Question about paragraph 5:

_____

_____

_____

Practice Exercise

Question about paragraph 6:

_____

_____

_____

Practice Exercise

Question about paragraph 7:

_____

_____

_____

Practice Exercise

Question about paragraph 8:

_____

_____

("walking around") of the stupa. Thus, on the outside of the Great Stupa of Sanchi we see a railed pathway, where pilgrims could take the ritual clockwise walk following the Path of Life around the World Mountain. Elsewhere the stupa is embellished richly with carvings and sculpture evoking scenes from the Buddha's life. Every part of the stupa is geared to the pursuit of personal enlightenment and transcendence.

9   If the Buddhist temple is dedicated to private worship, then its extreme opposite can be found in the total encompassment of a community religious experience: the medieval Christian cathedral. And the supreme example of that ideal is the Cathedral of Notre Dame de Chartres, in France. Chartres Cathedral was built, rebuilt, and modified over a period of several hundred years, but the basic structure, which is in the Gothic style, was established in the 13th century. A cathedral—as opposed to a church—is the bishop's domain and therefore is always in a town or a city. This one fact is crucial to understanding the nature of Chartres and the role it played in the people's lives.

10   The cathedral towers magnificently over the surrounding city, much as the Parthenon does over Athens, but here the resemblance ends. Whereas the Parthenon is above and apart from the city, accessible only by a steep path, Chartres Cathedral is very much a living presence *within* the city. In the Middle Ages houses and shops clustered right up to its walls, and one side of the cathedral formed an edge of the busy marketplace. The cathedral functioned as a hub of all activities, both sacred and secular, within the town.

11   Medieval France had one dominant religion, and that was the Christianity of Rome. One could assume that almost every resident of the town of Chartres professed exactly the same faith, and so the church was an integral part of everyday life. Its bells tolled the hours of waking, starting work, praying, and retiring for the evening rest. Its feast days were the official holidays. Chartres Cathedral and its counterparts served the populace not only as a setting for religious worship but as meeting hall, museum, concert stage, and social gathering place. Within its walls business

The Great Stupa, Sanchi, India. Third century B.C. to first century A.D. *(Superstock)*

Practice Exercise

Question about paragraph 9:

_____

_____

Practice Exercise

Question about paragraph 10:

_____

_____

Practice Exercise

Question about paragraph 11:

_____

_____

Chartres Cathedral, France.
c. 1194-1260.
(Adam Woolfitt/Corbis)

deals were arranged, goods were sold, friends met, young couples courted. Where else but inside the cathedral could the townsfolk hear splendid music? Where else would they see magnificent art?

12   Three religious structures: the Parthenon, the Great Stupa, and Chartres Cathedral. Each was built in the service of religion but for each we can find another slightly different purpose. For the Parthenon the purpose is also *political;* ·for the Great Stupa there is the purely *private* observance of religion; and for Chartres the *social* role is as important as the religious.

Practice Exercise

Question about paragraph 12:

_____

_____

Source: Rita Gilbert, "Art in the Service of Religion," in *Living with Art,* 3d ed., McGraw-Hill, New York, 1992, pp. 63–65. Reproduced with permission of McGraw-Hill.

Comprehension Quiz

Directions: For each comprehension question below, use information from the selection to determine the correct answer. You may refer to the selection as you answer the questions. Write your answer in the space provided.

True or False

_____ **1.** Throughout history, art has served religion in three important ways.

_____ **2.** The Parthenon was built as a temple to the Greek goddess Diana.

_____ **3.** Greek citizens gathered inside the Parthenon to worship their gods.

_____ **4.** Many consider the Parthenon the most splendid building ever constructed.

_____ **5.** The Buddhist religion and its architecture were developing in India at approximately the same time as the Parthenon was being constructed in Greece.

_____ **6.** "Circumambulation" is a Buddhist religious ritual that involves walking clockwise around a stupa, a Buddhist shrine.

Multiple-Choice

_____ **7.** Which of the following does not describe early Buddhism?
   a. It is a personal religion.
   b. It requires individual contemplation and a search for enlightenment.
   c. It requires communal worship.
   d. It involves a ritual of walking.

_____ **8.** One of the finest Buddhist shrines, the Great Stupa of Sanchi in India, is characterized by all of the following except which?
   a. It contains a railed pathway.
   b. It resembles the cosmos with its moundlike form.
   c. It does not contain any carving or sculptures.
   d. It houses relics of the Buddha.

_____ **9.** In medieval France, the cathedral served as a
   a. place of worship.
   b. concert stage and meeting hall.
   c. museum housing fine religious paintings and sculpture.
   d. all of the above

_____ **10.** Chartres Cathedral in France was built, rebuilt, and modified over a period of
   a. 25 years.
   b. 50 years.
   c. 100 years.
   d. several hundred years.

SELECTION **3-3**

Art Appreciation

Extend Your Vocabulary by Using Context Clues

Directions: Context clues are words in a sentence that allow the reader to deduce (reason out) the meaning of an unfamiliar word in that sentence. For each vocabulary item below, a sentence from the selection containing an important word (*italicized, like this*) is quoted first. Next, there is an additional sentence using the word in the same sense and providing another context clue. Use the context clues from both sentences to deduce the meaning of the italicized word. *Be sure the answer you choose makes sense in both sentences.* If you discover that you must use a dictionary to confirm an answer choice, remember that the meaning you select must still fit the context of both sentences. To indicate your answer, write the letter in the space provided.

Pronunciation key: ă pat ā pay âr care ä father ĕ pet ē be ĭ pit
ī tie îr pier ŏ pot ō toe ô paw oi noise ou out ŏŏ took
ōō boot ŭ cut yōō abuse ûr urge th thin *th* this hw which
zh vision ə about
Stress Mark: ′

_____ 1. First, artists have erected the sacred temples where believers join to *profess* their faith and follow the observances faith requires.

Although the visiting scientists tried to *profess* loyalty to the host country, they were nevertheless deported as spies.

profess (prə fĕs′) means:
   a. discuss
   b. lie about
   c. deny
   d. declare

_____ 2. In ancient Greece, *veneration* of the gods was closely allied to the political and social ideals of a city-state that celebrated its own greatness.

In Asian cultures older people, such as grandparents, are treated with great respect and *veneration.*

veneration (vĕn ə rā′ shən) means:
   a. reverence
   b. courtesy
   c. fondness
   d. patience

_____ 3. All four walls of the exterior were decorated with sculptures high up under the roof, and originally, portions of the marble *facade* were painted a vivid blue and red.

The architect updated the *facade* of the old hotel by adding a beautiful new brick exterior and elegant bronze doors.

facade (fə säd′) means:

a.   front of a building

b.   decorative trim

c.   columns; pillars

d.   steps or stairs

_____   **4.** Although of noble birth, the Buddha *renounced* his princely status and life of ease.

When my brother became a Catholic priest, he *renounced* all of his worldly possessions and took a vow of poverty.

renounced (rĭ nounst′) means:

a.   ignored

b.   gave up, especially by formal announcement

c.   described in someone else's words

d.   collected; gathered together

_____   **5.** He began with the *supposition* that humans are predisposed to live out lives of suffering, to die, then to be reborn and repeat the pattern.

Under the American judicial system, we begin with the *supposition* that a person is considered innocent until proven guilty.

supposition (sŭp ə zĭsh′ ən) means:

a.   scientific conclusion

b.   religious belief

c.   assumption

d.   hope

_____   **6.** Like the Parthenon, the Great Stupa turns more outward than inward, but its moundlike form is more sculptural, intended as a representation of the *cosmos*.

Because human beings have always wondered how life began, every culture has its own explanation of the creation of the *cosmos*.

cosmos (kŏz′ məs) means:

a.   city

b.   mountains

c.   the universe regarded as an orderly, harmonious whole

d.   life after death

_____   **7.** Buddhist shrines—the word "stupa" means "shrine"—often housed *relics* of the Buddha, and worship rituals called for circumambulation ("walking around") of the stupa.

The museum presented a splendid exhibit of Russian icons, altar pieces, and other religious *relics.*

relics (rĕl′ ĭks) means:

a. objects of religious veneration

b. pieces of art

c. personal belongings

d. paintings

_____ **8.** Elsewhere the stupa is *embellished* richly with carvings and sculpture evoking scenes from the Buddha's life.

The Sistine Chapel in Rome is *embellished* with magnificent frescoes by Michelangelo.

embellished (ĕm bĕl′ ĭsht) means:

a. made colorful and bright

b. painted

c. made in a shape of a bell

d. adorned; made beautiful

_____ **9.** Every part of the stupa is geared to the pursuit of personal enlightenment and *transcendence.*

The monk spent his days in solitude, meditation, and prayer as a way of seeking *transcendence.*

transcendence (trăn sĕn′ dĕns) means:

a. suffering

b. existence above or independent of the material universe

c. a change from one physical place to another

d. recognition; honor

_____ **10.** *Medieval* France had one dominant religion, and that was the Christianity of Rome.

Our favorite childhood stories were about *medieval* kings, queens, and castles.

medieval (mē dē ē vəl) means:

a. pertaining to the Middle Ages, a 1,000-year period of European history between antiquity and the Renaissance

b. pertaining to the period of American history between the Civil War and the present

c. pertaining to a period in European history between the fourteenth and sixteenth centuries, a time of revived intellectual and artistic achievement

d. pertaining to a period in European history characterized by absence of artistic achievement

SELECTION **3-3**

Art Appreciation

Collaboration Option

Respond in Writing

Directions: Refer to the selection as needed to answer the essay-type questions below.

Option for collaboration: Your instructor may direct you to work with other students or, in other words, to work *collaboratively.* In that case, you should form groups of three or four students as directed by your instructor and work together to complete the exercises. After your group discusses each item and agrees on the answer, have a group member record it. Every member of your group should be able to explain all of your group's answers.

1. The Great Stupa of Sanchi was designed strictly for the private observance of religion by individuals. However, the Parthenon and Chartres Cathedral served other purposes besides private observance. In addition to religious worship, what *other purposes* did each of them serve?

Parthenon:

_____

_____

Chartres Cathedral:

_____

_____

2. Overall main idea. What is the overall main idea the author wants the reader to understand about religious structures like the Parthenon, the Great Stupa of Sanchi, and Chartres Cathedral? Answer this question in one sentence.

_____

_____

_____

_____

Read More about It on the World Wide Web

To learn more about the topic of this selection, visit these websites or use your favorite search engine (such as Yahoo ®). Whenever you go to any website, it is a good idea to evaluate it critically. Are you getting good information—information that is accurate, complete, and up-to-date? Who sponsors the website? How easy is it to use the features of the website?

http://www.greatbuildings.com

This is one of the leading architecture sites on the Web. Great Buildings Online *is a gateway to architecture around the world and across history. It documents 1,000 buildings and hundreds of leading architects; it includes photographic images, architectural drawings, three-dimensional models, commentaries, bibliographies, Web links, and more. Type in Parthenon, Chartres Cathedral, and Great Stupa of Sanchi.*

http://www.biblicalarts.org/

This is the home page for the Biblical Arts Center, *a nondenominational art museum. Its goal is to help people of all faiths envision the places, events, and people of the Bible.*

http://www.mhhe.com/catalogs/007913212x.mhtml

This site gives an overview for the textbook, Living with Art, *5th edition, by Rita Gilbert, which is an art appreciation textbook used in numerous colleges and universities.*

http://www.refdesk.com

Click on site map, then choose World Religions under the Facts Subject Index.

Comprehension

*Understanding College
Textbooks by Reading for Ideas*

© PhotoDisc

C H A P T E R

4

Determining the Topic
and the Stated Main Idea

CHAPTER OBJECTIVES

In this chapter you will learn the answers to these questions:

- Why is it important to determine the topic of a paragraph?

- How can I determine the topic of a paragraph?

- Why is the stated main idea of a paragraph important?

- How can I locate the stated main idea sentence of a paragraph?

189

SKILLS

The Topic of a Paragraph

- What Is the Topic of a Paragraph, and Why Is It Important?

- Determining and Expressing the Topic

The Stated Main Idea of a Paragraph

- What Is a Stated Main Idea, and Why Is It Important?

- Locating the Stated Main Idea Sentence

- How to Tell if You Have Identified the Stated Main Idea Sentence

- Stated Overall Main Ideas in Longer Passages

A Word about Standardized Reading Tests: Topics and Stated Main Ideas

CREATING YOUR SUMMARY

Developing Chapter Review Cards

READINGS

Reading is to the mind like exercise is to the body.

Sir Richard Steele

A person who does not read has no advantage over a person who cannot read.

THE TOPIC OF A PARAGRAPH

What Is the Topic of a Paragraph, and Why Is It Important?

KEY TERM
Topic

Word, name, or phrase that tells who or what the author is writing about.

The topic is also known as the *subject,* or the *subject matter.*

Every paragraph has a topic because every paragraph is written about something. That "something" is the topic. A **topic** is a word, name, or phrase that tells what the author is writing about in a paragraph. (There are other names for the topic of a paragraph. In a writing course or an English course, you may hear the topic referred to as the *subject* or *subject matter.* These are simply different terms for the topic.)

The topic is always expressed as a single word or a name (for instance, *procrastination* or *Bill Gates*) or as a phrase consisting of two or more words (for instance, *the increasing use of computers in education*). The topic is never a sentence. Each sentence in a paragraph should relate in some way to the topic (explain it, tell more about it, give examples of it, etc.). For this reason, the topic may be mentioned several times within a paragraph.

Determining the topic focuses your attention and helps you understand complex paragraphs precisely. It is the essential first step in understanding a passage that you are reading and studying. As you will learn later in this chapter, it is also the key to the main idea of the paragraph.

Determining and Expressing the Topic

Comprehension Monitoring Question for Determining the Topic

Who or what is this paragraph about?

You know from Chapter 2 that effective readers are active and interactive readers who ask questions as they read. When you read a paragraph, you can determine its topic by asking yourself, "Who or what is this paragraph about?" and then answering this question. Paragraphs, especially paragraphs in textbooks, contain various clues that will help you answer that question.

One or more of the following clues often make the topic of a textbook paragraph obvious. The topic is a word, name, or phrase that:

- appears as a *heading* or *title*
- appears in *special type* such as **bold print,** *italics,* or color
- is *repeated* throughout the paragraph
- appears at the beginning of the paragraph and is then referred to throughout the paragraph by *pronouns* (or other words)

A paragraph does not usually contain all of these clues, but every paragraph has at least one of them. Let's look at each clue in more detail.

191

Determining the topic is the essential first step in understanding a passage that you are reading and studying. (Emma Lee/Life File/Photo Disc)

The Topic Is Often Used as a Heading or Title

Textbook authors typically use the topic of a section as the heading or title for that section. The following paragraph from a textbook on business communications illustrates this clue (as well as some others). Read the paragraph and use its heading (and other clues) to determine its topic.

Doing Business and Learning about a Culture through Its Language

The best way to prepare yourself to do business with people from another culture is to study their culture in advance. If you plan to live in another country or do business there repeatedly, learn the language. The same holds true if you must work closely with a subculture that has its own language, such as Vietnamese-Americans or Hispanic-Americans. Even if you end up doing business with foreigners in your own language, you may show respect by making the effort to learn their language. In addition, you will learn something about the culture and its customs in the process. If you do not have the time or opportunity to actually learn a new language, at least learn a few words.

Source: Adapted from Courtland Bovée and John Thill, *Business Communication Today,* 3d ed., McGraw-Hill, New York, 1992, p. 570. Reproduced with permission of McGraw-Hill.

Stop and Annotate

Go back to the textbook excerpt above. Underline or highlight the heading, which indicates the topic.

Notice that in this excerpt, the heading *Doing Business and Learning about a Culture through Its Language* tells you its topic. This phrase describes everything that is discussed in the paragraph: it expresses the topic that all the sentences in the paragraph have in common. (Notice also that the words *business, language, culture,* and *learn* are repeated throughout the paragraph.)

It is important to understand that although the heading of a paragraph is often a clue to the topic, it may not always express the topic completely or accurately. To determine the topic, do not rely *only* on headings; you must also read the paragraph and ask yourself, "Who or what is this paragraph about?"

The Topic Often Appears in Special Print

A second clue to the topic of a paragraph is the use of special print (such as **bold** print, *italics,* or color) to emphasize a word, name, or phrase. The paragraph below is from a textbook on criminal justice. As you read this paragraph, watch for special print that indicates its topic.

> Written criminal codes in all jurisdictions make distinctions between felonies and misde-meanors, and sometimes lesser offenses called "violations" or "infractions." A **felony** is a serious crime with correspondingly harsh penalties including such civil disabilities as loss of voting privi-leges after conviction as well as criminal punishment of more than 1 year in prison. A **misdemeanor** is a minor offense, less serious than a felony, subject to penalties such as a fine or a jail term of less than 1 year.
>
> *Source:* Patrick R. Anderson and Donald J. Newman, *Introduction to Criminal Justice,* 5th ed., McGraw-Hill, New York, 1993, p. 7.

Stop and Annotate

Go back to the textbook excerpt above. Underline or highlight the words in bold print, which indicate the topic.

Notice the words in bold print: **felony** and **misdemeanor.** These words, to-gether, indicate the topic; the paragraph discusses *felonies and misdemeanors.* Keep in mind that the topic can also appear in italics, and that in many college textbooks such key words are printed in color. Special print, then, can often help you identify the topic.

The Topic Is Often Repeated throughout the Paragraph

A third clue to the topic is repetition of a word, name, or phrase throughout a paragraph. Read the paragraph below from a psychology textbook and use this clue to determine its topic.

> Claustrophobia. Acrophobia. Xenophobia. Although these sound like characters in a Greek tragedy, they are actually members of a class of psychological disorders known as phobias. Phobias are intense, irrational fears of specific objects or situations. For example, claustrophobia is a fear of enclosed places, acrophobia a fear of high places, and xenophobia a fear of strangers. Although the objective danger posed by an anxiety-producing stimulus is typically small or nonexistent, to the indi-vidual suffering from the phobia it represents great danger, and a full-blown panic attack may follow exposure to the stimulus.
>
> *Source:* Robert S. Feldman, *Understanding Psychology,* 3d ed., McGraw-Hill, New York, 1993, p. 562.

Stop and Annotate

Go back to the textbook excerpt above. Underline or highlight the repeated words which indicate the topic.

Notice that the word *phobias* or *phobia* appears three times in this para-graph, indicating that this is the topic. In addition, three specific types of pho-bias are given as examples.

The Topic Sometimes Appears Only Once, but Is Then Referred to by Pronouns or Other Words

A fourth clue to the topic of a paragraph is a word, name, or phrase that ap-pears near the beginning of the paragraph and is then referred to throughout the paragraph by a pronoun (such as *he, she, it, they, his, her, its,* etc.) or other words. Here is a paragraph from a physics textbook. Use this clue to determine the topic of the paragraph.

> Before the age of 30, Isaac Newton had invented the mathematical methods of calculus, demonstrated that white light contained all the colors of the rainbow, and discovered the law of grav-itation. Interestingly, this mathematical genius led a lonely and solitary life. His father died before he

was born, and after his mother remarried, he was raised by an aged grandmother. In 1661, he was admitted to Cambridge University, where he worked for the next eight years, except for one year at home to escape the plague. During those years, he made his major discoveries, although none were published at that time. His genius was nonetheless recognized, and in 1669 he was appointed Lucasion Professor of Mathematics at Cambridge University, a position he retained until 1695. His major scientific work was completed prior to 1692, when he suffered a nervous breakdown. After his recovery, he determined to lead a more public life, and soon became the Master of the Mint in London. He was elected president of the Royal Society in 1703, and held that position until his death.

Source: Adapted from Frederick Bueche, *Principles of Physics,* 5th ed., McGraw-Hill, New York, 1988, p. 70.

Stop and Annotate

Go back to the textbook excerpt above. Underline or highlight the topic, the pronouns, and other words that refer to the topic.

Notice that Newton's name appears only in the first sentence, but it is obvious from the words *This mathematical genius,* and the pronouns *he* and *his,* that the rest of the paragraph continues to discuss him. Therefore, *Isaac Newton* is the topic of this paragraph.

Be sure you understand that authors sometimes present the topic (a word, name, or phrase) at or near the beginning of a paragraph, but then refer to the topic by one or more *other* words, rather than just by pronouns. For instance, a paragraph might began "Pneumonia is . . ." and then might say something such as "This disease is characterized by . . ." and "The condition worsens when . . ." and "The disorder is typically treated by . . ." In this case, the words *disease, condition,* and *disorder* refer to *pneumonia* and indicate that pneumonia is the topic of the paragraph. (And, in the example above, you saw *Isaac Newton* referred to as *this mathematical genius* as well as by pronouns.)

It is important to be precise when you describe the topic of a paragraph. If you use words that are too general or too specific, they will not describe the topic accurately. A topic described in terms that are *too general,* or too broad, will go beyond what is discussed in the paragraph. A topic described in terms that are *too specific,* or too narrow, will fail to cover everything discussed in the paragraph. Suppose, for instance, that the topic of a paragraph is *causes of gang violence.* The word *gangs* or *violence,* or the phrase *gang violence,* would be too general to express this topic precisely. The paragraph could be about many different things that pertain to gangs or violence. On the other hand, the phrase *lack of parental supervision as a cause of gang violence* would be too specific, even though "lack of parental supervision" might be mentioned in the paragraph as one of the causes.

Keep in mind that it is often possible to express a topic correctly in more than one way. For example, the topic of a paragraph could be correctly expressed as *Winston Churchill's childhood, the childhood of Winston Churchill, Churchill's life as a child, Churchill's boyhood,* or *Churchill's youth,* since these all mean the same thing.

Determining a topic precisely is the starting point in comprehending as you read. It is also a key to locating the main idea sentence in a paragraph, as you will see in the next section of this chapter.

THE STATED MAIN IDEA OF A PARAGRAPH

What Is a Stated Main Idea, and Why Is It Important?

Every paragraph has a main idea. A **stated main idea** is a sentence within a paragraph that contains both the topic and the author's single most important point about this topic. (There are various terms for a stated main idea. In a writing course or an English course, the main idea sentence of a paragraph may be called the *topic sentence.*) Unlike the topic, which is always a single word, name, or phrase, the main idea is always expressed as a complete sentence.

Do not select a question from a paragraph as the main idea, because the stated main idea is always written as a statement (a sentence). The stated main idea is *never* written in the form of a question. The stated main idea sentence, however, will often be the *answer* to a question the author presents at the beginning of a paragraph.

As you learned at the beginning of this chapter, the topic of a paragraph tells who or what the paragraph is about. It is always a word, name, or phrase, never a sentence. A main idea, however, is always a *sentence.* It goes further than the topic because this sentence expresses *the author's one most important point about the topic.* For example, the main idea sentence in a paragraph whose topic is *procrastination* might be, "Procrastination is the major cause of stress for college students." This sentence includes the topic, *procrastination,* and tells the important point the author is making about *procrastination.* Because the word *main* means "most important," there can be only *one* main, or most important, idea in any paragraph. This is only logical: two or three different sentences can't all be the one most important sentence.

A main idea is called a *stated main idea* when the author presents it (in other words, *states* it) as one of the sentences in the paragraph. An author can place his or her stated main idea sentence anywhere in the paragraph: at the beginning, end, or even in the middle.

In this chapter, you will practice only with paragraphs that contain stated main ideas. Sometimes, however, an author does not state the main idea of a paragraph directly. In that case, the main idea is called an *implied main idea,* and the reader must create a sentence that states the author's main point. (Implied main ideas are discussed in Chapter 5.)

There are several reasons why it is important to determine main ideas when you are studying:

* To increase your comprehension
* To enable you to mark textbooks effectively and take notes as you study
* To enable you to write summaries and outlines
* To help you identify and remember important material for tests

For these reasons, effective readers focus on main ideas.

Locating the Stated Main Idea Sentence

Steps to Follow

Since a stated main idea is one of the sentences in the paragraph, your task is simply to determine *which* sentence is the main idea. Often, the stated main idea will be obvious. To identify the stated main idea sentence, find the sentence that contains both the topic and the most important point about it.

To locate the stated main idea, follow these two steps:

- **Step 1.** After you have read the paragraph, determine the topic by asking yourself, "Who or what is the passage about?" and then answering this question. (Use the clues you learned in the first part of this chapter for determining the topic.)

- **Step 2.** Locate the main idea sentence by asking yourself, "What is the single most important point the author wants me to understand about the topic of this paragraph?" Then search the paragraph for the sentence that answers this question. That sentence is the stated main idea.

Comprehension Monitoring Question for Stated Main Idea

"What is the single most important point the author wants me to understand about the topic of this paragraph?"

Here is a simple formula that gives the essential parts of any stated main idea sentence:

$$\boxed{\text{The } \textit{topic}} \quad + \quad \boxed{\text{Author's } \textit{most important point} \text{ about the topic}} \quad = \quad \boxed{\text{Main idea sentence}}$$

Authors can put a stated main idea sentence anywhere in a paragraph. However, they usually put it at the beginning of a paragraph. The next most common place is at the end of a paragraph. Of course, a stated main idea can also be placed within the paragraph as well. Let's look at examples of each.

Where a Stated Main Idea Sentence May Appear

Authors often put their stated main idea sentence at the beginning of the paragraph. Although they could put the sentence anywhere in the paragraph, they often put it first because it can make it easier for the reader to comprehend the paragraph.

The following excerpt from a textbook on career planning is an example in which the main idea has been stated at the beginning of the paragraph. The topic of this paragraph is *beginning a new job*. Read the paragraph and ask yourself, "What is the most important point the authors want me to understand about beginning a new job?" The sentence that answers this question, the first sentence, is the main idea.

Beginning a new job is always exciting and sometimes intimidating. There is an invigorating feeling of a fresh start and a clean slate. You face new challenges and draw on a renewed sense of energy as you approach them. But you may also feel apprehensive about this new adventure. Will it actually turn out as well as you hope? You are entering a strange environment, and you must learn to work with new associates. If you were fired from your last job, you may feel particularly sensitive. "What if it happens again?" you ask yourself.

Source: William Morin and James Cabrera, *Parting Company: How to Survive the Loss of a Job and Find Another,* Harcourt, Brace, San Diego, Calif., 1982, p. 238.

Stop and Annotate

Go back to the textbook excerpt above. Underline or highlight the stated main idea sentence.

The first sentence in the excerpt is a general one which mentions two different types of feelings people often have as they start a new job. Since the most important thing the authors want you to understand is that people may have *both* types of feelings, this sentence is the main idea of the paragraph: *Beginning a new job is always exciting and sometimes intimidating.* The rest of the paragraph presents specific details that support this sentence as the main idea: the first half of the paragraph explains why starting a new job is *exciting,* and the last half of the paragraph explains why it can be *intimidating.* In this paragraph, then, the first sentence states the main idea, and the rest of the sentences are details that tell us more about it.

The author may place a stated main idea sentence at the end of a paragraph. Frequently, the *last sentence* of a paragraph is the stated main idea. Authors sometimes like to lead up to their main point, and so they place it at the end of the paragraph. They know it can be helpful to the reader if they first give an explanation, provide background information or present examples, and then state their main idea.

Read the excerpt below, from a sociology textbook. The topic of this paragraph is *ethnocentrism.* As you read the paragraph, ask yourself, "What is the most important point the authors want me to understand about the term *ethnocentrism?*" The sentence that answers this question, the last sentence, is the stated main idea.

When members of a dominant culture become suspicious of subcultures and seek to isolate or assimilate them, it is often because the members of the dominant culture are making value judgments about the beliefs and practices of the subordinate groups. Most Anglo-Americans, for instance, see the extensive family obligations of Hispanics as a burdensome arrangement that inhibits individual freedom. Hispanics, in contrast, view the isolated nuclear family of Anglo-Americans as a lonely institution that cuts people off from the love and assistance of their kin. This tendency to view one's own cultural patterns as good and right and those of others as strange or even immoral is called **ethnocentrism.**

Source: Craig Calhoun, Donald Light, and Susanne Keller, *Sociology,* 6th ed., McGraw-Hill, New York, 1994, p. 65.

Stop and Annotate

Go back to the textbook excerpt above. Underline or highlight the stated main idea sentence.

In this paragraph, the first sentence is an introductory one that explains how and why members of a dominant culture may react to members of subcultures. It is followed by two examples. However, the last sentence of the paragraph is the main idea because it states the authors' most important point: that *ethnocentrism* is the term used to describe the tendency to view one's own cultural patterns as superior and other cultures' patterns as inferior or wrong. Notice that this stated main idea sentence contains the topic, and that the topic is in bold print.

Authors sometimes put the stated main idea sentence within the paragraph. Sometimes the stated main idea sentence is neither the first nor the last sentence of a paragraph, but rather one of the other sentences in the paragraph. That is, the stated main idea appears *within* the paragraph. Sometimes authors begin a paragraph with an introductory comment or question designed to get the reader's attention, or with some background information. Then they present their main idea. The rest of the information in the paragraph then explains or tells more about the main idea, or gives examples. (Helpful hint: whenever a paragraph begins with a question, expect the author to then answer that important question. Moreover, the "answer" is often the main idea of the paragraph.)

Here is a paragraph from a government textbook in which the second sentence is the main idea sentence. The topic is *television commercials and presidential campaigns.* As you read this paragraph, ask yourself, "What is the most important point the author wants me to understand about television commercials and presidential campaigns?"

> The television campaign includes political advertising. Televised commercials are by far the most expensive part of presidential campaigns. Since 1976, political commercials on television have accounted for about half of the candidates' expenditures in the general election campaign. In 1992 Bush and Clinton each spent more than $30 million on advertising in the general election, and Perot spent even more. Perot relied heavily on "infomercials"—30-minute and hour-long commercials that emphasized substance over slogans.
>
> *Source:* Thomas E. Patterson, *The American Democracy,* 3rd ed., McGraw-Hill, New York, 1996, p. 398.

Stop and Annotate

Go back to the textbook excerpt above. Underline or highlight the stated main idea sentence.

The author's second sentence presents his most important point: *Televised commercials are by far the most expensive part of presidential campaigns.* Each of the other sentences presents facts or examples that demonstrate how expensive televised campaign commercials have become.

How to Tell If You Have Identified the Stated Main Idea Sentence

Stated Main Idea Checklist

How can you tell if you have *correctly* identified an author's stated main idea sentence in a paragraph? You have found the stated main idea sentence if:

- The sentence contains the topic.
- The sentence states the *single* most important point about the topic.
- The sentence is general enough to cover all the information in the paragraph.
- The other sentences explain or tell more about the main idea sentence.
- The sentence makes complete sense by itself (in other words, a reader could understand it without having to read the rest of the paragraph).

For example, the following sentence would not be meaningful by itself, since the reader would not know who "him" refers to: *Most historians consistently rank him among the five greatest presidents of the United States.* Therefore, this sentence could not be a correct main idea sentence. On the other hand, this sentence could be a main idea sentence, since it makes sense by itself: *Most historians consistently rank Abraham Lincoln among the five greatest presidents of the United States.*

How to Avoid Two Common Errors in Locating a Stated Main Idea

You have learned that a stated main idea sentence is most often the first or last sentence of a paragraph, and so you may be tempted to try to take a shortcut by reading only the first and last sentences. This is a common mistake you should avoid. You must read the entire paragraph to identify the main idea accurately. You will not be able to compare the sentences to evaluate which is the most important unless you read the whole paragraph. You may miss a stated main idea sentence that occurs somewhere in the middle.

A second common error can occur when a paragraph is difficult. In this case, you may be tempted to select a sentence as the main idea simply because it contains familiar or interesting information, or because it seems to "sound important." These are not good reasons for choosing a sentence as the stated main idea. To avoid this mistake, remind yourself that the stated main idea sentence must always answer the question, "What is the *single most important point* the author wants me to understand about the topic of this paragraph?"

Stated Overall Main Ideas in Longer Passages

Locating stated main ideas is a skill that can also be applied to passages longer than a single paragraph, such as sections of a textbook chapter, short reading selections, and essays. You will sometimes discover a sentence in a longer passage (usually an introductory or concluding sentence) that expresses the most important point or the overall message of the *entire passage*. The chapter reading selections in *Opening Doors* include an exercise called Respond in Writing, which gives you practice in determining the main idea (the overall message) of the entire selection.

A WORD ABOUT STANDARDIZED READING TESTS: TOPICS AND STATED MAIN IDEAS

Many college students are required to take standardized reading tests as part of an overall assessment program, in a reading course, or as part of a state-mandated "basic skills" test. A standardized reading test typically consists of a series of passages followed by multiple-choice questions, to be completed within a specified time limit. Included in Part Two of *Opening Doors* are tips that should help you earn higher scores on standardized reading tests. The tips below have to do with determining topics and stated main ideas.

To begin with, you should be aware that students sometimes miss questions on reading tests because they do not realize what they are being asked. If the wording of an item is even slightly unfamiliar, they may not recognize that they are being asked to apply a reading comprehension skill they already know. Therefore, you should learn to recognize certain types of questions no matter how they are worded, just as you recognize your friends no matter what they are wearing.

You are being asked to identify the topic of a passage when the test question begins:

The best title for this selection is . . .

This passage discusses . . .

This passage focuses mainly on . . .

The topic of this passage is . . .

This passage is mainly about . . .

This passage mainly concerns . . .

The problem the author is discussing in this passage is . . .

The author is explaining the nature of . . .

To find the right answer, simply ask yourself, "Who or what is this passage about?" Then see which of the choices offered most closely matches your answer. Remember to use the four clues for determining topics: titles or headings; words emphasized in special print; repetition; and mention of the topic that is then referred to by pronouns or other words.

You are being asked to identify the main idea when the question is worded:

The author's main point is that . . .

The principal idea of this passage is that . . .

Which of the following best expresses the main idea of this paragraph?

Which of the following is the main idea of the last paragraph? (or some specified paragraph)

Which of the following best expresses the main idea of the entire passage?

To find the right answer, ask yourself, "What is the single most important point the author wants me to understand about the topic?" Next, search the paragraph or passage for a single sentence that answers this question. Finally, read each of the choices and select the one that is the same as the sentence you selected or means essentially the same thing even if the wording is different.

DEVELOPING CHAPTER REVIEW CARDS

Review cards, or summary cards, are an excellent study tool. They are a way to select, organize, and review the most important information in a textbook chapter. The process of creating review cards helps you organize information in a meaningful way and, at the same time, transfer it into long-term memory. The cards can also be used to prepare for tests (see Part Three). The review card activities in this book give you structured practice in creating these valuable study tools. Once you have learned how to make review cards, you can create them for textbook material in your other courses.

Now, complete the seven review cards for Chapter 4 by answering the questions or following the directions on each card. When you have completed them, you will have summarized: (1) what the topic of a paragraph is and (2) how to determine it; (3) what a stated main idea sentence is and (4) how to locate it; (5) where the stated main idea sentence of a paragraph may appear; (6) how to tell if you have identified a stated main idea sentence correctly; and (7) how to avoid two errors in identifying stated main idea sentences.

The Topic of a Paragraph

1. What is the topic of a paragraph? (See page 191.)

_____

_____

2. Why is determining the topic important? (See page 191.)

_____

_____

3. To determine the topic, what question should you ask yourself? (See page 191.)

_____

_____

Card 1   **Chapter 4: Determining the Topic and the Stated Main Idea**

Determining the Topic of a Paragraph

What four clues will help you determine the topic? (See page 191.)

1. _____

   _____

2. _____

   _____

3. _____

   _____

4. _____

   _____

Card 2   **Chapter 4: Determining the Topic and the Stated Main Idea**

The Stated Main Idea of a Paragraph

1. What is a stated main idea sentence? (See page 195.)

   _____

   _____

2. What are four reasons why it is important to determine a stated main idea? (See page 195.)

   Reason: _____

   _____

   Reason: _____

   _____

   Reason: _____

   _____

   Reason: _____

Card 3   **Chapter 4: Determining the Topic and the Stated Main Idea**

Locating a Stated Main Idea Sentence

What are two steps to follow in locating a stated main idea sentence? (See page 196.)

Step 1: _____

_____

Step 2: _____

_____

What is a formula for the essential parts of a stated main idea sentence? (See page 196.)

Formula:

Card 4   **Chapter 4: Determining the Topic and the Stated Main Idea**

Where a Stated Main Idea Sentence May Appear

Where in a paragraph may the stated main idea sentence appear? List three places. (See pages 196–198.)

1. _____

_____

2. _____

_____

3. _____

_____

Card 5   **Chapter 4: Determining the Topic and the Stated Main Idea**

Checking Your Identification of a Stated Main Idea Sentence

List five ways you can tell if you have identified the stated main idea sentence correctly. (See page 198.)
You have selected the stated main idea sentence if:

1. _____

   _____

2. _____

   _____

3. _____

   _____

4. _____

   _____

5. _____

   _____

Card 6   **Chapter 4: Determining the Topic and the Stated Main Idea**

Avoiding Errors in Determining a Stated Main Idea Sentence

What are two common errors in determining stated main idea sentence? Describe how each can be avoided. (See page 199.)

Error: _____

_____

How to avoid it: _____

_____

Error: _____

_____

How to avoid it: _____

_____

_____

_____

Card 7   **Chapter 4: Determining the Topic and the Stated Main Idea**

SELECTION **4-1**
Magazine Article

THE NEW WORKFORCE
From *Business Week*
By Michelle Conlin

Prepare Yourself to Read

Directions: Do these exercises *before* you read Selection 4-1.

1. Magazine articles are typically written in a straightforward journalistic style. Preview this selection by reading the following:

   Introduction
   Title
   First paragraph (paragraph 1)
   First sentence of each paragraph
   Last paragraph (paragraph 20)

2. After you have previewed the selection, answer these questions:

   Who do you think the "new workforce" might be?

   _____

   Why do you think these people are now entering the workforce in large numbers?

   _____

Apply Comprehension Skills

Directions: Do the Annotation Practice Exercises as you read Selection 4-1. Apply two skills from this chapter:

Determine the topic.   When you read a paragraph, ask yourself, "Who or what is this about?"

Identify the stated main idea.   As you read, ask yourself, "What is the most important point the author wants me to understand about the topic?" Then search for the sentence that answers this question.

Complete the Annotation Practice Exercises. In these exercises, you will work only with paragraphs that have stated main ideas.

THE NEW WORKFORCE

Did you know that one out of every six people in the United States has a disability? This means that there are currently 54 million American men, women, and children who are disabled. Ready for an even more shocking figure? According to researchers' estimates, as the population ages, one in every three persons in our country will become disabled in some way. Some will experience a temporary disability; for others, the disability will be permanent. The disability may be present at birth, may come on gradually (as with a progressive illness), or may occur suddenly (from an accident, for example). This means that virtually all of us will know disability either firsthand or through the experience of family members, friends, or coworkers. Fortunately, attitudes toward the disabled, especially in the workforce, are changing for a variety of reasons. The article below, from Business Week *magazine, explores why this change is occurring and examines some barriers that still remain between the disabled and a good job.*

1   The Gap's emporium of affordable chic in midtown Manhattan throbs with New Economy action. Salesclerks sporting headsets race across the store to wait on tourists and time-starved New Yorkers. Stockboys heave huge boxes overflowing with clothes. At the center of this retail hubbub is Gap's "wild man in a wheelchair," supersalesman Wilfredo "Freddy" Laboy, a fast-talking, goateed 36-year-old who lost his legs when he fell off a freight train at age 9. Freddy dances across the store, popping wheelies and spinning himself around to the bouncy pop music. Little kids stare as he hops off his chair and onto the floor to grab a tangerine-colored T-shirt and then pulls himself up on his stump to reach for another pair of khakis. Instead of using the elevator, he prefers to horrify colleagues by scooting himself down the stairs. "It's faster," he says.

2   Freddy loves the Gap, and the Gap loves Freddy. But just six months ago, the story was altogether different. An amateur wheelchair basketball star who pulled himself through the New York City Marathon, Freddy was used to letting nothing stand in his way. But even with New York City's unemployment level at record lows, he couldn't find a job. Once prospective employers caught sight of his legless torso, they lost interest.

3   Still, on a whim, Freddy wheeled himself into the Gap last October. To his astonishment, they hired him. "I finally got accepted somewhere because they didn't just see the wheelchair," says the married father of three. "They saw me."

4   Freddy may well be at the cusp of a huge change rocking the world of the workplace,

Annotation Practice Exercises

Directions: For each exercise below,

- Write the topic of the paragraph on the lines beside the paragraph.

- Underline or highlight the stated main idea sentence of the paragraph.

This will help you remember the topic and the stated main idea.

marking the first time in history that people with disabilities have been poised to enter Corporate America en masse—many of them with the help of wheelchairs and seeing-eye dogs.

5   Facing the worst labor shortage in modern history, recruiters are tapping the kinds of workers they would have easily blown off just 10 years ago: prepubescent wireheads, grandmothers—even convicted murderers. Next up are the disabled, who may prove to be the last great hope—if only because they're the only labor pool that hasn't been completely drained. At the same time, groundbreaking technology is creating ways for people with disabilities to better perform jobs, helping to erase the deep divisions that once existed between them and everybody else.

6   Sure, a few companies have a long record of hiring workers with disabilities. In the 1980s—still the Dark Ages of the movement—Marriott International Inc. was doing the unheard-of: paying adults with Down's Syndrome $7 an hour to work 40 hours a week cleaning rooms and sweeping floors. But that was the exception. Despite the Americans with Disabilities Act (ADA), passed a decade ago this July, only 25% of the country's 15 million disabled who are also of working age are employed. Of the 75 percent who aren't working, Harris Polls indicate that two-thirds of them wish they could be. Says Paul H. Wehman, director of the rehabilitation research center at Virginia Commonwealth University: "The dirty little secret of the welfare-to-work movement is that people with disabilities got left out."

7   That may be about to change. Never before has it been so easy and made so much economic sense for companies to invest in workers with disabilities by making accommodations for them. "We can use new technologies to contribute to society in ways that weren't really possible when I started 25 years ago," says Michael Coleman, IBM's vice-president for global operations. Coleman, who lost both his hands in Vietnam when he was trying to defuse a bomb, is IBM's top-ranking disabled worker. He is also chairing the company's task force to find ways to employ more workers with disabilities.

8   Crestar Bank has already found ways to make that happen. Newfangled voice-activated technology means that callers to the bank never know that customer service representative Chris Harmon is a

Salesman extraordinaire Freddy Laboy couldn't find a job until he wheeled himself into a Gap in Midtown Manhattan.
(John Abbott)

Annotation Exercise

- Topic of paragraph 7:

  Investing in disabled workers.

- Underline or highlight the stated main idea of paragraph 7.

quadriplegic. He is so disabled that the recruiter who hired him had to stick a pen in his mouth so he could sign the employment application. At the company's Richmond (Va.) call center, he simply tells his computer what to do and the information appears on the screen in a flash.

9 Crestar is one of a growing list of businesses that is mining the ranks of the disabled to solve labor crises they say would otherwise have been catastrophic. Turns out that what began as a last-ditch maneuver to stem this worker drought has yielded an unexpected boon that veteran employers of people with disabilities have long known about: The disabled are often more proficient, productive, and efficient than "normies," according to researchers.

10 A 30-year study by DuPont revealed that job performance by workers with disabilities was equal to or better than that of fully functioning peers. The disabled had a 90% above-average job performance, with safety and attendance records that were far above the norm, too. Perhaps most enticing to human-resource heads pulling their hair out over the dot-com-induced worker exodus is the fact that people with disabilities can often be far more loyal to the employers who gave them a break and are therefore less likely to be lured away by a boss dangling a bigger paycheck.

11 But until recently, the disabled were actually penalized for finding a job because even a minimum-wage gig flipping burgers or mopping floors meant the automatic loss of Medicaid benefits. That huge barrier to employment fell in December when President Clinton signed the Workers Incentives Improvement Act, clearing the path for states to change Medicaid laws to let the disabled hang on to much-needed benefits while entering the workforce.

12 The move comes none too soon. Already, temporary agency Manpower Inc. is raiding the ranks of the disabled to fill its employee rolls. The National Disability Council reports a 50% jump in requests for workers with disabilities from companies as diverse as Merrill Lynch & Co. and Microsoft Corp.

13 In fact, Microsoft is so eager to hire such workers that the software company is spearheading the Able to Work program, a consortium of 22 businesses scrambling to find the best ways to place disabled people in jobs. Says Microsoft's

---

Annotation Exercise

• Topic of paragraph 10:

  Better Job Performance

• Underline or highlight the stated main idea of paragraph 10.

director of diversity, Santiago Rodriguez: "Until now, the whole country has been at a loss as to how to do this."

14 To many advocates for the disabled, this confusion is a disappointment. The ADA was passed with great hopes of creating jobs and access for America's disabled population of 54 million. It prohibited employers from refusing to hire qualified applicants who also had disabilities. It also mandated that the disabled have access to telecommunications equipment and public transportation.

15 But barriers standing between most people with disabillities and a good, solid job haven't exactly been wiped out by employee sensitivity training courses and curb-cut accessible sidewalks. Those and other strides have helped, but problems still abound. Cities such as Chicago and New Orleans face lawsuits for failing to bring their public transportation systems into compliance.

16 There are also, disability advocates say, still too many lawsuits like the one brought on behalf of a mentally retarded janitor, Don Perkl, who loved scrubbing toilets for Chuck E. Cheese in Madison, Wis. A district manager, a lawsuit alleges, fired him after saying "We don't hire people like that." The pizza parlor's local manager and two other employees quit in protest because they claimed the perennially upbeat Perkl was doing such a stellar job. Last year, a jury in federal court in the Western District of Wisconsin agreed with them, slapping the company with $13 million in punitive damages—the largest ADA award ever for a single plaintiff. A judge is still reviewing the jury's verdict. Chuck E. Cheese claims that Perkl "wasn't dismissed due to his disability but because he couldn't perform the job," says company spokesman Jon Rice.

17 Plenty of other lawsuits brought under the ADA have caused critics to question its scope. Some worry that the act is not broad enough, pointing to a recent Supreme Court ruling that established that people with treatable disabilities don't qualify for protection. Others say the ADA is straying into the realm of the absurd, noting such cases as the employee with bad body odor who argued she should be protected from getting fired because her glandular problem qualified her as disabled.

18 But most of the country's workers with disabilities face challenges that are far more

---

Annotation Exercise

- Topic of paragraph 15:

  Accessible Area

- Underline or highlight the stated main idea of paragraph 15.

Annotation Exercise

- Topic of paragraph 17:

  ADA Protection law

  law sue

- Underline or highlight the stated main idea of paragraph 17.

clear-cut: They are deaf, blind, paralyzed, or emotionally impaired. Some have been burdened with disabilities since they were born. Others, like Booz, Allen & Hamilton Inc. principal Jeffrey Schaffer, are new to the minority—a group that one in three people will be a part of during their lives. Three years ago, Schaffer's car was in a head-on collision with another vehicle that swerved into his lane on a windy back road in West Virginia. It took paramedics an hour to cut him from the wreckage.

19   After learning he would be confined to a wheelchair, Schaffer says, the thought of returning to work was the thing that kept him going. "Getting back to work was critical to my sense of well-being," says Schaffer from the bed of a hospital where he has just undergone his sixth operation since the accident. "Work ends up being a defining characteristic for self-worth."

20   For worker-starved companies, spreading that kind of self-worth around is looking more and more like the only answer to today's labor-shortage woes. Still, the real test will be when the economy cools and companies can afford to get picky about choosing between applicants with disabilities and everyone else. By then, though, it may be a lot harder to tell the difference.

Source: Michelle Conlin, *Business Week,* March 20, 2000, pp. 64–68.

SELECTION **4-1**

Magazine Article

Comprehension Quiz

Directions: For each comprehension question below, use information from the selection to determine the correct answer. You may refer to the selection as you answer the questions. Write your answer in the space provided.

True or False

_____ 1. The Americans with Disabilities Act has been highly effective in helping disabled Americans enter the workforce.

_____ 2. People with disabilities tend to be more loyal than other workers to employers who give them a chance.

_____ 3. Seventy-five percent of disabled Americans who are not working wish they could be.

_____ 4. One study revealed that 90 percent of disabled workers had an above-average job performance, but their safety and attendance records were far below the norm.

Multiple-Choice

_____ 5. More disabled people are now entering the workforce because of the
   a. new economy.
   b. worst labor shortage in modern history.
   c. new technologies that make it easier for companies to accommodate workers with disabilities.
   d. all of the above.

_____ 6. Until recently the disabled were actually penalized for finding a job because
   a. they were paid less than other workers.
   b. they lost their Medicaid benefits if they entered the workforce.
   c. their disabilities made the workplace less safe for them.
   d. they had to work harder than "normies."

_____ 7. The number of disabled Americans is
   a. 54 million.
   b. 36 million.
   c. 22 million.
   d. 15 million.

_____ **8.** How many people will become disabled during their lives?
  a.   three in four
  b.   one in two
  c.   one in three
  d.   four in five

_____ **9.** Which of the following would be a violation of the Americans with Disabilities Act?
  a.   refusing to hire qualified applicants who have disabilities
  b.   lack of accessible telecommunications equipment
  c.   unavailability of public transportation
  d.   all of the above

_____ **10.** Companies' attitudes toward hiring the disabled
  a.   have not changed in decades.
  b.   have worsened.
  c.   have improved dramatically.
  d.   should begin to change with the next decade.

SELECTION **4-1**

Magazine Article

Extend Your Vocabulary by Using Context Clues

Directions: Context clues are words in a sentence that allow the reader to deduce (reason out) the meaning of an unfamiliar word in that sentence. For each vocabulary item below, a sentence from the selection containing an important word (*italicized, like this*) is quoted first. Next, there is an additional sentence using the word in the same sense and providing another context clue. Use the context clues from *both* sentences to deduce the meaning of the italicized word. *Be sure the answer you choose makes sense in both sentences.* If you discover that you must use a dictionary to confirm an answer choice, remember that the meaning you select must still fit the context of *both* sentences. To indicate your answer, write the letter in the space provided.

Pronunciation key: ă pat   ā pay   âr care   ä father   ĕ pet   ē be   ĭ pit
ī tie   îr **pier**   ŏ pot   ō toe   ô paw   oi noise   ou out   ŏŏ took
ōō **boot**   ŭ cut   yōō abuse   ûr **urge**   th **thin**   *th* **this**   hw **which**
zh vision   ə about
Stress mark: ′

_____ **1.** Once *prospective* employers caught sight of his legless torso, they lost interest.

Prospective students are often invited to visit and take a tour of a college they are considering attending.

prospective (prə spĕk ′ tĭv)
a. highly intelligent
b. likely to be or become
c. inclined to be competitive
d. tending to be selfish

_____ **2.** Newfangled voice-activated technology means that callers to the bank never know that customer service representative Chris Harmon is a *quadriplegic.*

After the mountain climber broke his neck in a fall and became a *quadriplegic,* all he could move was his head.

quadriplegic (kwŏd rə plē′ jĭk)
a. person who is completely paralyzed from the neck down
b. person whose lower body is paralyzed
c. person whose arms are paralyzed
d. person whose vocal cords are paralyzed

_____ **3.** Crestar is one of a growing list of businesses that is mining the ranks of the disabled to solve labor crises that they say would otherwise be *catastrophic.*

The entire town was destroyed by the *catastrophic* tornado.

catastrophic (kă tə strŏ′ fĭk)
a. having an unknown outcome
b. having a disastrous outcome
c. having an undetermined outcome
d. having a unexpectedly pleasant outcome

_____ **4.** Turns out that what began as a last-ditch maneuver to stem the worker drought has yielded an unexpected *boon* that veteran employers have long known about: The disabled are often more proficient, productive, and efficient than "normies," according to researchers.

Receiving the scholarship was a real *boon* to Luis because it enabled him to quit work and go to school full time.

boon (bo͞on)
a. side effect
b. problem
c. benefit
d. hindrance

_____ **5.** Perhaps most *enticing* to human-resource heads pulling their hair out over the dot-com-induced worker exodus is the fact that people with disabilities are often far more loyal to the employers who gave them a break and are therefore less likely to be lured away by a boss dangling a bigger paycheck.

The aroma of the fresh-baked cookies was so *enticing* that we went into the bakery and bought a dozen.

enticing (ĕn tī′ sĭng)

a. upsetting

b. causing puzzlement or confusion

c. attracting by arousing desire

d. misunderstood

_____ **6.** Perhaps the most enticing to human-resource heads pulling their hair out over the dot-com-induced worker *exodus* is the fact that people with disabilities are often far more loyal to the employers who gave them a break and are therefore less likely to be lured away by a boss dangling a bigger paycheck.

When rumors began to spread of a possible terrorist attack, there was an *exodus* from the city.

exodus (ĕk′ sə dəs)

a. general, widespread panic

b. a closing off or enclosing

c. redistribution of people

d. departure of a large number of people

_____ **7.** It also *mandated* that the disabled have access to telecommunications equipment and public transportation.

Desegregation of public schools was *mandated* in 1954 by the Supreme Court decision in a case known as *Brown* v. *Board of Education of Topeka*.

mandated (măn′ dā təd)

a. required

b. overturned

c. questionable

d. changed

_____ **8.** But the barriers standing between most people with disabilities and a good, solid job haven't exactly been wiped out by employee sensitivity training courses and curb-cut *accessible* sidewalks.

Wheelchair ramps, electric door openers, and elevators were added to make the public library *accessible* to the elderly and the disabled.

accessible (ăk sĕs′ ə bəl)

a. off-limits

b. more pleasing

c. more attractive

d. easily approached or entered

_____ **9.** Cities such as Chicago and New Orleans face lawsuits for failing to bring their public transportation systems into *compliance.*

The company reviewed its accounting procedures to be sure they were in *compliance* with the new laws.

compliance (kəm plī′ əns)

a. disagreement

b. agreement with a demand

c. popularity

d. good repair

_____ **10.** There are also, disability *advocates* say, still too many lawsuits like the one brought on behalf of a mentally retarded janitor, Don Perkl, who loved scrubbing toilets for Chuck E. Cheese in Madison, Wis.

Advocates for animal rights staged a demonstration in front of the department store to protest the sale of fur coats.

advocates (ăd′ və kəts)

a. protesters

b. advisers

c. teachers

d. supporters

SELECTION **4-1**

Magazine Article

Collaboration Option

Respond in Writing

Directions: Refer to the selection as needed to answer the essay-type questions below.

Option for collaboration: Your instructor may direct you to work with other students, or in other words, to work *collaboratively.* In that case, you should form groups of three or four students as directed by your instructor and work together to complete the exercises. After your group discusses each item and agrees on the answer, have a group member record it. Every member of your group should be able to explain all of your group's answers.

1. How would you react to seeing an obviously disabled person such as Freddy Laboy working in a Gap store? How would the presence of such an employee influence your opinion the store?

_____

_____

_____

2. Some able-bodied people treat the disabled as if they were invisible. Why do you think this happens?

    _____

    _____

    _____

3. What are some ways that technology could be used to adapt the workplace for disabled workers? Give at least 3 examples.

    _____

    _____

    _____

4. According to the selection, one-third of all Americans will become disabled to some extent during their lives. List at least 5 ways in which a person could become disabled.

    _____

    _____

    _____

    _____

    _____

5. Overall main idea. What is the overall main idea the author wants you to understand about the "new workforce?" Answer this question in one sentence. Be sure that your overall main idea sentence includes the topic (*disabled people* or *the new workforce*) and tells the overall most important point about it. Do *not* begin your sentence with "The overall main idea is . . ." or "The author wants us to understand . . .". Just *state* the overall main idea.

    _____

    _____

    _____

    _____

Read More about It on the World Wide Web

To learn more about the topic of this selection, visit these websites or use your favorite search engine (such as Yahoo®). Whenever you go to *any* website, it is a good idea to evaluate it critically. Are you getting good information—information that is accurate, complete, and up-to-date? Who sponsors the website? How easy is it to use the features of the website?

http://www.nod.org

This is the website for the National Organization on Disability (NOD), which promotes full and equal participation in all aspects of life by America's 54 million men, women, and children with disabilities. NOD is the only national disability network organization concerned with all disabilities, all age groups, and all issues related to disability.

http://icanonline.net

iCan brings together content, community and resources one place and is easy to navigate. It is for those who face the daily challenges of living with a disability, but also for people who have a personal connection to the disability community. Contains information on travel and transportation, sports and leisure, legislation, caregivers, and employment, among others.

http://www.ablelink.org

Ability OnLine is a friendly and safe computer friendship network (electronic bulletin board) where young people with disabilites or chronic illnesses connect to each other as well as to their friends, family members, caregivers and supporters. Free and easy to use.

http://janweb.icdi.wvu.edu

The Job Accommodation Network (JAN) is not a job placement service, but an international toll-free consulting service that provides information about job accommodations and the employablity of people with disabilities. JAN also provides information regarding the Americans with Disabilites Act (ADA). More that 250 links.

SELECTION **4-2**

Sociology

LATINOS

From *Sociology: An introduction*

By Richard J. Gelles and Ann Levine

Prepare Yourself to Read

Directions: Do these exercises *before* you read Selection 4-2.

1. First, read and think about the title. What are the countries of origin of the Latinos who live in your city or closest to the area in which you live?

   _____

   _____

2. Latinos have made many contributions to our country's culture—in the arts, literature, politics, science, medicine, the military, sports, and music and other entertainment fields. Who are some distinguished or famous Latinos you are already aware of?

   _____

   _____

   _____

3. Next, complete your preview by reading the following:

   > Introduction (in *italics*)
   > All of the first paragraph (paragraph 1)
   > First sentence of each paragraph
   > Charts
   > Map
   > All of the last paragraph (paragraph 7)

   On the basis of your preview, what does the selection now seem to be about?

   _____

   _____

Apply Comprehension Skills

Directions: Do the Annotation Practice Exercises as you read Selection 4-2. Apply the skills from this chapter:

Determine the topic. When you read a paragraph, as yourself, "Who or what is this about?"

Identify the stated main idea.   As you read, ask yourself, "What is the most important point the authors wants me to understand about the topic?" Then search for the sentence that answers this question.

Complete the Annotation Practice Exercises. In these exercises, you will work only with paragraphs that have stated main ideas.

LATINOS

Latinos constitute the fastest-growing minority in the United States. It is estimated that by 2010 one out of every five Americans will be Latino. Although Latinos represent a rapidly growing segment of our population, many people are still unaware of their achievements and contributions to our culture. Latinos have made contributions in science and medicine, literature and the arts, politics and government, education, the military, sports, and entertainment. Nevertheless, Latinos as a whole are among the less educated and less well-to-do in our society. Their increasing impact on American life and culture, however, underscores the need for young Latinos to educate themselves for professional careers and to prepare themselves for the leadership roles which many of them will be called upon to assume.

Latinos have immigrated to the United States from Mexico, Central America, South America, Cuba, and Puerto Rico, and they live in virtually every state in the United States. The selection below, from a sociology textbook, gives an overview of this increasingly important segment of our population.

1   Latinos are the second-largest minority in the United States and will outnumber African Americans early in the twenty-first century, in part because of immigration, and in part because many Latinos are in their childbearing years and tend to have larger families than non-Hispanics. People of Spanish heritage have lived in what is now the United States since the sixteenth century, but nearly two-thirds of those who identify themselves as Latino or Hispanic today are immigrants or the children of immigrants. A diverse population, they come from varied national backgrounds and social classes and have followed different immigration and settlement patterns. Latinos may have European, Amerindian, or African ancestors or—perhaps most often—some combination thereof. Latinos have been described as the "in-between" minority, whose ethnic status lies between European Americans and African Americans.

2   In socioeconomic terms, Latinos are among the most disadvantaged groups in our society. Many Latino families are solidly middle-class: one in five has a household income of $50,000 or more, about the same percentage as for African Americans. But more than one-quarter (28 percent) have incomes below the poverty level. Latinos have the lowest rates of high school and college graduation of any major population group. On average, Mexican Americans have the lowest education levels and incomes, and Cuban Americans the highest (though below levels for non-Hispanic whites). Why do Latinos have such low

Annotation Practice Exercises

Directions: For each exercise below,

- Write the topic of the paragraph on the lines beside the paragraph.

- Underline or highlight the stated main idea sentence of the paragraph.

This will help you remember the topic and the stated main idea.

Annotation Exercise

- Topic of paragraph 2:

  Second-class authority

- Underline or highlight the stated main idea of paragraph 2.

incomes and high poverty levels? Many are re-cent immigrants who have few marketable skills, speak little English, and work for entry-level salaries at low-level jobs. Many face discrimination in the workplace, particularly if they are dark-skinned and have strong accents. In school, Latino young people face numerous barriers, including limited proficiency in English, low expectations on the part of teachers, and overcrowded and poorly funded schools. Although Latinos make up 11 percent of the population, in 1997 only 1 percent of all elected officials and 17 members of Congress were Latino.

3   The Latino population includes three main ethnic groups (as well as many smaller ones, including many recent immigrants from Central and South America). The largest group, Mexican Americans, are concentrated in the southwest. Some trace their ancestry to colonial days, while others are recent immigrants. Up through the 1960s, a majority worked as agricultural laborers. The Anglo majority viewed Mexican Americans as "peasants" and "foreigners," and little effort was made to assimilate them. In the 1970s and 1980s, Mexican Americans began moving into cities, where eight out of ten reside today. But the pattern of low levels of education and low-wage employment, especially among recent immigrants, has continued.

4   The second-largest group is Puerto Ricans, most of whom live in New York City. Puerto Ricans were declared American citizens in 1917, but the first large wave of immigrants did not arrive until the 1950s, when airlines introduced relatively inexpensive flights between the island and the mainland. By 1970 there were half as many Puerto Ricans on the mainland as in Puerto Rico, but migration back and forth is common. Owing to low levels of education, poor English, recent entry into the labor force, and discrimination, especially against those who are dark-skinned, Puerto Ricans are among the poorest Latinos.

5   Another prominent group of Latinos in the United States is Cuban Americans, who began arriving in 1959, the year Fidel Castro seized control of the Cuban government. The first large group of refugees to move to the United States en masse, Cuban Americans have also been one of the most successful non-English-speaking immigrant groups.

Latinos are the second-largest minority in the United States.
(Bob Daemmrich / Stock Boston)

Latino Americans.

Although a majority of Latino immigrants are from Mexico, immigration from countries in Central and South America is increasing.

Source: R. J. Gelles and A. Levine. *Sociology: An Introduction,* 6th ed. New York: McGraw-Hill, 1999, p. 348.

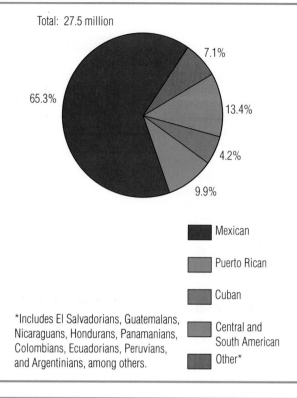

Total: 27.5 million

65.3%
7.1%
13.4%
4.2%
9.9%

Mexican

Puerto Rican

Cuban

Central and South American

Other*

*Includes El Salvadorians, Guatemalans, Nicaraguans, Hondurans, Panamanians, Colombians, Ecuadorians, Peruvians, and Argentinians, among others.

Countries of origin of Hispanic immigrants, 1980s and 1990s.

Source: J. del Pinal and A. Singer. "Generations of Diversity:Latinos in the United States." *Population Bulletin* 52 (3), October 1997, p. 10, fig. 8.

NORTH AMERICA

Mexico
Cuba
Dominican Republic
Puerto Rico
Guatemala
Honduras
El Salvador
Nicaragua
Panama
Venezuela
Colombia
Ecuador
Peru
SOUTH AMERICA

N

Argentina

6   Cuban Americans differ from Mexican Americans and Puerto Ricans in a number of ways. Many of the early Cuban refugees were educated urban business owners and professionals. They arrived not as poor individuals but as a relatively well-off group with established social networks. As political refugees, they had access to government programs not available to other immigrants. A majority settled in Miami, where they established an economic enclave with businesses run by and catering to Cubans. As a result they did not have to learn a new language and new ways of doing business or to accept entry-level jobs in the mainstream economy. Subsequent waves of Cuban (and other Latino) immigrants supplied both the labor and the consumers to maintain and expand this enclave.

7   Second- and third-generation Latinos tend to be "bicultural" as well as bilingual. Although Americanized in some ways, they have maintained their language, religion (Roman Catholicism), family traditions, and contacts with their homelands over the generations.

Source: Richard J. Gelles and Ann Levine, *Sociology, An Introduction,* 6th ed., McGraw-Hill, Boston, Mass., 1999, pp. 347–349.

Annotation Exercise

- Topic of paragraph 6:

  Cuban American

- Underline or highlight the stated main idea of paragraph 6.

Annotation Exercise

- Topic of paragraph 7:

  Roman Catholicism

- Underline or highlight the stated main idea of paragraph 7.

SELECTION **4-2**

Sociology

Comprehension Quiz

Directions: For each comprehension question below, use information from the selection to determine the correct answer. You may refer to the selection as you answer the questions. Write your answer in the space provided.

True or False

_T_ **1.** Nearly two-thirds of those who today identify themselves as Latino or Hispanic are immigrants or children of immigrants.

_T_ **2.** One out of every five Latino families in the United States has a household income of $50,000 or more.

_F_ **3.** Puerto Ricans were declared American citizens in 1970.

_T_ **4.** There have been people of Spanish heritage living in what is now the United States since the sixteenth century.

_F_ **5.** In 1997 only 11 members of the United States Congress were Latino.

Multiple-Choice

_C_ **6.** Latinos will outnumber African Americans in the United States early in the twenty-first century, in part because of immigration, and in part because
   a. Latinos are the "in-between" minority.
   b. many young Latinos will bring their older relatives here from other countries.
   c. many Latinos are in their childbearing years, and Latinos tend to have larger families than non-Hispanics.
   d. many Latino families are now middle-class.

_B_ **7.** Today eight out of ten Mexican Americans
   a. have incomes below the poverty level.
   b. live in cities.
   c. live in rural areas.
   d. work as agricultural workers.

8. The largest ethnic group within the Latino population is the
   a. Mexican Americans.
   b. Puerto Ricans.
   c. Cuban Americans.
   d. Latinos from Central and South America.

9. The first large wave of Puerto Rican immigrants arrived
- *a.* in 1917.
- *b.* in 1970.
- *c.* after Fidel Castro seized control of the government.
- *d.* when airlines introduced relatively inexpensive flights between the island and the mainland.

10. The percent of Latino Americans who are from Puerto Rico is
- *a.* 4.2%.
- *b.* 7.1%
- *c.* 9.9%.
- *d.* 13.4%.

SELECTION **4-2**

Sociology

Extend Your Vocabulary by Using Context Clues

Directions: Context clues are words in a sentence that allow the reader to deduce (reason out) the meaning of an unfamiliar word in the sentence. For each vocabulary exercise below, a sentence from the reading selection containing an important word (*italicized, like this*) is quoted first. Next, there is an additional sentence using the word in the same sense and providing another context clue. Use the context clues from *both* sentences to deduce the meaning of the italicized word. *Be sure the answer you choose makes sense in both sentences.* (If you discover that you must use a dictionary to confirm an answer choice, remember that the meaning you select must still fit the context of *both* sentences.)

Pronunciation key: ă pat ā pay âr care ä father ĕ pet ē be ĭ pit
ī tie îr pier ŏ pot ō toe ô paw oi noise ou out ŏŏ took
ōō boot ŭ cut yōō abuse ûr urge th thin *th* this hw which
zh vision ə about
Stress mark: '

---

1. People of Spanish *heritage* have lived in what is now the United States since the sixteenth century, but nearly two-thirds of those who identify themselves as Latino or Hispanic today are immigrants or the children of immigrants.

Several of Johann Sebastian Bach's children received the strong musical *heritage* of their gifted father and they, too, became musicians or composers.

heritage (hĕr′ ĭ tĭj)

a. specialized training

b. highly negative influence

c. origin

d. something acquired through birth

_____A_____ **2.** Many are recent immigrants who have few *marketable* skills, speak little English, and work for entry-level salaries at low-level jobs.

The first electric-powered cars were not *marketable,* because they were too expensive and were not practical for driving long distances.

marketable (mär′ kĭt ă bəl)

a. in demand by buyers or employers

b. appealing in appearance

c. related to technology

d. pertaining to a high level of performance

_____D_____ **3.** In school, Latino young people face numerous barriers, including limited *proficiency* in English, low expectations on the part of teachers, and overcrowded and poorly funded schools.

My cousin received a university scholarship because of his *proficiency* in foreign languages.

proficiency (prə fĭsh′ ən sē)

a. extensive training

b. deep love for

c. limited ability

d. high ability or skill

_____C_____ **4.** The largest group, Mexican Americans, are *concentrated* in the southwest.

Many of the best-paying careers are *concentrated* in the fields of computer science and information technology.

concentrated (kŏn′ sən trāt d)

a. related to

b. disappearing from

c. gathered

d. undeveloped

_____C_____ **5.** The Anglo majority viewed Mexican Americans as "peasants" and "foreigners," and little effort was made to *assimilate* them.

Many Native Americans take great pride in their own culture and have resisted attempts of others to completely *assimilate* them into mainstream American culture.

assimilate (ə sĭm′ ə lāt)

a.   soak up

b.   educate

c.   take in and make similar

d.   retrain

6. Another *prominent* group of Latinos in the United States is Cuban Americans, who began arriving in 1959, the year Fidel Castro seized control of the Cuban government.

    Microsoft's founder Bill Gates, one of the most *prominent* businessmen of all times, is also becoming recognized throughout the world for his charitable giving.

    prominent (prŏm′ ə nənt)

    a.   distinguished

    b.   widely known

    c.   ruthless

    d.   humorous

7. Another prominent group of Latinos in the United States is Cuban Americans, who began arriving in 1959, the year Fidel Castro seized control of the Cuban government. The first large group of refugees to move to the United States *en masse,* Cuban Americans have also been one of the most successful non-English-speaking immigrant groups.

    When the workers were denied a pay raise for the third year in a row, all 200 of them resigned *en masse.*

    en masse (ŏn măs′)

    a.   as a group

    b.   in a formal ceremony

    c.   for political reasons

    d.   after a meeting held in a church

8. A majority settled in Miami, where they established an economic *enclave* with businesses run by and catering to Cubans.

    The center of the city is now an *enclave* of stately old homes surrounded by dozens of new office and government buildings.

    enclave (ĕn′ klāv)

    a.   suburb of a large city

    b.   an area enclosed within a larger area

    c.   industrial area

    d.   restricted area

_____ 9. *Subsequent* waves of Cuban (and other Latino) immigrants supplied both the labor and the consumers to maintain and expand this enclave.

I made a low score on my first history test, but I have scored well on all *subsequent* tests this semester.

subsequent (sŭb′ sĭ kwĕnt)

a. advanced

b. unexpected

c. following

d. harder

_d_ 10. Second- and third-generation Latinos tend to be *"bicultural"* as well as bilingual. Although Americanized in some ways, they have maintained their language, religion (Roman Catholicism), family traditions, and contacts with their homelands over the generations.

Montreal is considered a *bicultural* city because it has strong influences from both the French and the English.

bicultural (bī kŭl′ chûr əl)

a. pertaining to the arts

b. pertaining to two distinct cultures

c. pertaining to manners

d. able to speak two languages

SELECTION **4-2**

Sociology

Collaboration Option

Respond in Writing

Directions: Refer to the selection as needed to answer the essay-type questions below.

Option for collaboration: Your instructor may direct you to work with other students, in other words, to work *collaboratively*. In that case, you should form groups of three or four students as directed by your instructor and work together to complete the exercises. After your group discusses each item and agrees on the answer, have a group member record it. Every member of your group should be able to explain all of your group's answers.

1. Name any Latino groups represented in your school, city, or region of the country.

_____

_____

2. What are some of the advantages and disadvantages of being an "in-between" or "bicultural" group such as the Latinos? Does every group that is new to a country experience being an "in-between" or "bicultural group?" (Be sure to answer both questions.)

   _____

   _____

   _____

   _____

3. What can any group of immigrants do to assimilate itself into the culture of the country to which it has immigrated?

   _____

   _____

   _____

4. In what ways do immigrants who settle in a country enrich that country's culture? List at least 4 ways.

   _____

   _____

   _____

   _____

5. Give the names and describe the achievements of at least four famous Americans of Latino descent. These individuals may have lived in the past or may be living presently. (If necessary, you may do research to answer this question.)

   _____

   _____

   _____

   _____

6. Overall main idea. What is the overall main idea the author wants the reader to understand about Latinos? Answer this question in one sentence. Be sure that your overall main idea sentence includes the topic (*Latinos*) and tells the overall most important point about it.

   _____

   _____

Read More about It on the World Wide Web

To learn more about the topic of this selection, visit these websites or use your favorite search engine (such as Yahoo ®). Whenever you go to *any* website, it is a good idea to evaluate it critically. Are you getting good information—information that is accurate, complete, and up-to-date? Who sponsors the website? How easy is it to use the features of the website?

http://www.hisp.com/links.html

This site provides links to Latino news and politics. There is also information about Latino arts, entertainment, lifestyles, and interests, and resources for business, careers, and education. and other resources.

http://www.latintrade.com

LatinTrade.com provides a neutral, secure marketplace for companies to find the right customers, sell goods, and acquire everything necessary.

http://www.zonalatina.com

"Zona Latina" is a site that contains links to media and marketing. There are virtually thousands of media Web links: newspapers, magazines, radio, and television. Also included are resources on individual Latin American countries, music, children's resources, book reviews, and more! Most sites are in English, but there are also many in español.

http://www.mundolatino.org/

Esta sitio contiene enlaces a los siguientes sectores: educatión, cultura, noticias, empleo, correo electrónico, y mucho otros. Disponible solamente en español.

MUHAMMAD
From *The 100: A Ranking of the Most Influential Persons in History*
By Michael K. Hart

Prepare Yourself to Read

Directions: Do these exercises *before* you read Selection 4-3.

1. First, read and think about the title. What do you already know about Muhammad?

   _____

   _____

2. Next, complete your preview by reading the following:

   Introduction (in *italics*)
   First paragraph (paragraph 1)
   First sentence of each paragraph
   Words in *italics*
   Last paragraph (paragraph 9)

   On the basis of your preview, what information about Muhammad does this selection seem to present?

   _____

   _____

Apply Comprehension Skills

Directions: Do the Annotation Practice Exercises as you read Selection 4-3. Apply two skills from this chapter:

Determine the topic.   When you read a paragraph, ask yourself, "Who or what is this about?"

Identify the stated main idea.   As you read, ask yourself, "What is the most important point the author wants me to understand about the topic?" Then search for the sentence that answers this question.

Complete the Annotation Exercises. In these exercises, you will work only with paragraphs that have stated main ideas.

MUHAMMAD

Of the billions of human beings who have populated the earth, which ones do you think have most influenced the world and the course of history? The historian Michael Hart attempts to answer this fascinating question in his book, The 100: A Ranking of the Most Influential Persons in History. *He emphasizes that he was seeking to identify the "most influential" persons in history, not necessarily the "greatest." On his list of the top 100, the first ten are: (1) Muhammad, (2) Isaac Newton, (3) Jesus Christ, (4) Buddha, (5) Confucius, (6) St. Paul, (7) Ts'ai Lun, (8) Johannes Gutenberg, (9) Christopher Columbus, (10) Albert Einstein. Perhaps you were surprised to see Muhammad listed first. In the selection below, Hart explains why he considers Muhammad to be the "most influential person in history."*

This selection will be especially useful to you if you do not already know who Muhammad is. Every well-educated person should be familiar with the names and accomplishments of individuals who have significantly influenced the history and culture of the world.

Keep in mind that it does not matter whether or not you agree with Michael Hart that Muhammad is the most influential person in history. Michael Hart does not expect everyone to agree with him. As you read, your goal should be to understand and consider the reasons Michael Hart gives for his selection of Muhammad as the most influential person who has ever lived.

1   My choice of Muhammad to lead the list of the world's most influential persons may surprise some readers and may be questioned by others, but he was the only man in history who was supremely successful on both the religious and the secular level.

2   Of humble origins, Muhammad founded and promulgated one of the world's great religions, and became an immensely effective political leader. Today, thirteen centuries after his death, his influence is still powerful and pervasive.

3   The majority of the persons in this book had the advantage of being born and raised in centers of civilization, highly cultured and politically pivotal nations. Muhammad, however, was born in the year 570, in the city of Mecca, in southern Arabia, at that time a backward area of the world, far from the centers of trade, art, and learning. Orphaned at age six, he was reared in modest surroundings. Islamic tradition tells us that he was illiterate. His economic position improved when, at the age of twenty-five, he married a wealthy widow. Nevertheless, as he approached forty, there was little outward indication that he was a remarkable person.

4   Most Arabs at that time were pagans, who believed in many gods. There were, however, in Mecca, a small number of Jews and Christians; it

Annotation Practice Exercises

Directions: For each exercise below,

• Write the topic of the paragraph on the lines beside the paragraph.

• Underline or highlight the stated main idea sentence of the paragraph.

This will help you remember the topic and the stated main idea.

Annotation Exercise

• Topic of paragraph 4:

_____

_____

• Underline or highlight the stated main idea of paragraph 4.

was from them no doubt that Muhammad first learned of a single, omnipotent God who ruled the entire universe. When he was forty years old, Muhammad became convinced that this one true God (Allah) was speaking to him, and had chosen him to spread the true faith.

5   For three years, Muhammad preached only to close friends and associates. Then, about 613, he began preaching in public. As he slowly gained converts, the Meccan authorities came to consider him a dangerous nuisance. In 622, fearing for his safety, Muhammad fled to Medina (a city some 200 miles north of Mecca), where he had been offered a position of considerable political power.

6   The flight, called the Hegira (hĕj′ər ə, hĭ jī′rə), was the turning point of the Prophet's life. In Mecca, he had had a few followers. In Medina, he had many more, and he soon acquired an influence that made him a virtual dictator. During the next few years, while Muhammad's following grew rapidly, a series of battles were fought between Medina and Mecca. This war ended in 630 with Muhammad's triumphant return to Mecca as conqueror. The remaining two and one-half years of his life witnessed the rapid conversion of the Arab tribes to the new religion. When Muhammad died, in 632, he was the effective ruler of all of southern Arabia.

7   How, then, is one to assess the overall impact of Muhammad on human history? Like all religions, Islam exerts an enormous influence upon the lives of its followers. It is for this reason that the founders of the world's great religions all figure prominently in this book. Since there are roughly twice as many Christians as Moslems in the world, it may initially seem strange that Muhammad has been ranked higher than Jesus. There are two principal reasons for that decision. First, Muhammad played a far more important role in the development of Islam than Jesus did in the development of Christianity. Although Jesus was responsible for the main ethical and moral precepts of Christianity (insofar as these differed from Judaism), St. Paul was the main developer of Christian theology, its principal prose-lytizer, and the author of a large portion of the New Testament.

8   Muhammad, however, was responsible for both the theology of Islam and its main ethical

Muhammad. 570–632 A.D.
(Bettmann/Corbis)

Annotation Exercise

• Topic of paragraph 6:

_____

_____

• Underline or highlight the stated main idea of paragraph 6.

and moral principles. In addition, he played the key role in proselytizing the new faith, and in establishing the religious practices of Islam. Moreover, he is the author of the Moslem holy scriptures, the *Koran,* [Qu'ran], a collection of certain of Muhammad's insights that he believed had been directly revealed to him by Allah. Most of these utterances were copied more or less faithfully during Muhammad's lifetime and were collected together in authoritative form not long after his death. The Koran, therefore, closely represents Muhammad's ideas and teachings and to a considerable extent his exact words. No such detailed compilation of the teachings of Christ has survived. Since the Koran is at least as important to Moslems as the Bible is to Christians, the influence of Muhammad through the medium of the Koran has been enormous. It is probable that the relative influence of Muhammad on Islam has been larger than the combined influence of Jesus Christ and St. Paul on Christianity. On the purely religious level, then, it seems likely that Muhammad has been as influential in human history as Jesus.

9   Furthermore, Muhammad (unlike Jesus) was a secular as well as a religious leader. In fact, as the driving force behind the Arab conquests, he may well rank as the most influential political leader of all time.

Annotation Exercise

- Topic of paragraph 9:

  _____

  _____

- Underline or highlight the stated main idea of paragraph 9.

Source: Michael Hart, *The 100: A Ranking of the Most Influential Persons in History,* Carol Publishing Group, Secaucus, New Jersey, 1978, from pp. 33–39. Copyright © 1978 by Hart Publishing Company, Inc. Published by arrangement with Carol Publishing Group. A Citadel Press Book.

SELECTION **4-3**

History

Comprehension Quiz

Directions: For each comprehension question below, use information from the selection to determine the correct answer. You may refer to the selection as you answer the questions. Write your answer in the space provided.

True or False

___F___ **1.** The author believes that everyone will agree with his choice of Muhammad as the most influential person in history.

___F___ **2.** The author chose Muhammad solely because of Muhammad's success as a religious leader.

___F___ **3.** Muhammad was born and raised in what was then called Arabia, a highly cultured and pivotal nation.

___T___ **4.** According to the author, Muhammad learned about a single, all-powerful God from the small number of Christians and Jews living in Mecca.

Multiple-Choice

___D___ **5.** Muhammad began preaching that Allah was the one true God when Muhammad was
  a. still in his teens.
  b. 26 years old.
  c. 30 years old.
  d. 40 years old.

___B___ **6.** The *Hegira* was Muhammad's flight
  a. from Arabia.
  b. from Medina to Mecca.
  c. from Mecca to Medina.
  d. to southern Arabia.

___A___ **7.** Since there are roughly twice as many Christians as Muslims, why does the author rank Muhammad higher than Jesus, the founder of Christianity?
  a. The author feels that Muhammad played a larger role in the development of Islam than Jesus did in the development of Christianity.
  b. The author is a Muslim.
  c. More books have been written about Muhammad than about Jesus.
  d. Muhammad, who died at age 62, lived longer than Jesus did.

_____C_____   **8.** The Koran is

    a. the Bible translated into Arabic.

    b. another name for the Hegira.

    c. the Muslim holy scriptures.

    d. Muhammad's family name.

_____C_____   **9.** Of the statements below about Muhammad's life, which one is *not* true?

    a. He was orphaned at age 6.

    b. He preached to close friends for 3 years and then began preaching in public.

    c. He never married.

    d. He was a driving force behind Arab conquests.

_____D_____   **10.** The author maintains that Muhammad should top the list of the world's most influential persons because

    a. Muhammad was responsible for the theology of Islam and its main principles.

    b. In Mecca, he became a virtual dictator.

    c. Muhammad was a great military leader.

    d. Muhammad was an influential religious leader and secular leader.

SELECTION **4-3**

History

Extend Your Vocabulary by Using Context Clues

Directions: Context clues are words in a sentence that allow the reader to deduce (reason out) the meaning of an unfamiliar word in that sentence. For each vocabulary item below, a sentence from the selection containing an important word (*italicized, like this*) is quoted first. Next, there is an additional sentence using the word in the same sense and providing another context clue. Use the context clues from *both* sentences to deduce the meaning of the italicized word. *Be sure the answer you choose makes sense in both sentences.* If you discover that you must use a dictionary to confirm an answer choice, remember that the meaning you select must still fit the context of both sentences. To indicate your answer, write the letter in the space provided.

Pronunciation key: ă pat   ā pay   âr care   ä father   ĕ pet   ē be   ĭ pit
ī tie   îr pier   ŏ pot   ō toe   ô paw   oi noise   ou out   ŏŏ took
ōō boot   ŭ cut   yōō abuse   ûr urge   th thin   *th* this   hw which
zh vision   ə about
Stress mark: ´

_____ **1.** Of humble origins, Muhammad founded and *promulgated* one of the world's great religions, and became an immensely effective political leader.

In the State of the Union speech, the President *promulgated* the new administration's policy on gun control.

promulgated (prŏm′ əl gāt əd) means:
- *a.* reversed or changed
- *b.* made known or put into effect by public declaration
- *c.* refused to reveal
- *d.* denounced as untrue

_____ **2.** Today, thirteen centuries after his death, his influence is still powerful and *pervasive.*

The drug problem in the United States is difficult to deal with because it is so *pervasive.*

pervasive (pər vā′sĭv) means:
- *a.* important
- *b.* widespread
- *c.* decreasing or diminishing
- *d.* popular

_____ **3.** The majority of the persons in this book had the advantage of being born and raised in centers of civilization, highly cultured or politically *pivotal* nations.

Supreme Court Justice O'Connor's opinion was the *pivotal* one that reversed the lower court's decision.

pivotal (pĭv′ ə təl) means:
- *a.* causing rotation or spinning
- *b.* pertaining to religion or theology
- *c.* determining a direction or effect; crucial
- *d.* going in two different directions

_____ **4.** Orphaned at age six, he was reared in *modest* surroundings.

Even after the Smiths won the lottery, they continued to live in a *modest* apartment and take the subway to work.

modest (mŏd′ ĭst) means:
- *a.* plain rather than showy
- *b.* shy or reserved
- *c.* luxurious
- *d.* rural; pertaining to the country

_C_   **5.** *Islamic* tradition tells us that Muhammad was illiterate.

Mosques are *Islamic* houses of worship.

Islamic (ĭs läm′ ĭc) means:
a. pertaining to the Christian religion based on the teachings of Jesus
b. pertaining to the Buddhist religion based on the teachings of Buddha
c. pertaining to the Muslim religion based on the teachings of Muhammad
d. pertaining to the Confucian religion based on the teaching of Confucius

_D_   **6.** Furthermore, Muhammad (unlike Jesus) was a *secular* as well as a religious leader.

While some people view abortion as a religious issue, others view it as a purely *secular* issue.

secular (sek′ yə lər) means:
a. private
b. pertaining to worship
c. spiritual
d. not related to religion

_A_   **7.** There were, however, in Mecca, a small number of Jews and Christians; it was from them no doubt that Muhammad first learned of a single, *omnipotent* God who ruled the entire universe.

Hitler's goal was to conquer all of Europe and Russia; he was a madman who thought he could be *omnipotent.*

omnipotent (ŏm nĭp′ ə tənt) means:
a. having unlimited power or authority
b. having limited power or authority
c. having authority given by the citizens of a country
d. having no power or authority

_B_   **8.** As he slowly gained *converts,* the Meccan authorities came to consider him a dangerous nuisance."

The new political party in India rapidly gained *converts.*

converts (kŏn′ vûrts) means:
a. people who revert to previously held beliefs
b. people who adopt a new religion or belief
c. people who cling to long-held beliefs
d. people who have no religious beliefs

9. Although Jesus was responsible for the main ethical precepts of Christianity, St. Paul was the main developer of Christian *theology,* its principal proselytizer, and the author of a large portion of the New Testament.

Although my uncle decided not to become a minister and left the seminary, he continued to read ancient and modern Christian *theology* throughout his life.

theology (thē ŏl′ ə jē) means:

a. system or school of opinions about God and religious questions

b. study of beliefs throughout the world

c. study of ancient religious rituals

d. study of the lives of saints

10. In addition, Muhammad played the key role in *proselytizing* the new faith, and in establishing the religious practices of Islam.

The evangelists went door to door *proselytizing,* telling anyone who was willing to listen about their religious beliefs.

proselytizing (prŏs′ ə lə tīz ĭng) means:

a. speaking loudly or shouting

b. deceiving with trickery

c. declaring false or untrue

d. attempting to convert people from one belief or faith to another

SELECTION **4-3**

History

Collaboration Option

Respond in Writing

Directions: Refer to the selection as needed to answer the essay-type questions.

Option for collaboration: Your instructor may direct you to work with other students or, in other words, to work *collaboratively.* In that case, you should form groups of three or four students as directed by your instructor and work together to complete the exercises. After your group discusses each item and agrees on the answer, have a group member record it. Every member of your group should be able to explain all of your group's answers.

1. List three reasons the author chose Muhammad as the most influential person in history.

Reason 1:

_____

_____

_____

Reason 2:

_____

_____

Reason 3:

_____

_____

_____

2. Michael Hart, the author of *The 100: A Ranking of the Most Influential Persons in History,* selected 99 other important people for his book. List 5 names *you* would include in a list of the world's most influential people, and state your reasons for including them. Remember, these must be people who have influenced the *world,* not just you. They must be actual *people* who have lived or are currently living. They should be people who have had the *most* influence, regardless of whether their influence on the world was positive or negative. (Choose people who are *not* in Hart's top 10.)

Person 1: _____

Reason: _____

Person 2: _____

Reason: _____

Person 3: _____

Reason: _____

Person 4: _____

Reason: _____

Person 5: _____

Reason: _____

3. Overall main idea. What is the overall main idea the author wants the reader to understand about Muhammad? Answer this question in one sentence. Be sure that your overall main idea sentence includes the topic (*Muhammad*) and tells the overall most important point about it.

_____

_____

Read More about It on the World Wide Web

To learn more about the topic of this selection, visit these websites or use your favorite search engine (such as Yahoo®). Whenever you go to *any* website, it is a good idea to evaluate it critically. Are you getting good information—information that is accurate, complete, and up-to-date? Who sponsors the website? How easy is it to use the features of the website?

http://www.britannica.com/bcom/eb/article/0/0,5716,108142+1+105853,00 .html

This is the Encyclopaedia Britannica *website. There is a direct Web address for detailed biographical information on Muhammad.*

http://www.usc.edu/dept/MSA/fundamentals/prophet

This website contains links to biographical information about Muhammad, examples of his teachings and sayings, his last sermon, and quotations from others about him. Try clicking on What He Was Like.

http://biography.com

Type in Muhammad *in the search box, then click on* Muhammad see: Mohammed, *and read a short biography of the founder of Islam.*

http://www.unn.ac.uk/societies/islamic

The goal of this site is to provide accurate information about Islamic beliefs and Islamic history and civilization for Muslims and non-Muslims.

© PhotoDisc

C H A P T E R **5**

Formulating Implied Main Ideas

CHAPTER OBJECTIVES

In this chapter you will learn the answers to these questions:

- What is an implied main idea of a paragraph?

- Why is formulating implied main ideas important?

- How can I formulate implied main idea sentences?

- How can I know when a formulated main idea sentence is correct?

SKILLS

CREATING YOUR SUMMARY

READINGS

If you want to climb mountains, do not practice on molehills.

If you want to be a better writer, become a better reader.

IMPLIED MAIN IDEAS IN PARAGRAPHS

What Is an Implied Main Idea?

Every paragraph has a main idea, of course, but not every paragraph includes a *stated* main idea sentence. When an author gives you the information needed to understand the main point without stating it directly as a single sentence, the main idea is *implied.* When an author implies the main idea, *you,* the reader, must use information in the paragraph to *infer* (reason out) the main idea and *formulate* (create) a sentence that expresses it. In other words, the **implied main idea** is a sentence formulated by the reader that expresses the author's main point about the topic.

Sometimes you must infer that essential information needs to be added to an existing sentence to formulate the complete main idea. At other times, you must infer that information from two or more sentences in the paragraph has to be *combined* to formulate one complete main idea sentence. At still other times, you will have to formulate a *general* sentence that expresses the most important (but unstated) point the author is trying to illustrate or prove. That is, if a paragraph presents facts, descriptions, explanations, or examples that only *suggest* the main point the author wants you to understand, it is up to you to infer and formulate the main idea. When you grasp the main idea in these ways, you are *inferring* it.

KEY TERM
Implied Main Idea

A sentence formulated by the reader that expresses the author's main point about the topic.

An implied main idea is also known as an *unstated main idea,* an *indirectly stated main idea,* and a *formulated main idea.*

Why Is Formulating Implied Main Ideas Important?

Your comprehension will be limited unless you understand main ideas, regardless of whether they are stated or implied. Just as you must be able to identify the main idea when it is stated, you must be able to formulate it when the author implies it. Of course, this will increase your comprehension, but you will also remember material better if you take the time to formulate main ideas whenever they are implied. College instructors assume that students read carefully enough to understand paragraphs with implied main ideas. Instructors base test items on implied main ideas, just as they base items on more obvious stated main ideas.

To be an effective reader, then, you must be able to identify stated main ideas and be able to formulate main idea sentences for any paragraphs in which the main idea is implied.

When the author does not state the main idea, the reader must *formulate* the author's main idea by "piecing together" important information.
(Stone/Stuart McClymont)

FORMULATING AN IMPLIED MAIN IDEA

Steps to Follow

Of course, you will not know until you read a paragraph whether its main idea is stated or implied. Whenever you cannot locate a stated main idea sentence, formulate the implied main idea by following these steps:

Comprehension Monitoring Question for Implied Main Idea

"What is the single most important point the author wants me to *infer* about the topic of this paragraph?"

- **Step 1.**   First, after you have read the paragraph, *determine the topic* by asking yourself, "Who or what is this passage about?"
- **Step 2.**   Next, *determine the main idea* by asking yourself, "What is the single most important point the author wants me to *infer* about this topic of this paragraph?"
- **Step 3.**   Then, use information in the paragraph to *formulate a main idea sentence* that answers the question in step 2. The sentence you formulate will be the main idea.

Three Methods for Using Information in a Paragraph to Formulate the Main Idea

Even when authors do not directly state a main idea as one sentence, they still provide you with all information you need to infer and formulate the main idea yourself. Authors may provide such information in three ways, and those three ways are the basis for three "formulas" for creating main idea sentences. The three formulas and examples of their application are presented below.

As always, you must begin by reading the paragraph and determining its topic. Next, ask yourself the comprehension monitoring question, "What is the single most important point the author wants me to infer about the topic of this paragraph?" Then use one of the three formulas explained below to help you create the formulated main idea sentence. How can you determine which formula to use? The particular formula you will need to use will depend of the type of information presented in the paragraph.

Formula 1: Add an Essential Word or Phrase to a Sentence Already in the Paragraph

Sometimes, an author may express most of the main idea in one sentence of the paragraph, yet that sentence lacks some essential piece of information—a piece of information that you must insert to make the sentence a *complete* main idea sentence. To put it another way, a paragraph may contain a sentence that *almost* states the author's main idea, but you must add certain information to that sentence to make it express the main idea completely. For instance, a sentence may need to have the topic inserted to make it express the complete main idea.

When a sentence in the paragraph almost states the main idea but lacks essential information, use **formula 1** to create a main idea sentence:

Sentence that *almost* states the main idea	+	Essential word or phrase that needs to be added	=	Formulated main idea sentence

Here is an example of how an implied main idea sentence can be formulated using formula 1. The following paragraph is from a sociology textbook. The topic of this passage is *ethnocentrism*. The last sentence almost states the authors' most important point—the definition of ethnocentrism—but it lacks the topic, the word *ethnocentrism*. A complete main idea sentence can be formulated by adding *ethnocentrism* (the topic) to the last sentence of the paragraph. This formulated main idea sentence will express the most important point the authors want you to understand about ethnocentrism, its definition.

Each person is born into a particular society that has its own particular culture. At an early age, children begin to learn many aspects of this culture, such as language, standards of behavior, and beliefs. They also begin to learn many of the group's values concerning judgments of good and bad, proper and improper, and right and wrong. This learning continues into and throughout adulthood as people internalize, accept, and identify with their group's way of living. This feeling is called **ethnocentrism.** It is the basic inclination to judge other cultures in terms of the values and norms of one's own culture.

Formulated Main Idea Sentence

_____

_____

_____

_____

_____

_____

Source: Daniel Hebding and Leonard Glick, *Introduction to Sociology,* McGraw-Hill, New York, 1992, p. 62.

Stop and Annotate

Go back to the textbook
excerpt above. Write the
formulated main idea
sentence in the space
provided by adding essential
information to the sentence
that almost states the main
idea.

The last sentence becomes a complete main idea sentence when the essential word *ethnocentrism* is added: *Ethnocentrism is the basic inclination to judge other cultures in terms of the values and norms of one's own culture.*

Formula 2: Combine Two Sentences from the Paragraph into a Single Sentence

You know that the main idea must always be written as a single sentence. Sometimes, however, an author puts *parts* of the main idea in two different sentences. He or she assumes that the reader will understand that they each contain part of the important information and that the sentences, *together,* convey the main point. Therefore, whenever an author does not state the main idea in a single sentence, *you* must combine these two sentences to formulate one sentence that expresses the complete main idea. This is because both sentences contain important information, yet neither sentence by itself expresses the complete main idea. The two sentences may follow one another, or they may be separated. (For example, the first sentence of the paragraph may present part of the main idea, and the last sentence may give the rest of the main idea.)

When you realize that two sentences in a paragraph each give part of the main idea, use **formula 2** to combine then into a single sentence that is the complete main idea:

Sentence that expresses *part* of the main idea	+	Sentence that expresses *rest* of the main idea	=	Formulated main idea sentence

Here is an example of formula 2. The paragraph below is from a textbook on sociology. Its topic is *tastes.* A main idea sentence for this paragraph can be formulated by combining its last two sentences into a single sentence. This formulated main idea sentence will express the most important point the authors want you to understand about tastes.

Tastes—we all have them. You prefer certain styles of art, certain kinds of food and clothing, certain types of music, certain ways of decorating your room. The list could go on and on. *De gustibus non est disputandum,* the old Latin saying goes—there is no accounting for taste. Tastes just seem to spring from somewhere inside us, rather mysteriously. We can't really say why we prefer rock to Mozart, burgers to pâté, jeans to neatly pressed slacks. Tastes are simply part of us, our individual selves. But tastes are also part of culture, which is a broader social phenomenon.

Formulated Main Idea Sentence

_____

_____

_____

_____

_____

Source: Craig Calhoun, Donald Light, and Susanne Keller, *Sociology,* 6th ed., McGraw-Hill, New York, 1994, p. 68.

Stop and Annotate

Go back to the textbook excerpt above. Write the formulated main idea sentence in the space provided by combining the two sentences in the paragraph that together express the main idea completely.

The two important sentences in the paragraph are the last two: "Tastes are simply part of us, our individual selves" and "But tastes are also part of culture, which is a broader social phenomenon." Neither sentence by itself expresses the complete main idea. The first sentence addresses taste on a personal level; the other sentence addresses it as part of culture. You must combine the sentences to formulate a complete main idea sentence: *Tastes are simply part of us, our individual selves, but tastes are also part of culture, which is a broader social phenomenon.* (Of course, it would be equally correct to express this same main idea in other ways, such as, *Although tastes are simply part of us, our individual selves, tastes are also part of culture, which is a broader social phenomenon.*)

Formula 3: Summarize Important Ideas in One Sentence or Write One Sentence that Gives a General Inference Based on the Details

With some paragraphs that have implied main ideas, you will either have to formulate a main idea sentence that *summarizes* the important information in the paragraph *or* formulate a sentence that gives a *general inference* based on the details. Which of these you do will depend upon the type of information you are given in the paragraph. When you create this kind of formulated main idea sentence, you will often have to use some of your own words along with certain important words from the paragraph.

Sometimes a paragraph consists only of details. When this is the case, you must formulate a main idea sentence by inferring the *general* point the author is illustrating or proving with the details, and then express this idea as a single sentence. This is not a matter of rewriting the details as one long sentence, but rather of writing a sentence that *sums up* the details the author presents. In other words, you have to create a general sentence that *summarizes* the details. When you write this formulated main idea sentence, you will usually have to use some of your own words.

When a paragraph has important ideas included in several sentences or the paragraph consists only of details, **formula 3** should be used to formulate a main idea sentence.

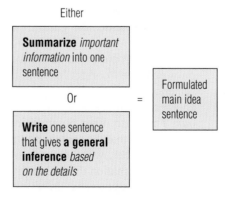

Here is an example of formulating an implied main idea using formula 3. The following excerpt is from a special section in an algebra textbook that introduces interesting information to be used in solving verbal problems. The topic of this paragraph is *pesticides*. The paragraph has an implied main idea that can be formulated from information given throughout the paragraph. As you read the paragraph, try to reason out (infer) the most important general point the authors are making about pesticides.

	Formulated Main Idea Sentence
Pesticides kill plants and animals other than the pests they are intended for. Pesticides pollute water systems. Some pests develop immunity to frequently used pesticides. Some pesticides such as DDT and its relatives can remain in the environment for many years beyond the time necessary to do their intended job. Some pesticides have been linked to cancer and other health problems in humans.	_____ _____ _____ _____ _____ _____

Source: James Streeter, Donald Hutchison, and Louis Hoelzle, *Beginning Algebra,* 3d ed., McGraw-Hill, New York, 1993, p. 370.

In this paragraph, you must write a general statement that is based on the important information in *several* sentences to formulate a main idea sentence. You need to examine the information, think about it, and ask yourself, "What is the most important general point the authors want me to understand about pesticides?" To answer that question, you will need to use some of your own words.

Although the phrase *dangerous effects* does not appear in this paragraph, it is obviously describing dangerous effects of pesticides. It is up to the reader to infer (reason out or deduce) the main idea and use a general phrase such as *dangerous effects*. An example of a correctly formulated main idea sentence for the paragraph would be: *Pesticides can have dangerous, unintended effects on the environment, plants, animals, and human beings.* This formulated main idea sentence expresses the general point the authors want you to understand about pesticides.

The example given above for the formulated main idea sentence is not the only possible "correct" formulation. Another possible formulated main idea sentence would be: *Pesticides have several unintended, dangerous effects.* Still another possibility is: *Certain unintended side effects of pesticides are dangerous.* There are other possibilities as well. What is important is not the exact wording but that the sentence express the authors' main point.

Remember, when formulating implied main ideas, you must look at the type of information the author gives in the paragraph. The following chart summarizes what you must do to formulate the implied main idea once you determine what the author has given you to work with in the paragraph.

Stop and Annotate

Go back to the textbook excerpt above. Formulate a general main idea sentence that summarizes the important information from several sentences into a single sentence and write it in the space provided.

THREE WAYS TO FORMULATE IMPLIED MAIN IDEA SENTENCES

What the Author Gives You to Start with in the Paragraph	What You Must Do with the Information in Order to Formulate the Implied Main Idea
A sentence that *almost* states the main idea, but lacks some essential piece of information (usually the topic)	*Use Formula 1.* *Add* the essential piece of information that is missing to that sentence. *How to apply the formula:* You can use the sentence from the paragraph and simply add or insert the information. *or* You can write the main idea in your own words as long as the meaning is the same.
Two sentences in the paragraph that each present *part* of the main idea	*Use Formula 2.* *Combine* them into one sentence (since the main idea must always be written as a single sentence). *How to apply the formula:* You will probably have to add a word or two in order to connect the two sentences (usually words such as *and, but, although,* etc.). *or* You can write the main idea in your own words, as long as the meaning is the same.
Details only	*Use Formula 3.* Write a *general sentence* that "sums up" the details or expresses the overall point the author is making. *How to apply the formula:* The sentence you write will consist mostly of your own words.

Requirements for Correctly Formulated Main Idea Sentences

When you formulate an implied main idea sentence (in other words, when you use one of the formulas above), there is a way to check to be sure that your formulated main idea sentence is correct. A *correctly* formulated implied main idea sentence is one that meets the requirements for *any* main idea (stated *or* implied).

- *A formulated main idea must be a complete sentence that includes the topic of the paragraph.*
- *A formulated main idea must express the author's most important general point about the topic.* In other words, if the formulated main idea sentence is placed at the beginning of the paragraph, the details will explain, prove, or tell more about it.
- *A formulated main idea must make complete sense by itself (without having to read the rest of the paragraph).* As you learned in Chapter 4, a main idea sentence must be meaningful by itself (even if the reader could not see the rest of the paragraph).

Remember that an implied main idea sentence can be expressed in various ways, as long as the sentence meets the three requirements. Keep in mind, however, that the formulated main idea sentence you write should simply tell the author's most important point. There are many extraneous, or extra, words that you should *not* include in your formulated main idea sentence. For example, if the author's main idea is *Pesticides have several unintended dangerous effects,* you should write only that. You should *not* write a formulated main idea sentence with extraneous words such as the italicized ones shown here:

The author's main idea is that pesticides have several unintended dangerous effects.

The author says that pesticides have several unintended dangerous effects.

What the author wants us to understand is pesticides have several unintended dangerous effects.

The author is trying to say is that pesticides have several unintended dangerous effects.

What the author means is that pesticides have several unintended dangerous effects.

It is enough merely to write the most important point the author wants readers to understand.

Implied Overall Main Ideas in Longer Passages

Of course, the ability to formulate implied main ideas is a skill that can be applied not only to paragraphs but also to longer passages, such as a section of a textbook chapter, a short reading selection, or an essay. In fact, you will often want to formulate the main idea of an entire passage in order to express its most important point, its overall message. Throughout this book, each chapter reading selection includes a Respond in Writing exercise that will give you practice in formulating a main idea sentence for the entire selection.

A WORD ABOUT STANDARDIZED READING TESTS: IMPLIED MAIN IDEAS

Many college students are required to take standardized reading tests as part of an overall assessment program, in a reading course, or as part of a state-mandated "basic skills" test. A standardized reading test typically consists of a series of passages followed by multiple-choice questions, to be completed within a specified time limit. Here are some tips about formulating implied main ideas that should help you score as high as possible on standardized tests.

Remember that test items about implied main ideas may be worded in several different ways. Possible wordings of the question stems include:

The author's main point is that . . .

The principal idea of this passage is that . . .

Which of the following best expresses the main idea of the entire passage?

Which of the following best expressed the main idea of this paragraph? (or a specifically identified paragraph)

To answer test items such as these, first determine the subject matter of the passage: the topic. Then ask yourself, "What is the most important idea the author wants me to understand about the topic?" If you cannot find a single sentence in the passage that answers this question, write your own formulation of the main idea on scratch paper or in the margin next to the passage. Next, examine the choices offered as answers, comparing each choice with your own formulation. Look for a choice that is similar *in meaning* to your own answer, but remember that the wording may be different. If none of the choices is at least partially similar to your formulation, you may need to reread the passage and make another attempt at formulating the main idea.

DEVELOPING CHAPTER REVIEW CARDS

Review cards, or *summary cards,* are an excellent study tool. They are a way to select, organize, and review the most important information in a textbook chapter. The process of creating review cards helps you organize information in a meaningful way and, at the same time, transfer it into long-term memory. The cards can also be used to prepare for tests (see Part Three). The review card activities in this book give you structured practice in creating these valuable study tools. Once you have learned how to make review cards, you can create them for textbook material in your other courses.

Now, complete the five review cards for Chapter 5 by answering the questions or following the directions on each card. When you have completed them, you will have summarized important information about implied main ideas: (1) what they are and why they are important, (2) what steps and (3) what formulas to follow in formulating them, (4) how to check to see if your formulations are correct, and (5) how to formulate main ideas in longer passages.

Implied Main Ideas

1. What is an implied main idea? (See page 247.)

_____

2. Why is formulating implied main ideas important? (See page 247.)

_____

_____

Card 1   **Chapter 5: Formulating Implied Main Ideas**

Steps to Follow in Formulating an Implied Main Idea Sentence

What are three general steps to follow in formulating an implied main idea sentence? (See page 248.)

Step 1: _____

_____

_____

Step 2: _____

_____

_____

Step 3: _____

_____

_____

Card 2   **Chapter 5: Formulating Implied Main Ideas**

Formulas for Creating Implied Main Idea Sentences

What are three formulas for creating implied main idea sentences? (See pages 249–251.)

Formula 1: _____

Formula 2: _____

Formula 3: _____

_____

Card 3   **Chapter 5: Formulating Implied Main Ideas**

Requirements for Correctly Formulated Main Idea Sentences

What are three requirements for a correctly formulated main idea sentence? (See page 253–254.)

Requirement 1: _____

_____

Requirement 2: _____

_____

Requirement 3: _____

_____

Card 4   **Chapter 5: Formulating Implied Main Ideas**

Implied Overall Main Ideas in Longer Passages

1. The skill of formulating implied main ideas can be applied to longer reading assignments, such as: (See page 253–254.)

_____

2. A purpose of formulating the main idea of an entire passage is to do the following: (See page 254.)

_____

Card 5   **Chapter 5: Formulating Implied Main Ideas**

SELECTION 5-1

Magazine Article

LAUGH YOUR STRESS AWAY

By Stephen Lally

Prepare Yourself to Read

Directions: Do these exercises *before* you read Selection 5-1.

1. First, read and think about the title. What are your greatest sources of stress as a college student? What strategies do you currently use to cope with stress?

   _____

   _____

   _____

   _____

2. Next, complete your preview by reading the following:

   > Introduction (in *italics*)
   > First paragraph (paragraph 1)
   > Headings
   > First sentence of each paragraph

   On the basis of your preview, what advice is the author going to give about handling stress?

   _____

   _____

Apply Comprehension Skills

Directions: Do the Annotation Practice Exercises as you read Selection 5-1. Apply the skills from this chapter:

Formulate implied main ideas. Follow these general steps: first determine the topic; then ask what the author's most important point about the topic is; then create a sentence that expresses the author's most important point. Use the appropriate formula to "formulate" an implied main idea sentence based on information in the paragraph.

Check your formulated main idea sentences. Be sure each of your main idea sentences meets the requirements on page 254.

In these exercises, you will work only with paragraphs that have implied main ideas.

261

LAUGH YOUR STRESS AWAY

Headaches. Backaches. Skin rashes. Indigestion. Fatigue. High blood pressure. Lowered resistance to infection. What do all these ailments have in common? All can be caused by chronic stress.

Stress is a response to events that threaten or challenge us. Each of us must deal with stress in our lives. In one study, at least 80 percent of the respondents identified the top three sources of stress as "not enough time," "too many things to do," and "troubling thoughts about the future." Every college student can certainly identify with those stressors.

How can you cope with stress? There are many ways, of course—exercise, relaxation techniques, meditation, and yoga, to name just a few—but the author of this selection offers a novel approach. In some situations, perhaps laughter is really the best medicine.

1   Humor is one of the best on-the-spot stress busters around. It's virtually impossible to belly-laugh and feel bad at the same time. If you're caught in a situation you can't escape or change (a traffic jam, for example), then humor may be the healthiest form of temporary stress release possible.

2   Even when you *can* change the situation, humor helps. Research by Alice M. Isen, Ph.D., a psychologist at Cornell University, in Ithaca, New York, shows that people who had just watched a short comedy film were better able to find creative solutions to puzzling problems than people who had either just watched a film about math or had just exercised. In other studies, Dr. Isen found that shortly after watching or experiencing comedy, people were able to think more clearly and were better able to "see" the consequences of a given decision.

3   The physiological effects of a good laugh work against stress. After a slight rise in heart rate and blood pressure during the laugh itself, there's an immediate recoil: Muscles relax and blood pressure sinks below prelaugh levels, and the brain may release endorphins, the same stress reducers that are triggered by exercise. A hearty ha-ha-ha also provides a muscle massage for facial muscles, the diaphragm, and the abdomen. Studies show that it even temporarily boosts levels of immunoglobulin A, a virus-fighter found in saliva.

4   While our cave-dwelling ancestors were stressed by actual life-threatening situations like bumping into a woolly mammoth, times have

Annotation Practice Exercises

Directions: For each exercise below,

- Write the topic of the paragraph on the lines provided.

- Formulate the implied main idea of the paragraph and write it on the lines provided.

This will help you remember the topic and the main idea.

changed. "Nowadays, stress is usually not caused by the situation itself, but by how we perceive that situation," says Allen Elkin, Ph.D., program director of Manhattan's Stress Management and Counseling Centers. Getting a new perspective is what comedy is all about. Several philosophers and writers have pointed out that comedy and tragedy are different ways of looking at the same stressful event.

5 Comedy works by stepping back from a situation and playing up its absurdities. The same kind of disinterested observation makes the tale of your disastrous vacation seem funny—after you get safely home. For stress busting, the trick is to find ways to laugh at the situation *while it's happening*. Even if you don't consider yourself much of a comedian, here are a few simple techniques you can use:

The Bart Simpson Maneuver

6 How would your favorite cartoon character or comedian react to the situation? "Imagining what would happen can give you a chuckle, making the situation less annoying. You can even pretend *you're* the star of a TV comedy, and this frustrating episode is tonight's plot," says Steve Allen Jr., M.D., an assistant professor of family medicine at SUNY Health Science Center, Syracuse (yes, he's the son of well-known comedian Steve Allen).

Ballooning

7 In your mind, consciously exaggerate the situation: Blow it completely out of proportion and into absurdity—into a comedy routine. In that long, long checkout line, don't say "This waiting is killing me; I hate this." Say: "I'll *never* get to the front of this line. The woman ahead of me is covered in cobwebs. The guy in front of her grew a beard standing in line. The cashier must be part snail. The continental drift moves faster." This maneuver helps take the edge off the situation, redirects your tension, and helps you see things as not so impossible after all. Your running commentary, however, is probably best kept to yourself. If people stare at you because you seem to

Cartoon character Bart Simpson, for whom the "Bart Simpson maneuver" (paragraph 6) is named.
(© 20th Century Fox)

Annotation Exercise

- Topic of paragraph 6:

_____

_____

- Formulate the implied main idea of paragraph 6:

_____

_____

_____

be laughing for no reason, pretend you're reading the scandal sheets. You don't have to be a master of one-liners to be funny. There are gentler forms of humor that can defuse anxiety in a group without making anyone feel like the butt of a joke.

Pick a Safe Subject

8   Making fun of your own foibles can save face in an embarrassing situation—you'll have people laughing *with* you, rather than *at* you. Inanimate sources of frustration, like computers and copying machines, are also safe objects of humor.

Lay It on the Line

9   Sometimes just telling the truth or pointing out the obvious can get a laugh. People are accustomed to exaggeration and truth bending (too many TV commercials, perhaps), so plain speaking can come as a refreshing shock. For example, after delivering a series of lengthy explanations during a question-and-answer period, some people have been known to put everyone in stitches by simply replying to the next question with "Gee, I don't know." This kind of humor is a way of fighting stress by accepting our shortcomings," says Joel Goodman, Ed.D., director of the HUMOR Project in Saratoga Springs, New York.

Clip a Cartoon

10   Keep a file of jokes and cartoons that make *you* laugh. Paste a few up where you're likely to need them—at work, on the refrigerator, wherever.

Source: Stephen Lally, "Laugh Your Stress Away," *Prevention,* June 1991, from pp. 50–53. Reprinted by permission of *Prevention* magazine.

Annotation Exercise

- Topic of paragraph 7:

_____

_____

- Formulate the implied main idea of paragraph 7:

_____

_____

_____

Annotation Exercise

- Topic of paragraph 9:

_____

_____

- Formulate the implied main idea of paragraph 9:

_____

_____

_____

_____

_____

Comprehension Quiz

Directions: For each comprehension question below, use information from the selection to determine the correct answer. You may refer to the selection as you answer the questions. Write your answer in the space provided.

True or False

_____ **1.** The author believes that humor may be the healthiest way to relieve stress.

_____ **2.** During a good laugh, there is a slight rise in heart rate and blood pressure.

_____ **3.** After a good laugh, blood pressure rises steadily.

_____ **4.** Our cave-dwelling ancestors were stressed by life-threatening situations.

_____ **5.** The trick to stress-busting is find ways to laugh at the situation after it has happened.

_____ **6.** Getting a new perspective is what comedy is all about.

Multiple-Choice

_____ **7.** Alice Isen, Ph.D., concluded that after watching or experiencing comedy, people
 a. felt better temporarily but then became depressed again.
 b. were able to think more clearly and see the consequences of a given decision.
 c. reported no difference.
 d. gradually became more relaxed and cheerful.

_____ **8.** The physiological effects of a good laugh include
 a. relaxation of the muscles.
 b. lowering of blood pressure.
 c. release of endorphins.
 d. all of the above.

_____ **9.** The Bart Simpson maneuver for reducing stress is to imagine
 a. yourself removed from the stressful situation.
 b. yourself as Bart Simpson.
 c. how your favorite cartoon character or comedian would react.
 d. none of the above.

_____ **10.** Ballooning, a technique to reduce stress, consists of

   a. seeing yourself attached to a balloon that is floating away from the stressful situation.

   b. consciously exaggerating the situation by blowing it out of proportion into absurdity.

   c. releasing your tension by inhaling and exhaling deeply.

   d. visualizing your stress as a balloon that explodes and disappears.

SELECTION **5-1**

Magazine Article

Extend Your Vocabulary by Using Context Clues

Directions: Context clues are words in a sentence that allow the reader to deduce (reason out) the meaning of an unfamiliar word in that sentence. For each vocabulary item below, a sentence from the selection containing an important word *(italicized, like this)* is quoted first. Next, there is an additional sentence using the word in the same sense and providing another context clue. Use the context clues from *both* sentences to deduce the meaning of the italicized word. *Be sure the answer you choose makes sense in both sentences.* If you discover that you must use a dictionary to confirm an answer choice, remember that the meaning you select must still fit the context of both sentences. To indicate your answer, write the letter in the space provided.

Pronunciation key: ă pat   ā pay   âr care   ä father   ĕ pet   ē be   ĭ pit
ī tie   îr pier   ŏ pot   ō toe   ô paw   oi noise   ou out   o͝o took   o͞o boot
ŭ cut   yo͞o abuse   ûr urge   th thin   *th* this   hw which   zh vision
ə about
Stress mark: ʹ

_____ **1.** The *physiological* effects of a good laugh work against stress.

   Because exercise has both *physiological* and psychological benefits, you feel better physically and mentally after a workout.

   physiological (fĭz ē ə lŏjʹ ə kəl) means:
   a. pertaining to the emotions
   b. pertaining to the body
   c. pertaining to nutrition
   d. pertaining to the lifespan of an organism

_____ **2.** After a slight rise in heart rate and blood pressure during the laugh itself, there's an immediate *recoil*.

   After he fired the powerful shotgun, the *recoil* knocked him backward.

recoil (rē′ koil) means:

a.   clicking sound

b.   winding something in loops

c.   increase

d.   drop or movement backward

_____   **3.**   Muscles relax and blood pressure sinks below prelaugh levels, and the brain may release *endorphins,* the same stress reducers that are triggered by exercise.

A pleasant effect of exercising, eating chocolate, and being in love is that each releases *endorphins* in the body.

endorphins (ĕn dôr′ fĭnz) means:

a.   hormones in the brain that cause hunger

b.   chemicals in the brain that cause drowsiness and confusion

c.   hormones in the body that cause feelings of sadness and depression

d.   chemicals in the brain that reduce pain and produce a sense of well-being

_____   **4.**   Muscles relax and blood pressure sinks below prelaugh levels, and the brain may release endorphins, the same stress reducers that are *triggered* by exercise.

The rioting in the city was *triggered* by the judge's unfair ruling.

triggered (trĭg′ ərd) means:

a.   activated; initiated

b.   pulled a trigger

c.   prevented

d.   decreased; diminished

_____   **5.**   While our cave-dwelling ancestors were stressed by actual life-threatening situations like bumping into a woolly *mammoth,* times have changed.

Scientists do not know for sure why the *mammoth* disappeared millions of years ago.

mammoth (măm′ əth) means:

a.   type of large moth

b.   animal that looks similar to a human being

c.   extinct type of elephant once found throughout the northern hemisphere

d.   rare bird

_____   **6.**   The same kind of *disinterested* observation makes the tale of your disastrous vacation seem funny—after you get safely home.

To be effective, referees and umpires must be *disinterested* regarding who wins the games they officiate.

disinterested (dĭs ĭn′ trĭ stĭd) means:

   a.   deeply interested

   b.   overly concerned

   c.   knowledgeable

   d.   impartial or free from bias

—————   **7.** The *continental* drift moves faster.

During World War II, *continental* warfare enveloped nearly all of Europe.

continental (kŏn tə nĕn′ tl) means:

   a.   pertaining to a continent or principal landmass of the earth

   b.   pertaining to water or the ocean

   c.   related to travel

   d.   pertaining to technology

—————   **8.** This *maneuver* helps take the edge off the situation, redirects your tension, and helps you see things as not so impossible after all.

I tried to talk the police officer out of giving me a speeding ticket by being friendly and polite, but the *maneuver* failed.

maneuver (mə nü′ vər) means:

   a.   joke

   b.   strategy

   c.   excuse

   d.   mistaken idea

—————   **9.** Making fun of your own *foibles* can save face in an embarrassing situation—you'll have people laughing with you, rather than at you.

He was a practical joker and a nonstop talker, but he was so talented that we overlooked these *foibles*.

foibles (foi′ bəlz) means:

   a.   admirable qualities in one's character

   b.   unforgivable mistakes

   c.   minor weaknesses of character

   d.   humiliating experiences

————— **10.** *Inanimate* sources of frustration, like computers and copying machines, are also safe objects of humor.

The actor's performance was so stiff that he seemed almost *inanimate*.

inanimate (ĭn ăn′ ə mĭt) means:

   a.   unfamiliar

   b.   lively; spirited

   c.   like a cartoon character

   d.   lacking lifelike qualities

Collaboration Option

Respond in Writing

Directions: Refer to the selection as needed to answer the essay-type questions below.

Option for collaboration: Your instructor may direct you to work with other students or, in other words, to work *collaboratively.* In that case, you should form groups of three or four students as directed by your instructor and work together to complete the exercises. After your group discusses each item and agrees on the answer, have a group member record it. Every member of your group should be able to explain all of your group's answers.

1. Consider the following situation:

    The selection states that stress is not usually caused by the situation itself, but by how we perceive the situation. Suppose that you are to give a presentation in one of your classes. A few minutes before class, someone spills coffee on you in the cafeteria. You have a large coffee stain on your shirt, but there is no time to change before class.

    Explain at least two ways you could perceive this situation.

    _____

    _____

    _____

    _____

    Now explain how you could apply one or more of Lally's five stress-busting techniques to help you deal with the situation.

    _____

    _____

    _____

    _____

    _____

2. Develop an original technique for stress-busting. (It must be safe and legal!)

    _____

    _____

    _____

    _____

    _____

    _____

3. Overall main idea. What is the overall main idea the author wants the reader to understand about stress? Answer this question in one sentence. Be sure that your overall main idea sentence includes the topic (*stress*) and tells the overall most important point about it.

_____

_____

_____

_____

_____

_____

Read More about It on the World Wide Web

To learn more about the topic of this selection, visit these websites or use your favorite search engine (such as Yahoo ®). Whenever you go to *any* website, it is a good idea to evaluate it critically. Are you getting good information—information that is accurate, complete, and up-to-date? Who sponsors the website? How easy is it to use the features of the website?

http://www.humorproject.com

The Humor Project, Inc., *seeks to help people get more "smileage" out of their lives and jobs by applying the practical, positive power of humor and creativity.*

http://www.mother.com/JestHome/

This is a website for Jest for the Health of It, *a company dedicated to the promotion and development of therapeutic humor skills.*

http://www.humormatters.com/

This is the Humor Matters *website, which is dedicated to the power and practice of positive therapeutic humor. The goal of this site is to educate, inform, and help you network and locate related resources.*

SELECTION **5-2**

Sociology

THE CHANGING ROLES OF MEN AND WOMEN

By Merrill McLoughlin with Tracy L. Shryer, Erica E. Goode, and Kathleen McAliffe

Prepare Yourself to Read

Directions: Do these exercises *before* you read Selection 5-2.

1. First, read and think about the title. What do you think the changes in the roles of men and women might be?

_____

_____

2. Next, complete your preview by reading the following:

Introduction (in *italics*)	First sentence of each paragraph
First paragraph (paragraph 1)	Words in **bold print** and *italics*
Headings	Last paragraph (paragraph 7)

On the basis of your preview, what do you think the authors seem to suggest about how the roles of men and women are changing?

_____

_____

Apply Comprehension Skills

Directions: Do the Annotation Practice Exercises as you read Selection 5-2. Apply the skills from this chapter:

Formulate implied main ideas.   Follow these general steps: first determine the topic; then ask what the author's most important point about the topic is; then create a sentence that expresses the author's most important point. Use the appropriate formula to "formulate" an implied main idea sentence based on information in the paragraph.

Check your formulated main idea sentences.   Be sure each of your main idea sentences meets the requirements on page 254.

In these exercises, you will work only with paragraphs that have implied main ideas.

THE CHANGING ROLES OF MEN AND WOMEN

Undoubtedly you have heard people refer to the "gender gap." However, many stereotypes about the differences between men and women are incorrect. What are the real differences research studies have found between men and women in terms of personality traits, management styles, behavior in small groups, and political views? In this selection you can read the conclusions of sociologists and compare them with your current opinions.

In Politics and Management, the "Gender Gap" Is Real

1   There is one difference between the sexes on which virtually every expert and study agree: Men are more aggressive than women. It shows up in 2-year-olds. It continues through school days and persists into adulthood. It is even constant across cultures. And there is little doubt that it is rooted in biology—in the male sex hormone testosterone.

2   If there's a feminine trait that's the counterpart of male aggressiveness, it's what social scientists awkwardly refer to as "nurturance." Feminists have argued that the nurturing nature of women is not biological in origin, but rather has been drummed into women by a society that wanted to keep them in the home. But the signs that it is at least partly inborn are too numerous to ignore. Just as tiny infant girls respond more readily to human faces, female toddlers learn much faster than males how to pick up nonverbal cues from others. And grown women are far more adept than men at interpreting facial expressions: A recent study by University of Pennsylvania brain researcher Ruben Gur showed that women easily read emotions such as anger, sadness, and fear. The only such emotion men could pick up was disgust.

3   What difference do such differences make in the real world? Among other things, women appear to be somewhat less competitive—or at least competitive in different ways—than men. At the Harvard Law School, for instance, female students enter with credentials just as outstanding as those of their male peers. But they don't qualify for the prestigious *Law Review* in proportionate numbers, a fact some school officials attribute to women's discomfort in the incredibly competitive atmosphere.

4   Students of management styles have found fewer differences than they expected between

Annotation Practice Exercises

Directions: For each exercise below,

- Write the topic of the paragraph on the lines provided.
- Formulate the implied main idea of the paragraph and write it on the lines provided.

This will help you remember the topic and the main idea.

Annotation Exercise

- Topic of paragraph 1:

  _____

  _____

- Formulate the implied main idea of paragraph 1:

  _____

  _____

  _____

  _____

Annotation Exercise

- Topic of paragraph 4:

  _____

  _____

- Formulate the implied main idea of paragraph 4:

  _____

  _____

  _____

  _____

men and women who reach leadership positions, perhaps because many successful women deliberately imitate masculine ways. But an analysis by Purdue social psychologist Alice Eagly of 166 studies of leadership style did find one consistent difference: Men tend to be more "autocratic"— making decisions on their own—while women tend to consult colleagues and subordinates more often.

5   Studies of behavior in small groups turn up even more differences. Men will typically dominate the discussion, says University of Toronto psychologist Kenneth Dion, spending more time talking and less time listening.

The roles of men and women are changing.
(Jack Hollingsworth/ PhotoDisc)

Political Fallout

6   The aggression-nurturance gulf even shows up in politics. The "gender gap" in polling is real and enduring: Men are far more prone to support a strong defense and tough law-and-order measures such as capital punishment, for instance, while women are more likely to approve of higher spending to solve domestic social problems such as poverty and inequality. Interestingly, there is virtually no gender gap on "women's issues," such as abortion and day care; in fact, men support them slightly *more* than women. . . .

7   Applied to the female of the species, the word "different" has, for centuries, been read to mean "inferior." At last, that is beginning to change. And in the end, of course, it's not a question of better or worse. The obvious point—long lost in a miasma of ideology—is that each sex brings strengths and weaknesses that may check and balance the other; each is half of the human whole.

Annotation Exercise

•   Topic of paragraph 7:

_____

_____

•   Formulate the implied main idea of paragraph 7:

_____

_____

_____

_____

_____

Source: Merrill McLoughlin with Tracy Shryer, Erica Goode, and Kathleen McAliffe, "Men versus Women," in Daniel Hebding and Leonard Glick, *Introduction to Sociology,* McGraw-Hill, New York, 1992, from pp. 111–112. Abridged from an excerpt from *U.S. News and World Report,* August 8, 1988, pp. 50–56, from *Men versus Women.* Copyright 1988, U.S. News and World Report. Reprinted by permission.

Comprehension Quiz

Directions: For each comprehension question below, use information from the selection to determine the correct answer. You may refer to the selection as you answer the questions. Write your answer in the space provided.

True or False

_____ **1.** The one difference between the sexes that experts seem to agree on is that men are more aggressive than women.

_____ **2.** Feminists argue that "nurturance" (the nurturing nature of women) has been drummed into women by a society that wants to keep them at home.

_____ **3.** According to recent studies, women are far more adept than men at interpreting facial expressions.

_____ **4.** Women appear to be less competitive than men, or at least competitive in a different way from men.

_____ **5.** Researchers who study management styles have found more differences than they expected between men and women who reached leadership positions.

Multiple-Choice

_____ **6.** After analyzing 166 studies of leadership style, Alice Eagly found that
    a. men tended to make more decisions on their own.
    b. women tended to consult colleagues and subordinates less often.
    c. men and women were similar in the amount of time they spent talking and listening.
    d. there were no differences between men and women.

_____ **7.** Polls on political issues report that
    a. men are less prone to support strong defense and tough law-and-order measures.
    b. women are less likely to approve of higher spending to solve domestic social problems.
    c. there is a definite "gender gap" on "women's issues."
    d. none of the above.

_____ **8.** Applied to the female of the species, the word *different* has, for centuries, been interpreted to mean
    a. physically different.
    b. inferior.
    c. more nurturing.
    d. all of the above.

———— **9.** Studies of men and women in small groups have found that

   a. men typically dominate the discussion and spend less time listening.

   b. women typically dominate the discussion and spend less time listening.

   c. there are no differences between men and women.

   d. there is no consistent pattern.

———— **10.** The authors of this selection conclude that

   a. differences between the sexes will continue to create difficulties for the societies of the world.

   b. each sex brings strengths and weaknesses that may check and balance the other, since each is half of the human whole.

   c. no further research is needed.

   d. there is essentially no difference between the sexes.

SELECTION **5-2**

Sociology

Extend Your Vocabulary by Using Context Clues

Directions: Context clues are words in a sentence that allow the reader to deduce (reason out) the meaning of an unfamiliar word in that sentence. For each vocabulary item below, a sentence from the selection containing an important word (*italicized, like this*) is quoted first. Next, there is an additional sentence using the word in the same sense and providing another context clue. Use the context clues from *both* sentences to deduce the meaning of each italicized word. *Be sure the answer you choose makes sense in both sentences.* If you discover that you must use a dictionary to confirm an answer choice, remember that the meaning you select must still fit the context of both sentences. To indicate your answer, write the letter in the space provided.

Pronunciation key: ă **pat**   ā **pay**   âr **care**   ä **father**   ĕ **pet**   ē **be**   ĭ **pit**
ī **tie**   îr **pier**   ŏ **pot**   ō **toe**   ô **paw**   oi **noise**   ou **out**   ŏŏ **took**   ōō **boot**
ŭ **cut**   yōō **abuse**   ûr **urge**   th **thin**   *th* **this**   hw **which**   zh **vision**
ə **about**
Stress mark: ʹ

———— **1.** In politics and management, the "*gender* gap" is real.

By using certain medical tests, it is possible to determine the *gender* of a baby before it is born.

gender (jĕn′ dər) means:
a. pertaining to business
b. pertaining to classification by sex
c. pertaining to males
d. pertaining to females

_____ 2. Feminists have argued that the *nurturing* nature of women is not biological in origin, but rather has been drummed into women by a society that wanted to keep them at home.

A *nurturing* teacher can often help timid children overcome their shyness.

nurturing (nûr′ chər ing) means:
a. constantly busy
b. quiet
c. new; inexperienced
d. supportive; fostering growth

_____ 3. Just as tiny infant girls respond more *readily* to human faces, female toddlers learn much faster than males how to pick up nonverbal cues from others.

When confronted with the stolen articles, the shoplifter gave herself up and *readily* admitted her guilt.

readily (rĕd′ l ē) means:
a. promptly
b. happily
c. reluctantly
d. coldly

_____ 4. At the Harvard Law School, for instance, female students enter with *credentials* just as outstanding as those of their male peers.

He tried to get a job as a realtor, but he lacked experience and the necessary *credentials*.

credentials (krĭ dən′ shəlz) means:
a. qualifications
b. applications
c. certificates
d. goals and objectives

_____ 5. But women don't qualify for the *prestigious* Law Review in proportionate numbers.

The late Supreme Court Justice Thurgood Marshall received many *prestigious* awards for his lifetime of outstanding service.

prestigious (prĕ stĭj´ əs) means:

a. little known

b. highly esteemed; valued

c. competitive

d. existing for many years

_____ **6.** Men tend to be more "*autocratic*"—making decisions on their own—while women tend to consult colleagues and subordinates more often.

The citizens hated many of the policies of their country's *autocratic* dictator.

autocratic (ô tō krǎ´tĭc) means:

a. irrational

b. unfair

c. friendly

d. making decisions without consulting others

_____ **7.** Men tend to be more "autocratic"—making decisions on their own—while women tend to consult colleagues and *subordinates* more often.

The district manager is able to work effectively both with her superiors and with the *subordinates* in the department she manages.

subordinates (sə bôr´ də nĭts) means:

a. people of lower rank or under the authority of another

b. people of equal rank; peers

c. supervisors

d. people whose rank is not known or cannot be determined

_____ **8.** The aggression-nurturance *gulf* even shows up in politics.

After their terrible argument, there was a great *gulf* between the father and his son.

gulf (gŭlf) means:

a. wide gap; separating distance

b. large body of water that is partially enclosed by land

c. ill-will or hostility

d. confusion

_____ **9.** Men are far more *prone* to support a strong defense and tough law-and-order measures such as capital punishment.

Lee is an impulsive person who is *prone* to act without thinking first.

prone (prōn) means:

a. lying face down

b. opposed to

c. unwilling

d. having a tendency; likely

_____ **10.** Women are more likely to approve higher spending to solve *domestic* social problems such as poverty and inequality.

Rather than focusing on international affairs, the president concentrated on *domestic* issues such as welfare, the national economy, and education.

domestic (də měs′ tĭk) means:

a. pertaining to business

b. pertaining to women

c. pertaining to a country's national or internal affairs

d. pertaining to pets and farm animals

SELECTION **5-2**

Sociology

Collaboration Option

Respond in Writing

Directions: Refer to the selection as needed to answer the essay-type questions below.

Option for collaboration: Your instructor may direct you to work with other students or, in other words, to work *collaboratively*. In that case, you should form groups of three or four students as directed by your instructor and work together to complete the exercises. After your group discusses each item and agrees on the answer, have a group member record it. Every member of your group should be able to explain all of your group's answer.

1. Complete the chart below, which compares and contrasts the six characteristics the authors present for women and those they present for men.

Men	*Women*
1. _____	Nurturing
2. Competitive	_____
3. _____ _____ _____	Likely to consult subordinates and colleagues in decision-making
4. Likely to dominate small-group discussions	_____ _____
5. _____ _____	In favor of higher government spending on domestic problems
6. Tend to support women's issues	_____

2. Overall main idea. What is the overall main idea the authors want the reader to understand about the roles of men and women? Answer this question in one sentence. Be sure that your overall main idea sentence includes the topic (*the roles of men and women*) and tells the overall most important point about it.

_____

_____

_____

_____

_____

_____

_____

_____

_____

_____

_____

Read More about It on the World Wide Web

To learn more about the topic of this selection, visit these websites or use your favorite search engine (such as Yahoo ®). Whenever you go to *any* website, it is a good idea to evaluate it critically. Are you getting good information— information that is accurate, complete and up-to-date? Who sponsors the website? How easy is it to use the features of the website?

http://www.informationweek.com/731/salsurve3.htm
> *This is an article entitled, "Gender Gap Is Smaller in Technology," on the Information Week Online Web page. This article asserts that women appear to be making more progress in pay equity in the information technology arena than in other industries.*

http://www.menstuff.org
> *An educational website with information on more than 100 topics related to men's issues, such as divorce, fathers, and sexuality.*

http://www.now.org
> *Homepage for the National Organization for Women (NOW). Features press releases and articles, as well as the history of NOW. Also provides a search form that allows you to locate a specific topic at NOW's site.*

SELECTION **5-3**
Sociology

DEMOGRAPHY
From *Sociology: An Introduction*
By Richard J. Gelles and Ann Levine

Prepare Yourself to Read

Directions: Do these exercises *before* you read Selection 5-3.

1. First, read and think about the title. What do you already know about demography?

_____

_____

2 Next, complete your preview by reading the following:

> Introduction (in *italics*)
> Headings
> All of the first paragraph (paragraph 1)
> First sentence of each of the other paragraphs
> Charts

On the basis of your preview, what does the selection now seem to be about?

_____

_____

Apply Comprehension Skills

Directions: Do the Annotation Practice Exercises as you read Selection 5-3. Apply the skills from this chapter:

Formulate implied main ideas. Follow these general steps: first determine the topic; then ask what the author's most important point about the topic is; then create a sentence that expresses the author's most important point. Use the appropriate formula to "formulate" an implied main idea sentence based on information in the paragraph.

Check your formulated main idea sentences. Be sure each of your main idea sentences meets the requirements on page 254.

In these exercises, you will work only with paragraphs that have implied main ideas.

DEMOGRAPHY

The United Nations designated October 12, 1999, as "Y6B," the day the world's population reached 6 billion. The exact day, of course, will never be known, but it certainly occurred before the end of 1999. Experts estimate that worldwide, 370,000 babies are born daily. In 1900, the world's population stood at 2 billion. Between 1900 and 1999—only one hundred years—the human population tripled. There is great concern that humans are quickly consuming natural resources and are ruining the environment and the planet. And nearly half of the babies born will be born into poverty. If the overall rate of population growth in the developing countries remains stable, their populations will double in only forty years.

In our own country, the state of California is expected to increase its population by 18 million by the year 2025, raising its population to 50 million. That means that California will be adding one resident every 45 seconds—the biggest population explosion in the nation's history. The other most populous states also face significant population increases. (Those states, in order, are: Texas, New York, Florida, Pennsylvania, Illinois, Ohio, Michigan, New Jersey, and North Carolina.) Also, the U.S. population is getting older and more Hispanic. (See Selection 4-2.) The problems raised by population growth and by the rapid increases in certain segments of the population—problems such as health care, poverty, education, traffic, streets and road repair, housing, utilities, city services, and pollution, to name a few—will affect all of us. The goal of the United States census in the year 2000 was to count every person in this country: without reliable figures, it is difficult to plan for the future. It is easy to see why the work of demographers is so important. The selection below, from a sociology textbook, explains what demography is and the population changes that occurred as western nations shifted from being agricultural nations to industrialized nations.

Demography: The Study of Population

1   The scientific study of population is known as *demography.* The word comes from the Greek for "measuring people." But counting heads is only a small part of what demographers do. They also attempt to calculate the growth rate of a population and to assess the impact of such things as the marriage rate and life expectancy, the sex ratio (the proportions of males to females), and the age structure (the proportions of young, middle-aged, and older people) on human behavior and the structure of society. They are interested in the distribution of population and in movements of people (migration). Put another way, demographers study the effects of such numbers on social trends.

2   Demographers use a number of standard measures in translating a locality's raw totals— births, deaths, the number of those moving in and out—into general statistics that allow them to identify trends. The birthrate is the number of births per 1,000 people in a given year. Suppose there were 900 births in a city of 50,000 in a spe-

Annotation Practice Exercises

Directions: For each exercise below,

- Write the topic of the paragraph on the lines provided.

- Formulate the implied main idea of the paragraph and write it on the lines provided.

This will help you remember the topic and the main idea.

cific year. Demographers calculate the birthrate for the city by dividing the number of births (900) by the population (50,000) and multiplying the result (0.018) by 1,000 to get 18. The birthrate in developed countries is 1.6; in less developed countries (excluding China) it is 4.0. The death rate is the number of deaths per 1,000 people in a given year. (The death rate is calculated in the same way as the birthrate.) The fertility rate is the number of live births per 1,000 women of the world. As mentioned earlier, population and population growth rates are highest in developing nations and lower in western nations. These rates are also complicated by mass movements of refugees to and from certain countries. By 1994 the population of refugees was over 23 million, up from about 10 million refugees worldwide in 1983. Mass movements of people into and out of Afghanistan, Somalia, Bosnia, and Mozambique have contributed to this sharp increase. Famine and political upheaval are usually behind these mass exoduses. (See Table 1 and Figure 1.)

In the United States, demographers analyze data gathered by the census. *(Spencer Grant/Photo Edit)*

The Demographic Transition

3   The term *demographic transition* refers to a pattern of major population changes that accompanied the transformation of western nations from agricultural into industrial societies. The demographic transition occurred in three stages. (See Figure 2.)

4   In *Stage I,* birthrates were high, but death rates were also high. As a result, the population growth rate was low. Thus in eighteenth-century Europe, birthrates were high, but many infants did not survive childhood and many adults did not reach old age. High infant mortality, epidemics, famines, and wars kept the population growth rate low.

5   In *Stage II,* which began in Europe in the late eighteenth century, birthrates remained high, but death rates began to fall. Why? Improvements in agricultural technology, the spread of new and hardier crops (such as the potato), and increased food production. Improvements in transportation facilitated food distribution: people were no longer dependent on local supplies or devastated by local crop failures. Better nutrition meant that people were more able to resist and survive disease. During the nineteenth century improvements in

Annotation Exercise

- Topic of paragraph 4:

  _____

- Formulate the implied main idea of paragraph 4:

  _____

  _____

  _____

| | | **TABLE 1** | | |
| | | **WORLD POPULATION CLOCK, 1997** | | |

Measure	World	Developed Countries	Developing Countries	Developing Countries (Excluding China)
Population:	5,840,433,000	1,174,792,000	4,665,641,000	3,428,948,000
Births per:				
Year	139,366,897	13,450,155	125,916,742	104,917,695
Month	11,613,908	1,120,846	10,493,062	8,743,141
Week	2,680,133	258,657	2,421,476	2,017,648
Day	381,827	36,850	344,977	287,446
Hour	15,909	1,535	14,374	11,977
Minute	265	26	240	200
Second	4.4	0.4	4.0	3.3
Deaths per:				
Year	53,353,684	12,006,985	41,346,699	33,233,993
Month	4,446,140	1,000,582	3,445,558	2,769,499
Week	1,026,032	230,904	795,129	639,115
Day	146,174	32,896	113,279	91,052
Hour	6,091	1,371	4,720	3,794
Minute	102	23	79	63
Second	1.7	0.4	1.3	1.1
Natural increase per:				
Year	86,013,213	1,443,170	84,570,043	71,683,702
Month	7,167,768	120,264	7,047,504	5,973,642
Week	1,654,100	27,753	1,626,347	1,378,533
Day	235,653	3,954	231,699	196,394
Hour	9,819	165	9,654	8,183
Minute	164	3	161	136
Second	2.7	0.0	2.7	2.3
Infant deaths per:				
Year	8,166,650	116,131	8,050,519	7,391,149
Month	680,534	9,678	670,877	615,929
Week	157,051	2,233	154,818	142,137
Day	22,374	318	22,056	20,250
Hour	932	13	919	844
Minute	16	0.2	15	14
Second	0.3	0.0	0.3	0.2

Source: Population Reference Bureau. *Population Today,* May 1997, p. 2.

Through most of human history, the population was more or less stable. In modern times, however, world population has skyrocketed.

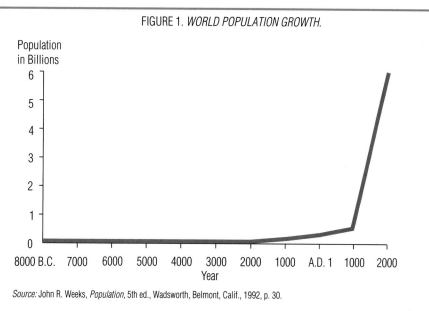

FIGURE 1. *WORLD POPULATION GROWTH.*

Population in Billions

Source: John R. Weeks, *Population,* 5th ed., Wadsworth, Belmont, Calif., 1992, p. 30.

In Stage I, birthrates and death rates were both high; population growth (the purple line) was slow. In Stage II, death rates declined faster than birthrates, so population growth continued to climb. Only when birthrates and death rates are both low, Stage III, does population growth slow down.

FIGURE 2. *DEMOGRAPHIC TRANSITION IN WESTERN NATIONS.*

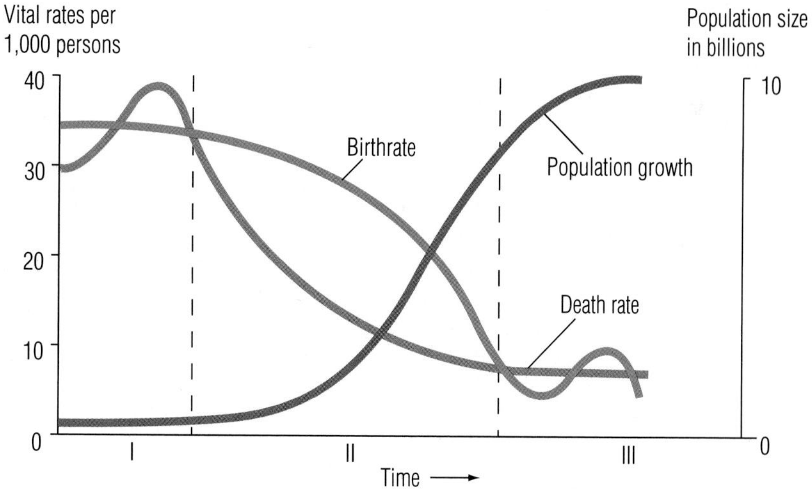

Vital rates per 1,000 persons

Population size in billions

Birthrate

Population growth

Death rate

Time ⟶

Source: John R. Weeks, *Population,* 5th ed., Wadsworth, Belmont, Calif., 1992, p. 76.

5 public health and sanitation (cleaner water, better sewage disposal, pasteurized milk) and advances in modern medicine contributed further to the decline in death rates. Many more women survived into their childbearing years. The population growth rate soared. (*Note:* The eighteenth-century population explosion was due to lower death rates, not to higher birthrates.)

6   In *Stage III,* which began in the mid-nineteenth century in western nations, birthrates started to fall. Stage III is associated with industrial development. In agricultural societies, children are an economic asset: the more hands, the better. In urban, industrial societies, however, children become an "economic burden." They are financially dependent on their parents for an extended period. Large families mean crowded living quarters, additional household expenses, and a lower family standard of living. Four additional factors that contributed to falling birthrates in the west in the twentieth century were the decline in infant mortality (which meant that a couple did not have to produce five or six children to ensure that three or four would live), government-sponsored Social Security programs in the 1930s and 1940s (which meant that parents did not have to depend on their children to support them in old age), access to modern birth control devices in the late 1950s and early 1960s, and postponement of the age of marriage. By the 1960s families with only two or three children had become the norm. Today birthrates in most western nations have stabilized at replacement levels, while death rates have continued to decline. (Half of the Americans now alive would have been dead if the death rate had remained at 1900 levels.) Thus the balance between birthrates and death rates has been restored; as in Stage I the population growth rate is low.

Source: Richard J. Gelles and Ann Levine, *Sociology: An Introduction,* McGraw-Hill, Boston, Mass., pp. 594–597.

Annotation Exercise

• Topic of paragraph 5:

_____

• Formulate the implied main idea of paragraph 5:

_____

_____

Annotation Exercise

• Topic of paragraph 6:

_____

• Formulate the implied main idea of paragraph 6:

_____

_____

_____

SELECTION **5-3**

Sociology

Comprehension Quiz

Directions: For each comprehension question below, use information from the selection to determine the correct answer. You may refer to the selection as you answer the questions. Write your answer in the space provided.

True or False

_____ **1.** The scientific study of population trends is known as the *fertility* rate.

_____ **2.** *Life expectancy* is the potential life span of the average member of any given population.

_____ **3.** Population growth rates are highest in western nations and lower in developing nations.

_____ **4.** According to the Population Reference Bureau, in 1997 there were a total of 381,827 births each day worldwide.

Multiple-Choice

_____ **5.** Demographers
   a. are interested in the distribution of population and in movements of people.
   b. assess the impact of such things as life expectancy and the marriage rate.
   c. count people and calculate the growth rate of a population.
   d. all of the above

_____ **6.** In a given year, the birthrate in less developed countries (excluding China) is
   a. 18 per 1,000 people.
   b. 4.0 per 1,000 people.
   c. 1.6 per 1,000 people.
   d. 0.018 per 1,000 people.

_____ **7.** Population growth slows down only when
   a. birth rates are low.
   b. death rates are high.
   c. both birth rates and death rates are low.
   d. both birth rates and death rates are high.

_____ **8.** World population began to skyrocket about
   a. 2000 B.C.
   b. 1000 B.C.
   c. A.D. 1000
   d. A.D. 2000

_____ **9.** During Stage III of the demographic transition in western nations, birthrates declined because

    a. infant mortality increased.

    b. access to modern birth control devices became available in the late 1950s and early 1960s.

    c. fewer people postponed marriage.

    d. couples began having children earlier.

_____ **10.** In 1997 there were 26 births per minute in developed countries, while in developing countries the number of births per minute was

    a. 240

    b. 265

    c. 932

    d. 4,720

Extend Your Vocabulary by Using Context Clues

SELECTION **5-3**

Sociology

Directions: Context clues are words in a sentence that allow the reader to deduce (reason out) the meaning of an unfamiliar word in the sentence. For each vocabulary exercise below, a sentence from the reading selection containing an important word (*italicized, like this*) is quoted first. Next, there is an additional sentence using the word in the same sense and providing another context clue. Use the context clues from *both* sentences to deduce the meaning of the italicized word. *Be sure the answer you choose makes sense in both sentences.* If you discover that you must use a dictionary to confirm an answer choice, remember that the meaning you select must still fit the context of *both* sentences. To indicate your answer, write the letter in the space provided.

Pronunciation key: ă pat   ā pay   âr care   ä father   ĕ pet   ē be   ĭ pit
ī tie   îr pier   ŏ pot   ō toe   ô paw   oi noise   ou out   ŏŏ took   ōō boot
ŭ cut   yōō abuse   ûr urge   th thin   *th* this   hw which   zh vision
ə about
Stress mark: ′

_____ **1.** They also attempt to calculate the growth rate of a population and to assess the impact of such things as the marriage rate and life *expectancy.*

Insurance rates are based on life *expectancy:* the younger the person, the lower the rate.

expectancy (ĭk spĕk′ tən sē)

a. length

b. a known quantity or amount

c. an expected amount calculated on the basis of statistical data

d. a quantity or amount that cannot be determined or estimated

_____ **2.** They are interested in the *distribution* of population and in movements of people (migration).

The *distribution* of saguaro cactus is limited to the southwestern part of the United States and northern Mexico.

distribution (dĭ strĭ byoo′ shŭn)

a. disappearance; extinction

b. planting

c. geographic occurrence or range

d. destruction

_____ **3.** Demographers use a number of *standard* measures in translating a locality's raw totals—births, deaths, the number of those moving in and out—into general statistics that allow them to identify trends.

Nutritionists have established the *standard* amount of fats, carbohydrates, and protein adults need in their diet.

standard (stăn′ dərd)

a. acknowledged measure

b. imprecise

c. incomplete

d. ambiguous

_____ **4.** Demographers use a number of standard measures in translating a *locality's* raw totals—births, deaths, the number of those moving in and out—into general statistics that allow them to identify trends.

Because the population in our suburb is increasing, there are many new businesses moving into our *locality*.

locality (lō kăl′ ĭ tē)

a. voting precinct

b. school district

c. state

d. a particular place

_____ **5.** *Mass* movements of people into and out of Afghanistan, Somalia, Bosnia, and Mozambique have contributed to this sharp increase.

Most large cities have subway systems, bus systems, or other forms of *mass* transit.

mass (măs)

a.   pertaining to religion

b.   relating to a large number of people

c.   relating to citizens of a country

d.   related to high speed

_____   **6.**   Famine and political *upheaval* are usually behind these mass exoduses.

The earthquake caused a complete *upheaval* of life in the peaceful mountain village.

upheaval (ŭp hē′ vəl)

a.   improvement

b.   elevation

c.   sudden, violent disruption

d.   gradual change

_____   **7.**   Famine and political upheaval are usually behind these mass *exoduses.*

Historians report that seeking refuge from war, religious persecution, and epidemics are three major reasons for *exoduses.*

exoduses (ēk′ sə dəs əz)

a.   trips or journeys

b.   departures of large numbers of people

c.   refusals to leave

d.   planned absences

_____   **8.**   High infant *mortality,* epidemics, famines, and wars kept the population growth rate low.

Child *mortality* is higher in poor countries because health care for children is so inadequate.

mortality (môr tăl′ ĭ tē)

a.   correct behavior

b.   heart attacks

c.   death rate

d.   protection

_____   **9.**   Improvements in transportation *facilitated* food distribution: people were no longer dependent on local supplies or devastated by local crop failures.

The new, computerized traffic signals *facilitated* the smooth flow of traffic during rush hour.

facilitated (fə sĭl′ ĭ tāt ĕd)

a. made easier

b. slowed down

c. directed

d. authorized

_____ **10.** Today birthrates in most western nations have *stabilized* at replacement levels, while death rates have continued to decline.

Once the paramedics *stabilized* the victim's erratic breathing and heart rate, they rushed her to the emergency room for treatment.

stabilized (stā′ bə līzd)

a. resuscitated

b. decreased

c. stopped

d. became steady or stable

SELECTION **5-3**

Sociology

Collaboration Option

Respond in Writing

Directions: Refer to the selection as needed to answer the essay-type questions below.

Option for collaboration: Your instructor may direct you to work with other students—in other words, to work *collaboratively.* In that case, you should form groups of three or four students as directed by your instructor and work together to complete the exercises. After your group discusses each item and agrees on the answer, have a group member record it. Every member of your group should be able to explain all of your group's answers.

1. The world's population growth is not expected to slow down for the next 50 years. What are the implications of this for you and your family (or your future family)?

_____

_____

_____

_____

2. In China, the government enforces a policy that permits most couples to have only one child. Given the overpopulation problem the world is facing, do you think all countries should limit the number of children couples are allowed to have? Explain why or why not.

_____

_____

_____

3. If the number of children couples could have were restricted by law, should couples be allowed to have an additional child if they can pay the government a special fee? Why or why not?

_____

_____

_____

4. Are there any *advantages* to having so many more people in the world today? Try to think of at least two.

_____

_____

_____

_____

_____

5. If there were a birth control pill for men, do you think the worldwide birthrate would decline? Explain why or why not.

_____

_____

_____

6. Use the information from the table in the selection to complete this summary chart:

	Per Minute			
	World	**Developed**	**Undeveloped**	**Without China**
Births				
Deaths				
Increase				
Infant Deaths				

7. Overall main idea. What is the overall main idea the authors want the reader to understand about demography? Answer this question in one sentence. Be sure that your overall main idea sentence includes the topic (*demography*) and tells the overall most important point about it.

_____

_____

_____

_____

Read More About It on the World Wide Web

To learn more about the topic of this selection, visit these websites or use your favorite search engine (such as Yahoo ®). Whenever you go to *any* website, it is a good idea to evaluate it critically. Are you getting good information— information that is accurate, complete, and up-to-date? Who sponsors the website? How easy is it to use the features of the website?

http://www.census.gov

This is the U.S. Census Bureau *website. The goal of the Census Bureau is to provide the best mix of timelines, relevance, quality, and cost for the data it collects and the services it provides.*

http://www.ssc.wisc.edu/cde/

Center for Demography and Ecology (CDE) *at the University of Wisconsin at Madison is one of the world's leading centers of social science.*

http://www.demographics.com

American Demographs, *a monthly Intertec magazine with a circulation of 30,000, covers human population patterns and consumer trends in behavior and attitude. Intertec publishes 100 magazines, produces more than 30 trade shows, and publishes 450 books and directories serving professionals in agribusiness, communications, electrical and public services, entertainment, industry, marketing, professional services, apparel, and transportation.*

© PhotoDisc

C H A P T E R

6

Identifying Supporting Details

CHAPTER OBJECTIVES

In this chapter you will learn the answers to these questions:

- What are supporting details in a paragraph?

- Why is it useful to understand supporting details?

- How can I identify supporting details in paragraphs?

- How can I list supporting details clearly?

- What are major and minor details, and what is the difference between them?

SKILLS

Supporting Details in Paragraphs

- What Are Supporting Details?

- Why Are Supporting Details Important?

Identifying and Listing Supporting Details

Major and Minor Details and How to Tell the Difference

A Word about Standardized Reading Tests: Supporting Details

CREATING YOUR SUMMARY

Developing Chapter Review Cards

READINGS

When we read too fast or too slowly, we understand nothing.

Blaise Pascal

Little by little does the trick.

SUPPORTING DETAILS IN PARAGRAPHS

What Are Supporting Details?

A paragraph consists of more than a topic and a main idea. In a paragraph with a stated main idea, the other sentences in the paragraph present supporting details. Even paragraphs with implied main ideas include details. The topic and the main idea are essential to understanding the paragraph, but the **supporting details** provide additional information that helps you understand the main idea *completely.* In other words, supporting details explain, illustrate, or prove the main idea.

Supporting details typically consist of:

KEY TERM
Supporting Details

Additional information in the paragraph that helps you understand the main idea completely.
Supporting details are also known as *support* or *details.*

- Names
- Descriptions
- Dates
- Statistics
- Places
- Other information explaining, illustrating, or proving the main idea.

Be careful not to confuse the main idea with the supporting details. Details pertain to the main idea, but they are not the same thing. The main idea expresses an important *general* point that is based on the supporting details or is explained by them.

Why Are Supporting Details Important?

As noted above, the supporting details in a paragraph have an important connection with the main idea. They obviously help explain the main idea; and, often, supporting details also lead you to the stated main idea. Similarly, supporting details contain important information that can help you formulate the main idea when it is implied.

In addition, it is useful to identify and understand supporting details because they can help you grasp the *organization* of a paragraph. And if you understand *how* the supporting details are organized to explain, illustrate, or support the main idea of the paragraph, that makes it easier to remember the material, to take notes, and to mark your textbooks effectively. As you will learn in Chapter 7, details are usually organized according to one of several common writing patterns. Specific types of supporting details that authors use to organize ideas into paragraphs include lists of characteristics, things, places, etc. (called a *list pattern*); items in a series or steps in a process (called a *sequence pattern*); similarities, differences, or both (called a *comparison-contrast pattern*), or reasons and results (called a *cause-effect pattern*).

297

Supporting details are important to include on study cards because the details explain, illustrate, or prove main ideas.
(David Young-Wolff/PhotoEdit)

Listing the supporting details on paper after you finish reading can help you find and remember all of them. Therefore, when you are studying there will be many instances when you will want to list supporting details in order to learn and remember them. For example, you might want to list important supporting details from a history textbook on chapter review cards. Instructors often ask test questions based on supporting details—examples, names, dates, places, and other important information. Along with determining the topic and the main idea, then, identifying supporting details will help you become a more successful reader and student.

The following diagram shows the relationship between a main idea and its supporting details:

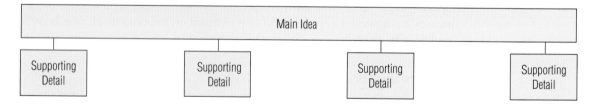

IDENTIFYING AND LISTING SUPPORTING DETAILS

Comprehension Monitoring Question for Identifying Supporting Details

"What additional information does the author provide to help me understand the main idea completely?"

To identify the supporting details of a paragraph, ask yourself, "*What additional information* does the author provide to help me understand the main idea completely?" One way to approach this is by turning the main idea sentence into a question, using the word *who, what, where, when, why,* or *how,* and then seeking the information that answers this question.

For example, suppose that the stated main idea of a paragraph is: *In a corporation, the chief financial officer is responsible for many basic functions.* You could change this sentence into the question, "*What* are the basic functions of a chief financial officer?" That question would lead you to the details that describe the basic functions and, therefore, explain the main idea.

Often, you will find that supporting details are introduced by signal words such as *first, second, next, also, in addition,* and *moreover.* Watch for numbers (1, 2, 3) and letters (*a, b, c*) that signal lists of details. Watch for information introduced by the phrases *for example* and *to illustrate,* since examples are always details.

Here is an excerpt from a music appreciation textbook. Its topic is *the role of American colleges and universities in our musical culture.* The first sentence is the main idea: *American colleges and universities have played an unusually vital role in our musical culture.* Turn this main idea into the question, "*What* role have American colleges and universities played in our musical culture?" After you have read the paragraph, identify the details that answer this question.

> American colleges and universities have played an unusually vital role in our musical culture. They have trained and employed many of our leading composers, performers, and scholars. Music courses have expanded the horizons and interests of countless students. And since the middle of the century, many universities have sponsored performing groups specializing in twentieth-century music. In addition, they have housed most of the electronic music studios.
>
> *Source:* Roger Kamien, *Music: An Appreciation,* 5th ed., McGraw-Hill, New York, 1992, p. 444.

Here is a list of the four details that answer the question, "*What* role have American colleges and universities played in our musical culture?"

1. They trained and employed many leading composers, performers, and scholars.
2. They expanded the horizons and interests of students through music courses.
3. Since mid-century, they have sponsored performing groups specializing in twentieth-century music.
4. They have housed most of the electronic music studios.

The following diagram shows the relationship between the main idea and the supporting details in this paragraph.

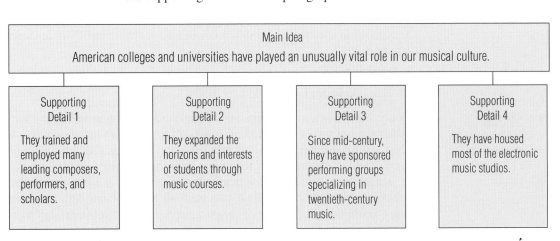

Stop and Annotate

Go back to the excerpt above. Locate the four supporting details and number them with a small ①, ②, ③, and ④. Underline or highlight the signal words *And* and *In addition* that helped you identify the last two details.

Notice that in this list, the supporting details are not written out exactly as they appear in the paragraph. When you are listing supporting details, you will often want to use some of your own words in order to keep them brief. Restating an author's material in your own words is called **paraphrasing.** Notice also, in this excerpt, the words *And* and *In addition* in the last two sentences. These words signal to the reader that two separate details are being given. But notice that not every detail is introduced by a signal word.

Since you are responsible for understanding the supporting details in a textbook paragraph, you will also find it helpful after you have read the paragraph to go back and insert a *number* next to each detail. Numbering the supporting details is helpful for at least three reasons. First, it helps you locate all the details. Second, it helps you remember how many details there were in the paragraph. Third, it prevents you from overmarking the paragraph by underlining or highlighting too much. (You may also find it helpful to number the details when you list them in your notes.)

In the next excerpt, the topic is *Richard Feynman* (fīn′ mən), an American physicist and writer. Feynman was a Nobel laureate who worked on the atomic bomb, reinvented quantum mechanics (the mathematics describing atomic processes), and exposed the fatal error by NASA that caused the explosion of the space shuttle *Challenger* in 1985. The first sentence of the paragraph is the stated main idea: *Mr. Feynman was one of the great characters of modern physics.* Change this main idea sentence into the question, "*Why* was Feynman considered a 'character'?" (As it is used in this paragraph, the word *character* refers to a peculiar or eccentric person.) Then read the paragraph to identify the details that answer this question.

> Mr. Feynman was one of the great characters of modern physics. He was a jokester who figured out how to crack safes in Los Alamos offices while working on atomic bomb research in World War II. He was a computational wizard, once beating early computers in a contest to track a rocket launch. He could demolish other physicists whose presentation contained an error or humiliate them by producing in minutes a complicated calculation that took them weeks or months.
>
> *Source:* Tom Siegfried, "Exploring the Mind of a Genius," *Dallas Morning News,* October 25, 1992, sec. J.

The question "*Why* was Feynman considered a 'character'?" is answered by these two details:

1. He was a jokester.
2. He was a computational wizard.

Stop and Annotate

Go back to the excerpt above. Locate the two supporting details and number them with a small ① and ②.

Notice how briefly these supporting details can be written and how clearly they stand out when they are listed on separate lines. Listing the supporting details this way makes it easy to see the information that explains why Feynman was considered a "character." (The contest with the computer and his "demolishing" other physicists are minor details that give proof of his computational ability.) As mentioned above, when you are listing supporting details it is not necessary to use the exact words of the paragraph, and it is not necessary to use complete sentences. Finally, did you notice that there were no signal words in this paragraph to indicate the supporting details?

The next excerpt is from a book on English composition. It has a number of important details. The topic of this paragraph is *careless writing and readers who get lost,* and the stated main idea is: *If the reader is lost, it's usually because the writer hasn't been careful enough.* Turn the main idea into the question, "*What* are some ways careless writers cause readers to get lost?" Now read the paragraph to find the supporting details that answer this question.

> It won't do to say that the reader is too dumb or too lazy to keep pace with the train of thought. If the reader is lost, it's usually because the writer hasn't been careful enough. The carelessness can take any number of forms. Perhaps a sentence is so excessively cluttered that the reader, hacking through the verbiage, simply doesn't know what it means. Perhaps a sentence has been so shoddily constructed that the reader could read it in several ways. Perhaps the writer has switched pronouns in mid-sentence, or has switched tenses, so the reader loses track of who is talking or when the action took place. Perhaps Sentence B is not a logical sequel to Sentence A—the writer, in whose head the connection is clear, has not bothered to provide the missing link. Perhaps the writer has used an important word incorrectly by not taking the trouble to look it up.
>
> *Source:* Adapted from William K. Zinsser, *On Writing Well,* 5th ed., Harper and Row, New York, 1994, pp. 9, 12.

Here is a list of the five details that answer the question, "*What* are some ways careless writers cause readers to get lost?"

1. Careless writers clutter sentences with too many words.
2. They write sentences that can be read in several ways.
3. They switch pronouns or tenses.
4. They don't supply links between sentences.
5. They use words incorrectly.

Stop and Annotate

Go back to the excerpt above. Locate the five supporting details and number them with a small ①, ②, ③, ④ and ⑤. Underline or highlight the signal words *perhaps* to help you identify all five details.

Notice that some of the details listed above have been paraphrased to make them easier to understand and remember. Notice also that none of the common signal words (such as *also, and,* and *another*) were used in this paragraph. Instead, repeated use of the words *perhaps* signals each supporting detail in the paragraph. Inserting small numbers next to the details would make them easy to locate, even though the details are spread throughout the paragraph.

The next sample paragraph is from a health textbook. As the heading indicates, its topic is *water.* Its implied main idea is: *Water serves many important functions in the body.* Turn this main idea into the question, "*What* important functions does water serve in the body?" Then read the paragraph to find the details that answer this question.

Water

Like fiber, water has no nutritional value, yet is a very important food component. It is used to transport nutrients to the cells and to remove cellular waste products. In addition, it acts as a medium for digestion, regulates body temperature, and helps cushion the vital organs. An inadequate water intake will restrict the function of all body systems. Finally, water and some of the chemicals it carries are responsible for bodily structure, since, on average, 60 percent of the body is water.

Source: Marvin Levy, Mark Dignan, and Janet Shirreffs, *Targeting Wellness: The Core,* McGraw-Hill, New York, 1992, p. 52. Reproduced with permission of McGraw-Hill.

Here is a list of the eight details that answer the question, "What important functions does water serve in the body?" Notice that they have been paraphrased and shortened.

1. an important food component
2. transports nutrients to cells
3. removes cellular waste
4. acts as a medium for digestion
5. regulates body temperature
6. helps cushion vital organs
7. inadequate intake restricts functions of all body systems
8. partly responsible for body structure because the body is 60 percent water

Stop and Annotate

Go back to the excerpt above. Locate the eight supporting details and number each with a small number. Underline or highlight the signal words *In addition* and *Finally*, which helped you identify two of the details.

As you can see, a single sentence can contain more than one supporting detail. In this paragraph, although there are five sentences, there are eight supporting details. The second sentence contains two details, and the third sentence contains three. There are two signals in the paragraph, *In addition* and *Finally*. (There are other ways besides listing to organize supporting details you want to learn. These techniques are presented in Chapter 10.)

MAJOR AND MINOR DETAILS AND HOW TO TELL THE DIFFERENCE

All the details in a paragraph ultimately support the main idea by explaining, illustrating or proving it in some way. In each of the examples presented earlier, all the details *directly* supported (explained) the main idea. Details that directly support the main idea are called **major details** (these are also known as *primary details*). However, there are paragraphs in which some details support or explain *other details*. These are called **minor details** (they are also known as *secondary details*).

KEY TERMS
Major Details

Details that directly support the main idea.
Major details are also known as *primary details*.

The following diagram shows the relationship between the main idea, major details and minor details.

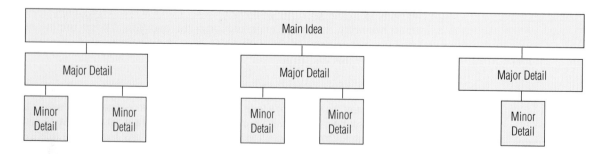

Here is a simple paragraph that has been created to illustrate major and minor details. Its topic is *uses of pepper*. Its stated main idea is the first sentence,

KEY TERMS
Minor Details

Details that support other details.

Minor details are also known as *secondary details*.

Throughout history, pepper has been used many different ways besides as a way to season food. There are three major details that explain important uses of pepper. The other sentences are minor details which explain the major details.

> Throughout history, pepper has had many other uses besides as a way to season food. Pepper was also one of the first ways of preserving meat. During the Crusades pepper was used to preserve sausages. Pepper is still used to preserve meat today. Pepper has also been used as a medicine. In medieval times peppercorns were prescribed to cure aches and pains. Native Americans today use pepper to cure toothaches. Today, pepper is also used to control insects. For example, the French and Dutch use pepper to kill moths and to repel other insects.

The following diagram shows the relationship between the main idea and the major and minor details for this paragraph.

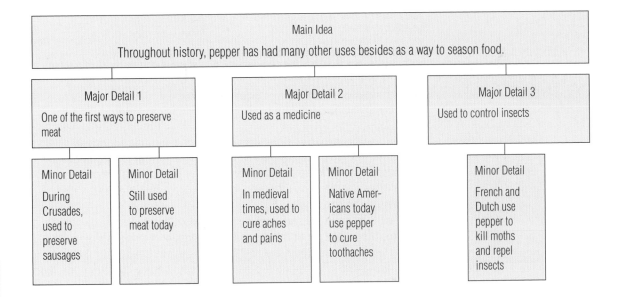

Stop and Annotate

Go back to the excerpt above. Locate the three major details and number them with a small ①, ②, and ③.

Again, notice that only three details directly answer the main idea question, "How has pepper been used in different ways throughout history besides as a way to season food?" Therefore, these three details are major details. The passage would make sense with only the main idea and those details. However, the author explains even more fully by giving examples of the three ways. Therefore, those details, which explain other details, are minor details.

Remember, to identify the supporting details of a paragraph, ask yourself, "What *additional information* does the author provide to help me understand the main idea completely?" Change the main idea into a question; then look for the major details that answer the question. Be aware that the author might also include minor details to increase your understanding even more. Don't spend too much time worrying about whether a detail is major or minor. The important thing is simply that you distinguish between the main idea and the details.

A WORD ABOUT STANDARDIZED READING TESTS: SUPPORTING DETAILS

Many college students are required to take standardized reading tests as part of an overall assessment program, in a reading course, or as part of a state-mandated "basic skills" test. A standardized reading test typically consists of a series of passages followed by multiple-choice questions to be completed within a specified time limit.

Standardized reading tests always include questions about supporting details. The purpose of such questions is to see if you can locate and comprehend specific information stated in a passage.

Questions about **supporting details** often begin with phrases such as the following:

According to the passage . . .

According to the information in the passage . . .

The author states . . .

The author states that . . .

Questions may also refer to **specific information** in a passage, as in the following examples:

One function of water in the body is . . .

The museum mentioned in the passage is located in . . .

World War I began in the year . . .

The height of the tower was . . .

To answer an item about supporting details, read the question carefully to determine exactly what information you need (for instance, a place, a person's name, or a date). Then *skim* the passage, looking for that information. When you come to the part of the passage that has what you are looking for, slow down and read it more closely.

Don't be fooled by a correct answer that is worded somewhat differently from the way the information appeared in the passage. For instance, a passage might state that a child was rescued by a "police officer," but the correct answer choice might be "an officer of the law." Or a passage might specifically mention "the Vanderbilts and the Rockefellers," but the correct answer choice might be "two wealthy eastern families." Remember, you need to look for information in the answer choices that *means the same thing* as the information in the passage, even if the words themselves are different.

DEVELOPING CHAPTER REVIEW CARDS

Review cards, or *summary cards,* are an excellent study tool. They are a way to select, organize, and review the most important information in a textbook chapter. The process of creating review cards helps you organize information in a meaningful way and, at the same time, transfer it into long-term memory. The cards can also be used to prepare for tests (see Part Three). The review card activities in this book give you structured practice in creating these valuable study tools. Once you have learned how to make review cards, you can create them for textbook material in your other courses.

Now, complete the five review cards for Chapter 6 by answering the questions or following the directions on each card. When you have completed them, you will have summarized: (1) what supporting details are, (2) why they are important, (3) how to find them in a paragraph, (4) how to list them, and (5) how to mark them.

What Supporting Details Are

Define *supporting details.* (See page 297.)

_____

_____

Supporting details may consist of: (See page 297.)

_____

_____

_____

_____

_____

Card 1   **Chapter 6: Identifying Supporting Details**

Why Supporting Details Are Important

Describe three reasons why supporting details are important. (See pages 297–298.)

1. _____
_____
_____

2. _____
_____
_____

3. _____
_____
_____

Card 2   **Chapter 6: Identifying Supporting Details**

How to Find Supporting Details

To identify supporting details in a paragraph, what question should you ask yourself? (See page 298.)

_____
_____

List some signal words that can introduce supporting details. (See page 299.)

_____
_____

Besides signal words, what are two other ways authors indicate supporting details? (See page 299.)

_____
_____

Is every supporting detail introduced by a signal of some sort? (See page 300.)

_____

Card 3   **Chapter 6: Identifying Supporting Details**

How to Write Down Supporting Details

When you write down supporting details, what should you do to make each supporting detail stand out clearly? (See page 300.)

_____

Define *paraphrasing.* (See page 300.)

_____

_____

Why is paraphrasing useful when you are writing down supporting details? (See page 300.)

_____

_____

_____

Card 4　**Chapter 6: Identifying Supporting Details**

How to Mark Supporting Details

How can you make supporting details easier to locate in a paragraph after you have read the paragraph? (See page 300.)

_____

_____

Give three reasons why this is a helpful technique. (See page 300.)

Reason 1: _____

_____

Reason 2: _____

_____

Reason 3: _____

_____

Card 5　**Chapter 6: Identifying Supporting Details**

BENJAMIN FRANKLIN: MAN FOR ALL REASONS

From the *Dallas Morning News*

By Mary L. Sherk

Prepare Yourself to Read

Directions: Do these exercises *before* you read Selection 6-1.

1. First, read and think about the title. What do you already know about Ben Franklin?

_____

_____

2. Next, complete your preview by reading the following:

> Introduction (in *italics*)
> Skim the entire article

On the basis of your preview, what does the selection now seem to be about?

_____

_____

Apply Comprehension Skills

Directions: Do the Annotation Practice Exercises as you read Selection 6-1. Apply the skills from this chapter:

Determine the topic.   When you read a paragraph, ask yourself, "Who or what is this about?"

Locate or formulate the main idea.   As you read, ask yourself, "What is the most important point the author wants me to understand about the topic?"

Identify and list supporting details.   As you read, ask yourself, "What additional information does the author provide to help me understand the main idea completely?" Then, list the supporting details.

BENJAMIN FRANKLIN: MAN FOR ALL REASONS

Benjamin Franklin (1706–1790), whose portrait appears on the U.S. hundred-dollar bill, achieved what few people have done: he was supremely successful in several areas. He excelled as a scientist and inventor; a writer and publisher; a politician, legislator, and diplomat; and a businessman. This dedicated patriot is known, among other things, for flying a kite with a metal key attached in a thunderstorm to prove that lightning is electricity. Although he came from a family of very limited means, he made himself prosperous. And, despite his limited formal schooling, he taught himself four languages. His autobiography is considered one of the greatest autobiographies ever written, and he left a legacy of often-quoted maxims (sayings). Franklin lived a long life, and it was a life well spent.

1   Historians call Benjamin Franklin a jack-of-all-trades and master of many. His interests ranged from statesmanship to soapmaking, book printing to cabbage growing, the rise of tides to the fall of empires. He was the only man to sign all four documents important to the birth of the United States of America.

2   By the time he was 24 years old, he owned a printing business and a newspaper. Twenty years later, he retired from printing to pursue "philosophic studies," at which time he actually began his better-known roles as politician, statesman and diplomat.

3   Born in Boston, he was the youngest son of 17 children from his father's two marriages. Though his brothers were apprenticed to different trades, Ben went to grammar school when he was 8 years old, his father hoping he'd become a clergyman.

4   In his autobiography, he said, "I do not remember when I could not read." The habit of reading everything he could lay his hands on stayed with him all his life.

5   Ben's father couldn't afford to continue his schooling, so at age 10 he was in the family candle-making business, which he did not like. Though he talked of going to sea as one brother had, his father disapproved. At age 12, he apprenticed as a printer to an older brother, and he stayed until he left Boston for Philadelphia.

6   Within six years, he purchased the newspaper where he worked, and, in 1732, he began publishing *Poor Richard's Almanack*. In 1730, he married Deborah Read, whom he met when he

Annotation Practice Exercises

Directions: For each paragraph indicated, in the spaces provided:

- Write the main idea sentence.
- List the supporting details on separate lines.

Doing this will help you remember main ideas and supporting details.

Annotation Exercise

- Main idea sentence of paragraph 1:

_____

_____

- Supporting details

_____

_____

_____

_____

_____

_____

_____

first came to Philadelphia. Though he proposed in 1724, they decided not to marry until he returned from a trip to England. Although he stayed away a year and a half, he sent her one letter.

7   When he came back, she had married someone else, though she never lived with the man or assumed his name. Fortuitously, the man disappeared and reportedly died in the West Indies, so she and Franklin signed a marriage agreement in 1730. They were apart much of their marriage; he was in London or Paris for years at a time. There were four children, two boys and two girls. Son William became governor of New Jersey.

8   Franklin believed "a person's highest duty is to serve others." He discovered or invented many things. He urged sharing "useful knowledge," and education for all, including girls. But he would not patent his ideas or profit from them, preferring that they be used for everyone's comfort and convenience.

9   His inventions were likely to add to his own comfort: a mechanical arm to retrieve books from high shelves, a chair seat lifted to reveal a stepladder, another chair with a foot-operated fan, a combination chair-table. He contrived a way to lock his bedroom door with a cord. When vision blurred with age, he made bifocal spectacle lenses.

10   During 50 years as a Philadelphian, Franklin helped launch the first fire-fighting company, street lighting and paving, a local militia, and the first hospital, and he reorganized the town watch.

11   On the square behind Independence Hall a sign on a building reads: "Curtis Publishing Company. The *Saturday Evening Post* began as Franklin's *Poor Richard's Almanack.*" He cofounded the Philadelphia Academy (now the University of Pennsylvania), the first subscription library, and the American Philosophical Society.

12   Franklin was one of the first to experiment with electricity. He also studied the movement of the Gulf Stream in the Atlantic, and he favored summer daylight-saving time. His stove improved indoor heating. Clearly, Franklin's interests were broad.

13   Politically, Franklin favored local control for Pennsylvania, not control by the absentee Penn family, and he represented the colonies in London in their differences with the crown.

Annotation Exercise

- Main idea sentence of paragraph 8:

_____

_____

- Supporting details

_____

_____

_____

_____

_____

_____

Annotation Exercise

- Main idea sentence of paragraph 12:

_____

_____

- Supporting details

_____

_____

_____

_____

_____

_____

_____

¹⁴   This led to his Revolutionary role, when he drafted a Plan of Union for the colonies. Utilizing wide-ranging interests and talents, he organized the colonial Post Office, went to Canada to seek cooperation against the British, and discussed strategy with General Washington. In 1775, the Continental Congress picked him as postmaster general.

¹⁵   Though he was 81 when the Constitutional Convention convened, Franklin helped draft the Declaration of Independence and negotiate treaties with France. His last five years were spent in his home in Franklin Court.

Benjamin Franklin. 1706–1790.
(Francis G. Mayer/Corbis)

Source: Adapted from Mary L. Sherk, *Dallas Morning News,* July 4, 1999, p. 8G.

Comprehension Quiz

Directions: For each comprehension question below, use information from the selection to determine the correct answer. You may refer to the selection as you answer the questions. Write your answer in the space provided.

True or False

_____ **1.** Benjamin Franklin's formal education ended when he was 16 years old.

_____ **2.** Franklin's role in the Revolution included his drafting of a Plan of Union for the colonies and helping draft the Declaration of Independence.

_____ **3.** Franklin and his wife Deborah Read had 17 children.

_____ **4.** During his 50 years of living in Philadelphia, Franklin helped create its first police department and its first academy for girls.

_____ **5.** Benjamin Franklin served as the third president of the United States.

Multiple-Choice

_____ **6.** A well-known publication of Franklin's was
  a. *Journal of the American Philosophical Society.*
  b. *The Philadelphian* newspaper.
  c. *The Saturday Evening Post.*
  d. *Poor Richard's Almanack.*

_____ **7.** Because he believed that each person had a duty to serve others, Franklin
  a. worked very hard at a young age.
  b. created inventions that were very unusual.
  c. would not patent his ideas or profit from them.
  d. was apprenticed as a printer at age 12 to an older brother.

_____ **8.** Franklin was born in
  a. Philadelphia.
  b. London.
  c. Boston.
  d. the West Indies.

_____ **9.** Although Benjamin Franklin had varied talents, history remembers him most because of his contributions as
  a. a printer.
  b. a diplomat, statesman, and politician.
  c. an inventor.
  d. a city planner and co-founder of the Pennsylvania Academy.

_____ **10.** One reason Franklin achieved so much was that

    a. he received an excellent education at the University of Pennsylvania.

    b. he was apprenticed to several of the best craftsmen in Philadelphia.

    c. he read constantly throughout his life.

    d. the Continental Congress selected him to organize the colonial Post Office and serve as its first postmaster general.

Extend Your Vocabulary by Using Context Clues

Directions: Context clues are words in a sentence that allow the reader to deduce (reason out) the meaning of an unfamiliar word in the sentence. For each vocabulary exercise below, a sentence from the reading selection containing an important word (*italicized, like this*) is quoted first. Next, there is an additional sentence using the word in the same sense and providing another context clue. Use the context clues from *both* sentences to deduce the meaning of the italicized word. *Be sure the answer you choose makes sense in both sentences.* If you discover that you must use a dictionary to confirm an answer choice, remember that the meaning you select must still fit the context of *both* sentences.

Pronunciation key: ă pat   ā pay   âr care   ä father   ĕ pet   ē be   ĭ pit   ī tie
îr pier   ŏ pot   ō toe   ô paw   oi noise   ou out   ŏŏ took   ōō boot   ŭ cut
yōō abuse   ûr urge   th thin   *th* this   hw which   zh vision   ə about
Stress mark: ′

_____ **1.** Historians call Benjamin Franklin a *jack-of-all-trades* and master of many.

An apartment handyman must be a *jack-of-all-trades* who can do electrical and plumbing repairs as well as deal with many other types of problems.

jack-of-all-trades (jăk əv ôl trādz)

    a. unemployed or laid-off worker

    b. person who can do many different kinds of work

    c. inventor

    d. person who has specialized training in a particular craft

_____ **2.** At age 12, he *apprenticed* as a printer to an older brother, and he stayed until he left Boston for Philadelphia.

My sister *apprenticed* with a master stone carver for three years, and eventually she learned enough to do some of the carving on the new cathedral.

apprenticed (ə prĕn′ tĭsd)

    a. worked with a skilled person in order to learn a trade

    b. ignored by

    c. influenced by a well-known person

    d. retained by a specialist

_____ **3.** *Fortuitously,* the man disappeared and reportedly died in the West Indies, so she and Franklin signed a marriage agreement in 1730.

The copilot had a heart attack during the flight, but *fortuitously,* one of the passengers was a doctor who could provide emergency medical treatment.

fortuitously (fôr tōō′ ĭ təs lē)

a. happening by chance

b. done by force

c. happening by design

d. unfortunately

_____ **4.** But he would not *patent* his ideas or profit from them, preferring they be used for everyone's comfort and convenience.

Both inventors developed a new type of modem, but the one who was able to *patent* it first was the one who made millions of dollars from it.

patent (păt′ nt)

a. to be denied the legal right to make, use, and sell an invention for a set period of time

b. to refuse the legal right to make, use, or sell an invention for a set period of time

c. to obtain the legal right to make, use, and sell an invention for a set period of time

d. to ignore the legal right to make, use, or sell an invention for a set period of time

_____ **5.** He *contrived* a way to lock his bedroom door with a cord.

Because the prisoners of war were forbidden to speak to each other, they *contrived* several ways to communicate secretly.

contrived (kən trīvd′)

a. failed at

b. were tricked or deceived by

c. were praised for

d. devised; planned with cleverness

_____ **6.** During 50 years as a Philadelphian, Franklin helped *launch* the first fire-fighting company, the first fire insurance company, street lighting and paving, a local militia, and the first hospital, and he reorganized the town watch.

Their plan was to *launch* a new computer magazine that was unlike anything that had been published before.

launch (lônch)

a.   sell to investors

b.   bring into existence; introduce to the public

c.   advertise

d.   put into orbit

_____   **7.**   During 50 years as a Philadelphian, Franklin helped launch the first fire-fighting company, the first fire insurance company, street lighting and paving, a local *militia,* and the first hospital, and he reorganized the town watch.

In colonial days, the townsmen who were members of the local *militia* had no uniforms, and each man had to supply his own rifle.

militia (mə lĭsh´ ə)

a.   highly trained military unit

b.   army consisting of highly trained volunteers

c.   army composed of ordinary citizens rather than professional soldiers

d.   officers in an army

_____   **8.**   Politically, Franklin favored local control for Pennsylvania, not by the *absentee* Penn family, and he represented the colonies in London in their differences with the crown.

Apartment buildings with a landlord on-site are usually better managed than those with *absentee* landlords.

absentee (ăb sən tē´)

a.   completely incompetent; incapable

b.   arrogant; conceited

c.   informal

d.   not in residence; not present

_____   **9.**   This led to his Revolutionary role, when he *drafted* a Plan of Union for the colonies.

The attorney *drafted* a will for the couple and sent it to them for their approval.

drafted (drăft´ ēd)

a.   reviewed

b.   prepared a final copy

c.   drew up a preliminary version of

d.   forced to join the military

———— **10.** Though he was 81 when the Constitutional Convention *convened,* Franklin helped draft the Declaration of Independence and negotiate treaties with France.

The congregation of the church *convened* last night to discuss building the new, half-million-dollar educational wing.

convened (kən vēnd′)

a. prayed silently

b. assembled formally

c. canceled

d. met in private

SELECTION **6-1**

Newspaper Article

Collaboration Option

Respond in Writing

Directions: Refer to the selection as needed to answer the essay-type questions below.

Option for collaboration: Your instructor may direct you to work with other students—in other words, to work *collaboratively.* In that case, you should form groups of three or four students as directed by your instructor and work together to complete the exercises. After your group discusses each item and agrees on the answer, have a group member record it. Every member of your group should be able to explain all of your group's answers.

1. On the basis of what you learned about Benjamin Franklin in the selection, what profession do you think he might be in if he were alive today? Explain why you think that.

———————————————————————————

———————————————————————————

———————————————————————————

2. In addition to his many talents and abilities, what personal qualities (such as patience) must Franklin have had in order to have been so successful in so many ways?

———————————————————————————

———————————————————————————

———————————————————————————

———————————————————————————

3. Think of at least one person in the last 100 years who was (or is) a versatile and multitalented person like Franklin. Tell who the person is, and tell the talents and achievements of the person.

_____

_____

_____

_____

_____

_____

_____

4. Overall main idea. What is the overall main idea the author wants the reader to understand about Ben Frankin? Answer this question in one sentence. Be sure that your overall main idea sentence includes the topic (*Ben Franklin*) and tells the overall most important point about it.

_____

_____

_____

Read More about It on the World Wide Web

To learn more about the topic of this selection, visit these websites or use your favorite search engine (such as Yahoo ®). Whenever you go to *any* website, it is a good idea to evaluate it critically. Are you getting good information—information that is accurate, complete, and up-to-date? Who sponsors the website? How easy is it to use the features of the website?

http://library.thinkquest.org/22254/about.htm
Ben Franklin: An Enlightened American *is an educational and research site. Intended for use by students of all ages, the site uses integrated links within the text to provide definitions of related words and descriptions of important events and people. This website touches on all aspects of Franklin's life.*

http://sln.fi.edu/franklin/
This is a Franklin Institute Online *website. Click on links to learn about Ben Franklin and see how his ideas are still relevant today.*

COMMUNICATION CLOSE-UP AT BEN AND JERRY'S HOMEMADE

From *Business Communication Today*

By Courtland Bovée and John Thill

Prepare Yourself to Read

Directions: Do these exercises *before* you read Selection 6-2.

1. First, read and think about the title. What do you already know about Ben and Jerry's as a company? What do you know about its ice cream?

_____

_____

2. Next, complete your preview by reading the following:

Introduction (in *italics*)
First paragraph (paragraph 1)
First sentence of each paragraph
Last paragraph (paragraph 10)

On the basis of your preview, what does the selection seem to be about?

_____

_____

Apply Comprehension Skills

Directions: Do the Annotation Practice Exercises as you read Selection 6-2.

Determine the topic. When you read a paragraph, ask yourself, "Who or what is this about?"

Locate or formulate the main idea. As you read, ask yourself, "What is the most important point these authors want me to understand about the topic?"

Identify and list supporting details. As you read, ask yourself, "What additional information do the authors provide to help me understand the main idea completely?" Then, list the supporting details.

COMMUNICATION CLOSE-UP AT BEN AND JERRY'S HOMEMADE

Cherry Garcia. Phish Food. New York Super Fudge Chunk. Chunky Monkey. Southern Pecan Pie. Wavy Gravy. Chubby Hubby. Totally Nuts. Bovinity Divinity. Chocolate Chip Cookie Dough. Orange and Cream. Different types of desserts? No—just some of the 50 great ice cream, frozen yogurt, and sorbet products made by Ben and Jerry's Homemade. Anyone who has ever tasted these premium, all-natural products knows that this is no ordinary ice cream. Neither is Ben and Jerry's an ordinary company. There really is a Ben, and there really is a Jerry.

The company was started by two friends in a renovated gas station. After its first year of business, the company began giving away ice cream cones one day a year at all of its "scoop shops." In 2000 it gave away a million ice cream cones worldwide. That alone tells you what an unusual company it is!

Over the years, Ben and Jerry's has donated millions of dollars to causes related to children and families, disadvantaged groups, and the environment. A board of nine employees decides the causes to which the funds will be donated. In April 2000, Ben and Jerry's Homemade was acquired by Unilever, one of the world's largest multinational consumer products companies. (Unilever makes personal care and home products, as well as food products. Among other things, it is the largest ice cream producer in the world.) Although owned by Unilever, Ben and Jerry's will remain an independent company. By combining their company with Unilever, Ben and Jerry hope "to create an even more dynamic, socially positive ice cream business with global reach." Not bad for a company that started in an old gas station!

The selection below tells Ben and Jerry's fascinating story and describes one of the keys to this unusual company's success.

---

1   Down at the factory in Waterbury, Vermont, they're known as "the boys." They are Ben Cohen and Jerry Greenfield, arguably America's most famous purveyors of ice cream and certainly two of America's most colorful entrepreneurs. They've been friends since seventh grade and business partners since 1978, when they opened their first scoop shop, using techniques gleaned from a $5 correspondence course on how to make ice cream. Their firm, Ben & Jerry's Homemade, sold more than $76 million worth of super premium ice cream in 1990 and employs around 300 people, give or take a few, depending on the season.

2   Ben and Jerry have stong personalities and strong opinions. They believe that work should be fun, or else it isn't worth doing. They also believe in helping the unfortunate, protecting the environment, and treating people fairly. They want their company to be a happy, humanitarian place where everybody feels good about coming to work and producing a top-notch product.

3   One person who helps the company accomplish this goal is Maureen Martin, the coordinator of employee communication. Her job is to see

Annotation Practice Exercises

Directions: For each paragraph indicated, in the spaces provided:

• Write the main idea sentence.

• List the supporting details on separate lines.

Doing this will help you remember main ideas and supporting details.

Annotation Exercise

• Main idea sentence of paragraph 1:

_____

_____

_____

• Supporting details:

_____

_____

_____

_____

that everyone knows what's going on at the company's two production plants, five company-owned retail outlets, and 82 franchised scoop shops. The theory at Ben & Jerry's is that sharing information builds trust and helps people do their jobs better. To that end, Martin publishes a monthly newsletter and organizes staff meetings, which are held every six to eight weeks at each of the two factories. Additionally, she handles internal publicity for a variety of special events and activities.

4   The staff meetings are an important channel of communication because they give all the employees a chance to interact directly with top management. The feedback gives Ben and Jerry insight into what the employees are thinking. According to Martin, the meetings combine the qualities of a "pep rally" and a financial briefing. Most are designed to convey information about Ben & Jerry's performance and operating plans, but some are held to deal with a specific agenda or to obtain employee input. "We sometimes break up into small discussion groups so that employees can express their opinions," Martin explains. "One meeting was held to discuss the topic of improving employee communications. We talked about what was working and what wasn't and possible solutions." Martin tries to keep the style of the meetings light and upbeat, and she uses a variety of media—sound effects, videotapes, and overhead transparencies.

5   To publicize special events, Martin relies on a combination of written and oral communication. She might send out a memo, post notices on bulletin boards, run an article in the newsletter, and pass the word informally as she talks with people about various matters. The repetition in various formats gives the message maximum exposure and builds anticipation.

6   The special events are, in themselves, a form of communication in that they express management's concept of a desirable working environment. Many of the events are dreamed up by the Joy Gang, an official, but informal, group headed by Jerry Greenfield himself, whose title is now Minister of Joy. (Greenfield has partially distanced himself from day-to-day management.) The committee's function is to spread cheer and build camaraderie. One of the group's recent events was Elvis Day, held in honor of Presley's

Ben Cohen and Jerry Greenfield, founders of Ben and Jerry's Homemade, enjoying some of their company's ice cream. *(Christine Boyd/FSP/Gamma Liaison)*

_____

_____

_____

_____

Annotation Exercise

•   Main idea sentence of paragraph 4:

_____

_____

_____

•   Supporting details:

_____

_____

_____

_____

_____

_____

_____

_____

_____

birthday. "A bunch of people dressed up like Elvis, and we played Elvis tunes all day long," Martin explains. "We even served Elvis's favorite food at lunch." At various times, the Joy Gang has also hired a masseuse to take the kinks out of weary production workers, rented a synchroenergizer to induce mental tranquillity, and purchased roller skates so that employees would not wear themselves out running around.

7   In many respects, actions speak louder than words at Ben & Jerry's. Plenty of companies publicize their commitment to community service, but very few match Ben & Jerry's financial contribution to charity. The firm donates 7.5 percent of its annual pretax profits to a foundation that funds environmentalists, the disadvantaged, and children.

8   Actions also telegraph Ben & Jerry's commitment to an egalitarian work environment: the open office arrangement, the bright colors, the pictures of cows and fields hanging on warehouse walls, the employee committees (so many that Maureen Martin is publishing a directory), the casual clothes, the first-name relationships, the compressed pay scale that keeps executive salaries in balance with lower-level compensation, the free health club memberships for everyone, the upcoming on-site day-care facility. And the free ice cream. Three pints a day per person. Now that's communication at its best!

9   Whether you work for a free-spirited company like Ben & Jerry's or a more conventional organization, you will discover that when all is said and done, what's done is more important that what's said. Action is the ultimate form of communication. It speaks with an unmistakable voice. The diaper changing tables in both the men's and women's rooms at Ben & Jerry's say more about the company's commitment to family values than any pronouncement in a policy manual possibly could. At the same time, when Ben Cohen tears his remaining hair and laments that the company is growing too fast, the employees give each other knowing looks and hustle to meet production targets. They've noticed that for

Annotation Exercise

• Main idea sentence of paragraph 6:

_____

_____

_____

• Supporting details:

_____

_____

_____

_____

_____

_____

_____

a man who hates growth, Ben sure sells a lot of ice cream.

10   Perhaps a certain amount of inconsistency between words and actions is unavoidable. Life is full of ambiguities, and most of us have mixed feelings about things from time to time. We don't always say what we really mean; in fact, we don't always *know* what we really mean. Under the circumstances, no wonder we sometimes have trouble figuring out all the surface and underlying messages that we send and receive. Unraveling the mysteries of communication requires perception, concentration, and an appreciation of the communication process.

Source: Courtland Bovée and John Thill, "Communication Close-Up at Ben & Jerry's Homemade," in *Business Communication Today,* 4th ed., McGraw-Hill, New York, 1996, pp. 28–30. Reproduced with permission of McGraw-Hill.

Comprehension Quiz

Directions: For each comprehension question below, use information from the selection to determine the correct answer. You may refer to the selection as you answer the questions. Write your answer in the space provided.

True or False

_____ **1.** Ben and Jerry feel that communication is less important than other aspects of their business.

_____ **2.** Ben and Jerry personally handle all the communication responsibilities for their company.

_____ **3.** The authors of this selection believe that unraveling the mystery of communication requires perception, concentration, and luck.

_____ **4.** The authors state that we do not always say what we really mean, and that we do not always know what we really mean.

_____ **5.** The authors' position is that action is the ultimate form of communication.

Multiple-Choice

_____ **6.** Ben Cohen and Jerry Greenfield
   a. were experienced in the ice cream business before they started their own company.
   b. became friends after college and then became business partners later.
   c. started their business in Maine.
   d. none of the above.

_____ **7.** Ways of facilitating communication at Ben and Jerry's Homemade include
   a. monthly newsletters and employee committees.
   b. staff meetings every 6 to 8 weeks.
   c. special events dreamed up by the "Joy Gang."
   d. all of the above.

_____ **8.** The authors describe Ben and Jerry's Homemade as a business that is
   a. pleasant but conventional.
   b. in need of revitalization.
   c. free-spirited.
   d. an example of poor business communication.

_____ **9.** Special activities at Ben and Jerry's Homemade have included
   a. having an "Elvis Day."
   b. buying roller skates for employees.
   c. hiring a masseuse for the employees.
   d. all of the above.

_____ **10.** Employees at Ben and Jerry's have expressed a need for

    a. a free health club.

    b. more casual dress at work.

    c. brighter, more pleasant working conditions.

    d. none of the above.

SELECTION **6-2**

Business

Extend Your Vocabulary by Using Context Clues

Directions: Context clues are words in a sentence that allow the reader to deduce (reason out) the meaning of an unfamiliar word in that sentence. For each vocabulary item below, a sentence from the selection containing an important word (*italicized, like this*) is quoted first. Next, there is an additional sentence using the word in the same sense and providing another context clue. Use the context clues from *both* sentences to deduce the meaning of the italicized word. *Be sure the answer you choose makes sense in both sentences.* If you discover that you must use a dictionary to confirm an answer choice, remember that the meaning you select must still fit the context of *both* sentences. To indicate your answer, write the letter in the space provided.

Pronunciation key: ă pat ā pay âr care ä father ĕ pet ē be ĭ pit
ī tie îr pier ŏ pot ō toe ô paw oi noise ou out ŏŏ took ōō boot
ŭ cut yōō abuse ûr urge th thin *th* this hw which zh vision
ə about
Stress mark: ʹ

_____ **1.** They are Ben Cohen and Jerry Greenfield, *arguably* America's most famous purveyors of ice cream.

AIDS is *arguably* the most dangerous health crisis facing the world today.

arguably (arʹ gyōō əb lē) means:

    a. by quarreling or bickering

    b. by defeating someone in a dispute

    c. illogically

    d. able to be supported with reasons in an argument

_____ **2.** They are Ben Cohen and Jerry Greenfield, arguably America's most famous *purveyors* of ice cream.

British firms take great pride in serving as *purveyors* of fine goods to the royal family.

purveyors (pər vā′ ərz) means:

a. people who supply or furnish something

b. people who purify something

c. people who invent something

d. people who ship or send something

3. They opened their first scoop shop using techniques *gleaned* from a $5 correspondence course on how to make ice cream.

By searching through state and local records and old newspaper clippings, Martha *gleaned* some information about her great-grandparents.

gleaned (glēnd) means:

a. sneaked or stole

b. learned in depth

c. collected bit by bit

d. misinterpreted

4. They want their company to be a happy, *humanitarian* place where everybody feels good about coming to work and producing a top-notch product.

The Red Cross is perhaps the most famous *humanitarian* organization in the world.

humanitarian (hyo͞o măn ĭ târ′ ē ən) means:

a. devoted to human welfare

b. devoted to improving working conditions

c. pertaining to life in poor countries

d. devoted to helping people during disasters

5. The repetition in various formats gives the message maximum *exposure* and builds anticipation.

Political candidates often appear on local and national talk shows in order to gain as much free public *exposure* as possible.

exposure (ĭk spō′ zher) means:

a. being subjected to light

b. being subjected to humiliation

c. being liked

d. being made known

6. The committee's function is to spread cheer and build *camaraderie.*

The *camaraderie* among the members of the swimming team lasted long after they had all finished college.

camaraderie (kä mə rä′ də rē) means:

a. happiness

b. skill or talent

c. goodwill among friends

d. competitiveness

———— **7.** At various times, the Joy Gang has also hired a *masseuse* to take the kinks out of weary production workers.

A *masseuse* accompanied the United States women's track team to the Olympics to treat their sore muscles.

masseuse (mă soez′) means:

a. woman who monitors employees' health

b. woman trained in relaxation techniques

c. woman who trains athletes

d. woman who gives massages professionally

———— **8.** Actions also telegraph Ben and Jerry's commitment to an *egalitarian* work environment: the open office arrangement, the employee committees, the casual clothes, the first-name relationships, the compressed pay-scale that keeps executive salaries in balance with lower-level compensation, and the free health club memberships for everyone.

Community colleges are *egalitarian* institutions that are open to any qualified member of the community.

egalitarian (ĭ găl ĭ târ′ ē ən) means:

a. favoring or advocating equality for all

b. pertaining to things that are not alike

c. favoring certain groups

d. pertaining to education

———— **9.** The diaper changing tables in both the men's and the women's rooms at Ben and Jerry's say more about the company's commitment to family values than any *pronouncement* in a policy manual could.

The surgeon general's *pronouncement* about the dangers of secondhand smoke is proving to be correct.

pronouncement (prə nouns′ mənt) means:

a. formal declaration or statement

b. words articulated clearly

c. guide to pronunciation

d. posted statement of an official or an employer

———— **10.** Life is full of *ambiguities,* and most of us have mixed feelings about things from time to time.

We were puzzled and amused by one of the *ambiguities* in her previous employer's reference letter: "You will be lucky if you can get her to work for you."

ambiguities (ăm bĭ gyōo′ ĭ tēz) means:

a. statements that can cause pain

b. statements that can be interpreted in more than one way

c. statements that can cause frustration

d. statements that are easy to comprehend

Collaboration Option

Respond in Writing

Directions: Refer to the selection as needed to answer the essay-type questions below.

Option for collaboration: Your instructor may direct you to work with other students or, in other words, to work *collaboratively.* In that case, you should form groups of three or four students as directed by your instructor and work together to complete the exercises. After your group discusses each item and agrees on the answer, have a group member record it. Every member of your group should be able to explain all of your group's answers.

1. The authors use Ben and Jerry's Homemade as an illustration of a company with effective communication strategies. Develop a list of the communication techniques and strategies described in the selection. You may paraphrase them (put them in your own words).

_____

_____

_____

_____

_____

_____

2. In your opinion, can socially responsible companies (who care about employees, the environment, and humanitarian causes) be truly profitable? Or is Ben & Jerry's Homemade an exception? Explain why you hold the opinion that you do.

_____

_____

_____

3. Overall main idea. What is the overall main idea the authors want the reader to understand about *Ben and Jerry's* and *effective communication*? Be sure to include the topic in your sentence. Answer this question in one sentence.

_____

_____

_____

_____

_____

_____

_____

Read More about It on the World Wide Web

To learn more about the topic of this selection, visit these websites or use your favorite search engine (such as Yahoo ®). Whenever you go to *any* website, it is a good idea to evaluate it critically. Are you getting good information—information that is accurate, complete, and up-to-date? Who sponsors the website? How easy is it to use the features of the website?

http://benjerry.com
> *This website is the commercial site for Ben and Jerry's Homemade, Inc. Visit this lively website and read descriptions of their flavors and learn about their charitable activities and their innovative business approach.*

SELECTION **6-3**
Economics

FROM *A BEGINNER'S GUIDE TO THE WORLD ECONOMY*

By Randy Charles Epping

Prepare Yourself to Read

Directions: Do these exercises *before* you read Selection 6-3.

1. First, read and think about the title. Do you have any knowledge of the "world economy"? What approach do you think a "beginner's guide" might take?

_____

_____

2. Why do you think it might be important or useful for the average person to know something about the world economy?

_____

_____

_____

3. Next, complete your preview by reading the following:

   Introduction (in *italics*)
   First paragraph (paragraph 1)
   Section headings
   Last paragraph (paragraph 17)
   Diagrams

On the basis of your preview, what three aspects of the Third World will be discussed?

_____

_____

Apply Comprehension Skills

Directions: Do the Annotation Practice Exercises as you read Selection 6-3.

Determine the topic.   When you read a paragraph, ask yourself, "Who or what is this about?"

Locate or formulate the main idea.   As you read, ask yourself, "What is the most important point this author wants me to understand about the topic?"

Identify and list supporting details.   As you read, ask yourself, "What additional information does the author provide to help me understand the main idea completely?" Then, list the supporting details.

331

A BEGINNER'S GUIDE TO THE WORLD ECONOMY

Poverty in Third World countries is exacerbated by natural disasters. In 2000, the worst flooding in 50 years occurred in Mozambique, Africa. Nearly a million people in this poor country were left homeless, and much of the country's crops, roads and bridges were washed away. In the Horn of Africa (Ethiopia, Eritrea, Somalia, and Kenya) as many as 16 million people are at risk of starving because of the most severe drought since the mid-1980s. In all these countries the disasters have also caused widespread disease. What will be the ultimate fate of "third world" countries such as these? How can the poorest of the poor countries survive? This selection will give you a basic understanding of the economic concept of "Third World," the roots of third world poverty, and what can be done to improve the situation.

What Is the Third World?

1   The term *Third World* was based on the idea that the "first" and "second" worlds were made up of the free-market and centrally planned countries with advanced industrial economies. This developed world was seen to include most of the countries of Eastern and Western Europe as well as Australia, New Zealand, Japan, the United States, and Canada.

2   The developing and relatively poor countries that are said to make up the Third World can be divided into three groups: those developing rapidly, those developing moderately, and the poorest few whose economies are not developing at all.

3   At the top of the list of Third World nations are the rapidly developing countries called Newly Industrialized Countries (NIC). Most lists of NICs include Brazil, Argentina, Hong Kong, Israel, Singapore, South Africa, South Korea, Taiwan, and Thailand. These "lucky few" are seen to be on their way to joining the ranks of the advanced economies of the world.

4   The bulk of the Third World consists of a large group of moderately developing economies that includes most of the countries in Africa, Asia, and Latin America. The most populous countries in this group are India, China, Indonesia, and Malaysia, which together comprise more than half of the world's population.

5   At the bottom of this list are the world's poorest countries, found mainly in sub-Saharan Africa, which have so few resources and so little money that it is virtually impossible for them to develop at all. In Somalia and Sudan, for example, there are essentially no natural resources on

Annotation Practice Exercises

Directions: For each paragraph indicated, in the spaces provided:

•   Write the main idea sentence.

•   List the supporting details on separate lines.

Doing this will help you remember main ideas and supporting details.

Annotation Exercise

•   Main idea sentence of paragraph 1:

_____

_____

_____

_____

•   Supporting details:

_____

_____

_____

_____

_____

_____

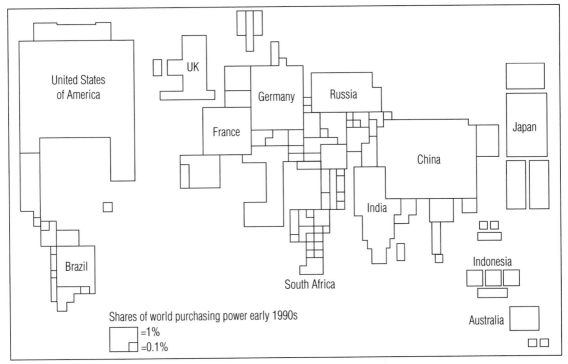

Purchasing power.

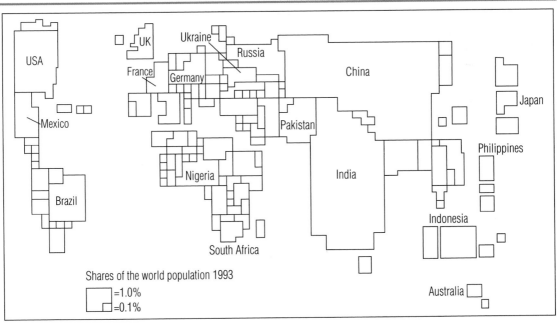

Population.

Source: *A Beginner's Guide to the World Economy*, 2nd ed., 1995, p. XIX.

which to base economic growth. This group is sometimes called the "Fourth World."

6   Although the Third World comprises three quarters of the world's population and 90 percent of the world's population growth, it provides only 20 percent of the world's economic production. And even though the Third World holds much of the world's natural resources—including vast petroleum reserves in Latin America, Asia, and the Middle East—many raw materials from the Third World are shipped abroad for consumption in the world's wealthier and more developed countries.

What Are the Roots of Third World Poverty?

7   Economic and political misjudgment can be blamed for much of the Third World's poverty, but an important factor has also been the population explosion. This caused many developing countries to see their populations double in as little as twenty years. The growth was due mainly to lack of birth control, to improved medical care, and to declining mortality rates.

8   Extreme poverty in the Third World has led many parents to create ever larger families, hoping that their children could work and increase family income. But the economic opportunities were often not available, and unemployed children and their parents ended up moving into already overcrowded Third World cities in a fruitless search for work.

9   By the end of the 1980s, most Third World nations found themselves in a vicious circle of poverty and overpopulation, with no hope in sight. The flood of poor families into major Third World cities put additional strains on the economic infrastructure. Growing urban areas like Bombay, São Paulo, and Shanghai became centers of glaring poverty and unemployment with extensive slums and squatter settlements ringing overgrown and polluted city centers.

10   Saddled with enormous debt payments, hyperinflation, surging populations, and mounting unemployment, many Third World countries in the late 1980s struggled just to keep their economies afloat. In many cases, with no money available for investment, even the infrastructure, such as roads and water systems, literally began to fall apart. The solution for many overburdened Third World

---

Annotation Exercise

- Main idea sentence of paragraph 7:

_____

_____

_____

_____

- Supporting details:

_____

_____

_____

_____

_____

_____

governments was to simply increase debt in order to keep money flowing. But rampant inflation often ends up eroding most of these efforts, creating an ever-widening gap between the Third World's poorest and richest nations.

11   While many economies in Latin America, Africa, and Asia stagnated, the economies of the elite developing countries of the Pacific Rim rose to levels that rivaled Japan's in the 1960s. The success of many Third World countries in growing their way out of poverty can be traced largely to effective economic policy. By efficiently producing and exporting manufactured goods, countries such as Taiwan and Korea earned enormous amounts of money that they have been able to reinvest in their growing economies.

What Can Be Done to Promote Third World Development?

12   Economic growth cannot possibly solve all the problems facing the billions of poor and undernourished people in the Third World, but because of rapid population growth, their problems would almost certainly get worse without it.

13   In order to provide the basic food, clothing, and shelter for their citizens, the underdeveloped Third World countries need to stimulate their stagnating economies caught in a vicious circle of low growth and declining export earnings. One of the first steps in encouraging development would be to reduce the Third World [nations'] debt and supply additional funds to revive their moribund economies. One such plan was formulated in the 1980s by U.S. Treasury Secretary Nicholas Brady, who called for the commercial banks to forgive part of the debt owed to them and to increase new lending. The basic goal of the Brady plan was to encourage economic growth in the Third World.

14   The Brady Plan also called upon the world's major development banks and funds, such as the World Bank and the International Monetary Fund, to provide substantial "project loans" to rebuild the infrastructure in the Third World. In addition, continued bank lending in the form of "adjustment loans" would help with the payment of interest and principal on previous loans. Basically, the Brady Plan called for a net transfer of funds back to the developing countries.

Annotation Exercise

- Main idea sentence of paragraph 11:

  _____

  _____

  _____

  _____

  _____

- Supporting details:

  _____

  _____

  _____

  _____

  _____

15   Another way to promote Third World development is to increase development funds provided by regional development banks with the backing of the developed countries. The Inter-American Development Bank, for example, was set up to provide low-interest loans to developing countries in the Western Hemisphere. In this way, funds from wealthy countries can be channeled to less-developed nations in the form of "development loans."

16   Wealthy creditor governments also have the option of writing off their debt, accepting that it will never be repaid. France, for example, decided in the 1980s that most of its development loans to African countries need not be repaid, in an effort to encourage further economic growth in the region.

17   In order to provide further assistance to Third World debtors, the world's wealthy countries can also work through specialized organizations such as the Lomé Convention, which channels development aid from the European Community to poor Third World countries; and the Paris Club, which helps governments of debtor nations "reschedule" or delay repayment of their loans until their economies are in better shape.

Source: From Randy Charles Epping, *A Beginner's Guide to the World Economy,* Vintage/Random House, New York, 1992, pp. 83–86, 93–94. Copyright © 1992 by Randy Charles Epping. Reprinted by permission of Random House, Inc.

SELECTION **6-3**

Economics

Comprehension Quiz

Directions: For each comprehension question below, use information from the selection to determine the correct answer. You may refer to the selection as you answer the questions. Write your answer in the space provided.

True or False

_____ **1.** The *first* and *second worlds* are defined as the free-market countries and the centrally planned countries with advanced industrial economies.

_____ **2.** The first and second worlds were considered to include most of the countries of eastern and western Europe, Australia, New Zealand, Japan, the United States, and Canada.

_____ **3.** The author believes that the economic problems of Third World countries cannot be solved.

_____ **4.** The Third World can be divided into three groups: countries with rapidly developing economies, countries with moderately developing economies, and countries whose economies are not developing at all.

_____ **5.** The bulk of the Third World consists of a large group of moderately developing countries.

_____ **6.** According to the author, economic growth cannot solve all the problems faced by billions of undernourished people in the Third World.

Multiple-Choice

_____ **7.** Newly Industrialized Countries (NIC) that seem to be on their way to joining the rank of advanced economies include
 a. Somalia and Sudan.
 b. India, China, Indonesia, and Malaysia.
 c. South Africa, South Korea, Taiwan, and Thailand.
 d. all of the above.

_____ **8.** Third World poverty is caused by
 a. economic and political misjudgment.
 b. enormous debt payments.
 c. overpopulation.
 d. all of the above.

_____ **9.** According to the author, Third World development will require that
 a. Third World countries pay off their debts completely.
 b. commercial banks press hard for debt payment from Third World countries.

    c.   wealthy countries discontinue making development loans to Third World countries.

    d.   none of the above.

————— **10.**   The author believes that wealthy creditor nations can aid Third World development by

    a.   agreeing to follow the Brady Plan.

    b.   channeling funds in the form of development loans.

    c.   writing off the debt owed by Third World countries.

    d.   all of the above.

SELECTION **6-3**

Economics

Extend Your Vocabulary by Using Context Clues

Directions: Context clues are words in a sentence that allow the reader to deduce (reason out) the meaning of an unfamiliar word in that sentence. For each vocabulary item below, a sentence from the selection containing an important word *(italicized, like this)* is quoted first. Next, there is an additional sentence using the word in the same sense and providing another context clue. Use the context clues from *both* sentences to deduce the meaning of the italicized word. *Be sure the answer you choose makes sense in both sentences.* If you discover that you must use a dictionary to confirm an answer choice, remember that the meaning you select must still fit the context of *both* sentences. To indicate your answer, write the letter in the space provided.

Pronunciation key: ă pat   ā pay   âr **care**   ä father   ĕ pet   ē be   ĭ pit
ī tie   îr **pier**   ŏ pot   ō toe   ô paw   oi **noise**   ou **out**   ŏŏ **took**   ōō **boot**
ŭ **cut**   yōō abuse   ûr **urge**   th **thin**   *th* **this**   hw **which**   zh vision
ə **about**
Stress mark: ʹ

————— **1.**   The term Third World was based on the idea that the "first" and "second" worlds were made up of the *free-market* and centrally planned countries with advanced industrial economies.

Currently, several countries are struggling to shift from a planned economy which the government controlled to a competitive *free market* economy.

free market (frē mär′ kĭt) means:

    a.   pertaining to a market in which everything is free

    b.   pertaining to an economic system in which resources are allocated by private decisions rather than by the government

    c.   pertaining to a completely unregulated economy

    d.   pertaining to an economic system in which the government is free to do whatever it pleases

_____ **2.** At the top of the list of Third World nations are the rapidly developing countries called Newly *Industrialized* Countries (NIC).

Advanced technology is characteristic of highly *industrialized* countries such as Japan and Germany.

industrialized (ĭn dŭs′ trē ə līzd) means:

a. having highly developed industries that produce goods and services

b. struggling

c. controlled by industries

d. busy or hardworking

_____ **3.** And even though the Third World holds much of the world's natural resources, many raw materials from the Third World are shipped abroad for *consumption* in the world's wealthier and more developed countries.

The level of energy *consumption* in the United States has risen dramatically during the twentieth century.

consumption (kən sŭmp′ shən) means:

a. use of consumer goods or serivces

b. spending

c. ingestion of food

d. debilitating illness

_____ **4.** The flood of poor families into major Third World cities put additional strains on the economic *infrastructure.*

The president pledged to improve two parts of the nation's *infrastructure:* public transportation and health care.

infrastructure (ĭn′ frə strŭk chər) means:

a. government buildings

b. hospitals

c. construction in rural areas

d. basic services and facilities needed by a society

_____ **5.** Saddled with enormous debt payments, *hyperinflation,* surging populations, and mounting unemployment, many Third World countries in the late 1980s struggled just to keep their economies afloat.

When Germany experienced *hyperinflation* in the 1920s, it took a wheelbarrow full of money to buy a single loaf of bread.

hyperinflation (hī pər ĭn flā′ shən) means:

a. decrease in inflation

b. rapid input of air

c. excessive rate of increase in consumer prices

d. rapid accumulation of debt

————   **6.** Saddled with enormous debt payments, hyperinflation, *surging* populations, and mounting unemployment, many Third World countries in the late 1980s struggled just to keep their economies afloat.

When the storm hit, the *surging* sea water flooded the beaches and low-lying areas of the city.

surging (sûrj′ ĭng) means:

a. decreasing

b. angry

c. increasing suddenly

d. poor

————   **7.** But *rampant* inflation often ends up eroding most of these efforts, creating an ever-widening gap between the Third World's poorest and richest nations.

In poverty-stricken areas of many large cities, crime is *rampant.*

rampant (răm′ pənt) means:

a. tolerated or accepted

b. decreasing

c. controlled

d. growing or spreading unchecked

————   **8.** While many economies in Latin America, Africa, and Asia *stagnated,* the economies of the elite developing countries of the Pacific Rim rose to levels that rivaled Japan's in the 1960s.

The actor's career had *stagnated* for several years, but after he starred in a blockbuster movie, he received many offers for leading roles.

stagnated (stăg′ nā təd) means:

a. rotted

b. improved

c. smelled bad

d. failed to change or develop

————   **9.** One of the first steps in encouraging development would be to reduce the Third World nations' debt and supply additional funds to revive their *moribund* economies.

The doctor summoned the family to the bedside of the *moribund* woman when she had only moments to live.

moribund (môr′ ə bŭnd) means:

a. abundant

b. dead

c. almost at the point of death

d. ill

——— **10.** Wealthy *creditor* governments also have the option of writing off their debt, accepting that it will never be repaid.

Because the Newtons charged too many purchases on their credit cards and were unable to pay their debts, they were hounded by countless *creditor* calls and letters.

creditor (krĕd′ ĭ tər) means:
a. one to whom money is owed
b. one who deserves financial credit
c. one who is trustworthy
d. one who owes money

SELECTION **6-3**

Economics

Collaboration Option

Respond in Writing

Directions: Refer to the selection as needed to answer the essay-type questions below.

Option for collaboration: Your instructor may direct you to work with other students or, in other words, to work *collaboratively.* In that case, you should form groups of three or four students as directed by your instructor and work together to complete the exercises. After your group discusses each item and agrees on the answer, have a group member record it. Every member of your group should be able to explain all of your group's answers.

1. The author presents three essential questions that he expects you to be able to answer after you have read this selection. In the spaces below and on the following page, write a complete answer to each question.

What is the Third World?

(Note: Before reading this selection, you may not have known exactly what the *Third World* is. Now that you have read the selection, define this term in your own words.)

_____

_____

_____

_____

_____

What are the roots of Third World poverty?

_____

_____

_____

_____

_____

What can be done to promote Third World development?

_____

_____

_____

_____

_____

2. Could the United States ever become a Third World country? (In other words, are there circumstances that could cause a "first" or "second" world country to become a Third World country?) Explain your answer.

_____

_____

_____

_____

_____

3. Third World countries fall into three categories (newly industrialized countries, moderately developed countries, and the world's poorest countries—"fourth world" countries). What would a Third World country have to do to become a "first" or "second" world country? Is there anything a "fourth world" country could do to improve its situation?

_____

_____

_____

_____

_____

_____

_____

4. Which two countries have the greatest purchasing power? (Use the diagram on page 333 to answer this question.)

_____

5. Overall main idea. What is the overall main idea the author wants the reader to understand about the Third World and its economy? Answer this question in one sentence. Be sure that your overall main idea sentence includes the topic (*the Third World and its economy*) and tells the overall most important point about it.

_____

_____

_____

_____

_____

_____

_____

_____

Read More about It on the World Wide Web

To learn more about the topic of this selection, visit these websites or use your favorite search engine (such as Yahoo ©). Whenever you go to *any* website, it is a good idea to evaluate it critically. Are you getting good information—information that is accurate, complete, and up-to-date? Who sponsors the website? How easy is it to use the features of the website?

http://alcazar.com/wwwvl_idc/
> *This is the* World Wide Web Virtual Library: International Development Cooperation *website. It has many links, reports, and articles pertaining to world economy and development.*

http://www.wcinet.com/th/News/101798/National/127847.htm
> *This is a short article entitled, "U.N. Blames Poverty on Policies, Stinginess."*

© *PhotoDisc*

C H A P T E R

7

Recognizing Authors' Writing Patterns

CHAPTER OBJECTIVES

In this chapter you will learn the answers to these questions:

- What is meant by authors' writing patterns?

- Why is it helpful to be aware of writing patterns?

- How can I recognize list, sequence, definition, comparison-contrast, and cause-effect patterns when I read?

- What are mixed patterns?

- How can I recognize each writing pattern?

SKILLS

Patterns of Writing

- What Are Authors' Writing Patterns?

- Why Is Recognizing Writing Patterns Important?

Recognizing Authors' Writing Patterns

- List Pattern

- Sequence Pattern

- Definition Pattern

- Comparison-Contrast Pattern

- Cause-Effect Pattern

- Mixed Patterns

A Word about Standardized Reading Tests: Writing Patterns

CREATING YOUR SUMMARY

Developing Chapter Review Cards

READINGS

The more you read, the more you'll know.
The more you know, the farther you'll go.

Dr. Seuss

If you don't know where you're going, you may end up somewhere else.

PATTERNS OF WRITING

KEY TERM
Writing Patterns

Ways authors organize the information they present. Writing patterns are also known as *organizational patterns, patterns of development, rhetorical patterns* and *thinking patterns.*

In this chapter you will learn another skill to help you improve your reading comprehension: recognizing authors' patterns of writing. **Writing patterns** are authors' ways of organizing information they present. You may hear writing patterns referred to as *organizational patterns, patterns of development, rhetorical patterns,* and *thinking patterns.* These are all names for the same thing.

What Are Authors' Writing Patterns?

All of us use certain patterns to organize our thoughts in ways that seem logical to us. When people write, they use these same patterns to organize information in ways that seem logical to them. If you can identify the pattern a writer is using and "think along" with the author as you read, then you will find it easier to comprehend what he or she is saying. The specific pattern an author uses depends on the relationship among the ideas he or she wants to emphasize. In this chapter you will be introduced to five writing patterns commonly used by textbook authors.

- List
- Sequence
- Definition
- Comparison-contrast
- Cause-effect

You will also be introduced to what are called *mixed patterns,* a combination of two or more patterns in the same paragraph or passage.

It is important for you to understand that, as mentioned above, the patterns that authors use are the same thinking patterns that you use every day. The box on page 348 gives examples of how college students might use these patterns in typical comments they make. You use these patterns yourself when you speak or write, but you still may not be aware of them when you read. This chapter will show you how to recognize the patterns when you read.

347

EXAMPLES OF THINKING PATTERNS IN EVERYDAY COMMENTS

"I'm taking four courses this semester: history, psychology, reading, and math." **(list)**

"I have a history paper due on Monday, a math quiz on Wednesday, a vocabulary quiz in reading on Thursday morning, and a psychology test Thursday afternoon!" **(sequence)**

"To me, success means always giving your best effort, even if the results aren't perfect." **(definition)**

"Psychology focuses on the behavior of the individual, but sociology focuses on human behavior in groups." **(comparison-contrast)**

"When I stick to my study schedule, I learn more, do better on tests, and feel less stress." **(cause-effect)**

Why Is Recognizing Writing Patterns Important?

Recognizing authors' writing patterns as you read provides several advantages:

- **Improved comprehension.**   You will comprehend more because you will be able to follow the writer's ideas more accurately and more efficiently.

- **More accurate predictions.**   As soon as you identify a pattern, you can make predictions about what is likely to come next in a paragraph. As you learned in Chapter 2, effective readers are active readers who make logical predictions.

- **Easier memorization.**   You can memorize information more efficiently when you understand the way it is organized. If you can grasp an author's pattern of organization, you will not only learn the information more quickly but also retain it more easily.

- **Improvement in your own writing.**   Using these patterns yourself will enable you to write better, more organized paragraphs. For example, you can write better answers on essay tests when you use appropriate patterns to organize the information.

RECOGNIZING AUTHORS' WRITING PATTERNS

Comprehension Monitoring Question for Recognizing Authors' Writing Patterns

"What pattern did the author use to organize the main idea and the supporting details?"

Five common writing patterns are described below, with textbook excerpts that illustrate each pattern. As you may already know, every pattern has certain words and phrases that are associated with it and serve as signals of it. Moreover, the main idea sentence often contains clues about which pattern is being used. As you read, ask yourself, "What pattern did the author use to organize the main idea and supporting details?"

List pattern.
(Stone/Bruce Rogovin)

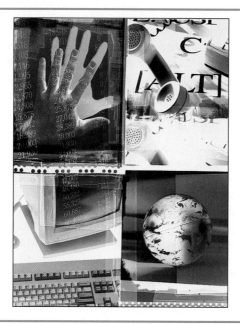

List Pattern

As its name indicates, the **list pattern** (sometimes called a *listing pattern*) presents a list of items in no specific order. The order of the items is not important. If the items listed in the paragraph were presented in a different order or rearranged, it would not matter.

Clues in a paragraph that typically indicate a listing pattern are *and, also, another, moreover, in addition,* and words such as *first, second, third, fourth, last,* and *finally.* Sometimes authors use numbers (1, 2, 3) or letters *(a, b, c),* even though the order is not important. Watch for words or numbers that announce *categories (two types, five ways, several kinds).* Sometimes bullets (•) or asterisks (*) are used to set off individual items in a list. Their purpose is to ensure that the reader will notice each separate item as well as the total number of items. It is important to remember that your task is to identify *all* the items in the list, even when not all of them (or perhaps any of them) are "signaled."

Here is a paragraph from an economics textbook. The topic is *the financing of corporate activity.* The first sentence states the main idea: *Generally speaking, corporations finance their activity in three different ways.* The authors have listed details that help you understand more about this main idea. Notice that these details are in no special order. As you read this paragraph, ask yourself, "What are the *three different ways* that corporations finance their activity?"

Generally speaking, corporations finance their activity in three different ways. First, a very large portion of a corporation's activity is financed internally out of undistributed corporate profits. Second, like individuals or unincorporated businesses, corporations may borrow from financial institutions. For example, a small corporation which wants to build a new plant or warehouse may obtain the funds from a commercial bank, a savings and loan institution, or an insurance company. Also, unique to corporations, common stocks and bonds can be issued.

Source: Campbell McConnell and Stanley Brue, *Economics: Principles, Problems, and Policies,* McGraw-Hill, New York, 1990, p. 110.

Stop and Annotate

Go back to the textbook excerpt above. Underline or highlight the words that signal the items in the list. Then number each supporting detail.

In this paragraph, the authors use the phrase *three different ways* and the clue words *first, second,* and *also* to signal that the reader should expect a list of three supporting details: three ways of financing corporate activities. The order in which the items are listed is not important. What is important is that there are three different ways, and what those ways are.

The next excerpt is from a health and fitness textbook. It illustrates the listing pattern in a very obvious way: the items in the list are numbered. The topic of the paragraph is *signs of alcoholism,* and its implied main idea (which must be formulated by the reader) is: *The diagnosis of alcoholism is often imprecise and difficult for nonprofessionals to make, but there are certain changes in behavior that can warn of possible alcoholism.* On the basis of the topic and the main idea, what do you predict will be listed?

Signs of Alcoholism

The diagnosis of alcoholism is not something that can be precise, and it is often difficult for nonprofessionals to make. The disease carries such a stigma that the alcoholic, friends, and family often postpone seeking treatment. Meanwhile, it is not unusual for the alcoholic to deny the problem and rationalize continued drinking. Certain changes in behavior that warn of possible alcoholism include:

1. Surreptitious, secretive drinking
2. Morning drinking (unless that behavior is not unusual in the person's peer group)
3. Repeated, conscious attempts at abstinence
4. Blatant, indiscriminate use of alcohol
5. Changing beverages in an attempt to control drinking
6. Having five or more drinks daily
7. Having two or more blackouts while drinking

Source: Martin Levy, Mark Dignan, and Janet Shirreffs, *Targeting Wellness: The Core,* McGraw-Hill, New York, 1992, p. 251.

Stop and Annotate

Go back to the textbook excerpt above. Underline or highlight the clues that signal a list.

At the end of this paragraph, the list of warnings of possible alcoholism is actually set off from the text, indicated by a colon (:), and announced by the phrase *Certain changes in behavior that warn of possible alcoholism include . . . .* The topic *signs of alcoholism* in the heading and the words *certain changes* in the main idea sentence help readers predict that a list will be given. The authors list seven supporting details (behavioral changes) and number these details even though they are not in any particular order. The numbers are included to make sure that the reader notices each separate item. (Numbering items in a list is referred to as *enumeration.*)

Sequence pattern
(Stone/Rich Iwasaki)

Sequence Pattern

KEY TERM
Sequence Pattern

A list of items presented in a specific order because the order is important.
The sequence pattern is also known as *time order, chronological order, a process, or a series.*

The **sequence pattern** presents a list of items *in a specific order* because the order is important. The sequence pattern is a type of list, but it differs from a simple list because the order of the items is significant. A very common type of sequence is based on occurrence of events in time, and therefore a sequence pattern is often called *time order* or *chronological order.* The sequence pattern is also known as *a process* or *a series.* Sets of directions are examples of sequences that students encounter daily.

Words that signal a sequence pattern include *first, second, third, then, next,* and *finally.* Words that refer to time, such as dates and phrases like *during the eighteenth century* or *in the last decade,* may also signal sequences. Watch also for enumeration (1, 2, 3, etc.), letters (*a, b, c,* etc.), and signal words such as *sequence, steps, stages, phases, progression,* and *series.*

Following is an excerpt in which authors use a sequence pattern to show the order in which certain events occur. The topic of this paragraph is *the alcohol continuum.* Read the paragraph and notice the list of details and the order in which they are given.

The Alcohol Continuum

Alcoholism is a progressive disease that develops as a series of stages through which any drinker may pass. At one end of the spectrum is occasional and moderate social drinking with family or friends on special occasions. At the other end is long-term, frequent, uncontrollable drinking with severe physical, psychological, and social complications. The full continuum can be summarized as follows:

1. **Occasional drinker** drinks in small quantities only on special occasions.
2. **Light drinker** drinks regularly in small and nonintoxicating quantities.
3. **Social drinker** drinks regularly in moderate and nonintoxicating quantities.
4. **Problem drinker** drinks to intoxication with no pattern to episodes, gets drunk without intending to or realizing it.
5. **Binge drinker** drinks heavily in recurrent episodes, often brought on by disturbances in work, home, or social life.
6. **Excessive drinker** experiences frequent episodes of uncontrollable drinking affecting work, family, and social relationships.
7. **Chronic alcoholic** is in serious trouble from long-term, frequent, and uncontrollable drinking; experiences physical complications including organic dysfunction, tolerance, and dependence; and develops severe work, home, and social problems.

Source: Martin Levy, Mark Dignan, and Janet Shirreffs, *Targeting Wellness: The Core,* McGraw-Hill, New York, 1992, pp. 250–256.

Stop and Annotate

Go back to the textbook excerpt above. Underline or highlight the clues that signal a sequence.

The details in this paragraph are numbered, announced by a colon, and clearly listed after the phrase *can be summarized as follows.* But there are other clues indicating that a sequence pattern is being used: the words *progressive, continuum, series of stages,* and *spectrum.* In this paragraph, the order of the information is obviously important.

Now read this excerpt from a music textbook, in which the author also uses the sequence pattern. Notice the dates that are associated with important events in the Beatles' career.

The Beatles

The Beatles—the singer-guitarists Paul McCartney, John Lennon, and George Harrison, and the drummer Ringo Starr—have been the most influential performing group in the history of rock. Their music, hairstyle, dress, and lifestyle were imitated all over the world, resulting in a phenomenon known as Beatlemania. All four Beatles were born during the early 1940s in Liverpool, England, and dropped out of school in their teens to devote themselves to rock. Lennon and McCartney, the main songwriters of the group, began working together in 1956 and were joined by Harrison about two years later. In 1962 Ringo Starr became their new drummer. The group gained experience by performing in Hamburg, Germany, and in Liverpool, a port to which sailors brought the latest American rock, rhythm-and-blues, and country-and-western records. In 1961, the Beatles made their first record, and by 1963 they were England's top rock group. In 1964, they triumphed in the United States, breaking attendance records everywhere and dominating the record market. Audiences often became hysterical, and the police had to protect the Beatles from their fans. Beatle dolls, wigs, sweatshirts, and jackets flooded the market. Along with a steady flow of successful records, the Beatles made several hit movies: *A Hard Day's Night, Help!* and *Yellow Submarine.*

Source: Roger Kamien, *Music: An Appreciation,* 5th ed., McGraw-Hill, New York, 1992, p. 608.

Stop and Annotate

Go back to the textbook excerpt above. Underline or highlight the clues that signal a sequence.

The details supporting the main idea—that the Beatles have been the most influential performing group in the history of rock—are given in chronological order: the order in which they occurred. The author uses dates throughout the paragraph to tell when each important event occurred. In addition, the phrases *were born during the early 1940s* and *dropped out of school in their teens* indicate the sequence of events in the Beatles' history.

Definition Pattern

The **definition pattern** presents the meaning of an important term that is discussed throughout the passage. The details in the rest of the paragraph discuss or illustrate the term.

Definitions are easy to identify because the terms being defined often appear in **bold print,** *italics,* or color. Moreover, they are typically introduced by signal words: *is, is defined as, means, is known as, refers to, the term, is called,* and so forth.

Sometimes an author will use a synonym (a word or phrase with a similar meaning) in order to define a term. The synonym will be signaled by words such as *or, in other words,* or *that is.* Take, for example, the sentence, "Many women perceive a **glass ceiling,** or barrier of subtle discrimination, that keeps them from the top position in business." The term that is being defined (glass ceiling) appears in bold print. The word *or* introduces words that define the meaning of glass ceiling: a "barrier of subtle discrimination."

Also, definitions can be signaled by certain punctuation marks. All the examples below define *anorexia nervosa.* Use the punctuation clues to help you find the definition.

- **Commas (,)**
  Anorexia nervosa, an eating disorder that can lead to starvation, occurs most often in teenage girls.
  Teenage girls are the most common victims of anorexia nervosa, an eating disorder that can lead to starvation.

- **Parentheses ( )**
  Anorexia nervosa (an eating disorder that can lead to starvation) occurs most often in teenage girls.

- **Brackets [ ]**
  Anorexia nervosa [an eating disorder than can lead to starvation] occurs most often in teenage girls.

- **Dashes (—)**
  Anorexia nervosa—an eating disorder that can lead to starvation—occurs most often in teenage girls.

- **Colon (:)**
  An illness affecting primarily teenage girls is anorexia nervosa: an eating disorder that can lead to starvation.

Here is a paragraph from a business textbook in which the authors define two forms of *sexual harassment* in the workplace. Notice that the entire paragraph defines sexual harassment.

Another sensitive issue concerning primarily women in the workplace is **sexual harass-ment.** As defined by the Equal Employment Opportunity Commission, sexual harassment takes two forms: the obvious request for sexual favors with an implicit reward or punishment related to work, and the more subtle creation of a sexist environment in which employees are made to feel un-comfortable by off-color jokes, lewd remarks, and posturing.

Source: David Rachman, Michael Mescon, Courtland Bovée, and John Thill, *Business Today,* McGraw-Hill, New York, 1993, p. 110.

Stop and Annotate

Go back to the textbook excerpt above. Underline or highlight the clues that signal a definition.

In this paragraph, the phrases *as defined by* and *takes two forms* signal to the reader that there are two distinct definitions of sexual harassment in the workplace. Notice that a colon (:) announces the two definitions. Notice also that although the term *sexual harassment* appears in the first sentence, it is actu-ally defined in the following sentence.

Below is an excerpt from a psychology textbook in which the author presents a definition as the main idea and then goes on to explain it more fully by giving an example. The term the author is defining is *the foot-in-the-door principle.*

Foot-in-the-Door Principle

People who sell door-to-door have long recognized that once they get a foot in the door, a sale is almost a sure thing. To state the **foot-in-the-door principle** more formally,   a person who agrees to a small request is later more likely to comply with a larger demand. Evidence suggests, for in-stance, that if someone asked you to put a large, ugly sign in your front yard to promote safe driving, you would refuse. If, however, you had first agreed to put a small sign in your window, you would later be much more likely to allow the big sign to be placed in your yard.

Source: Dennis Coon, *Essentials of Psychology,* 5th ed., West Publishing Company, St. Paul., Minn., 1991, p. 627. Copyright © 1991 by West Publishing Company. All rights reserved.

Stop and Annotate

Go back to the textbook excerpt above. Underline or highlight the clues that signal a definition.

In this paragraph the author gives the definition of the foot-in-the-door principle within the main idea sentence: *a person who agrees to a small request is later more likely to comply with a larger demand.* To announce to the reader that the foot-in-the-door effect is being defined precisely, the author uses the phrase *To state the **foot-in-the-door principle** more formally.* . . . Did you no-tice that the definition is set off by a comma, and that the important term ap-pears in the heading and in bold print within the paragraph?

KEY TERM
Comparison-contrast Pattern

Similarities (comparisons) between two or more things are presented, differences (contrasts) between two or more things are presented, or both similarities and differences are presented. The comparison-contrast pattern is also known as *ideas in opposition.*

Comparison-Contrast Pattern

Often writers want to emphasize comparisons and contrasts. A *comparison* shows how two or more things are similar or alike. A *contrast* points out the differences between them. The **comparison-contrast pattern** presents similari-ties (comparisons) between two or more things, differences (contrasts) between two or more things, or both. The comparison-contrast pattern is also known as *ideas in opposition.*

To signal comparisons, authors use the words *similarly, likewise, both, same,* and *also.* To signal contrasts, authors use clues such as *on the other hand, in con-trast, however, while, whereas, although, nevertheless, different, unlike,* and *some . . . others.* Contrasts are also signaled by words in a paragraph that have oppo-site meanings, such as *advantages* and *disadvantages* or *assets* and *liabilities.*

Comparison-contrast pattern
(Stone/David Allan Brandt)

In the following excerpt from an art textbook, the author presents important information about the advantages and disadvantages of the very slow rate at which oil paint dries. Read the paragraph to determine what she says about the positive and negative aspects of this characteristic.

> The outstanding characteristic of oil paint is that it dries very slowly. This creates both advantages and disadvantages for the artist. On the plus side, it means that colors can be blended very subtly, layers of paint can be applied on top of other layers with little danger of separating or cracking, and the artist can rework sections of the painting almost indefinitely. This same asset becomes a liability when the artist is pressed for time—perhaps when an exhibition has been scheduled. Oil paint dries so very slowly that it may be weeks or months before the painting has truly "set." Another great advantage of oil is that it can be worked in an almost infinite range of consistencies, from very thick to very thin.
>
> *Source:* Adapted from Rita Gilbert, *Living with Art,* 3d ed., McGraw-Hill, New York, 1992, p. 200.

Stop and Annotate

Go back to the textbook excerpt above. Underline or highlight the clues that signal a comparison-contrast pattern.

In this paragraph, *advantages, disadvantages, on the plus side, asset,* and *liability* are clues or signals that the author is presenting both the positive and the negative aspects of the slow rate at which oil paint dries.

Here is another paragraph from the same art textbook, which also uses the comparison-contrast pattern. (It appears in Selection 3-3 of *Opening Doors.*) Notice that the author presents similarities and differences between a Buddhist shrine and a medieval Christian cathedral.

> Buddhist shrines—the word stupa means "shrine"—often housed relics of the Buddha, and worship rituals called for circumambulation ("walking around") of the stupa. Thus, on the outside of the Great Stupa of Sanchi we see a railed pathway, where pilgrims could take the ritual clockwise walk following the Path of Life around the World Mountain. Elsewhere the stupa is embellished richly with carvings and sculpture evoking scenes from the Buddha's life. Every part of the stupa is geared to the pursuit of personal enlightenment and transcendence. If the Buddhist temple is dedicated to private worship, then its extreme opposite can be found in the total encompassment of a community religious experience: the medieval Christian cathedral. And the supreme example of that ideal is the Cathedral of Notre Dame de Chartres, in France. Chartres Cathedral was built, rebuilt, and modified over a period of several hundred

years, but the basic structure, which is in the Gothic style, was established in the thirteenth century. A cathedral—as opposed to a church—is the bishop's domain and therefore is always in a town or a city. This one fact is crucial to understanding the nature of Chartres and the role it played in the people's lives.

Source: Rita Gilbert, *Living with Art,* 3d ed., McGraw-Hill, New York, 1992, pp. 64–65.

Stop and Annotate

Go back to the textbook excerpt above. Underline or highlight the clues that signal a comparison-contrast pattern.

In the middle of this passage, the author signals the major difference she is presenting between the Great Stupa and Chartres Cathedral by the words *extreme opposite.* She wants the reader to understand that these two structures were built to serve different religious purposes. More specifically, she wants the reader to understand that Buddhist stupas were designed for *personal enlightenment* and *private worship,* whereas Christian cathedrals were designed for a *community religious experience.* In this passage, the words *personal* and *private* are used in contrast to *community.* (Incidentally, there is an additional contrast in this excerpt. Near the end of the excerpt, a distinction is made between a cathedral and a church. The phrase *as opposed to* points out the difference.)

Cause-Effect Pattern

KEY TERM
Cause-effect Pattern

Reasons (causes) and results (effects) of events or conditions are presented.

The **cause-effect pattern** presents *reasons* (causes) and results (effects) of events or conditions. Authors often use these words to indicate a cause: *because, the reasons, causes, reasons why, is due to, is caused by.* These words are often used to indicate an effect: *therefore, consequently, thus, as a consequence, led to, the results, as a result, the effect was, resulted in.*

The following excerpt from a health textbook uses the cause-effect pattern. Its topic is *lung cancer and the way an individual smokes.* The verb *affects* and the phrase *depending on* signal the cause-effect pattern.

> The way an individual smokes affects the chances of developing lung cancer. The risk increases depending on how many cigarettes are smoked each day, how deeply the smoker inhales, and how much tar and nicotine are contained in the cigarettes. People who started smoking early in their lives are also at greater risk than those who have only smoked for a few years.
>
> *Source:* Adapted from Martin Levy, Mark Dignan, and Janet Shirreffs, *Targeting Wellness: The Core,* McGraw-Hill, New York, 1992, p. 261.

Stop and Annotate

Go back to the textbook excerpt above. Underline or highlight the clues that signal a cause-effect pattern.

In this paragraph, the authors present four *causes* that contribute to one *effect,* the smoker's increased risk of lung cancer: (1) how many cigarettes are smoked daily, (2) how deeply the smoker inhales, (3) the amount of tar and nicotine in the cigarettes, and (4) the age at which a person starts smoking. (Notice that three causes are mentioned in a single sentence.)

Here is an excerpt from a physics textbook which uses the cause-effect pattern. It explains *why* many people enjoy physics.

Many People Enjoy Physics. Why?

> There are several reasons physicists and many of those who study physics find it enjoyable. First, it is a joy to find out how the world behaves. Knowledge of the laws of nature allows us to look on the world with a fuller appreciation of its beauty and wonder. Second, we all enjoy discovering

Cause-effect pattern.
(Stone/Zigy Kaluzny)

something new. Scientists take great satisfaction in exposing a facet of nature that was previously not seen or perhaps not understood. Imagine how Columbus must have felt when he sighted America. Scientists share a similar excitement when their work results in the discovery of a new aspect of nature. Fortunately, it seems that the more we discover about nature, the more there is to discover. The excitement of discovery drives science forward. Third, most of us enjoy the successful completion of a demanding task. That is why people of all ages work puzzles. Each question or problem in science is a new puzzle to be solved. We enjoy the satisfaction of success. Fourth, science benefits humanity. A substantial fraction of those who embark on scientific work do so because they wish to contribute to the progress of civilization. Call it idealistic, perhaps, but ask yourself what medical tools we would have today without the work of countless scientists in physics, chemistry, biology, and the related sciences. Our present civilization is heavily indebted not only to those in science but also to those in the general populace who know enough about science to support its progress.

Source: Frederick J. Bueche, *Principles of Physics*, 5th ed., McGraw-Hill, New York, 1988, p. 3.

Stop and Annotate

Go back to the textbook excerpt above. Underline or highlight the clues that signal a cause-effect pattern.

In the main idea sentence (the first sentence), this author uses the clue words *several reasons.* Then he uses *first, second, third,* and *fourth* to announce the four reasons which explain his main idea: *There are several reasons physicists and many of those who study physics find it enjoyable.* Even the word *Why?* in the title tells readers to expect a list of reasons (causes).

In the following excerpt from a business textbook, the authors present several effects (results) of employee assistance programs. This paragraph does not contain signal words such as *results* or *effects.* Instead, the authors assume that the reader will understand the relationship between these programs and their results. The phrase *Such programs have been reported to reduce . . .* implies that employee assistance programs have certain effects. Read the paragraph and notice the four effects the authors present.

A number of companies have also instituted **employee assistance programs** (EAPs) for employees with personal problems, especially drug or alcohol dependence. Such programs have been reported (on the average) to reduce absenteeism by 66 percent, health-care costs by 86 percent, sickness benefits by 33 percent, and work-related accidents by 65 percent. Participation in EAPs is voluntary and confidential. Employees are given in-house counseling or are referred to outside therapists or treatment programs.

Source: David Rachman, Michael Mescon, Courtland Bovée, and John Thill, *Business Today,* McGraw-Hill, New York, 1993, pp. 283–284.

Stop and Annotate

Go back to the textbook excerpt above. Underline or highlight the phrase that signals a cause-effect pattern.

In a single sentence, these authors present four beneficial *effects* of employee assistance programs: reductions in (1) absenteeism, (2) costs of health care, (3) costs of sickness benefits, and (4) work-related accidents. (Notice that all four effects are given in a single sentence.)

In this chapter so far, you have learned about five common paragraph patterns textbook authors use: list, sequence, definition, comparison-contrast, and cause-effect. The following chart summarizes the signals and clue words for each of these five patterns.

SUMMARY OF PARAGRAPH PATTERN SIGNALS AND CLUE WORDS

1. List Pattern

and	a, b, c . . .
also	bullets (•)
another	asterisks (*)
moreover	words that announce lists
in addition	(such as *categories, kinds, types, ways,*
first, second, third	*classes, groups, parts, elements,*
finally	*characteristics, features,* etc.)
1, 2, 3 . . .	

2. Sequence Pattern

first, second, third	*series*
now, the, next, finally	*stages*
dates	*when*
1, 2, 3 . . .	*before, during, after*
a, b, c . . .	*at last*
steps	*process, spectrum, continuum*
phases	*heirarchy*
progression	instructions and directions
words that refer to time	

3. Definition Pattern

words in bold print

words in italics

words in color

is defined as

means

refers to, is referred to as

the term

is called

in other words

is, is known as

in other words

that is (i. e.)

by this we mean

or (preceding a synonym)

punctuation that sets off a definition
  or synonym, : () [] —

examples that illustrate the definition or meaning
  of a term

4. Comparison-Contrast Pattern

Comparisons:

similarly

likewise

both

same

also

resembles

parallels

in the same manner

in the same way

words that compare
  (adjectives that describe
  comparisons, such as *safer,
  slower, lighter, more
  valuable, less toxic*, etc.)

Contrasts:

in contrast

however

on the other hand

whereas

while

although

nevertheless

instead (of)

different

unlike

conversely

rather than

as opposed to

some . . . others

opposite words

5. Cause-Effect Pattern

Causes:

The reason(s)

the causes(s)

because

is due to (cause)

Effects:

the result(s)

the effect(s)

the outcome

the final product

(Continued on next page)

(Continued from previous page)

was caused by (<u>cause</u>)	*therefore*
(<u>cause</u>) *led to*	*thus*
resulted from (<u>cause</u>)	*consequently*
since	*as a consequence*
	hence
	on that account
	resulted in, results in (<u>effect</u>)
	(<u>effect</u>) *was caused by*
	(<u>effect</u>) *is due to*
	led to (<u>effect</u>)
	(<u>effect</u>) resulted from

<u>Both the cause and the effect:</u>
- (<u>effect</u>) *is due to* (<u>cause</u>)
- (<u>effect</u>) *resulted from* (<u>cause</u>)
- (<u>effect</u>) *was caused by* (<u>cause</u>)
- (<u>cause</u>) *led to* (<u>effect</u>)
- (<u>cause</u>) *results in* (<u>effect</u>)

<u>Some questions that indicate cause-effect:</u>
- *What causes* (effect)? (Answer will be the cause)
- *Why does* (effect) *occur?* (Answer will be the cause)
- *What is the reason for* (effect)? (Answer will be the cause)
- *How can* (effect) *be explained?* (Answer will be the cause)
- *What does* (cause) *lead to?* (Answer will be the effect)

Avoid Seeing Everything as a "List"

When you are first learning to identify authors' writing patterns, you may mistakenly view every paragraph as having a "list pattern," since the same clue words can signal more than one pattern. For example, you may have noticed that some of the cause-effect clue words in the excerpt on physics (page 356) are the same clue words that could signal a simple list. The passage about physics, however, uses the clue words *first, second, third,* and *fourth* to present a list of *reasons.* Since these reasons demonstrate a cause-effect relationship that the author wants to emphasize, this excerpt should be considered to have a cause-effect pattern, not a list pattern.

Whenever you encounter what appears to be a list, ask yourself, "A list of *what?*" Your answer should help you realize if the author is using one of the other patterns instead. For instance,

- If your answer is "a list of *events in a particular order,*" then the paragraph has a sequence pattern.

- If your answer is "a list of *similarities* or *differences,*" the paragraph has a comparison-contrast pattern.

- If your answer is "a list of *causes, reasons,* or *results,*" then the paragraph has a cause-effect pattern.

View a paragraph as having a list pattern only when you are certain that no other pattern can be used to describe the way the ideas are organized.

Mixed Patterns

Each of the textbook excerpts presented so far in this chapter has been used to illustrate only one writing pattern, but you should be aware that authors frequently use two or more of the patterns in the same paragraph or passage. Such a combination of two or more writing patterns in the same paragraph or passage is called a **mixed pattern.**

**KEY TERM
Mixed Pattern**

Combination of two or more writing patterns in the same paragraph or passage.

Below is an example of a *mixed pattern in a single paragraph.* This excerpt, from a health and fitness textbook, uses both the definition pattern and the cause-effect pattern. The paragraph presents a definition of passive smoking, and it also presents effects of passive smoking.

Passive Smoking and the Rights of Nonsmokers

Reports from the U.S. surgeon general's office suggest that tobacco smoke in enclosed indoor areas is an important air pollution problem. This has led to the controversy about **passive smoking**—the breathing in of air polluted by the secondhand tobacco smoke of others. Carbon monoxide levels of sidestream smoke (smoke from the burning end of a cigarette) reach a dangerously high level. True, the smoke can be greatly diluted in freely circulating air, but the 1 to 5 percent carbon monoxide levels attained in smoke-filled rooms can cause health problems in people with chronic bronchitis, other lung disease, or cardiovascular disease. As a result, nicotine also builds up in the blood of nonsmokers exposed to cigarette smoke hour after hour. It has been estimated that passive smoking can give nonsmokers the equivalent in carbon monoxide and nicotine of one to ten cigarettes per day.

Source: Adapted from Martin Levy, Mark Dignan, and Janet Shirreffs, *Targeting Wellness: The Core,* McGraw-Hill, New York, 1992, pp. 262–263.

Stop and Annotate

Go back to the textbook excerpt above. Underline or highlight the clues that signal the definition pattern and the cause-effect pattern.

In this paragraph, the bold print and the dash (**passive smoking**—) are clues that the authors are defining a term. The clue words that signal cause-effect are *cause* and *as a result.* Therefore, this paragraph can be described as a mixed pattern because it includes both a definition *and* a cause-effect relationship.

Here is an excerpt from a textbook on American government that is an example of a *mixed pattern in a longer passage.* It consists of four paragraphs in which the author uses three patterns. In the first paragraph, the author presents a *definition* of regionalism (the tendency of people in a particular geographic area to defend their interests against those of people in other geographic areas). In the second paragraph, the author uses the *comparison-contrast* pattern to emphasize differences between two regions of the United States, the "Sunbelt" and the "Frostbelt." In the third paragraph, the author uses the *cause-effect* pattern to explain the conflict over federal aid that resulted from a shift of economic influence to the Sunbelt. In the fourth paragraph, the author again uses a *cause-effect* pattern to explain a shift of political influence (an increased number of seats in Congress) from the northeastern and midwestern (Frostbelt) to the southern and western states (Sunbelt). (Although the passage includes several references to time—*past two decades, in the first half of the 1980s,* etc.—the author is not emphasizing a sequence relationship.)

The Resurgence of Regionalism

An important characteristic of intergovernmental politics today is **regionalism,** the tendency of people in a particular geographic area to defend their interests against those of people in other geographic areas. Historic regionalism pitted North against South, as we saw, for example, in examining the conflicts at the Constitutional Convention. One central regional issue today is the competition between Sunbelt and Frostbelt for federal moneys.

The so-called **Sunbelt** region (the states of the South and Southwest) has experienced significant increases in population and economic development over the past two decades. During the same time, the Northeastern and Midwestern states of the so-called **Frostbelt** saw both their population and their economic growth lag behind that of the nation at large. In the first half of the 1980s, the North Central region actually lost more jobs than it gained. Southwestern oil states such as Texas and Oklahoma were also hit hard in the middle 1980s by the collapse of the oil boom. Nevertheless, the Sunbelt has grown in economic influence relative to the rest of the nation.

This shift of economic influence from the Frostbelt to the Sunbelt has led to a sharp conflict between these regions in seeking greater amounts of federal aid. Frostbelt leaders have charged that their region pays more income taxes into the federal treasury than comes back in the form of grants-in-aid, and they subsequently have pressured Congress to rewrite funding formulas so that they will be more favorable to the Frostbelt. Faced with this challenge, Sunbelt leaders have also begun to lobby Washington for their version of how federal aid ought to be distributed.

The rise of the South and the West is seen not only in economic influence but in political influence as well. The reapportionment of congressional seats after the 1990 census resulted in a dramatic shift of congressional seats from the Northeast and Midwest to fast-growing Southern and Western states such as Florida and California.

Source: Adapted from John Harrigan, *Politics and the American Future,* McGraw-Hill, New York, 1992, pp. 72–73.

Stop and Annotate

Go back to the textbook excerpt above. Underline or highlight the clues that signal the three patterns used in this mixed pattern.

Here is another excerpt, from a business textbook, that illustrates the use of a mixed pattern in longer passage. In this excerpt, which discusses *crisis management,* the authors have used four patterns: *definition, cause-effect, comparison-contrast,* and *sequence.* As you read this excerpt, look for clue words that indicate which pattern is being used in each paragraph.

Crisis Management

The most important goal of any business is to survive. But any number of problems may arise, some threatening the very existence of the company. An ugly fight for control of a company, a product failure (such as Microsoft's first two versions of the Windows program), breakdowns in an organization's routine operations (as a result of fire, for example)—any surprising event may develop into a serious and crippling crisis. **Crisis management,** the handling of such unusual and serious problems, goes a long way toward determining the company's future. For example, Johnson & Johnson is widely thought to have done a good job of coping with the two Tylenol poisoning scares, moving quickly to remove capsules from the shelves and to publicize the problem. As a result, the effects of the first scare had been almost completely overcome by the time the second hit.

In contrast, H.J. Heinz handled a crisis so badly that the future of its Canadian subsidiary of StarKist Foods was in doubt. StarKist was accused of shipping 1 millions cans of "rancid and decomposing" tuna, which were first rejected by Canadian inspectors but later passed by a high government official. Under the prodding of Canadian news media, the prime minister finally had the tainted tuna seized. All along, Heinz and StarKist maintained a story silence over "Tunagate," and their mishandling of the crisis cost plenty: The company that once controlled half of the Canadian tuna market watched its revenues fall 90 percent. After being closed for almost three years, the StarKist plant reopened in August 1988. Due to the economic downturn in 1989, StarKist closed the plant for good.

Companies that experience a crisis for which they are ill prepared seem to make a series of mistakes. First, warnings about possible problems are ignored at one or several management levels. Then the crisis hits. Under pressure, the company does the worst thing it could do: It denies the severity of the problem or it denies its own role in the problem. Finally, when the company is forced to face reality, it takes hasty, poorly conceived action.

A better way does exist. Management experts caution that the first 24 hours of a crisis are critical. The first move is to explain the problem—both to the public and to the company's employees. Simultaneously, the offending product is removed from store shelves, and the offending action is stopped, or the source of the problem (whatever it is) is brought under control to the extent possible.

Source: David Rachman, Michael Mescon, Courtland Bovée, and John Thill, *Business Today,* McGraw-Hill, New York, 1993, pp. 169–170. Reproduced with permission of McGraw-Hill.

Stop and Annotate

Go back to the textbook excerpt above. Underline or highlight the clues that signal the four patterns used in this mixed pattern.

A WORD ABOUT STANDARDIZED READING TESTS: AUTHORS' WRITING PATTERNS

Many college students are required to take standardized reading tests as part of an overall assessment program, in a reading course, or as part of a state-mandated "basic skills" test. A standardized reading test typically consists of a series of passages followed by multiple-choice questions, to be completed within a specified time limit.

Questions about organization of material in a passage may be worded several different ways. Sometimes you are asked to identify the *type* of pattern; sometimes you are asked about specific *information* that has been listed, presented in a sequence, defined, compared or contrasted, or discussed in terms of causes and effects.

Here are some examples of typical wording of questions about authors' writing patterns:

Which of the following organization patterns does the author use to present information in the passage?

In this passage the author presents . . . (*a comparison, a sequence of events,* etc.)

How is the information in the selection organized?

In this passage, what is compared with . . . ?

According to this passage, what are effects of . . . ?

This passage explains *(two, three, four)* similarities between . . .

Which of the following is an effect of . . . ?

Paragraph 3 contrasts childhood aggression with . . .

The second step in the process of carbon filtration is . . .

To answer questions about organization, watch for clue words that signal each of the patterns. When you find clue words in a passage, *circle them* so that you can clearly see relationships among the ideas presented. You will also find it helpful to *number* items in lists and sequences, causes and effects, and similarities and differences so that you do not overlook any of them. Remember, too, that words in a stated main idea sentence may suggest a pattern (such words include ways, *factors, causes, reasons, series, stages, differences, similarities,* etc.).

DEVELOPING CHAPTER REVIEW CARDS

Review cards, or *summary cards,* are an excellent study tool. They are a way to select, organize, and review the most important information in a textbook chapter. The process of creating review cards helps you organize information in a meaningful way and, at the same time, transfer it into long-term memory. The cards can also be used to prepare for tests (see Part Three). The review card activities in this book give you structured practice in creating these valuable study tools. Once you have learned how to make review cards, you can create them for textbook material in your other courses.

Now, complete the three review cards for Chapter 7, following the directions on each card. When you have completed them, you will have summarized: (1) names and definitions of five writing patterns, (2) advantages of recognizing authors' patterns as you read, and (3) clues that serve to signal writing patterns.

Authors' Writing Patterns

Name and describe five writing patterns commonly used by authors. (See pages 349–358.)

Pattern: _____

   Description: _____

Pattern: _____

   Description: _____

Pattern: _____

   Description: _____

Pattern: _____

   Description: _____

Pattern: _____

   Description: _____

Card 1   **Chapter 7: Recognizing Authors' Writing Patterns**

Advantages of Identifying Writing Patterns

To recognize an author's writing pattern, what question should you ask yourself? (See page 348.)

_____

What are four advantages of identifying writing patterns as you read? (See page 348.)

1. _____

_____

2. _____

_____

3. _____

_____

4. _____

_____

Card 2   **Chapter 7: Recognizing Author's Writing Patterns**

Clues to Writing Patterns: Signal Words

List several clues or signal words that identify each of the five writing patterns described in this chapter. (See pages 358–360.)

1. List _____

_____

2. Sequence: _____

_____

3. Definition: _____

_____

4. Comparison-contrast: _____

_____

5. Cause-effect: _____

_____

Card 3   **Chapter 7: Recognizing Authors' Writing Patterns**

SELECTION **7-1**
Personal finance

CAREER CHOICE

From *Personal Finance*

By Jack R. Kapoor, Les R. Dlabay, and Robert Hughes

Prepare Yourself to Read

Directions: Do these exercises *before* you read Selection 7-1.

1. First, read and think about the title. What do you already know about choosing a career?

_____

_____

2. Describe any steps you have taken (or plan to take) to explore your career options.

_____

_____

_____

3. Next, complete your preview by reading the following:

> Introduction (*in italics*)
> The first paragraph (paragraph 1)
> Headings
> First sentence of each paragraph
> Chart
> Diagram
> The last paragraph (paragraph 16)

On the basis of your preview, what does the selection now seem to be about?

_____

_____

Apply Comprehension Skills

Directions: Do the Annotation Practice Exercises as you read Selection 7-1.

Determine topics and main ideas. When you read a paragraph, ask yourself what it is about (the topic) and the most important point the author wants you to understand about the topic (the main idea).

Identify supporting details.   As you read, ask yourself what else the author wants you to know so that you can understand the main idea.

Recognize the authors' writing pattern.   As you read, ask yourself, "What pattern did the authors use to organize the main idea and the supporting details?" Watch for clue words that signal the pattern.

CAREER CHOICE

If you are a young adult attending college, perhaps you are just beginning to think seriously about a career. Or perhaps you are an adult who has come to college or returned to college in order to improve your career options. Some people say that the career you choose, along with the person you marry (if you choose to marry), are the two biggest decisions in your life because so much of your happiness will depend on these decisions.

Tom Peters, a nationally known business writer, predicts that 90 percent of the white-collar jobs (professional and salaried jobs that do not involve manual labor) that existed in 2000 will be completely transformed or nonexistent by 2010. According to the Bureau of Labor Statistics, the hottest job opportunities of the twenty-first century are related to technology and to the aging population (such as health care aides, physical therapists, and medical assistants). What factors should you take into consideration when choosing a career? This selection examines some of those factors.

1   Have you ever wondered why some people find great satisfaction in their work while others want only to put in their time? As with other personal financial decisions, career selection and professional growth require planning. The average person changes jobs about seven times during a lifetime. Most likely, therefore, you will reevaluate your choice of a job on a regular basis.

2   The lifework you select is a key to your financial well-being and personal satisfaction. You may select a **job,** an employment position obtained mainly to earn money. Many people work in one or more jobs during their lives without considering their interests or opportunities for advancement. Or you may select a **career,** a commitment to a profession that requires continued training and offers a clear path for occupational growth.

Annotation Practice Exercises

Directions: For each exercise, use the spaces provided to write:

* Main idea sentence of the paragraph
* Authors' pattern for organizing the supporting details (writing pattern)

Annotation Exercise

* Main idea sentence of paragraph 2:

_____

_____

_____

* Writing pattern:

_____

Most colleges and universities offer career counseling to students.
(Carl J. Single/The Image Works)

3   In many career areas, opportunities for advancement provide strong financial potential. However, entry-level salaries may be low. In contrast, strong earnings potential may not be available in jobs where the position and duties are more fixed. Workers may have to change jobs to improve their long-term financial capacity.

Trade-Offs of Career Decisions

4   While many factors affect daily living habits and financial choices, your employment situation probably affects them the most. Your income level, business associates, and available leisure time are a direct result of the work you do. Some people work so they can pursue their hobbies and recreational activities, while others have a chosen career field that reflects their interests, values, and goals.

5   Like other decisions, career choice and professional development alternatives have risks and opportunity costs. In recent years, many people in our society have placed family values and personal fulfillment above monetary reward and professional recognition. Career choices require a continual evaluation of trade-offs related to personal, social, and economic factors. For example:

- Some people select employment that is challenging and offers strong personal satisfaction rather than employment in which they can make the most money.
- Some people refuse a transfer or a promotion that would require moving their families to a new area or reducing leisure time.
- Many parents opt for part-time employment or flexible hours to allow more time for their children.
- Many people give up secure job situations because they prefer to operate their own · businesses.

Your ability to assess your personal values, needs, and goals will be an important basis for evaluating the personal and financial opportunity costs of your career choice.

Annotation Exercise

- Main idea sentence of paragraph 4:

  _1_ _____

  _____

  _____

  _____

- Writing pattern:

  Cause and effect

Figure 1. Education and income.

As of the late-1990s, estimated lifetime earnings for workers, based on the completed level of education, was:

Non-high school graduate

High school graduate

Some college

College graduate (bachelor's degree)

Professional degree

Source: U.S. Bureau of the Census.

Career Training and Skill Development

6   Your level of formal training affects your financial success. Figure 1 shows the influence of education on income. The statistics in this exhibit do not mean you will automatically earn a certain amount because you have a college degree. They imply that more education increases your *potential* earning power. However, other factors, such as field of study, also influence future income.

7   In addition to formal career training, successful managers, employers, and career counselors stress the importance of traits adaptable to most work situations. While some of these traits can be acquired in school, others require experiences in other situations. The traits that successful people usually possess include:

- An ability to work well with others in a variety of settings.

| **Annotation Exercise** |

- Main idea sentence of paragraph 6:

  _____

  _____

  _____

  _____

- Writing pattern:

  Cause and effect

- A desire to do tasks better than they have to be done.
- An interest in reading a wide variety of materials.
- A willingness to cope with conflict and adapt to change.
- An awareness of accounting, finance, and marketing fundamentals.
- A knowledge of technology and computer software such as word processing, spreadsheet, database, Web search, and graphics programs.
- An ability to solve problems creatively in team settings.
- A knowledge of research techniques and library resources.
- Well-developed written and oral communication skills.
- An understanding of both their own motivations and the motivations of others.

These competencies give people flexibility, making it easy to move from one organization to another and to successfully change career fields.

Personal Factors

8   You might be able to identify a satisfying career using guidance tests that measure your abilities, interests, and personal qualities. Aptitude tests, interest inventories, and other types of career assessment tests are available at school career counseling offices. You can use a book that allows you to take these tests at home. For a fee, testing services will mail you the results of your completed test.

9   **What Do You Do Best?** *Aptitudes* are natural abilities that people possess. The ability to work well with numbers, problem-solving skills, and physical dexterity are examples of aptitudes.

10   **What Do You Enjoy?** *Interest inventories* determine the activities that give you satisfaction. These instruments measure qualities related to various types of work. People with strong social tendencies may be best suited for careers that involve dealing with people, while people with investigative interests may be best suited for careers in research areas.

Practice Exercise

- Main idea sentence of paragraph 8:

  Carrer choices

- Writing pattern:

  listing

Practice Exercise

- Main idea sentence of paragraph 10:

  carrer satisficion

- Writing pattern:

  Cause and effect

11   **Does a Dream Job Exist?** Test results will not tell you which career to pursue. They will only give you an indication of your aptitudes and interests. Another important dimension of career selection is your personality. Do you perform best in structured or high-pressure situations, or do you prefer unstructured or creative work environments? The financial aspects of the career are also likely to be a concern.

DID YOU KNOW?

Prospective workers who are most desirable to employers possess technical skills (such as computer use and financial analysis), have the ability to communicate, and are team players.

12   Some experts say the best job is the one you look forward to on Monday morning. You want a job in which financial rewards, location, and work satisfaction are balanced. Some people adapt to any work situation, while others constantly think the next job will be the best. A vital ingredient in career choice is flexibility, since change will be a constant part of your work life and the job market.

13   Many people are able to obtain employment based on various interests and experiences. A person with volunteer experience might be hired as executive director of a community organization. Or a person who enjoys planning parties and other events may work as a meeting planner.

Career Decision Making

14   Changing personal and social factors will require you to continually assess your work situation. Figure 2 provides an approach to career planning and advancement.

15   As you can see, the different entry points depend on your personal situation. Your career goals will also affect how you use this process. If you desire more responsibility on the job, for example, you may obtain advanced training or change career fields.

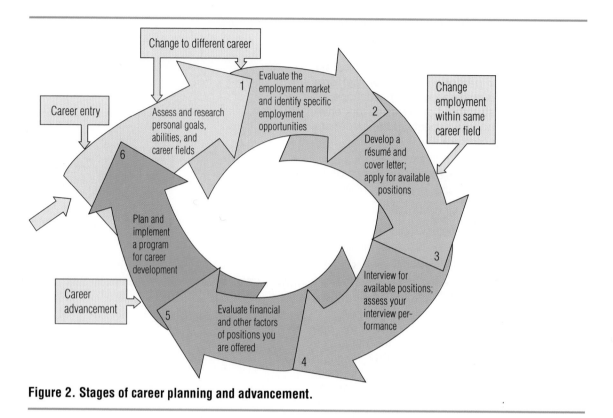

Figure 2. Stages of career planning and advancement.

16   This process is a suggested framework for planning, changing, or advancing in a career. Your specific strategies will depend on opportunity costs, the alternatives you identify, and your career area. Methods for obtaining employment are quite different for a college professor, an accountant, a computer sales representative, and a government social worker. Talking to people in your field of interest can be very valuable to career planning.

Source: Jack R. Kapoor, Les R. Dlabay, and Robert J. Hughes, *Personal Finance,* 5th ed., Irwin McGraw-Hill, Boston, pp. 31–34.

SELECTION **7-1**

Personal Finance

Comprehension Quiz

Directions: For each comprehension question below, use information from the selection to determine the correct answer. You may refer to the selection as you answer the questions. Write your answer in the space provided.

True or False

1. Examples of aptitudes are physical dexterity, problem-solving skills, and the ability to work well with numbers.

2. The average person changes jobs four times during a lifetime.

3. Many career areas that offer opportunities for occupational growth and advancement have low entry-level salaries.

4. Career choices require a continual evaluation of trade-offs related to personal, social, and economic factors.

5. Lifetime earnings for those who earn a bachelor's degree are more than twice as high as for those who do not graduate from high school.

Multiple-Choice

6. Traits that successful people usually possess include:
   a. an interest in reading a wide variety of materials.
   b. well-developed written and oral communication skills.
   c. a knowledge of technology and computer software such as word processing, spreadsheet, database, Web search, and graphics programs.
   d. all of the above.

7. The more traits of successful people that you possess, the easier it will be for you to
   a. move from one organization to another and to successfully change career fields.
   b. find jobs at the top of the pay scale.
   c. earn a college degree in the highest-paying job fields.
   d. evaluate entry-level jobs.

8. Once you interview for available positions, assess your performance during the interviews, and receive job offers, you should
   a. develop a résumé and cover letter.
   b. evaluate the employment market.
   c. evaluate financial and other factors of the positions that you are offered.
   d. change to a different career.

9. A job differs from a career in that
    a. jobs do not require college degrees.
    b. careers require college degrees and specialized preparation.
    c. entry-level salaries in careers are always lower than entry-level salaries for jobs.
    d. jobs are obtained mainly to obtain money, while careers offer paths for occupational growth.

10. It has been said that you have found the best job for you if
    a. it has a variety of health and retirement benefits.
    b. you look forward to going to it on Monday morning.
    c. it will be a constant part of your work life.
    d. you took tests to determine if your aptitudes are suited to the job.

S E L E C T I O N **7-1**

Personal Finance

Extend Your Vocabulary by Using Context Clues

Directions: Context clues are words in a sentence that allow the reader to deduce (reason out) the meaning of an unfamiliar word in the sentence. For each vocabulary exercise below, a sentence from the reading selection containing an important word (*italicized, like this*) is quoted first. Next, there is an additional sentence using the word in the same sense and providing another context clue. Use the context clues from *both* sentences to deduce the meaning of the italicized word. *Be sure the answer you choose makes sense in both sentences.* If you discover that you must use a dictionary to confirm an answer choice, remember that the meaning you select must still fit the context of *both* sentences.

Pronunciation key: ă pat   ā pay   âr care   ä father   ĕ pet   ē be   ĭ pit
ī tie   îr pier   ŏ pot   ō toe   ô paw   oi noise   ou out   ŏŏ took
ōō boot   ŭ cut yōō abuse   ûr urge   th thin   *th* this   hw which
zh vision   ə about
Stress mark: ʹ

1. In many career areas, opportunities for advancement provide strong financial *potential.*

We invested in the stock because it seemed to offer extraordinary *potential* for profit, so we were devastated when we lost all our money.

potential (pə tĕnʹ shəl)
    a. stability
    b. public appeal
    c. possibility
    d. variability

_____ **2.** However, *entry-level* salaries may be low.

Marie had never worked before, so she had to take an *entry-level* job as a receptionist because it required no special training or skills.

entry-level (ĕn′ trē lĕv əl)

a. incentive-based
b. appropriate for skilled workers
c. based on commission from sales to new customers
d. appropriate for or accessible to one who is inexperienced in a field

_____ **3.** In recent years, many people in our society have placed family values and personal fulfillment above *monetary* reward and professional recognition.

Many couples argue over *monetary* matters, such as how much money to save each month and how much to charge on credit cards.

monetary (mŏn′ ĭ tĕr ē)

a. relating to money
b. relating to family
c. relating to married life
d. relating to emotions

__C__ **4.** These *competencies* give people flexibility, making it easy to move from one organization to another and to successfully change career fields.

Before they are allowed to enroll in certain credit courses, some college students are required to pass a test to demonstrate certain *competencies* in reading, writing, and math.

competencies (kŏm′ pĭ tən sēs)

a. previous training
b. enjoyment of
c. skill, knowledge, or abilities
d. improvement

__B__ **5.** Aptitude tests, interest *inventories,* and other types of career assessment tests are available at school career counseling offices.

Because the computerized cash registers automatically make *inventories* of the merchandise sold in each department, our store always knows which items need to be reordered.

inventories (ĭn′ vən tôr ēs)

a. markdowns in prices
b. evaluations or surveys
c. listing of recently sold items
d. changes in prices

6. These *instruments* measure qualities related to various types of work.

Psychologists use IQ tests, personality tests, and other psychological *instruments* to determine whether a defendant is competent to stand trial.

instruments (ĭn' strə mənts)
a. devices used to make music
b. tools and implements made of metal
c. reports
d. devices for measuring; means by which something is done

7. People with strong social tendencies may be best suited for careers that involve dealing with people, while people with *investigative* interests may be best suited for careers in research areas.

Because my sister is highly curious and is very skilled at research, she wants to become either a detective or an *investigative* reporter for our local television station.

investigative (ĭn vəs' tĭ gā tĭv)
a. pertaining to a successful, lucrative career
b. pertaining to uncovering hidden information
c. pertaining to legal activities
d. pertaining to public issues

8. Test results will not tell you which career to pursue. They will only give you an indication of your *aptitudes* and interests.

I have many *aptitudes,* such as the ability to sing and dance, but I have no artistic or mechanical abilities.

aptitudes (ăp' tĭ tōods)
a. inherent or inborn abilities or talents
b. distinct preferences
c. hobbies or pastimes
d. deep and long-standing interests

9. Do you perform best in *structured* or high-pressure situations, or do you prefer unstructured or creative work environments?

The children followed a *structured* schedule at summer camp: arts and crafts in the morning; horseback riding, swimming, and other sports in the afternoon.

structured (strŭk' chərd)
a. highly organized
b. flexible
c. constantly changing
d. dull; boring

_____ C _____ **10.** In addition to formal career training, successful managers, employers, and career counselors stress the importance of traits *adaptable* to most situations.

The benefit of a four-wheel-drive sport utility vehicle is that it is *adaptable* for driving off-road on rough terrain.

adaptable (ə dăpt′ ə bəl)

a. inappropriate for a specific use or situation

b. ruined by

c. able to be made suitable for a specific use or situation

d. incompatible with a specific use or situation

Collaboration Option

Respond in Writing

Directions: Refer to the selection as needed to answer the essay-type questions below.

Option for collaboration: Your instructor may direct you to work with other students—in other words, to work *collaboratively.* In that case, you should form groups of three or four students as directed by your instructor and work together to complete the exercises. After your group discusses each item and agrees on the answer, have a group member record it. Every member of your group should be able to explain all of your group's answers.

1. Would you rather have a job or a career? Tell which, and explain the reasons for your choice.

_____

_____

_____

2. List at least 3 *aptitudes* that you have.

_____

_____

_____

List at least 3 *interests* of yours.

_____

_____

_____

Describe the kind of *environment* in which you would prefer to work (for example, in a group or alone; in a high-pressure or low-stress environment; in an informal situation or a formal one; in a structured environment or a creative one; indoors or out-of-doors).

_____

_____

_____

On the basis of the information above, describe at least three jobs or careers that you think might be "dream jobs" for you.

_____

_____

_____

3. List at least five jobs that you would *never* want to have. Explain your reason for not wanting each of the jobs.

_____

_____

_____

_____

_____

_____

_____

_____

_____

4. In what ways do you think college can prepare a person for a career instead of just a job?

_____

_____

_____

_____

_____

5. Most people change jobs or even careers several times in their lives. What are some of the advantages and disadvantages of changing jobs or careers more than once during a lifetime? What are some ways in which a person could prepare himself or herself for the possibility of several job or career changes?

_____

_____

_____

_____

_____

_____

6. Overall main idea. What is the overall main idea the author wants the reader to understand about choosing a career? Answer this question in one sentence. Be sure that your overall main idea sentence includes the topic (*choosing a career*) and tells the overall most important point about it.

_____

_____

_____

_____

Read More about It on the World Wide Web

To learn more about the topic of this selection, visit these websites or use your favorite search engine (such as Yahoo ®). Whenever you go to *any* website, it is a good idea to evaluate it critically. Are you getting good information—information that is accurate, complete, and up-to-date? Who sponsors the website? How easy is it to use the features of the website?

http://members.aol.com/jocrf19/index2.html
> *The* Johnson O'Connor Research Foundation, Inc. *is a nonprofit scientific and educational organization with two primary commitments: to study human abilities and to provide people with knowledge about their aptitudes in order to help them make decisions about school and work.*

http://campus.monster.com
> *This website is designed especially for college students. It allows users to explore their career options and refine their career objectives.*

http://www.experienceonline.com/

> Experience.com *is a resource for students and young professionals who are just beginning their careers. From researching a company and finding a job to reading about the latest workplace trends,* experience.com *has it all.*

http://www.aegonsmg.com/getgo/

> Getting Past Go *is a World Wide Web resource for new and recent college graduates. Everybody knows it's hard to find and land a good job, but there's plenty of help for job seekers in cyberspace—if you know where to look. This site brings together a great deal of useful information in one place. Links will help you write résumés, look for work, decide where to locate, keep your health coverage current, and stay wired to the Net.*

SELECTION **7-2**

Health

THE DECISION TO MARRY

From *Targeting Wellness: The Core*

By Marvin Levy, Mark Dignan, and Janet Shirreffs

Prepare Yourself to Read

Directions: Do these exercises *before* you read Selection 7-2.

1. First, read and think about the title. In your opinion, why do most people people decide to marry?

_____

_____

2. How much consideration do you think most people really give to their reasons for marrying?

_____

_____

_____

3. Next, complete your preview by reading the following:

> Introduction (in *italics*)
> First paragraph (paragraph 1)
> Headings in *italics*
> First sentence of each paragraph
> Words in *italics*
> Last paragraph (paragraph 9)

On the basis of your preview, what three aspects of the decision to marry does this selection seem to be about?

_____

_____

Apply Comprehension Skills

Directions: Do the Annotation Practice Exercises as you read Selection 7-2.

Determine topics and main ideas. When you read a paragraph, ask yourself what it is about (topic) and what the author wants you to understand (main idea) about the topic.

Identify supporting details.   As you read, ask yourself what else the author wants you to know so that you can understand the main idea.

Recognize the authors' writing pattern.   As you read, ask yourself, "What pattern did the author use to organize the main idea and supporting details?" Watch for clue words that signal the pattern.

THE DECISION TO MARRY

Today, half of all marriages fail. Part of this can be attributed to getting married for the wrong reasons or marrying someone who is incompatible. What are poor reasons for getting married? What characterizes a successful, high-quality marriage? What determines a couple's compatibility? This textbook selection answers these questions.

1   Marriage is an institution that is changing. Traditionally, marriage has been an economic arrangement in which husbands have worked outside the home to provide financial security for their families, while wives have cared for the children and run the home. Today, however, this arrangement is changing. The roles of husband and wife are not as clearly defined as in the past, especially when both partners work and earn money for the family. Many people today expect and get more from marriage than economic benefits. They look to their spouses for sharing, emotional support, and intimacy. Happily married people often identify the spouse as their best friend.

2   **Why do people marry?**   The pressures for a couple to marry can be enormous. This pressure often comes from parents and other relatives as well as from the media. Sometimes the members of a family, ethnic group, or religious group may pressure individuals to marry so that a new generation can be raised in the teaching and values of the group.

3   Aside from these pressures, people marry for a variety of reasons. Some still marry for economic reasons. For others, marriage is viewed as the only acceptable framework in which to enjoy sex freely. Some people marry to escape from an unhappy home life, on the rebound from another relationship, or to avoid loneliness.

4   Researchers have identified several patterns in "high-quality," or well-balanced marriages. Some of these married people tend to focus their energies on joint activities. Their strongest wish is to spend time together, yet they also strike a balance between privacy and togetherness. Other couples focus their energies on being parents and on raising their children.

Annotation Practice Exercises

Directions: For each exercise, use the spaces provided to write:

*   Main idea sentence of the paragraph
*   Author's pattern for organizing the supporting details (writing pattern)

Annotation Exercise

Main idea sentence of paragraph 2:

_____

_____

_____

_____

_____

Writing pattern:

_____

Annotation Exercise

Main idea sentence of paragraph 4:

_____

_____

_____

_____

Writing pattern:

_____

Some dual-career couples, although they spend much of their energy on their individual careers, develop intimacy by sharing what is going on in their work. It thus seems that the desire to spend time together, raise children, and share other aspects of life and career are all healthy reasons for marrying.

5   **Love and romance**   A basic element in most marriages is the love one person feels for another. There are many different types of love between persons, including parental love, fraternal love, and romantic love. Each requires caring and respect. Romantic love includes the qualities of deep intimacy and passion and begins with a feeling of intense attraction between two people.

6   Although most marriages are based on romantic love, few couples sustain that romance as the years go by. Romantic love often develops into a less intense, less all-consuming type of love known as companionate love. A companionate love relationship is steadier than romantic love and is based on trust, sharing, affection, and togetherness. Maintaining the love in a marriage requires considerable effort and commitment. Married partners who succeed in communicating, giving physical warmth, and sharing interests and responsibilities are more likely to remain in love.

7   **Assessing compatibility**   When people are looking for a mate, they tend to be attracted to potential partners whose ethnic, religious, economic, and educational background is similar to their own. Certain physical attributes are also significant factors. They are least likely to match up with a similar person in the area of compatibility of personality. Personality factors are not always easy to observe. Sometimes people do not reveal their true selves during courtship. Moreover, people with opposite personality types often attract each other, perhaps because one personality rounds out the other.

8   Unfortunately, great differences in personality can often lead to conflict later on. One study found that a source of marital dissatisfaction among husbands was a feeling that their wives were too possessive, neglectful, and openly admiring of other men. Dissatisfied wives complained that their husbands were possessive, moody, and openly attracted to other women.

Annotation Exercise

Main idea sentence of paragraph 6:

_____

_____

_____

_____

Writing pattern:

_____

The study also found that sex is a source of great difficulties for unhappy married men and women. It found that women see sex as following from emotional intimacy, while men see it as a road to intimacy. As a result, men complain that their wives withhold sex from them and women complain that their husbands are too sexually aggressive.

9   How can people be sure they are marrying people with whom they are truly compatible? One way is by taking plenty of time to get to know the other person. Researchers have found that couples seem to go through three stages in this process. First, each person tries to measure his or her good and bad qualities against those of the other person. People tend to be drawn to others who seem to have about the same assets and liabilities they themselves possess. Second, people look for compatible beliefs, attitudes, and interests to support the initial attraction. It is not until the third stage that people reveal to each other how they handle responsibility, react to disappointment, and cope with a wide variety of situations. The key to compatibility is for the couple to be sure that they have arrived at this last stage before they think seriously about marriage. Such people are less likely to be unpleasantly suprised than are those who marry quickly.

Since antiquity, the marriage ceremony has provided a formal setting in which a couple can publicly affirm their love for and commitment to each other.
(*Buccina Studios/PhotoDisc*)

Source: Marvin Levy, Mark Dignan, and Janet Shirreffs, "The Decision to Marry," in *Targeting Wellness: The Core,* McGraw-Hill, New York, 1992, pp. 122–123. Reproduced with permission of McGraw-Hill.

Comprehension Quiz

Directions: For each comprehension question below, use information from the selection to determine the correct answer. You may refer to the selection as you answer the questions. Write your answer in the space provided.

True or False

_____ **1.** Marriage is an unchanging institution.

_____ **2.** People can experience enormous pressure to marry.

_____ **3.** Pressure to marry can come from many sources.

_____ **4.** Sometimes people do not reveal their true selves during courtship.

_____ **5.** As years go by in a marriage, most couples are able to sustain the intense attraction of romantic love.

_____ **6.** People with opposite personality types will not attract each other.

Multiple-Choice

_____ **7.** Which of the following is *not* a characteristic of companionate love?
   a.   steadiness
   b.   all-consuming intensity of feeling
   c.   mutual trustworthiness
   d.   shared areas of responsibility

_____ **8.** Which of the following is *not* a characteristic of "high quality" marriages?
   a.   Energy is focused on the economic benefits of marriage.
   b.   Energy is focused on joint activities.
   c.   Energy is focused on being parents and raising children.
   d.   A balance is struck between privacy and togetherness.

_____ **9.** Which of these is a source of marital dissatisfaction?
   a.   husbands' feeling that wives are too possessive, neglectful, and openly admiring of other men
   b.   wives' feeling that husbands are possessive, moody, and openly attracted to other women
   c.   conflicts over sex
   d.   all of the above

_____ **10.** Researchers have found that people seem to go through three stages in the process of selecting a mate. Which of the following is *not* a stage?

  a. A person measures his or her good and bad qualities against those of the other person.

  b. People evaluate the physical attractiveness of a possible partner.

  c. People look for compatible beliefs, attitudes, and interests in the other person.

  d. People reveal how they handle responsibility and disappointment.

Extend Your Vocabulary by Using Context Clues

Directions: Context clues are words in a sentence that allow the reader to deduce (reason out) the meaning of an unfamiliar word in that sentence. For each vocabulary item below, a sentence from the selection containing an important word (*italicized, like this*) is quoted first. Next, there is an additional sentence using the word in the same sense and providing another context clue. Use the context clues from *both* sentences to deduce the meaning of the italicized word. *Be sure the answer you choose makes sense in both sentences.* If you discover that you must use a dictionary to confirm an answer choice, remember that the meaning you select must still fit the context of both sentences. To indicate your answer, write the letter in the space provided.

Pronunciation key: ă **pat** ā **pay** âr **care** ä **father** ĕ **pet** ē **be** ĭ **pit**
ī **tie** îr **pier** ŏ **pot** ō **toe** ô **paw** oi **noise** ou **out** ŏŏ **took**
ōō **boot** ŭ **cut** yōō **abuse** ûr **urge** th **thin** *th* **this** hw **which**
zh **vision** ə **about**
Stress mark: ʹ

_____ **1.** Marriage is an *institution* that is changing.

  The family is an *institution* that has been studied extensively by researchers.

  institution (ĭn stĭ tōōʹ shən) means:

  a. building

  b. written agreement

  c. political decision

  d. established custom or practice

_____   **2.** Some people marry to escape from an unhappy home life, on the *rebound* from another relationship, or to avoid loneliness.

The senator was quickly on the *rebound* after losing the election, and soon began making plans to enter a new career.

rebound (rē′ bound) means:

a. recovery from disappointment

b. capture of something

c. sideways movement

d. ground

_____   **3.** There are many different types of love between persons, including parental love, *fraternal* love, and romantic love.

He joined a *fraternal* organization to make new friends and enjoy social activities.

fraternal (frə tûr′ nəl) means:

a. pertaining to friendship

b. pertaining to business

c. pertaining to hobbies

d. none of the above

_____   **4.** Although most marriages are based on romantic love, few couples *sustain* that romance as the years go by.

Although he was in an irreversible coma, his family asked the doctors to do everything possible to *sustain* his life.

sustain (sə stān′) means:

a. prevent

b. alter

c. end

d. maintain

_____   **5.** Romantic love often develops into a less intense, less all-*consuming* type of love known as companionate love.

Sailing has become such a time-*consuming* hobby for Bob that he never has time for anything else on weekends.

consuming (kən sōōm′ ĭng) means:

a. engrossing; absorbing

b. confusing

c. wasting

d. saving

_____ **6.** Sometimes people do not reveal their true selves during *courtship.*

Lynn and Pat's *courtship* lasted for six years before they decided to marry.

courtship (kôrt′ shĭp) means:

a. court case

b. voyage at sea

c. legal separation

d. seeking someone's affection with the hope of marrying him or her

_____ **7.** One study found that a source of *marital* dissatisfaction among husbands was a feeling that their wives were too possessive, neglectful, and openly admiring of other men.

Please indicate your *marital* status: single, married, divorced, or widowed.

marital (măr′ ĭ tl) means:

a. pertaining to fighting

b. pertaining to marriage

c. pertaining to divorce

d. pertaining to a wedding

_____ **8.** People tend to be drawn to others who seem to have about the same assets and *liabilities* they themselves possess.

Not knowing how to use computers and lack of rapport with others are *liabilities* for anyone who plans to enter the business world.

liabilities (lĭ ə bĭl′ ĭ tēz) means:

a. handicap; something that holds one back

b. advantages, benefits

c. business skills

d. lies, deceptions

_____ **9.** Second, people look for compatible beliefs, attitudes, and interests to support the *initial* attraction.

The doctor changed her *initial* diagnosis after she received the patient's test results.

initial (ĭ nĭsh′ əl) means:

a. professional

b. inappropriate

c. first

d. puzzling

_____ **10.** The key to *compatibility* is for the couple to be sure that they have arrived at this last stage before they think seriously about marriage.

In families with step-children, psychological counseling can promote *compatibility* and make family life more pleasant.

compatibility (kəm păt ə bĭl′ ə tē) means:

a. an interesting marriage

b. financial security

c. a harmonious or agreeable combining

d. achievement of career goals

SELECTION **7-2**

Health

Collaboration Option

Respond in Writing

Directions: Refer to the selection as needed to answer the essay-type questions below.

Option for collaboration: Your instructor may direct you to work with other students or, in other words, to work *collaboratively*. In that case, you should form groups of three or four students as directed by your instructor and work together to complete the exercises. After your group discusses each item and agrees on the answer, have a group member record it. Every member of your group should be able to explain all of your group's answer.

1. List several reasons mentioned in paragraphs 2 and 3 of the selection that are *inappropriate* reasons for marrying.

_____

_____

_____

_____

_____

_____

2. In paragraph 4, what three reasons do the authors say are *healthy* reasons for marrying? First healthy reason:

_____

_____

Second healthy reason:

_____

_____

Third healthy reason:

_____

_____

3. In addition to the inappropriate reasons for marrying that are discussed in the selection, describe at least one other reason that can cause marriages to fail.

_____

_____

_____

4. Suppose that two people are attracted to each other, and they share similar ethnic, religious, economic, and educational backgrounds. However, because their personalities are quite different, they are not sure they are compatible. According to the selection, what three stages should they go through to determine whether their personalities are truly compatible?

_____

_____

_____

_____

_____

_____

_____

5. Overall main idea. What is the overall main idea the author wants the reader to understand about the decision to marry? Answer this question in one sentence. Be sure that your overall main idea sentence includes the topic (*the decision to marry*) and tells the overall most important point about it.

_____

_____

_____

_____

_____

Read More about It on the World Wide Web

To learn more about the topic of this selection, visit these websites or use your favorite search engine (such as Yahoo ®). Whenever you go to *any* website, it is a good idea to evaluate it critically. Are you getting good information—information that is accurate, complete, and up-to-date? Who sponsors the website? How easy is it to use the features of the website?

http://www.uwyo.edu/ag/ces/family/BEN/Marriage/time.htm
This website provides links to four excellent articles on marriage.

http://www.family.org/married/
This is part of a magazine-format website that contains articles and links pertaining to different aspects of marriage.

SELECTION 7-3

Psychology

REACTIONS TO IMPENDING DEATH

From *Essentials of Psychology*

By Dennis Coon

Prepare Yourself to Read

Directions: Do these exercises *before* you read Selection 7-3.

1. First, read and think about the title. What do you already know about dying people's reactions to impending death?

   _____

   _____

2. Next, complete your preview by reading the following:

   Introduction (in *italics*)
   First paragraph (paragraph 1)
   Headings
   First sentence of each paragraph
   Words in **bold print** and *italics*
   Last paragraph (paragraph 16)

   On the basis of your preview, what does this selection seem to be about?

   _____

   _____

Apply Comprehension Skills

Directions: Do the Annotation Practice Exercises as you read Selection 7-3.

Determine topics and main ideas.   When you read a paragraph, ask yourself what it is about (topic) and what the author wants you to understand (main idea) about the topic.

Identify supporting details.   As you read, ask yourself what else the author wants you to know so that you can understand the main idea.

Recognize the author's writing pattern.   As you read, ask yourself, "What pattern did the author use to organize the main idea and supporting details?" Watch for clue words that signal the pattern.

REACTIONS TO IMPENDING DEATH

"It's not that I'm afraid to die; I just don't want to be there when it happens," Woody Allen once quipped. Although he was making a joke, his comment reflects our culture's squeamish attitude towards death. Kahlil Gibran, author of The Prophet, *had a very different view: "For life and death are one, even as the river and the sea are one."*

Because the topic of death makes many people in our society uncomfortable, it tends not to be discussed. Yet death is a reality, the natural, inevitable end of life, and not talking about it only makes death more difficult for those who are dying and for the survivors who will grieve for them. Fortunately, extensive, thorough, and thoughtful research on terminally ill patients' reactions to their impending deaths was done by Dr. Elisabeth Kübler-Ross. We now know that certain reactions are normal and predictable. Kübler-Ross's findings have proved extraordinarily helpful to the terminally ill, to those who love them, to others who provide them emotional support, and to those who provide their health care.

In this selection from a psychology textbook, the author presents Kübler-Ross's findings, as well as helpful information on hospices and bereavement. This selection will provide you with valuable insights that will benefit you in a variety of ways.

---

1   A direct account of emotional responses to death comes from the work of Elisabeth Kübler-Ross (1975). Kübler-Ross is a **thanatologist** (one who studies death) who spent hundreds of hours at the bedsides of the terminally ill. She found that dying persons tend to display several emotional reactions as they prepare for death. Five basic reactions are described here:

1. **Denial and isolation.** A typical first reaction to impending death is an attempt to deny its reality and to isolate oneself from information confirming that death is really going to occur. Initially the person may be sure that "It's all a mistake," that lab reports or X-rays have been mixed up, or that a physician is in error. This may proceed to attempts to ignore or avoid any reminder of the situation.

2. **Anger.** Many dying individuals feel anger and ask, "Why me?" As they face the ultimate threat of having everything they value stripped away, their anger can spill over into rage or envy toward those who will continue living. Even good friends may temporarily evoke anger because their health is envied.

3. **Bargaining.** In another common reaction the terminally ill bargain with themselves or with God. The dying person thinks, "Just let me

Annotation Practice Exercises

Directions: For each exercise, use the spaces provided to write:

*   Main idea sentence of the paragraph

*   Author's pattern for organizing supporting details (writing pattern)

Annotation Exercise

Main idea sentence of paragraph 1:

_____

_____

_____

Writing pattern:

_____

_____

live a little longer and I'll do anything to earn it." Individuals may bargain for time by trying to be "good" ("I'll never smoke again"), by righting past wrongs, or by praying that if they are granted more time they will dedicate themselves to their religion.

4. **Depression.** As death draws near and the person begins to recognize that it cannot be prevented, feelings of futility, exhaustion, and deep depression may set in. The person recognizes that he or she will be separated from friends, loved ones, and the familiar routines of life, and this causes a profound sadness.

5. **Acceptance.** If death is not sudden, many people manage to come to terms with dying and accept it calmly. The person who accepts death is neither happy nor sad, but at peace with the inevitable. Acceptance usually signals that the struggle with death has been resolved. The need to talk about death ends, and silent companionship from others is frequently all that is desired.

As cultural rituals, funerals encourage a release of emotion and provide a sense of closure for survivors, who must come to terms with the death of a loved one.
(A. Ramey/Photo Edit)

2   Not all terminally ill persons display all these reactions, nor do they always occur in this order. Individual styles of dying vary greatly, according to emotional maturity, religious beliefs, age, education, the attitudes of relatives, and so forth. Generally, there does tend to be a movement from initial shock, denial, and anger toward eventual acceptance of the situation. However, some people who seem to have accepted death may die angry and raging against the inevitable. Conversely, the angry fighter may let go of the struggle and die peacefully. In general, one's approach to dying will mirror his or her style of living.

3   It is best not to think of Kübler-Ross's list as a fixed series of stages to go through in order. It is an even bigger mistake to assume that someone who does not show all the listed emotional reactions is somehow deviant or immature. Rather, the list describes typical and appropriate reactions to impending death. It is also interesting to note that many of the same reactions accompany any major loss, be it divorce, loss of a home due to fire, death of a pet, or loss of a job.

*Question: How can I make use
of this information?*

4   First, it can help both the dying individual and survivors to recognize and cope with periods of depression, anger, denial, and bargaining. Second, it helps to realize that close friends or relatives of the dying person may feel many of the same emotions before or after the person's death because they, too, are facing a loss.

5   Perhaps the most important thing to recognize is that the dying person may have a need to share feelings with others and to discuss death openly. Too often, the dying person feels isolated and separated from others by the wall of silence erected by doctors, nurses, and family members. Adults tend to "freeze up" with a dying person, saying things such as, "I don't know how to deal with this."

6   Understanding what the dying person is going through may make it easier to offer support at this important time. A simple willingness to be with the person and to honestly share his or her feelings can help bring dignity, acceptance, and meaning to death. In many communities these goals have been aided by the hospice movement.

Hospice

7   A **hospice** is basically a hospital for the terminally ill. The goal of the hospice movement is to improve the quality of life in the person's final days. Hospices typically offer support, guidance, and companionship from volunteers, other patients, staff, clergy, and counselors. Pleasant surroundings, an atmosphere of informality, and a sense of continued living help patients cope with their illnesses. Unlimited around-the-clock visits are permitted by relatives, friends, children, and even pets. Patients receive constant attention, play games, make day trips, have pre-dinner cocktails if they choose, and enjoy entertainment. In short, life goes on for them.

8   At present most larger cities in the United States have hospices. They have been so successful that they are likely to be added to many more communities. At the same time, treatment for the terminally ill has dramatically improved in

Annotation Exercise

Main idea sentence of paragraph 6:

_____

_____

_____

Writing pattern:

_____

Annotation Exercise

Main idea sentence of paragraph 7:

_____

_____

_____

Writing pattern:

_____

hospitals—largely as a result of pioneering efforts in the hospice movement.

Bereavement

9   After a friend or relative has died, a period of grief typically follows. Grief is a natural and normal reaction to death as survivors adjust to loss.

10   Grief tends to follow a predictable pattern. Grief usually begins with a period of **shock** or numbness. For a brief time the bereaved remain in a dazed state in which they may show little emotion. Most find it extremely difficult to accept the reality of their loss. This phase usually ends by the time of the funeral, which unleashes tears and bottled-up feelings of despair.

11   Initial shock is followed by sharp **pangs of grief.** These are episodes of painful yearning for the dead person and, sometimes, anguished outbursts of anger. During this period the wish to have the dead person back is intense. Often, mourners continue to think of the dead person as alive. They may hear his or her voice and see the deceased vividly in dreams. During this period, agitated distress alternates with silent despair, and suffering is acute.

12   The first powerful reactions of grief gradually give way to weeks or months of **apathy, dejection,** and **depression.** The person faces a new emotional landscape with a large gap that cannot be filled. Life seems to lose much of its meaning, and a sense of futility dominates the person's outlook. The mourner is usually able to resume work or other activities after 2 or 3 weeks. However, insomnia, loss of energy and appetite, and similar signs of depression may continue.

13   Little by little, the bereaved person accepts what cannot be changed and makes a new beginning. Pangs of grief may still occur, but they are less severe and less frequent. Memories of the dead person, though still painful, now include positive images and nostalgic pleasure. At this point, the person can be said to be moving toward **resolution.**

14   As was true of approaching death, individual reactions to grief vary considerably. In general, however, a month or two typically passes before the more intense stages of grief have run their

Annotation Exercise

Main idea sentence of paragraph 10:

_____

_____

Writing pattern:

_____

course. As you can see, grief allows survivors to discharge their anguish and to prepare to go on living.

Question: Is it true that suppressing grief leads to more problems later?

15   It has long been assumed that suppressing grief may later lead to more severe and lasting depression. However, there is little evidence to support this idea. A lack of intense grief does not usually predict later problems. Bereaved persons should work through their grief at their own pace and in their own way—without worrying about whether they are grieving too much or too little. Some additional suggestions for coping with grief follow.

Coping with Grief

- Face the loss directly and do not isolate yourself.
- Discuss your feelings with relatives and friends.
- Do not block out your feelings with drugs or alcohol.
- Allow grief to progress naturally; neither hurry nor suppress it.

16   The subject of death brings us full circle in the cycle of life.

SELECTION **7-3**

Psychology

Comprehension Quiz

Directions: For each comprehension question below, use information from the selection to determine the correct answer. You may refer to the selection as you answer the questions. Write your answer in the space provided.

True or False

_____ **1.** Elisabeth Kübler-Ross found that every terminally ill patient displays five basic reactions to dying.

_____ **2.** Kübler-Ross's list of reactions represents a fixed series of stages.

_____ **3.** Many of the reactions outlined by Kübler-Ross also accompany major losses such as divorce, loss of a job, and loss of a home in a fire.

_____ **4.** The primary goal of the hospice movement is to provide advanced medical treatment for the dying person.

_____ **5.** The hospice movement has had no effect on the quality of care that terminally ill patients receive in hospitals.

_____ **6.** Patients in a hospice may have a pre-dinner cocktail if they choose to.

Multiple-Choice

_____ **7.** A thanatologist is one who studies

    a. hospital care.

    b. diseases.

    c. death.

    d. psychology.

_____ **8.** The author states that individual styles of dying are influenced by all the following factors *except* the

    a. attitude of relatives.

    b. gender of the dying person.

    c. age of the dying person.

    d. emotional maturity of the dying person.

_____ **9.** Which of the following does *not* illustrate the value of Kübler-Ross's findings?

    a. We can assume that someone who does not exhibit all the emotional reactions described by Kübler-Ross is immature.

    b. The dying person who is familiar with Kübler-Ross's theory may be able to recognize, cope with, and discuss the various stages.

    c. As survivors, we can better understand and support the terminally ill person.

    d. Doctors and nurses may have a better understanding of the feelings of the terminally ill person.

_____ **10.** Hospice care is characterized by

    a. restricted visits.

    b. a hospital-like environment.

    c. day trips, entertainment, and visits by the family (even pets), if the patient is able.

    d. care, guidance, and support by doctors and staff only.

SELECTION **7-3**

Psychology

Extend Your Vocabulary by Using Context Clues

Directions: Context clues are words in a sentence that allow the reader to deduce (reason out) the meaning of an unfamiliar word in that sentence. For each vocabulary item below, a sentence from the selection containing an important word (*italicized, like this*) is quoted first. Next, there is an additional sentence using the word in the same sense and providing another context clue. Use the context clues from *both* sentences to deduce the meaning of the italicized word. *Be sure the answer you choose makes sense in both sentences.* If you discover that you must use a dictionary to confirm an answer choice, remember that the meaning you select must still fit the context of both sentences. To indicate your answer, write the letter in the space provided.

Pronunciation key: ă pat   ā pay   âr care   ä father   ĕ pet   ē be   ĭ pit
ī tie   îr pier   ŏ pot   ō toe   ô paw   oi noise   ou out   ŏŏ took
ōō boot   ŭ cut yōō abuse   ûr urge   th thin   *th* this   hw which
zh vision   ə about
Stress mark: ʹ

_____ **1.** As death draws near and the person begins to recognize that it cannot be prevented, feelings of *futility,* exhaustion, and deep depression may set in.

When they saw how vast the forest fire was, the firefighters realized the *futility* of their efforts to put it out and simply tried instead to prevent it from spreading.

futility (fyo͞o tĭl′ ĭ tē) means:

a. reasonableness; sensibleness

b. uselessness; lack of useful results

c. cheerfulness

d. helpfulness

_____ **2.** Acceptance usually signals the struggle with death has been *resolved.*

My parents always *resolved* their problems by discussing them.

resolved (rĭ zōlvd′) means:

a. found a solution to; settled

b. ignored; paid no attention to

c. made known publicly

d. kept secret

_____ **3.** It is an even bigger mistake to assume that someone who does not show all the listed emotional reactions is somehow *deviant* or immature.

Children who are abused often exhibit *deviant* behavior later in their lives.

deviant (dē′ vē ənt) means:

a. kind, gentle

b. illegal; against the law

c. difficult to diagnose

d. differing from accepted standards

_____ **4.** Rather, the list describes typical and appropriate reactions to *impending* death.

We knew from the dark clouds that the *impending* storm could hit at any minute.

impending (ĭm pĕn′ dĭng) means:

a. about to take place

b. severe, harsh

c. delayed; later than expected

d. soothing

_____ **5.** For a brief time the *bereaved* remain in a dazed state in which they may show little emotion.

The *bereaved* widow of the police officer received hundreds of letters expressing sympathy over the loss of her courageous husband.

bereaved (bĭ rēvd′) means:
a. peaceful; serene
b. young; childlike
c. suffering the loss of a loved one
d. suffering from a serious illness

_____ **6.** This phase usually ends by the time of the funeral, which *unleashes* tears and bottled-up feelings of despair.

When a hurricane *unleashes* its fury, it can cause millions of dollars of damage.

unleashes (ŭn lēsh′ əz) means:
a. releases
b. controls
c. calms; soothes
d. prevents

_____ **7.** Initial shock is followed by sharp *pangs* of grief.

We had not eaten since morning, and our hunger *pangs* increased when we smelled the delicious aroma coming from the campfire that night.

pangs (păngz) means:
a. strong desires
b. strong, sudden sensations
c. sad, despondent feelings
d. strong dislikes

_____ **8.** During this period, agitated distress alternates with silent despair, and suffering is *acute.*

Everyone in the search party felt *acute* relief when the missing child was found.

acute (ə kyōōt′) means:
a. intense
b. mild
c. moderate
d. not noticeable

_____ **9.** The first powerful reactions of grief gradually give way to weeks or months of apathy, *dejection,* and depression.

We could tell from their *dejection* that they had lost the final game of the baseball playoffs.

dejection (dǐ jĕkt′ shən) means:

a. agitation; nervousness

b. energy; liveliness

c. discouragement or low spirits

d. happiness; elation

_____ **10.** Life seems to lose much of its meaning, and a sense of futility *dominates* the person's outlook.

The rumor of the president's resignation *dominates* the media this week.

dominates (dŏm′ ə nāts) means:

a. controls or occupies

b. treats harshly

c. treats as unimportant

d. is excluded from

Collaboration Option

Respond in Writing

Directions: Refer to the selection as needed to answer the essay-type questions below.

Option for collaboration: Your instructor may direct you to work with other students or in other words, to work *collaboratively.* In that case, you should form groups of three or four students as directed by your instructor and work together to complete exercises. After your group discusses each item and agrees on the answer, have a group member record it. Every member of your group should be able to explain all of your group's answer.

1. The thanatologist Elisabeth Kübler-Ross found five basic reactions to death (or any major loss). Give examples of how each of these reactions might manifest itself in a person's behavior. You may add examples of your own to any the author gives. (For instance, one possible behavior accompanying the first emotional reaction is avoiding calling to get results of medical tests.)

Emotional reaction   *Possible behaviors accompanying the reaction*

Denial and isolation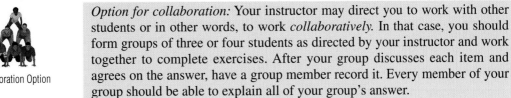

Anger

Bargaining

_____

_____

_____

Depression

_____

_____

_____

_____

_____

Acceptance

_____

_____

_____

_____

2. What are two important ways a person could benefit from knowing about the five reactions Kübler-Ross describes?

_____

_____

_____

_____

_____

_____

_____

_____

3. How does a hospice differ from a hospital? In your answer, use words that signal contrasts (see page 359 for these words).

_____

_____

_____

_____

_____

_____

_____

4. With the exception of the "bargaining stage," there is a predictable pattern of grief, just as there is a predictable pattern of reactions to impending death. Review this comparison (presented at the end of the selection) and complete the table on the opposite page. (To get you started, the answers to be inserted opposite *Denial and isolation* are "shock or numbness" and "difficulty accepting the reality of the loss." Write them in the spaces provided.)

Reactions to death or loss	*Reactions to grief*
Denial and isolation	_____
	_____
Anger	_____
	_____
Bargaining	(No equivalent reaction)
Depression	_____
Acceptance	_____

5. Think of a situation in which you or someone you know experienced a significant loss (such as the loss of a valued job, divorce, loss of a home through fire or a natural disaster, or the death of a pet). Describe any of the reactions mentioned in the selection that you or the person who experienced the loss went through.

_____

_____

_____

_____

_____

6. In his best-selling book *Tuesdays with Morrie,* the journalist Mitch Albom chronicles the final months of his favorite college professor's life. Morrie Schwartz, a sociology professor, was dying from amyotrophic lateral sclerosis (ALS), a terminal illness that gradually moves up the body, destroying the nerves and eventually rendering a person unable to move, swallow, or breathe. Morrie tells Mitch, "Death ends a life, not a relationship" and "Learn how to die and you learn how to live." Take one of these "lessons" of Morrie's and explain why you agree or disagree with it.

_____

_____

_____

_____

_____

7. Overall main idea. What is the overall main idea the author wants the reader to understand about reactions to impending death? Answer this question in one sentence. Be sure that your overall main idea sentence includes the topic (*reactions to impending death*) and tells the overall most important point about it.

_____

_____

_____

_____

_____

_____

_____

Read More about It on the World Wide Web

To learn more about the topic of this selection, visit these websites or use your favorite search engine (such as Yahoo ®). Whenever you go to *any* website, it is a good idea to evaluate it critically. Are you getting good information—information that is accurate, complete, and up-to-date? Who sponsors the website? How easy is it to use the features of the website?

http://www.wic.org/bio/eross.htm
> *This website contains a concise educational and professional profile of Dr. Elisabeth Kübler-Ross's accomplishments.*

http://www.amazon.com
> *In the search box, select "Books," then type in, "Tuesdays With Morrie." This website will give you information on the book* Tuesdays With Morrie, *a story about important lessons learned from a dying college professor by one of his former students.*

© PhotoDisc

C H A P T E R

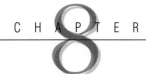

8

Reading Critically

CHAPTER OBJECTIVES

In this chapter you will learn the answers to these questions:

- What is critical reading?

- How can I determine an author's purpose?

- How can I determine an author's intended audience?

- How can I determine an author's point of view or bias?

- How can I determine an author's tone and intended meaning?

SKILLS

What Is Critical Reading?

Critical Reading Skills

- Determining an Author's Purpose and Intended Audience

- Determining an Author's Point of View, Tone, and Intended Meaning

A Word About Standardized Reading Tests: Critical Reading

CREATING YOUR SUMMARY

Developing Chapter Review Cards

READINGS

The end of reading is not more books, but more life.

Holbrook Jackson

To disagree with something without understanding it is impertinent.
To agree with something without understanding it is inane.

WHAT IS CRITICAL READING?

KEY TERM
Critical Reading

Gaining insights and understanding that go beyond comprehending the topic, main idea, and supporting details.

Going beyond basic comprehension to gain insights as you read is called **critical reading.** Whenever you read, of course, you should identify basic information: topic, main idea, and supporting details. However, to gain greater understanding, you will need to go beyond these basic elements.

Reading critically requires you to ask certain questions *after* you read a passage and to think carefully about what you have read. Critical reading requires you to understand implied (suggested) and figurative (nonliteral) meanings in addition to literal (stated) meanings. As you will learn in Chapter 9, this also means taking time to reread and reconsider an author's message so that you can make careful evaluations and judgments about what you are reading.

CRITICAL READING SKILLS

The important, interrelated critical reading skills presented in this chapter are:

- Determining an author's purpose
- Determining an author's intended audience
- Determining an author's point of view
- Determining an author's tone and intended meaning

Because these skills are *interrelated,* they are presented together in this chapter. As you will learn in this chapter, an author's *purpose* causes him or her to present certain facts and opinions, and to use a certain *tone* to convey a *point of view* and an *intended meaning* to an *intended audience.*

Determining an Author's Purpose and Intended Audience

KEY TERM
Purpose

An author's reason for writing.

Authors write for specific purposes. An author's **purpose** is simply his or her reason for writing. The author's purpose may be to *inform,* to *instruct,* to *entertain,* or to *persuade* the reader to believe something or take a certain action. Most textbook authors write for the purpose of informing (giving information) or instructing (explaining how to do something). However, some authors, such as movie critics, newspaper editors, and political writers, write to give their opinion or to persuade. Finally, other writers, such as humorists or certain newspaper columnists, write for the purpose of entertaining. They may entertain readers, for example, with humorous stories or with enjoyable descriptions.

411

Reading critically involves asking yourself certain questions *after* you read a passage and thinking carefully about what you have read.
(Stewart Cohen/Index Stock)

Sometimes an author will state his or her purpose. For example, the author of a biology textbook might write, "The purpose of this section is to define and explain the two types of cell division." At other times, the author may feel that the purpose is obvious and assume that the reader can infer it. Understanding an author's purpose means that you are aware of his or her motive for writing. It is important to understand an author's motive for writing so that you can prevent yourself from being unknowingly influenced by the author.

To determine an author's purpose, think carefully about the words he or she has used. Authors often choose certain words precisely because those words can direct or influence the reader's thinking.

For example, authors sometimes use phrases such as these when they want to *inform* you of important information:

The important point is . . .
Be sure you know . . .
It is important to understand . . .
Remember that . . .

When authors want to *instruct,* they may include phrases such as:

Follow these directions . . .
You must do the following . . .
The steps below explain how to . . .
These instructions tell how to . . .
This is the procedure for . . .

Authors may use phrases such as these when they want to *persuade:*

The only intelligent choice, then, is . . .
Any reasonable person will agree that . . .
Only an uninformed person would believe that . . .
Those who understand the issue will certainly agree . . .

When authors are writing to *entertain* readers, they may use phrases such as:

You'll never believe what happened to me when I . . .

The funny thing about . . .

And then the oddest thing happened . . .

I'll never forget the day I . . .

Comprehension Monitoring Question for Determining an Author's Purpose

"Why did the author write this?"

Looking at the words the author has chosen is one way to determine the author's purpose. Another way to determine an author's purpose is to examine whether or not both sides of a controversial issue have been presented. That is, check to see whether important information has been left out. Authors frequently choose to leave out information that does not support their point of view. Keep in mind that although an author may appear to be neutral on an issue, his or her real purpose may be to persuade you to support one side.

Remember, then: To read critically, you must determine the author's purpose by asking yourself, "Why did the author write this?"

KEY TERM
Intended Audience

People an author has in mind as his or her readers.

Authors also have specific audiences in mind when they write. An author's **intended audience** consists of the people the author has in mind as readers; that is, the people he or she is writing for. For instance, a psychologist writing a textbook may assume that his or her audience will be students taking an introductory psychology course. The psychologist will have these students in mind while writing, and this will shape decisions about the material to be included and about the level of difficulty. "Who did the author intend to read this?" is a question critical readers always ask themselves.

Comprehension Monitoring Question for Determining an Author's Intended Audience

"Who did the author intend to read this?"

Sometimes, of course, an author will state who the intended audience is. However, when you must determine an author's intended audience, examine these three things: the topic being discussed (Is it of *technical* or of *general interest?*), the level of language used (Is it *simple, sophisticated,* or *specialized?*), and the purpose for writing (Is it to *instruct, inform, persuade,* or *entertain?*).

Following is a paragraph from an article in *Prevention* magazine entitled "Laugh Your Stress Away" (Selection 5-1). After you read this paragraph, ask yourself, "Why did the author write this?" and "Who did the author intend to read this?"

Humor is one of the best on-the-spot stress busters around. It's virtually impossible to belly laugh and feel bad at the same time. If you're caught in a situation you can't escape or change (a traffic jam, for example), then humor may be the healthiest form of temporary stress release possible.

What is the author's purpose?

_____

Who is the author's intended audience?

_____

Source: Steven Lally, "Laugh Your Stress Away," *Prevention,* June 1991, p. 284. Reprinted by permission of *Prevention* magazine.

Stop and Annotate

Go back to the excerpt above. Determine the *author's purpose* and *intended audience,* and write your responses in the spaces provided.

In this paragraph, the author's purpose is simply to *inform* the reader that humor can be an effective way to temporarily reduce stress. You can see that the author uses simple language and short sentences. Notice that the author uses informal language: *stress busters* and *belly laugh.* He also chooses a simple example: being stuck in a traffic jam. Because his topic requires no special prior knowledge and because his approach is uncomplicated, you can assume that the author's intended audience is *the general public.* Practically anyone could understand and benefit from the information he presents. Of course, the source of the passage, *Prevention* magazine, helps confirm that the general public is the intended audience.

Now read a passage from a business communication textbook to determine the authors' purpose and the audience they had in mind.

Think about the people you know. Which of them would you call successful communicators? What do these people have in common? Chances are, the individuals on your list share five qualities:

• *Perception.* They are able to predict how their message will be received. They anticipate your reaction and shape the message accordingly. They read your response correctly and constantly adjust to correct any misunderstanding.

• *Precision.* They create a "meeting of the minds." When they finish expressing themselves, you share the same mental picture.

• *Credibility.* They are believable. You have faith in the substance of their message. You trust their information and their intentions.

• *Control.* They shape your response. Depending on their purpose, they can make you laugh or cry, calm down, change your mind, or take action.

• *Congeniality.* They maintain friendly, pleasant relations with the audience. Regardless of whether you agree with them, good communicators command your respect and goodwill. You are willing to work with them again, despite your differences.

What sets good communicators apart is their ability to overcome the main barriers to communication. They do this by creating their messages carefully, minimizing noise in the transmission process, and facilitating feedback.

Source: Courtland Bovée and John Thill, *Business Communication Today,* 3d ed., McGraw-Hill, New York, 1992, p. 44. Reproduced by permission of McGraw-Hill.

What is the authors' purpose?

_____

Who is the authors' intended audience?

_____

_____

_____

_____

_____

_____

Stop and Annotate

Go back to the excerpt above. Determine the *authors' purpose* and *intended audience,* and write your responses in the spaces provided.

In this excerpt, the authors' purpose is also to *inform.* The authors list specific elements that characterize good communicators and describe how these people interact with others. The authors' intended audience is *students in a business communications course* or *adults who want to know about characteristics of effective communication.*

Here is a passage from a health textbook whose purpose and audience are easy to determine. In this passage, the authors use simple, factual language to describe to the reader the proper procedure to follow when someone is choking.

Choking

If a person who seems to be choking on food or a foreign object can speak, do not interfere with that individual's attempt to cough up the object. If the person is unable to speak, it is appropriate to provide emergency care by using the Heimlich maneuver. Stand behind the victim and place both arms around his or her waist. Grasp one fist with the other hand and place the thumb side of the fist against the victim's abdomen, slightly above the navel and below the rib cage. Press your fist into the victim's abdomen with a quick inward and upward thrust. Repeat this procedure until the object is dislodged. The Heimlich maneuver should not be used with infants under one year of age.

Source: Marvin Levy, Mark Dignan, and Janet Shirreffs, *Targeting Wellness: The Core,* McGraw-Hill, New York, 1992, pp. 284–285.

What is the authors' purpose?

_____

Who is the authors' intended audience?

_____

_____

_____

_____

Stop and Annotate

Go back to the excerpt above. Determine the *authors' purpose* and *intended audience,* and write your responses in the spaces provided.

The purpose of the passage is to *instruct.* The paragraph describes the steps necessary for performing the Heimlich maneuver. The intended audience is *students in a health course* or *people who are interested in learning the Heimlich maneuver.* (In Chapter 7 you learned that sets of instructions are sequences. When the author's purpose is to instruct, watch for a sequence.)

Here is a short paragraph from an article entitled "The Time Message" (Selection 8-1). After you have read it, ask yourself, "Why did the author write this?" and "Who did the author intend to read this?"

Time is dangerous. If you don't control it, it will control you! If you don't make it work for you, it will work against you. You must become the master of time, not the servant. In other words, as a college student, time management will be your number-one problem.

Source: E. N. Chapman, "The Time Message," in Frank Christ, ed., *SR/SE Resource Book,* SRA, Chicago, Ill., 1969, p. 3.

What is the author's purpose?

_____

Who is the author's intended audience?

_____

Stop and Annotate

Go back to the excerpt above. Determine the *author's purpose* and *intended audience*, and write your responses in the spaces provided.

Although the author of this paragraph informs the reader about the importance of controlling time, his primary purpose is to *persuade* the reader to deal with this potentially "dangerous" problem. The author also used an exclamation point in the second sentence to emphasize the importance of dealing with time so that you are not "controlled" by it. The author's intended audience is clearly stated in the last sentence of the paragraph: the *college student,* especially one who has not yet mastered time management.

Here is a paragraph written for a completely different purpose. It is from the best-seller *Having Our Say: The Delany Sisters' First 100 Years* (Selection 8-2.) In this excerpt, 103-year-old Bessie Delany describes her nearly fatal bout with typhoid fever when she was 15 years old.

When I got out of the hospital, I looked like death. They had cut off my hair, real short, and I weighed next to nothing. I could not get enough to eat. Mama was so worried that she fixed a small basket of fruit each morning for me to carry with me all day, so I could eat whenever I wanted. For a long time I was on crutches, and I was not expected to recover fully. They used to say that typhoid fever left its mark on people. Well, nothing has shown up yet, so I guess I'm in the clear!

What is the author's purpose?

_____

Who is the author's intended audience?

_____

Source: Sarah and Elizabeth Delany with Amy Hill Hearth, *Having Our Say,* Dell, New York, 1993, p. 83.

Stop and Annotate

Go back to the excerpt above. Determine the *authors' purpose* and *intended audience*, and write your responses in the spaces provided.

As the humor in the last sentence suggests, the purpose of this paragraph is to *entertain* the reader. At 103 years of age Bessie Delany "guesses" she's "in the clear" and no longer needs to worry that any aftereffects of her bout with typhoid fever will show up. The intended audience of this passage is *the general public* who would enjoy reading about a centenarian's recollection of her childhood.

Remember, part of critical reading involves asking yourself these two questions in order to determine the author's purpose and intended audience: "Why did the author write this?" and "Who did the author intend to read this?"

Determining an Author's Point of View, Tone, and Intended Meaning

KEY TERM
Point of View

An author's position (opinion) on an issue.

Point of view is also known as the *author's argument* or the *author's bias.*

Point of view refers to an author's position on an issue. In other words, an author's point of view is his or her opinion about that topic. It is the position he or she hopes to convince the reader to accept or believe. An author's point of view is also known as the *author's argument* or the *author's bias.*

Even though authors are generally experts in their fields, they do not always agree on every topic and issue. Because authors may have different points of view and may disagree with other experts, it is important that you recognize what each author's point of view is. For example, one author's point of view might be, "Gun control is necessary if we are to have a safe society." The point of view of an author with the opposite bias would be, "Gun control would only make society less safe." A neutral point of view would be, "Gun control has both advantages and disadvantages."

Notice the use of the word bias in the preceding paragraph. In everyday conversation, people often use the word bias to mean *prejudice;* that is, they mean that a biased person has taken a position without thinking it through and without examining the evidence. For this reason, the word bias sometimes has a negative connotation. However, with regard to written material, an author's **bias** simply represents his or her *preference* for one side of an issue over the other. There is nothing wrong with this. Many thoughtful writers weigh the evidence carefully, then adopt the point of view that makes the most sense to them. When you read, you must try to determine whether the author has a bias. A bias may cause an author to slant the facts and not be objective.

Sometimes the author states his or her bias directly. For example, an author might state that he or she has a bias against home schooling. At other times, authors expect the reader to recognize their bias, on the basis of the information they include (or leave out) and the way they present the information. Consider the following sample paragraph, in which the author clearly expresses a bias against using a cell phone while driving.

> There should be a law against using a cell phone when driving. In spite of what they say, drivers become distracted reaching for the phone, dialing it, or answering it. The conversation itself can also take their attention away from the road. Suppose a driver having a conversation gets upset or angry with the caller. In that case, is the driver's full concentration really on the road? Drivers who are busy with their cell phones are involved in more accidents than drivers who do not use cell phones. They cause more accidents that kill and injure not only themselves, but other innocent, unsuspecting drivers. The bumper sticker says it all: "Hang up and drive!"

Incidentally, you should be aware of your *own* biases whenever you are reading about a controversial issue. If you have a strong bias on a subject and an author has the opposite bias, you might be tempted to reject the author's point of view without giving it serious consideration. Do not let your own bias cause you to automatically close your mind to an author's point of view just because it is different from yours. (For example, readers who favor being able to use cell phones while driving might automatically close their minds after reading the first sentence of the sample paragraph above.)

To determine the author's point of view, critical readers ask themselves, "What is the author's position on this issue?" Look for words that reveal the author's point of view, such as:

Supporting this new policy is *essential* because . . .

The proposed legislation *will benefit* all the citizens of Dade county because . . .

It is *not in the best interest* of the country to . . .

Voters *should oppose* the creation of a state lottery because . . .

An author's **tone** is a manner of writing that reveals or reflects his or her attitude toward a topic, just as tone of voice reveals a speaker's attitude. When someone is speaking, you can generally tell by the tone if he or she is serious,

KEY TERM
Author's Bias

The side of an issue an author favors; an author's preference for one side of an issue over the other.

Comprehension Monitoring Question for Determining an Author's Point of View

"What is the author's position on this issue?"

KEY TERM
Tone

Manner of writing (choice of words and style) that reveals an author's attitude toward a topic.

sarcastic, sympathetic, enthusiastic, etc. To convey a tone, a speaker relies on pitch, volume, and inflection, along with choice of words. For example, if someone says, "I made a C on my biology test," you would need to know the speaker's tone to know whether he or she was excited, relieved, or disappointed.

**Comprehension
Monitoring Question for
Determining an Author's
Tone**

"What do the author's choice
of words and style of writing
reveal about his or her
attitude toward the topic?"

Authors use tone just as speakers do. Authors, however, must rely on style of writing and choice of words to reveal their tone. They select words and writing styles that fit their purposes for writing (to inform, instruct, persuade, or entertain) and their point of view (for example, in favor of or opposed to something). In other words, they use a certain tone (informal, serious, sincere, humorous, etc.) to help convey their intended meaning. You can determine an author's tone by examining his or her choice of words and style of writing. To determine an author's tone, ask yourself, "What do the author's choice of words and style of writing reveal about his or her attitude toward the topic?"

As just noted, choice of words—or *word choice*—is one way authors reveal their tone. For example, when talking about a politician, one writer might use the word *lie* to convey a critical, disapproving, or bitter tone; another author might choose the word *exaggerate* instead to convey a tolerant or even an amused tone. Compare the following two sentences; they contain the same message (taxpayers' money will be used to help the unemployed), but the word choice makes their tone very different:

> Once again, the American taxpayers have to foot the bill for those who are too lazy or unmotivated to work.

> Once again, American taxpayers are showing their generosity by helping those who are unable to find employment.

Note the disapproving tone conveyed by the word choice in the first sentence (*foot the bill* and *too lazy or unmotivated to work*). A more positive, compassionate tone is conveyed by the choice of words in the second sentence (*showing their generosity by helping* and *unable to find employment*).

Now consider how an author's writing style also conveys a tone. Compare these two sentences; they contain the same message (the field of virtual reality is expanding rapidly), but the writing style makes their tone quite different:

> Since there will be a significant increase in employment opportunities in the field of "virtual reality," computer science majors would be wise to investigate this fast-growing area.

> VR is becoming a really hot career option, so check it out!

These two sentences present essentially the same information, but the first sentence has a more formal, factual tone. It is the type of sentence you might find in a career brochure or a computer science textbook. In the second sentence, however, the use of the abbreviation "VR," the phrase *really hot career option,* and the expression *check it out!* convey an informal and enthusiastic tone. This kind of sentence might appear in a computer magazine or in an advertisement for computer job training.

Although an author's tone is often obvious, there may be times when the tone is less clear and requires careful thought on your part. If you misunderstand an author's tone, you may misinterpret the message. For example, if you read a short story and you miss the author's ironic or sarcastic tone, you will mistakenly think his or her meaning is the opposite of what it actually is. When authors use **irony,** they create a deliberate contrast between their apparent meaning and their intended meaning; their words say one thing but mean the opposite. That is, the words are intended to express something different from their literal meaning. You use irony every day in conversation. For example, you might say, "Well, that test was a breeze!" but your ironic tone makes it clear how difficult the test actually was. Another form of irony occurs when there is incongruity between what might be expected and what actually occurs. For example, it would be ironic if you won a new car in a contest on the same day that you bought a new one. Students sometimes confuse irony with sarcasm. **Sarcasm** is a cutting, often ironic remark that is intended to convey contempt or ridicule. Sarcasm is always meant to hurt; irony is not intended to be hurtful.

For many students, especially those for whom English is a second language, it can be challenging to detect sarcasm in written material. When you are reading, you can concentrate so much on following what the author is saying that you forget to think about how sensible it is and whether the author really expects you to take the words literally. It is often helpful to "step back" and think about whether the author is being sarcastic. If the author is using sarcasm, his or her true meaning will be the opposite of what the words appear to be saying. For example, suppose you read this letter from a school principal to a newspaper editor about students who cheat in school:

> As a high school principal, I strongly believe that there shouldn't be any penalties for students who are caught cheating. After all, everyone does it. Besides, cheating in school will help prepare these same students to cheat on their employers later on, to cheat on their spouses when they marry, and to cheat on their taxes. In fact, we could help students even more if we offered a course on how to cheat.

The fact that you feel surprised, shocked, or confused at what the writer is saying should alert you to the fact that he or she is being sarcastic. Does the writer, a high school principal, really mean that it is fine for students to cheat in school? No, of course not. To make a point, the writer is saying the *opposite* of what he or she actually means. Sometimes an author is deliberately ridiculous. The author's words are so absurd, in fact, that their absurdity makes it clear that the author does not mean at all what the words appear to be saying. In the example above, the author expects readers to understand that students who are caught cheating in school *should* be punished. Otherwise, those who cheat in school without any consequences will turn out to be dishonorable adults who continue to cheat in a variety of ways and think that there is nothing wrong with it. Would it really make sense to think that a school principal, the writer of the letter, would advocate cheating? Of course not. However, if you are not reading critically and you fail to notice the writer's sarcasm, you might go away feeling puzzled and mistakenly believing that the high school principal who wrote the letter thinks it is all right for students to cheat.

There are additional clues that can help you detect sarcasm in written material. First, pay attention when authors use words that seem inappropriate for what they are describing, such as an obvious exaggeration or an obvious understatement. For example, an author might exaggerate by saying that if the city's baseball team ever won a single game, the entire population would turn out on the streets for a weeklong celebration. Or in describing a bitter legal case over property rights that has gone on for years, the writer might deliberately understate and describe it as "that unfriendly little property dispute." A second way to detect sarcasm is to think about how a passage would sound if the author *spoke* the words rather than wrote them. You may even want to read the passage aloud yourself and listen to your tone of voice. Can you hear any sarcasm in it?

As noted earlier, irony involves using words that seem straightforward but that actually contain a different, hidden meaning. In the year 2000, just before the Academy Awards, there were many complaints that the program the preceding year has lasted entirely too long—four hours. In spite of this, the 2000 Academy Awards lasted even longer—four and a half hours! The emcee, Billy Crystal, made an ironic comment when he said he didn't understand why anyone was complaining because "the 2000 Academy Awards ceremony was the shortest one of the millennium." His comment was ironic because technically he was right, since that evening's ceremony was the *only* ceremony in this millennium. Therefore, regardless of how long the ceremony was, it was automatically the "shortest one of the millennium."

Another form of irony occurs when there is incongruity or difference between what is expected and what actually occurs. (The cartoon on page 422 illustrates this form of irony.) For example, it would be ironic if you got on an airplane to make a surprise visit to friend in another city, and your friend was not there because he was making a trip to pay a surprise visit to you in your city!

Satire is a type of writing in which the author sometimes uses sarcasm or irony for a specific purpose. To be precise, **satire** is a style of writing in which the author uses sarcasm, irony, or ridicule to attack or expose human foolishness, corruption, or stupidity. When authors are being satirical (using satire), they expect readers to pick up on it and understand their real message. Many famous writers have used satire to expose weaknesses in human society and morals. When you read a selection, ask yourself if the writer is trying to expose some problem by making fun of it. Here is an example of a passage in which the author uses satire to expose a politician's corrupt nature:

> Would our distinguished state senator ever accept bribes from large corporations in exchange for his vote on important issues? Certainly not! He was never convicted when those charges were brought against him twice in the past. Is he a corrupt man who would accept illegal campaign contributions? Absolutely not. When it was revealed that he had accepted several questionable donations, he eventually returned all of them. Would the noble senator ever fail to report income on his tax form? Ridiculous. Although he has refused to release any of his tax returns, he obviously has nothing to hide. Would this fine man ever accept trips or other expensive gifts from lobbyists? Definitely not. Even though he cannot afford them on his salary, he shouldn't have to explain how he paid for all those expensive golf and ski vacations or how he is able to afford a vacation home in the country. After all, he's told us he hasn't done anything wrong, and as we all know, the senator is an honorable man.

You can almost hear the writer's voice drip with sarcasm. To show us how "honorable" the senator is, the writer tells us that the senator:

Has twice had charges brought against him of selling his votes for bribes

Returned certain campaign contributions when it was revealed to the public that they might be illegal

Refuses to make his income tax returns available to the public

Refuses to explain how he can afford certain very expensive luxuries on his salary

By mentioning one questionable matter after another that the senator has been involved in or accused of, and pretending to discount them, the writer reveals the senator's dishonest nature. The writer refers to the senator as "distinguished," "noble," and "honorable," although his (let's assume the writer is male) sarcasm makes it clear that he believes the senator is none of these. In response to accusations about the senator's behavior, the writer vigorously declares, "Certainly not," "Absolutely not," "Ridiculous," and "Definitely not." Again, though, his overly strong denials make it clear he thinks the senator is guilty of the charges. If readers fail to recognize that the writer is satirizing the senator, they would come away with a complete misunderstanding of the writer's real point of view: the senator is corrupt.

It is not so important that you be able to distinguish among sarcasm, irony, and satire. What is important is that you pick up on clues that authors use to signal that their intended meaning is different from what their words *appear* to be saying.

If you overlook irony or sarcasm you may think authors are being serious when they are actually joking; that they are calm when, in fact, they are angry; or that they are in favor of something when, in reality, they oppose it. **Author's intended meaning** is what an author wants readers to understand even when his or her words seem to be saying something different. Determining the author's tone correctly will enable you to grasp the author's intended meaning, even when the author's words appear on the surface to be saying something different. Critical readers ask themselves, "What is the author's *real* meaning?"

There are many words that can be used to describe an author's tone. Several of these are listed and defined below. You should familiarize yourself with ones that are new to you.

KEY TERM
Intended Meaning

What an author wants readers to understand even when his or her words seem to be saying something different.

Comprehension Monitoring Question for Determining an Author's Intended Meaning

"What is the author's *real* meaning?"

ambivalent	having opposite feelings or attitudes at the same time
amused	feeling entertained or occupied in a pleasant manner
approving	expressing approval or agreement
arrogant	giving oneself an undue degree of importance; haughty
authoritative	speaking in a definite and confident manner
bitter	characterized by sharpness, severity, or cruelty
cautious	wary; careful; not wanting to take chances
compassionate	sympathetic; merciful
concerned	caring deeply about an issue or person

This cartoon illustrates situational irony since it is the *bug* that is being bitten. (The FAR SIDE © 1993 FarWorks, Inc. Used by permission. All rights reserved.)

THE FAR SIDE   By GARY LARSON

"Wow. ... That's ironic. I think something bit me."

conciliatory	willing to give in on some matters
critical	inclined to criticize or find fault
defiant	resisting authority; intentionally contemptuous
disapproving	passing unfavorable judgment upon; condemning
disbelieving	not believing; refusing to believe
encouraging	showing support
enthusiastic	showing excitement
evasive	intentionally vague or ambiguous; not giving a direct answer
grim	stern; fearsome
impassioned	showing warmth of feeling; characterized by passion or zeal
indifferent	appearing to have no preference or concern
indignant	wrathful; irate; feeling wrath or anger
intolerant	not allowing difference of opinion or sentiment
ironic	humorously sarcastic or mocking
irreverent	not showing the respect that is deserved
malicious	intended to cause harm or suffering; with wicked or mischievous intentions or motives
mocking	treating with scorn or contempt
nostalgic	bittersweet longing for things, persons, or situations in the past

optimistic	expecting the best; having a positive outlook
pessimistic	expecting the worst; having a negative attitude; gloomy
positive	in favor of; supportive; optimistic
remorseful	feeling regret
sarcastic	making cutting remarks to show scorn or contempt
satirical	using sarcasm, irony or caustic wit to expose or ridicule human folly, vice or stupidity
self-pitying	feeling sorry for oneself
sentimental	based on emotions rather than reason
skeptical	reluctant to believe; doubting or questioning everything
solemn	stately; ceremonious
straightforward	direct; free from ambiguity; without evasion
supportive	showing support or assistance
sympathetic	inclined to sympathy; showing pity; empathic
tolerant	showing respect for the rights, or opinions, or practices of others
urgent	calling for immediate attention; instantly important

To be sure you understand an author's intended meaning, you must understand the author's tone. Ask yourself the questions critical readers ask: "What do the author's choice of words and style of writing reveal about his or her attitude toward the topic?" and "What is the author's *real* meaning?"

Here is an excerpt from an essay by George Will, a well-known political commentator and columnist. The topic of this excerpt is legal gambling (state lotteries and betting on the sport of jai alai). As you read, notice that his disapproving tone helps convey his negative point of view toward legal forms of gambling.

Last year, Americans legally wagered $15 billion, up 8 percent over 1976. Lotteries took in 24 percent more. Stiffening resistance to taxes is encouraging states to seek revenues from gambling, and thus to encourage gambling. There are three rationalizations for this:

- State-run gambling controls illegal gambling.
- Gambling is a painless way to raise revenues.
- Gambling is a "victimless" recreation, and thus is a matter of moral indifference.

Actually, there is evidence that legal gambling increases the respectability of gambling, and increases public interest in gambling. This creates new gamblers, some of whom move on to illegal gambling, which generally offers better odds. And as a revenue-raising device, gambling is severely regressive.

Gamblers are drawn disproportionately from minority and poor populations that can ill afford to

What is the author's point of view?

_____

_____

_____

What is the author's tone?

_____

_____

_____

gamble, that are especially susceptible to the lure of gambling, and that especially need a government that will not collaborate with gambling entrepreneurs, as in jai alai, and that will not become a gambling entrepreneur through a state lottery.

A depressing number of gamblers have no margin for economic losses and little understanding of the probability of losses. Between 1975 and 1977 there was a 140 percent increase in spending to advertise lotteries—lotteries in which more than 99.9 percent of all players are losers. Such advertising is apt to be especially effective, and cruel, among people whose tribulations make them susceptible to dreams of sudden relief.

Grocery money is risked for such relief. Some grocers in Hartford's poorer neighborhoods report that receipts decline during jai alai season. Aside from the injury gamblers do to their dependents, there is a more subtle but more comprehensive injury done by gambling. It is the injury done to society's sense of elemental equities. Gambling blurs the distinction between well-earned and "ill-gotten" gains.

State-sanctioned gambling institutionalizes windfalls, whets the public appetite for them, and encourages the delusion that they are more frequent than they really are. Thus do states simultaneously cheat and corrupt their citizens.

Source: George F. Will, "Lotteries Cheat, Corrupt the People," © 1994, *Washington Post* Writers' Group. Reprinted with permission.

This passage clearly shows George Will's point of view: *he opposes legal gambling* because he believes it harms the public in a variety of ways. His tone is *disapproving.* His disapproval of legal gambling is revealed by his deliberate choice of these words:

rationalization (instead of *reasons*)

collaborating with (which suggests helping someone do something wrong)

the *lure* of gambling

a *depressing* number of gamblers

cruel

dreams of sudden relief (which probably will not happen)

injury

ill-gotten gains

encourages the *delusion*

cheat and corrupt their citizens

Stop and Annotate

Go back to the excerpt above. Determine the author's *point of view* and *tone,* and write your responses in the spaces provided.

In addition, George Will's style of writing conveys his tone and point of view. He appears extremely knowledgeable about his subject. He uses factual support and presents a convincing, well-reasoned argument against gambling. There is no intended meaning beyond what he has stated. His meaning is exactly as he presents it: states cheat and corrupt their citizens when they allow legal gambling.

In the passage below from a study skills textbook, the authors' tone is completely different. Its purpose is to define concentration and explain why it is a complex process. After you read this paragraph, ask yourself, "What is the author's position on this issue?" and "What do the author's choice of words and style of writing reveal about his or her attitude toward the topic?"

Psychologically defined, concentration is the process of centering one's attention over a period of time. In practical application, however, concentration is not as simple to cope with as the definition may imply. For this reason, it is important to keep the following points in mind:

- Your attention span varies.
- Your attention span is short.
- When you truly concentrate, you are paying attention to only one thing at a time.
- Distractors to concentration can be both physical and psychological.
- Emotions are the most powerful psychological distractors.

Source: Adapted from William Farquar, John Krumboltz, and Gilbert Wrenn, "Controlling Your Concentration," in Frank Christ, ed., *SR/SE Resource Book,* SRA, Chicago, 1969, p. 119.

What is the authors' point of view?

_____

_____

What is the authors' tone?

_____

_____

_____

Stop and Annotate

Go back to the excerpt above. Determine the authors' *point of view* and *tone,* and write your responses in the spaces provided.

In this paragraph, the authors' tone is *factual and straightforward* rather than emotional and persuasive. The authors' point of view is that *concentration is not as simple a process as it might seem.* Since this is factual material presented in a straightforward manner, the authors' intended meaning is exactly what it appears to be.

Remember, part of reading critically involves asking yourself, "What is the author's position on this issue?" "What do the author's choice of words and style of writing reveal about his or her attitude toward the topic?" and "What is the author's *intended* meaning?"

It is obvious from the two examples above that an author's tone is related to his or her purpose and point of view: being aware of the author's tone will help you determine that purpose and point of view. The chart on page 426 shows the *interrelationship* among author's purpose, tone, point of view, intended meaning, and intended audience.

HOW THE CRITICAL READING SKILLS ARE INTERRELATED

The author's purpose causes him or her to use a certain tone to convey a point of view to an intended audience.

- The author decides on a *purpose* (reason) for writing:

  to inform   to instruct   to persuade   to entertain

- To accomplish this purpose, the author uses an appropriate *tone;* for example:

  serious   formal   sincere   enthusiastic

  disapproving   sympathetic   informal   humorous

  ironic

- To convey his or her main idea or *point of view* (position on an issue):

  point of view (*in favor of* or *opposed to*) or argument

- To an *intended audience:*

  the general public   a specific group   a particular person

The chart below illustrates the application of critical reading skills to a review of an imaginary movie. It is designed to show that critical reading skills are related and that they can be applied to reading tasks that you encounter daily.

EXAMPLE OF CRITICAL READING APPLIED TO A CRITIC'S REVIEW OF A MOVIE

Here is a critic's review of *Cyberpunk,* a new science fiction movie:

Do you enjoy violence? Do you like vulgar language? Do you appreciate painfully loud sound effects? What about watching unknown actors embarrass themselves? Or sitting for three hours and ten minutes without a break? If so, and you've got $7.50 to burn, then *Cyberpunk* is the movie for you!

Critical Reading Questions	Answers
What is the author's purpose?	To present a persuasive evaluation of a new movie
Who is the author's intended audience?	The moviegoing public
What is the author's point of view?	The movie is terrible.
What is the author's tone?	Sarcastic
What is the author's intended meaning?	Don't waste your money or your time on this movie.

A WORD ABOUT STANDARDIZED READING TESTS: CRITICAL READING

Many college students are required to take standardized reading tests as part of an overall assessment program, in a reading course, or as part of a state-mandated "basic skills" test. A standardized reading test typically consists of a series of passages followed by multiple-choice questions, to be completed within a specified time limit.

Here are some examples of typical wording about critical reading:

Questions about the *author's purpose* may be worded:

The author's purpose for writing this passage is to . . .

The reason the author wrote this passage is . . .

It is likely that the author wrote this in order to . . .

The reason the author wrote this selection is primarily to . . .

The author wrote this passage in order to . . .

Questions about the *author's intended audience* may be worded:

The author intended this passage to be read by . . .

The author's intended audience is . . .

The author expects this passage to be read by . . .

Questions about the *author's point of view* may be worded:

The passage suggests that the author's point of view is . . .

The author's opinion about . . . . is . . .

It is clear that the author believes . . .

The passage suggests that the author's opinion about . . . is . . .

Questions about the *author's tone* may be worded:

The tone of this passage is . . . (factual, ironic, etc.)

The tone of this passage can be described as . . .

Which of the following words best describes the tone of the passage?

Questions about the *author's intended meaning* may be worded:

The author wants the reader to understand that . . .

The author's use of sarcasm suggests that . . .

The author's meaning is . . .

The author's use of irony indicates . . .

In this passage, the author intended the reader to understand that . . .

Although the author states that . . ., she means that . . .

Although the author appears to be supporting . . ., he actually wants the reader to . . .

DEVELOPING CHAPTER REVIEW CARDS

Review cards, or *summary cards,* are an excellent study tool. They are a way to select, organize, and review the most important information in a textbook chapter. The process of creating review cards helps you organize information in a meaningful way and, at the same time, transfer it into long-term memory. The cards can also be used to prepare for tests (see Part Three). The review card activities in this book give you structured practice in creating these valuable study tools. Once you have learned how to make review cards, you can create them for textbook material in your other courses.

Now, complete the five review cards for Chapter 8 by answering the questions or following the directions on each card. When you have completed them, you will have summarized: (1) what critical reading is, (2) author's purpose, (3) author's intended audience, (4) author's point of view, and (5) author's tone and intended meaning.

Critical Reading

Define *critical reading.* (See page 411.)

_____

_____

List the skills of critical reading. (See page 411.)

1. _____

_____

2. _____

_____

3. _____

_____

4. _____

_____

Card 1   **Chapter 8: Reading Critically**

Author's Purpose

Define the *author's purpose*. (See page 411.)

_____

List four common purposes for writing. (See page 411.)

1. _____

2. _____

3. _____

4. _____

What are two ways to determine an author's purpose? (See pages 412–413.)

1. _____

2. _____

To determine an author's purpose, what question should you ask yourself? (See page 413.)

_____

Card 2   **Chapter 8: Reading Critically**

Author's Intended Audience

Define *intended audience*. (See page 413.)

_____

_____

To determine an author's intended audience, what question should you ask yourself? (See page 413.)

_____

_____

What are three things you can examine in order to determine the author's intended audience? (See page 413.)

1. _____

2. _____

3. _____

Card 3   **Chapter 8: Reading Critically**

Author's Point of View

Define *point of view*. (See page 416.)

_____

Give some examples of words that reveal an author's point of view. (See page 417.)

_____

_____

_____

_____

To determine an author's point of view, what question should you ask yourself? (See page 417.)

_____

Define author's *bias*. (See page 417.)

_____

_____

_____

Card 4   **Chapter 8: Reading Critically**

Author's Tone and Intended Meaning

Define *tone*. (See page 417)

_____

What are two things you can examine in order to determine an author's tone? (See page 418.)

1. _____

2. _____

To determine an author's tone, what question should you ask yourself? (See page 418.)

_____

_____

Define *intended meaning*. (See page 421.)

_____

_____

To determine an author's intended meaning, what question should you ask yourself? (See page 421.)

_____

What is *irony?* (See page 419.)

_____

_____

What is *sarcasm?* (See page 419.)

_____

Card 5   **Chapter 8: Reading Critically**

THE TIME MESSAGE

By Elwood N. Chapman

Prepare Yourself to Read

Directions: Do these exercises *before* you read Selection 8-1.

1. First, read and think about the title. What do you already know about time management?

    _____

    _____

2. Next, complete your preview by reading the following:

    > Introduction (in *italics*)
    > First paragraph (paragraph 1)
    > Headings
    > All of the last paragraph (paragraph 20)

    On the basis of your preview, what aspects of time management do you think will be discussed?

    _____

    _____

Apply Comprehension Skills

Directions: Do the Annotation Practice Exercises as you read Selection 8-1. Read critically: Think about the author's purpose, intended audience, point of view, tone, and intended meaning.

THE TIME MESSAGE

In this chapter from a college orientation handbook, Chapman discusses what he calls the number one problem of college students: time management. Read each of Chapman's ten messages to determine which ones you might need to apply for more efficient management of your time.

1   You may have been exposed to this idea before, but this time try to hear. Pull out your earplugs! Turn up the volume! There is a message that is trying to reach you, and it is important that it get through loud and clear. It's beamed to all college freshmen. The message?

2   Time management!

3   Time is elusive and tricky. It is the easiest thing in the world to waste—the most difficult to control. When you look ahead, it may appear you have more than you need. Yet it has a way of slipping through your fingers like sand. You may suddenly find that there is no way to stretch the little time you have left to cover all your obligations. For example, as a beginning student looking ahead to a full semester or quarter you may feel that you have an oversupply of time on your hands. But toward the end of the term you may panic because time is running out. The answer?

4   Control.

5   Time is dangerous. If you don't control it, it will control you! If you don't make it work for you, it will work against you. You must become the master of time, not the servant. In other words, as a college student you'll find that time management will be your number one problem.

6   Study hard and play hard is an old adage, but it still makes sense. You have plenty of time for classes, study, work, and play if you use your time properly. It is not how much time you allocate for study that counts but how much you learn when you do study. Remember! You won't have a good time when you do go out on the town if you have a guilty feeling about your studies.

7   Too much wasted time is bad medicine. The more time you waste, the easier it is to continue wasting time. Soon, doing nothing becomes a habit you can't break. It becomes a drug. You are hooked and out of control. When this happens, you lose your feeling of accomplishment and you fall by the wayside. A full schedule is a good schedule.

Annotation Practice Exercises

Directions: For each of the exercises below, read critically to answer the questions. This will help you gain additional insights as you read.

Annotation Exercise

What is the author's *tone* in paragraph 5?

_____

_____

What is the author's *point of view* in paragraph 5?

_____

_____

8   Some students refuse to hear the time message. They refuse to accept the fact that college life demands some degree of time control. There is no escape. So what's the next step? If you seriously wish to get the time message, this chapter will give it to you. Remember—it will not only improve your grades but also free you to enjoy college life more.

Message 1. Time is valuable—control it from the beginning.

9   Time is today, not tomorrow or next week. Get in the driver's seat now. Start your plan at the beginning of the term and readjust it with each new project. Thus you can spread your work time around a little.

Message 2. Get the notebook habit.

10   Go to the student bookstore today and buy a pocket-size appointment notebook. There are many varieties of these special notebooks. Select the one you like best. Use it to schedule your study time each day. You can also use it to note important dates (such as announced exams or deadlines for papers), appointments, addresses, and telephone numbers (in case you need to check with professors or classmates about assignments). Keep it with you at all times.

Message 3. Prepare a weekly study schedule.

11   The main purpose of the notebook is to help you prepare a weekly study schedule. Once it is prepared, follow the same pattern every week with minor adjustments. Sunday is an excellent day to make up your schedule for the following week. Write in your class schedule first. Add your work hours, if any. Then write in the hours each day you feel you must allocate for study. Keep it simple.

Message 4. Be realistic.

12   Often you know from experience how long it takes you to write a 500-word composition, to study for a quick quiz, to prepare a speech, or to review for a final. When you plan time for these things, be realistic. Don't underestimate. Overestimate, if possible, so that emergencies that arise don't hang you up. Otherwise your entire routine may get thrown off balance while you devote night and day to crash efforts.

As a college student, you may find that time management is your number one problem. *(David Young-Wolff/Photo Edit).*

Message 5. Make study time fit the course.

13   Some authorities say you should schedule three hours of study for every hour in class; others say two hours of preparation should be sufficient. How much study time you schedule for each classroom hour depends on four factors: (1) your ability, (2) the difficulty of the class, (3) the grades you hope to achieve, and (4) how well you use your study time. One thing, however, is certain: you should schedule a minimum of one hour of study for each classroom hour. In many cases, more will be required.

Message 6. Keep your schedule flexible.

14   It is vital that you replan your schedule on a weekly basis so that you can keep a degree of flexibility as you move through a semester. For example, as you approach midterms or final exams you will want to juggle your schedule to provide more time for review purposes. When a research project is assigned, you will want to provide an additional block of time to squeeze it in. A good schedule must have a little give so that special projects can be taken care of properly. Think out and prepare your schedule each week, and do not become a slave to an inflexible pattern. Adjust it as you deem necessary. Experiment. A schedule is nothing more than a predetermined plan to make the best possible use of your time. Don't permit it to handcuff your ability to meet unexpected demands.

Message 7. Use the 20-20-20 formula.

15   For those students who must work about twenty hours each week and take a full college load, the 20-20-20 formula makes sense. This means you will be in classes (or labs) approximately 20 hours each week, you will work 20 hours, and you will study a minimum of 20 hours.

Message 8. Study first—fun later.

16   You will enjoy your fun time more after you have completed your study responsibilities. So, where possible, schedule your study hours in advance of fun activities. This is a sound principle to follow, so keep it in mind as you prepare your first schedule.

Who is the author's *intended audience* in this selection?

_____

_____

Message 9. Study some each class day.

17 Some concentrated study each day is better than many study hours one day and nothing the next. As you work out your individual schedule, attempt to include a minimum of two study hours each day. This will not only keep the study habit alive but also keep you up to date on your class assignments and projects.

Message 10. Free on Saturday—study on Sunday.

18 Many students think that it is psychologically good to back away from all study endeavors for one full day. Most students choose Saturday because of work, sporting events, or social activities. Sunday, on the other hand, seems to be an excellent study day for many students. It is a good day to catch up on back reading and other assignments. Give it some thought; it may be best for you too. Such a plan has the added advantage of warming you up for getting back into the weekday swing.

19 Few beginning freshmen can control their time effectively without a written schedule, so why kid yourself into thinking you don't need one? You do. Later on, when you have had more experience and you have the time-control habit, you may be able to operate without it. Of course the schedule is only the first step. Once you have it prepared, you must stick with it and follow it faithfully. You must push away the many temptations that are always present, or your schedule is useless. Your schedule will give you control only if you make it work.

20 Here's the message once more: You have plenty of time to take a full college load, study, work up to twenty hours a week, get sufficient sleep, take care of personal responsibilities, and have a good, healthy social life—if you control your time. It's your decision, and your life. So no excuses, please.

Source: Elwood N. Chapman, "The Time Message," in Frank Crist, ed., *SR/SE Resource Book,* SRA, Chicago, Ill., 1969; abridged from chap. 1, pp. 3–8.

Practice Exercise

What is the author's *purpose* in paragraph 20?

_____

_____

What is the author's *point of view* in paragraph 20?

_____

_____

_____

Comprehension Quiz

Directions: For each comprehension question below, use information from the selection to determine the correct answer. You may refer to the selection as you answer the questions. Write your answer in the space provided.

True or False

_____ **1.** According to the author, few beginning college students can control their time effectively without a written schedule.

_____ **2.** "Study hard and play hard" is an adage that the author believes no longer makes sense.

_____ **3.** All college students realize the importance of controlling their time.

_____ **4.** The more time you waste, the easier it is to continue wasting time.

_____ **5.** According to the selection, many college students think it is psychologically beneficial to back away from all study tasks for two full days on the weekend.

_____ **6.** Some concentrated study each day is better than many study hours one day and nothing the next.

Multiple-Choice

_____ **7.** The author wrote this article to persuade students that
　　a. they must become masters of their time.
　　b. time is the easiest thing in the world to waste.
　　c. time management is the number one problem of college students.
　　d. all of the above

_____ **8.** Your weekly study schedule for college classes should have all of the following characteristics *except* that
　　a. the same pattern must be followed exactly every week.
　　b. the same pattern should be followed every week with only minor adjustments.
　　c. some concentrated study for each class should be included each day.
　　d. a pocket-size calendar should be used to record your study schedule.

_____ **9.** The author believes that a college student should schedule
　　a. a minimum of 1 hour study time for each classroom hour.
　　b. 2 hours of study each day.
　　c. a minimum of 3 hours of study each day.
　　d. 3 hours of study for every hour in class.

_____ **10.** According to the selection, how much study time you schedule for each classroom hour depends on all of the following *except*

    a. your ability.

    b. the difficulty of class assignments and tests.

    c. your work schedule.

    d. how well you use your time.

S E L E C T I O N **8-1**

Study Skills

Extend Your Vocabulary by Using Context Clues

Directions: Context clues are words in a sentence that allow the reader to deduce (reason out) the meaning of an unfamiliar word in that sentence. For each vocabulary item below, a sentence from the selection containing an important word (*italicized, like this*) is quoted first. Next, there is an additional sentence using the word in the same sense and providing another context clue. Use the context clues from *both* sentences to deduce the meaning of the italicized word. *Be sure the answer you choose makes sense in both sentences.* If you discover that you must use a dictionary to confirm an answer choice, remember that the meaning you select must still fit the context of *both* sentences. To indicate your answer, write the letter in the space provided.

Pronunciation key: ă pat ā pay âr care ä father ĕ pet ē be ĭ pit
ī tie îr pier ŏ pot ō toe ô paw oi noise ou out ŏŏ took
ōō boot ŭ cut yōō abuse ûr urge th thin *th* this hw which
zh vision ə about
Stress Mark: ʹ

_____ **1.** You may have been *exposed* to these ideas before, but this time try to hear.

College students are *exposed* to many new concepts and different points of view.

exposed (ĭk spōzdʹ) means:

    a. convinced

    b. made aware of

    c. displayed

    d. repeated frequently

_____ **2.** Time is *elusive* and tricky.

Because certain mathematical concepts are *elusive,* it can take considerable thought to comprehend them.

elusive (ĭ lōo ′ sĭv) means:

a. easy

b. unable to be captured

c. difficult to grasp

d. impossible to understand

_____ **3.** Study hard and play hard is an old *adage,* but it still makes sense.

My grandmother's favorite *adage* is, "To have a friend, you must be one."

adage (ăd′ ĭj) means:

a. proverb or short saying

b. saying used only in a family

c. proverb made up by a famous person

d. saying whose origin in unknown

_____ **4.** It is not how much time you *allocate* for study that counts but how much you learn when you do study.

Tom and Margaret *allocate* approximately one-third of their monthly income to pay for housing and utilities.

allocate (ăl′ ə kāt) means:

a. assign; allot

b. waste; throw away

c. misuse

d. earn

_____ **5.** Once the schedule is prepared, follow the same pattern each week with *minor* adjustments.

My professor said that my paper was well written and needed only *minor* corrections.

minor (mī′ nĕr) means:

a. weekly

b. done on a regular basis

c. small in amount, size, or importance

d. done by a professional

_____ **6.** When you plan time for these things, be realistic. Don't *underestimate.*

The soccer players tended to *underestimate* the ability of their opponents.

underestimate (ŭn dər ĕs′ tə māt) means:

a. judge a value or amount too low

b. guess wildly

c. predict accurately

d. value highly

_____ 7. Think out and prepare your schedule each week, and do not become a slave to an *inflexible* pattern.

Professor Little is so *inflexible* that he will not make any exceptions to his course requirements or his grading policies.

inflexible (ĭn flĕk′ sə bəl) means:
   a.   variable; changing
   b.   rigid; unalterable
   c.   unpleasant
   d.   difficult

_____ 8. A schedule is nothing more than a *predetermined* plan to make the best possible use of your time.

Some insurance companies insist that each doctor publish a list of *predetermined* charges for medical services.

predetermined (prĕ dĭ tûr′ mĭnd) means:
   a.   decided by a group of people
   b.   incapable of being changed
   c.   determined or decided in advance
   d.   incapable of being known or determined

_____ 9. This is a sound *principle* to follow, so keep it in mind as you prepare your first schedule.

Isaac Newton is credited with formulating the *principle* of gravity.

principle (prĭn′ sə pəl) means:
   a.   basic truth, law, or assumption
   b.   person who directs a public school
   c.   false belief
   d.   reason

_____ 10. Many students think that it is psychologically good to back away from all study *endeavors* for one full day.

Because he works so hard, my father is highly successful in nearly all of his business *endeavors*.

endeavors (ĕn dĕv′ ərz) means:
   a.   sessions
   b.   routines
   c.   carefully made plans
   d.   attempts or efforts

Collaboration Option

Respond in Writing

Directions: Refer to the selection as needed to answer the essay-type questions below.

Option for collaboration: Your instructor may direct you to work with other students or, in other words, to work *collaboratively.* In that case, you should form groups of three or four students as directed by your instructor and work together to complete the exercises. After your group discusses each item and agrees on the answer, have a group member record it. Every member of your group should be able to explain all of your group's answers.

1. Which of the "time messages" mentioned in the article do you use now? What *other* things do you do that help you manage your time effectively?

_____

_____

_____

_____

_____

_____

_____

_____

2. What are some problems that prevent you from using your time as productively as you would like?

_____

_____

_____

_____

_____

_____

_____

_____

What solutions do you propose for the problems listed above?

_____

_____

_____

_____

_____

_____

_____

3. The author calls time management the number one problem of college students. Is this true for you? Explain why you agree or disagree with the author's statement. If you disagree, describe what you consider *your* number one problem. Is that problem in any way *related* to time management?

_____

_____

_____

_____

_____

4. Overall main idea. What is the overall main idea the author wants the reader to understand about time? Answer this question in one sentence. Be sure that your overall main idea sentence includes the topic (*time*) and tells the overall most important point about it.

_____

_____

_____

_____

_____

_____

Read More about It on the World Wide Web

To learn more about the topic of this selection, visit these websites or use your favorite search engine (such as Yahoo ®). Whenever you go to *any* website, it is good idea to evaluate it critically. Are you getting good information—information that is accurate, complete, and up-to-date? Who sponsors the website? How easy is it to use the features of the website?

http://www.uoguelph.ca/csrc/learning/tmres-b.htm

This website is the Time Management *Web page, which is part of Learning Services at the University of Guelph in Ontario, Canada. "Time management for university students" provides details on Guelph's semester system and how students can develop a time planning system that will be effective for them, their needs, and their program.*

http://daytimer.com/

This website offers the tools needed to build a time management system that works for you.

http://www.mindtools.com/tmintro.html

This set of articles explains time management as set of related, commonsense skills that help you use your time as effectively and productively as possible.

FROM *HAVING OUR SAY: THE DELANY SISTERS'* *FIRST 100 YEARS*

By Sarah L. Delany and A. Elizabeth Delany with Amy Hill Hearth

Prepare Yourself to Read

Directions: Do these exercises *before* you read Selection 8-2.

1. First, read *only* the title, the introduction, and the first three paragraphs.

    What comes to your mind when you read the title *Having Our Say: The Delany Sisters' First 100 Years?*

    _____

    _____

    _____

2. Do you personally know anyone who is 100 years (or more) of age? When you think of think of him or her, what comes to mind?

    _____

    _____

    _____

    _____

    _____

3. As you read the rest of the selection, keep in mind which sister is speaking.

Apply Comprehension Skills

Directions: Do the Annotation Practice Exercises as you read Selection 8-2. Read critically: Think about the author's purpose, intended audience, point of view, tone, and intended meaning.

FROM *HAVING OUR SAY*

What would it be like to live for more than 100 years? To be nearly half as old as the United States itself? Sarah ("Sadie") Delany was born in 1889; her sister Elizabeth ("Bessie") was born in 1891. Neither sister ever married, and the two lived together nearly all of their lives. Sadie Delany said that she and her sister probably know each other "better than any two human beings on this Earth." Their book, Having Our Say, *was published in 1993 and quickly went onto the New York Times best-seller list. In their book, they are described this way: "Sarah Delany and Dr. Elizabeth Delany were born in Raleigh, North Carolina, on the campus of St. Augustine's College. Their father, born into slavery, and freed by the Emancipation, was an administrator at the college and America's first elected black Episcopal bishop. Sarah received her bachelor's and master's degrees from Teachers College at Columbia University and was New York City's first appointed black home economics teacher on the high school level. Elizabeth received her degree in dentistry from Columbia University and was the second black woman licensed to practice dentistry in New York City. The sisters retired to Mount Vernon, New York." [Note: Bessie Delany died in 1996 at the age of 104. Sadie died in 1999 at the age of 109].*

1   Both more than one hundred years old, Sarah ("Sadie") Delany and her sister, Annie Elizabeth ("Bessie") Delany, are among the oldest living witnesses to American history. They are also the oldest surviving members of one of the nation's preeminent black families, which rose to prominence just one generation after the Civil War.

2   Few families have ever achieved so much so quickly. Henry Beard Delany, the sisters' father, was born into slavery but eventually became the first elected "Negro" bishop of the Episcopal Church, U.S.A. All ten of his children were college-educated professionals at a time when few Americans—black or white—ever went beyond high school.

3   The Delany creed centered on self-improvement through education, civic-mindedness, and ethical living, along with a strong belief in God. The family motto was, "Your job is to help somebody." According to Bessie and Sadie Delany, this code applied to anyone who needed help, regardless of color. Their accomplishments could not shield them from discrimination and the pain of racism, but they held themselves to high standards of fair-minded idealism.

Sadie

4   One thing I've noticed since I got this old is that I have started to dream in color. I'll remember that someone was wearing a red dress or a

Annotation Practice Exercises

Directions: For each of the exercises below, read critically to answer the questions. This will help you gain additional insights as you read.

pink sweater, something like that. I also dream more than I used to, and when I wake up I feel tired. I'll say to Bessie, "I sure am tired this morning. I was teaching all night in my dreams!"

5   Bessie was always the big dreamer. She was always talking about what she dreamed the night before. She has this same dream over and over again, about a party she went to on Cotton Street in Raleigh, way back when. Nothing special happens; she just keeps dreaming she's there. In our dreams, we are always young.

6   Truth is, we both forget we're old. This happens all the time. I'll reach for something real quick, just like a young person. And realize my reflexes are not what they once were. It surprises me, but I can't complain. I still do what I want, pretty much.

7   These days, I am usually the first one awake in the morning. I wake up at six-thirty. And the first thing I do when I open my eyes is smile, and then I say, "Thank you, Lord, for another day!"

8   If I don't hear Bessie get up, I'll go into her room and wake her. Sometimes I have to knock on her headboard. And she opens her eyes and says, "Oh, Lord, another day?" I don't think Bessie would get up at all sometimes, if it weren't for me. She stays up late in her room and listens to these talk-radio shows, and she doesn't get enough sleep.

9   In the mornings, Monday through Friday, we do our yoga exercises. I started doing yoga exercises with Mama about forty years ago. Mama was starting to shrink up and get bent down, and I started exercising with her to straighten her up again. Only I didn't know at that time that what we were actually doing was "yoga." We just thought we were exercising.

10   I kept doing my yoga exercises, even after Mama died. Well, when Bessie turned eighty she decided that I looked better than her. So she decided she would start doing yoga, too. So we've been doing our exercises together ever since. We follow a yoga exercise program on the TV. Sometimes, Bessie cheats. I'll be doing an exercise and look over at her, and she's just lying there! She's a naughty old gal.

11   Exercise is very important. A lot of older people don't exercise at all. Another thing that is terribly important is diet. I keep up with the latest news about nutrition. About thirty years ago,

Bessie and Sadie Delany at home in Mount Vernon, New York.
(Photo by Brian Douglas/copyright 1993 Amy Hill Hearth)

Annotation Exercise

In paragraph 7, what is the author's (Sadie's) *point of view* about being alive?

_____

Annotation Exercise

In paragraph 8, what is the author's (Sadie's) *point of view* regarding Bessie?

_____

_____

Bessie and I started eating much more healthy foods. We don't eat that fatty Southern food very often. When we do, we feel like we can't move!

12   We eat as many as seven different vegetables a day. Plus lots of fresh fruits. And we take vitamin supplements: Vitamin A, B complex, C, D, E, and minerals, too, like zinc. And Bessie takes tyrosine when she's a little blue.

13   Every morning, after we do our yoga, we each take a clove of garlic, chop it up, and swallow it whole. If you swallow it all at once, there is no odor. We also take a teaspoon of cod liver oil. Bessie thinks it's disgusting, but one day I said, "Now, dear little sister, if you want to keep up with me, you're going to have to start taking it, every day, and stop complainin'." And she's been good ever since.

14   As soon as we moved to our house in 1957, we began boiling the tap water we use for our drinking water. Folks keep telling us that it's not necessary, that the City of Mount Vernon purifies the water. But it's a habit and at our age, child, we're not about to change our routine.

15   These days, I do most of the cooking, and Bessie does the serving. We eat our big meal of the day at noon. In the evening, we usually have a milk shake for dinner, and then we go upstairs and watch "MacNeil Lehrer" on the TV.

16   After that, we say our prayers. We say prayers in the morning and before we go to bed. It takes a long time to pray for everyone, because it's a very big family—we have fifteen nieces and nephews still living, plus all their children and grandchildren. We pray for each one, living and dead. The ones that Bessie doesn't approve of get extra prayers. Bessie can be very critical and she holds things against people forever. I always have to say to her, "Everybody has to be themselves, Bessie. Live and let live."

Bessie

17   I wonder what Mr. Miliam would think of his granddaughters living this long. Why, I suppose he'd get a kick out of it. I know he'd have lived longer if Grandma hadn't died and it broke his heart. Sometimes, you need a reason to keep living.

18   Tell you the truth, I wouldn't be here without sister Sadie. We are companions. But I'll tell you

---

Annotation Exercise

What is the author's (Sadie's) *tone* in paragraph 14?

_____

_____

something else. Sadie has taken on this business of getting old like it's a big *project*. She has it all figured out, about diet and exercise. Sometimes, I just don't want to do it, but she is my big sister and I really don't want to disappoint her. Funny thing about Sadie is she rarely gets—what's the word?—depressed. She is an easygoing type of gal.

19   Now, honey, I get the blues sometimes. It's a shock to me, to be this old. Sometimes, when I realize I am 101 years old, it hits me right between the eyes. I say, "Oh Lord, how did this happen?" Turning one hundred was the worst birthday of my life. I wouldn't wish it on my worst enemy. Turning 101 was not so bad. Once you're past that century mark, it's just not as shocking.

20   There's a few things I have had to give up. I gave up driving a while back. I guess I was in my late eighties. That was terrible. Another thing I gave up on was cutting back my trees so we have a view of the New York City skyline to the south. Until I was ninety-eight years old, I would climb up on the ladder and saw those tree branches off so we had a view. I could do it perfectly well; why pay somebody to do it? Then Sadie talked some sense into me, and I gave up doing it.

21   Some days I feel as old as Moses and other days I feel like a young girl. I tell you what: I have only a little bit of arthritis in my pinky finger, and my eyes aren't bad so I know I could still be practicing dentistry. Yes, I am sure I could still do it.

22   But it's hard being old, because you can't always do everything you want, exactly as *you* want it done. When you get old as we are, you have to struggle to hang onto your freedom, your independence. We have a lot of family and friends keeping an eye on us, but we try not to be dependent on any one person. We try to pay people, even relatives, for whatever they buy for us, and for gasoline for their car, things like that, so that we do not feel beholden to them.

23   Longevity runs in the family. I'm sure that's part of why we are still here. As a matter of fact, until recently there were still five of us, of the original ten children. Then, Hubert went to Glory on December 28, 1990, and Hap, a few weeks later, in February 1991. Laura, our dear baby sister, passed on in August 1993. That leaves just me and Sadie.

Annotation Exercise

What is the author's (Bessie's) *point of view* about growing old?

_____

_____

Annotation Exercise

What is the author's (Bessie's) *intended meaning* when she says, "Hubert went to Glory?"

_____

Annotation Exercise

What is the authors' (the Delany sisters') *purpose* in telling their story?

_____

_____

Annotation Exercise

Who is the *intended audience* of this selection?

_____

_____

24   Now, when Hubert died, that really hurt. He was just shy of ninety years old. It never made a bit of difference to me that Hubert became an assistant United States attorney, a judge, and all that. He was still my little brother.

25   Same way with Hap. You know what? Even when he was ninety-five years old, Sadie and I still spoiled him. When he didn't like what they were cooking for dinner at his house, he would get up and leave the table and come over here and we'd fix him what he liked to eat.

26   Good ol' Hap knew he was going to Glory and he was content. He said, "I've had a good life. I've done everything I wanted to do. I think I've done right by people." We Delanys can usually say that when our time comes.

Source: Sarah L. Delany and A. Elizabeth Delany with Amy Hill Hearth, *Having Our Say: The Delany Sisters 100 Years,* New York, Dell, 1993, pp. 3, 5, 287–290, 296–298.

SELECTION **8-2**

Literature

Comprehension Quiz

Directions: For each comprehension question below, use information from the selection to determine the correct answer. You may refer to the selection as you answer the questions. Write your answer in the space provided.

True or False

1. The Delany sisters have similar outlooks on living and growing older.

2. Bessie can be pessimistic at times.

3. The Delany sisters attribute their longevity to hard work and luck.

4. Sadie is more optimistic and easygoing than Bessie.

5. The Delany sisters pray twice each day.

Multiple-Choice

6. Bessie Delany believes that one reason for her longevity is
   a. determination.
   b. genetics.
   c. independence.
   d. assistance from family members.

7. Bessie Delany started doing yoga exercises when she was
   a. a young girl.
   b. a teenager.
   c. in her forties.
   d. quite old.

8. In addition to exercise and eating healthy foods, the Delany sisters also
   a. take vitamin supplements.
   b. eat a clove of garlic every day.
   c. take a teaspoon of cod liver oil each day.
   d. all of the above.

9. The reason the Delany sisters still boil the tap water they use for drinking is that
   a. it has simply become a habit.
   b. their city does not have a water purification system.
   c. it is cheaper than buying bottled water.
   d. all of the above.

_____ **10.** For Bessie Delany, one difficult part of old age is
     a. fighting boredom.
     b. worrying about financial security.
     c. struggling to maintain independence.
     d. staying in contact with other family members.

SELECTION **8-2**

Literature

Extend Your Vocabulary by Using Context Clues

Directions: Context clues are words in a sentence that allow the reader to deduce (reason out) the meaning of an unfamiliar word in that sentence. For each vocabulary item below, a sentence from the selection containing an important word (*italicized, like this*) is quoted first. Next, there is an additional sentence using the word in the same sense and providing another context clue. Use the context clues from *both* sentences to deduce the meaning of the italicized word. *Be sure the answer you choose makes sense in both sentences.* If you discover that you must use a dictionary to confirm an answer choice, remember that the meaning you select must still fit the context of *both* sentences. To indicate your answer, write the letter in the space provided.

Pronunciation key: ă pat ā pay âr care ä father ĕ pet ē be ĭ pit
ī tie îr pier ŏ pot ō toe ô paw oi noise ou out ŏŏ took
ōō boot ŭ cut yōō abuse ûr urge th thin *th* this hw which
zh vision ə about
Stress Mark: ʹ

_____ **1.** They are also the oldest surviving members of one of the nation's *preeminent* black families, which rose to prominence just one generation after the Civil War.

Pearl Buck, William Faulkner, John Steinbeck, Ernest Hemingway, and Saul Bellow are *preeminent* twentieth-century American writers who have each won both the Pulitzer Prize and the Nobel Prize in literature.

preeminent (pre ĕmʹ ə nənt) means:
     a. possessing unusual academic skills
     b. college-educated
     c. unknown by the general public
     d. outstanding; superior

_____ **2.** They are also the oldest surviving members of one of the nation's preeminent black families, which rose to *prominence* just one generation after the Civil War.

A former California governor, Earl Warren gained national *prominence* as Chief Justice of the Supreme Court and as the leader of a government commission that investigated the assassination of President John F. Kennedy.

prominence (prŏm′ ə nəns) means:

a. limited power or influence

b. vast wealth

c. being superior and widely known

d. great popularity

_____ **3.** The Delany *creed* centered on self-improvement through education, civic-mindedness, and ethical living, along with a strong belief in God.

Two important aspects of the architect Frank Lloyd Wright's innovative *creed* were uniting buildings with their surroundings and integrating technology into his structures.

creed (krēd) means:

a. slogan or motto

b. quotation whose source is unknown

c. selfishness and greed

d. system of beliefs, principles, or opinions

_____ **4.** The Delany creed centered on self-improvement through education, civic-mindedness, and *ethical* living, along with a strong belief in God.

Because of their honesty and integrity, George Washington and Abraham Lincoln are considered two of the most *ethical* men ever to serve as president of the United States.

ethical (ĕth′ ĭ kəl) means:

a. exceedingly popular

b. in accordance with other people's beliefs

c. plain; not fancy

d. in accordance with the accepted principles of right and wrong; moral

_____ **5.** Their accomplishments could not shield them from discrimination and the pain of racism, but they held themselves to high standards of fair-minded *idealism.*

The ruthlessness of the corporate world quickly destroyed the young employee's *idealism.*

idealism (ī dē′ ə lĭz əm) means:

a. pursuit of honorable or worthy principles or goals

b. enthusiasm; excitement

c. racial prejudice or biogotry

d. unhelpful, misguided beliefs

_____ **6.** We have a lot of family and friends keeping an eye on us, but we try not to be *dependent* on any one person.

If you have *dependent* children for whom you provide the primary financial support, you must indicate this when you file your income tax.

dependent (dĭ pĕn′ dənt) means:

a. unreasonable

b. grateful; appreciative

c. relying on or requiring the aid of another for support

d. dependable; reliable

_____ **7.** We try to pay people, even relatives, for whatever they buy for us, and for gasoline for their car, things like that, so that we do not feel *beholden* to them.

Because my wonderful parents helped pay for my college education, I will always be *beholden* to them.

beholden (bĭ hōl′ dən) means:

a. holding tightly to someone or something

b. owing something, such as gratitude, to another; indebted

c. feeling guilty; guilt-ridden

d. hostile

_____ **8.** *Longevity* runs in the family.

My 90-year-old grandmother attributes her *longevity* to a healthy lifestyle and positive attitude.

longevity (lŏn jĕv′ ĭ tē) means:

a. long life; great duration of life

b. being unusually tall

c. illness characterized by weakened muscles

d. addiction to harmful substances

_____ **9.** As a matter of fact, until recently, there were still five of us, of the *original* ten children.

Were you able to locate the *original* documents or only the later versions of them?

original (ə rĭj′ ə nəl) means:

a. creative or unusual in nature

b. new

c. there at the beginning

d. fresh

_____ **10.** Good ol' Hap knew he was going to Glory and he was *content.*

After serving twelve years as her company's chief executive, she was *content* to turn the role over to her capable vice president.

content (kən tĕnt′) means:

a. full; complete

b. dissatisfied

c. angry; resistant

d. willing; ready to accept

Collaboration Option

Respond in Writing

Directions: Refer to the selection as needed to answer the essay-type questions below.

Option for collaboration: Your instructor may direct you to work with other students, or in other words, to work *collaboratively.* In that case, you should form groups of three or four students as directed by your instructor and work together to complete the exercises. After your group discusses each item and agrees on the answer, have a group member record it. Every member of your group should be able to explain all of your group's answers.

1. What was the most surprising or interesting thing you learned about either or both of the Delany sisters?

_____

_____

_____

_____

_____

_____

_____

_____

2. In what ways are Sadie and Bessie Delany alike? In what ways are they different?

_____

_____

_____

_____

_____

_____

_____

3. Bessie states that "longevity runs in the family." In addition to heredity, however, to what else do you think contributed to Delanys' long lives?

_____

_____

_____

_____

_____

_____

_____

4. Being educated made a significant difference in the Delanys' lives. How do you think *you* will look back on the time you spent in college? What difference do you think it might make in your life?

_____

_____

_____

_____

_____

_____

_____

5. Assuming that you were able to maintain good health, what do you think would be some of the *best* things about being 100 years old?

_____

_____

_____

_____

_____

_____

_____

6. Overall main idea. What is the overall main idea the author wants the reader to understand about the Delany sisters and their lives? Answer this question in one sentence. Be sure that your overall main idea sentence includes the topic *(the Delany sisters)* and tells the overall most important point about it.

_____

_____

_____

_____

Read More about It on the World Wide Web

To learn more about the topic of this selection, visit these websites or use your favorite search engine (such as Yahoo ®). Whenever you go to *any* website, it is a good idea to evaluate it critically. Are you getting good information—information that is accurate, complete, and up-to-date? Who sponsors the website? How easy is it to use the features of the website?

http://www.startext.com/news/doc/1047/1:ENTNEWS25/1:ENTNEWS250 20199.html

> *This website presents an article from* Star-telegram.com *by the Associated Press reporter Martha Waggoner. The article highlights the life and death of Sadie Delany.*

http://www.cnn.com/US/9509/bessie_delany

> *This is a CNN website, which posted the article entitled,* "Paying Tribute to Bessie Delany." *The article highlights her life, and there are tributes from those who knew and were inspired by her. Pictures are included on this website.*

THE JOY LUCK CLUB

From *The Joy Luck Club* by Amy Tan

Prepare Yourself to Read

Directions: Do these exercises *before* you read Selection 8-3.

1. First, read and think about the title. What kind of a club do you think the Joy Luck Club might be?

   _____

   _____

2. Next, complete your preview by reading the following:

   Introduction (in *italics*)

   All of the first and second paragraphs (paragraph 1 and 2)

   All of the last paragraph (paragraph 9)

   _____

   On the basis of your preview, what does the selection now seem to be about?

   _____

   _____

Apply Comprehension Skills

Directions: Do the Annotation Practice Exercises as you read Selection 8-3. Read critically: Think about the author's purpose, intended audience, point of view, tone, and intended meaning.

THE JOY LUCK CLUB

In The Joy Luck Club, *the novelist Amy Tan tells the story of four Chinese women who have immigrated to the United States after the Second World War. In the novel, the narrator's mother starts a "club" with three other recent immigrant women. They meet once a week to play a game called mah jong, eat special Chinese foods, "say" stories, and keep each others' spirits up. In the selection below, the narrator's mother explains how she first created a "Joy Luck Club" many years ago in China during a time when conditions were awful and how it helped them have hope that things would get better.*

Amy Tan was born in California two and a half years after her own parents immigrated to the United States from China. The Joy Luck Club, *Tan's first novel, was an immediate best-seller and a finalist for both the prestigious National Book Award and the National Book Critics Circle Award. Tan is also the author of three other novels,* The Kitchen God's Wife, The Hundred Secret Senses, *and* The Bonesetter's Daughter. *Her work is characterized by insight into family relationships and into the challenges facing those who come to a new country, and their children. Her essays and fiction have been published in many well-known magazines.*

---

1   "My idea was to have a gathering of four women, one for each corner of my mah jong table. I knew which women I wanted to ask. They were all young like me, with wishful faces. One was an army officer's wife, like myself. Another was a girl with very fine manners from a rich family in Shanghai. She had escaped with only a little money. And there was a girl from Nanking who had the blackest hair I have ever seen. She came from a low-class family, but she was pretty and pleasant and had married well, to an old man who died and left her with a better life.

2   "Each week one of us would host a party to raise money and to raise our spirits. The hostess had to serve special *dyansyin* foods to bring good fortune of all kinds—dumplings shaped like silver money ingots, long rice noodles for long life, boiled peanuts for conceiving sons, and of course, many good-luck oranges for a plentiful, sweet life.

3   "What fine food we treated ourselves to with our meager allowances! We didn't notice that the dumplings were stuffed mostly with stringy squash and that the oranges were spotted with wormy holes. We ate sparingly, not as if we didn't have enough, but to protest how we could not eat another bite, we had already bloated ourselves from earlier in the day. We knew we had luxuries few people could afford. We were the lucky ones.

4   "After filling our stomachs, we would then fill a bowl with money and put it where everyone could see. Then we would sit down at the mah jong table. My table was from my family and was of a very fragrant red wood, not what you call rosewood, but *hong mu,* which is so fine there's no English word for it. The table had a very thick pad, so

Directions: For each of the exercises below, read critically to answer the questions. This will help you gain additional insights as you read.

Annotation Exercise

In paragraph 3, what is the author's *intended meaning* when she describes the food as "fine" and then mentions it was "stringy" and "wormy"?

_____

_____

_____

that when the mah jong *pai* were spilled onto the table the only sound was of ivory tiles washing against one another.

5   "Once we started to play, nobody could speak, except to say *'Pung!'* or *'Chr!'* when taking a tile. We had to play with seriousness and think of nothing else but adding to our happiness through winning. But after sixteen rounds, we would again feast, this time to celebrate our good fortune. And then we would talk into the night until the morning, saying stories about good times in the past and good times yet to come.

6   "Oh, what good stories! Stories spilling out all over the place! We almost laughed to death. A rooster that ran into the house screeching on top of dinner bowls, the same bowls that held him quietly in pieces the next day! And one about a girl who wrote love letters for two friends who loved the same man. And a silly foreign lady who fainted on a toilet when firecrackers went off next to her.

7   "People thought we were wrong to serve banquets every week while many people in the city were starving, eating rats and, later, the garbage that the poorest rats used to feed on. Others thought we were possessed by demons—to celebrate when even within our own families we had lost generations, had lost homes and fortunes, and were separated, husband from wife, brother from sister, daughter from mother. Hnnnh! How could we laugh, people asked.

8   "It's not that we had no heart or eyes for pain. We were all afraid. We all had our miseries. But to despair was to wish back for something already lost. Or to prolong what was already unbearable. How much can you wish for a favorite warm coat that hangs in the closet of a house that burned down with your mother and father inside of it? How long can you see in your mind arms and legs hanging from telephone wires and starving dogs running down the streets with half-chewed hands dangling from their jaws? What was worse, we asked among ourselves, to sit and wait for our own deaths with proper somber faces? Or to choose our own happiness?

9   "So we decided to hold parties and pretend each week had become the new year. Each week we could forget past wrongs done to us. We weren't allowed to think a bad thought. We feasted, we laughed, we played games, lost and won, we told the best stories. And each week, we could hope to be lucky. That hope was our only joy. And that's how we came to call our little parties Joy Luck."

Award-winning writer Amy Tan, the author of *The Joy Luck Club.* *(Reuters/Robert Giroux/Archive Photos)*

Annotation Exercise

What is the author's *purpose* in writing this selection?

_____

_____

Annotation Exercise

Who is the author's (not the narrator's) *intended audience* in this selection?

_____

_____

Annotation Exercise

In paragraph 9, how does the author describe her mother's *point of view* about finding happiness in life in the United States?

_____

_____

Source: Amy Tan, *The Joy Luck Club,* New York: G.P. Putnam's Sons, 1989, pp. 23–25.

Comprehension Quiz

Directions: For each comprehension question below, use information from the selection to determine the correct answer. You may refer to the selection as you answer the questions. Write your answer in the space provided.

True or False

_____ 1. The Joy Luck Club got its name because hoping to be lucky was the only joy of the four women in the club.

_____ 2. The four women in the club enjoyed telling stories and eating while they played mah jong.

_____ 3. At meetings of the Joy Luck Club, *dyansyin* foods were served to remind the women of all their misfortunes.

Multiple-Choice

_____ 4. There were four members of the Joy Luck Club because
   a.   that is how many people are needed to play mah jong.
   b.   the speaker wanted one player for each corner of her mah jong table.
   c.   the speaker only wanted to include her very best friends.
   d.   several women refused to join the club.

_____ 5. The hostess of the Joy Luck Club served all of the following except
   a.   dumplings.
   b.   oranges.
   c.   roast duck.
   d.   long rice noodles.

_____ 6. The speaker started the Joy Luck Club
   a.   to raise money for her family and the families of her friends.
   b.   to be sure she and her friends could eat a nice meal at least once a week.
   c.   to make the most of her new mah jong table.
   d.   to provide herself and her friends with a distraction from the terrible conditions in which they lived.

_____ 7. The members of the Joy Luck Club did all of the following except
   a.   play mah jong.
   b.   sing traditional songs.
   c.   tell stories.
   d.   raise money.

_____ **8.** The speaker's mah jong table is made of

   a. glass.

   b. ivory.

   c. red wood.

   d. marble.

_____ **9.** All of the Joy Luck Club members

   a. had great sadness in their lives in China.

   b. learned to speak fluent English.

   c. were elderly women when the club began.

   d. came from upper-class families.

_____ **10.** The Joy Luck Club held its parties

   a. daily.

   b. weekly.

   c. monthly.

   d. twice a year.

SELECTION **8-3**

Literature

Extend Your Vocabulary by Using Context Clues

Directions: Context clues are words in a sentence that allow the reader to deduce (reason out) the meaning of an unfamiliar word in the sentence. For
each vocabulary exercise below, a sentence from the reading selection containing an important word *(italicized, like this)* is quoted first. Next, there is
an additional sentence using the word in the same sense and providing another context clue. Use the context clues from *both* sentences to deduce the
meaning of the italicized word. *Be sure the answer you choose makes sense
in both sentences.* If you discover that you must use a dictionary to confirm
an answer choice, remember that the meaning you select must still fit the
context of *both* sentences.

Pronunciation key: ă pat ā pay âr care ä father ĕ pet ē be ĭ pit
ī tie îr pier ŏ pot ō toe ô paw oi noise ou out ŏŏ took
ōō boot ŭ cut yōō abuse ûr urge th thin *th* this hw which
zh vision ə about
Stress Mark: ´

_____ **1.** What fine food we treated ourselves to with our *meager* allowances!

   In spite of a *meager* salary, John managed to save enough money to buy a car.

meager (mē′ gər)

a.   large or excessive

b.   generous

c.   increased

d.   insufficient in quantity

_____ **2.** We ate *sparingly,* not as if we didn't have enough, but to protest how we could not eat another bite, we had already bloated ourselves from earlier in the day.

During the drought citizens were encouraged to use water *sparingly.*

sparingly (spar′ ĭng lē)

a.   with enthusiasm

b.   often, but in small amounts

c.   whenever possible

d.   in small amounts

_____ **3.** We ate sparingly, not as if we didn't have enough, but to protest how we could not eat another bite, we had already *bloated* ourselves from earlier in the day.

I wasn't used to eating such a large dinner and afterwards, I felt so *bloated* that I had to loosen my belt.

bloated (blōt′ əd)

a.   made abnormally large

b.   obliged to eat excessive amounts

c.   starved

d.   embarrassed

_____ **4.** My table was from my family and was of a very *fragrant* red wood, not what you call rosewood, but hong mu, which is so fine there's no English word for it.

The corsage was beautiful, but it was a little too *fragrant* and Sally found herself sneezing all evening.

fragrant (frā′ grənt)

a.   moldy

b.   having an odor

c.   cracked or rotting

d.   likely to decay

_____ **5.** But to *despair* was to wish back for something already lost.

Our team was behind by fifteen points in the fourth quarter, but the coach told us not to *despair.*

despair (di spâr′)

a. to lose hope

b. to win

c. to quit

d. to try harder

_____ **6.** What was worse, we asked among ourselves, to sit and wait for our own deaths with proper *somber* faces? Or to choose our own happiness?

My younger brother looked particularly *somber* on the last day of his summer vacation.

somber (sŏm′ bər)

a. unlikely to change

b. excited

c. gloomy or depressed

d. pale

_____ **7.** People thought we were wrong to serve *banquets* every week while many people in the city were starving, eating rats and, later, the garbage that the poorest rats used to feed on.

It took my mother and grandmother three days to prepare the food for my sister's wedding *banquet.*

banquet (ban′ kwət)

a. an informal party with no host

b. any family gathering

c. a long and involved performance

d. an elaborate meal, often in honor of a person (or people)

_____ **8.** The hostess had to serve special dyansyin foods to bring good luck of all kinds—dumplings shaped like silver money *ingots,* long rice noodles for long life, boiled peanuts for conceiving sons, and of course, many good-luck oranges for a plentiful, sweet life.

When we toured the United States Mint in Philadelphia we saw row after row of stacked silver *ingots* that would eventually be melted and used to make certain coins.

ingots (ĭng′ gəts)

a. metal that is cast into bars for storage or shipment

b. flat, irregular-shaped blocks

c. ancient coins

d. molds used to shape metal

_____ **9.** The hostess had to serve special dyansyin foods to bring good luck of all kinds—dumplings shaped like silver money ingots, long rice noodles for long life, boiled peanuts for conceiving sons, and of course, many good-luck oranges for a *plentiful,* sweet life.

The survivors of the shipwreck did not starve on the island because of the *plentiful* coconuts and tropical fruits.

plentiful (plĕn′ tĭ fəl)

a. lucky; filled with good fortune

b. fully as much as one needs or desires

c. excessive

d. easy to obtain

_____ **10.** We *feasted,* we laughed, we play games, lost and won, we told the best stories.

At the dinner following the wedding ceremony, guests *feasted* on chicken cordon bleu, asparagus in hollandaise sauce, chocolate mousse, and champagne.

feasted (fēs′ təd)

a. heartily ate a large, elaborately prepared meal

b. prepared a large, elaborate meal

c. delighted in

d. greedily gulped down a large meal

SELECTION **8-3**

Literature

Collaboration Option

Respond in Writing

Directions: Refer to the selection as needed to answer the essay-type questions below.

Option for collaboration: Your instructor may direct you to work with other students—in other words, to work *collaboratively.* In that case, you should form groups of three or four students as directed by your instructor and work together to complete the exercises. After your group discusses each item and agrees on the answer, have a group member record it. Every member of your group should be able to explain all of your group's answers.

1. People of all ages join clubs. Children often form neighborhood clubs or join church groups, athletic clubs, or organizations such as Boy Scouts and Girl Scouts. Teenagers often join organizations at their schools; some join gangs. College students join school clubs and social organizations such as fraternities and sororities. Adults belong to many kinds of clubs and organizations, such as country clubs, hobby clubs, and civic groups such as the Lions Club or Rotary Club. Why is it people are drawn to join clubs?

List at least three reasons why you think people join clubs and organizations.

_____

_____

_____

_____

2. There can be disadvantages to joining clubs and organizations. List at least three negative aspects of joining or belonging to a club.

_____

_____

_____

_____

_____

_____

3. What clubs and organizations have you been a member of or do you currently belong to? Have you belonged to any of them for a long time? Have your experiences been positive? If so, why? If not, why not?

_____

_____

_____

_____

4. In this selection the narrator's mother recounts to her daughter the story of how she created the Joy Luck Club. Describe briefly a story that one of your parents or grandparents told you about an important event in his or her early life (or his or her life before you were born).

_____

_____

_____

5. Overall main idea. What is the overall main idea the author wants the reader to understand about her mother's creating the Joy Luck Club? Answer this question in one sentence. Be sure that your overall main idea sentence includes the topic (*the Joy Luck Club*) and tells the overall most important point about it.

_____

_____

Read More about It on the World Wide Web

To learn more about the topic of this selection, visit these websites or use your favorite search engine (such as Yahoo ®). Whenever you go to *any* website, it is a good idea to evaluate it critically. Are you getting good information—information that is accurate, complete, and up-to-date? Who sponsors the website? How easy is it to use the features of the website?

http://asianamculture.miningco.com
> *A website dedicated to nearly all aspects of Asian American culture. It also contains links to relevant sites.*

http://www.luminarium.org/contemporary/amytan/
> *Contains links to bibliographical information, interviews, essays, reviews, synopses, excerpts from Tan's writings, and more. Interestingly, this page was created by someone who is "just a fan" of Amy Tan's work.*

© PhotoDisc

C H A P T E R

Thinking Critically

In this chapter you will learn the answers to these questions:

- What is critical thinking?

- How can I distinguish between facts and opinions?

- How can I make inferences and draw logical conclusions?

- What is the difference between deductive and inductive reasoning?

- How can I evaluate an author's argument?

- What are propaganda devices?

SKILLS

What Is Critical Thinking and Why Is It Important?

Critical Thinking Skills

- Why Readers Fail to Think Critically

- Distinguishing Facts from Opinions and Determining Whether Opinions Are Well Supported

- Making Inferences and Drawing Logical Conclusions

- Distinguishing between Deductive and Inductive Reasoning

- Evaluating an Author's Argument

- Identifying Propaganda Devices

A Word about Standardized Reading Tests: Critical Thnking

CREATING YOUR SUMMARY

Developing Chapter Review Cards

READINGS

It is not enough to have a good mind. The main thing is to use it well.

René Descartes

Don't be down on something you're not up on.

WHAT IS CRITICAL THINKING, AND WHY IS IT IMPORTANT?

KEY TERM
Critical Thinking

Thinking in an organized way about material you have read in order to evaluate it accurately.
Critical thinking is also referred to as *critical reasoning* or *critical analysis*.

Critical thinking means thinking in an organized way about material that you have read in order to evaluate it accurately. Before you can think critically about material that you have read, you must first understand the main idea, the supporting details, and the pattern of organization. Only when you understand this basic information are you ready to think critically about what you have read.

You may be wondering why it is necessary to think critically rather than just accept the author's information and leave it at that. After all, thinking critically about information you have read can, quite frankly, be hard work. However, the consequences of *not* thinking critically and of *not* evaluating ideas for yourself can be costly. Failing to think critically can result, for example, in your choosing a college major that does not really suit you, accepting a job that you are ill-suited for, signing a contract or credit agreement you do not fully understand, making the wrong decision as a member of a jury, being misled or defrauded, supporting a cause that later turns out to be an embarrassment, and even marrying the wrong person! Most professors would agree that learning to think critically, along with learning how to learn, is one of the most important skills any college student can acquire.

Rather than accept everything you read as true, you should question it to see if it stands up to the test of critical thinking: thinking critically can help you avoid the kinds of problems mentioned above and other painful, unpleasant experiences. Moreover, thinking critically will not only help you when you read, but it will also help you when you write. This is because reading and writing are both forms of the thinking process. To improve your reading and writing, you must improve the quality of your *thinking*. Although thinking critically may seem difficult at times, it simply means applying certain reading and thinking skills in a systematic, thorough fashion. In other words, critical thinking means consistently asking certain additional questions and applying logic when you read.

CRITICAL THINKING SKILLS

You must apply these three skills in a systematic, careful manner in order to think critically when you read:

- Distinguishing facts from opinions, and determining how well supported the opinions are
- Making inferences and drawing logical conclusions
- Evaluating an author's argument accurately

471

Thinking critically involves thinking in an organized way about material you have read in order to evaluate it accurately.
(Matt Klicker / The Image Works)

In this chapter, each of these three important skills will be explained and demonstrated. These skills can also be applied to things you hear, but our focus in this chapter is on applying them to material that you read.

Why Readers Fail to Think Critically

If critical thinking simply means applying thinking skills in a systematic, careful manner, why do people not do it more often when they read? Actually, besides mental laziness, there are at least five reasons:

1. **We let "experts" and "authorities" do our thinking for us.** Rather than think through a complex issue, we just accept the information or judgment of someone or something we perceive as an authority. This might be a parent or other relative; a college adviser; a doctor or therapist; a minister, priest or rabbi. We may accept the beliefs or positions of a political entity (such as a political party or the government itself) or the beliefs and rules of a religious or social institution without thinking critically about them. (This is not to say that all experts and authorities are wrong, only that you should think through what they have written or said, rather than accepting their words without question.) For example, you might accept the advice of a favorite uncle who is a highly successful realtor that you should also become a realtor—even though you may prefer to work by yourself at a computer rather than sell to the public.

2. **We want things to be different from the way they are.** In other words, we deny reality and refuse to see what is really there. Denial is based on emotion, not on reason. Perhaps a person you have just begun dating is attractive, yet has a serious drinking problem. But because you like dating someone who is attractive, you ignore obvious facts and deny to yourself that the person is alcoholic. Or, for example, you are not making any systematic effort to save money each month, yet you are hoping that you will somehow have enough money by the time you graduate to pay for a new car and a trip to Europe.

3. **We put things into one of two mutually exclusive categories.** This means that we mistakenly view things as "either-or." Another way of putting this is "seeing everything as either black or white." Needless to say, very few things in life are simple enough to fall into only one of two categories. Thinking of everything in terms of good or bad, beautiful or ugly, fair or unfair, generous or selfish, conservative or liberal, immature or mature, and so forth, prevents us from thinking critically about issues.

4. **We view things too much in light of our culture and past experience.** We are all ethnocentric, which means that we accept that whatever our cultural group believes or does is the proper way. Whether it is encouraging large or small families, eating with a fork or chopsticks or one's fingers, or celebrating events and holidays in certain ways, we consider anything different from what we do to be odd or even wrong. Viewing things only in light of our culture and past experience prevents us from looking at new ideas and considering them objectively. With regard to personal experience, for example, someone who had a happy experience being a stepchild would have a very different view of blended families from someone who had an unhappy experience as a stepchild.

5. **We stereotype and label.** The world can be overwhelming and confusing. One way we try to make sense of it is to put things and people into categories. While this is helpful, it also has some negative effects. It prevents us from seeing situations and individuals as unique because we assume things about them that may not be true. For example, on the first day of the semester, suppose you notice a classmate who is very physically fit and is wearing a baseball cap. You might be inclined to make an automatic judgment (stereotype) about him and what he is like as a person: that he is a "jock" (or even a "dumb jock"). Consequently, you decide he is not worth taking the time to get to know. Perhaps he is a straight-A student who has a full academic scholarship, and whose goal is to become a dentist. You will never know unless you think critically enough to question your assumptions and the stereotypes you hold.

Which of these reasons prevent you from thinking critically when you read? (Think critically about this!) Becoming aware of these tendencies in yourself is essential in order for you to think critically.

Distinguishing Facts from Opinions and Determining Whether Opinions Are Well Supported

Many students mistakenly believe that anything that appears in print, especially in textbooks, must be a fact. Although most college textbooks do consist largely of facts, textbooks typically include many useful and valuable opinions as well.

KEY TERM
Fact

Something that can be proved to exist or to have happened.

What is the difference between a fact and an opinion? A **fact** is something that can be proved to exist or to have happened. An example would be: *In 1620 the Pilgrims landed in what is now Plymouth, Massachusetts.* In addition, a fact can be something that is generally assumed to exist or to have happened. An example would be: *Thousands of years ago, early people migrated from Asia to the North American continent by walking from Siberia to Alaska across the frozen Bering Strait.* The process of proving that something is a fact (that it is true) is called *verification.* Verification requires experimentation and research or direct experience and observation.

KEY TERM
Opinion

Something that cannot be proved or disproved; a judgment or a belief.

An **opinion,** on the other hand, is a judgment or belief that cannot be proved or disproved. When information in a statement cannot be proved to be either factual or false, it represents an opinion. It is important to realize, however, that although opinions cannot be proved, they can be supported by valid reasons and plausible evidence. Therefore, well-supported opinions are useful, since they are based on facts or on the ideas of knowledgeable people. Opinions in textbooks typically represent this type of valuable opinion, since they are the well-reasoned beliefs of the author or other experts. Scientific theories are also examples of "expert opinions." (If a theory could be proved, then it would no longer be a theory, of course. It would become a fact.) Needless to say, poorly supported or unsupported opinions are not useful.

Students sometimes mistake incorrect information for an opinion because they assume if something is not a fact, it must automatically be an opinion. However, information can be one of three things: it can be a fact (it is correct information); it can be an opinion (it represents someone's belief); or it can be a *false statement of fact* (it is not a fact or an opinion; it is simply incorrect information). *January follows February* and *Water freezes at 212° F* are examples of false statements of fact. Since they can be *proved* incorrect, they are not facts or opinions.

Comprehension Monitoring Question for Thinking Critically to Evaluate Whether Statements in Written Material Are Facts or Opinions

"Can the information the author presents be proved, or does it represent a judgment?"

Critical readers ask themselves, "Can the information the author presents be proved, or does it represent a judgment?" When an author includes opinions, it is important for you to evaluate them, because not all opinions are valid or useful. An opinion is of little value if it is poorly supported (that is, if the author does not give good reasons for it.) A well-supported opinion, on the other hand, can be as important and as useful as a fact. To repeat: Even though opinions cannot be proved, they are valuable when supported by facts and other well-reasoned opinions; poorly supported opinions are of little value, even if the author writes persuasively. For example, consider the following two sets of support for this statement: *Anna Garcia has excellent qualifications for serving as governor.* (This statement is an opinion, of course, because of the use of the word *excellent.*) Note how both facts and opinions are used to support the statement. Also, note the important difference between the quality of the two sets of facts and opinions given as support for the statement.

Opinion: Anna Garcia has excellent qualifications for serving as governor.

Well-reasoned support:
She has a law degree from Harvard. (fact)
She was chief legal counsel of a Fortune 500 company for six years. (fact)
She served 12 years as a state senator. (fact)

She is extremely ethical. (opinion)

She is strongly committed to family values. (opinion)

She is an effective problem-solver. (opinion)

Poor support:

Her father served as an ambassador. (fact)

Her brother is a millionaire. (fact)

She has been married to the same man for twenty years. (fact)

She has smart, beautiful children. (opinion)

She is attractive. (opinion)

She comes across well on TV. (opinion)

A critical reader would be much more likely to accept the opinion that "Anna Garcia has excellent qualifications for serving as governor" if it were supported with good reasons (the first set of support) rather than with poor reasons (the second set). Critical readers know that support is convincing if it consists of relevant facts and well-reasoned opinions. Don't ignore a statement simply because it is an opinion or is supported with other opinions. They may all be valuable, pertinent opinions.

How can you tell when you are reading an opinion rather than a fact? Because opinions represent judgments, beliefs, or interpretations, authors often use certain words or phrases to indicate that they are presenting an opinion. The following words and phrases are typical of those that signal an opinion:

perhaps	many experts believe
apparently	many people think that
presumably	it seems likely
one possibility is	this suggests
one interpretation is	in our view
in our opinion	in the opinion of

In addition, words that indicate value judgments can signal opinions. These include descriptive words such as:

better	interesting
more	outdated
less	beautiful
safer	wealthy
most	incompetent
greatest	successful
worst	irresponsible
best	dangerous
excellent	fascinating
harmful	effective

These words signal opinions because people will often disagree about what is considered "successful," "fascinating," etc. For example, in the sentence *Adults must have a college degree in order to be successful,* the word *successful* could mean successful financially, personally, socially, or in all these ways. Because there are different interpretations of what *successful* means, it would be impossible to prove a statement like this (although it could be supported with certain facts about college graduates). Consequently, the statement expresses an opinion. (Even though this may be a widely held opinion, it is still an opinion.) As you read, then, watch for value judgment—words that can be interpreted in different ways by different people.

The flowchart below summarizes the process for determining whether statements are facts, incorrect information, or opinions. Use this process to distinguish between facts, incorrect information, and well-supported opinions (which are valuable) and unsupported or poorly supported opinions (which are of no value).

DETERMINING WHETHER A STATEMENT REPRESENTS A FACT, INCORRECT INFORMATION, OR AN OPINION

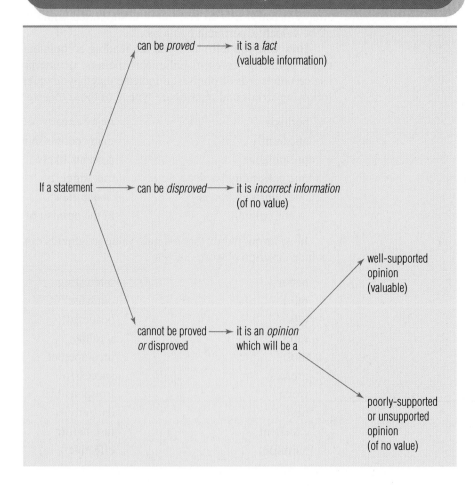

To distinguish between facts and opinions by thinking critically, ask yourself these questions in this order:

1. *Can the information in the statement be proved?*
If so, it is correct information: a fact.

2. *Can the information in the statement be disproved?*
If so, it is incorrect information.

3. *Is the information in the statement something that cannot be proved or disproved?*
If so, it is an opinion.

When the statement is opinion, ask yourself these additional questions:

- *Is the opinion well-supported?* (That is, is it based on valid reasons and plausible evidence?) If so, it is a valuable opinion.

- *Is the opinion poorly supported or unsupported?* If so, it is of little or no value.

Following are two excerpts from *The Autobiography of Malcolm X* (Selection 1-3, "Saved"). The first contains *facts* that can be verified about the prison in which Malcolm X served time.

The Norfolk Prison Colony's library was in the school building. A variety of classes was taught there by instructors who came from such places as Harvard and Boston universities. The weekly debates between inmate teams were also held in the school building.

List the facts in this excerpt.

_____

_____

_____

_____

_____

_____

_____

_____

Source: Alex Haley, *The Autobiography of Malcolm X,* Ballantine, New York, 1992, p. 173. Copyright © 1964 by Alex Haley and Malcolm X and copyright © 1965 by Alex Haley and Betty Shabazz. Reprinted by permission of Random House, Inc.

Stop and Annotate

Go back to the excerpt above. In the space provided, list on separate lines the *facts* contained in the excerpt.

Notice that this passage contains information that can be verified by objective proof: the location of the prison library, some of the universities the instructors came from, and that weekly debates were held in the school building.

In the next passage, Malcolm X states his *opinions* about the new vistas that reading opened to him:

Reading had changed forever the course of my life. As I see it today, the ability to read awoke inside me some long dormant craving to be mentally alive.

List the opinions in this excerpt.

_____

_____

_____

_____

_____

_____

_____

Source: Adapted from Alex Haley, *The Autobiography of Malcolm X,* Ballantine, New York, 1992, p. 179. Copyright © 1964 by Alex Haley and Malcolm X and copyright © 1965 by Alex Haley and Betty Shabazz. Reprinted by permission of Random House, Inc.

Stop and Annotate

Go back to the excerpt above. In the space provided, list on separate lines the *opinions* contained in the excerpt.

Malcolm X's opinions are that reading changed the course of his life forever, and that it awoke in him a craving to be mentally alive. These are statements that reflect Malcolm X's judgment about reading; they cannot be proved or disproved. He even introduces one of his opinions with, "As I see it today."

The next excerpt, from an American government textbook, discusses how historians and political scientists rank presidents of the United States. The excerpt includes a table that summarizes the results of three surveys. As this passage shows, experts often agree in their opinions. When such agreement exists, the opinions are especially valuable.

Scholars Rank the Presidents

Several surveys have asked American historians and political scientists to rank the presidents from best to worst. Although some presidential reputations rise or fall with the passage of time, there has been remarkable consistency in whom the scholars rank as the best and worst presidents. The consistency of these results suggests that scholars use some unspoken criteria when assessing the presidents. At least four criteria stand out: the effectiveness of presidential policy, the president's vision of the office, the president's handling of crises, and the president's personality.

In three surveys conducted in the 1980s, scholars were asked to rank the presidents. The results below show only those presidents who clearly and consistently ranked near the top or bottom. The surveys included all presidents except Reagan (who was still in office and thus could not be assessed dispassionately), Bush

What is the opinion of these historians and political scientists as to which presidents have been the greatest?

_____

_____

_____

_____

_____

and Clinton (who had not yet served), and William Harrison and James Garfield (whose terms were too short to be realistically assessed).

Greatest presidents (in top five on all three surveys)	Failures (in bottom five in all three surveys)
Abraham Lincoln	James Buchanan
George Washington	U.S. Grant
Franklin Delano Roosevelt	Warren G. Harding
Thomas Jefferson	Richard M. Nixon
Theodore Roosevelt	

Near-greats (in top ten on all three surveys)	Near-failures (in bottom ten on all three surveys)
Woodrow Wilson	Calvin Coolidge
Andrew Jackson	Millard Fillmore
Harry S. Truman	Andrew Johnson
	John Tyler
	Franklin Pierce

Sources: John J. Harrigan, *Politics and the American Future,* 3rd ed., McGraw-Hill, New York, 1992, pp. 282–283. Table: 1982 poll of forty-nine scholars in *Chicago Tribune Magazine,* January 10, 1982, pp. 8–13, 15, 18 (Copyrighted 1982 Chicago Tribune Company, all rights reserved, used with permission); and poll of forty-one scholars by David L. Porter in 1981, reprinted in Robert K. Murray and Tim H. Blessing, "The Presidential Performance Study: A Progress Report," *Journal of American History* 70, no. 3 (December 1983): 535–555.

Stop and Annotate

Go back to the excerpt above. In the space provided, list the presidents historians and political scientists who, in the opinion of all the scholars surveyed, feel have been the greatest presidents.

As you can see from the information listed in the table, five presidents have been judged, in the opinion of all the scholars surveyed, to be the greatest: Abraham Lincoln, George Washington, Franklin Delano Roosevelt, Thomas Jefferson, and Theodore Roosevelt.

Here are two additional points about facts and opinions: First, you should remember that although some paragraphs contain only facts or only opinions, a paragraph may contain *both* facts and opinions (it may even present both facts and opinions in the same sentence). Second, you should realize that it may seem difficult at times to distinguish opinions from facts. This is because authors sometimes present opinions in ways that make them seem like facts. For example, a writer might introduce his or her opinion by stating, "The fact is . . ." (For example, "The fact is, Hawaii's weather makes it the perfect place for your winter vacation." This statement is really an opinion about winter vacations and Hawaii's weather.) Stating that something is a fact, however, does not make it a fact. (Hawaii isn't the perfect place for your winter vacation if you want to go snow skiing.) Ideally, of course, an author would always express an opinion in a way that makes it clear that it *is* an opinion. ("In this writer's opinion, Hawaii's weather makes it the perfect place for your winter vacation.") But authors do not always do this, and it is your job to *think critically* as you read, being alert for opinions. When you identify an opinion, continue reading to determine whether or not the opinion is well supported. Although you should not accept an opinion unless it is well supported, you should be open to accepting opinions that *are* well supported.

Making Inferences and Drawing Logical Conclusions

Thinking critically as you read also entails understanding not only what the author states directly, but also what the author *suggests*. In other words, it is the responsibility of critical readers to make inferences and draw conclusions about what they have read. An **inference** is a logical conclusion based on what an author has stated. A **conclusion** is a decision that is reached after thoughtful consideration of information the author presents. The information leads up to the conclusion that should be drawn. Needless to say, any inferences or conclusions you draw will be affected by your experience, your prior knowledge (or lack of it), and your own biases.

Making inferences is not new to you. In fact, you make inferences continually in your daily life. You draw conclusions based on descriptions, facts, opinions, experiences, and observations. Assume, for example, that a woman in your class arrives late. She seems frustrated and upset, and her hands are covered with grease and grime. It would be logical to infer that she has had a flat tire or some other trouble with her car and that she had to fix the problem herself. Your inference would be based on your observations. Similarly, you make inferences every day about things you read. For instance, suppose that your roommate leaves you a note saying, "Hope you didn't need your brown jacket today. It looks great with my new jeans." You would infer that your roommate has borrowed—and is probably wearing—your brown jacket. This is your roommate's intended meaning ("I borrowed your jacket, and I'm wearing it"), even though this information does not appear in the message.

In fact, jokes and cartoons (including editorial and political cartoons) are funny only if the listener or reader makes the correct inference. Take, for example, the editorial cartoon on page 481. It comes from *Business Week* magazine. What inferences does the cartoonist expect readers to make about the fuel efficiency and size of the SUV (sport utility vehicle)? What inference could be made about the cartoonist's (and the publication's) position regarding SUVs?

You have also had opportunities to make inferences earlier in the book. The skills in Chapter 5, "Formulating Implied Main Ideas," involve making inferences. You learned that when authors *suggest* a main idea but do not state it directly, they are *implying* it. When readers comprehend an implied main idea, they are *inferring* it (making an inference about it). The writer implies the main idea; the reader infers it. Some of the skills in Chapter 8, "Reading Critically," also involve making inferences. In that chapter you learned, for example, how an author's tone can help you infer his or her intended meaning. You learned that after determining the author's purpose, you can conclude who the intended audience was.

KEY TERM
Inference

A logical conclusion based on what an author has stated.

KEY TERM
Conclusion

A decision that is reached after thoughtful consideration of information the author presents.

Critical thinking involves making inferences and drawing logical conclusions, although there are times when an author simply states his or her conclusion. When the author does state the conclusion, it typically appears at the end of the passage, and it is often the main idea of a paragraph or the overall main idea of the entire selection. Authors use phrases such as these to announce a conclusion: *In conclusion, Consequently, Thus,* and *Therefore.* Stated conclusions are important, so pay careful attention to them.

When the author states the conclusion, you do not need to infer it, of course. However, when there is a conclusion to be drawn, and the author does not state it, then it is up to the reader to infer it. An inference goes beyond what the author states but must always be *based on* what the author has said. That is, your inferences are conclusions you have made on the basis of what is stated in the passage. Remember that you cannot use as an inference anything *stated* by the author. For example, if the author states that "The *Titanic* sank because it hit an iceberg," you cannot give as an inference, "The *Titanic* sank because it hit an iceberg" because it has been directly stated. This is logical: if the author has already stated it, there is no reason for you to infer it. Nor are you making an inference if you merely paraphrase information that is presented in the paragraph. For example, you cannot give an inference, "An iceberg caused the *Titanic* to sink" because it is merely a paraphrase of information that was given by the author. You could, however, make the inference that "The water in which the *Titanic* sank was extremely cold." This is a logical inference, since the author states that there were icebergs in the water.

When you read, you should ask yourself, "What logical inference (conclusion) can I make, based on what the author has stated?" To draw a conclusion, the reader must deduce (reason out) the author's meaning. That is, readers must use the "evidence" and facts the author presents in order to arrive at the conclusion or inference the author wants them to make. Readers must make a connection between what an author says and what the author wants them to conclude.

Comprehension Monitoring Question for Making Inferences

"What logical inference (conclusion) can I make, based on what the author has stated?"

For example, a writer might describe the benefits of regular exercise but not state directly that you should exercise. The writer expects you to make the inference (draw the conclusion) that you should exercise regularly because he or she has presented the facts needed in order for you to conclude that exercise is beneficial.

You can understand more about how to make logical inferences by studying examples of correct inferences. Here is an excerpt from a business communications textbook about a well-known ice cream company, Ben and Jerry's Homemade (Selection 6-2). After reading this excerpt, you will see that you can draw some inferences about how employees feel about working at Ben and Jerry's.

What logical conclusions could you make about the employees at Ben and Jerry's Homemade?

_____

_____

_____

_____

_____

_____

Down at the factory in Waterbury, Vermont, they're known as "the boys." They are Ben Cohen and Jerry Greenfield, arguably America's most famous purveyors of ice cream and certainly two of America's most colorful entrepreneurs. They've been friends since seventh grade and business partners since 1978 when they opened their first scoop shop, using techniques gleaned from a $5 correspondence course on how to make ice cream. Their firm, Ben & Jerry's Homemade, sold more than $76 million worth of super premium ice cream in 1990 and employs around 300 people, give or take a few, depending on the season.

Ben and Jerry have strong personalities and strong opinions. They believe that work should be fun, or else it isn't worth doing. They also believe in helping the unfortunate, protecting the environment, and treating people fairly. They want their company to be a happy, humanitarian place where everybody feels good about coming to work and producing a top-notch product.

Actions also telegraph Ben & Jerry's commitment to an egalitarian work environment: the open office arrangement, the bright colors, the pictures of cows and fields hanging on warehouse walls, the employee committees, the casual clothes, the first-name relationships, the compressed pay scale that keeps executive salaries in balance with lower-level compensation, the free health club memberships for everyone, the upcoming on-site day-care facility. And the free ice cream. Three pints a day per person. Now that's communication at its best.

Source: Courtland Bovée and John Thill, *Business Communication Today,* 3rd ed., McGraw-Hill, New York, 1992, pp. 26, 28.

Because the owners of Ben and Jerry's Homemade provide their employees with a fair, supportive, informal, and comfortable work environment, it is logical to conclude that:

Employees are happy to work there.

They appreciate the company's philosophy.

They do not feel a high level of stress.

They are likely to remain employees of Ben and Jerry's.

The following details from the passage are the ones on which these inferences are based:

Employees call Ben and Jerry "the boys."

Ben and Jerry believe that work should be fun.

Ben and Jerry are interested in protecting the environment.

They believe in treating people fairly.

They want their company to be a happy, humanitarian place.

They have an open office arrangement.

They use bright colors.

There are pictures on warehouse walls.

Employees wear casual clothes.

First names are used.

There is a compressed pay scale.

There is a free health club.

There will soon be an on-site day-care facility.

Employees receive free ice cream daily.

Stop and Annotate

Go back to the excerpt above. In the space provided, write the *logical conclusions* that can be made about the employees at Ben and Jerry's Homemade.

You could draw other logical conclusions from these details as well. For example, you could conclude that companies can be humane and humanitarian yet still be extremely profitable. You could conclude that the public appreciates a high-quality product and is willing to pay for it. You might even conclude that you would like to work at Ben and Jerry's.

Here is another textbook excerpt in which conclusions must be inferred by reading and thinking critically. The passage is from a health textbook, and its topic is *passive smoking.*

Passive Smoking

Reports from the U.S. surgeon general's office suggest that tobacco smoke in enclosed indoor areas is an important air pollution problem. This has led to the controversy about ***passive smoking***—the breathing in of air polluted by the secondhand tobacco smoke of others. Carbon monoxide levels of sidestream smoke (smoke from the burning end of a ciga-

What logical conclusions can you make about nonsmokers and smokers?

_____

_____

_____

_____

rette) reach a dangerously high level. True, the smoke can be greatly diluted in freely circulating air, but the 1 to 5 percent carbon monoxide levels attained in smoke-filled rooms can be sufficient to harm the health of people with chronic bronchitis, other lung disease, or cardiovascular disease.

_____

_____

_____

_____

_____

Source: Martin Levy, Mark Dignan, and Janet Shirreffs, *Targeting Wellness: The Core*, McGraw-Hill, New York, 1992, pp. 262–263.

Stop and Annotate

Go back to the excerpt above. In the space provided, write the *logical conclusions* that can be made about both nonsmokers and smokers.

The authors want the reader to conclude that nonsmokers, especially those with certain health conditions, should avoid enclosed indoor areas in which there is cigarette smoke. Smokers should also conclude that they ought to refrain from smoking around others in an enclosed area. These are conclusions the authors want the reader to infer, even though they do not state them. These inferences are based on the statements that "carbon monoxide levels of sidestream smoke reach dangerously high levels" and that these levels "can be sufficient to harm the health of people with chronic bronchitis, other lung disease, or other cardiovascular disease."

When you read, remember to ask yourself, "What logical conclusion can I draw, based on what the author has stated?"

The chart below illustrates the application of critical thinking skills to a review of an imaginary movie. (This is the same movie review that appeared in Chapter 8, "Reading Critically.") It is designed to show that critical thinking skills are related and that they are applicable to reading tasks that you encounter daily.

EXAMPLE OF CRITICAL THINKING APPLIED TO A CRITIC'S REVIEW OF A MOVIE

Here is a critic's review of *Cyberpunk,* a new science fiction movie:

Do you enjoy violence? Do you like vulgar language? Do you appreciate painfully loud sound effects? What about watching unknown actors embarrass themselves? Or sitting for three hours and ten minutes without a break? If so, and you've got $7.50 to burn, then "Cyberpunk" is the movie for you!

Critical Reading Questions	**Answers**
What is the author's purpose?	To present a persuasive evaluation of a new movie
Who is the author's intended audience?	The movie-going public
What is the author's point of view?	*Cyberpunk* is a terrible movie.

Critical Reading Questions	Answers
What is the author's tone?	Sarcastic
What is the author's intended meaning?	Don't waste your money or your time on this movie.
Does the author include facts, opinions, or both?	Both
What logical inference (conclusion) does the author expect you to make?	Don't waste your time or your money on this movie.

Distinguishing between Deductive and Inductive Reasoning

No discussion of critical thinking would be complete without explaining the difference between deductive reasoning and inductive reasoning. As a college student, you should know the difference between the two. ***Deductive reasoning*** refers to reasoning by taking a generalization and seeing how it applies to a specific situation. It is often called "reasoning from the general to the specific." This is the type of reasoning that is used when a judge or an attorney applies a general law or legal precedent to a particular, specific legal case. It is also the type of reasoning that is used when a general theorem in geometry is applied to a specific problem, or a general algebraic formula is applied to a specific problem. It is the kind of reasoning you apply when you take a general principle or value you hold, such as being honest, and apply it in a particular situation ("I need to find the owner of this billfold and return it").

The opposite of deductive reasoning is inductive reasoning. ***Inductive reasoning*** refers to drawing a general conclusion that is based on specific details or facts. It is also called "reasoning from the specific to the general." You use inductive reasoning whenever you read a paragraph that consists only of details, and on the basis of these details, you reason out the general point the author is making (the implied main idea). Or, a doctor might examine specific case histories of several patients with similar symptoms and draw the general conclusion that a certain toxic chemical was the common factor that caused their illness.

Students sometimes get deductive and inductive reasoning mixed up. Here is a memory peg that may help you avoid this problem:

- With *deduct*ive reasoning, you are going from something larger and more general to smaller, more specific things (deduct = take away).
- With *in*ductive reasoning, the smaller parts or specific details lead *in* to the larger generalization (induct = lead into).

The chart on pages 486–487 presents three examples of deductive and inductive reasoning in textbook paragraphs.

KEY TERM
Deductive Reasoning

A process of reasoning in which a general principle is applied to a specific situation.

KEY TERM
Inductive Reasoning

A process of reasoning in which a general principle is developed from a set of specific instances.

Deductive Reasoning

Here is an example of a paragraph that opens with a general statement (which also happens to be the main idea). The rest of the paragraph explains specific ways reading can enrich a person's life.

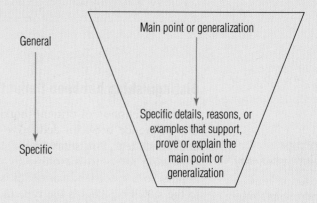

Example:

Being a good reader can enrich your life in many ways. Of course, reading is a key to doing well in school. But once you leave school, reading allows you to continue learning throughout your life. Many satisfying, high-paying careers, such as law and medicine, require the ability to read and comprehend large amounts of information. And reading is a wonderful pastime, an enjoyable way to relax and escape from the stresses of everyday life.

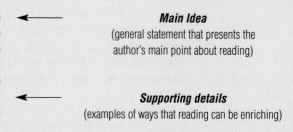

In this example of deductive writing, the author begins with a general principle, then presents specific examples to illustrate it.

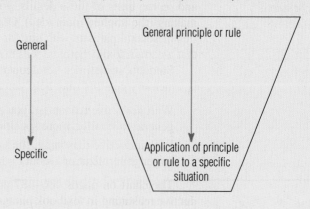

Example:

According to the Miranda ruling, if a person is not informed of his or her legal rights at the time of an arrest, the charges may be dropped. A woman charged of shoplifting may have the charges against her dropped if she is not informed when she is arrested, "You have the right to remain silent" and "Anything you say can be used against you in court." Or someone accused of assault may have the charges dismissed if the arresting officers fail to inform him, "You have the right to talk to an attorney before we ask you any questions and to have an attorney with you during questioning." A homeless person could have legal charges against her dismissed if the arresting officer neglects to tell her, "If you cannot afford an attorney, one will be provided for you before any questioning, if you wish."

◄───── ***Main Idea***
(general statement that presents the author's main point about being informed at the time of arrest about legal rights according to the Miranda ruling)

◄───── ***Supporting details***
(specific examples of Miranda violations)

Inductive Reasoning

In this example of inductive writing, the author presents specific examples that lead to a general statement that sums them up.

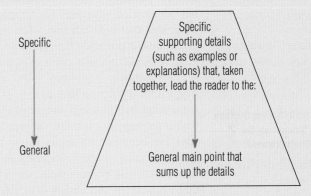

Specific

General

Specific supporting details (such as examples or explanations) that, taken together, lead the reader to the:

General main point that sums up the details

Example:

When most people hear the word "abuse," they think of *physical abuse,* such as hitting or kicking someone. However, there is also *sexual abuse,* in which the abuser forces the victim to engage in sexual acts against his or her will. *Emotional (psychological) abuse* is still another form of abuse. In this form of abuse there is a continual eroding of the victim's self-esteem and mental well-being. And many people forget that abuse can also be *verbal,* in which the abuser uses words to inflict severe emotional pain and damage. **It is important to recognize that abuse can take many forms.**

◄───── ***Supporting Details***
(examples of four specific forms of abuse)

◄───── ***Main idea***
(general statement that sums up the author's general point about abuse)

Evaluating an Author's Argument

You now know that critical thinking includes the skills of distinguishing between facts and opinions and making logical inferences. Now you will learn how to use these two skills (along with the critical reading skills you learned in Chapter 8) to *evaluate* material you read. The steps below describe the process for evaluating an author's argument.

Step 1: Identify the Issue

Critical Thinking Question for Identifying the Issue

"What controversial topic is this passage about?"

The first step, of course, is to identify the issue. An *issue* is simply a controversial topic. In other words, an issue is a topic that people have differing opinions about. To identify the issue, ask yourself: "What controversial topic is this passage about?" Examples of issues are: *whether there should be regulation of pornographic websites, whether government-subsidized health care should be provided for all Americans,* and *whether day-trading is too risky for inexperienced investors.*

Step 2: Determine the Author's Argument

KEY TERM

Author's Argument

The author's position on an issue.
The author's argument is also known as the author's *point of view.*

The second step is to determine the author's argument. An **author's argument** is the author's position on an issue. That is, an author's argument is his or her opinion on an issue. (In fact, the author's argument is simply an overall main idea that is an opinion.) The author's argument is what the author believes and wants to persuade the reader to believe (or do). You may also hear an argument referred to as the *point of view.*

An author's "argument" is not the same as an oral disagreement or dispute. The author's purpose in a written argument is to persuade the reader to believe something by "arguing" (presenting) a case for it. An author "argues" for it in the same way an attorney "argues" his or her client's side of a case during a trial. For example, an author might argue that *All college students should be required to take at least one computer course.* To persuade the reader to accept (believe) his or her argument, the author typically presents support or evidence that backs it up. An author does this in the same way that an attorney presents evidence to support his or her case. To determine the author's argument, ask yourself, "What is the author's position on this issue?"

Critical Thinking Question for Determining the Author's Argument

"What is the author's position on the issue?"

Part of understanding an author's argument is recognizing the **author's bias** in favor of one side of an issue. For example, if the author's argument is *All college students should be required to take at least one computer course,* then the author's bias is that he or she *favors* computer literacy for college students. If an author's argument is *Our government should not impose any restrictions on gun ownership,* then the author's bias is that he or she *opposes* gun control.

KEY TERM

Author's Bias

The side of an issue an author favors; an author's preference for one side of the issue over the other.

Authors who have a bias in favor of one side of a controversial issue support that side: they are *for* it. For example, the term *pro-environmental* would describe an author who favors legislation to protect the environment. Authors who have an opposing bias take the opposite position: they are *against* it. For example, the term *anti-environmental* would describe an author who opposes efforts or legislation to protect the environment.

Critical Thinking Question for Determining the Author's Bias

"Which side of the issue does the author support?"

How can you tell whether an author has a bias when the author does not directly state his or her position? The best way is to examine the support the author gives. Ask yourself, "Does the author present support and information about both sides of the issue?" If not, ask yourself, "Which side of the issue does the author present support for?" This will reveal the author's bias.

By the way, part of thinking critically involves asking yourself whether *you* have a bias about an issue. If you do, you will have to make an extra effort to be open-minded and objective when you evaluate an author's argument. Otherwise, you may reject the author's argument without seriously considering it or without considering it objectively.

Of course, there will be times when an author chooses not to take a position on an issue. That is, the author will be *neutral* on an issue. The author does not take a position because his or her purpose is to present *both* sides of an issue objectively. The author wants to present relevant support for both sides of an issue so that reader can make their own informed decision about the matter. Most of the time, however, authors *do* have a point of view.

Step 3: Identify the Assumptions on Which the Author Bases His or Her Argument

KEY TERM
Author's Assumption

Something the author takes for granted without proof.

When authors present an argument, they typically base it on certain assumptions. An *assumption* is something that is taken for granted or assumed to be true. That is, it is accepted as true without proof that it is actually true (although it is often very logical).

Critical Thinking Question for Identifying the Author's Assumptions

"What does the author take for granted?"

To identify an author's assumptions, ask yourself, "What does the author take for granted?" To illustrate, suppose an author's argument is, "Society must do more to protect young children from abuse." In order to make this argument, the author would have to have made these assumptions:

- Young children are worth protecting.
- Young children are not being protected adequately at present.
- Young children are not able to protect themselves.
- There are things society can and should do to protect young children.

These are all valid assumptions because they are reasonable and logical. Sometimes, though, an author bases an argument on illogical, unreasonable, or even incorrect assumptions. For example, an author's argument might be, *The minimum age for obtaining a driver's license should be 20.* In this case, the author's assumptions might be:

- Teenagers are irresponsible.
- If people are older when they begin driving, they will be better drivers.

It is incorrect to assume that all teenagers are irresponsible, or that if people are older when they begin driving, they will automatically be better drivers.

When you read an author's argument, you must think critically about assumptions the author makes to be sure that they are not incorrect assumptions and so that you are not manipulated by the author. Let's say that an author's argument is, "We should hire Margaret Jones as our city manager because only a woman cares enough about the city's historic district to preserve it." Two of the assumptions this argument is based on are:

A man would not care about the city's historic district.

A man is not capable of saving the city's historic district.

The author also assumes that saving the city's historic district is the sole or most important issue upon which the selection of the city manager should be based. These are illogical and incorrect assumptions, of course. Readers who do not question the author's assumptions might be manipulated into believing the author's argument.

Critical Thinking Question for Identifying Support

"What types of support does the author present?"

Step 4: Identify the Types of Support the Author Presents

Examine the supporting details to see if the author give facts, examples, case studies, research results, or expert opinions. Is the author himself or herself an expert? Does he or she cite personal experience or observations, make comparisons, give reasons or evidence? Ask yourself, "What types of support does the author present?"

Critical Thinking Question for Deciding Whether an Author's Support Is Relevant

"Does the support pertain directly to the argument?"

Step 5: Decide Whether the Support Is Relevant

Support is *relevant* when it pertains directly to the argument. In other words, the support is meaningful and appropriate, and it relates directly to the argument. Ask yourself, "Does the support pertain directly to the argument?" For example, the author might argue that *All states should lower the blood alcohol level used to determine when drivers are legally drunk.* Statistics that show a decrease in traffic accidents and deaths in the states that already have a lower blood alcohol level would be relevant support. Sometimes, however, an author will try to persuade readers by using support that is irrelevant. If the author mentions that many drivers damage their own vehicles after drinking a large amount of alcohol, it would not be relevant support for this argument.

Critical Thinking Questions for Evaluating Whether an Author's Argument Is Objective and Complete

"Is the argument based on facts and other appropriate evidence?" "Did the author leave out information that might weaken or disprove the argument?"

Step 6: Determine Whether the Author's Argument Is Objective and Complete

The term *objective* means that an argument is based on facts and evidence instead of on the author's feelings or unsupported opinions. Suppose the author who is arguing that *All states should lower the blood alcohol level used to determine when drivers are legally drunk* knows someone who was injured by a drunk driver and is angry because the inebriated driver was not penalized. As support for his argument, the author talks about how angry drunk drivers make him. This would not be objective support; it would be *subjective* support (support based on emotion). Ask yourself, "Is the author's argument based on facts and other appropriate evidence?" An author's support should be objective, not merely personal or emotional.

The term *complete* means that an author has not left out information simply because it might weaken or even disprove his or her argument. Suppose an author's argument is *Our city would benefit from a new sports arena.* Perhaps the author mentions that a new arena would boost the city's image and increase civic pride, but does not mention that a special bond would have to be passed by voters in order to pay for the arena, or that the new arena would cause major traffic congestion whenever sporting events were held. Particularly when an author has a bias, he or she may deliberately leave out important information that would weaken the argument. When evaluating the completeness of an author's argument, ask yourself, "Did the author leave out information that might weaken or disprove the argument?" To be fully convincing, an author's argument should be objective and complete.

Step 7: Evaluate the Overall Validity and Credibility of the Author's Argument

The term *valid* means that an argument was correctly reasoned and its conclusions follow logically from the information, evidence, or reasons that were presented. You must evaluate the author's logic, the quality of his or her thinking. To evaluate the validity of an author's argument, ask yourself, "Is the author's argument logical?" You should not accept an author's argument if it is not valid. Before you can determine whether an argument is valid, you must consider your answers to the questions mentioned in the previous steps:

- "What does the author take for granted?"
- "What type of support does the author present?"
- "Does the support pertain directly to the argument?"
- "Is the argument objective and complete?"

Critical Thinking Question for Evaluating if an Author's Argument Is Valid and Credible

"Is the author's argument logical and believable?"

Finally, you must evaluate the credibility of the author's argument. The term *credibility* refers to how believable an author's argument is. To be believable, the author's argument must be based on logic or relevant evidence. You must once again consider the author's assumptions, the types and relevance of the support, objectivity, completeness, and validity to determine the believability of the author's argument. To evaluate the credibility of an author's argument, ask yourself, "Is the argument believable?" An argument that has credibility is a convincing one. You must think critically about an author's argument in order to evaluate it. You should reject any argument that lacks validity and credibility, but you should be just as open to accepting one that is valid and credible.

Let's look at an example of how an author's argument could be evaluated critically. Consider the argument, *All college students should be required to take at least one computer science course.* To evaluate its credibility, you would first examine the assumptions the author has made. For example, he or she obviously assumes that it is valuable to know about computers, that computers will continue to be important in people's personal and professional lives, etc. The types of support the author gives might include facts and research findings about the growing use of computers, several examples of ways college students could benefit from computer skills, and his or her personal experience with computers. As a reader, you would then have to decide whether or not the support is relevant (directly supports the argument), whether it is complete (whether information that might support the other side of the issue was omitted), whether it is objective (based on facts and other appropriate evidence), and whether it is valid (logical). Consideration of these elements would enable you to evaluate whether or not the author's argument has validity and credibility.

Now read and evaluate an excerpt from a wellness textbook. This excerpt (from Selection 7-2, "The Decision to Marry") discusses the compatibility of married couples who have great differences in personality. After you have read this passage, apply the seven steps above to evaluate it critically.

Unfortunately, great differences in personality can often lead to marital conflict later on. For example, one study found that a source of marital dissatisfaction among husbands was a feeling that their wives were too possessive, neglectful, and openly admiring of other men. Dissatisfied wives complained that their husbands were possessive, moody, and openly attracted to other women. The study also found that sex is a source of great difficulties for unhappy married men and women. It found that women see sex as following from emotional intimacy, while men see it as a road to intimacy. As a result, men complain that their wives withhold sex from them and women complain that their husbands are too sexually aggressive.

Evaluating an Author's Argument

Issue:
"What controversial topic is this passage about?"

_____

_____

_____

Authors' argument:
"What is the authors' position on the issue?"

_____

_____

_____

Authors' assumptions:
"What do the authors take for granted?"

_____

_____

_____

_____

_____

_____

Type of support:
"What type of support do the authors present?"

_____

_____

_____

Relevance of support:
"Does the support pertain directly to the argument?"

_____

_____

_____

_____

_____

Objectivity and completeness:
"Is the argument based on facts and other appropriate evidence?" and *"Did the author leave out information that might weaken or disprove the argument?"*

_____

_____

Validity and credibility:
"Is the argument logical and believable?"

_____

_____

_____

_____

Source: Adapted from Marvin Levy, Mark Dignan, and Janet Shirreffs, "The Decision to Marry," *in Targeting Wellness: The Core,* McGraw-Hill, New York, 1992, p. 123.

The issue in this passage is *personality differences and marital conflict.* The authors' argument is stated in the first sentence: *Unfortunately, great differences in personality can often lead to marital conflict later on.*

The authors assume that personality traits can be accurately measured and that they remain consistent throughout people's lives. Also, the authors would not bother to present the information unless they assume that people can make better decisions in selecting a spouse if they are aware of the effects of personality differences on relationships. Their assumptions seem reasonable and logical.

The support the authors present is the result of a research study that compares husbands' and wives' sources of dissatisfaction with each other.

Some of the support is relevant; some of it is not. The first finding of the study *does* support the argument that personality differences can lead to conflict later on (since possessiveness, moodiness, and aggressiveness can be viewed as personality traits). On the other hand, the second finding of the study (on sex as a source of difficulties for unhappy married couples) does *not* directly support the authors' argument (since it is differences in attitudes toward sex rather than personality differences that appear to cause the problems). Moreover, the differing attitudes of husbands and wives appear to be related to gender rather than to personality. Therefore, this second finding of the study is not as relevant to the authors' argument.

The argument is objective, but it is not complete. It is objective because the authors present research rather than merely giving their own unsupported opinions. Although the authors present the findings from one study, their argument would have been more complete had they presented several sets of research findings.

Although the argument could have been made stronger had the authors included additional relevant support, their argument nevertheless appears to have some validity, and therefore some credibility as well.

Stop and Annotate

Go back to the excerpt above. In the spaces provided, answer the critical thinking questions for evaluating an author's argument.

An evaluation of the author's argument could be summed up as follows: The authors' argument (that great differences in personalities can lead to conflict between a married couple) does have some validity and credibility. This is because the authors' argument is based on logical assumptions and is supported with a relevant finding from a research study.

Now look at two short selections that both address the issue of legalizing drugs that are currently illegal. As you read, think about which side presents the better argument. (Before you begin reading, think about whether *you* already have a bias on this issue.)

Pro-Legalization: Weighing the Costs of Drug Use

For over 100 years this society has made the use of certain drugs illegal and has penalized illegal drug use. But during that time the use of marijuana, heroin and other opiates, and cocaine has become an epidemic. Most recently, Americans have spent billions of dollars on arresting and imprisoning sellers and importers of crack cocaine, with almost no effect on the supply or street price of the drug.

The societal costs of illegal drugs are immense. They include the costs of law enforcement, criminal proceedings against those arrested, and jails and prisons. They also include the spread of deadly diseases such as AIDS and hepatitis through the use of shared needles; the cost to society of raising "crack babies," children poisoned by drugs even before birth; and the

Evaluating an Author's Argument

Issue:
"What controversial topic is this passage about?"

_____

_____

_____

Authors' argument:

"What is the authors' position on the issue?"

_____

_____

cost of raising a generation of young people who see illegal drug selling and violence as their only escape from poverty and desperation. Finally, the societal costs include the emotional cost of the violence that no one can now escape.

Legalizing drug use in this country would eliminate many of these costs. Billions of dollars would be saved. This money could be spent on treatment of addicts, job training, and education programs to help many disadvantaged young people assume valuable roles in society. The government could make drug use legal for adults but impose severe penalties on anyone who sells drugs to young people. Drug sales could be heavily taxed, thus deterring drug purchases and giving society the benefit of tax revenues that could be used for drug treatment and education.

Authors' assumptions:

"What do the authors take for granted?"

———————————————

———————————————

———————————————

Type of support:

"What type of support do the authors present?"

———————————————

———————————————

———————————————

Relevance of support:

"Does the support pertain directly to the argument?"

———————————————

———————————————

———————————————

Objectivity and completeness:

"Is the argument based on facts and other appropriate evidence?" and *"Did the author leave out information that might weaken or disprove the argument?"*

———————————————

———————————————

———————————————

———————————————

———————————————

Validity and credibility:
"Is the argument logical and believable?"

_____

_____

_____

_____

_____

_____

Source: Richard Schlaad and Peter Shannon, "Legalizing Drugs," in Marvin Levy, Mark Dignan, and Janet Shirreffs, *Targeting Wellness: The Core,* McGraw-Hill, New York, 1992, p. 235.

Anti-Legalization: Providing a Positive Role Model

Certain drugs are illegal because they are dangerous and deadly and provide no societal value. To make their possession or use legal would send a message to young people that using drugs is acceptable and that drugs are not treacherous or life-destroying.

Making drugs illegal has not increased the number of drug users or sellers, just as making alcohol legal after Prohibition did not reduce the number of people who drank. Recent law enforcement efforts have indeed made a difference. Over the past few years, as law enforcement efforts have sent more and more people to jail, the number of young people who use illegal drugs has steadily declined. Furthermore, education about the ill effects of drug use has begun to deter people from buying and using illegal drugs.

Recently, the incidence of drug-related deaths and violence has begun to level off even in the areas of the most hard-core drug use. This is proof that strict law enforcement is working. This country has begun to turn the corner on this drug epidemic.

Evaluating an Author's Argument

Issue:
"What controversial topic is this passage about?"

_____

_____

_____

Authors' argument:
"What is the authors' position on the issue?"

_____

_____

_____

Authors' assumptions:
"What do the authors take for granted?"

_____

_____

_____

_____

Type of support:
"What type of support do the authors present?"

_____

_____

_____

_____

Relevance of support:
"Does the support pertain directly to the argument?"

_____

_____

_____

Objectivity and completeness:
"Is the argument based on facts and other appropriate evidence?" and *"Did the author leave out information that might weaken or disprove the argument?"*

_____

_____

_____

_____

Validity and credibility:
"Is the argument logical and believable?"

_____

_____

_____

_____

_____

_____

_____

_____

_____

Source: Richard Schlaad and Peter Shannon, "Legalizing Drugs," in Marvin Levy, Mark Dignan, and Janet Shirreffs, *Targeting Wellness: The Core,* McGraw-Hill, New York, 1992, p. 235.

Stop and Annotate

Go back to the two selections above. In the spaces provided, answer the two sets of critical thinking questions for evaluating an author's argument.

Of the two selections, the pro-legalization argument (the first argument) is stronger. The authors give five distinct "costs" of illegal drugs and then explain how legalizing drugs (and the revenue from taxing them) could be directed at treating the problem. Further, the authors make it clear that there could still be strong penalties for any adults who sell drugs to young people. The anti-legalization article is very general and is less convincing. Of course, the issue of drug legalization is a complex one, and this is not to say that all drugs should be legalized immediately. Still, of the two selections, the stronger argument was made in the pro-legalization selection.

Identifying Propaganda Devices

KEY TERM

Propaganda Devices

Techniques authors use in order to unfairly influence the reader to accept their point of view.

Examining support is a crucial element in evaluating an author's argument. Readers must be aware that authors sometimes use unfair techniques in order to persuade readers to believe their argument. Authors with a bias may use what are known as "propaganda" techniques to try to unduly influence the reader to accept their point of view. This means that the "support" they present is in some way inadequate, misleading, or flawed. You are more likely to encounter propaganda in editorials, advertisements, and certain other types of writing than in textbooks, of course. Still, you must think critically to detect whether propaganda is offered as support. If you are not alert to propaganda devices, you may find yourself being manipulated by them.

Comprehension Monitoring Question for Thinking Critically to Identify Propaganda Devices

"Has the author tried to unfairly influence me to accept his or her point of view?"

There are too many types of propaganda to describe all of them, but here are brief descriptions and examples of several of the most common ones. Although speakers often use these same propaganda techniques, our focus is on authors' use of them. In either case, and as the explanations show, each propaganda device is based either on emotion or on flawed reasoning. To think critically and identify propaganda devices, ask yourself, "Has the author tried to unfairly influence me to accept his or her point of view?"

Authors often try to appeal to readers' emotions, such as appeals to fear, guilt, greed, status, vanity, sympathy, tradition, and so forth, rather than to reason. Some examples of appeals to emotion are:

Appeal to fear. The author tries to manipulate readers by frightening them into accepting his or her point of view.

Examples

"If you don't know how to use a computer, you might as well give up any hope of having a good career."

"Afraid to smile? Embarrassed by dingy yellow teeth? Don't let yellow teeth stand between you and an active social life. Brush with Gleam-O-Dent twice daily and in just three weeks, you'll no longer be afraid to smile."

Volvo: "Pay more for a car and live to see why."

Appeal to sympathy. The author tries to manipulate readers by making them feel sorry for someone or something.

Examples

"Adopt a pet today. There's nothing more heartbreaking than a sad, lonely kitten or puppy in need of a loving home."

"Thousands of innocent children will die if our readers do not donate at least half a million more dollars to our fund by the end of the year."

"Yes, some athletes and scholarship students cheat on tests, but they are under tremendous pressure to maintain a certain GPA. If they do not maintain their average, they will lose their eligibility or their scholarships. They will have to drop out of college, and after that, they will never have any chance of getting a good job or being successful in life."

Appeal to vanity. The author tries to manipulate readers by making them feel that they are special or superior to other people.

Examples

"Discriminating buyers insist on a Cadillac."

"Connoisseurs of fine wine insist on Grape Arbor Chardonnay."

"You'll be the envy of everyone when you glide down the street in your sleek, new, Snobmobile. Your refined sense of taste and elegance will be obvious to all. Move up to a Snobmobile and drive the car you deserve."

Army: "Be all you can be."

Marines: "The few. The proud. The Marines."

L'Oréal: "L'Oréal . . . because I'm worth it."

Appeal to tradition. The author tries to manipulate readers by telling them that they should do or believe something because that is the way it has always been done in the past, or that they can create a new tradition.

Examples

"In this part of the state, we've always voted for conservative candidates."

DeBeers: "A diamond is forever."

Bandwagon.   The author says, in effect, that everyone believes, accepts, or does what he is describing and therefore the reader should "get on the bandwagon" too. In other words, the author says you should believe something just because "everyone else" believes it. The author knows that this strategy appeals to people's desire to be part of the crowd and their fear of being different or feeling left out.

> *Example*
>
> "We all want to be in great shape nowadays, so join the millions of Americans who have bought the home Exer-Gym. Everyone agrees that it's the only piece of exercise equipment you'll ever need, that it's the world's best, and that it's the most enjoyable way to get in shape. Join the Exer-Gym crowd now!"

Appeal to Authority.   The author tries to influence the reader to accept his argument or point of view by citing some authority who believes it.

> *Examples*
>
> "Dr. Doe, my psychology teacher, believes that there was once life on Mars. If he believes it, it must be right. He is well-educated and has read many books about extraterrestrial life."
>
> "Three out of four dentists who recommend mouthwash recommend Rinse-O-Dent to their patients."

Testimonial.   This is similar to the appeal to authority. In this case, a famous person endorses an idea or product in order to influence others to believe or buy it. Many times, however, the person endorsing the product has no special knowledge about it or experience with it, so the testimonial is not worth very much. Testimonial is also called ***endorsement.***

> *Examples*
>
> A celebrity such as an actor, model, sports figure, or entertainer endorses a certain brand of automobile or a particular line of clothing.
>
> Michael Jordan and the cartoon characters Tweety Bird and Elmer Fudd have been used to endorse MCI telephone service.
>
> "Golf pros like Tiger Woods know that Nike athletic products are the best money can buy!"

Straw Man.   The author misrepresents what an opponent believes, then attacks that belief.

> *Examples*
>
> "Our college cafeteria has awful food. Obviously, the cafeteria's manager doesn't care at all about students' preferences or their health. The college administration needs to replace the current cafeteria manager with someone who actually cares about cafeteria customers."

Either-Or. The author puts everything into one of two mutually exclusive categories and acts as if there are no other possibilities besides one category or the other.

Examples

"Either install a Blammo Home Security System or pay the consequences."

"There are cultivated people who like opera and there are uncultivated ones who don't."

"Yes, there is an alternative to calcium supplements. It's called osteoporosis."

False Analogy. The author makes a comparison that is either inaccurate or inappropriate.

Examples

"Taking a shower with Spring Burst soap is like a refreshing romp in the surf."

"Everyone knows that professional athletes are just overgrown spoiled children."

Circular Reasoning. The author merely restates the argument or conclusion rather than providing any real support. This is also called ***begging the question.***

Example

"Vote for Bob Griggs for senator. He's the best person for the job because there is no one else who's better!"

"Fourth World countries could improve their economic situation by making their economies better."

Transfer. The author transfers the good or bad qualities of one person or thing to another in order to influence the reader's perception of it.

Examples

"Mother Teresa would have supported the legislation we are proposing to help the country's homeless."

"Our candidate is another JFK!"

"This old car gets about the same gas mileage as an army tank!"

Sweeping Generalization. The author presents a broad general statement that goes far beyond the evidence. (*Stereotyping* is one form of sweeping generalization.)

Examples

BMW:"The best-handling car in America. The ultimate driving machine."

"All women are bad drivers."

"No man will ever admit he's lost."

"All jocks are dumb."

"The homeless are lazy, unmotivated people who would rather ask for a handout than work for a living."

Hasty Generalization.   The author jumps to a conclusion that is based on insufficient proof or evidence.

Examples

"Sudzo made all my clothes spotless and bright again. It'll work on all your laundry too!"

"My brother was a Boy Scout and loved it. Any boy would find that becoming a Boy Scout is one of the best decisions he could ever make!"

"If you care at all about animals, you'll make a generous donation to the Ferret Fund."

Plain Folks.   The author appeals to readers by presenting himself or herself as someone who is just like the readers.

Examples

Shimano fishing reels: "For the rich, there's therapy. For the rest of us, there's bass. The Cariolus reel is built with care and precision by people who, just like you, would go crazy if they couldn't fish."

"Why should we hardworking, middle-class folks have to carry the tax burden in this country? We work hard, but we never get ahead. It's time Congress gave us middle-class citizens the tax break we deserve."

Ad Hominem.   The author attacks the person rather than the views or ideas the person presents.

Example

"My opponent once lied about serving in the military when he was a young man. Why should you believe him now when he says he will reduce taxes if you elect him? He's a liar and every campaign promise he makes is just another lie."

PROPAGANDA TECHNIQUES EXERCISE

Directions: Here is a list of propaganda techniques. Decide which type of propaganda technique is used in each of the examples that follow. The first one has been completed for you.

appeal to authority	bandwagon	straw man
appeal to tradition	circular reasoning	sweeping generalization
appeal to sympathy	either-or	testimonial
appeal to fear	false analogy	transfer
appeal to vanity	hasty generalization	ad hominem
	plain folks	

1. Insist on Best Brand Turkeys—because Thanksgiving Day is too important to ruin.

   appeal to fear

2. The victims of the tornado need more than your pity. They need you to roll up your sleeve and donate blood.

3. Gold Star Butter—it's not for just anyone.

4. Christmas just wouldn't be Christmas without Creamy-Smooth Eggnog! It's been America's number one choice for more than half a century.

5. Each year more than one million Americans trust Nationwide Realty to sell their homes. Shouldn't you?

6. Parents are justified in doing whatever it takes to keep themselves informed about their child if they think their child is doing something wrong. Dr. Laura says it's OK for parents to search their teenagers' rooms, read their diaries, and even make them take drug tests.

7. I've been a radio talk show host for fifteen years now, and I've never found an arthritis pain reliever more effective than Salvo.

8. The governor opposes legislation that mandates safety locks on guns. Obviously, he has no problem with innocent children being killed from playing with guns. It's time to vote the governor out of office!

9. You can either buy a Health Trip exercise bicycle or continue to be overweight and out of shape.

10. Having a career in multimedia production is like being able to print money!

11. America will have better-educated citizens when fewer students drop out of school.

12. Princess Diana would have donated her time and energy to this worthy cause.

13. All of today's youth are self-centered and irresponsible.

14. Blue Label Beer—the working man's brew!

15. Senator Bledsoe is opposed to campaign funding reform. He's just the type of person who would solicit illegal contributions! I'll bet that over the last decade he's taken in hundreds of thousands of dollars illegally.

16. If you like being near the beach, you'll love living in Hawaii.

Many college students are required to take standardized reading tests as part of an overall assessment program, in a reading course, or as part of a state-mandated "basic skills" test. A standardized reading test typically consists of a series of passages followed by multiple-choice questions, to be completed within a specified time limit.

Here are some examples of typical wording of questions about **critical thinking:**

Questions about *fact and opinion* may be phrased:

Which of the following statements represents an opinion of the author's?

Which of the following statements expresses an opinion rather than a fact?

Which of the following sentences from the passage represents a fact?

Which of the following sentences from the passage represents an opinion?

In dealing with questions about fact and opinion, watch for words (such as *perhaps, apparently, it seems, experts believe*) that signal opinions. Watch also for judgmental words (such as *best, worst* or *beautiful*), which also indicate opinions.

Questions about *inferences and logical conclusions* may be worded:

Which of the following conclusions could be made about . . . ?

On the basis of information in this passage, the reader could conclude . . .

It can be inferred from the passage that . . .

The passage implies that . . .

In dealing with questions on inferences and logical conclusions, remember that an inference must be logical and must be based on information in the passage.

Questions about the *author's argument* may be worded:

The author's argument about . . . is . . .

In this selection, the author argues that . . .

The author's position on this issue is . . .

The author's point of view is . . .

The passage suggests that the author believes . . .

Questions about the *author's credibility* may be worded:

The author has credibility because . . .

The author establishes his credibility by . . . (by presenting data, giving examples, etc.)

The author's argument is believable because . . .

The author is believable because . . .

Questions about the *author's assumptions* may be worded:

The author bases his (or her) argument on which of the following assumptions?

Which of the following assumptions underlies the author's argument?

The author's argument is based on which of the following assumptions?

Questions about *types of support* the author presents may be worded:

The author presents which of the following types of support?

The author includes all of the following types of support except . . .

CREATING YOUR SUMMARY

DEVELOPING CHAPTER REVIEW CARDS

Review cards, or *summary cards,* are an excellent study tool. They are a way to select, organize, and review the most important information in a textbook chapter. The process of creating review cards helps you organize information in a meaningful way and, at the same time, transfer it into long-term memory. The cards can also be used to prepare for tests (see Part Three). The review card activities in this book give you structured practice in creating these valuable study tools. Once you have learned how to make review cards, you can create them for textbook material in your other courses.

Now, complete the eight review cards for Chapter 9 by answering the questions or following the directions on each card. When you have completed them, you will have summarized: (1) what critical thinking is, (2) distinguishing facts from opinions, (3) making logical inferences and drawing logical conclusions, (4) deductive and inductive reasoning, (5) the steps in evaluating an author's argument, (6) the definition of author's argument, author's bias and author's assumptions, (7) critical thinking questions to ask yourself, and (8) propaganda devices.

Critical Reading

Define *critical thinking.* (See page 471.)

_____

List the skills of critical thinking. (See page 471.)

1. _____

2. _____

3. _____

Card 1   **Chapter 9: Thinking Critically**

Distinguishing Facts and Opinions

What is a *fact?* (See page 473.)

_____

What is an *opinion?* (See page 474.)

_____

To distinguish facts from opinions, what question should you ask yourself? (See page 474.)

_____

What are some typical clue words and phrases that signal an opinion? (See page 475.)

_____

_____

_____

What makes an opinion valuable? (See page 474.)

_____

Card 2   **Chapter 9: Thinking Critically**

Making Logical Inferences and Drawing Conclusions

What is an *inference?* (See page 480.)

_____

_____

What is a *conclusion?* (See page 480.)

_____

_____

In order to make an inference, what question should you ask yourself? (See page 481.)

_____

_____

Card 3   **Chapter 9: Thinking Critically**

Deductive and Inductive Reasoning

Define *deductive reasoning.* (See page 485.)

_____

_____

Define *inductive reasoning.* (See page 485.)

_____

_____

Card 4   **Chapter 9: Critical Thinking**

Steps in Evaluating an Author's Argument

List the seven steps you must take to evaluate an author's argument. (See pages 488–491.)

1. _____

2. _____

3. _____

4. _____

5. _____

6. _____

7. _____

Card 5   **Chapter 9: Thinking Critically**

Author's Argument, Bias and Assumptions

Define *author's argument.* (See pages 488.)

_____

_____

Define *author's bias.* (See pages 488.)

_____

_____

Define *author's assumption.* (See pages 489.)

_____

_____

Card 6   **Chapter 9: Thinking Critically**

Critical Thinking Questions for Evaluating an Author's Argument

What are the questions you should ask yourself in order to complete the seven steps for evaluating an author's argument? (See pages 488–491.)

1. _____

2. _____

3. _____

4. _____

5. _____

6. _____

   _____

7. _____

Card 7   **Chapter 9: Thinking Critically**

Identifying Propaganda Devices

What are propaganda devices? (See page 498.)

_____

List sixteen types of propaganda devices. (See pages 498–502)

_____   _____

_____   _____

_____   _____

_____   _____

_____   _____

_____   _____

_____   _____

_____   _____

Card 8   **Chapter 9: Thinking Critically**

SPORT UTILITY VEHICLES: HOW DO I HATE THEE?
LET ME COUNT THE WAYS

From the *Dallas Morning News*

By Geneva Overholser

Prepare Yourself to Read

Directions: Do these exercises *before* you read Selection 9-1.

1. First, read and think about the title. Do you own an SUV or have you had an unpleasant experience with an SUV someone else was driving? How do you feel about SUVs?

   _____

   _____

2. Next, complete your preview by reading the following:

   > Introduction (in *italics*)
   > Skim the entire editorial

   On the basis of your preview, what does the editorial seem to be about?

   _____

   _____

Apply Comprehension Skills

Directions: Do the Annotation Practice Exercises as you read Selection 9-1. Think critically:

Distinguish between facts and opinions.
Make logical inferences and draw conclusions as you read.
Evaluate the author's argument.

SPORT UTILITY VEHICLES: HOW DO I HATE THEE? LET ME COUNT THE WAYS

Today sport utility vehicles (SUVs) are ubiquitous—they're in every parking lot and on every highway. In fact, in 1999 SUV sales exceeded car sales for the first time ever. Millions of Americans have fallen in love with these vehicles, and perhaps just as many detest them. What is your opinion of SUVs? As the title suggests, the author has a strong opinion on this issue. Read the selection to see why she feels the way she does.

1   Let me say out front that sport utility vehicles drive me nuts. No one need waste time writing to tell me I sound like a raving lunatic about this. I feel like a lunatic about SUVs, and I hereby invite you to join me in raving.

2   Of course, you already may be among the hordes of Americans who have purchased one of these inexplicably popular extravagances. Or you may be among what surely must be the equally fast-growing numbers who seethe over the idiocy of buying mammoth, highly engineered off-road vehicles in order to go the drugstore. But on the off chance you remain uncommitted, I offer three reasons that SUVs' growing popularity should alarm and infuriate you.

3   First, gasoline. Anyone of age in the 1970s will remember when our great nation was brought to its knees by something called OPEC. This international oil cartel—the Organization of Petroleum Exporting Countries—was able to cripple our economy because of our then-shameful reliance on others for 36 percent of our oil.

4   Once OPEC put the fear of the Lord into us, we admirably changed our ways. We began insulating our homes and businesses, turning out lights, buying energy-efficient appliances and—most important—switching to smaller cars that burned less gasoline.

5   What a difference a quarter-century makes. Now, our cars' gas mileage no longer is improving. We are driving more. Fuel consumption keeps rising. And these nonsensical, gas-guzzling behemoths are the fastest-growing segment of the vehicle market. Depending on driving conditions, the six most popular SUVs get as low as 13 miles to the gallon.

6   In case you think nothing like what happened in the 1970s could happen again, you should know that OPEC's members, concerned about

Annotation Practice Exercises

Directions: For each of the exercises below, think critically to answer the questions. This will help you gain additional insights as you read.

low oil costs, got together in March in Vienna and decreed a cut in production of about 3 percent. And guess how much of our oil we import nowadays? It is 56 percent.

7   The good news here is that in 1999 Vice President Al Gore proposed that automakers triple SUV fuel efficiency by 2007. More power to him.

8   If energy dependence doesn't concern you, how about safety? Begin with a news story in February, when Ford Motor Co. introduced a design change to make its new SUVs a little safer in crashes. Its newest SUV, the Excursion, will have steel bars below its bumpers so it won't ride over other cars during collisions.

9   The Excursion, please note, is nearly 7 feet tall and weighs more than three tons. Ford tested it with its own Taurus and found that in a head-on collision, the SUV would ride over the normal car's hood and strike the base of the Taurus windshield, causing "tremendous damage to the passenger compartment," as the *New York Times* delicately put it.

10   The National Highway Traffic Safety Administration says the size of SUVs makes them responsible for 2,000 deaths a year more than conventional cars would have caused in the same collisions.

11   Not concerned about gasoline or accidents? Perhaps you worry about the environment or like to breathe. Carbon dioxide emissions from cars and trucks make up about a third of this country's generous contribution to global warming. And SUVs are the carbon-dioxide-spewing champs: The new SUVs send out 70 tons per year, compared with the average car's 50 tons.

12   There is modest good news here, too. The Clinton administration proposed rules that would force most SUVs to meet the same emissions standards as cars. If the proposals survive the public comment period, the new standards would be phased in over five years, beginning in 2004— a reasonable enough expectation.

13   But apparently not reasonable to everyone. Opponents began weighing in immediately. The often sensible Sen. Dick Lugar of Indiana, for example, complained about "cracking down on automobiles that are popular with the American people."

14   Heaven forbid we would seek to do anything to control America's appetite for vehicles that spew pollution and guzzle gas, weigh twice as

John Branch/*San Antonio Express-News*

Practice Exercise

Does the author present a *fact* or an *opinion* in paragraph 10?

_____

_____

Practice Exercise

In paragraph 13, what *conclusion* can you draw about Senator Lugar's position on SUVs?

_____

_____

_____

much as normal cars, shine their headlights directly into everyone's rearview mirrors, and run over hoods in collisions.

15   If a nation increasingly full of SUV drivers who never even go off-road is sane, I am proud to sound otherwise. I only hope you will join me.

Evaluating the Author's Argument

Issue:
"What controversial topic is this passage about?"

_____

_____

_____

_____

Author's argument:
"What is the author's position on the issue?"

_____

_____

_____

_____

Author's assumptions:
"What does the author take for granted?"

_____

_____

_____

_____

Type of support:
"What type of support does the author present?"

_____

_____

_____

_____

Practice Exercise

Does the author present *facts* or *opinions* in paragraph 15?

_____

Relevance of support:
"Does the support pertain directly to the argument?"

_____

_____

_____

_____

Objectivity and completeness:
"Is the argument based on facts and other appropriate evidence?" and *"Did the author leave out information that might weaken or disprove the argument?"*

_____

_____

_____

Validity and credibility:
"Is the argument logical and believable?"

_____

_____

_____

Source: Geneva Overholser, *Dallas Morning News,* May 13, 1999, p. 23A.

SELECTION **9-1**

Editorial

Comprehension Quiz

Directions: For each comprehension question below, use information from the selection to determine the correct answer. You may refer to the selection as you answer the questions. Write your answer in the space provided.

True or False

1. One-third or all carbon dioxide emissions released into the atmosphere comes from cars and trucks.

2. Today the United States imports less oil than it did in 1970.

3. Sport utility vehicles are the fastest-growing segment of the vehicle market.

4. Because of the size of sport utility vehicles, 2,000 more people die in collisions with them each year then would have died in collisions with conventional cars.

Multiple-Choice

5. According to the author, sport utility vehicles are
   a. acceptable.
   b. extravagances.
   c. becoming less popular.
   d. a help to large families.

6. In response to the OPEC cartel in 1970, many people in the United States
   a. switched to smaller cars.
   b. bought energy-efficient appliances.
   c. turned off unnecessary lights and began insulating their homes.
   d. all of the above.

7. How much carbon dioxide does a new sports utility vehicle send out into the atmosphere each year?
   a. 3 tons
   b. 7 tons
   c. 50 tons
   d. 70 tons

8. The author hopes that
   a. sports utility vehicle owners will use their vehicles only for off-road driving.
   b. the government will force cars to have the same emission standards as sports utility vehicles.
   c. more people will oppose sports utility vehicles.
   d. raving lunatics will stay off our roads.

9. Many sports utility vehicles cause unnecessary deaths in collisions because they
   a. run over normal cars' hoods.
   b. shine their headlights directly into everyone else's rearview mirrors.
   c. are engineered to go off-road.
   d. send out so much carbon dioxide into the atmosphere.

10. The author believes that the growing popularity of sport utility vehicles should alarm and infuriate everyone because
   a. sports utility vehicles cause more deaths in collisions than conventional cars.
   b. the most popular sports utility vehicles get as low as 13 miles to the gallon.
   c. sports utility vehicles pollute more than ordinary cars.
   d. all of the above

S E L E C T I O N **9-1**

Editorial

Extend Your Vocabulary by Using Context Clues

Directions: Context clues are words in a sentence that allow the reader to deduce (reason out) the meaning of an unfamiliar word in the sentence. For each vocabulary exercise below, a sentence from the reading selection containing an important word (*italicized, like this*) is quoted first. Next, there is an additional sentence using the word in the same sense and providing another context clue. Use the context clues from *both* sentences to deduce the meaning of the italicized word. *Be sure the answer you choose makes sense in both sentences.* If you discover that you must use a dictionary to confirm an answer choice, remember that the meaning you select must still fit the context of *both* sentences.

Pronunciation key: ă pat   ā pay   âr care   ä father   ĕ pet   ē be   ĭ pit
ī tie   îr pier   ŏ pot   ō toe   ô paw   oi noise   ou out   oŏ took
ōō boot   ŭ cut   yōō abuse   ûr urge   th thin   *th* this   hw which
zh vision   ə about
Stress mark: ʹ

---

1. Let me say out front that sport *utility* vehicles drive me nuts.

Besides blades, a Swiss Army knife has a screwdriver, scissors, and other features that enhance its *utility.*

utility (yōō tĭlʹ ĭ tē)
   a. fashion
   b. low price

    c. usefulness

    d. difficulty of use

_____ **2.** No one need waste time writing to tell me I sound like a raving *lunatic* about this.

The man was standing naked in the middle of the busy intersection singing, hopping around, and flapping his arms like a *lunatic.*

lunatic (lo͞o′ nə tĭk)

    a. person who is insane

    b. traffic officer

    c. athletic person

    d. ballet dancer

_____ **3.** Of course, you already may be among the *hordes* of Americans who have purchased one of these inexplicably popular extravagances.

Hordes of last-minute shoppers jammed the mall on Christmas Eve.

hordes (hôrds)

    a. a smattering

    b. large groups or crowds

    a. small but steady number

    b. troops

_____ **4.** Of course, you already may be among the hordes of Americans who have purchased one of these *inexplicably* popular extravagances.

Everyone thought the company president was satisfied with his job, so we were shocked when he *inexplicably* resigned last week and joined the Peace Corps.

inexplicably (ĭn ĕk′ splĭ kəb lē)

    a. difficult or impossible to explain

    b. understandably

    c. predictably

    d. without any warning

_____ **5.** Or you may be among what surely must be the equally fast-growing numbers who *seethe* over the idiocy of buying mammoth, highly engineered off-road vehicles in order to go to the drugstore.

It makes me *seethe* when reckless drivers endanger others by running red lights.

seethe (sē*th*)

    a. feel unhappy

    b. feel pleasure or enjoyment

_c._ feel violently agitated

_d._ feel deep sadness

_____ **6.** Or you may be among what surely must be the equally fast-growing numbers who seethe over the idiocy of buying _mammoth,_ highly engineered off-road vehicles in order to go to the drugstore.

Mammoth Caves, the largest caves in the state, are a popular tourist attraction.

mammoth (măm′ əth)

_a._ dark; gloomy

_b._ having a distinctive shape

_c._ brightly colored

_d._ of enormous size; huge

_____ **7.** This international oil _cartel_—the Organization of Petroleum Exporting Countries—was able to cripple our economy because of our then-shameful reliance on others for 36 percent of our oil.

The Colombian drug _cartel_ controls most of the heroin and cocaine traffic from South America to the United States.

cartel (kär těl′)

_a._ organizations working together to regulate the production, pricing, and marketing of goods

_b._ police

_c._ processing company

_d._ a group of victims

_____ **8.** You should know that OPEC's members, concerned about low oil costs, got together in March in Vienna and _decreed_ a cut in production of about 3 percent.

The mayor _decreed_ that until the water shortage was over, homeowners would be allowed to water their lawns only once a week.

decreed (dĭ krēd′)

_a._ worried intensely

_b._ hoped fervently

_c._ was unable to comprehend

_d._ issued an order that has the force of law

_____ **9.** And SUVs are the carbon-dioxide-_spewing_ champs: The new SUVs send out 70 tons per year, compared with the average car's 50 tons.

The radiator hose suddenly broke, _spewing_ boiling water like a fountain.

spewing (spyōō′ ĭng)

_a._ sending out in a stream; ejecting forcefully

_b._ soaking up

c. trickling down and melting

d. releasing

_____ **10.** Heaven forbid we would seek to do anything to control America's *appetite* for vehicles that spew pollution and guzzle gas, weigh twice as much as normal cars, shine their headlights directly into everyone else's rearview mirrors, and run over hoods in collisions.

The public's *appetite* for violence is reflected in the popularity of violent movies and video games.

appetite (ăp′ ĭ tīt)

a. hostility toward

b. a strong wish or desire for

c. tolerance for

d. disgust with

SELECTION **9-1**

Editorial

Collaboration Option

Respond in Writing

Directions: Refer to the selection as needed to answer the essay-type questions below.

Option for collaboration: Your instructor may direct you to work with other students—in other words, to work *collaboratively.* In that case, you should form groups of three or four students as directed by your instructor and work together to complete the exercises. After your group discusses each item and agrees on the answer, have a group member record it. Every member of your group should be able to explain all of your group's answers.

1. The author presents three reasons not to own or drive an SUV. On the other side of the issue, what are at least 3 *advantages* of owning or driving a sport utility vehicle?

_____

_____

_____

_____

2. Besides the drawbacks mentioned in the article, what are some *other* problems associated with sport utility vehicles? (The drawbacks can be either for the owners or for other drivers.)

_____

_____

_____

_____

_____

_____

_____

_____

3. Males between the ages of 16 and 25 tend to be involved in more accidents than other drivers, and collisions between sport utility vehicles and conventional cars tend to result in an increased number of deaths to drivers of the conventional cars. On the basis of these statistics, should these young male drivers be prohibited from driving SUVs? Explain your position.

_____

_____

_____

4. Overall main idea. What is the overall main idea the author wants the reader to understand about SUVs? Answer this question in one sentence. Be sure that your overall main idea sentence includes the topic (*SUVs*) and tells the overall most important point about it.

_____

_____

_____

_____

Read More about It on the World Wide Web

To learn more about the topic of this selection, visit these websites or use your favorite search engine (such as Yahoo ®). Whenever you go to *any* website, it is a good idea to evaluate it critically. Are you getting good information—information that is accurate, complete, and up-to-date? Who sponsors the website? How easy is it to use the features of the website?

http://www.howard.net/ban-suvs.htm

> *This is the website for* The Sport Utility Vehicle Anti-Fan Club, *which is an international club aimed at the eradication of sports utility vehicles.*

http://www.auto.com/reviews/sportutility_index.htm

> *Auto.com is a website for SUV lovers. It contains links that list reviews, services, auto shows, and news about SUVs.*

SELECTION 9-2

Government

WHY VOTE? POLITICIANS ARE ALL THE SAME

From *American Politics in a Changing World*

by Janet Flammang, Dennis Gordon, Timothy Lukes, and Kenneth Smorsten

Prepare Yourself to Read

Directions: Do these exercises *before* you read Selection 9-2.

1. First, read and think about the title. When was the last time you voted? If you have never voted, why not?

_____

_____

2. Do you think most 18- to 20-year-olds really care about political issues and voting? Why or why?

_____

_____

3. Next, complete your preview by reading the following:

> Introduction (in *italics*)
> First paragraph (paragraph 1)
> First sentence of each paragraph
> Last paragraph (paragraph 5)

On the basis of your preview, what do you think this selection is about?

_____

_____

Apply Comprehension Skills

Directions: Do the Annotation Practice Exercises as you read Selection 9-2. Think critically:

> Distinguish between facts and opinions.
> Make logical inferences and draw conclusions as you read.
> Evaluate the authors' argument.

WHY VOTE? POLITICIANS ARE ALL THE SAME

The United States lags far behind European and other western nations in both number of voters and voter turnout. About one-third of all eligible voters (70 million Americans) are not registered to vote, even in presidential elections. Moreover, only about a third of eligible voters turn out in non-presidential elections. (In other western nations 70 to 85 percent of all citizens vote regularly.) Who does vote in America? Three trends are evident: college graduates are much more likely to vote than people with eight years or less of education; senior citizens are much more likely to vote than 18- to 24-year-olds; and people in higher-income groups tend to vote more often.

On the other hand, why do people vote even when they know that their vote will not influence the outcome of the election? Why should people vote even if they know their vote probably will not influence the outcome of the election? Read this selection from a government text to find the reasons the authors give.

1   Given the fact that each person is only one of approximately 90 million voters in this country, does it make sense to believe that one person's participation, one vote, will have any impact on a major election? Simply to raise the question "What if everyone felt the same way?" does not remove the lingering impression that a single person is dwarfed by the enormous number of people who do trek to the polls, especially in a national election.

2   Supporters of the ruling elite theory insist that even though voters are given a choice among candidates, their choice is restricted to a narrow range of similar-minded individuals sanctioned by the ruling elite. Elections do not express what most people want or need, nor do they provide guidance for politicians (even if they want it) on what policies to enact. In this view, elections are primarily just rituals that perform a symbolic function for society.

3   Still, since most people continue to show their faces at the polls at one time or another, what arguments can be made in favor of voting? One argument is that voting does have significance, if not in individual impact, then in group pressure. Because citizens collectively have the power to give or withhold votes, they directly control the tenure of elected officials. Even if the choice is between Tweedledee and Tweedledum, Tweedledee knows that a day of reckoning is fixed by law and that minimally he or she must strive to avoid displeasing the constituents or lose the job.

4   But political efficacy and impact in voting are not the only considerations anyway. People

Annotation Practice Exercises

Directions: For each of the exercises below, think critically to answer the questions. This will help you gain additional insights as you read.

Annotation Exercise

Does the author present *facts, opinions,* or both in paragraph 4?

do not vote only to influence policy. Millions go to the effort to register and vote for a variety of other reasons as well. Some people may participate just to avoid feeling guilty about not voting. They may have been taught that is their patriotic duty to vote and that they have no right to complain about the outcome if they stay at home. Still others may vote to derive satisfaction from feeling that they are somehow participants, not just spectators, in an exciting electoral contest.

5   Even if their one vote may not be crucial to the outcome, it nevertheless affirms their role in and support for the political process. Indeed, perhaps it is this final need that fuels the desire for full democratic participation among people in many nations of the world.

Many college students exercise their right to vote. Unfortunately, however, many more college-age people who are eligible to vote do not bother to vote.
(Charles Gypton/Steck Boston)

Annotation Exercise

On the basis of the selection, what *logical conclusion* do the authors want you to draw about voting?

_____

_____

_____

Evaluating the Author's Argument

Issue:
"What controversial topic is this passage about?"

_____

_____

_____

_____

Authors' argument:
"What is the authors' position on the issue?"

_____

_____

_____

_____

_____

Authors' assumptions:
"What do the authors take for granted?"

_____

_____

_____

_____

Type of support:
"What type of support do the authors present?"

_____

_____

_____

_____

_____

_____

_____

_____

_____

_____

Objectivity and completeness:
"Is the argument based on facts and other appropriate evidence?" and *"Did the author leave out information that might weaken or disprove the argument?"*

_____

_____

_____

_____

_____

_____

Relevance of support:
"Does the support pertain directly to the argument?"

_____

_____

_____

Validity and credibility:
"Is the argument logical and believable?"

_____

_____

_____

Source: Janet Flammang, Dennis Gordon, Timothy Lukes, and Kenneth Smorsten, "Why Vote? Politicians Are All the Same," from *American Politics in a Changing World,* 3d ed., Wadsworth, Belmont, CA, 1990, p. 304. Used by permission of Wadsworth Publishing Company.

SELECTION **9-2**

Government

Comprehension Quiz

Directions: For each comprehension question below, use information from the selection to determine the correct answer. You may refer to the selection as you answer the questions. Write your answer in the space provided.

True or False

_____ **1.** The writers of this passage believe that an American should still vote even though that person is only one of approximately 9 million voters.

_____ **2.** Voters may vote a politician out of office if he or she displeases the constituents.

_____ **3.** Voting does have significance, if not in individual impact, then in group pressure.

_____ **4.** Voters go to the polls for a single reason.

_____ **5.** Most people believe that elections are primarily just rituals that perform a symbolic function for society.

_____ **6.** Voters cannot directly control the tenure of elected officials.

Multiple-Choice

_____ **7.** Supporters of the ruling elite theory believe that
  a. people vote as a way to influence policy.
  b. elections express what people want and need.
  c. there is a narrow range of similar-minded candidates for voters to choose from.
  d. voters find electoral contests exciting.

_____ **8.** People continue to vote for all of the following reasons *except* that they
  a. feel their one vote is crucial to the outcome of the election.
  b. want to avoid feeling guilty about not voting.
  c. feel it is patriotic to do so.
  d. feel as if they are participants in the electoral process and not just spectators.

_____ **9.** The example of the twins Tweedledum and Tweedledee (characters in the book *Alice in Wonderland*) is used by these writers to illustrate that
  a. the world of politics is a "wonderland."
  b. voters do not control how long a candidate will be in office.
  c. people need to vote.
  d. voters sometimes have to choose between remarkably similar candidates.

_____ **10.** The authors believe that in the final analysis, eligible voters

    a. vote because they have overcome doubts that their one vote counts.

    b. do not vote, because they have not overcome their doubts.

    c. vote because voting affirms their role in and supports the political process.

    d. vote because they have strong ties to the political party of their choice.

SELECTION **9-2**

Government

Extend Your Vocabulary by Using Context Clues

Directions: Context clues are words in a sentence that allow the reader to deduce (reason out) the meaning of an unfamiliar word in that sentence. For each vocabulary item below, a sentence from the selection containing an important word (*italicized, like this*) is quoted first. Next, there is an additional sentence using the word in the same sense and providing another context clue. Use the context clues from *both* sentences to deduce the meaning of the italicized word. *Be sure the answer you choose makes sense in both sentences.* If you discover that you must use a dictionary to confirm an answer choice, remember that the meaning you select must still fit the context of *both* sentences. To indicate your answer, write the letter in the space provided.

Pronunciation key: ă pat ā pay âr care ä father ĕ pet ē be ĭ pit
ī tie îr pier ŏ pot ō toe ô paw oi noise ou out o͝o took
o͞o boot ŭ cut yo͞o abuse ûr urge th thin *th* this hw which
zh vision ə about
Stress mark: ′

_____ **1.** Supporters of the ruling elite theory insist that even though voters are given a choice among candidates, their choice is restricted to a narrow range of a similar-minded individuals sanctioned by the ruling *elite.*

The *elite* usually live in large homes, are well educated, hold positions of power in their jobs, shop at expensive stores, eat in fine restaurants, and drive luxury cars.

elite (ĭ lēt′) means

    a. men in a social group

    b. older members of a social group

    c. superior members of a social group

    d. new members of a social group

_____ **2.** Elections do not express what most people want or need, nor do they provide guidance for politicians (even if they want it) on what policies to *enact.*

Congress must go through a lengthy process to *enact* a piece of proposed legislation.

enact (ĕn ăkt′) means:

a. make a bill into a law

b. act out on a stage

c. pretend

d. write

_____ **3.** Because citizens *collectively* have the power to give or withhold votes, they directly control the tenure of elected officials.

The club members believed, *collectively,* that their treasurer should resign; and because they all felt that way, he turned in his resignation.

collectively (kə lĕk′ tĭv lē) means:

a. in a manner pertaining to a collection of objects

b. for a reason

c. in a manner pertaining to a country

d. by a number of individuals acting as one group

_____ **4.** Because citizens collectively have the power to give or withhold votes, they directly control the *tenure* of elected officials.

Because Supreme Court justices have a lifetime *tenure,* they serve until they retire, resign, or die.

tenure (tĕn′ yər) means:

a. power held by a person in office

b. length of time a person holds office

c. salary paid to a person who holds office

d. success of a person who holds office

_____ **5.** Even if the choice is between Tweedledee and Tweedledum, Tweedledee knows that the day of reckoning is fixed by law and that *minimally* he or she must strive to avoid displeasing the constituents or lose the job.

With just a high school diploma, he was only *minimally* prepared to start a career.

minimally (mĭn′ ə məl ē) means:

a. to the greatest degree or amount possible

b. to the same amount or degree

c. to an unknown amount or degree

d. to the least amount or degree

_____ **6.** Even if the choice is between Tweedledee and Tweedledum, Tweedledee knows that the day of reckoning is fixed by law and that minimally he or she must strive to avoid displeasing the *constituents* or lose the job.

Because the *constituents* were unhappy with the mayor's performance, they did not reelect him.

constituents (kən stĭch′ o͞o ənts) means:

a. people who are represented by an elected official

b. people who favor an elected official

c. people who vote in every election

d. people who plan to seek public office

_____ **7.** But perhaps political *efficacy* and impact in voting are not the only considerations anyway.

Carlos was thankful for the *efficacy* of the new medicine; it stopped his terrible headaches.

efficacy (ĕf′ kə sē) means:

a. prescription

b. weakness

c. ability to produce a desired effect

d. formula

_____ **8.** Still others may vote to *derive* satisfaction from feeling that they are somehow participants, not just spectators, in an exciting electoral contest.

With a positive attitude, you can *derive* enjoyment even from ordinary day-to-day tasks.

derive (dĭ rīv′) means:

a. wish for

b. avoid

c. delay

d. obtain

_____ **9.** Still others may vote to derive satisfaction from feeling that they are somehow participants, not just spectators, in an exciting *electoral* contest.

Many people criticize the *electoral* process, but voting by the public is still one of the fairest systems for choosing government officials.

electoral (ĭ lĕk′ tər əl) means:

a. pertaining to an election

b. pertaining to Congress

c. pertaining to political campaigns

d. pertaining to luck

_____ **10.** Even if their one vote may not be crucial to the outcome, it nevertheless *affirms* their role in and support for the political process.

The homeless man says that people's kindness to him since his accident *affirms* his faith in human goodness.

affirms (ə fûrmz′) means:

a. reduces or eliminates

b. declares or maintains to be true

c. proves wrong or inappropriate

d. reveals or shows

Collaboration Option

Respond in Writing

Directions: Refer to the selection as needed to answer the essay-type questions below.

Option for collaboration: Your instructor may direct you to work with other students or, in other words, to work *collaboratively.* In that case, you should form groups of three or four students as directed by your instructor and work together to complete the exercises. After your group discusses each item and agrees on the answer, have a group member record it. Every member of your group should be able to explain all of your group's answers.

1. According to the selection, what are three of the reasons that people *do* vote?

   _____

   _____

   _____

   _____

   _____

   _____

   _____

2. List the three reasons the authors present for why people do *not* vote.

   _____

   _____

   _____

   _____

   _____

   _____

   _____

   _____

3. Suppose that only a very small number of citizens in the United States
    voted in presidential elections. Discuss what you think might happen to our
    country by the year 2010 if only a very small percent of qualified voters
    bothered to vote.

    _____

    _____

    _____

    _____

    _____

    _____

    _____

    _____

    _____

    _____

    _____

    _____

4. When members of a group (such as the poor or the young) do not vote,
    they become even more powerless. What does this suggest about the
    members of groups that *do* vote (such as senior citizens and those who are
    better educated)?

    _____

    _____

    _____

5. Overall main idea. What is the overall main idea the author wants the
    reader to understand about voting? Answer this question in one sentence.
    Be sure that your overall main idea sentence includes the topic (*voting*) and
    tells the overall most important point about it.

    _____

    _____

    _____

    _____

    _____

Read More about It on the World Wide Web

To learn more about the topic of this selection, visit these websites or use your favorite search engine (such as Yahoo ®). Whenever you go to *any* website, it is a good idea to evaluate it critically. Are you getting good information—information that is accurate, complete, and up-to-date? Who sponsors the website? How easy is it to use the features of the website?

http://www.rockthevote.org/
> *Rock the Vote is dedicated to protecting freedom of expression and helping young people realize and utilize their voting power to create change in the civic and political lives of their communities.*

http://www.igc.apc.org/cvd/
> *Center for Voting and Democracy researches how voting systems affect participation, representation, and governance. Click on Voter Turnout.*

SELECTION **9-3**

Magazine Article

TAKE OUT THE TRASH, AND PUT IT . . . WHERE?

From *Parade Magazine*

By Bernard Gavzer

Prepare Yourself to Read

Directions: Do these exercises *before* you read Selection 9-3.

1. First, read and think about the title. What do you think this article will be about?

   _____

   _____

2. Next, complete your preview by reading the following:

   > Introduction (in *italics)*
   > Skim the entire article
   > Charts and graphs

   On the basis of your preview, what problem do you think will be discussed in this article?

   _____

   _____

Apply Comprehension Skills

Directions: Do the Annotation Practice Exercises as you read Selection 9-3. Think critically:

Distinguish between facts and opinions.

Make logical inferences and draw conclusions as you read.

Evaluate the author's argument.

TAKE OUT THE TRASH, AND PUT IT . . . WHERE?

Perhaps you had to take out the garbage when you were younger. Did you ever wonder where the garbage went after it was picked up? Did you ever wonder whether we might eventually run out of places to put garbage? Read this magazine article to find out the answers to these troubling questions.

1   "Dealing with America's cascade of garbage is as vital an issue as Social Security, or Medicare, or maintaining a defense structure," says Denis Hayes, president of Seattle's non-profit Bullitt Foundation and one of the founders of Earth Day in 1970. "We need to be an Heirloom Society instead of a Throw-Away Society."

2   Governor George E. Pataki of New York says, "Americans have to be made more aware of the value of recycling and pass that knowledge on to our children."

3   From Maine to California, from Seattle to Miami, increasingly Americans are confronted by our remarkable capacity to create *garbage.* Fresh Kills Landfill, on New York City's Staten Island, is one of the largest man-made constructions in the world (and one of the highest points of land on the eastern seaboard). The Environmental Protection Agency estimates that, on average, we each produce 4.4 pounds of garbage a day, for a total of 217 million tons in 1997. The cost of handling garbage is the fourth biggest item—after education, police, and fire protection—in many city budgets.

4   But where does each of our 4.4 pounds per day go? Some is recycled, some is incinerated, but the majority of it is laid to rest in the more than 2,300 landfills in operation in the United States today. And that's where the problem starts.

5   In examining garbage in America, *Parade* found these unsettling facts:

- Landfills produce leachate, which is runoff that can contaminate ground water.
- Incinerators, no matter how sophisticated, have risky emissions.

Landfills: Are They Safe?

6   "We have learned that it is only a matter of time until even the best engineered landfill with

Annotation Practice Exercises

Directions: For each of the exercises below, think critically to answer the questions. This will help you gain additional insights as you read.

Practice Exercise

Does the first statement by Denis Hayes in paragraph 1 represent a *fact* or an *opinion*?

Our Garbage Problem Is Growing and Growing

The annual production of municipal solid waste in the U.S. has more than doubled since 1960.

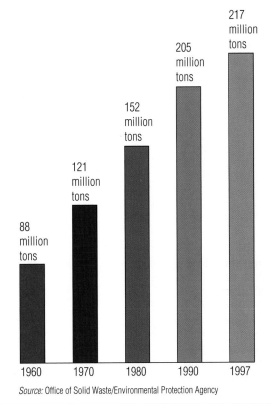

88 million tons — 1960

121 million tons — 1970

152 million tons — 1980

205 million tons — 1990

217 million tons — 1997

Source: Office of Solid Waste/Environmental Protection Agency

What's in our garbage?

Paper and paperboard 38.6%

Yard waste 12.8%

Food waste 10.1%

Plastics 9.9%

Metals 7.7%

Glass 5.5%

Wood 5.3%

Other materials such as rubber, leather, textiles, etc. 10.1%

Source: EPA, 1997.

Who makes the most garbage?

California makes more garbage than any other state, according to *BioCycle* magazine. It generated 56 million tons in 1998. Texas made 33.8 million tons, followed by New York (30.2 million), Florida (23.8 million), Michigan (19.5 million), Illinois (13.3 million), North Carolina (12.6 million) and Ohio (12.3 million).

Illinois
13.3 million tons

Michigan
19.5 million tons

Ohio
12.3 million tons

New York
30.2 million tons

North Carolina
12.6 million tons

California
56 million tons

Texas
33.8 million tons

Florida
23.8 million tons

state-of-the-art design will leak," says Stephen Lester, science director of the Center for Health, Environment, and Justice in Falls Church, Virginia. "Even the very best landfill liners made with tough high-density polyethylene are vulnerable to chemicals found in most household garbage."

7   Toxic elements can be carried into groundwater by leachate, which is water that becomes contaminated when it seeps through waste. It's often called "garbage juice." Environmental advocates estimate that New York's Fresh Kills Landfill produces 1 million gallons per day of leachate. Even after the landfill closing on December 31, 2001, New York City must treat the leachate to stop it from leaking into New York Harbor.

What Is Garbage?

8   "It certainly isn't just food scraps and stuff you throw in a garbage pail," says William Rathje, an archeologist at the University of Arizona and coauthor of *Rubbish!* and *Use Less Stuff.* "Garbage, in order of its volume, consists mainly of cardboard, paper, yard trimmings, and food waste."

9   There is also commercial garbage, mainly from construction and demolition, as well as hazardous, radioactive, medical, and nuclear waste. Sludge from sewage treatment plants and toxic waste may end up in some municipal solid waste landfills, but generally they require special disposal.

10   Rathje, who is known as "the garbology professor" because of his exploration of landfills, says his studies have put an end to the notion that things decompose and degenerate in the landfill. "The thought that after 30 or so years newspapers and food would disintegrate is off-track," Rathje says. "Things become mummified. We found hot dogs that could be recooked and perfectly legible newspapers." Gerald Backhaus, a waste management director in Chandler, Arizona, says, "Landfills are like giant Tupperware bowls, preserving the trash."

Not in My Backyard!

11   Communities have an almost universal resistance to having a landfill nearby. But the fact is that nearly every state engages in exporting and importing garbage. The landfills receive "tipping" fees—$10 a ton in Wyoming to $65 a ton and higher in Vermont—for the waste they handle.

Practice Exercise

What logical *conclusion* can you draw about whether landfills are safe?

_____

_____

_____

The tipping fees are used by communities to reduce taxes on the people who live near where the garbage is buried.

12   New York has to find a place for garbage, since it must shut down its 50-year-old Fresh Kills Landfill soon. Every day, 18 Sanitation Department barges, each carrying 700 tons of garbage, go from the city's marine transfer stations to Fresh Kills. Trucks then haul the trash to the landfill site, accompanied by an estimated 40,000 seagulls that swoop perilously close to bulldozers to snatch food scraps. In all, Fresh Kills gets the bulk of the city's daily generation of 13,200 tons of municipal waste. The city's businesses, using private carters, dispose of another 13,000 tons a day. This waste goes to private landfills or incinerators outside the city.

Can We Burn It?

13   The idea of burning waste to create energy seemed to make a lot of sense. But in practice it hasn't turned out that way because of the very high cost and problems of environmental pollution.

14   According to the EPA, there are 110 plants in the United States that burn municipal waste to get rid of it or use it as fuel to generate power. The word "incinerator" dismays industry representatives at the Integrated Waste Services Association, in Washington, D.C., who prefer the label "waste-to-energy plants." Maria Zannes, the association president, says the plants that burn municipal garbage to create steam and electricity are "one of the cleanest sources of power in the world. The process destroys bacteria, pathogens, and other harmful elements usually found in garbage, and burning cuts its volume by about 90 percent." Incinerators now dispose of 16 percent of the waste stream, with tipping fees ranging from $80 a ton in Alaska to $34 a ton in California and $27 in Indiana.

15   But incinerators produce bottom ash, which sifts through the grate at the bottom of the furnace; and fly ash, which is collected by air-pollution-control devices. Inevitably, some fly ash escapes.

16   "The fly ash is very toxic," says Paul Connett, a professor of chemistry at St. Lawrence University in Canton, New York. He adds that although ash by-products pass toxicity tests, the way such tests are conducted can invalidate the results.

Practice Exercise

What can logical *conclusion* can you make about what New York will do with its garbage?

_____

_____

_____

Reduce, Reuse, Recycle

17   The most practical solution to our waste problem, says Professor Connett, "is not to perfect the destruction of our waste, but to find ways to avoid making it in the first place."

18   The Bullitt Foundation's Denis Hayes, an environmentalist who studies waste problems, agrees. "Think of how much could be saved just by cutting down the vast amount of cardboard and paper that goes into packaging," he says.

19   "The fact is, you use 96 percent less energy when you make aluminum from aluminum cans rather than bauxite; you save half the amount of energy when you recycle paper as opposed to using virgin timber," says Allen Hershkowitz, senior scientist of the Natural Resources Defense Council in New York.

20   One of the most optimistic views of the future of garbage in America comes from Jerome Goldstein, publisher and editor of *BioCycle* magazine in Emmaus, Pennsylvania, which has conducted annual reports on America's garbage for 11 years. He says: "Many places in North America have come up with a new way of thinking about garbage—creating systems that sort trash into recyclables, compostables, and disposables. These systems can keep 60 to 70 percent of what was trash out of landfills and incinerators."

Practice Exercise

Does Allen Hershkowitz's statement in paragraph 19 represent a *fact* or an *opinion?*

_____

_____

Evaluating the Author's Argument

Issue:
"What controversial topic is this passage about?"

_____

_____

_____

_____

Author's argument:
"What is the authors' position on the issue?"

_____

_____

_____

_____

Author's assumptions:
"What do the authors take for granted?"

_____

_____

_____

_____

Type of support:
"What type of support do the authors present?"

_____

_____

_____

_____

Relevance of support:
"Does the support pertain directly to the argument?"

_____

_____

_____

Validity and credibility:
"Is the argument logical and believable?"

_____

_____

_____

Objectivity and completeness:
"Is the argument based on facts and other appropriate evidence?" and *"Did the author leave out information that might weaken or disprove the argument?"*

_____

_____

_____

_____

Source: Adapted from Bernard Gavzer, *Parade Magazine,* June 13, 1999, pp. 4–6.

SELECTION **9-3**

Magazine Article

Comprehension Quiz

Directions: For each comprehension question below, use information from the selection to determine the correct answer. You may refer to the selection as you answer the questions. Write your answer in the space provided.

True or False

_____ **1.** Since 1960, the yearly production of municipal solid waste has doubled.

_____ **2.** The cost of handling garbage is the biggest item in many city budgets.

_____ **3.** Newspapers and food dumped into a landfill will decompose in less than ten years.

Multiple-Choice

_____ **4.** On average, each person in the United States produces how many pounds of garbage each day?
  a. 44 pounds
  b. 14 pounds
  c. 4.4 pounds
  d. less than 3 pounds

_____ **5.** Most of our garbage consists of
  a. food waste.
  b. plastics.
  c. materials such as rubber, leather, and textiles.
  d. paper and paperboard.

_____ **6.** Which two states generate the most garbage?
  a. New York and Texas
  b. New York and Florida
  c. New York and California
  d. Texas and California

_____ **7.** What is "garbage juice"?
  a. water that has become contaminated as it seeps through waste in a landfill
  b. toxic substances found in most household garbage
  c. fuel made from recycled garbage
  d. purified water

_____ **8.** The majority of the garbage in the United States ends up in
  a. open dumps.
  b. state-of-the-art incinerators.

       c.   modern landfills.

       d.   recycling plants.

_____ **9.** The problem with landfills is that

       a.   we are running out of land for them.

       b.   eventually they leak.

       c.   they release toxic emissions.

       d.   they cause tipping fees to rise.

_____ **10.** According to Jerome Goldstein of *BioCycle* magazine, we could reduce the amount of garbage sent to landfills and incinerators by 60 to 70 percent by

       a.   sorting trash and then processing recyclables and compostables.

       b.   constructing landfills with leak-proof polyethylene linings.

       c.   increasing landfill tipping fees.

       d.   incinerating only those materials that do not produce fly ash.

SELECTION **9-3**

Magazine Article

Extend Your Vocabulary by Using Context Clues

Directions: Context clues are words in a sentence that allow the reader to deduce (reason out) the meaning of an unfamiliar word in the sentence. For each vocabulary exercise below, a sentence from the reading selection containing an important word *(italicized, like this)* is quoted first. Next, there is an additional sentence using the word in the same sense and providing another context clue. Use the context clues from *both* sentences to deduce the meaning of the italicized word. *Be sure the answer you choose makes sense in both sentences.* If you discover that you must use a dictionary to confirm an answer choice, remember that the meaning you select must still fit the context of *both* sentences.

Pronunciation key: ă pat ā pay âr care ä father ĕ pet ē be ĭ pit
ī tie îr pier ŏ pot ō toe ô paw oi noise ou out ŏŏ took
ōō boot ŭ cut yōō abuse ûr urge th thin *th* this hw which
zh vision ə about
Stress mark: ´

_____ **1.** Dealing with America's *cascade* of garbage is as vital an issue as Social Security or Medicare or maintaining a defense structure.

When we opened the storage cabinet in my grandfather's garage, we were flooded with *cascade* of forty years' worth of *National Geographic* magazines.

cascade (kă skād´)

    a.   small, steady trickle

    b.   large, compacted block of material

    c.   limited amount

    d.   something thought to resemble a waterfall

_____ **2.**   We need to be an *Heirloom* Society instead of a Throw-Away Society.

I treasure this hand-carved baby crib, an *heirloom* made by my great-great-grandfather.

heirloom (ār′ lo͞om)

    a.   a possession that belongs to a relative

    b.   valued possession passed down in a family through succeeding generations

    c.   property specified in a will

    d.   furniture that has been restored

_____ **3.**   Some is recycled, some is *incinerated,* but the majority of it is laid to rest in the more than 2,300 landfills in operation in the United States today.

The passengers' baggage was *incinerated* by the explosion and fire that raged in the plane's cargo hold.

incinerated (ĭn sĭn′ ə rā təd)

    a.   burned slightly

    b.   burned completely

    c.   damaged

    d.   scorched

_____ **4.**   Even the very best landfill liners made with tough high-density polyethylene are *vulnerable* to chemicals found in most household garbage.

People with weakened immune systems are more *vulnerable* to infections.

vulnerable (vŭl′ nər ə bəl)

    a.   susceptible to

    b.   unaffected by

    c.   resistant to

    d.   killed by

_____ **5.**   Environmental *advocates* estimate that New York's Fresh Kills Landfill produces 1 million gallons per day of leachate.

Advocates of free speech believe that nothing on the Internet should be regulated or censored.

advocates (ăd′ və kātz)

    a.   supporters of something

    b.   those who oppose something

c.   protestors

d.   terrorists

_____   **6.**   Things become *mummified.*

When excavated from the pyramid after nearly 3,000 years, the *mummified* body of the Egyptian pharaoh was still remarkably intact.

mummified (mŭm′ mĭ fīd)

a.   disintegrated

b.   badly damaged

c.   destroyed

d.   dried up and preserved

_____   **7.**   In all, Fresh Kills gets the bulk of the city's daily *generation* of 13,200 tons of municipal waste.

Both solar and nuclear energy can be used for the *generation* of electricity.

generation (jĕn ə rā′ shən)

a.   destruction

b.   conversion

c.   production

d.   reduction

_____   **8.**   According to the EPA, there are 110 plants in the United States that burn *municipal* waste to get rid of it or use it as fuel to generate power.

Our *municipal* government consists of a mayor and a 12-member city council.

municipal (myo͞o nĭs′ ə pəl)

a.   uncontrollable

b.   pertaining to a city

c.   unspecified

d.   pertaining to a state

_____   **9.**   The fly ash is very *toxic.*

Botulism is a form of severe, sometimes fatal, food poisoning caused by *toxic* bacteria.

toxic (tŏk′ sĭk)

a.   difficult to detect

b.   easy to identify

c.   having a distinct odor

d.   capable of causing injury or death

_____ **10.** Although ash by-products pass toxicity tests, the way such tests are conducted can *invalidate* the results.

When the private investigator discovered new evidence, he was able to *invalidate* the police officer's theory about the murder.

invalidated (ĭ văl′ ĭ dā təd)

a. made unnecessary

b. improved the quality of; enhanced

c. publicized widely

d. canceled the value of; nullified

SELECTION **9-3**

Magazine Article

Respond in Writing

Directions: Refer to the selection as needed to answer the essay-type questions below.

Collaboration Option

Option for collaboration: Your instructor may direct you to work with other students—in other words, to work *collaboratively.* In that case, you should form groups of three or four students as directed by your instructor and work together to complete the exercises. After your group discusses each item and agrees on the answer, have a group member record it. Every member of your group should be able to explain all of your group's answers.

1. What recycling efforts does your college currently make? If your college does not participate in recycling at present, what recycling measures could it implement?

_____

_____

_____

2. How does your city dispose of its garbage after it is collected? Does your city have a recycling program? (You may need to do some research to answer these questions.)

_____

_____

_____

3. Give at least three examples of materials or products that can be recycled. Tell what the material is and the products into which it could be recycled.

_____

_____

_____

_____

_____

4. Describe at least 4 uses for old tires or old telephone poles that would allow them be recycled into something "new." Be creative!

_____

_____

_____

_____

_____

_____

5. Overall main idea. What is the overall main idea the author wants the reader to understand about dealing with our garbage? Answer this question in one sentence. Be sure that your overall main idea sentence includes the topic *(dealing with our garbage)* and tells the overall most important point about it.

_____

_____

_____

Read More about It on the World Wide Web

To learn more about the topic of this selection, visit these websites or use your favorite search engine (such as Yahoo ®). Whenever you go to *any* website, it is a good idea to evaluate it critically. Are you getting good information—information that is accurate, complete, and up-to-date? Who sponsors the website? How easy is it to use the features of the website?

http://www.kab.org/
> *This is the Keep America Beautiful, Inc. website. Its mission is to empower individuals to take greater responsibility for enhancing their community's environment.*

http://www.earthchair.com/
> *Earthchair.com's mission is to create opportunities for individual participation in waste management in order to raise the collective environmental consciousness.*

http://www.enviroweb.org/issues/landfills/
> *Basics of Landfills is a site with extensive information and links to articles, questions, and related resources.*

PART THREE

Systems for Studying Textbooks

Developing a System that Works for You

© PhotoDisc

C H A P T E R

10

Selecting and Organizing Textbook Information

In this chapter you will learn the answers to these questions:

- How can I select important textbook information?

- Why should I organize textbook information as I read?

- How can I use textbook features to make my studying more efficient?

- What are effective ways to mark textbooks?

- How can I take notes from textbooks by outlining, mapping, and summarizing?

- How can I interpret graphic material correctly?

549

SKILLS

- Guidelines for Mapping
- Guidelines for Summarizing

Interpreting Graphic Material

- Bar Graphs
- Line Graphs
- Pie Charts
- Flowcharts
- Tables

CREATING YOUR SUMMARY

Developing Chapter Review Cards

READING

Selection 10-1 *(Speech Communications)*
"Intercultural Communication"
from *Human Communication*
by Stewart L. Tubbs and Sylvia Moss

SKILLS

One of the toughest things to learn is the ability to make yourself do the thing you have to do, when it ought to be done, whether you like it or not.

Thomas Huxley

Without the mind to engage it, the eye inevitably wanders.

STUDYING BETTER RATHER THAN HARDER

Chapter 1 of this book emphasized that it can take considerable time to learn the information in your textbooks. Although experienced college students know this, new students sometimes do not. Beginning students often have unrealistic expectations about the amount of time it will take to read and study textbooks and prepare for tests. In fact, they may be shocked to discover just how much time studying requires; and they may also conclude, mistakenly, that *they* are the only ones who have to spend so much time.

You already know, then, that one of the things it takes to be successful is allowing sufficient study time. However, you also need to recognize that simply

Effective students learn to study better, not just harder or longer. To do this, they develop a systematic way of approaching their college reading assignments. *(Patrick Clark / PhotoDisc)*

spending large amounts of time studying will not by itself guarantee success: what you *do* during your study times is equally important.

Staring at a book is not the same as reading, and sitting at a desk is not the same as studying. Some students who claim they are studying often are only daydreaming. (Studying a little and daydreaming a lot do not add up to studying.) Other students really do invest many hours in studying yet are disappointed in the results. Still other students are successful at studying but feel discouraged because it seems to take them too much time. You yourself have undoubtedly had the experience of finishing an assignment, realizing that you did it the "hard way," and feeling frustrated because you know you worked harder and longer than you needed to. You are probably wondering, "Isn't there a better, more efficient way?"

The answer is yes: there *is* a better, more efficient way to study. This chapter and the next one describe specific techniques to help you read your textbooks more efficiently and learn to study *better,* rather than harder or longer. Often, what makes the difference between a successful student and a less successful one is *applying these study skills in a systematic way.*

You may already be familiar with some of these study techniques, or you may be learning them for the first time. In either case, by mastering and using these skills you can become a more effective student. These skills will serve you well in all your courses, adding new techniques to your study repertoire. They will also help you in a variety of other learning situations. There will always be situations in college and in the workplace in which you must organize, learn, and remember information.

Remember, however, that these study skills are not "magic." They simply allow you to study better rather than harder. The truth is that being a successful student demands time, effort, and dedication. You can become a better and better student each semester, but only if you are willing to invest enough time and effort, and if you bring enough dedication to the task.

THREE KEYS TO STUDYING COLLEGE TEXTBOOKS

The strategies in this chapter and Chapter 11 are based on three essentials of studying: three *keys* to studying better. The three keys are *selecting* essential information to study, *organizing* that information in a meaningful way, and *rehearsing* it in order to remember it. As you will see, selectivity, organization, and rehearsal are interrelated and interdependent.

Key 1: Selectivity

Selectivity is the first essential key to understanding and remembering what you read. Too many students think that they can (and must) learn and remember everything in their textbooks, but this is a mistaken idea that leads only to frustration. Generally, *it is necessary to identify and remember only main ideas and important supporting details.* Therefore, you must be selective as you read and study.

Chapters 4 through 9 (Part Two, the "comprehension core,") explained how to read selectively by focusing on main ideas and details. The techniques in the present chapter will further increase your ability to be selective: you will learn about textbook features, textbook marking, and textbook notes.

Key 2: Organization

Organization is the second key to learning and remembering what you read. The reason is simple: *organized material is easier to learn, memorize, and recall* than unorganized material.

Part Two explained how to see relationships between main ideas and supporting details by identifying authors' patterns of writing. Those skills make learning and remembering easier. In this chapter, you will learn additional skills of organization. Using textbook features, along with your own textbook marking and note-taking, will help you to organize material more effectively.

Key 3: Rehearsal

Rehearsal, a concept introduced in Chapter 3, is the third key to learning and remembering textbook material. Rehearsal involves saying aloud or writing down material you want to memorize. It is *not* merely rereading, nor is it a casual overview. Rehearsal is a way of reviewing material that puts the material into your memory. Particularly with complex material, it is necessary to *rehearse information to transfer it to long-term (permanent) memory.*

It is important to understand that comprehending and remembering are two separate tasks. The fact that you comprehend textbook material does not necessarily mean that you will remember it. To *remember* material as well as understand it, you must take additional steps; that is, you must rehearse. Just as actors begin to memorize their lines long before a performance, students need to rehearse textbook material frequently, long before a test. (Rehearsal is discussed in detail in Chapter 11.)

SUMMARY OF THE THREE-STEP PROCESS FOR STUDYING COLLEGE TEXTBOOKS

Step 1: Prepare to read

Overview to see what the selection contains and how it is organized.

Assess your prior knowledge.

Plan your reading and study time.

Step 2: Ask and answer questions to guide your reading.

Use questions to guide your reading.

Read actively, looking for answers.

Record the answers to your questions.

Step 3: Review by rehearsing your answers.

Review the material by *rehearsing,* to transfer it to long-term memory.

Selectivity, organization, and rehearsal are the foundation for the study techniques in this chapter and in Chapter 11. At this point, however, it will be useful to look back at the three-step process for reading and studying textbooks presented in Chapter 3, since we will now be adding specific study skills to that general approach. The three-step process is shown again in the box.

USING TEXTBOOK FEATURES

Using textbook features will help you locate, select, and organize material you want to learn. Taking advantage of textbook features is one way to study better rather than harder.

KEY TERM
Textbook Feature

Device used by an author to emphasize important material and show how it is organized.

A **textbook feature** is a device an author uses to emphasize important material or to show how material is organized. It is a way authors help readers get the most out of a textbook. Another term for *textbook feature* is *learning aid.*

There are many kinds of textbook features, and in this section you will look at some of the most important. Though no single college textbook is likely to include all of these features, many of your textbooks will have several of them.

Keep in mind that different authors may call the same feature by different names. For example, what one author may call a *chapter summary* another may call a *chapter review, chapter highlights, key points, points to remember, a look back,* or *summing up.*

Be sure to take advantage of textbook features as you study; they are there to help you locate, select, and organize the material you must learn.

Prefaces

KEY TERM
Preface

Introductory section in which
authors tell readers about the
book.

At the beginning of a textbook, you will usually find one or more kinds of introductory material. A **preface** (such as the example below from a communications textbook) is a section in which the author tells readers about the book. It is an important message from the author. Whether a preface is addressed to students, to instructors, or to both, it is likely to provide helpful information. It typically describes the author's approach to the subject, explains how the book is organized, and mentions special features the book contains. The author may also explain how the current edition of a book improves on the previous edition.

Regardless of what a preface is called (*Preface, To the Student, A Word to Students*), you should read it before you read anything else, because it gives important information and advice. For instance, in the example from a composition text on the next page, the authors explain the value of the list of words and definitions following each reading.

In *Opening Doors,* the section "To the Student" is a preface; it appears on pages xxii–xxxi. Did you read it? If not, you should do so now.

Preface

Human Communication is designed for introductory communication courses. Since it was first published twenty years ago, it has been used by over 125,000 students—a figure that makes us feel both humbled and encouraged. As in earlier editions, our commitment is to present students with a comprehensive theoretical base, an understanding of how modern communication has evolved and continues to change and grow, and a grasp of its immediate and long-term applications to their own lives.

Once again we focus on the traditional concerns of speech communication and link together contexts as various as two-person communication and mass communication. Our approach is to fuse current and classic communication theory, fundamental concepts, and important skills. Despite its complexities, we believe we can present our subject to introductory students without over-simplification, in language that is clear, vivid, and precise.

We have tried, as in previous editions, to create a text that is sensitive to diversity, one that reflects our long-term interest in gender and cultural issues. Thus, throughout our book we integrate examples and references that represent a wide variety of backgrounds, ages, and ethnic and cultural groups.

Source: Stewart L. Tubbs and Sylvia Moss, *Human Communication,* 7th ed., McGraw-Hill, New York, 1994, from p. xiii. Reproduced with permission of McGraw-Hill.

TO THE STUDENT

We have chosen these readings primarily to provide you with helpful models of style and structure. At the same time, we have tried hard to select pieces that you will enjoy and find enlightening. The idea is to encourage in you a fondness for language and a sharp eye for technique, both of which will serve to make you a more skillful writer.

The selections include poetry and stories as well as essays, and the writing assignments sometimes ask you to do what might be called "creative writing." You may want to know why you should ponder a poem or describe a fantasy when the writing you will need to do in the working world consists of ordering parts from the Acme Showcase Company, reporting on water damage from burst pipes, or describing right-of-way specifications for a city street. Although these quite different kinds of writing appear to have little in common, the creative exercises will stretch your imagination and bolster your confidence. Any practice that helps you to realize fully your power over words will prove worthwhile. The ease of expression you develop during creative writing (when no rules apply) will carry over into anything you choose to write. Of course, every writer has times when the words stubbornly have minds of their own, kicking each other in the shins and refusing to stand nicely in line; but the more you think about and practice writing, the briefer these little rebellions will be.

Many students feel confident that they can understand an essay, but turn into quivering masses of uncertainty when given a poem to read. Don't let yourself be intimidated by the unusual word patterns of poets. If the meaning is unclear on first reading, go over it again—aloud this time. Give yourself the pleasure of puzzling out the meaning. Assume an open, relaxed approach to the literary selections, and you will find that you can learn from them as much about rhetoric as you can from a comfortably paragraphed page of prose.

Your task will be made easier by the list of words and definitions following each reading. These definitions supply only the meaning of the word in the context of that selection. The words defined are those that may be new to you (like *interlocutor* or *vacuity*), those that carry a different meaning in the selection from the usual one (*exact* used as a verb, for example), and those that have changed meaning over time (*fancy* meaning "imagination," for instance).

Your most taxing work in using this text involves thinking. You will need to think critically in analyzing the selections, and you will have to think hard in planning and practicing your writing. But you should find, as you progress, that the line between work and pleasure grows steadily less distinct.

Source: Susan Day and Elizabeth McMahan, *The Writer's Resource: Readings for Composition,* 4th ed., McGraw-Hill, New York, 1994, p. xxv. Reproduced with permission of McGraw-Hill.

Tables of Contents

Another feature at the beginning of a textbook is a **table of contents.** This may simply be a list of chapter titles, or (like the example on page 558) it may be more detailed, including major chapter headings. Some tables of contents show chapter subheadings as well. The table of contents is your first chance to get an overview of the organization of the textbook as a whole: the "big picture." Notice, in the example on the next page, that this history textbook is divided into major parts. Each part is in turn divided into chapters ("1/, 2/," etc.). The order of the chapters seems to be based on both chronology (time) and geography.

In addition to the main table of contents at the beginning of a textbook, there may also be a separate listing of some special sections or features. The example below, from a sociology text, lists "boxes" (a feature that will be discussed on page 567–568).

LIST
OF BOXES

BOX

Source: Richard T. Schaefer and Robert P. Lamm, *Sociology: A Brief Introduction,* McGraw-Hill, New York, 1994, p. xiii. Reproduced with permission of McGraw-Hill.

CONTENTS

Source: Richard E. Sullivan, Dennis Sherman, and John B. Harrison, *A Short History of Western Civilization,* 8th ed., McGraw-Hill, New York, 1994, p. iv. Reproduced with permission of McGraw-Hill.

Part Openings

As you have just seen, chapters in a textbook may be grouped into larger sections or parts. *Opening Doors,* for example, has three major parts. **Part openings** are often useful features. A part opening may list the chapters contained in that part (as in *Opening Doors*), or it may present an opening statement or briefly describe each of its chapters (like the example from a sociology text on the next page). This gives you a quick overview of the material that will be covered by all chapters in the part and also suggests how those chapters are connected or interrelated.

Sometimes, important text material is given in the part opening, as in the example below from a theater textbook. (Note the definition of *Renaissance,* the dates, and the general historical background.) Information mentioned in a part opening may actually appear in several different chapters; by consolidating this information at the beginning of the part, the authors clarify it and make it easier to remember.

PART TWO

THEATERS OF THE RENAISSANCE

The Renaissance was an age of humanism, discovery, and exceptional art. *Renaissance* is a French word meaning "rebirth," and during this historical period—from roughly 1400 to 1650—European culture is said to have been reborn. Its rebirth included a rediscovery of earlier cultures, but equally important was a new view of human possibilities. In the Middle Ages, human beings had been seen as small, insignificant figures on the lower rungs of a sort of universal ladder, with the deity and other divinities at the top. In the Renaissance, people began to regard the individual as important and as having enormous potential.

A significant aspect of the Renaissance was, of course, the rediscovery of the civilizations of Greece and Rome. For the first time in several centuries, the heritage of these civilizations—their art, literature, and philosophy—became available, largely through the rediscovery of ancient manuscripts. The achievements and ideas of Greece and Rome struck a sympathetic chord in men and women of fourteenth-century Italy and France, who hoped to create a new classical civilization that would equal the old.

Other things were happening in addition to this rediscovery of the past. The major distinction between the Middle Ages and the Renaissance was a secularization of society—that is, a move away from religion. The dominance of the Roman Catholic church was eroded as Renaissance society became more concerned with "this world" than with the "next world," the afterlife in heaven.

Source: Edwin Wilson and Alvin Goldfarb, *Living Theater: A History, 2d ed.,* McGraw-Hill, New York, 1994, from pp. 136–137. Reproduced with permission of McGraw-Hill.

P A R T

A sociologist can make a reasonably accurate prediction about where a child will end up in life on the basis of a few simple facts: the child's parents' incomes and education; whether the child is black, Hispanic, Asian American, or Anglo-American; and whether the child is male or female. To be sure, some youngsters will escape the sociologist's crystal ball. But most will not. The "crystal ball" in this case is an understanding of social stratification.

Chapter 8 explores the origins and consequences of social stratification. This chapter describes social class differences in the United States, with special emphasis on the poor, and shows how these differences affect not just how well people live but how long they live.

Chapter 9 examines inequalities based on race and ethnicity. This chapter begins by looking at intergroup relations in cross-cultural perspective; then traces the history of racial and ethnic inequality in the United States; analyzes where black, Hispanic, Native, and Asian Americans stand today; and suggests why efforts to reduce racial and ethnic inequality have proven so disappointing.

Chapter 10 focuses on gender and age. Clearly the roles women play in our society have changed dramatically in the past quarter century. But are American women better off than their mothers were? If not, why not? The position the elderly occupy in our society has also changed, in many ways for the better. What explains these two different patterns?

SOCIAL
INEQUALITY

Source: Michael S. Bassis, Richard J. Gelles, and Ann Levine, *Sociology: An Introduction,* 4th ed., McGraw-Hill, New York, 1991, p. 213. Reproduced with permission of McGraw-Hill.

Chapter Outlines

A **chapter outline** is a list of chapter topics or headings in their order of appearance in the chapter. It provides a preliminary overview of the chapter. This feature helps you see the content and organization of the entire chapter. It lets you know in advance not only what topics the chapter will cover, but how they fit together. Trying to read or study a chapter without first seeing its outline is like trying to solve a jigsaw puzzle without looking at the picture on the box. It can be done, certainly, but it takes longer and is much more difficult!

Chapter outlines may be called by various names, such as *Chapter Contents, Chapter Topics, Preview, Overview,* or *In This Chapter;* or they may have no title at all. They can also take various forms. They may or may not actually be set up in outline style, and they may be general or detailed.

Chapter outlines in *Opening Doors,* for instance, appear on separate pages, include headings and subheadings, and also list reading selections. The example on the next page (from a criminology text) is also in outline style; notice that next to it, in the second column, the chapter itself begins. The example shown below (from a text on social behavior) looks very different: it must be read "across," and subheadings are indicated by *italics* rather than indentations.

5

Some Interesting Differences in the Elements of Subjective Culture

❖

The Sapir-Whorf Hypothesis ◆ Gender Inequalities across the World ◆
Foragers ◆ *Horticultural Societies* ◆ *Pastoral Societies* ◆ *Agrarian Societies* ◆
Industrial Societies ◆ *Socialist Societies* ◆ *The Third World* ◆ *Information
Societies* ◆ What Is Functional Is Good ◆ Cultural Differences in
Attributions ◆ Cultures and Dealing with Time ◆ Culture and Marriage ◆
Culture and Social Distance ◆ Culture and Stereotypes ◆
Sex Stereotypes ◆ Summary

Source: Harry C. Triandis, *Culture and Social Behavior,* McGraw-Hill, New York, 1994, p. 120. Reproduced with permission of McGraw-Hill.

CHAPTER 18

Corrections: Prisons and Alternatives to Prisons

We like to think of ourselves as a civilized and humane society even with respect to criminals. Indeed, we call our prisons ''correctional'' institutions, presumably placing corrected behavior as the central goal. Surveys show that individual deterrence, reaffirmation of norms, and rehabilitation rank higher in American public opinion than do retribution, incapacitation, and revenge (Jacoby and Dunn, 1987). Yet the United States currently has the largest prison population in its history.

Criminologists generally believe that they approach the issues of punishment and imprisonment in a rational and humane way. For instance, they usually refer to punishment in terms of ''just deserts,'' deterrence, selective incapacitation, rehabilitation, restitution, and community service. In fact, most studies of criminal punishment rarely employ the word **penology** (the study of punishment); rather they use the term ''corrections.'' Again, the implication is that the punishment system is structured to change or reform the criminal's behavior.

Social scientists of both liberal and conservative orientations are skeptical of any reformative claims made by the penal system. If anything, there is at present a retributive mood among many policymakers and some scientists (Casper, 1988). Today the rehabilitation ideology is hardly mentioned in a positive light.

Source: Lydia Voigt, William E. Thornton, Jr., Leo Bartile, and Jerrold M. Seaman, *Criminology and Justice,* McGraw-Hill, New York, 1994, p. 518. Reproduced with permission of McGraw-Hill.

Chapter Objectives and Introductions

Authors often use a list of **chapter objectives** at the beginning of a chapter to tell you what you should know or be able to do after studying the chapter. Objectives appear in various forms and may also be called *Preview Questions, What You'll Learn, Goals,* etc. In the example below left (from a communication text), the authors state directly, "After finishing this chapter, you should be able to . . ." and they state the objectives like test items. Note the directions *define, explain, compare and contrast,* and *describe.* In the example below right (from a sociology text), the objectives are called "Looking Ahead" and are phrased as questions. In *Opening Doors,* chapter objectives are also written as questions.

A **chapter introduction** is an opening passage which describes the overall purpose, major topics and their sequence, or how this chapter is linked to preceding chapters. Or it may "set the scene" by giving, for instance, a case study or an anecdote. A chapter introduction may (like the example at the top of the next page) actually be called *Introduction,* or (like the other example on the next page) it may be indicated by special type or a large ornamental letter at the beginning of the first word. Read chapter introductions carefully; they are a helpful guide to what lies ahead.

After finishing this chapter, you should be able to:

Define *listening*

Explain the nature of serial communication

State how much time you spend listening

Compare and contrast helpful and harmful listening habits

Distinguish between the processes of hearing and listening

Explain the "listening level–energy involvement" scale

Define *feedback*

Describe how feedback affects communication

Use different types of evaluative and nonevaluative feedback

Focus your attention while listening

Set appropriate listening goals

Listen to understand ideas

Listen to retain information

Listen to evaluate and analyze content

Listen empathically

Source: Teri Kwal Gamble and Michael Gamble, *Communication Works,* 4th ed., McGraw-Hill, New York, 1993, p. 141. Reproduced with permission of McGraw-Hill.

LOOKING AHEAD

- How are girls socialized to be "feminine" and boys to be "masculine"?
- How are gender roles apparent in everyday conversations between men and women?
- Why is it that, despite outnumbering men, women are viewed as a subordinate minority by sociologists?
- How pervasive is sex-typing of jobs? Are there many jobs viewed either as "men's work" or as "women's work"?
- When married women work outside the home, do their husbands assume equal responsibility for housework and child care?
- Why is it said that women from racial and ethnic minorities face a kind of "double jeopardy"?
- How does the world view of feminists involved in defending abortion rights differ from that of antiabortion activists?

Source: Richard T. Schaefer and Robert P. Lamm, *Sociology,* 4th ed., McGraw-Hill, New York, 1992, p. 324. Reproduced with permission of McGraw-Hill.

Introduction

In this chapter, you will be reading longer passages because college reading isn't limited to single paragraphs. Fortunately, one of the hallmarks of a mature reader is the ability to deal with increasingly longer, more complex textbook passages. For example, a reader moves from comprehending a sentence to comprehending a paragraph. The reader then connects the information in a paragraph with the information in the next paragraph, and the next (all the while following the writer's main ideas). Soon the reader has followed the writer's thoughts throughout the chapter and subsequently throughout all the chapters of the book.

In one sense, reading longer passages is easier. You can see the *overall subject matter* and the *overall main idea* instead of just smaller parts. Seeing the overall organization of a longer section of a textbook chapter (or even the entire chapter) promotes comprehension and recall.

In this chapter you will learn how to determine the overall subject matter and the overall main idea for a longer passage. You will also learn how to write a summary of a longer textbook selection. But first, you will find out how to read and study a textbook assignment in an organized, intelligent manner.

Source: Joe Cortina, Janet Elder, and Katherine Gonnet, *Comprehending College Textbooks,* 2d ed., McGraw-Hill, New York, 1992, p. 320. Reproduced with permission of McGraw-Hill.

C onflict is an inevitable part of the life of any group, and sooner or later it touches all group members. A conflict can be started by anyone and can occur at any point in a group's existence. Opposed or contradictory forces within us can create inner conflicts, or we can find ourselves experiencing tension as external forces build and create interpersonal conflicts. Thus, a conflict can originate within a single group member or between two or more group members.

A group experiences *conflict* whenever a member's thoughts or acts limit, prevent, or interfere with his or her own thoughts or acts or with those of any other member. If you think about your recent group experiences, you will probably discover that you have been involved in conflicts. Some involved only you; some involved you and another. Probably, some were mild and subtle; others were intense and hostile. In any case, probably all of them were interesting.

Our goal in this chapter is to explore what conflict is, how it arises, how it affects us as group members, and how we can handle it productively. In doing so, we will develop skills to help us deal more effectively with group problem solving and decision making.

Source: Teri Kwal Gamble and Michael Gamble, *Communication Works,* 4th ed., McGraw-Hill, New York, 1994, p. 283. Reproduced with permission of McGraw-Hill.

Lists and Sequences

KEY TERM
Lists and Sequences

Textbook feature in which important material are set off from a paragraph in some special way.

When **lists and sequences** of important material are set off from a paragraph in some special way, they become helpful textbook features. A list or sequence is presented in this way in order to draw your attention to it. Items in a list sequence may be set in a row or rows (like the example below left, from a sociology text), numbered (like the example at the top of page 566, from a music text), or lettered. The example below right is set in **boldface** and shows a symbol for each planet. The items in the sequence at the bottom of page 566 (from a journalism text) have small marks called *bullets* (which are also used in *Opening Doors*). Notice also that the important stages here (*Phase 1, Phase 2,* etc.) are in a special typeface.

Note, too, that the authors of the astronomy text suggest a *mnemonic device* (memory aid). Mnemonic devices are often a good method to use with lists and sequences.

Cultural Universals

Like the hominids, human beings have made dramatic cultural advances. Despite their differences, all societies have attempted to meet basic human needs by developing cultural universals. *Cultural universals,* such as language, are general practices found in every culture.

Anthropologist George Murdock (1945:124) compiled a list of cultural universals. The examples identified by Murdock include the following practices:

Athletic sports	Housing
Bodily adornment	Language
Calendar	Laws
Cooking	Marriage
Courtship	Medicine
Dancing	Music
Decorative art	Myths
Family	Numerals
Folklore	Personal names
Food habits	Property rights
Food taboos	Religion
Funeral ceremonies	Sexual restrictions
Games	Surgery
Gestures	Toolmaking
Gift giving	Trade
Hairstyles	Visiting

Source: Richard T. Schaefer and Robert P. Lamm, *Sociology: A Brief Introduction,* McGraw-Hill, New York, 1994, p. 34. Reproduced with permission of McGraw-Hill.

A Survey of the Planets

The solar system is defined as the sun, its nine orbiting planets, their own satellites, and a host of small interplanetary bodies, such as asteroids and comets. Starting in the center of the solar system, the major bodies and their symbols are:

⊙ **Sun**

☿ **Mercury**

♀ **Venus**

⊕ **Earth**

♂ **Mars**

♃ **Jupiter**

♄ **Saturn**

♅ **Uranus**

♆ **Neptune**

♇ **Pluto**

The symbols, mostly derived from ancient astrology, are sometimes used as convenient abbreviations today. A traditional memory aid for this outward sequence is "*Men Very Early Made Jars Stand Upright Nicely, Period.*" Surely today's students can do better![1] To avoid confusion about the positions of Saturn, Uranus, and Neptune, remember that the *SUN* is a member of the system, too.

Source: William K. Hartman, *Astronomy: The Cosmic Journey,* Wadsworth, Belmont, Calif., 1988, p. 106. Reprinted by permission.

CHARACTERISTICS OF MUSIC SINCE 1950

Accurately describing the relatively recent past is a difficult task. Yet any overview of music since 1950 must include these major developments:

1. Increased use of the *twelve-tone system*
2. *Serialism*—use of the techniques of the twelve-tone system to organize rhythm, dynamics, and tone color
3. *Chance music*, in which a composer chooses pitches, tone colors, and rhythms by random methods, or allows a performer to choose much of the musical material
4. *Minimalist music*, characterized by a steady pulse, clear tonality, and insistent repetition of short melodic patterns
5. Works containing deliberate *quotations* from earlier music.
6. A *return to tonality* by some composers
7. *Electronic music*
8. *"Liberation of sound"*—greater exploitation of noiselike sounds
9. *Mixed media*
10. New concepts of *rhythm* and *form*

Source: Roger Kamien, *Music: An Appreciation*, 2d Brief ed., McGraw-Hill, New York, 1994, p. 305. Reproduced with permission of McGraw-Hill.

PHASES OF A DEVELOPING STORY

Whenever a major news event occurs, all the daily media strive to keep their audiences as up to date as possible. A story can be developed for hours or for months, and it is usually covered in four phases:

- *Phase 1.* The story first breaks. Journalists rush to the scene to report the news as it is happening, or they work the phones to put together an initial breaking story. They work on the story full time, and their primary function is to tell their audiences *what* happened, *when, where* and to *whom.* The story is front-page news. Reporters will usually write *mainbars*, primary stories that report the *breaking news;* and *sidebars*, supplemental stories that explain the news or report the human element.

- *Phase 2.* Journalists try to explain the *why* and *how* of the story, but they also continue to report late-breaking developments, such as cleanup operations or a final casualty count. This means that the story is likely to remain front-page news. *Second-day stories*, which report the latest news as well as summarize the earlier news, and sidebars are written to put the news into perspective for an audience.

- *Phase 3.* The story is no longer front-page news, unless something unusual happens to warrant front-page treatment, but reporters are still covering it full time or routinely. They look for something fresh, but they also analyze and continue to humanize the story. Follow-ups and features may be written for days afterward.

- *Phase 4.* Few reporters are working on the story full time any longer, but there may be a few pursuing specific angles. Reporters still make routine checks. Weeks or months later, there may be a major development as officials release their findings or investigative reporters come up with something. The story could become front-page news again.

Source: Bruce D. Itule and Douglas Anderson, *News Writing and Reporting for Today's Media*, 3d ed., McGraw-Hill, New York, 1994, p. 121. Reproduced with permission of McGraw-Hill.

Boxes

KEY TERM
Boxes

A textbook feature consisting of supplementary material separated from the regular text.
A box is also called a *sidebar.*

A **box,** or *sidebar,* is supplementary material that is separated from the regular text. It may appear at the bottom or top of a page of text (like the example below) or on one or more pages by itself. "Box" material may or may not be in an actual box; it may be set off in columns, in a different typeface, or by color.

Boxes can contain a variety of information: case studies, research studies, biographical sketches, interviews, excerpts from other works, controversial issues, practical applications—the possibilities are almost endless. Boxes may be numbered, and authors often create box titles to fit the subject matter: for example *Points to Ponder, Issues and Debate, Close-Up, Speaking Out, Current Research,* and *What Do You Think?*

Pay close attention to boxes: they clarify important points, provide vivid examples, and broaden and deepen your understanding of the material.

● CULTURE AND COMMUNICATION

A REFUSAL TO COMPETE

A new teacher—let's call her Mary—arrived at a Navaho Indian reservation. Each day in her classroom, something like this would occur. Mary would ask five of her young Navaho students to go to the chalkboard and complete a simple mathematics problem from their homework. All five students would go to the chalkboard, but not one of them would work the problem as requested. Instead, they would all stand silent and motionless.

Mary, of course, wondered what was going on. She repeatedly asked herself if she might possibly be calling on students who could not do the assigned problems. "No, it couldn't be that," she reasoned. Finally, Mary asked her students what the problem was. Their answer displayed an understanding not many people attain in a lifetime.

Evidently, the students realized that not everyone in the class would be able to complete the problems correctly. But they respected each other's uniqueness, and they understood, even at their young age, the dangers of a "win-lose" approach. In their opinion, no one would "win" if anyone was embarrassed or humiliated at the chalkboard, and so they refused to compete publicly with each other. Yes, the Navaho students wanted to learn—but not at the expense of their peers.

Where do you stand? In your opinion would typical American schoolchildren behave similarly? Why or why not? Should they behave like the Navahos?

Source: Teri Kwal Gamble and Michael Gamble, *Communication Works,* 4th ed., McGraw-Hill, New York, 1994, p. 290. Reproduced with permission of McGraw-Hill.

MARITAL POWER

Sociologists Robert Blood, Jr., and Donald Wolfe (1960) developed the concept of *marital power* to describe the manner in which decision making is distributed within families. They defined power by examining who makes the final decision in each of eight important areas that, the researchers argue, traditionally have been reserved entirely for the husband or for the wife. These areas include what job the husband should take, what house or apartment to live in, where to go on vacation, and which doctor to use if there is an illness in the family. Using this technique, Blood and Wolfe (1960:22–23) surveyed families in the Detroit area and concluded that the "aggregate balance of power falls slightly in the husband's direction." They added that, in general, it seemed appropriate to "label these as relatively egalitarian couples."

Recent research suggests that money plays a central role in determining marital power. Money has different meanings for members of each sex: for men it typically represents identity and power; for women, security and autonomy. Apparently, money establishes the balance of power not only for married couples but also for unmarried heterosexual couples who are living together. Married women with paying work outside the home enjoy greater marital power than full-time homemakers do (Blumstein and Schwartz, 1983; Godwin and Scanzoni, 1989; Kaufman, 1985).

Labor not only enhances women's self-esteem but also increases their marital power, because some men have greater respect for women who work at paying jobs. Sociologist Isik Aytac (1987) studied a national sample of households in the United States and found that husbands of women holding management positions share more of the domestic chores than other husbands. In addition, as a wife's proportional contribution to the family income increases, her husband's share of meal preparation increases. Aytac's research supports the contention that the traditional division of labor at home can change as women's position in the labor force improves and women gain greater marital power.

Comparative studies have revealed the complexity of marital power issues in other cultures. For example, anthropologist David Gilmore (1990) examined decision making in two rural towns in southern Spain. These communities—one with 8000 residents and the other with 4000—have an agricultural economy based on olives, wheat, and sunflowers. Gilmore studied a variety of decision-making situations, including prenuptial decisions over household location, administration of domestic finances, and major household purchases. He found that working-class women in these communities—often united with their mothers—are able to prevail in many decisions despite opposition from their husbands.

Interestingly, wives' control over finances in these towns appears to lessen with affluence. Among the wealthier peasants, husbands retain more rights over the family purse strings, especially in terms of bank accounts and investments. In some cases, they make investments without their wives' knowledge. By contrast, in the working class—where surplus cash is uncommon and household finances are often based on borrowing and buying on credit because of the uncertainties of household employment—it is the wife who "rules" the household economy, and the husband accepts her rule.

Some marital relationships may be neither male-dominated nor female-dominated. The third type of authority pattern, the *egalitarian family,* is one in which spouses are regarded as equals. This does not mean, however, that each decision is shared in such families. Mothers may hold authority in some spheres, fathers in others. In the view of many sociologists, the egalitarian family has begun to replace the patriarchal family as the social norm. A study of Detroit families by Robert Blood, Jr., and Donald Wolfe (1960) supports this contention (see Box 9-1).

Source: Richard T. Schaefer and Robert P. Lamm, *Sociology: A Brief Introduction,* McGraw-Hill, New York, 1994, p. 237. Reproduced with permission of McGraw-Hill.

Tables

A **table** consists of material arranged in rows and columns. Tables contain words, numbers, or both. They may also include symbols, calculations, diagrams, and other types of information.

A table is an important textbook feature because it summarizes a great deal of information in a clear, concise, and organized way, as you can see from the examples here. To understand a table, it is necessary to read its title and the headings of the rows and columns. (Later in this chapter is a section on interpreting graphic material.)

TABLE 14.1
Summary of Findings Concerning Child Abuse

	Infancy	Toddler and pre-school period	Middle childhood	Adolescence
Interpersonal				
Social	Insecure attachment: Mother — Child Rejecting; — Avoidant hostile — (Type A) Neglecting — Ambivalent — (Type C) Rejecting & — Avoidant & neglecting — ambivalent — (Type D)	Avoids familiar people;* aggressive response to positive overtures;* ambivalent approach;* aggressive or distressed response to distress*	Fewer social and communicative skills; fewer friends; difficulty decentering; less empathy	Less competent; dysfunctional family
Play		Less mature, less group and parallel play; aggressive;* withdrawn;† interacts with teachers†		
Intrapersonal				
Adjustment			Increased internalizing and externalizing of problems; less initiative	Increased internalizing and externalizing of problems
Self		Visual recognition delayed and affectless; fewer words for own and others' inner states		

* Physically Abused
† Neglected

Source: Charles Wenar, *Developmental Psychopathology*, 3d ed., McGraw-Hill, New York, 1994, p. 386. Reproduced with permission of McGraw-Hill.

TABLE 19-2   FUNDAMENTAL BOSONS

Field	Particle	Mass	Spin	Couples to:
Electromagnetic	Photon	0	1	Charge
Strong nuclear	Gluon	0	1	Color
Weak nuclear	$W^\pm$	80,130	1	} All
	Z^0	91,180	1	} fermions
Gravity	Graviton?	0	2	Energy
Higgs?	Higgs?	?	0	Rest mass

Source: Robert H. March, *Physics for Poets*, 3d ed., McGraw-Hill, New York, p. 247. Reproduced with permission of McGraw-Hill.

TABLE 1–4
FOUR PERSPECTIVES ON HUMAN DEVELOPMENT

Perspective	Important Theories	Basic Belief	Technique Used
Psychoanalytic	Freud's psychosexual theory	Freud: Behavior is controlled by powerful unconscious urges.	Clinical observation
	Erikson's psychosocial theory	Erikson: Personality develops throughout life in a series of stages.	
Mechanistic	Behaviorism, or traditional learning theory (Pavlov, Skinner, Watson) Social-learning theory (Bandura)	Behaviorism: People are responders; concern is with how the environment controls behavior. Social-learning theory: Children learn in a social context, by observing and imitating models; person is an active contributor to learning.	Rigorous and scientific (experimental) procedures
Organismic	Piaget's cognitive-stage theory	There are qualitative changes in the way children think that develop in a series of four stages between infancy and adolescence. Person is an active initiator of development.	Flexible interviews; meticulous observation
Humanistic	Maslow's self-actualization theory	People have the ability to take charge of their lives and foster their own development.	Discussion of feelings

Source: Diane E. Papalia and Sally Wendkos Olds, *Human Development*, 5th ed., McGraw-Hill, New York, 1992, p. 22. Reproduced with permission of McGraw-Hill.

Graphic Aids

Graphic aids, or *illustrations,* consolidate information and present it more clearly than would be possible with words alone. Graphic aids include figures, cartoons, and photographs.

Figures include maps, charts, diagrams, graphs, and "how-to" processes. They also include anatomical drawings (like the example below left) and drawings of laboratory apparatus (like the example below right).

Textbook figures are often numbered for reference (for example, "Figure 6a," "Figure 10-2"). They typically have *legends:* titles, descriptions, and explanations that appear above, below, or alongside the illustration. To understand a figure, you must read the legend and any labels within the figure. To understand a graph, be sure to read the *axes* (the labels that appear on the sides and bottom of the graph).

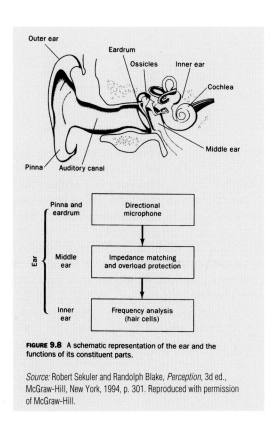

FIGURE 9.8 A schematic representation of the ear and the functions of its constituent parts.

Source: Robert Sekuler and Randolph Blake, *Perception,* 3d ed., McGraw-Hill, New York, 1994, p. 301. Reproduced with permission of McGraw-Hill.

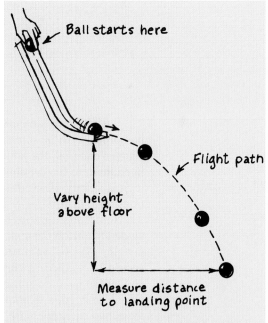

Figure 2-2 *Galileo's apparatus for studying projectile motion.*

Source: Robert H. March, *Physics for Poets,* 3d ed., McGraw-Hill, New York, 1992, p. 23. Reproduced with permission of McGraw-Hill.

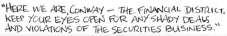
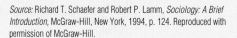

"HERE WE ARE, CONWAY — THE FINANCIAL DISTRICT. KEEP YOUR EYES OPEN FOR ANY SHADY DEALS AND VIOLATIONS OF THE SECURITIES BUSINESS."

Source: Richard T. Schaefer and Robert P. Lamm, *Sociology: A Brief Introduction,* McGraw-Hill, New York, 1994, p. 124. Reproduced with permission of McGraw-Hill.

Developmental tests are designed to chart the progress of infants and toddlers.

(SW Productions/PhotoDisc)

Cartoons are a popular feature because they can make a point quickly and humorously. To be sure the reader will understand how a cartoon relates to the chapter material, the author may provide a legend (a comment or explanation) in addition to the caption (as in the example above left). Often, however, a cartoon is simply allowed to "speak for itself," and the reader must infer its relationship to the text.

Some photographs in textbooks (like the example above right) are included to enrich the text, to provide an example of a concept or situation, or to give the "flavor" of a time or place. Other photographs are informational and should be studied as carefully as the text itself: photos of paintings, statues, and buildings in an art appreciation text (like Selection 3-3 in *Opening Doors*) would be a good example. Of course, photos often fall somewhere between these two categories. Be sure to read photo legends (the words accompanying the photograph).

KEY   TERMS

ambient system	dynamic visual acuity	group movement
apparent motion	element movement	induced motion
critical flicker frequency (CFF)	flicker	motion aftereffect
	focal system	motion capture
direction–selective cell	global motion	optic ataxia

Vocabulary Aids

Among the most common and most helpful textbook features are **vocabulary aids,** devices that highlight important terms and definitions. Authors highlight vocabulary in a variety of ways. Important terms may be set in **boldface,** *italic,* or color. They may also be printed in the margins (like *Key Terms* in *Opening Doors,* one of which appears here). There may be a list of terms, perhaps with definitions, at the end of a chapter (like the example at the top of this page) or after reading a selection (like the example below). These lists can also appear at the beginning of a chapter or reading. They may be called *Key Terms, Basic Terms, Terms to Know, Vocabulary, Terms to Remember,* and so on.

A list of important terms and definitions from the entire textbook may appear near the end of the book in a mini-dictionary, the *glossary.* (Shown on page 574 is the first page of the glossary of a psychology text.)

It is important to pay attention to vocabulary aids, because instructors expect you to know important terms, and often include them on tests.

VOCABULARY

delineate	to explain point by point
dialect	a manner of speaking common only to people from, or living in, a specific area
eloquent	able to speak (or write) in an especially moving and effective way
envoy	a messenger from, or representative of, a higher authority
flunkie	a person who does small, boring, or meaningless tasks at the orders of someone else; a "go-fer" (also spelled "flunky," "flunkey")
heresy	a belief or action that contradicts the official or strongly held beliefs of a society or organization, especially a church
japonica	a shrub that flowers profusely in spring
relentless	untiring, unwavering, ceaseless, persistent
sepulchral	like a tomb; having a tomblike atmosphere
whence	from which; where something came from
writ	a legal document, usually ordering some specific action

GLOSSARY

absolutist view of deviance The view that deviance is intrinsic to certain actions. In this view, right and wrong exist independently of arbitrary, human-created social judgments.

accounts Explanations that we offer for our behaviors. Accounts take four forms: excuses, justifications, concessions, and refusals.

additive task A task in which the performance of the group is measured in terms of the sum of the members' responses.

affect control theory (ACT) David Heise's theory offering a model of attitudes which suggests that the meanings we assign to identities and behaviors shape our social interactions. The theory uses the concepts of fundamental sentiments, transient sentiments, and deflection to describe the relationship between attitudes and behaviors.

affirmative action A government policy aimed at ending discriminatory practices by employers, as well as requiring them to take additional steps necessary to overcome the effects of past discrimination and give minorities "equal opportunity."

age grading The classification of individuals into age categories which divide the life course into meaningful stages and establish timetables for life events.

ageism Society's denial of privileges to a category of people because of their age.

agents of socialization The individuals, groups, and institutions that play a part in the transmission of culture to the new generation.

aggregate A unit of two or more persons whose interaction is minimal.

aggression Intentional harm done by one party to another.

alternative sources All the sources of rewards available to a person.

anticipatory socialization A phase of socialization in which individuals fan-

tasize about, experiment with, and try on the behaviors associated with role expectations for future roles.

attitude consistency The organization of attitudes in a harmonious manner so that attitudes are not in conflict with each other (inconsistency or imbalance). Attitude consistency theories suggest that we strive to maintain consistency and to avoid inconsistency, which is experienced as an uncomfortable psychological state.

attitude toward the behavior In the reasoned action model, the behavioral-intention factor consisting of a person's beliefs and evaluations of the possible outcomes of the behavior. It is estimated by summing the person's evaluations of the consequences of the behavior, weighted by the likelihood of each consequence.

audience task A task involving performance in the presence of others who are observing the behavior but not performing the same task.

authoritarian parenting style A style of parenting in which parents rely on a combination of normative, reward, and coercive resources to produce their children's strict obedience.

authoritative parenting style A style of parenting in which parents rely on a combination of expert, informational, reward, and coercive resources to persuade their children to behave in a certain manner, taking into account the child's explanation for noncompliance.

backchannel feedback Any subtle vocal or nonverbal response that a listener makes while a speaker is talking that signals to the speaker whether he or she is keeping the listener's interest and being understood.

balance Balance theory's term for attitude consistency.

balance theory The original formulation of attitude consistency theory, developed by Fritz Heider, which focused on three elements: (1) the per-

son who is the focus of attention, P; (2) some other person, O; and (3) an impersonal entity, X. The theory posits that P strives to maintain consistency among the attitudes connecting these elements, that is, P's attitude toward O, P's attitude toward X, and P's perception of O's attitude toward X.

behavioral intentions Our plans to perform a behavior. In the reasoned action model, behavioral intention is a function of the person's attitude toward the behavior and his or her subjective norm regarding it.

behavioral perspective An approach to social psychology proposing that our social behavior can best be understood by focusing on directly observable behavior and the environment that causes our behavior to change.

biological maturation The more or less automatic unfolding of biological potential in a set, predictable sequence.

birth cohort A category of people who were born in the same year or period and who age together.

body language The nonverbal communication of meaning through physical movements and gestures.

bonding The effort or desire to maintain a relationship.

catharsis A lessening of aggressive energy (anger) by discharging it through aggressive behavior.

civil inattention Form of body language in which we give others enough visual notice to signal to them that we recognize their presence, but then we quickly withdraw visual contact to show that we pose no threat to them and that we do not wish to interact with them.

coaction task A task involving performance in the presence of others with whom one has little interaction but who are performing the same task.

coalition An alliance of two or more parties who coordinate their efforts in order to achieve their ends against the

Sources: (Opposite page) Robert Sekuler and Randolph Blake, *Perception*, 3d ed., McGraw-Hill, New York, 1994, p. 25 *(top);* Susan Day and Elizabeth McMahan, *The Writer's Resource: Readings for Composition*, 4th ed., McGraw-Hill, New York, 1994 p. 340 *(bottom). (Above)* James A. Wiggins, Beverly B. Wiggins, and James Vander Zanden, *Social Psychology*, 5th ed., McGraw-Hill, New York, 1994, p. 551. Reproduced with permission of McGraw-Hill.

Study Questions and Activities

Many textbooks include **study questions and activities,** such as *exercises, drills,* and *practice sections.* These can be among the most important features you use, because they direct you to essential information you will be expected to know. Generally, if you are able to answer study questions and exercises, you will be able to do well on an actual test.

Study questions and activities may appear at the beginning or end of a chapter, a reading, or other subdivisions of the text. (In *Opening Doors,* for instance, questions appear preceding and following each reading selection.) In addition to the terms noted above, questions or activities may be called *Questions for Study and Review, Review, Ask Yourself, Self-Test, Check Your Mastery, Mastery Test, Learning Check, Check Your Understanding, Topics for Discussion, Problems,* etc. The examples shown here are typical.

Don't neglect study questions and activities; take the time to work on them. They provide valuable practice and give you a way to monitor your learning. Also, instructors often use these same items, or similar items, on tests.

PROBES

1 Briefly explain the objectives of the introduction.
2 Briefly describe five parts of an introduction.
3 Briefly describe five ways of getting the attention of the audience.
4 Describe three ways of preparing the audience for the body of the speech.
5 Briefly explain the objectives of the conclusion.
6 Describe four types of conclusions.
7 Briefly describe the idea of common ground.

APPLICATIONS

1 For each of the following subjects, create a method for getting the attention of the audience: (**a**) Preventing AIDS. (**b**) Date rape. (**c**) Applying first aid to a wound. (**d**) Joining the Peace Corps.
2 What kinds of conclusions could you use for each of the following topics? (**a**) Preventing child abuse. (**b**) Learning to use a computer. (**c**) Supporting affirmative action. (**d**) How to improve memory.
3 Read some issues of *Vital Speeches* and see how the speakers opened and closed their speeches.

Source: James A. Byrns, *Speaks for Yourself: An Introduction to Public Speaking,* McGraw-Hill, New York, 1994. p. 178. Reproduced with permission of McGraw-Hill.

QUESTIONS FOR CRITICAL READING, THINKING, DISCUSSION, AND WRITING

Analyzing Content and Technique

1. Why, according to Taylor, is television so concerned with depicting family life?
2. What were the main characteristics of the television families of the 1950s?
3. What did the television industry realize in the 1970s? How did this change the type of family shows being produced? What happened in the 1980s?
4. What are some of the differences between *All in the Family* and *The Cosby Show?* How does Taylor evaluate each show?
5. In her conclusion, Taylor states, "Today, the generous space that was opened up then for public discussion is again being narrowed . . . [to] sentimentality and a profound horror of argument." What evidence does she provide? Do you find her evidence adequate or inadequate? Explain.

Making Connections

1. Describe two or three current television shows about family life, analyzing the characters, the situations, and the implied values. What do these shows reveal to you about social trends? Which show do you prefer, and why?
2. Write an essay comparing and contrasting your own family with one specific television family. How realistic is the television family? Have you learned anything from it, either positive or negative, that you can apply to your own family situation?

Source: Chitra B. Divakaruni, *Multitude: Cross-Cultural Readings for Writers,* McGraw-Hill New Yorki, 1993, p. 86. Reproduced with permission of McGraw-Hill.

REVIEW QUESTIONS

1. Distinguish between passionate and companionate love. Describe how you feel physically and emotionally when in passionate love. Have you ever loved another passionately, only to have the passion fade? Explain.

2. Think of a romantic relationship you once had and draw a love triangle to represent the extent of your passion, intimacy, and decision/commitment. What shape does the triangle take? Which component—passion, intimacy, decision/commitment—was the most prominent; least prominent? Now draw your partner's love triangle. Which component was most prominent; least prominent? Are there differences between the two triangles? Do you think these differences had anything to do with the breakup of the relationship?

3. How does the "feminization of love" affect romantic relationships? What are some strategies couples might use to counteract this tendency in their own relationships?

4. Why is it important to self-disclose in relationships? What are the risks of self-disclosure? Have you ever been in a relationship in which your partner seemed to disclose too much, too soon? Describe the situation and how you felt. Is the relationship ongoing or did it end?

5. What is relationship equity? Equity theory? When an individual is underbenefitted in a relationship, how does he or she typically react?

6. What is the difference between normal and pathological jealousy? What causes a person to feel jealous? How does a person usually react when confronted by a jealous partner? Are there ways to keep normal jealous reactions under control?

Source: Gloria Bird and Keith Melville, *Families and Intimate Relationships,* McGraw-Hill New York, 1994, p. 84. Reproduced with permission of McGraw-Hill.

Chapter Summaries

A **chapter summary** is one of the most helpful textbook features because in it the author collects and condenses the most essential ideas. Many students find it useful to read a chapter summary both before and after studying a chapter. Of course, when you read a summary before you read the chapter, you may not understand it completely, but you will have a general idea of the most important material in the chapter.

Summaries can be short (like the first example below, from a public speaking text) or a full page or more in length (like the example on page 578, from a text on family life). A summary may also be called *Conclusion, Recapitulation, Looking Back, Summing Up, Key Points, Key Concepts,* etc. Summaries may be written as paragraphs or lists, and they may contain special aids. The second example below, from a sociology text, highlights key terms, for instance.

SUMMARY

Telling, showing, and doing are three important types of supporting information and should be used in every speech. Verbal channels include definitions, examples, stories and anecdotes, comparison and contrast, description, statistics, and testimony. Doing includes planning activities and leading groups through structured experiences.

SUMMARY

Culture is the totality of learned, socially transmitted behavior. This chapter examines the basic elements which make up a culture, social practices which are common to all cultures, and variations which distinguish one culture from another.

1 The process of expanding human culture has already been under way for thousands of years and will continue in the future.

2 Anthropologist George Murdock has compiled a list of general practices found in every culture, including courtship, family, games, language, medicine, religion, and sexual restrictions.

3 Societies resist ideas which seem too foreign as well as those which are perceived as threatening to their own values and beliefs.

4 *Language* includes speech, written characters, numerals, symbols, and gestures and other forms of non-verbal communication.

5 Sociologists distinguish between *norms* in two ways. They are classified as either *formal* or *informal* norms and as *mores* or *folkways*.

6 The most cherished *values* of a culture will receive the heaviest sanctions; matters that are regarded as less critical, on the other hand, will carry light and informal sanctions.

7 Generally, members of a *subculture* are viewed as outsiders or deviants.

8 From a conflict perspective, the social significance of the concept of the *dominant ideology* is that the most powerful groups and institutions in a society control the means of producing beliefs about reality through religion, education, and the media.

9 Advocates of *multiculturalism* argue that the traditional curricula of schools and colleges in the United States should be revised to include more works by and about African Americans, other racial and ethnic minorities, and women.

Sources: (Above) James A. Bryns, *Speak for Yourself: An Introduction to Public Speaking,* 3rd ed., McGraw-Hill, New York, 1994, p. 139 *(top)*; Richard T. Schaefer and Robert P. Lamm, *Sociology: A Brief Introduction,* McGraw-Hill, New York, 1994, p. 52 *(bottom)*.

SUMMARY POINTS

- There are three types of power: social power, latent power, and manifest power. Social power refers to cultural beliefs and norms that, through socialization, influence women and men to devalue women's status and assign them fewer resources and less power. Latent power is present when the less powerful partner anticipates the reaction of the more powerful partner and adjusts her or his course of action without the partner having to say a word. Manifest power relies on the use of particular tactics or strategies to bring issues forward or keep them from being raised.

- Power strategies fall into four general categories: direct-cooperative, direct-uncooperative, indirect-cooperative, indirect-uncooperative.

- Men more often rely on direct power strategies based on concrete resources that emphasize their individual competencies. Women more often use indirect strategies based on personal resources that exaggerate their powerlessness.

- Employed women typically have higher self-esteem, use more direct strategies, report that marital issues are settled more fairly, and indicate that their needs are more often taken into account during marital negotiation.

- Cooperative power strategies are the most beneficial to relationships and usually result in the greatest satisfaction of partners. When cooperative strategies (bargaining, reasoning) do not get results, competitive strategies (coercion, manipulation) may be used. Should these strategies also fail, some partners resort to threats. Finally, if verbal means of influence are not successful, physical means of asserting power may be employed.

- The First and Second National Violence Surveys carried out by Murray Straus and his colleagues are valuable sources of information about violence in the American family.

- These national surveys are one of the few sources of information about violence in both black and white families. Some scholars, however, caution that race is only one of the factors, and not among the most critical, to consider when trying to understand family violence.

- Violence is not limited to any particular social class.

- Use of alcohol or drugs is not a cause of abusive behavior in families. Rather, drinking and using drugs are socially accepted *excuses* for bad behavior.

- Violence is influenced by sociocultural factors and the family is where people get their "basic training" in the use of violence. The marriage license is considered by some to be a "hitting license."

- The Conflict Tactics Scales were developed by Murray Straus to assess marital violence. Although the scales have been criticized, they continue to be the instruments used most frequently in measuring violence in the family.

- Lenore Walker proposes that most incidents of wife battering proceed through three distinct stages: tension building, acute battering, and loving contrition. She calls this three-stage sequence of events the cycle of violence.

- Women stay in violent relationships for many reasons. Among them are social isolation from kin and friends; lack of reliable community support systems; fear that their abusive partner will find them and punish them if they leave; dependence on the partner for money, food, shelter, and love; and learned helplessness.

- Men who batter tend to downplay and trivialize the seriousness of their violent behavior. Potential batterers share some common identifiable characteristics, including advocating traditional gender roles, externalizing problems, being unreasonably jealous, handling life problems in a physically aggressive manner, believing that battered women cause their own abuse, and being impulsive and manipulative.

- When a woman reacts violently, it is usually to break out of her partner's grasp, to "fight back" during an abusive episode, or to protect herself from being more seriously injured by her batterer.

- Suzanne Steinmetz argues that no matter how small the percentage of female batterers compared to male batterers, all battering should be taken seriously because of its effects on the family. Men say that they stay in battering relationships to maintain their standard of living, out of a need to be good fathers and keep the family together, and, in some cases, to protect their children from the mother's abuse.

Source: Gloria Bird and Keith Melville, *Families and Intimate Relationships*, McGraw-Hill, New York, 1994, p. 340. Reproduced with permission of McGraw-Hill.

Appendixes

An **appendix** is a section at the end of a book which includes supplemental material or specialized information. (Information may be presented as an appendix so that it can be referred to conveniently, or because it is too long to be included in any single chapter, or because it relates to more than one chapter.) The appendix is a useful textbook feature because it presents additional information that you may need to refer to repeatedly.

In an American history or American government text, the Declaration of Independence and the Constitution may appear as appendixes. Physics and chemistry texts may have formulas in appendixes. In texts with self-tests, an answer key may appear as an appendix. A very helpful appendix in some history texts is a chronology or "time line" like the one shown on page 580. Shown below is the first page of an important appendix in a theater text that students would refer to often.

Opening Doors has four (appendixes, including a list of word parts and a glossary of key terms.)

APPENDIX 5
REALISM AND NONREALISM

The distinction between realism and nonrealism in theater becomes clearer when the two approaches are placed side by side. They are present in all aspects of theater, as the following table illustrates.

REALISTIC TECHNIQUES	NONREALISTIC TECHNIQUES
STORY	
Events which the audience knows have happened or might happen in everyday life: Blanche DuBois in Tennessee Williams's *A Streetcar Named Desire* goes to New Orleans to visit her sister and brother-in-law.	Events which do not occur in real life but take place only in the imagination: Emily in Thornton Wilder's *Our Town*, after she has died, returns to life for one day.
STRUCTURE	
Action confined to real places; time passes normally as it does in everyday life: in *The Little Foxes* by Lillian Hellman, the activity occurs over several days in Regina's house as she takes control of her family's estate.	Arbitrary use of time and place: in Strindberg's *The Dream Play*, walls dissolve and characters are transformed, as in a dream.
CHARACTERS	
Recognizable human beings, such as the family—mother, father, and two sons—in O'Neill's *Long Day's Journey into Night*.	Unreal figures like the Ghost of Hamlet's father in *Hamlet*, the Three Witches in *Macbeth*, and the people who turn into animals in Ionesco's *Rhinoceros*.

Source: Edwin Wilson, *The Theater Experience*, 6th ed., McGraw-Hill, New York, 1994, p. 455. Reproduced with permission of McGraw-Hill.

CHRONOLOGY $\left[\begin{array}{c}\text{APPENDIX}\\ \textbf{2}\end{array}\right]$

MIDDLE AGES (450–1450)

Musicians	Artists and Writers	Historical and Cultural Events
		Sack of Rome by Vandals (455)
		Reign of Pope Gregory I (590–604)
		First Crusade (1096–1099)
Perotin (late twelfth century)		Beginning of Notre Dame Cathedral in Paris (1163)
		King John signs Magna Carta (1215)
	Dante (1265–1321)	
	Giotto (1266–1337)	
Guillaume de Machaut (c. 1300–1377)		
	Boccaccio (1313–1375)	
	Chaucer (c. 1343–1400)	Hundred Years' War (1337–1453)
		Black death (1348–1350)

RENAISSANCE (1450–1600)

Musicians	Artists and Writers	Historical and Cultural Events
Guillaume Dufay (c. 1400–1474)		Fall of Constantinople (1453)
Josquin Desprez (c. 1440–1521)	Leonardo da Vinci (1452–1519)	Gutenberg Bible (1456)
		Columbus discovers America (1492)
	Michelangelo (1475–1564)	
	Raphael (1483–1520)	Martin Luther's ninety-five theses (1517)
	Titian (c. 1477–1576)	
	François Rabelais (c. 1494–c. 1553)	
Andrea Gabrieli (c. 1520–1586)		

Source: Roger Kamien, *Music: An Appreciation,* 2d Brief ed., McGraw-Hill, New York, 1994, p. 381.

Bibliographies, Suggested Readings, and Webliographies

KEY TERM
Bibliography

List of sources from which the author of the text has drawn information.

A **bibliography** (which usually appears near the end of a textbook) is a list of sources: books, articles, and other works from which the author of the text has drawn information. A bibliography may also be called *References, Works Cited,* or *Sources.* A bibliography sometimes lists works the author recommends for further (supplemental) reading, such as the one below. Or it may be called a *Select Bibliography* (like the example on page 582, from a theater text), *Selected Works,* etc. Of course, some bibliographies serve both functions and are called *Bibliography and Selected Readings* or *References and Bibliography.*

A list of **suggested readings** often appears at the end of chapters (or parts), where it may be called *Additional Readings, Suggestions for Further Reading, Supplementary Readings,* etc. Suggested readings may be annotated, like the example below. That is, the textbook author may provide brief descriptions and explain why each work is listed.

SUGGESTIONS FOR FURTHER READING

DeVito, Joseph A.: *The Elements of Public Speaking,* HarperCollins, New York, 1991. Helpful for speakers who find it difficult to select a topic.

Ehninger, Douglas, Bruce Gronbeck, Ray McKerrow, and Alan Monroe: *Principles and Types of Speech Communication,* HarperCollins, New York, 1992. Includes useful material on subjects for speeches and occasions for public speaking.

Fletcher, Leon: *How to Design and Deliver a Speech,* 4th ed., HarperCollins, New York, 1990. Offers step-by-step procedures for making a topic manageable.

Ilardo, Joseph: *Speaking Persuasively,* Macmillan, New York, 1981. Provides a detailed theory of topic selection.

Osborn, Michael, and Suzanne Osborn: *Public Speaking,* 2d ed., Houghton Mifflin, Boston, Mass., 1991. Provides helpful strategies for determining the purpose of a speech.

Source: Teri Kwal Gamble and Michael Gamble, *Communication Works,* 4th ed., McGraw-Hill, New York, 1993, p. 339.

SELECT BIBLIOGRAPHY

Allen, John: *Theatre in Europe,* J. Offord, Eastbourne, England, 1981.

Aristotle: *Aristotle's Poetics,* S. H. Butcher (trans.), Introduction by Francis Fergusson, Hill and Wang, New York, 1961.

Aronson, Arnold: *American Set Design,* New York, 1985.

Artaud, Antonin: *The Theater and Its Double,* Mary C. Richards (trans.), Grove, New York, 1958.

Atkinson, Brooks: *Broadway,* rev. ed., Macmillan, New York, 1974.

Austen, Gayle: *Feminist Theories for Creative Criticism,* University of Michigan Press, Ann Arbor, 1990.

Bartow, Arthur: *The Directors' Voice: 21 Interviews,* Theatre Communications Group, New York, 1988

Bay, Howard: *Stage Design,* Drama Book Specialists, New York, 1974.

Beckerman, Bernard: *Dynamics of Drama: Theory and Method of Analysis,* Drama Book Specialists, New York, 1979.

Benedetti, Jean: *Stanislavski: An Introduction,* Theatre Arts, New York, 1982.

Benedetti, Robert: *The Actor at Work,* Prentice-Hall, Englewood Cliffs, N.J., 1971.

Bentley, Eric: *The Life of the Drama,* Atheneum, New York, 1964.

—— (ed.): *The Theory of the Modern Stage,* Penguin, Baltimore, 1968.

Brecht, Bertolt: *Brecht on Theatre,* John Willett (trans.), Hill and Wang, New York, 1965.

Betsko, Kathleen, and Koenig, Rachel: *Interviews*

with Contemporary Women Playwrights, Beech Tree, New York, 1987.

Bradby, David, and Williams, David: *Director's Theater,* St. Martin's, New York, 1988.

Brockett, Oscar G.: *History of the Theatre,* 5th ed., Allyn & Bacon, Boston, 1991.

—— and Robert R. Findlay: *Century of Innovation: A History of European and American Theatre and Drama Since the Late 19th Century,* 2d ed., Allyn and Bacon, Boston, 1990.

Brook, Peter: *The Empty Space,* Atheneum, New York, 1968.

——: *The Shifting Point,* HarperCollins, New York, 1987.

Burns, Elizabeth: *Theatricality,* Harper & Row, New York, 1973.

Case, Sue-Ellen: *Feminism and Theatre.* Routledge, Chapman, and Hall, New York, 1987.

Chinoy, Helen K., and Jenkins, Linda W.: *Women in American Theatre,* rev. ed., Theatre Communications Group, New York, 1987.

Clark, Barrett H. (ed.): *European Theories of the Drama,* rev. ed., Crown, New York, 1965.

Clurman, Harold: *On Directing,* Macmillan, New York, 1972.

Cohen, Robert: *Acting Power,* Mayfield, Palo Alto, Calif., 1978.

Cole, Toby: *Playwrights on Playwriting,* Hill and Wang, New York, 1961.

——, and Helen Krich Chinoy: *Actors on Acting,* Crown, New York, 1970.

Corrigan, Robert (ed.): *Comedy: Meaning and Form,* Chandler, San Francisco, 1965.

Source: Edwin Wilson, *The Theater Experience,* 6th ed., McGraw-Hill, New York, 1994, p. 461. Reproduced with permission of McGraw-Hill.

KEY TERM
Webliography

List of websites which feature material related to a topic.

A **Webliography** is a list of websites which feature material related to a topic. A Webliography gives a list of Web "addresses" where pertinent material is located. Some Webliographies (such as the ones that accompany the reading selections in *Opening Doors*) are annotated. This means that there is a brief description of the type of material found at each website. Websites usually contain "links" which allow users to go directly to additional, related websites. In textbooks, Webliographies may be called by various names, such as "Read More about it on the World Wide Web," "Related websites," "Net Search," and "On the Web" (such as in the example, which comes from a study skills textbook).

Bibliographies, suggested readings, and Webliographies can be especially helpful for research assignments, such as papers and reports, or when you want or need to read other material to improve your understanding of the text.

On the Web

The following sites on the World Wide Web provide the opportunity to extend your learning about the material in this chapter. (Although the Web addresses were accurate at the time the book was printed, check the P.O.W.E.R. Learning Web site [http://mhhe.com/power] for any changes that may have occurred.)

http://www.basenet.net/~eagle/educate/1997/june97/list.html
Check out this list of 163 of the most classic titles in literature, called the "Ultimate Reading List." You're sure to find something that looks appealing.

http://www.ucc.vt.edu/stdysk/sq3r.html
This site introduces an approach to reading, and retaining, textual material.

http://www.cabsju.edu/academicadvising/help/eff-list/html
This site presents a series of tips on effective listening.

Source: Robert S. Feldman, *Power Learning,* McGraw-Hill, New York, 2000, p. 191.

Indexes

At the end of a textbook you will usually find one or more indexes. An **index** is an alphabetical listing of topics and names in the text, giving the specific pages on which you can find information about them. The index is a useful textbook feature because it helps you locate information quickly.

On the opposite page is an example of a general index, from a history text. Some textbooks have a separate *name index* and *subject index,* like the examples below from a psychology text. Anthologies and other textbooks with reading selections often have an *index of authors and titles.*

Indexes sometimes include special features. For instance, in the example from the history textbook, the notations *f* and *m* tell readers where they will find figures and maps. The index for *Opening Doors* begins on page 730.

Name Index

Abramson, L. Y., 27
Acocella, J. R., 261, 309
Adair, J. G., 49, 54
Addison, W. E., 104
Adjang, O. M. J., 88
Adler, A., 304
Adler, T., 31
Allison, M. G., 314–315
Alloy, L. B., 261, 309
Allport, G. W., 22, 298, 303
Altmann, J., 106
Altomari, M. G., 98, 101
American Psychiatric Association, 20
American Psychological Association, 5, 38–39, 62, 65, 165, 420–442
Anastasi, A., 136–137, 139, 142
Anderson, C. R., 46
Anderson, J. R., 27, 28
Anderson, K. J., 259
Anisfeld, M., 428
Arthur, J., 95, 101
Asch, S. E., 193–194
Ascione, F. R., 75
Asher, S. J., 201
Atkinson, R. C., 302, 331
Atwater, J. D., 358
Aubrey, L. W., 24
Ayllon, T., 314–315

Babbie, E., 125
Baer, D. M., 160, 319

Bailey, J., 244–246, 308
Baldwin, E., 50
Barash, D. P., 77, 99, 101
Barker, L. S., 87, 98
Barker, R. G., 87, 98
Barlow, D. H., 298, 304, 309, 311, 313, 316
Baron, J. N., 169
Bartholomew, G. A., 419
Bartlett, F. C., 74
Bass, B. M., 423
Bazerman, M., 151, 168–169
Bellack, A. S., 47, 57–58, 316
Benassi, V. A., 19–20
Benjamin, L. T., Jr., 442
Berch, D. B., 253, 260–261
Berk, R. A., 329, 348, 358
Bickman, L., 76, 83
Biggers, K., 95
Biglan, A., 95, 101
Blanck, P. D., 47, 50, 57–58
Bloom, B. L., 201
Bobo, L., 410
Bolgar, H., 298, 300, 304–305
Bollen, K. A., 169
Bond, C. F., Jr., 102
Booth, W., 59
Bootzin, R. R., 261, 309
Boring, E. G., 4–5, 8
Borkovec, T. D., 203
Bornstein, M. T., 316
Bornstein, P. H., 63
Bornstein, R. F., 288

Subject Index

ABAB (reversal) design, 311–314, 353–354
   natural settings and, 353–354
   (*See also* Single-case experimental designs)
ABBA counterbalancing, 219–220
Accidental sample, 118–119
Alpha (*see* Level of significance)
American Psychological Association (APA), 4–6, 31–32, 38–39, 60–61
American Psychological Society (APS), 6
Analysis of experiments, 193–198, 269–289
   computer-assisted, 273, Appendix A
   effect size, 286–287
   estimating error variation, 276–277, 279
   logic of, 193–198, 269–289
   meta-analysis, 287–289
   null hypothesis testing, 193–198, 273–276, 279
   power and, 285–286
   sensitivity, 178, 213, 285
   (*See also* Analysis of variance; Coding; Data reduction; Descriptive statistics; Appendix A)
Analysis of variance (*F*-test, ANOVA):
   analytical comparisons, 260–261, 263, 275–276, 280, 284–285
   complex designs, 280–285
   computer-assisted analyses, Appendix A
   critical values, Appendix A
   degrees of freedom, 274, 280–282
   effect size, 286–287
   error variation, 194, 269–270, 276–277, 279
   F-ratio, 270–273
   independent groups design, 270–276

Analysis of variance (*continued*)
   interaction effects, 259–264, 282–283
   main effect, 238, 243–244
   null hypothesis, 270–273
   omnibus *F*-test, 273, 280–282
   random groups design, 270–276
   residual variation, 277, 279–280
   simple comparisons, 263, 283–284
   simple main effect, 263, 282
   summary table, 273–275, 279–282
   table of critical values, Appendix A
   within-subjects designs, 276–280
   (*See also* Appendix A for computational procedures)
Analytical comparisons, 260–261, 263, 275–276, 284–285
ANOVA (*see* Analysis of variance)
Applied behavior analysis, 297, 308–309
Applied research, 295–363
   versus basic research, 328–329, 356–359
Archival data, 156–169
   content analysis and, 161–164
   illustrative uses of, 164–169
   problems and limitations of, 167–169
   rationale for use of, 156–160
   types of, 160–161

Balancing, 12, 180–183, 189–191
Baseline stage, 310
Basement (floor) effect, 256–257, 334–335
Basic vs. applied research, 328–329, 356–359
Behavior modification, 309
Behavior therapy, 309

Source: John J. Shaughnessy and Eugene B. Zechmeister, *Research Methods in Psychology,* 3d ed., McGraw-Hill, New York, 1994, pp. 489, 494. Reproduced with permission of McGraw-Hill.

INDEX

Note: Page numbers followed by the letter *f* or *m* indicate figures or maps, respectively.

Source: Richard E. Sullivan, Dennis Sherman, and John B. Harrison, *A Short History of Western Civilization*, 8th ed., McGraw-Hill, New York, 1994, p. I-1. Reproduced with permission of McGraw-Hill.

Additional Features and Supplements

There are numerous other types of textbook features. Many texts (such as *Opening Doors*) include *epigraphs,* quotations at the opening of chapters (or other sections) that suggest overall themes or concerns. Some texts put vivid or provocative quotations in the margins.

Depending on the subject matter, a text may include special *exhibits* or *examples* such as student papers, plot summaries, profit-and-loss statements, documents, forms, and printouts. Useful material (such as the periodic table of the elements in a chemistry text) may even appear on the inside of the cover. Sometimes a textbook has a unique feature, such as the chapter review cards in *Opening Doors.*

Finally, some textbooks have *supplements,* separate aids that accompany the text. These might include *study guides, supplemental readings, student workbooks,* and *computer diskettes.* Supplements are a good investment, since they have been developed to help you guide your own learning, test yourself, and check your progress.

All these textbook features can help you use your study time effectively and efficiently. Students often remark that in college textbooks "everything seems important." They find it hard to get a sense of how the facts and concepts add up to a coherent whole. Taking advantage of textbook features as you read can enable you to identify the essential information in a chapter and to understand its organization. Remember that authors and publishers want to help you study and learn from their textbooks. For this reason, they put a great deal of time, effort, and thought into designing textbook features.

STUDY TIPS FOR USING TEXTBOOK FEATURES

Prefaces

Read the preface to see what the book contains, how it is organized, and what its special features are.

Tables of contents

Use the table of contents, particularly if no chapter outlines are given. Your chapter study notes should cover each item listed in the table of contents. Pay attention to the size and type style, which indicate major and minor headings.

Part openings

Reading a part opening will help you understand the scope of what is contained in the section, how the section is organized, and how its chapters are interrelated.

Chapter outlines

Pay attention to major topics in a chapter outline. Your notes should also include all subtopics. The author has done some of your selecting for you, so take advantage of it.

Chapter objectives and introductions

Use objectives and introductions to test yourself on the chapter material. Try to write out the answers from memory.

Lists and sequences

Use mnemonic devices (memory devices) to help you remember information.

Boxes

Pay attention to boxed information. It helps you understand the text. Also, you may be tested on boxed material.

Tables

Pay attention to tables. They consolidate important information and help you understand relationships among ideas. Instructors may base test questions on them.

Graphic aids

Watch for graphic aids. Figures, cartoons, and photographs present important information or explain the text.

Vocabulary aids

Write down the definition for each term included in a vocabulary aid. It is your responsibility to learn the special vocabulary of each subject you study. Expect to be asked about these terms on tests.

Study questions and activities

Take the time to answer study questions and work on exercises, especially if your instructor has not provided study questions. Think carefully about discussion topics. Items like these may appear on tests.

Chapter summaries

Read the chapter summary both *before and after* you read the chapter itself.

Appendixes

Use appendixes for reference and as a source of additional information.

Bibliographies, suggested readings, and Webliographies

Use source lists when you are doing papers, reports, and other research assignments. You can also use supplementary readings to improve your understanding of the textbook.

Indexes

Indexes will help you find specific material quickly.

Additional features

Look for epigraphs (quotations), exhibits, and examples in the text. Don't neglect special reference material that may appear on the inside of the cover.

Supplements

Study guides, study guides with, supplemental readings, workbooks, and software accompanying your textbooks will usually prove to be a good investment. Use supplements like these to direct and focus your study, to test yourself, and to evaluate your learning.

MARKING TEXTBOOKS: UNDERLINING, HIGHLIGHTING, AND ANNOTATING

KEY TERM
Underlining and Highlighting

Techniques for marking topics, main ideas, and definitions.

KEY TERM
Annotation

Explanatory notes written in the margins of a textbook to organize and remember information.

It has been estimated that as much as 80 percent of the material in college tests comes from textbooks. For this reason alone, you need to be able to underline, highlight, and annotate your textbooks effectively.

Underlining and **highlighting** are techniques for marking topics, main ideas, and important definitions in reading materials. **Annotation** refers to explanatory notes you write *in the margins of your textbook* to help you organize and remember important information that appears within paragraphs. Taking a moment to annotate information (write or jot it down) also helps you concentrate. When you are reading a difficult textbook, you need to concentrate on one paragraph at a time. Effective students mark their textbooks by both underlining or highlighting *and* annotating.

Here are some considerations for *underlining and highlighting.* First, you need to avoid the most typical mistake students make in marking textbooks: *overmarking* (underlining or highlighting too much). Students often make this mistake because they try to underline or highlight *while* they are reading the material instead of *after* they have read it. The process of underlining and highlighting a textbook is very selective. Further, you cannot know what is important in a paragraph or section until you have *finished* reading it. Remember, for example, that the main idea sometimes does not appear until the end of a paragraph. Remember, too, that you may not be able to understand some paragraphs until you have read an entire section. The rule, then, is this: *Read first, and underline only after you have identified the important ideas.* A word of caution: Some students substitute underlining and highlighting for *thinking.* They mistakenly believe that if they have marked a lot in a chapter, they must have read it carefully and found the important information. To avoid this error, follow these steps: Read and *think; then* underline or highlight *selectively.*

Second, you need to know the kinds of things you *should* underline or highlight. As mentioned above, underline or highlight the *topic* of a paragraph. Underline or highlight the *main idea* of a paragraph if it is stated directly. Keep in mind that often you will not need to underline every word of a main idea sentence to capture the idea it is expressing. Underline or highlight important *definitions.* You may find it helpful to mark important terms as well.

Third, you need to know the kinds of things you should *not* underline or highlight. Do *not* underline or highlight supporting details, since this results in overmarking. (As you will see below, annotation can be used effectively to indicate supporting details.)

Once you have underlined and highlighted topics, main ideas, and important terms, you will want to *annotate:* that is, write explanatory notes and symbols in the margins. If a textbook has narrow margins, you may prefer to use notebook paper or even stick-on notes for your annotations, to give yourself more room.

The following box shows how a passage from a human development textbook (about different forms of marriage) could be underlined and annotated. Notice how relatively little is underlined and how helpful the annotations would be in preparing for a test on this material.

AN EXAMPLE OF UNDERLINING AND ANNOTATION

A life-style that apparently exists in all societies is marriage—a socially sanctioned union between a woman and a man with the expectation that they will play the roles of wife and husband. After studying extensive cross-cultural data, the anthropologist George P. Murdock (1949) concluded that reproduction, sexual relations, economic cooperation, and the socialization of offspring are functions of families throughout the world. We now recognize that Murdock overstated the matter, since there are a number of societies—for instance, Israeli kibbutz communities—in which the family does not encompass all four of these activities (Spiro, 1954; Gough, 1960). What Murdock describes are commonly encountered tendencies in family functioning in most cultures.

Societies differ in how they structure marriage relationships.
① Four patterns are found: monogamy, one husband and one
② wife; polygyny, one husband and two or more wives; polyandry,
③ two or more husbands and one wife; and group marriage, two
④ or more husbands and two or more wives. Although monogamy exists in all societies, Murdock discovered that other forms may be not only allowed but preferred. Of 238 societies in his sample, only about one-fifth were strictly monogamous.

Polygyny has been widely practiced throughout the world. The Old Testament reports that both King David and King Solomon had several wives. In his cross-cultural sample of 238 societies, Murdock found that 193 of them permitted husbands to take several wives. In one-third of these polygynous societies, however, less than one-fifth of the married men had more than one wife. Usually it is only the rich men in a society who can afford to support more than one family.

In contrast with polygyny, polyandry is rare among the world's societies. And in practice, polyandry has not usually allowed freedom of mate selection for women; it has often meant simply that younger brothers have sexual access to the wife of an older brother. Thus where a father is unable to afford wives for each of his sons, he may secure a wife for only his oldest son.

Source: James Vander Zanden, *Human Development*, Knopf, New York, 1985.

(def) marriage: socially sanctioned union of a woman and a man with the expectation they will play the roles of wife and husband

4 tendencies in functions of families:*
—reproduction
—sexual relations
—economic cooperation
—socialization of offspring

(def) Four patterns of marriage:*
—monogamy: 1 husband/1 wife
—polygyny: 1 husband/2+ wives
—polyandry: 2+ husbands/1 wife
—group marriage: 2+ husbands/2+ wives

Polygyny:
Old Testament kings with several wives:
—Solomon ⎫
—David   ⎬ ex.
—Murdock study: 193/238 societies permitted polygyny

—Usually only rich were polygynous

Polyandry:
—women not usually allowed to choose mates
—often simply means younger brothers have sexual access to wife of older brother

You may be wondering what types of annotations are helpful and why it is necessary to annotate as well as to underline or highlight. First, you may want to list the topics of certain paragraphs in the margin. This can help you grasp the sequence of the author's ideas.

Wouldn't it be convenient if a computer software program could automatically find and highlight main ideas in college textbooks?

CLOSE TO HOME   JOHN McPHERSON

CLOSE TO HOME © 2000 John McPherson. Reprinted with permission of UNIVERSAL PRESS SYNDICATE. All rights reserved.

Writing out an *important term* and a brief *definition* in the margin is also helpful. When your instructor uses these terms in class, you will recognize them and be able to record them more easily in your lecture notes. And, of course, you will remember the terms and definitions more clearly. You will need to know these terms for tests.

Also, you may choose to list essential *supporting details* in shortened form in the margin. Annotating is an effective, convenient, concise way to organize supporting details; and jotting details down in the margin will help you connect them with the main ideas they support.

Formulated main ideas are another type of helpful annotation. Your formulated main idea sentence can be written in the margin next to the paragraph.

Symbols and *abbreviations* are still another helpful form of annotation. Your symbols and abbreviations will enable you to locate important material quickly and (if necessary) return to passages that need further study. Here are a few examples of abbreviations and symbols you can use in the margins:

def	*Definition.* Use *def* when an important term is defined.
?	*Question mark.* Use this when you do not understand something and need to study it further or get help with it.
1, 2, 3 . . .	*Numbers.* Use numbers when an author gives items in a list or series.
*	*Asterisk.* Use an asterisk to mark important information.
ex	*Example.* Use *ex* to identify helpful examples.

TAKING NOTES FROM TEXTBOOKS: OUTLINING, MAPPING, AND SUMMARIZING

In addition to underlining, highlighting, and marginal annotations, *taking notes from textbooks* is another important study skill. Students who take notes and review them are four to five times more likely to recall important information during a test. In fact, you are much more likely to recall *any* idea that you have written out. Note-taking is your single greatest aid to successful test preparation later on. (Note-taking during a lecture is also your single greatest aid to concentration.) Three very useful forms of textbook note-taking are outlining, mapping, and summarizing.

Guidelines for Outlining

KEY TERM
Outlining

Formal way of organizing main ideas and supporting details to show relationships among them.

Outlining is a formal way of organizing main ideas and the supporting details that go with them. Even if you underline main ideas in your textbook and annotate supporting details in the margin, there may be times when it is helpful to outline a section or chapter. Outlines are especially useful for organizing complex material. Outlining is best done on separate paper rather than written in the textbook.

When should you outline? Obviously, you will not need to outline every section or every chapter. As mentioned above, outlining can be appropriate for complex material. It is also helpful when you need to condense a lengthy section or chapter in order to give yourself an overview. Because outlining condenses information and lets you see and understand how an entire section or chapter is organized, an outline makes the material easier to study and remember.

How do you create an outline of textbook material? To outline a paragraph, you need to write its main idea. Then, on separate, indented lines below the main idea, write the supporting details that go with it, like this:

I. Main idea sentence
   A. Supporting detail
   B. Supporting detail
   C. Supporting detail
   D. Supporting detail

For longer passages consisting of several paragraphs, continue your outline in the same way:

I. First main idea sentence
   A. Supporting detail for main idea I
   B. Supporting detail for main idea I
   C. Supporting detail for main idea I
   D. Supporting detail for main idea I
II. Second main idea sentence
   A. Supporting detail for main idea II
   B. Supporting detail for main idea II

III. Third main idea sentence

    A. Supporting detail for main idea III
    B. Supporting detail for main idea III
    C. Supporting detail for main idea III

    The purpose of your study outline is to show you how ideas are related. Making your outline look perfect is not as important as making sure that the relationships are clear to *you*. Main ideas should stand out, and it should be obvious which details go with each main idea. Roman numerals (I, II, III) are often used for main ideas, and uppercase letters (A, B, C, D) are used for supporting details. This notation helps you see how ideas are related.

    An outline can consist of phrases or sentences. However, when you have complex material, a sentence outline works well because it gives complete thoughts.

    The box below shows a sentence outline of a passage from Selection 7-3. Notice also the identifying title: *Reactions to Impending Death.*

    Use the same title for your outline as the one that appears in the original material. Do not entitle your outline "Outline." (It will be obvious that it is an outline!)

SAMPLE OUTLINE

Reactions to Impending Death

I. Elisabeth Kübler-Ross, a thanatologist, found in her research on the terminally ill that they tend to have certain basic emotional reactions as they prepare for death.

    A. There are five types of reactions: denial and isolation, anger, bargaining, depression, and acceptance.

    B. Different patients display different emotions.

    C. Reactions may occur in various orders, although the general pattern is shock, denial, anger, and acceptance.

    D. Several factors influence a person's type and sequence of emotional reactions.

    E. Overall, a person's approach to dying reflects his or her approach to living.

    F. These same emotions are characteristic of anyone who has experienced a major loss.

II. There are several uses of Kübler-Ross's research.

    A. It can be used to help the dying cope with their emotions by enabling them to discuss these emotions.

    B. It can be used to help survivors cope with the dying person's emotions as well as their own.

III. A hospice is a special hospital for the terminally ill.

   A. A hospice can enhance a dying person's final days.

   B. Life goes on more normally in this pleasant, informal environment.

   C. There are many supportive people, including personnel and family members.

IV. Survivors normally go through a period of grieving or bereavement following an ill person's death.

   A. Grief follows the pattern of shock or numbness; pangs of grief; apathy, dejection, and depression; and resolution.

   B. Survivors' reactions vary, but survivors are usually able to discharge their anguish by grieving, and thus prepare to go on living.

   C. Each person must grieve at his or her own pace and in his or her own way.

Using the Cornell Method of Note-Taking

The Cornell Method of note-taking is an organized way of taking notes that includes a built-in review column. Sheets of loose-leaf notebook paper are marked ahead of time with a line to rule off a review column on the left side of the page. (See the examples.) You record information on the main part of the page using outline form to organize main ideas and the supporting details that go with each of them. Read over your notes to make sure you will be able to understand them weeks from now. Write out words that are unclear and be sure you understand all your abbreviations. Add any words or phrases needed to clarify your notes, such a detail, an example, or a definition. Underline, circle, or star key points. (To evaluate your current note-taking skills, complete the "Checklist for Good Note-taking.")

After you have finished taking notes from your book or from a lecture, fill in the review column by writing clue words or questions. When you are ready to review, cover your notes so that only the review column shows. Try to answer the review column questions by reciting the information aloud. If you cannot remember, uncover the material, look at the answer, re-cover it, and try it again until you can recite it successfully. (An example of the information in Selection 7-3, "Reactions to Impending Death," in Cornell format is provided on page 595.)

The Cornell format for taking notes.

(Rule notebook paper off ahead of time.)

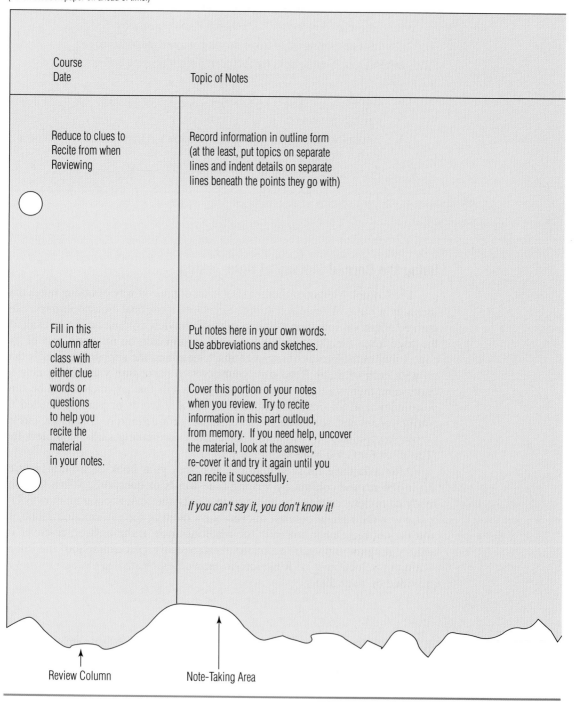

Course
Date   Topic of Notes

Reduce to clues to   Record information in outline form
Recite from when   (at the least, put topics on separate
Reviewing   lines and indent details on separate
                                      lines beneath the points they go with)

Fill in this   Put notes here in your own words.
column after   Use abbreviations and sketches.
class with
either clue
words or   Cover this portion of your notes
questions   when you review. Try to recite
to help you   information in this part outloud,
recite the   from memory. If you need help, uncover
material   the material, look at the answer,
in your notes.   re-cover it and try it again until you
                                      can recite it successfully.

                                      If you can't say it, you don't know it!

Review Column   Note-Taking Area

Recall Column ↓	**Record Section** ↓
November 14 (Psych 101)	Reactions to Impending Death
What are 5 general reactions of dying persons?	1. Thanatologist Elisabeth Kübler-Ross found terminally-ill patients have certain reactions as they prepare for death: • denial and isolation ("test results are wrong!") • anger (at God, at those who are healthy, etc.) • bargaining ("If you let me live, I'll be a better person.") • depression • acceptance (uses time left as well as possible)
Is there a set of sequence of reactions?	--not everyone has all 5 reactions or has them in that order
Uses of findings?	--helps both the dying and the survivors understand and cope with their reactions
What is a hospice?	2. Hospice = hospital for the terminally ill that seeks to improve the quality of life their final days: • supportive staff, clergy, counselors • pleasant surroundings • round-the-clock visits from everyone, including pets • constant attention, flexible rules
What is bereavement?	3. Bereavement = natural, normal period of grief after a death Grief follows predictable pattern:
What are the stages grief?	• shock or numbness (dazed; ends by time of funeral) • pangs of grief (painful yearning for person; suffering acute; may think person is still alive, see them in dreams) • apathy, dejection and depression (lasts weeks or months; person feels futility, but resumes activities) • resolution (acceptance; memories now include positive images and nostalgic pleasure)
Purpose of grief?	--Allows survivors to discharge anguish and prepare to go on living
Does suppressing grief lead to problems later on?	--Suppressing grief does not lead to depression later on; lack of intense grief does not predict problems late on; each person must grieve in his or her own way and at own pace.
↑ **Fill in questions after writing information in the Record section. Cover Record section so you can test yourself aloud.**	↑ **Record information here in an organized fashion.**

Because of its built-in "Recall Column," the Cornell Format is an effective way to take notes. This column is especially helpful when reviewing for tests.

CREATING A REVIEW SHEET USING THE CORNELL NOTE-TAKING FORMAT

- You should take your notes on loose-leaf notebook paper in Cornell format. Remove your notes and spread them out on a desk or table top so that only the review column of each page is exposed.

- Overlap the review columns so that you create a continuous review column for the material you want to review.

- Use this built-in review aid when you review for tests. Prepare by reciting the answers to questions you have written in the review column.

- As you answer each question in the review column, lift up the page to check whether your answer is complete and correct.

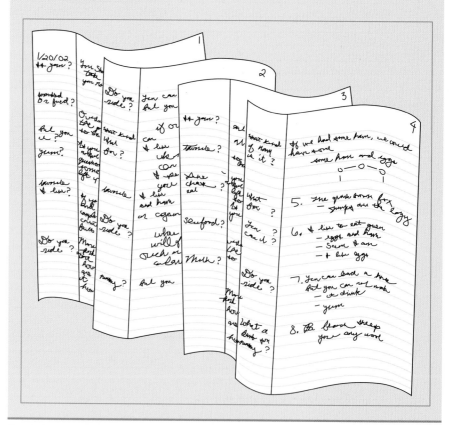

Sample of notes in Cornell format with only review columns showing.

CHECKLIST FOR GOOD NOTE-TAKING

Here are guidelines for evaluating notes you take from a classroom lecture or from your textbooks. Answer *yes* or *no* for each question.

When you take notes, do you:

Yes No

___ ___ **1.** use standard-sized loose-leaf notebook paper rather than a spiral notebook?

___ ___ **2.** rule off your paper ahead of time so that you can use the Cornell format for clear, organized notes?

___ ___ **3.** always label your notes with the name of the course, date (for lecture notes), or chapter and pages (for material from you text)?

___ ___ **4.** write the title or general topic of the notes at the top of the page?

___ ___ **5.** wait until a point shapes up before you write it down?

___ ___ **6.** write each major point on a separate line and skip a line or two before writing another major point?

___ ___ **7.** set off details and examples by indenting them beneath the main point they go with?

___ ___ **8.** add quick sketches or diagrams whenever they can help illustrate a point or aid recall later on?

___ ___ **9.** invent your own abbreviations to save time?

___ ___ **10.** strive for brief yet complete notes?

___ ___ **11.** edit your notes for readability, clarity, and completeness as soon as possible after you take them, and then review your notes within 24 hours?

___ ___ **12.** review again within a week to strengthen your recall later on?

Circle items to which you answered *no* and consider ways to change or improve your note-taking skills.

Guidelines for Mapping

Another form of textbook note-taking is mapping. **Mapping** is an informal way of organizing main ideas and supporting details by using boxes, circles, lines, arrows, and the like. The idea is to show information in a way that clarifies relationships among ideas. Like outlining, mapping is done on separate paper rather than in the margins of the textbook.

One simple type of map consists of the topic or main idea in a circle or box in the middle of the sheet of paper, with supporting details, radiating out from it. Another type has the main idea in a large box at the top of the paper, with supporting ideas in smaller boxes below it and connected to it by arrows or "leader lines." If the information is sequential (for instance, significant events in World War I), a map can take the form of a flowchart. Samples of these kinds of maps are shown on page 599.

There is no one right way to do maps. They are personal records of information you want to understand and remember. However, research on study maps (which are also called *concept maps, learning maps,* and *idea maps*) indicates that using different colors helps many students remember the material. It also seems to help if key words are written in bold capital letters and if simple sketches are included. Finally, when you make a map, you may find it helps to turn the page sideways, since this gives you more room.

A study map for the passage on reactions of dying patients is shown on page 600. It condenses all the important information on a single page. A complete study map like this requires considerable thought and effort.

Since outlines and study maps both show relationships among important ideas in a passage, how can you decide which to use for a particular passage? Your decision will depend on how familiar you are with each technique, and on how the passage itself is written. Keep in mind that mapping is an informal study technique, whereas outlining can be formal or informal. When you are asked to prepare a formal outline in a college course, do not assume that you can substitute a study map.

TYPES OF MAPPING

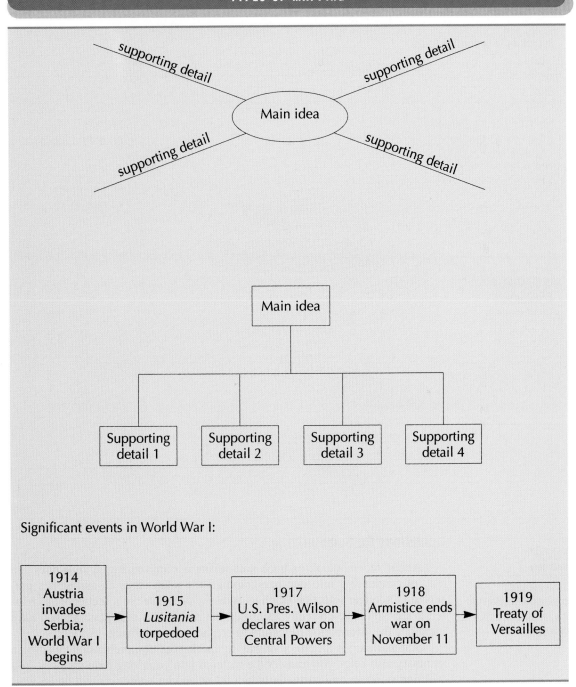

SAMPLE STUDY MAP

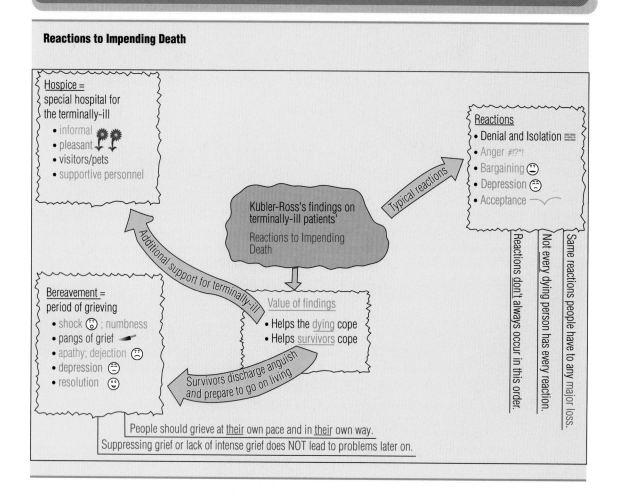

Reactions to Impending Death

Hospice =
special hospital for
the terminally-ill
 • informal
 • pleasant
 • visitors/pets
 • supportive personnel

Kübler-Ross's findings on
terminally-ill patients'
Reactions to Impending
Death

Additional support for terminally-ill

Typical reactions

Reactions
 • Denial and Isolation
 • Anger #!?*!
 • Bargaining
 • Depression
 • Acceptance

Reactions don't always occur in this order.

Not every dying person has every reaction.

Same reactions people have to any major loss.

Bereavement =
period of grieving
 • shock ; numbness
 • pangs of grief
 • apathy; dejection
 • depression
 • resolution

Value of findings
 • Helps the dying cope
 • Helps survivors cope

Survivors discharge anguish
and prepare to go on living

People should grieve at their own pace and in their own way.
Suppressing grief or lack of intense grief does NOT lead to problems later on.

KEY TERM
Summary

Single paragraph
condensation of all the main
ideas presented in a longer
passage.

Guidelines for Summarizing

A third technique of textbook note-taking is summarizing. A **summary** is a way of condensing into one paragraph all the main ideas an author has presented in a longer selection (such as an essay or article) or a section of a chapter. When you have correctly identified the main ideas in a passage, you have identified the information necessary to prepare your summary.

Summarizing is an effective way to check your comprehension. Writing a summary also helps you transfer the material into your long term memory. You will find summarizing particularly helpful when you know you will be answering essay questions on a test. Summarizing allows you to "rehearse" an answer you may have to write on the test.

Here are some things to keep in mind when you are preparing a summary:

- **Include all the main ideas.** You must include *all* the main ideas the author presents in the section. Include a supporting detail (such as the definition of an important term) if a main idea cannot be understood without it.
- **Do not add anything.** You must not add anything beyond the author's ideas (such as your own opinions).
- **Keep the original sequence.** Present the ideas in the same order that the author has used. In other words, you must keep the author's organization.
- **Reword as necessary, providing connections.** You must reword (paraphrase) the main ideas if necessary and supply clear connections among these ideas.
- **Give your summary a title.** Use the same title that appears in the original material. Do not entitle it "Summary."

The box below shows a sample summary for the passage on dying patients.

SAMPLE SUMMARY

Reactions to Impending Death

Elisabeth Kübler-Ross is a thanatologist whose research with terminally ill patients revealed that they tend to display several emotional reactions as they prepare for death. The five basic responses she found were *(1) denial and isolation, (2) anger, (3) bargaining, (4) depression, and (5) acceptance.* Different patients display different emotions. These may occur in various orders, although the general pattern is shock, denial, anger, and acceptance. Several factors influence a person's types and sequence of emotions. Overall, the individual's approach to dying reflects his or her approach to living. Emotions displayed by a dying person are the typical, appropriate ones that accompany any major loss. This information can be used to help dying persons and survivors cope with their emotional reactions. Most important, knowledge of these emotions can enable other to be supportive of dying people and help them discuss death and their feelings. The hospice, a hospital for the terminally ill, can enhance a dying person's last days. The ill person is offered emotional support and guidance from family as well as from other people. Life goes on more nearly as normal in this informal, pleasant environment. A period of bereavement (grieving) by survivors normally follows the death of the ill person. Grief also follows a pattern: *shock or numbness; pangs of grief; apathy, dejection, and depression; and resolution.* Survivor's reactions vary, but survivors are usually able to discharge their anguish by grieving, and thus prepare to go on living. Each person must grieve at his or her own pace and in his or her own way.

INTERPRETING GRAPHIC MATERIAL

Nearly every textbook contains graphic aids: tables, graphs (such as bar graphs, pie charts, and line graphs), time lines, diagrams, charts, maps, cartoons, photographs, flowcharts, and so forth. **Graphic aids** provide visual explanations of concepts and relationships in ways that are often more concise and easier to understand than words alone. For example, graphic aids can be used to illustrate numerical relationships (such as profits and losses), sequences (such as stages of cognitive development), processes (such as how a bill becomes a law), and spatial relationships (such as a floor plan). Writers include graphic aids precisely because they enable students to grasp and recall information more easily. When an author directs you to a graphic aid ("See Figure 1-3"), you should stop and look at it *at that very point,* and then resume reading. Authors mention graphic aids at the point where they think the graphic aids will help readers the most.

Although graphic aids contain important information, they can appear difficult unless you know how to interpret them. The following strategies will enable you to interpret graphic material more effectively and efficiently.

- Read the *title* and any *explanation* that accompanies the graphic aid. The title tells you what aspect of the writer's topic is being clarified or illustrated.

- Check the *source* of the information presented in the graphic aid to see if it seems current and reliable.

- Read all the *headings* in a table and all the *labels* that appear in a chart or a graph (such as those on the bottom and side of a graph) to determine what is being presented or measured. For example, the side of a bar graph may be labeled "Annual Income in Thousands of Dollars" and the bottom may be labeled "Level of Education."

- Examine the *units of measurement* in a graphic aid (for example, decades, percents, thousands of dollars, per hour, kilograms, per capita, milliseconds).

- Finally, use the information provided by the title and explanation (if any), the source, the headings and labels, and the units of measurement to help you determine the *important points or conclusions* that the author is conveying. Try to understand how the information in the graphic aid clarifies or exemplifies the written explanation. See if there are patterns or trends in the data that allow you to draw a general conclusion.

Here are explanations and examples of five commonly used graphic aids: bar graphs, line graphs, pie charts, flow charts, and tables. With bar graphs, line graphs and tables, look for trends. A *trend* is a steady, overall increase or decrease. Along with each graphic aid is a summary of its important elements as well as the conclusions that can be drawn from the graph.

Bar Graphs

A **bar graph** is a chart in which the length of parallel rectangular bars is used to indicate relative amounts of the items being compared. The bars in a bar graph may be vertical or horizontal. The bar graph here comes from a textbook on human development.

Title or explanation. Population of the United States aged 65 and over, 1900–2030 (projected).

Source. U.S. Bureau of the Census, 1992.

Headings and labels. Millions (of people), years (1900–2030; bar for 1990 differs from the other bars to indicate that figures beyond it are projections).

Units of measurement. Millions (increments of 10 million), years (20-year increments from 1900 to 1980; 10-year increments from 1980 to 2030), percents (of population aged 65 and over).

Important points or conclusions. Since the beginning of this century, the number of people aged 65 and over has continued to increase. This trend is expected to continue through the aging of the "baby boom" generation. The number of people 65 and over will more than double by 2030.

Population of the United States Aged 65 and Over
(*Source:* U.S. Bureau of the Census, 1992)

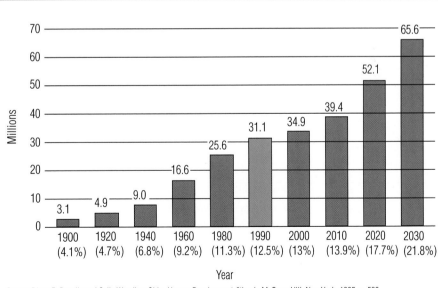

Source: Diane E. Papalia and Sally Wendkos Olds, *Human Development,* 6th ed., McGraw-Hill, New York, 1995, p. 528.

Percentage of the Labor Force in Various Sectors of the U.S. Economy.
(*Source:* U.S. Bureau of Labor Statistics)

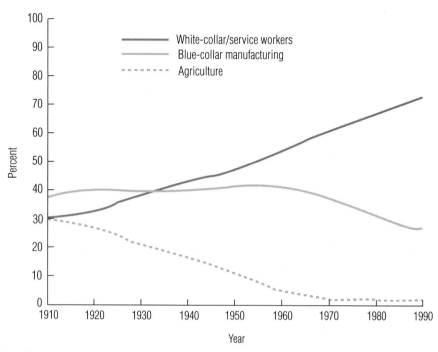

Source: Craig Calhoun, Donald Light, and Susanne Keller, *Sociology,* 6th ed., McGraw-Hill, New York, 1994, p. 420.

Line Graphs

A **line graph** is a diagram whose points are connected to show a relationship between two or more variables. There may be one line or several lines, depending on what the author wishes to convey.

Title or explanation. Percentage of the Labor Force in Various Sectors of the U.S. Economy, 1910–1990.

Source. Data from U.S. Bureau of Labor Statistics.

Headings and labels. Year, percent; Agriculture, Blue-collar manufacturing, White-collar/Service workers.

Units of measurement. Decades, percent in increments of ten.

Important points and conclusions. During this century there has been a sharp drop in agricultural work and manufacturing jobs, and a striking increase in white-collar/service jobs. These trends seem likely to continue. Therefore, Americans today need higher educational/training levels to enter and remain in the workforce.

People of Hispanic Origin in the United States
(*Source:* U.S. Dept. of Commerce and Bureau of the Census)

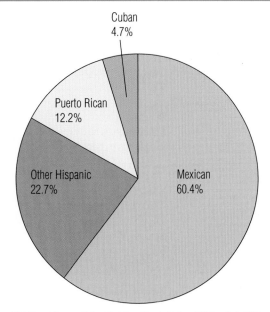

Source: Craig Calhoun, Donald Light, and Susanne Keller, *Sociology,* 6th ed., McGraw-Hill, New York, 1994, p. 64.

Pie Charts

A **pie chart,** as its name suggests, is a circle graph in which the sizes of the "slices" represent parts of the whole. Pie charts are a convenient way to show the relationship among component parts as well as the relationship of each part to the whole. The example here comes from a sociology textbook.

Title or explanation. People of Hispanic Origin in the United States.

Source. U.S. Department of Commerce, Bureau of the Census, Release CB91-216 (June 12, 1991).

Headings and labels. Mexican, Cuban, Puerto Rican, Other Hispanic.

Units of measurement. Percentage.

Important points and conclusions. The majority of people of Hispanic origin in the United States are of Mexican descent.

Flowcharts

A **flowchart** shows steps in procedures or processes by using boxes, circles, and other shapes that are connected with lines or arrows. The example here is from the *Dictionary of Cultural Literacy* and presents the legislative process (how a bill becomes a law).

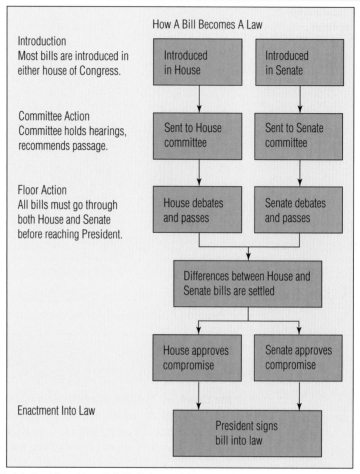

How A Bill Becomes A Law

Introduction
Most bills are introduced in either house of Congress.

Committee Action
Committee holds hearings, recommends passage.

Floor Action
All bills must go through both House and Senate before reaching President.

Enactment Into Law

Introduced in House → Introduced in Senate

Sent to House committee → Sent to Senate committee

House debates and passes → Senate debates and passes

Differences between House and Senate bills are settled

House approves compromise → Senate approves compromise

President signs bill into law

Source: E. D. Hirsch Jr., Joseph Kett, and James Trefil, *The Dictionary of Cultural Literacy,* Boston, Houghton-Mifflin, 1988, p. 319.

Title or explanation. How a Bill Becomes a Law.

Source. Hirsch, Kett and Trefil, *The Dictionary of Cultural Literacy,* 1988

Headings and labels. Introduction, Committee Action, Floor Action, Enactment into Law.

Units of measurement. None.

Important points and conclusions. Although bills can be introduced in either the House or the Senate, all bills must go through committee hearings and through floor action in both the House and Senate, before the bill is submitted to the president for enactment into law.

Tables

A **table** is a systematic listing of data in rows and columns. The example below, from a textbook on human development, presents data about how school-age children spend their time. (Textbook features, including tables, are discussed earlier in this chapter.)

Title or explanation. How School-Age Children Spend Their Time: Children's Top 10 Activities (Average Hours and Minutes Per Day).

Source. Adapted from Institute for Social Research, 1985.

Headings or labels. Activity, Weekdays/Weekends, Ages 6–8/Ages 9–11.

Units of measurement. Average Hours and Minutes per Day.

Important points and conclusions. Children spend about two-thirds of their time on necessary or required activities (sleeping, eating, school, personal care, housework, and religious observance). The two main things that children choose to do in their free time are playing and watching television. Both age groups watch more television on weekends, and amount of television watching increases with age.

TABLE 9-1

HOW SCHOOL-AGE CHILDREN SPEND THEIR TIME: CHILDREN'S TOP 10 ACTIVITIES, AVERAGE HOURS AND MINUTES PER DAY
(ADAPTED FROM INSTITUTE FOR SOCIAL RESEARCH, 1985)

Activity	Weekdays Ages 6–8	Ages 9–11	Weekends Ages 6–8	Ages 9–11
Sleeping	9.55	9.09	10:41	9:56
School	4:52	5:15	—	—
Television	1:39	2:26	2:16	3:05
Playing	1:51	1:05	3:00	1:32
Eating	1:21	1:13	1:20	1:18
Personal care	0:49	0:40	0:45	0:44
Household work	0:15	0:18	0:27	0:51
Sports	0:24	0:21	0:30	0:42
Religious observance	0:09	0:09	0:56	0:53
Visiting	0:15	0:10	0:08	0:13

Source: Diane E. Papalia and Sally Wendkos Olds, *Human Development,* 6th ed., McGraw-Hill, New York, 1995, p. 312.

INTERPRETING GRAPHIC AIDS EXERCISE

Directions: The source of the following four graphic aids is an advertising textbook. They pertain to computers and the Internet. Identify each type of graphic aid and answer the questions that follow.

Which activities do people take time from to spend time on the computer? (Note: Multiple responses accepted)

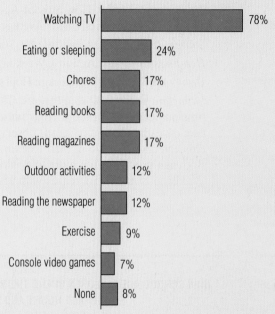

Activity	Percentage
Watching TV	78%
Eating or sleeping	24%
Chores	17%
Reading books	17%
Reading magazines	17%
Outdoor activities	12%
Reading the newspaper	12%
Exercise	9%
Console video games	7%
None	8%

Source: Arens, William F. *Contemporary Advertising,* 7th ed., Irwin/McGraw-Hill, Boston, 1999, p. 513.

1. What type of graphic aid is this? _____

2. What is the topic of this graphic aid?_____

3. Which is greater: the percentage of people who take time from watching TV to spend on the computer, or the total percentage of people who take time from reading books, magazines and newspapers?_____

_____

4. What important point or conclusion can be drawn about the activities people take time from to spend on the computer?

_____

_____

WHAT DO YOU DO WHEN YOU GO ONLINE?*

Activity	1997	1996
Gather news or information	87.8%	82.0%
Send e-mail	83.2	80.5
Conduct research	80.5	69.1
Surf various sites	75.3	66.9
Play games	33.7	23.8
Participate in chats	30.8	25.3
Post to bulletin boards	30.0	39.3
Shop	17.8	14.9

Notes: Respondents could choose more than one answer.
*Based on 584 U.S. residents who have been online in the past six months

Source: William F. Arens, *Contemporary Advertising,* 7th ed., Irwin/McGraw-Hill, Boston, 1999, p. 514.

5. What type of graphic aid is this?_____

6. What is the topic of this graphic aid?_____

7. What are the three column headings?_____

8. What is the only category of online activity that decreased between 1996 and 1997?_____

9. Of the top three online activities, in which category was there the greatest increase between 1996 and 1997? _____

_____

10. What important point or conclusion can be drawn about online activities between 1996 and 1997?_____

_____

_____

(Continued on next page)

(Continued from previous page)

Percentage of Total Sales on Online Product Mix in 2000

Note: Computer products, which total $2.1 billion, travel ($1.58 billion) and entertainment ($1.3 billion) will account for the lion's share.

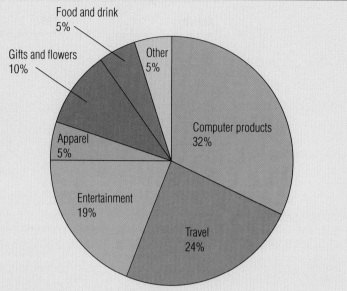

Source: William F. Arens, *Contemporary Advertising,* 7th ed., Irwin/McGraw-Hill, Boston, 1999, p. 512.

11. What type of graphic aid is this?_____

12. What is the topic of this graphic aid?_____

13. What category represents the third highest percentage of online sales?_____

14. Which is greater: online sales of food and drink or online sales of gifts and flowers? _____

15. What important point or conclusion can be drawn about types of online sales?_____

_____

_____

_____

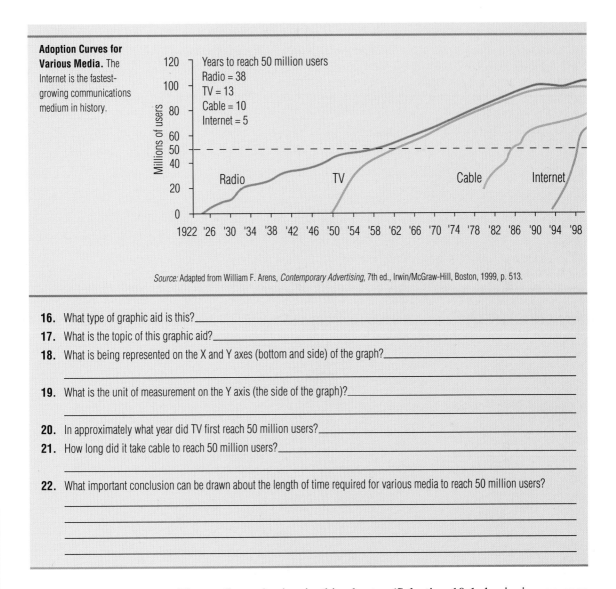

Adoption Curves for Various Media. The Internet is the fastest-growing communications medium in history.

Years to reach 50 million users
Radio = 38
TV = 13
Cable = 10
Internet = 5

Millions of users

Radio   TV   Cable   Internet

1922 '26 '30 '34 '38 '42 '46 '50 '54 '58 '62 '66 '70 '74 '78 '82 '86 '90 '94 '98

Source: Adapted from William F. Arens, *Contemporary Advertising,* 7th ed., Irwin/McGraw-Hill, Boston, 1999, p. 513.

16. What type of graphic aid is this?_____

17. What is the topic of this graphic aid?_____

18. What is being represented on the X and Y axes (bottom and side) of the graph?_____

_____

19. What is the unit of measurement on the Y axis (the side of the graph)?_____

_____

20. In approximately what year did TV first reach 50 million users?_____

21. How long did it take cable to reach 50 million users?_____

22. What important conclusion can be drawn about the length of time required for various media to reach 50 million users?

_____

_____

_____

_____

The reading selection in this chapter (Selection 10-1, beginning on page 617) is itself a complete chapter from a communications textbook. It will give you an opportunity to try out the study skills in Chapter 10, and it will also help you gain a realistic idea of how much time is needed to master a textbook chapter. Then, whenever a course involves mastering textbook information, you will know *how* to master it and will feel confident that you *can* master it.

DEVELOPING CHAPTER REVIEW CARDS

Review cards, or *summary cards,* are an excellent study tool. They are a way to select, organize, and review the most important information in a textbook chapter. The process of creating review cards helps you organize information in a meaningful way and, at the same time, transfer it into long-term memory. The cards can also be used to prepare for tests (see Chapter 11). The review card activities in this book give you structured practice in creating these valuable study tools. Once you have learned how to make review cards, you can create them for textbook material in your other courses.

Now, complete the seven review cards for Chapter 10 by supplying the important information about each topic. When you have completed them, you will have summarized important information about the skills in this chapter.

Three Keys to Studying College Textbooks

1. _____

2. _____

3. _____

Card 1   **Chapter 10: Selecting and Organizing Textbook Information**

Underlining and Highlighting Textbook Material

Card 2   **Chapter 10: Selecting and Organizing Textbook Information**

Annotating Textbooks

Card 3   **Chapter 10: Selecting and Organizing Textbook Information**

Outlining

Card 4   **Chapter 10: Selecting and Organizing Textbook Information**

Mapping

Card 5   **Chapter 10: Selecting and Organizing Textbook Information**

Summarizing Textbook Information

Card 6   **Chapter 10: Selecting and Organizing Textbook Information**

Interpreting Graphic Material

Card 7   **Chapter 10: Selecting and Organizing Textbook Information**

SELECTION **10-1**

**Speech
Communications**

INTERCULTURAL COMMUNICATION

From *Human Communication*
By Stewart L. Tubbs and Sylvia Moss

Prepare Yourself to Read

Directions: Do these exercises *before* you read Selection 10-1.

1. First, read and think about the title. What do you already know about the media in intercultural communication?

_____

_____

2. Next, complete your chapter preview by reading the following:

> Chapter objectives
> Section headings
> First sentence of each paragraph
> Words in **boldface** or *italic*
> Illustrations and their legends
> Chapter summary
> Review questions

On the basis of your preview, what aspects of intercultural communication does this chapter seem to be about?

_____

_____

Apply Comprehension Skills

Directions: Do these exercises as you read Selection 10-1.

• Budget your time for reading this selection. It has four sections. If you wish, divide the selection into shorter reading sessions.
• As you read, apply the skills of selectivity and organization you have learned in this chapter. To remember essential information, underline, highlight, annotate, and take notes.

*I*ntercultural Communication

CHAPTER OBJECTIVES

After reading this chapter, you should be able to:

1 Discuss how cultural groups differ from other groups with shared characteristics, and define "intercultural communication."

2 State three broad communication principles that have important implications for intercultural communication.

3 Identify and explain at least three ways in which language can interfere with communication between cultures.

4 Explain how nonverbal messages, including those that express emotion, vary from culture to culture and can be misinterpreted.

5 Describe how cultural roles and norms, including norms about conflict, affect intercultural communication.

6 Discuss the effects of differences in beliefs and values on people from different cultures.

7 Explain the concept of ethnocentrism and discuss two reasons for stereotyping of groups.

8 Describe some of the personal, political and social effects of intercultural communication.

9 Identify seven principles that would promote community building.

Source: Stewart L. Tubbs and Sylvia Moss, *Human Communication*, 7th ed., McGraw-Hill, New York, 1994, pp. 419–447 (Chap. 13). Reproduced with permission of McGraw-Hill. New York. (For additional sources, see page 646.)

*T*he 1965 revision of U.S. immigration policies is changing the character of some of our major cities. For example, during the last two decades over a million immigrants have come to New York City, most of them from the West Indies, Latin America, and Asia (Foner, 1987, p. 1). Today the other new leading immigrant city is Los Angeles, and other cities receiving large numbers of immigrants include Chicago, Houston, Miami, and San Francisco (p. 4). In *The Middleman and Other Stories* (1988), Bharati Mukherjee portrays some of these new immigrants "trying on their new American selves, shouldering into their new country." She is writing, she explains, of "the eagerness and enthusiasm and confidence with which the new immigrants chase the American dream. But sometimes they get the American codes wrong, by being too aggressive, for example" (quoted in Healy, 1988, p. 22).

When members of different cultures communicate, getting the codes wrong is a common experience. Throughout this book we have discussed cultural differences in connection with many aspects of communication. As we have seen, intercultural communication can occur in any of the contexts we have discussed in the past few chapters, from intimate two-person communication to formal organizational and mass communication. Whenever intercultural communication occurs, the differences in the participants' frames of reference make the task of communication more complicated and more difficult, especially since participants may not be aware of all aspects of each others' cultures. In fact, one reason intercultural communication has fascinated scholars in the past few years is that it reveals aspects of our own communication behavior that we might not otherwise notice as distinct, such as our attitude toward time.

From another perspective, adjustment to a foreign culture often includes experiences of *culture shock:* "feelings of helplessness, withdrawal, paranoia, irritability, and a desire for a home" (Koester, 1984, p. 251). To compound the problem, readjustment to one's home culture after an experience in another culture produces a shock of its own: *reverse culture shock*. This may result from changes in attitudes, ways of interacting, and the like. In fact, those of us who are most adaptable to the foreign culture will probably experience the greatest *unanticipated* reentry shock (Koester, 1984).

Over 20 million people from outside the United States visit each year, and during 1991 to 1992, the number of foreign students attending colleges and universities in the United States was 419,585. The five leading countries from which these students came were China, Japan, Taiwan, India, and the Republic of South Korea (Zikopoulos, 1992). As the amount of intercultural communication we engage in increases, it becomes more important for each of us to understand some of its problems and implications.

A DEFINITION OF CULTURE

In Chapter 1 we defined **intercultural communication** as *communication between members of different cultures (whether defined in terms of racial, ethnic,*

Intercultural communication can be enriching, yet barriers to intercultural communication can sometimes lead to misunderstandings.

or socioeconomic differences). As this definition suggests, the divisions between cultural groups are not established or absolute; we may choose one or more of a variety of characteristics to identify a group of people as having a common culture. We may, for instance, speak of natives of California, Nebraska, and New Hampshire as being from different regional cultures (West Coast, Midwest, and New England); we may identify each of them as a member of an urban or rural culture, or as a member of a Jewish or Irish culture; we may speak of them all as members of a broader Western culture. Although scholars disagree as to which of these designations may properly be said to be a cultural group, to a certain extent all of them are.

Culture is *a way of life developed and shared by a group of people and passed down from generation to generation.* It is made up of many complex elements, including religious and political systems, customs, and language as well as tools, clothing, buildings, and works of art. The way you dress, your relationships with your parents and friends, what you expect of a marriage and of a job, the food you eat, the language you speak are all profoundly affected by your culture. This does not mean that you think, believe, and act exactly as everyone else in your cultural group. Not all members of a culture share all its elements. Moreover, a culture will change and evolve over time. Still, a common set of characteristics is shared by the group at large and can be traced, even through great changes, over many generations.

Culture As Learned

A popular cartoon that appeared during a period when many Americans were adopting Vietnamese War orphans depicted a woman announcing to her husband that the daughter they had adopted as a Vietnamese infant had spoken her first words that day. "English or Vietnamese?" he asked. Language, like culture, is so much a part of us that we tend to think of it as genetically transmitted, like the more physiological characteristics of race and nationality. As we attempt to communicate with people from other cultures and reconcile our differences, it is important that we remember culture is *learned*.

Because culture is learned, not innate, an infant born in Vietnam of Vietnamese parents but brought to the United States and raised as an American will be culturally an American. Because culture is learned, it also changes as people come into contact with one another or as their experiences change their needs. *The Covenant,* a novel by James Michener, describes how various cultural groups in South Africa changed as they came in contact with one another. Influenced by the demands of the new world and by their contact with the tribes who were there before them, the early Dutch settlers and their descendants became a separate cultural group, distinct in their way of living and speaking, from the Dutch in the homeland they had left behind them.

Some of the reasons people have so many problems communicating across cultural boundaries is suggested in this definition of culture:

> A culture is a complex of values polarized by an image containing a vision of its own excellence. Such a "tyrannizing image" takes diverse forms in various cultures such as "rugged individualism" in America, an individual's "harmony with nature" in Japan, and "collective obedience" in China. A culture's tyrannizing image provides its members with a guide to appropriate behavior and posits a super-sensible world of meaning and values from which even its most humble members can borrow to give a sense of dignity and coherence to their lives. (Cushman and Cahn, 1985, p. 119)

In a sense, then, it is the culture that provides a coherent framework for organizing our activity and allowing us to predict the behavior of others. People from other cultures who enter our own way may be threatening because they challenge our system of beliefs. In the same way, we ourselves may become threatening to others as we enter a foreign culture and challenge the cultural foundations of their beliefs.

Distinctions among Cultures

Differences between two cultural groups range from the slight to the very dramatic. The culture of the Yanomami people, a Stone Age tribe in Brazil, has little in common with the highly industrialized cultures of Japan or the United States. Many Americans, with their heritage of sympathy for union organization and antipathy toward big business, are amazed at such Japanese work customs as employees' beginning the day by singing a company song and the expectation that employees will stay with one company for life.

In recent years many Europeans and Americans have been shocked by the continuing Islamic death threat against novelist Salman Rushdie because of his novel *Satanic Verses.* The book outraged followers of Islam, who considered it blasphemous. Rushdie, a British subject, has lived in hiding since 1989.

Radical differences among cultures usually occur when there has been little exchange between them or, in some cases, with other cultures in general. What distinguishes one cultural group from another, however, is not always so evident. A New Yorker and a Californian will have cultural differences and similarities. Both may celebrate Thanksgiving and the Fourth of July with much the same sense of tradition associated with those holidays. On a day-to-day basis, however, they are likely to eat somewhat different foods, although probably with the same kind of utensils. They are likely to speak the same language but with different accents and a few different words or phrases. Both will speak more or less the same language as people who have always lived in England and Ontario, and they may even share many of the same values, but cultural differences are likely to become more evident as the Americans, Canadians, and British communicate with one another. Similarly, differences among cultures do not occur abruptly at regional or national borders but gradually, over a range (Samovar and Porter, 1991*a*).

MEANS OF INTERCULTURAL COMMUNICATION

Because of the technological innovations of the last two decades, writes Gergen, "contemporary life is a swirling sea of social relationships" (1991, p. 61). In that sea we must place the growing number of intercultural relationships. A dramatic increase in intercultural communication has come about primarily through high-tech developments in both aviation and electronic communication networks.

Consider first the extraordinary rise in our use of air transportation. Once an experience for the privileged few, international air travel is now routine and accessible to millions. We vacation in foreign capitals, we attend professional conferences and trade fairs, we fly to business meetings. Students in high school as well as college participate in study-abroad programs. Members of the scientific community attend international conferences on medical and environmental issues. Tourist groups from Europe and Asia are a common sight in large American cities.

We have come to take for granted the use of telephone, radio, newspaper, books, wireless services, and network television. Now satellite technology has brought the immediacy of political events into our homes—whether it be in the unprecedented coverage of the Gulf War by CNN or in the televised images of Bosnia's suffering people. As we saw in Chapter 12, the expansion of a vast electronic communications network has linked peoples of the world many times over. And the technologies of computers, electronic mail, teleconferencing, and fax, we are told, are only the beginning.

New technology is creating many opportunities for intercultural communication.

OBSTACLES TO INTERCULTURAL COMMUNICATION

Although modern means of travel and communication have brought us into contact with virtually the whole world, the technical capacity to transmit and receive messages is not, in itself, enough to allow people who have vastly different cultures to communicate with one another. Dramatic improvements in the technological means of communication have in many instances outstripped our abilities to communicate effectively with people who have different languages, different beliefs and values, and different expectations of relationships. Repeatedly, interaction between people of different cultures has created far more misunderstanding than understanding.

Of the many principles used by theorists to describe the communication process, several clearly apply to intercultural exchanges. The first is *a shared code system*, which of course will have *two aspects—verbal and nonverbal*. Sarbaugh (1979) argues that without such a shared system, communication will be impossible. There will be degrees of difference, but the *less* a code system is shared, the *less* communication is possible.

In his work anthropologist Edward Hall makes the distinction between high- and low-context cultures (1976). We can think of them along a continuum as, for example, in Figure 13.1. High- and low-context cultures have several important differences in the way information is coded. Members of **high-context cultures** are more skilled in reading nonverbal behaviors "and in reading the environment"; and they assume that other people will also be able to do so. Thus they speak less than members of low-context cultures; and in general their communication tends to be indirect and less explicit. **Low-context cultures** on the other hand, stress direct and explicit communication: "verbal messages are extremely important . . . and the information to be shared is coded in the verbal message" (Samovar and Porter, 1991*b*, pp. 234–235; Gudykunst and Kim, 1992, pp. 44–45).

Among members of high-context cultures are the Chinese, Korean, and Japanese. Notice our own position in Figure 13.1—within the low-context end of the spectrum, yet not at the very bottom. In comparing Americans with

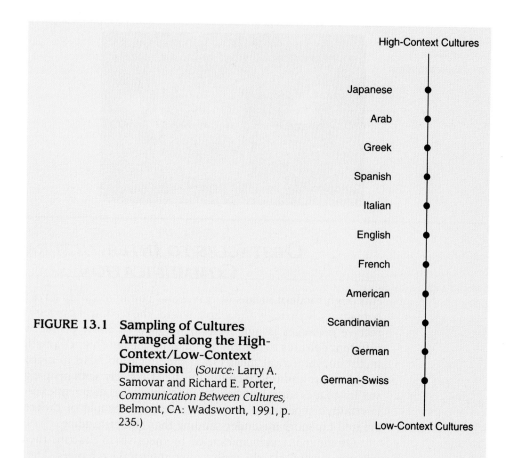

FIGURE 13.1   **Sampling of Cultures Arranged along the High-Context/Low-Context Dimension**   (*Source:* Larry A. Samovar and Richard E. Porter, *Communication Between Cultures,* Belmont, CA: Wadsworth, 1991, p. 235.)

Malays and Japanese, Althen offers a clear example of the high-context/low-context dimension:

> Americans focus on the words people use to convey their ideas, information and feelings. They are generally quite unskilled in "reading" other people's non-verbal messages. "Oh, you Americans!" said an exasperated Japanese woman who was being pressed to express some details about an unpleasant situation, "You have to say everything!" (Althen, 1992, p. 416)

Second, different *beliefs and behaviors* between communicators establish the basis for different assumptions from which to respond. In fact, our own beliefs and behaviors influence our perceptions of what other people do. Thus two people of different cultures can easily attribute different meanings to the same behavior. If this happens, the two behave differently with neither being able to predict the other's response. Yet as we saw in Chapter 7, predictions are an integral part of being able to communicate effectively. Writing of his trip to East Africa, American essayist Edward Hoagland described how Gabriel, who was from the Sudan, served him a drink:

> Gabriel explained that it was his duty as a host to make me want to share with him whatever he had. I suggested that it was foolish for us to argue about the nature of hospitality in our two countries. . . . This sufficed for a while, but because I was not drinking my share of the sherry he became agitated again that I was not participating in the ritual of being his guest. I didn't know whether the way he knitted his forehead was from a host's unease, from empathy with my discomfort with . . . [my] headache, or from real twinges of a kind of pain of his own. (1979, p. 213)

A third principle discussed by Sarbaugh that has important implications for intercultural communication is the *level of knowing and accepting the beliefs and behaviors of others*. Notice that there are two components: knowledge and acceptance. It isn't so much the catalogue of differences—that is, the knowledge of such differences—that creates a problem. It's also the level of your acceptance. For example, writing about a tribe of African hunters called the Ik, anthropologist Colin Turnbull tried to come to terms with his own feelings of repulsion. The Ik, he knew, were uprooted hunters and the violent way they now lived—stealing each other's food, killing, and so on—could be explained by the fact that their entire society had been uprooted. Turnbull *knew* a great deal about the beliefs and behaviors of the Ik, but he could not *accept* the people of that culture. As an anthropologist, however, he still brings to his perceptions a certain objectivity—simply in declaring his responses.

The degree to which we judge a culture by our own cultural values and refuse to consider other cultural norms will determine how likely it is that effective communication takes place. At one extreme, we have participants in a transaction who both know and accept the beliefs and behaviors of others; at the other, we have those who neither know nor accept. And in this instance the probability of a breakdown in communication is extremely high (Sarbaugh, 1979).

Adopting a shared code system, acknowledging differences in beliefs and behaviors, and learning to be tolerant of the beliefs and behaviors of others all contribute to effective communication.

American anthropologist Mary Catherine Bateson tells of visiting her husband's family in Beirut on her honeymoon and being frustrated because, although she spoke to them in Armenian, her in-laws kept responding in English:

> Then, on the fourth or fifth day of our visit, his mother set out to make *chee kufta,* a dish in which finely ground lamb is kneaded at length with bulgur wheat, parsley, and onions until the raw meat simply disappears into the wheat. It's one of those dishes, shaped by their mother's hands, that sons go home to eat. Greatly daring, I went into the kitchen and

took over the kneading. After that day, my in-laws began to answer me in Armenian, the handling of the meat and grain and the sharing of what I had prepared having transformed me into a different person. . . . (1990, p. 126)

Verbal Messages

The European Community's translation service in Brussels recently held an exhibition of signs that had been translated into English with some hilarious results including "Please leave your values at the front desk" (from a Paris hotel) and "Our wines leave you nothing to hope for" (this from a Swiss restaurant) (Goldsmith, 1992, B1). On a personal level, learning a foreign language improperly, even if just a few words are involved, can create immediate difficulties. For example, a Japanese businessman who was transferred to the United States explained his frustration in trying to find affordable housing; he kept asking about renting a "mansion," the word he had been taught instead of "apartment."

Language differences can go much deeper than simple translation ambiguities, however. Have you ever asked someone to translate a word from another language to you, only to have him say "Well, it doesn't translate into English exactly, but it means something like . . ."? As we saw in our discussion of the Whorf hypothesis in Chapter 3, languages differ more than strict word-for-word translations often indicate because the people who speak the languages have different needs.

Even when we can manage to translate from one language to another with literal accuracy, the deeper meanings are often lost because they are rooted in the culture of the language. Consider the following description of how the failure to understand the deeper meanings of words may interfere with communication between people who do not share a culture:

There may be no better example to illustrate cultural mistranslation than the word *Red*. To Westerners "the Reds" conjures up images of blood, fire, fierceness, e.g., *red with anger, . . . seeing red*, but the Russian translation *krasnyi* has a different aura. For example, to a Russian

krasnyi = beautiful
pryekrasnyi = exquisite
krasnaya ryiba = fine fish (e.g., salmon)
krasnoye zoloto = pure gold ("red" gold)
krasna devitza = beautiful girl

Rather than *Red*, a far, far better symbolic translation of this word into English is *Golden*, as in a *Golden opportunity, . . . The Golden Age*, etc.

No doubt a Russian might translate this word back into Russian to mean "the color of money!" . . .

I was once highly embarrassed when using our common term *Red Indian* (American Indian, in British usage) to an American audience, some of whom took it to refer to an Indian communist. Colors are no more translatable than words. (Cherry, 1971, pp. 16–17)

Literal translations from one language to another often create misunderstandings because they do not account for culture-based linguistic styles. The elaborate style used in Arabic with its rhetoric of exaggeration, compliment, and multiple extended metaphors is puzzling to those unfamiliar with it. Even a yes-or-no answer can be misconstrued:

An Arab feels compelled to overassert in almost all types of communication because others expect him to. If an Arab says exactly what he means without the expected assertion, other Arabs may still think that he means the opposite. For example, a simple "No" by a guest to a host's request to eat or drink more will not suffice. To convey the meaning that he is actually full, the guest must keep repeating "No" several times coupling it with an oath such as "By God" or "I swear to God." (cited in Gudykunst and Ting-Toomey, 1992, p. 227)

You can also get an inkling from this of how an Arab might interpret a single succinct "No" from someone speaking in English.

A grasp of the subtleties in language style is particularly important in matters of diplomacy. For example, Sir Hamilton Gibb of Oxford University suggests that "the medium in which the aesthetic feeling of the Arabs is mainly . . . expressed is that of word and language—the most seductive, it may be, and certainly the most unstable and even dangerous of all the arts" (cited in Kaplan, 1992, p. 41). In general, many career diplomats feel that our embassies need more foreign service officers proficient in foreign languages—particularly Arabic (p. 61).

When two cultures vary widely in their perceptions of how language functions in communication—and certainly this is true of high- and low-context cultures—there may even be differences in how the very act of *asking* a question is evaluated. For example, the person asking a question may think it necessary and innocuous; the person being asked may be offended and even avoid telling the truth. In Japanese business transactions, for example,

one avoids the direct question unless the questioner is absolutely certain that the answer will not embarrass the Japanese businessman in any way whatsoever. In Japan for one to admit being unable to perform a given operation or measure up to a given standard means a bitter loss of face. Given a foreigner so stupid, ignorant, or insensitive to ask an embarrassing question, the Japanese is likely to choose what appears to him the lesser of two evils. (Hall and Whyte, in Mortensen, 1979)

Nonverbal Messages

Kurt Vonnegut, in his novel *Jailbird*, describes a woman attempting to interview a refugee of undetermined national origin. She tries a number of languages, looking for one they might have in common, and as she changes from one language to another, she changes her gestures as well.

Nonverbal communication systems vary from culture to culture just as verbal systems do, but we often overlook the symbolic nature of nonverbal systems. Many American travelers abroad have been embarrassed when they discovered that the two-fingered gesture they use to mean "Give me two" is assigned a different, obscene meaning in many countries. They have also been mistaken when they assumed that a nod always means yes. In some countries, a nod means "no"; in others a nod, or yes, simply indicates that a person understood the question. In this country, the gesture for "okay" is made by forming a circle with the thumb and forefinger while the other fingers are held up. But in France this gesture means "you're worthless," and in Greece it's a vulgar sexual invitation (Ekman et al., 1984).

Confusion in nonverbal indicators may be much more complex. In Chapter 4 we considered some of the different ways that cultures regard such nonverbal factors as the use of time and space. As we discussed then, we rely on nonverbal cues to give us information about the meaning we are to assign to a verbal message. Because we often interpret these nonverbal cues unconsciously, the message received is often very different from the one the speaker intended.

As we noted in Chapter 4, vocal cues such as volume are used differently in different cultures. In the Arab countries, men are expected to speak loudly to indicate strength and sincerity, at a volume that Americans consider "aggressive, objectionable, and obnoxious." A Saudi Arab may also lower his voice to indicate respect to a superior. In an exchange between an American and an Arab, the confusion of signals is likely to be disastrous. If the Arab speaks softly to indicate respect, the American is likely to raise his voice, because in *his* culture, one asks another person to speak more loudly by raising one's own voice. The Arab, thinking the American is suggesting that he is not being respectful enough, will lower his voice even more. The American responds by raising his voice again, and the cycle continues until the American is shouting and the Arab is no longer audible. "They are not likely to part with much respect for one another" (Hall and Whyte, in Mortensen, 1979, pp. 408–409).

The expression of emotion is also regulated by culture. For example, a gesture that Americans often misunderstand is the Japanese smile, cultivated for use as a social duty in order to appear happy and refrain from burdening friends with one's unhappiness. There are several cross-cultural studies of attitudes toward the display of emotion. For example, one study of people in England, Italy, Japan, and Hong Kong (Argyle et al., 1986) found that the Italians and the English allow more expressions of distress and anger than the Japanese. In fact, another study found that Japanese children are slower than North American children to identify anger—probably because "Japanese are socialized from an early age to avoid the expression of emotions like anger" (Gudykunst and Ting-Toomey, 1988a, p. 386). Moreover, it seems that in some cultures the display of emotions is limited to emotions that are "positive" and do not disturb group harmony (p. 396).

One aspect of a shared code system that contributes to the smooth flow of conversation and ultimately to understanding is **synchrony,** *the sharing of rhythms* (Gudykunst and Kim, 1992; Douglis, 1987). When people speak, they develop a rhythm, a dancelike beat that emphasizes and organizes meaning during conversation—a phenomenon to be observed between family members, friends, and lovers—even business associates. It is during a beat or stress that a speaker will often reveal important information or introduce a new topic into the conversation. It seems that timing in conversation can be affected even by a few microseconds and speakers who stay in sync not only have better understanding but a better relationship.

This rhythmic pattern is also seen in the nonverbal behavior that accompanies conversation: Speaking patterns are accented by nonverbal gestures and movements that follow the beat. But when two people are from different cultures or linguistic backgrounds, even their expectations for speech rhythms and nonverbal behaviors may be vastly different. Consciousness about synchrony also seems to vary from culture to culture. Hall has found people from Northern Europe and North America less aware of such rhythms than people from Asia, Latin America, and Africa:

> The fact that synchronized rhythmic movements are based on the "hidden dimensions" of nonverbal behavior might explain why people in African and Latin American cultures (as high-context nonverbal cultures) are more in tune and display more sensitivity toward the synchronization process than people in low-context verbal cultures, such as those in Northern Europe and the United States. (Gudykunst and Ting-Toomey, 1992, p. 281)

Relationships: Norms and Roles

Cultures also vary in the contexts in which verbal and nonverbal systems are used. When we think of making friends with a foreign student or of working with people abroad in business situations, it is important to remember that personal and working relationships are not the same and do not develop the same way in every culture. People in different cultures expect different behaviors from one another in a relationship. One culture's friendly gesture might be considered aggressive or impertinent in another culture, for example, while a gesture of respect or deference might be interpreted as inappropriate reticence or as defiance, depending on the cultural context.

Norms

Norms, as we discussed in Chapter 7, are *established rules of what is accepted and appropriate behavior.* Although we often use these rules as if they are absolute or instinctive standards, they are actually culturally developed and transmitted. If you grew up in the United States, for instance, you were probably taught to "speak up" clearly and to look at a person who is speaking to you, and that mumbling and looking away when someone addresses you is disrespectful. These norms would seem natural and logical to you, but not all cultural groups interpret these behaviors as good manners. We have already seen that people in some cultures drop their voices as an indication of respect and deference. White American police officers patrolling Hispanic neighborhoods have often misinterpreted a similar gesture: Hispanic children are taught to lower their eyes, as a gesture of respect, when a person in authority addresses them. The police, who had been brought up with opposite norms, interpreted the gesture as sullen and resentful, and reacted accordingly.

"A smile is the same in any language," is a saying that was popular a few years ago and that still shows up occasionally. In fact, though, a smile and related attempts to be friendly are interpreted in cultural contexts. An American student's smile of greeting to a non-Western student might be interpreted as superficial, sexually suggestive, or even rude; the American student, in turn, is likely to interpret the other's failure to return the smile as unfriendly or even hostile (Samovar and Porter, 1991a, pp. 346–347).

Understanding **conflict norms** becomes particularly important when a disagreement seems to be brewing between two people from different cultures. Sillars and Weisberg (1987) identify at least two important variables that distinguish how members of a given culture view interpersonal and family conflicts: (1) expressivity, and (2) privacy and individuality.

Even in this country there is considerable cultural variation in the amount of emphasis placed on **expressive communication** about conflict. Studies have shown that "North American and Black American males may regard deep personal feelings as too personal to express openly"; that Jews frequently value discussion and analysis so highly that by "mainstream" standards they may seem argumentative; that Irish families in family therapy dealt with conflicts through allusion, sarcasm, and innuendo rather than engage in verbal confrontations. In each instance we see a set of assumptions about what constitutes conflict and how it should be negotiated or resolved—or perhaps ignored.

One reason we cannot apply the expressive norms of mainstream America to other groups is that so many cultures place far less value on individual self-disclosures. Talking about feelings and being open about one's dissatisfactions—even with a member of your family, for example—is not always considered appropriate behavior, and many of the suggestions for resolving conflict mentioned in Chapter 6 would be difficult to apply to intercultural contexts. In fact, in many cultures keeping problems to oneself is strongly favored, and a stoic attitude often develops. For example, in working-class families, problems are frequently regarded as "lying outside the family and within the realm of natural economic, social, and biological conditions that are futile for the family to address. Thus [family members] may adopt a passive problem-solving style that emphasizes family cohesion over active problem solving" (p. 159).

The direct expression of conflict is also considered inappropriate in cultures that deemphasize explicit verbal coding of information and pay more attention to subtle cues and indirect messages. In such cultures, discretion and indirectness are the norms for dealing with conflict, and they of course are upheld and understood by members. This is true, as we have seen, of the Chinese and Japanese (Chapter 6). So while we might perceive the indirect treatment of conflict as cowardly, members of another type of culture might view our more confrontational approach as lacking in taste (Gudykunst and Ting-Toomey, 1988*b*, p. 160).

Cultural norms about **privacy and individuality** are equally variable. In the two-person and familial relationships of mainstream America, a great deal of autonomy is expected—especially among the middle class. Thus during a conflict, advice from friends and others outside the immediate family may be looked upon as an infringement of privacy. They are certainly not expected to intervene. In extended families, however, there is a more public aspect of relationships: "Because extended networks promote communal and traditional norms, there are more definite guidelines for resolving conflicts" (p. 161). There are even times when conflicts are settled not through personal communication but through the intervention of a third party. In Japan this is sometimes the case.

According to Sillars and Weisberg's survey of research, emphasis on cooperation, affiliation, and dependence is stressed by such groups as Africans, Native Americans, Asians, West Indians, Japanese, Mexicans, Mormons, and Catholics. Their norms dictate that some conflicts will be minimized or even solved indirectly for the good of the group. For example, in the tribal meetings of Native Americans or native Alaskans, it is expected that the individual will put group goals before personal ones and reach consensus (pp. 160–162). Sometimes the mainstream American ideal of agreeing to disagree becomes "an impractical and even undesirable goal" (p. 162).

Roles

Roles, as we discussed in Chapter 7, are *sets of norms that apply to specific groups of people in a society.* Roles, too, vary markedly among cultures. Differences in the respective roles of men and women may represent some of the most apparent cultural differences in human relationships: how unmarried couples should behave and whether they should be chaperoned, how men and women should behave toward each other in business situations, what a husband's and wife's responsibilities are to one another and to their respective families.

Researchers from several disciplines acknowledge that dual-culture marriage is different from a marriage in which both partners share a common culture. For example, there are cultural differences in decision-making power and self-disclosure patterns, and there is general agreement that there is less use of self-disclosure among northern Europeans than among people from Mediterranean cultures. "Perhaps," writes Rohrlich, "what is lacking is a set of Johari windows . . . which graphically depict the amount of open, blind, hidden and unknown areas of disclosure representative of cultures" (1988, p. 41). The author stresses that to marry someone from another culture is, in effect, marrying that culture. When one spouse fails to communicate interest or assumes that the other is not attached to his or her culture, there may be serious problems. In this view, an awareness of cultural differences must precede the development of appreciation and sensitivity: "The cultural difference is what makes the fabric of the marriage more varied, interesting, and richer" (p. 42).

Many other roles are dictated culturally. For example, the director of a conversant program (a program in which foreign students learning English were matched with native-speaking American students for informal practice in the language) at a major U.S. university routinely cautioned American women students not to meet their male Algerian conversants alone in their homes because their (the Americans') intentions would be misconstrued.

Many international students who come to this country for graduate study support themselves with jobs as teaching assistants. In interviews with graduate students (TAs) from England, Thailand, Japan, and China, Ross and Krider (1992) found how different their expectations are about the roles of teacher and student and about procedures in the classroom. For example, the assistants were not prepared for the degree of verbal interaction between student and teacher that takes place in the American classroom. Although all thought this to be positive, some felt challenged. One teaching student said:

> I felt that sometimes with their comments, I was being made fun of and not taken seriously. . . . I always felt like they were trying to test my knowledge base with all their questions. (p. 284)

Accustomed to far greater formality in the university, assistants were also surprised to see students eating and drinking during class though some seem to have grown accustomed to the practice.

Beliefs and Values

Even if you've never traveled outside of the United States, you have heard stories about how American politicians and presidents have inadvertently insulted Polish or Latin American audiences when trying to speak to their audiences in the unfamiliar languages. Movies and television shows provide a glimpse of many ways of life, including the roles and norms of Hawaiian-American, Asian, Native American, and numerous other cultures. Although the portrayals are not always accurate, they help to give us a sense of some cultural differences.

It is much more difficult to comprehend and accept the values of another culture when they differ from our own. More than any other aspect of the culture taught us from birth, our values seem to be universal absolutes. Values determine what we think is right, good, important, beautiful; we find it difficult to accept that what is right or good is as relative to culture as the word for "book" or "stove," or as the way our food is prepared or our clothes are made. It may be difficult for a Westerner to adjust to the combinations or seasonings of an unfamiliar Middle Eastern or Asian cuisine. It is even more difficult to accept that some cultures eat plants or animals that we do not classify as food, and still more difficult to understand why, in the face of mass starvation in India, cattle wander the streets unrestrained, protected by religious taboos. People of other cultures, meanwhile, may be appalled at Americans' willingness to eat meat, or at the casualness with which we often have meals "on the run," without ceremony.

Nonetheless, living in another country over a long period of time sometimes leads to changes in value systems—particularly when people do not remain insulated within their own cultural group. In a recent study DiMartino (1991) examined the effect of culture on moral values—specifically, through the interpretation of moral and conventional dilemmas. Her subjects, Sicilian-American men and women, had all come to the United States as young adults. She found that the women relied more on reasoning and used more moral than conventional adjectives in their interpretations whereas Sicilian-American men seemed to "retain the thinking patterns acquired as children in Sicily" (p. 318). DiMartino explains that while the men seemed to have stayed within a "cultural cocoon," spending all their leisure and work time with other Sicilian Americans, their wives—because of their involvement with children and community—negotiated two different social systems and thus had to develop other values and moral standards (p. 318). In fact, these women often complained "that their husbands were too conservative and too tied to the 'old' ways" (p. 318).

Other recent cross-cultural research suggests that sometimes our system of beliefs and values can improve our ability to adapt to living in another country. A study of Tibetan refugees who resettled in India shows that they have been extremely successful in adjusting to their new environment and have made many economic and social gains. Mahmoudi (1992) found that Tibetan views and institutions concerning religion, government, economics, and education were critical to their adjustment. Most important, it seems, was the sense of community engendered by Tibetan religious beliefs:

> Mahayana Buddhism provides the Tibetans not only with a design for living but also with a rather positive, industrious, pragmatic, and balanced view of life. . . .
>
> [For the Tibetans] actions promote life affirmation based on the good deeds performed by the individual and the community. The Tibetan Buddhism worldview promotes a "can do" attitude with a healthy dose of cheerfulness. (p. 23)

Mahmoudi believes that Tibetans can provide a model for other international refugee populations.

BARRIERS TO INTERCULTURAL UNDERSTANDING

We cannot learn another language by simply memorizing its vocabulary and grammatical structures. A language is a complex system, intricately related to culture, and it cannot be mastered by simple substitutions. Nor can we master a culture by memorizing a list of symbols, norms, and values, even if it were possible to memorize all of them. The meaning of "red" and "gold," the proper amount of time to devote to a business transaction, the appropriate way to behave toward a person in authority—these are not isolated factors; they are all part of the intricate pattern of a culture (Hall, 1959, pp. 99–105). Learning aspects of a given culture, therefore, will not allow you to understand that culture in the same way you understand your own.

The book *Blue Collar Worker,* by John Coleman (1974), illustrates some of the difficulties of understanding another culture. Coleman, a university president, spent some months working at a number of menial jobs, including collecting garbage, digging ditches, and working in a restaurant kitchen. Although the jobs and his contact with the people he worked with (none of whom knew he was a university president) taught him a great deal about the way of life of an unskilled worker, his understanding was ultimately very limited. He lived on his wages from his blue-collar jobs, but his salaries from the university and from the companies on whose boards he served supported his family, paid his children's tuitions, and met his insurance payments; as a result, he had no firsthand experience of living on an unskilled worker's pay. He learned how a garbage collector is supposed to act and how his supervisors, coworkers, and the people whose garbage he collected behaved toward him, but the roles he played ultimately had little effect on his self-concept because when his leave from the university ran out, he would go back to his job as university president. In many ways, Coleman was never "really" a blue-collar worker.

If you have spent summers in an unskilled job in a restaurant or factory, you may have noticed that the summer-employed college students and the more regular, full-time employees tend to form separate groups at lunchtime and after work. Although both groups of people hold similar jobs at the same place, they generally feel they have little in common. If you are returning to school after some years of working in or outside your home, you may feel quite isolated from the younger students around you, at least at first. You probably feel that you have very different ways of life outside of class, different roles in your families, different ways of spending your leisure time, and different expectations of your education. Not all these differences are necessarily cultural, but in both cases, the groups of people are divided by more than a collection of differences; their entire ways of life are different.

The more diverse two cultures are, the wider the division between their people, and the less they can come to really understand one another. Coleman's blue-collar coworkers shared, in most cases, Coleman's language, many of his social and political values, and the same national heritage, yet Coleman could never understand what it was to be a blue-collar worker. The division between cultural groups who have less contact with one another is likely to be greater and even more difficult to reconcile. As much as a native United States citizen of non-Asian heritage may study Korean culture, for example, he or she can never really understand what it is to be brought up in that culture.

Ethnocentrism

We are not aware of the many aspects of our culture that distinguish it from others; in fact, many of the aspects of communication and culture discussed in this book came to be recognized not through the direct study of communication but through the study of other cultures. Culture, as Hall (1976) describes it, "can be understood only by painstaking or detailed analysis." As a result, a person tends to regard his or her own culture "as though it were innate. He is forced into the position of thinking and feeling that anyone whose behavior is not predictable or is peculiar in any way is slightly out of his mind, improperly brought up, irresponsible, psychopathic, politically motivated to a point beyond all reason, or just plain inferior" (p. 38).

The tendency to judge the values, customs, behaviors, or other aspects of another culture *"using our own group and our own customs as the standards for all judgments"* is **ethnocentrism**. Because culture is unconscious, it may be inevitable that we regard "our own groups, our own country, our own culture as the best, as the most moral" (Samovar and Porter, 1991*a*). Psychologist Roger Brown (1986) puts it another way: "It is not just the seeming universality of ethnocentrism that makes us think it ineradicable but rather that it has been traced to its source in individual psychology, and the source is the individual effort to achieve and maintain positive self-esteem. That is an urge so deeply human that we can hardly imagine its absence" (p. 534).

An Australian-born historian recalls her visit to England after graduating from the University of Sydney and writes of weekend visits with her English hosts:

> They could not have been kinder, but I resented their air of superiority toward Australians. . . . I came to wait for the ultimate compliment which could be counted on by Sunday breakfast. I knew the confidential smile and the inclination of the head would be followed by "You know, my dear, one would hardly know you were not English." I couldn't control the irritation produced by such accolades, and would usually begin by telling preposterous stories about life in the outback to emphasize how different I was. (Conway, 1990, p. 206)

In a recent study of intercultural anxiety, Stephan and Stephan (1992) looked at a group of American college students who had been in Morocco on a four-day visit. One finding was that students who tested high in ethnocentrism tended to have a higher level of anxiety. The researchers used these six statements to measure ethnocentrism, asking students to rate each response on a ten-point scale from strongly disagree to strongly agree:

1. Americans have been very generous in teaching other people how to do things in more efficient ways.

2. English should be accepted as the international language of communication.

3. Primitive people have unsophisticated social and political systems.

4. The fact that America was able to put a man on the moon is evidence of America's technological superiority.

5. Minority groups within a country should conform to the customs and values of the majority.

6. In many countries people do not place a high value on human life—to them, life is cheap. (Adapted from p. 93)

It seems that, to some degree, every group teaches its members to be ethnocentric.

Hall (1976) believes that ethnocentrism complicates intercultural communication even when both parties in the interaction attempt to keep open minds:

> Theoretically, there should be no problem when people of different cultures meet. Things begin, most frequently, not only with friendship and good will on both sides, but there is an intellectual understanding that each party has a different set of beliefs, customs, mores, values, or what-have-you. The trouble begins when people start working together, even on a superficial basis. Frequently, even after years of close association, neither can make the other's system work! . . . Without knowing it, they experience the other person as an uncontrollable and unpredictable part of themselves. (p. 210)

Stereotyping

As discussed in Chapter 2, we tend to impose stereotypes on groups of people, which limits our communication with those groups. It is almost impossible for us *not* to stereotype a group of people with whom we have no personal contact; furthermore, without personal contact, it is almost impossible for us to dispel the stereotypes we acquire about the group. We saw in

Chapter 2 that stereotypes are inadequate because they are generalizations based on limited experience. Certainly, the sources of our information about people of different cultures are often inaccurate. For example, Driessen (1992) writes about the stereotyping of people from Mediterranean cultures:

> The stereotype of the excessively gesticulating Spaniard linked to his spontaneous, emotional, quick-tempered and high-spirited disposition . . . persists in the images of Spain created by the tourist industry but also surfaces in recent ethnographies. (p. 242)

Gumpert and Cathcart (1984) identify our main source of information about foreigners as television. According to their finding, the stereotyped images from the media even influence our face-to-face interaction with people of other cultures. Along with French and Japanese teams, the two researchers conducted a cross-cultural study of television stereotyping of American, French, and Japanese people.

Recently, content analyses (Dominick, 1993) show that Arab men tend to be presented on television by one of three negative stereotypes:

> (1) terrorists (although only a miniscule amount of real Arabs fit this category, it is prevalent in the media); (2) oil sheik (not too many fit in here either); and Bedouin desert nomad (only 5 percent of Arabs in real life are Bedouin). (p. 515)

Theorists emphasize that in addition to creating expectations about how people will behave, stereotypes often set in motion self-fulfilling prophecies because we act on information we believe to be true (Hamilton et al., 1992). This is especially the case in intercultural communication, where our information about others tends to be so limited.

EFFECTS OF INTERCULTURAL COMMUNICATION

Effects on the Individual

Although intercultural communication increasingly affects the world we live in, most scholars agree that the obstacles to intercultural communication and understanding will probably always mean that little of that communication will occur at a personal level. Travel is easier and more feasible economically than it was for our parents and grandparents, for example, but few people travel extensively enough to have much personal acquaintance with people of other cultures.

Even within our own country we tend to stay within our own groups and subgroups. Today the needs and desires of people of many groups to affirm and preserve their cultures are reflected in demands for more bilingual education, multicultural programs and curriculums, and textbooks that better represent all cultural contributions to our literature and history. Among the swelling immigrant population in this country's largest cities we find ethnic groups clustering in their own neighborhoods. New York, for example, has its Russian, Korean, and Indian sections, as in "Little Bombay," a densely packed area with row on row of stores stocking Indian spices, saris, videos, newspapers—every imaginable evidence of this thriving culture.

For anyone who reads books and newspapers, who watches television and is concerned with international events, the world has grown larger. The mass media have brought us images of Chinese students demonstrating in Tiananmen Square, the events leading up to the dismantling of the Soviet Union, and a starving Somalian population. We can no longer escape knowledge of world hunger or turn away from the impact of international events.

Although it is often assumed that international understanding increases as a result of cultural and educational exchanges over an extended period of time, scholars believe that this hoped-for goal must be demonstrated empirically. Thus there have been several studies of student exchange programs. For example, Rohrlich and Martin (1991) studied the adjustment of U.S. college students to studying abroad as well as their readjustment to returning home; they found women to be more satisfied than men upon returning, perhaps because their life-style at home was more independent than when living with a host family (pp. 178–179). Another investigation (Carlson and Widaman, 1988) compared 450 students from the University of California who spent their junior year studying at a European university (Sweden, Spain, France, the Federal Republic of Germany, Italy, and the United Kingdom were the countries involved) with students who remained on campus during the junior year. At the end of the school year, the study-abroad group had higher levels of cross-cultural interest, international political concern, and cultural cosmopolitanism. And when compared with students who remained at home, students who studied abroad also reported significantly more positive and more critical attitudes toward their own country (p. 14)—a finding consistent with earlier research. So relatively long-term study abroad may contribute to more favorable attitudes and increased international understanding, but there is still much to be learned about how such attitudes develop.

Social and Political Effects

We are no longer limited to being members of our own small community; we are citizens of the world as well, affected by political, economic, and social changes.

Communications, banking, and manufacturing have become increasingly international. Companies that deal in many commodities usually have offices, factories, and distributors in several countries or all over the world. As a result, the economies of the world's nations have become more and more intertwined, and the goods available in the nations that trade freely are drawn from the world at large. American companies have built plants and oil wells and in doing so created jobs in other countries. Similarly, companies from many parts of the world have created jobs for people in the United States. There have been multinational manufacturing efforts, and consortiums involving goods and services of every kind. Airbus Industrie, for example, is a consortium made up of the English, the French, the Germans, the Spanish, and the Dutch. Now, that joint venture may be extended to include the United States—and perhaps other international partners: In 1993 Boeing and Airbus agreed to explore the possibility of building an 800 passenger "superjumbo" airliner.

Not all the implications of an international economy are positive, however. When Iraq invaded Kuwait in 1990, for instance, there was much concern that the world's oil would be restricted and increasingly subject to Iraq's political actions. Economic problems in many areas of the world have resulted in repeated incidents of racial and ethnic conflict. Following several years of

No amount of information we read about intercultural communication can substitute for face-to-face encounters with people of other cultures and backgrounds.

recession and widespread unemployment, U.S. attitudes toward Japan have become extremely negative with Japan bashing characterized by one writer as "the national sport" (Krauthammer, 1992), and in the last few years a number of books have been published that many critics feel demonize the Japanese.

Yet our interdependence is clear. The United Nations, one of the most famous international organizations, is far more than a forum for political debate. Like many other international agencies, it deals actively with "the mechanics of living," such as the needs for food, health care, and education in many countries. International organizations also work on behalf of international refugees who, according to U.N. statistics, number between 15 and 20 million. Some international organizations provide such services as literacy training, education in such areas as modern agricultural methods, and help in organizing the local craft production into profitable cottage industries that market their goods beyond the immediate community. These services help to increase productivity and raise standards of living.

Cultural Effects

From the earliest times, cultures have been affected by contact with one another. Traders and the Mongol invasions once brought gunpowder, macaroni, and other Asian goods from Asia to Europe; later, immigrants brought these and other goods and customs to the United States. The Norman invasion of England in the eleventh century permanently affected the English language, not only from contact with the French language but because French became the language of the aristocracy and English the language of the peasants. European explorers brought horses to Native Americans, Native Americans taught early settlers how to grow corn and tobacco, and those settlers and their descendants drove the Native Americans westward. These are only a few examples of how trade, war, conquest, and migration have affected cultures throughout history.

As intercultural communication becomes more common and widespread, the effects of cultural contact are more pronounced and rapid. These are evident in the increased availability of goods that once would have been available, if at all, only to the very rich: tea from India, coffee from Brazil, woolen cloth from Britain, wine from France and Italy. It is also apparent in the spread of Western technology, health care methods, and Hilton Hotels in the "underdeveloped" nations, and the spread of Japanese industry and business methods in the United States.

Most people would not question the value of some aspects of cultural exchange, such as the introduction of sanitation methods that curb epidemics, or agricultural methods that save thousands from starvation. But many, including a number of scholars of culture, question the value of other aspects of cultural exchange. They ask whether certain so-called Stone Age and aboriginal communities that have been isolated for hundreds of years truly benefit from sudden contact with the outside world—whether, for example, exposure to war as well as sources of illness and pollution might outweigh what we consider the "advances" of civilization. The possibilities raise many ethical questions.

Intercultural exchange leads to **cultural homogenization,** *the tendency for cultures in contact with one another to become increasingly similar to one another.* Cultural homogenization implies that some aspects of one culture will dominate and eliminate the corresponding aspects of the other. The "standard American" voices we hear on television, for instance, are responsible for a standard American dialect and the disparagement of nonstandard dialects spoken by people who live in specific regions of the country. As a result of mass communication and travel, columnist Ellen Goodman notes, "We dress alike, we eat alike, and I guess we are destined to sound alike" (1981).

But even if we are familiar with foods from all over the world and blue jeans are as popular in Russia as in the United States, emphasis today is increasingly on our diversity. It is *differences* that have become the issue in conflicts not only between racial and ethnic groups in our own country but in those of other countries. Robert Jay Lifton, a psychiatrist who has written on the holocaust, believes that our discomfort at seeing televised images of human suffering can be a catalyst for change by evoking empathy and compassion:

> The evidence is there, on the screens, and in millions of human minds. Televised images can change the world.
>
> As survivors by proxy, can our witness be transformed into life-enhancing action—in Bosnia in this case, but also in other areas of death and suffering such as the famine in Somalia? (1992, p. 24)

Given enough understanding of regional as well as national cultures, it is possible to preserve individual differences of many kinds and allow members of various subcultures or groups to coexist and flourish. Indeed, Gudykunst and Kim maintain that "cultural and ethnic diversity are necessary for community to exist" (1992, p. 255); and they propose seven principles for building community, principles for which each of us must be responsible:

1. *Be committed.* We must be committed to the principle of building community in our lives, as well as to the individuals with whom we are trying to develop community.

2. *Be mindful.* Think about what we do and say. Focus on the process, not the outcome.

3. *Be unconditionally accepting.* Accept others as they are; do not try to change or control them. . . . Value diversity and do not judge others based only on their diversity.

4. *Be concerned for both ourselves and others.* Avoid polarized communication and engage in dialogue whenever possible. Consult others on issues that affect them and be open to their ideas.

5. *Be understanding.* Recognize how culture and ethnicity affect the way we think and behave. Search for commonalities. . . . Balance emotion, anxiety, and fear with reason.

6. *Be ethical.* Engage in behavior that is not a means to an end but behavior that is morally right in and of itself.

7. *Be peaceful.* Do not be violent or deceitful, breach valid promises, or be secretive. Strive for harmony. (Adapted from pp. 267–268)

SUMMARY

In this chapter, we discussed intercultural communication, which has become increasingly prevalent in the last few decades. We defined "culture" as the way of life developed and shared by a people and passed down from generation to generation. Because cultures vary along a range, the differences between two cultures may be slight or very dramatic. Even when two cultural groups are very similar, however, the differences between them are likely to become more evident in intercultural communication.

Intercultural communication has increased rapidly because of technological advances that have made long-distance communication more feasible and more available to the general public. Despite the advances in the means of sending and receiving messages, however, there are still many obstacles to intercultural communication. Differences in cultural factors such as language, nonverbal communication systems, relational roles and norms (particularly conflict norms), and beliefs and values that are deeply rooted in the whole cultural system often lead to intercultural misunderstanding.

Because we are not aware of the aspects of our own cultures in ourselves, the barriers to intercultural communication are complex and formidable. Ethnocentrism and stereotyping both limit our ability to deal with people beyond our own communities.

REVIEW QUESTIONS

1. Explain the difference between culture shock and reverse culture shock.

2. How do cultural groups differ from other groups that have shared characteristics?

3. Why is it important for effective intercultural communication to understand that culture is learned, rather than innate?

4. Why do cultures vary along a range, rather than being clearly distinct from one another?

5. What are the two major reasons that intercultural communication has increased in the last decades?

6. State three communication principles with significant implications for intercultural communication.

7. Identify at least three aspects of culture.

8. Explain the major difference between high-context and low-context cultures.

9. Explain at least three ways in which language is an obstacle to intercultural communication.

10. Describe at least three aspects of nonverbal communication that vary from culture to culture.

11. How can cultural roles and norms affect communication between cultures?

12. What are two variables that influence how members of a culture view conflict. Give an example of each.

13. Explain how differences in beliefs and values can prove to be obstacles in intercultural communication.

14. What is ethnocentrism? Why does it interfere with intercultural communication? Give an example.

15. Give two reasons for the stereotyping of cultural groups.

16. Identify several personal, political, and social effects of intercultural communication.

17. What is meant by "cultural homogenization"?

18. Explain the need for community building and state seven principles that have been proposed.

EXERCISES

1. Make a list of some of the cultural groups in your own region or state, including the group (or groups) that founded your community. To what extent have these groups been in contact with one another? To what extent

have they remained distinct from one another? List some ways in which these cultural groups have affected your own culture, such as your traditions, religious beliefs, and language.

2. Find three current articles about a cultural group, such as a group in Japan or Saudi Arabia, that has recently come into extended business or diplomatic contact with the United States. List at least five ways in which that culture, or that of the United States, has been affected by this contact.

3. List at least eight cultures, both inside and outside the United States, with which you communicate in some way (through personal contact, your work or business communication, or mass media). With which of these groups is your communication personal? With which is it institutional? In at least one case in which your contact with the other culture is primarily institutional, describe some ways in which your understanding of the people in that group is limited by your communication with them.

4. Think of a group of people that you feel have specific, shared, cultural characteristics, for example, Californians, southerners, New Yorkers, blacks, whites, Amish, Japanese, Russians, Chinese. Describe the people as a group, and list the characteristics that you think distinguish that group from others. To what extent is your description a stereotype? What is the source of your information about the group? Can you think of some reasons why your stereotype might be inaccurate? Can you think of some ways in which it might affect your communication with individual members of that group?

5. Listen to a national newscaster report the news on television. Do you think that such newscasters' use of language has affected the way you speak? Do you think their use of language affects what you consider to be good English? Why?

SUGGESTED READINGS

Baldwin, James. "Stranger in the Village." In *The Price of the Ticket*. By James Baldwin. New York: St. Martin's, 1985.

This is a moving essay on the experience of a black American who comes to live in an isolated European village.

Barnlund, Dean C. *Communicative Styles of Japanese and Americans: Images and Realities*. Belmont, CA: Wadsworth, 1989.

A comparative study that is thorough and clear-sighted. The author examines many stereotypical notions about the Japanese and the Americans.

Carroll, Raymonde. *Cultural Misunderstandings.* Translated by Carol Volk. Chicago: University of Chicago Press, 1988.

The author, who is French, has written a fascinating analysis of many of the cultural differences between the French and the Americans that generate so much misunderstanding on both sides.

Cushman, Donald P., and **Dudley D. Cahn, Jr.** *Communication in Interpersonal Relationships.* Albany, NY: SUNY Press, 1985.

An excellent book for the advanced student. There are good summaries of intercultural material in Chapter 8, "Cultural Communication and Interpersonal Relationships," and Chapter 9, "Cross-cultural Communication and Interpersonal Relationships."

Foner, Nancy, ed. *New Immigrants in New York.* New York: Columbia University Press, 1987.

This collection of essays by scholars from several disciplines examines the influence of New York City on its new immigrants as well as their influence on city life.

Gudykunst, William B., and **Young Yun Kim.** *Communicating with Strangers: An Approach to Intercultural Communication.* 2d ed. New York: McGraw-Hill, 1992.

The authors approach this excellent introduction to intercultural communication by providing students with a solid grounding in theoretical issues. Building community through diversity is the subject of the final chapter.

Gudykunst, William B., and **Young Yun Kim,** eds. *Readings on Communicating with Strangers: An Approach to Intercultural Communication.* New York: McGraw-Hill, 1992.

These readings have been selected to illustrate concepts across cultures or ethnic groups. The editors have an interdisciplinary focus which makes the book an invaluable resource.

Hall, Edward T. *Beyond Culture.* Garden City, NY: Doubleday, 1976.

The author of this book, an anthropologist, is an important researcher in cultural aspects and differences and in their affects on intercultural communication in business and diplomacy.

Hall, Edward T. *The Silent Language.* New York: Doubleday, Anchor, 1973.

This is one of the earliest books on nonverbal communication and its relationship to culture. The author describes a number of aspects of culture, such as the use of time and space, and discusses their implications for intercultural communication.

Kaplan, Robert. "Tales from the Bazaar." *The Atlantic,* 270 (August 1992): 37–61.

A fascinating report on Arabists, U.S. diplomats in the Middle East, and the long-term effects of their immersion in Arab culture.

Samovar, Larry A., and **Richard E. Porter,** eds. *Intercultural Communication: A Reader.* 6th ed. Belmont, CA: Wadsworth, 1991.

An outstanding collection of readings. Coverage is comprehensive and timely.

Additional sources: Photo, p. 620, Gary Conner/Index Stock; photo, p. 623, Peter Turnley/Corbis; Figure 13-1, p. 624, used by permission; photo, p. 639, Gloria Karlson/Index Stock.

SELECTION **10-1**

Speech Communications

Collaboration Option

Comprehension Quiz: Textbook Chapter

Directions: Refer to Selection 10-1 as necessary to complete the following activities.

Options for collaboration: For some of these exercises, your instructor may prefer that you work collaboratively, that is, with other students. These exercises are identified in the margin. *If your instructor directs you to work collaboratively on any of these items,* form groups of three or four classmates to complete the exercise together. Discuss your answers with each other and have one member of the group record the answers. A member of the group may be asked to share the group's answers with the class.

1. Complete an outline or study map for *one* of these subsections in Selection 10-1.

   "A Definition of Culture" (pages 619–622)

   "Obstacles to Intercultural/Communication" (623–634)

   "Barriers to Intercultural Understanding" (634–637)

   "Effects of Intercultural Communication" (637–642)

   Note: Your instructor will give you specific instructions about this assignment.

2. Your instructor will distribute one or more quizzes on Selection 10-1. Use the materials you have prepared to study for it. You will be allowed to use your outlines or maps.

Read More about It on the World Wide Web

To learn more about the topic of this selection, visit these websites or use your favorite search engine (such as Yahoo ®). Whenever you go to *any* website, it is a good idea to evaluate it critically. Are you getting good information—information that is accurate, complete, and up-to-date? Who sponsors the website? How easy is it to use the features of the website?

http://www.webofculture.com

As the global economy continues to grow and our communications with neighbors worldwide become more frequent and flexible, there is an even greater need to understand other cultures. The Web of Culture *seeks to inform business professionals about cross-cultural communications. If you are planning to conduct business with foreign counterparts, the* Web of Culture *website should be your first stop.*

http://www.webofculture.com/refs/gestures.html

The same gestures can have different meanings in different countries. At this website you can examine "body etiquette" in the nations of the world on a country-by-country basis.

http://www.webofculture.com/refs/languages.html

Language is inherent in our cultural upbringing. This website includes charts of the languages spoken in each country, foreign dictionaries for travelers, and a foreign language resource center.

http://www.nmci.org/

NMCI's *mission is to increase communication, understanding, and respect among people of different racial, ethnic, and cultural backgrounds, and to provide a forum for discussion of the critical issues of multiculturalism facing our society.*

© PhotoDisc

C H A P T E R

11

Rehearsing Textbook Information and Preparing for Tests

In this chapter you will learn the answers to these questions:

- Why is rehearsal important to memory?

- What are important guidelines for test preparation?

- What is the five-day test review plan?

- How can I use review cards to prepare for a test?

- How can I consolidate important information on test review sheets?

649

SKILLS

Rehearsal and Memory

Studying for Tests

- General Guidelines

- Five-Day Test Review Plan

- Using Review Cards to Prepare for a Test

- Using Test Review Sheets

CREATING YOUR SUMMARY

Developing Chapter Review Cards

READING

Selection 11-1 *(Psychology)*
"Communication" from *Social Psychology*
by James A. Wiggins, Beverly B. Wiggins, and
James Vander Zanden

Little strokes fell great oaks.

Benjamin Franklin, *Poor Richard's Almanack,* 1750

No great thing is created suddenly.

Epictetus

REHEARSAL AND MEMORY

As you may have discovered, it is difficult to memorize information that you do not understand. This is why you must focus on understanding material before attempting to memorize it. Thorough comprehension enables you to memorize more efficiently.

Even when you understand material, however, you should not underestimate the time or effort needed to memorize it. To do well on tests, you must study information effectively enough to store it in **long-term memory,** or permanent memory. One serious mistake students make is leaving too little study time before the test to transfer material into long-term memory. Instead, they try to rely on **short-term memory.** However, as the term implies, material remains in short-term memory only temporarily. If you rely only on short-term memory (this kind of studying is called cramming), the information you need may not be there later when you try to recall it on a test.

To understand the difference between long-term and short-term memory, consider a telephone number that you have just heard on the radio. The number is only in your short-term memory and will be forgotten in a matter of minutes or even seconds *unless you do something to transfer it into long-term memory.* In other words, you will forget the number unless you "rehearse" it in some way.

Rehearsal refers to taking specific steps to transfer information into long-term memory. Typical steps include writing information down and repeatedly reciting it aloud. In the example above, for instance, rehearsing the telephone number would probably involve writing it, saying it aloud several times, or both. Consider how much information you already have stored in long-term memory: the alphabet; the multiplication tables; names of thousands of people, places, and things; meanings and spellings of thousands of words. You have successfully stored these in your long-term memory because you rehearsed them again and again.

As noted in Chapter 10, rehearsal is the third key to effective studying. When you are preparing for a test, you should study over several days, enough days to enable you to transfer information from short-term memory into long-term memory. Psychologists who study how people learn emphasize that both sufficient time and ample repetition are needed to accomplish this transfer.

Before you can rehearse the information in a textbook chapter efficiently, you need to *organize* it. Obviously, the better you organize material, the more efficiently you will be able to memorize it. If you organize the material in your assignments consistently as you study, right from the beginning of the semester,

KEY TERM
Long-term Memory

Permanent memory.

KEY TERM
Short-term Memory

Temporary memory.

KEY TERM
Rehearsal

Steps taken to transfer information into long-term memory; techniques include saying the information aloud and writing it down.

651

Effective rehearsal requires taking specific steps in order to transfer information into long-term memory. *(SuperStock)*

you will be prepared to rehearse and memorize material for each test. You can organize material by using any of these techniques:

- Underlining and annotating textbook material
- Outlining or mapping information
- Preparing summaries
- Making review cards
- Making test review sheets

Underlining, annotating, outlining, mapping, and summarizing are discussed in Chapter 10; review cards and sheets are discussed below. The very act of preparing these study tools helps you store information in long-term memory.

After you have organized material, you should *rehearse* by doing one or more of the following:

- Reciting from review cards
- Reciting from test review sheets
- Reciting from your notes
- Writing out information from memory

Too often, students try to review for a test simply by rereading their notes and their textbook over and over again. But rereading is a time-consuming process and does not automatically result in remembering. It has been estimated that 80 percent of the time spent studying for a test should be used for memorizing, that is, for transferring information into long-term memory. Here is an example of how you could apply this "80 percent rule." If you need 5 hours to study for a test, you should spend the first hour organizing the material and getting help with, or clarification of, things you do not understand. The remaining 4 hours would be spent rehearsing the material in order to memorize it.

You may be wondering, "How can I tell when I have successfully transferred information into long-term memory?" The way to find out is to test yourself. Try to write the information from memory on a blank sheet of paper. If material is in your long-term memory, you will be able to recall it and write it down. If you cannot write it, or if you are able to write only a part of it, then not all of the information is in your long-term memory yet; you need to rehearse it further.

These steps may sound like a lot of work, but they are necessary if you want to lock information into long-term memory. It is precisely this type of study effort that leads to mastery.

STUDYING FOR TESTS

General Guidelines

This chapter presents a five-day test review plan, but the day to begin studying for a test is actually the first day of the semester! That means taking good notes, reading every assignment, reviewing regularly, and attending all classes. The review plan described here is designed to complement your careful day-to-day preparation. No review plan can replace or make up for inadequate daily studying and preparation. Following are a few more points you should be aware of before you examine the review plan itself.

First, one reason for starting to review several days ahead of time is that the amount of material covered is too much to learn at the last minute. In fact, in college you are typically given new material right up to the day of a test.

Second, it is appropriate to ask your instructor what type of test will be given and what will be included on it. Usually, instructors are willing to give a fairly complete description of tests. Don't miss the opportunity to ask questions about a test. For example, you might ask:

- Will the test be based on textbook material, on class material (lectures, demonstrations, etc.), or on both?
- How many textbook chapters will the test cover?
- What will be the format of the test (multiple-choice questions, essay questions, etc.)?
- How many questions will be asked?
- Should certain topics be emphasized in studying?

Third, be realistic about "test anxiety," or "freezing up," when you take a test. Students often complain that they "go blank" on tests, but what really happens is that they discover during the test that they did not rehearse and learn the material well enough. They did not actually forget; after all, a person cannot forget something he or she never knew. Good daily preparation and an effective test review plan are the best ways to prevent test anxiety. Knowing what to expect on a test can also leave you feeling calmer, and this is another reason for asking questions about tests, as noted above.

KEY TERM
Distributed Practice

Study sessions that are spaced out over time; a more efficient study method than massed practice.

Fourth, research studies have found that **distributed practice** is more effective than *massed practice*. This simply means that studying and reviewing sessions which are spaced out over time are more effective than a single session done all at once. Above, *cramming* was described as trying to rely on short-term memory when you should be putting the information into long-term memory. It can also be thought of as massed rather than distributed practice. Frantic last-minute cramming usually results in faulty understanding, poor recall, increased anxiety, and lower grades.

Fifth, to study and review efficiently, you must be rested. Cramming typically involves going without sleep, but staying up late or all night can do more harm than good. Late-night or all-night cramming overtires you, increases stress, and contributes to test anxiety. Cramming forces you to rely on short-term memory, which can fail under the pressure of fatigue and stress. Try to get at least 8 hours of sleep the night before a test. On the day of the test, eat a good breakfast: for example, fruit or juice, whole-grain cereal or bread, yogurt, eggs, or low-fat milk. (It is especially important to get enough protein.) Don't rely on caffeine; avoid sugary, salty, or fatty foods. Getting enough rest and eating a nourishing breakfast will give you sustained energy and help you concentrate and think clearly.

A final word: Your attitude toward tests can make a big difference. Students often see tests as negative and threatening—even as punishment. Instead, try to think of a test as a learning experience. Try also to consider it an opportunity to demonstrate to yourself and your instructor how much you have learned. Remember that a test can tell you what you understand and how well you understand it. When you get a test back from an instructor, don't look at just the grade. Study the test carefully to see what you missed and why. A test also gives you an opportunity to evaluate the effectiveness of your test preparation techniques.

Five-Day Test Review Plan

Here is a detailed description of an effective five-day plan for preparing for a test. Although you may need more than five days, that is the least amount of time you should allow.

Five Days before the Test

Get an overview of all the material that will be on the test. This includes text material, class notes, handouts, etc. Identify important main ideas and details and prepare review cards and one or more test review sheets for the material to be covered. (Such cards and sheets summarize all the important points you expect to encounter on the test. You will learn to construct review cards and test review sheets later in this chapter.) You might also have a study guide that accompanies your textbook, or perhaps your instructor has given you a special review guide. In any case, try to anticipate questions that may be asked on the test. This is also the time to identify questions and problem areas you need further help on. By starting five days ahead, you will have allowed yourself enough time to get any help you need. You will have time to ask the instructor or a classmate, or to get help from a tutor. Plan to spend at least 2 hours studying. Take a 5- to 10-minute break after each hour.

Four Days before the Test

Briefly overview all the material that will be covered on the test; then review and rehearse the first third of the material in detail. First review all the material on your review cards and your test review sheet or sheets. Then, as you carefully study the first third of the material, use rehearsal techniques to memorize it and test yourself on it: that is, write and recite. Remember that you want to transfer the material into long-term (permanent) memory. Write the information; recite the information; test yourself by taking a blank sheet of paper and writing from memory what you have learned. Plan to spend at least 2 hours studying. If there are problem areas, get extra help or clarification from a tutor, a classmate, or your instructor.

Three Days before the Test

After a brief overview of all the material, review and rehearse the second third of the material in detail. Use the rehearsal techniques of writing and reciting to memorize and test yourself on the material. Plan to spend at least 2 hours studying. If any problem areas still remain, this is the time to clear them up. If you still don't understand, make another attempt at getting some additional help.

Two Days before the Test

After a brief overview of all the material, review and rehearse the last third of the material in detail. Use the rehearsal techniques of writing and reciting to memorize and test yourself on the material. Plan to spend at least 2 hours studying. Rehearse material in the problem areas that you cleared up earlier.

One Day before the Test

Make a final review of all of the material. Rehearse! Write! Recite! Test yourself! This is your final study session for the test, a full "dress rehearsal." Use this session to study your review cards and your test review sheet or sheets, covering all the important information in the material. At this point you should be feeling confident about the test. At the end of the day, right before you go to sleep, look through the material one last time; then get a good night's rest. Resist any temptation to relax or celebrate the completion of your review by watching television or going to a movie. These activities create interference that can make it harder to recall information when you take the test.

Using Review Cards to Prepare for a Test

As suggested above, one highly effective way to prepare for a test is to make review cards. You already have some experience with such cards, since you have been completing your chapter-by-chapter review cards throughout *Opening Doors.*

KEY TERM
Test Review Card

Index card with an important question on the front and the answer on the back.

Another kind of **review card,** especially useful in preparing for tests, is an index card with an important question on the front and the answer on the back. The question and answer may have to do with a single main idea and its supporting details, a term and its definition, a name and an identification, a mathematical or chemical formula, and so on. Review cards are an efficient, effective, and convenient way to study for tests. Review cards can be prepared from a textbook or from lecture notes.

The boxes on page 656 show an example of a review card for an important concept presented in a sociology textbook. Notice how this card focuses on one main idea and its two supporting details. Notice also the format of this card: one side presents a probable test question, and the other side answers the question.

SAMPLE REVIEW CARD: FRONT

Card 5

What are the two levels of sociological analysis?

SAMPLE REVIEW CARD: BACK

The two basic levels of sociological analysis are microsociology and macrosociology.

Microsociology: Small-scale analysis of data derived from the study of everyday patterns of behavior.

Macrosociology: Large-scale analysis of data in which overall social arrangements are scrutinized.

Just as outlining, mapping, and summarizing help you organize material, review cards allow you to arrange material clearly and concisely. Most students prefer to use 3- by 5-inch or 4- by 6-inch index cards. Cards of this size are convenient to carry and can be reviewed whenever you have spare moments. Index cards are available in several colors, and some students find it helpful to use a different color for each chapter or course. Other students use different colors for different categories of study material; for instance, vocabulary terms might be on cards of one color and key people on cards of another color. You may want to number your review cards so that they can be easily rearranged and then put back in order. For instance, you may want to set aside cards with especially difficult questions so that you can give them special attention before the test.

Review cards are helpful in numerous ways. First, since preparing these cards involves writing out certain information, the very act of making them will help you rehearse material and commit it to long-term memory. Do not assume, though, that simply making the review cards is a substitute for rehearsing the information on them.

Second, review cards let you concentrate on one small, manageable part of the material at a time. Lecture and textbook material can seem overwhelming if you try to review it all at once before a test or at the end of a semester, but it can be quite manageable in small parts.

Third, review cards can be especially useful for memorizing key terms, key people, formulas, and the like. For example, a college instructor might require students to learn math or chemistry formulas or to memorize a set of important terms. Learning 10 definitions, names, or formulas a week is much easier than trying to learn 150 of them just before a final exam.

Fourth, review cards can be a good way to review material with a study partner. When you are studying for a test, working with a partner can be highly effective. In fact, even when you use review cards by yourself, it is helpful to say the answers out loud, as you would if you had a partner.

Fifth, effective students try to anticipate test questions, and review cards are a good way to guide this effort. Writing an anticipated test question on the front of a card, with the answer on the back, allows you to test yourself on material before the instructor tests you.

Sixth, review cards can help you monitor your learning by measuring what you know and what you still need to learn or rehearse further.

To sum up, if you prepare your review cards carefully and use them to rehearse and learn information, they can be an important key to success.

Using Test Review Sheets

Suppose that you are going to be given a test in a sociology course. The test will cover a full chapter of your sociology textbook and the corresponding class sessions. Your instructor has announced that you will be allowed to prepare one sheet of notes (front *and* back) to use while you are taking the test. How could you consolidate an entire chapter's worth of information on one sheet of paper?

To begin with, consolidating all this information on a single test review sheet would *not* mean trying to recopy all the lecture notes, handouts, and textbook material in tiny handwriting. In other words, the question really is, "What kind of information would you include on this review sheet?" Preparing the sheet would mean being very selective; it would mean summarizing essential information from different sources, such as the chapter, your own class and textbook notes, and your instructor's handouts.

KEY TERM
Test Review Sheet

Single sheet of paper consolidating and summarizing, on its front and back, the most important information to be covered on a test.

This example is imaginary, but in fact you should create a real **test review sheet** whenever you prepare for a test. You should try to restrict yourself to a single sheet (front and back) consolidating all the crucial information you would bring to the test if you could. (If a test will cover several chapters, though, you might want to prepare several review sheets: one sheet for each chapter.) Preparing such a review sheet is in itself a way of selecting, organizing, and rehearsing the material you must learn.

Obviously, you need to start by identifying major topics that you know will be on the test. Remember that you must be selective, because you cannot include everything. If you have been preparing review *cards* as you went along, then you have already taken the first step in preparing a test review *sheet,* because you have already identified most of the important information you need for the sheet. However, you will probably have to condense this information even more to create your test review sheet.

Another way to proceed with the first step in making a test review sheet is to list the major topics and the most important points about each. If your instructor does not identify the major topics for you, you should check your lecture notes. You should also refer to the main table of contents or to the chapter-opening contents in the textbook for an overview of the material that will be covered. The main headings and subheadings of the chapter are the major topics. If there is no detailed main table of contents or chapter-opening contents, you will need to check the text itself for titles and headings.

Your next step is to organize the material that you will include on the sheet. There is no one "correct" way to organize a test review sheet. However, the chapter material itself may often suggest logical ways in which the sheet can be organized. For example, a test review sheet can be as simple as a list of major topics with key words beside or beneath each topic. It could also consist of a grid of rows and columns, a set of mapped notes, a list of formulas, important terms (with or without definitions), a diagram or sketch, or some combination of these. The key is to organize the test review sheet in some way that is meaningful to *you*. Moreover, since this is your personal review sheet, you should feel free to use abbreviations, symbols, and highlighting in different colors to make this review sheet as clear and helpful to you as possible.

The boxes on pages 658–660 show entries in a table of contents for one chapter of a sociology text (note the major headings and subheadings) and the front and back of a test review sheet that could be prepared for this chapter.

EXAMPLE: CHAPTER TABLE OF CONTENTS USED TO PREPARE A TEST REVIEW SHEET

Source: Donald Light, Susanne Keller, and Craig Calhoun, *Sociology*, 5th ed., Knopf, New York, 1989, pp. xi, 3–25.

SAMPLE TEST REVIEW SHEET (FRONT OF PAGE)

Chapter 1—Approaches to Sociology

1. SOCIOLOGICAL PERSPECTIVE

Social Facts & Social Causes

Sociology—systematic study of human societies & behavior in social settings

Sociological perspective—lets us see how our background, social position, time, & place affect how we view world & act—also, who we interact with & how others see us

Sociological facts—properties of group life that can't be explained by indiv traits, actions, or feelings. Soc facts emerge from social forces (e.g., concept of beauty, romantic love)

Sociological Imagination

Soc imag—ability to see personal experience in world (pers ex is limited, so we shouldn't make hasty generalizations)

Science, Sociology, & Common Sense

Scientific method used by sociologists—collect data (facts, statistics); develop theories

Theory—systematic formal explanation of how two or more phenomena are related. Local th = narrow aspect; middle-range th = broader; general th = most comprehensive (explain how several ths fit together). (Contrast w common sense— from pers ex, facts not checked, no organization into ths to be tested.)

Levels of Sociological Analysis

Microsociology—small-scale analysis of data from everyday behavior patterns.

Macrosociology—large-scale anal of data on overall social arrangements.

2. BASIC SOCIOLOGICAL QUESTIONS

What Holds Society Together?

Functional perspective—different parts of society contribute to whole

Power pers—those who control resources prob will shape society to their own advantage

What Is Relationship between Individuals & Society?

Structural perspective—indiv choices explained by forces arising from soc organization

Action pers—society shaped by people's actions

SAMPLE TEST REVIEW SHEET (BACK OF PAGE)

3. ORIGINS OF SOCIAL THEORY

Rational-Choice Th

Founder—<u>Adam Smith.</u> People choose & decide for own advantage; soc = self-regulating system; all parts act in own int; market forces mesh pts into whole. Expanded by <u>Jeremy Bentham</u>—govt intervention needed to help soc function & let people benefit from resources.

Th of Karl Marx

<u>Economic</u> system shapes soc life, breeds conflict; proletariat (workers) should overcome capitalists (oppressors—owners of resources)

Th of Émile Durkheim

Human behav explained by soc forces binding society (social solidarity); society held together by interrelated working of pts

Th of Max Weber

Power comes from dif factors—education, soc connections, etc.; society produced by actions of indivs. Stressed politics & culture (not only econ like Marx).

Interactionist Th

<u>George Herbert Mead</u>—people interact depending of how they interpret soc situations; we learn our place in world thru soc interactions. Th developed from phenomenology.

4. FOUNDING THEORIES & CONTEMPORARY SOCIOLOGY

Sociologists still influenced by ths above—have expanded orig ths to apply to modern issues.

Some to combine functional and power pres; structural & action-oriented pres.

DEVELOPING CHAPTER REVIEW CARDS

Review cards, or *summary cards,* are an excellent study tool. They are a way to select, organize, and review the most important information in a textbook chapter. The process of creating review cards helps you organize information in a meaningful way and, at the same time, transfer it into long-term memory. The cards can also be used to prepare for tests. The review card activities in this book give you structured practice in creating these valuable study tools. Once you have learned how to make review cards, you can create them for textbook material in your other courses.

Now, complete the five review cards for Chapter 11 by supplying the important information about each topic. When you have completed them, you will have summarized important material about the study skills in this chapter.

Rehearsal and Its Importance to Memory

_____

_____

_____

_____

_____

_____

_____

_____

Card 1   **Chapter 11: Rehearsing Textbook Information and Preparing for Tests**

Studying for Tests: General Guidelines

_____

_____

_____

_____

_____

_____

_____

_____

_____

Card 2   **Chapter 11: Rehearsing Textbook Information and Preparing for Tests**

Five-Day Test Review Plan

_____

_____

_____

_____

_____

_____

_____

_____

_____

_____

Card 3   **Chapter 11: Rehearsing Textbook Information and Preparing for Tests**

Test Review Cards

_____

_____

_____

_____

_____

_____

_____

_____

Card 4   **Chapter 11: Rehearsing Textbook Information and Preparing for Tests**

Test Review Sheets

_____

_____

_____

_____

_____

_____

_____

_____

Card 5   **Chapter 11: Rehearsing Textbook Information and Preparing for Tests**

SELECTION **11-1**

Psychology

COMMUNICATION

from *Social Psychology*

By James A. Wiggins, Beverly B. Wiggins, and James Vander Zanden

Prepare Yourself to Read

Directions: Do these exercises *before* you read Selection 11-1.

1. First, read and think about the title. What do you already know about communication?

   _____

   _____

2. Next, complete your chapter preview by reading the following:

   > First paragraph (chapter introduction)
   > Headings in each section
   > Words in **bold print** or *italics*
   > Illustrations and their legends
   > Chapter summary

   On the basis of your preview, what aspects of communication does this chapter seem to be about?

   _____

   _____

Apply Comprehension Skills

Directions: Do these exercises as you read Selection 11-1.

- Budget your time for reading this selection. It has four subsections. If you wish, divide your reading time into four sessions.
- To remember essential information, underline or highlight and annotate or take notes on a separate sheet of paper.
- Apply the skills you have learned in this chapter. Create test review cards for one or more of the four sections, making at least one card for every heading within each section. (Your instructor will give you specific directions.)

CHAPTER 5

COMMUNICATION

*I*n Chapter 4, "Social Relationships and Groups," we discussed how people are linked by social relationships — patterns of social interaction and sets of expectations (norms and roles) reflecting and shaping these interaction patterns. We noted that social relationships go through cycles of negotiation and renegotiation. But we said very little about *how* this is accomplished. In this chapter we will focus on the important contribution of **communication**, the process by which people interact and interpret their interactions.

Symbols

When people interact, much of the language, behavior, and appearance of each party constitutes **symbols** — objects or actions that, by social convention, stand for or represent something else. Symbols are *arbitrary* stand-ins for other things; their meanings are not *givens*. Rather, they come to have meaning by virtue of socially shared conventions, that is, understandings between users. For example, you and a friend might agree that if you wink at him at a party, the wink means you're having a good time and want to stay longer. You could just as easily agree that the wink means

you're bored and want to escape as soon as possible. Through socialization we learn the meanings assigned by our culture to many symbols. Spoken and written words, for example, are symbols, as are clothing styles and actions such as handshakes and frowns. The traditions and consensus within a society give symbols their meanings. As a result, many symbols have different meanings in different cultures.

Sometimes the parties to an interaction interpret aspects of it differently, and as a consequence, their interaction does not run smoothly. What interests social psychologists is how we negotiate meanings and the implications of this process for our continued interaction. Consider the following newspaper account:

Stockton, Calif. — The worst possible fate befell two young masked robbers last night. They tried to hold up a party of thirty-six prominent, middle-aged women, but couldn't get anybody to believe they were for real.

One of the women actually grabbed the gun held by one of the youths.

"Why," she said, "that's not wood or plastic. It must be metal."

"Lady," pleaded the man, "I've been trying to tell you, it is real. This is a holdup."

Source: James W. Wiggins, Beverly B. Wiggins, and James Vander Zanden, *Social Psychology,* 5th ed., 1994, pp. 135–170 (chap. 5). Reproduced with permission of McGraw-Hill. (For additional sources, see page 700.)

"Ah, you're putting me on," she replied cheerfully.

The robbers' moment of frustration came about 9:00 p.m. at the home of Mrs. Florence Tout . . . as she was entertaining at what is called a "hi-jinks" party. Jokes and pranks filled the evening. Thus not one of the ladies turned a hair when the two men, clad in black, walked in.

"All right now, ladies, put your rings on the table," ordered the gunman [the women were prominent in Stockton social circles].

"What for?" one of the guests demanded.

"This is a stickup. I'm serious!" he cried.

All the ladies laughed.

One of them playfully shoved one of the men. He shoved her back.

As the ringing laughter continued, the men looked at each other, shrugged, and left empty-handed. (*San Francisco Examiner*, April 4, 1968)*

In this example, interaction was problematic because the participants did not share meanings. The failure of the robbery attempt can be attributed to the *different meanings* that the robbers and the women at the party assigned to the robbers' message. The robbers thought that their symbols—masks, guns, and the words "This is a stickup"—would lead the partygoers to define the situation as a robbery and to give up their valuables.

But that's *not* how the women interpreted the symbols. They saw the masks and guns and heard the words, but these happened in the context of a "hi-jinks" party, where several pranks had already occurred. The women interpreted the robbers' symbols as part of still another joke. Moreover, in the women's minds, the joke did not call for them to actually hand over their valuables. In other words, the robbers and the women arrived at different meanings for the same symbols because they interpreted them in terms of different definitions of the situation. A **definition of the situation** is the meaning we give to an entire situation.

*Reprinted with permission from the *San Francisco Examiner*. © 1968 *San Francisco Examiner*.

DEFINITIONS OF THE SITUATION

What we are trying to arrive at when we send and receive various types of symbols is a definition of the situation. We might, for example, have definitions for such situations as a prayer meeting, a camping trip, an accident, an argument, a seduction, a friendly conversation, a tennis match, a robbery, a party, a social psychology class, and so forth. We use whatever information we can to help us define the situation we are in or are about to enter. Some of this information comes in the form of symbols provided by others—communication. Once we arrive at a definition of the situation, we interpret other information in terms of that definition. In other words, the definition of the situation constitutes a type of context for our interpretation of events. If we define the situation as a wedding, for example, and observe that a woman in the front row is weeping, we may interpret her tears as tears of joy. If we define the situation as a funeral, we may be more likely to define her tears as tears of grief.

Arriving at a definition of a situation gives us insight as to the roles people are going to play—allowing us to anticipate the actions of others and adjust our own actions accordingly. Much human interaction occurs among people who do not know one another and who, consequently, have no direct experience on which to base predictions about one another's behavior. *Scripts* are mental representations of sequences of interaction over a period of time. They allow us to quickly and easily fit our behavior with that of others in a situation. We feel quite comfortable going to an appointment with a new dentist, going to a new restaurant, or attending a class for the first time because we know the scripts. This allows us to take for granted certain expectations for our own behavior and the behavior of others in the situation.

When behavior follows a script, interaction proceeds smoothly. This is highlighted by cases in which we *don't* know the script for the situation. If we received an invitation to a state dinner at the White House and planned to attend, we would probably try to find out as much as we could about the script for state dinners. We'd want to know "who does what when?" (See the Student Observation: "Scripts.")

We are, of course, also interested in information not provided by the script for a particular definition of a situation. When visiting the dentist, for example, a patient might also be attentive to symbols indicating whether the dentist intended to carry out a complicated procedure, liked him, seemed competent and professional, or was in a bad mood. He would use this additional information to modify his interaction in that particular encounter with the dentist.

SIGNIFICANT SYMBOLS— SHARED MEANINGS

Because appearances and behaviors — indeed, all the things that can serve as symbols in communication — are interpreted, people may perceive and interpret the same information in different ways. Interpretation provides meaning for the symbol. When a symbol is interpreted similarly by several persons, the symbol is said to be a significant symbol. In other words, **significant symbols** are symbols whose meaning is *shared* by the parties in question. For example, for most Americans, the American flag stands for the country and our pride in it. But for some, it stands for aspects of the American government to which they object. When members of these two groups interact, the American flag will not be a significant symbol. In other words, they will not agree on its meaning.

Significant symbols are important because they allow us to anticipate one another's behavior and, therefore, to coordinate our behaviors. If the symbols we choose are *not* significant symbols — if their meanings are not shared — the chances of coordinating our actions with those of others is greatly diminished.

Subgroups within language groups often have specialized vocabularies or other symbols that emphasize the concepts that are most important to them. In this course, you are learning many of terms which social psychologists use regularly but which are relatively unknown to others. Similarly, physicists, farmers, truck drivers, cooks, physicians, and construction workers all have special vocabularies that allow them to efficiently communicate with one another about the things that are important to them.

STUDENT OBSERVATION

Scripts

People fail to realize how important scripts are until they come into a situation for which they don't have one. A few weeks ago I was reminded of this fact when I attended a retreat of the co-chairs of the committees of the Campus-Y. I was one of the very newest members of the Y, and I didn't know any of the other co-chairs. I had never been to one of the retreats before. When I arrived at the campground, I was painfully aware that I had no *script* — no mental representation of sequences of behavior over time — for this occasion. As all the other committee chairs boldly slung their bags and other gear in a corner of the big log cabin meeting room and laughed and hugged one another in a presumably Campus-Y co-chair fashion, *I was so uncomfortable*! I did not know what an appropriate greeting would be for me, a new, unfamiliar member, nor had I the faintest idea what to do with my camping stuff. I stood very awkwardly — scriptless — until a facilitator, someone who obviously had a script, introduced herself and kindly showed me where to put my backpack and sleeping bag. After watching the others for a while, I began to piece together a script so that I could fit my behavior to theirs. However, I was never more grateful for directions than I was those first minutes at the rustic retreat.

THE TWO SIDES OF WARSPEAK

During the 1991 Persian Gulf War, a *Time* magazine article pointed out that the top brass and the GIs seemed to be speaking two different languages, neither of them English. William Lutz, a Rutgers University English professor, noted that military strategists seemed to have adopted M.B.A.-style buzzwords that reflected an "emphasis on managerial skills," a depersonalization of the enemy, and a distancing from violence, while the men and women in the ranks adopted a more colorful and less distanced way of communicating. Here's a sampler:

Top Brass

Incontinent ordinance: Bombs and artillery shells that fall wide of their targets and hit civilians.
Area denial weapons: Cluster bombs with the ability to wreak great damage over a particular zone.
Ballistically induced aperture in the subcutaneous environment: A bullet hole in a human being.
Coercive potential: The capability of bombs to harm and demoralize soldiers.
Suppressing assets: The destruction of sites containing antiaircraft weaponry.
Unwelcome visit: British term for any foray into enemy territory.

Scenario-dependent, post-crisis environment: Conditions after the war.

Grunts

Echelons beyond reality: The source of orders from superior officers.
High speed, low drag: Phrase indicating that an operation went exactly according to plan.
Micks: Abbreviation of minutes, as in "Give me five micks."
9-4: A more chummy version of the traditional "10-4" radio sign-off.
Suicide circles: Nickname for Saudi traffic roundabouts. A number of allied soldiers died in road accidents in Saudi Arabia.
180 out: The coordinate-minded soldier's term for the wrong answer—180 degrees from the truth.
Strack: To get on the right track, or frame of mind, for battle.

Source: Reprinted from D. Ellis, "The Two Sides of Warspeak," *Time,* February 25, 1991 p. 13. Copyright 1991 Time, Inc. Reprinted by permission.

These special vocabularies are sometimes disparagingly referred to as *jargons*, because the meanings these words have are not shared by the larger population. Thus, although they increase the efficiency of communication among those who share them, they are not effective symbols for communication with those who don't. During the 1991 war against Iraq in the Persian Gulf, the public was exposed to military jargon during the many briefings on the progress of the war. Interested observers noted that the jargons of the commanders and those of the lower-level soldiers differed, perhaps reflecting the two groups' different concerns and perspectives on the situation (see the box "The Two Sides of Warspeak").

KINDS OF SYMBOLS—CHANNELS OF COMMUNICATION

Talking and listening are the activities that we most often associate with communicating. But speech is only one of the kinds of symbols we use to communicate with others. Besides using words, we communicate with qualities of our voices and through nonverbal channels—our facial expressions, body movements, the distances and orientations with which we position ourselves relative to others, and our physical appearance and such personal attributes as hair styles and clothing. Social psychologists and linguists note that these kinds of symbols constitute the *channels of communication* available to us. They distinguish between the verbal and nonverbal channels.

Verbal Symbols

Verbal symbols are of two main types: language and paralanguage. **Language** is our principal vehicle for communication, finding expression in speech and writing. Language allows us to denote abstract ideas and events that are distant in time or place. A single word may have a complex meaning. For example, you may associate the word "home" not only with the house you live in but also with your family and dinnertime, with conflict or happiness and security. So the word "home" may represent more than "bricks and mortar" if it pertains to these other things as well.

We learn words and their meanings from agents of socialization (see our discussion in Chapter 2, "Early Socialization," for details). Because these meanings are largely shared, we are able to communicate with others in our language group. However, we sometimes create new symbols, such as new words, or assign words new meanings that are shared only by members of a particular relationship or group. Such symbols are part of the internal culture of our relationships and groups. They are significant symbols for members of the group, but not for others. For example, you may have a special name for a loved one that stands for your special feelings for that person. (We discussed internal culture in Chapter 4, "Social Relationships and Groups.")

Paralanguage consists of the nonsemantic aspects of speech — the stress, pitch, and volume of speech — by which we communicate meaning. Paralanguage has to do with *how* we say something, not with *what* we say. Tone of voice, inflection, pacing of speech, silent pauses, and extralinguistic sounds (such as sighs, screams, laughs) constitute paralanguage. Paralanguage is what we are referring to when we say, "It wasn't *what* she said; it was the *way* she said it." Consider, for instance, the difference in the meaning of the response "Oh yeah" under the following circumstances:

1. As a retort to the threat "Stop it or I'll smash you!" (hostile intonation)

2. As a response to the sexual invitation "Let's make love." (seductive intonation)

3. As a response to the suggestion "Won't it work if you hold that button down?" (embarrassed acknowledgement)

4. As a response to the question "Are you coming with us?" (affirmation)

Baby talk is a type of paralanguage (Caporael, 1981, Caporael and Culbertson, 1986; DePaulo and Coleman, 1986). While baby talk contains unique words (for example, "choo-choo" for train

---

STUDENT OBSERVATION

Paralanguage

My roommate provides a good example of the use of paralanguage in his telephone conversations. When he talks to his relatives, he speaks at a higher volume than in normal conversation. He also uses a higher pitch and a very happy tone of voice. When he talks to his girlfriend, he raises his pitch still higher and slows his rate of speech. When speaking to friends, he lowers his pitch and varies his tone of voice more frequently. The variation in paralanguage is really evident when one of his male friends calls when he is expecting his girlfriend. He answers with a high-pitched "Hey!" — but quickly "corrects" his pitch and tone when he realizes who the caller actually is.

and "tum-tum" for stomach), it is also distinctive in its paralinguistic features, especially its high pitch and exaggerated intonations. Indeed, baby talk has been documented in numerous languages. The higher pitch of baby talk may serve to hold babies' attention. Studies show that babies prefer to listen to baby talk (Fernald, 1985). (Before reading further, see the Student Observation: "Paralanguage.")

Nonverbal Symbols

Suppose you can see, through a window across the street, a young man and woman interacting in an apartment. Because of the noise of the traffic below, you can't hear their words, or even their voices, but you can see their faces and movements quite clearly. Without any verbal or paralinguistic cues, do you think you could tell whether the couple was having an argument or beginning a romantic evening together? Your guess just might be correct. This is because, besides speech and paralanguage, we use several kinds of nonverbal symbols to convey or amend meaning. These include body language, interpersonal spacing, and physical characteristics and personal effects. (Before reading further, see the Student Observation: "Symbols.")

Body language (also called **kinesics**) is the nonverbal communication of meaning through physical movements and gestures. We tap our fingers to show impatience. We shrug our shoulders to indicate indifference. We nod our heads to mean "yes" or "um-hum, I'm paying attention." We scratch our heads in puzzlement. We maneuver our bodies to negotiate a crowded setting without touching others. We avoid eye contact to indicate an unwillingness to interact. Through the motions of our bodies, limbs, faces, and eyes we communicate information about our feelings, attitudes, and intentions. This is not to say that we easily decipher the motions, wiggles, and fidgets accompanying ordinary speech. A nonverbal behavior may represent many different meanings, depending on the context in which it occurs — its timing and intensity, and its combination with other verbal and nonverbal behaviors (Zuckerman et al., 1981; Harper, 1985; O'Sullivan et al., 1985).

Eye contact frequently functions as a type of body language. Depending on how people define the situation, eye contact may signal an aggressive or dominating intent, as in a staredown; intimacy or close bonding, as among lovers; or a fervent call for assistance, as with a prisoner of war ap-

STUDENT OBSERVATION

Symbols

When I was about four years old, I attended a wonderful playschool. However, one afternoon my mother was late picking me up. Of course, I was hysterical — I thought my mother was never coming back to get me! From that point on, the playschool was a terrifying place to me. I began to have temper tantrums in the mornings before going, and I cried all day until my mother came to pick me up. Finally, my mother figured out a plan to ease my fear of being left and forgotten. She devised a symbol to represent the fact that she wasn't going to forget about me in the afternoons — she might be late, but she wasn't going to forget and leave me.

The symbol was nothing but a simple lipstick kiss on the back of my hand. It may sound silly, but it worked. Every day when she left me at the playschool, my mother would kiss my hand and leave her lipstick print. This "silly" mark meant the world to me. It was a symbol of security, of my mother's love, and of her promise that she would never forget me.

STUDENT OBSERVATION

Civil Inattention

One interesting example of civil inattention takes place in automatic teller lines. In lines for other kinds of service, people tend to stand with about 1 or 2 feet between them. In automatic teller lines, however, the distance between the person completing the transaction and the next one in line greatly increases. The "next up" must stand at least 4 to 5 feet away and make an obvious effort to gaze at something other than the person completing the transaction, in effect saying, "Don't worry about me. I'm just waiting for my turn — I'm not trying to see your number or how much money you're taking out. I'm no threat."

The other day I was in one of these lines. The next-up man was obviously in a hurry and violated the interpersonal spacing norms either out of carelessness or an effort to hurry the woman completing her transaction. She looked over her shoulder with a sharp, nervous expression on her face, obviously perceiving the opposite of the benign, adequately spaced message: "I'm too close to be normal — I'm looking to see your number or how much money you are taking out. I'm a threat." As soon as he saw her look back, the man sheepishly backed up to the appropriate distance — now saying, "No, I'm really *not* a threat. Sorry!" — and concentrated on the bush to the left, looking embarrassed about having communicated such a threatening message unintentionally.

pearing before a television camera. Gazes come in many variations. We can glare, gawk, ogle, or leer. We alter the symbolism of a gaze by tilting our heads, widening or narrowing our eyes, or lowering or raising our eyebrows. For instance, we typically perceive the lowering of brows as more assertive and domineering than the raising of brows (Mazur et al., 1980).

Eye contact assumes considerable importance in public settings. We employ it to assess strangers and define their intentions. Consider our behavior on a city bus, a subway, or an elevator. We view these forms of public transportation as means of moving from one place to another. Therefore, within such contexts we usually aim to protect our own rights and to maintain a proper social distance from strangers.

One way to achieve these outcomes is through **civil inattention**: we give others enough visual notice to signal to them that we recognize their presence, but then we quickly withdraw visual contact to show that we pose no threat to them and that we do not wish to interact. We do this by cutting off eye contact, a maneuver of civil inattention that Erving Goffman dubs "a dimming of the lights" (1963*b*: 84). Thus, despite the closeness of our bodies and our mutual vulnerability, little focused interaction occurs, few of us are accosted, and few friendships arise. We project cues to ensure that these things *do not take place*. (See the Student Observation: "Civil Inattention.")

Social contexts vary in permissible *looking time* — the amount of time that we can hold another person's gaze without being rude, aggressive, or intimate. The permissible looking time is zero on an elevator; it is a little longer in a crowded subway or bus; and it is still longer out on the street. Apparently, greater leeway is permitted to pedestrians in "looking one another over."

Interpersonal spacing (also termed **proxemics**) is nonverbal communication involving the distances and angles at which people position themselves relative to others. We invite interaction by angling our bodies toward others and discourage it by angling away. We position ourselves closer to those we like and farther from those we don't like.

We also use *markers* — signs that communicate the fact of ownership or legitimate occupancy to keep others at a distance from the territory we want to claim. As markers we use symbols such as nameplates, fences, hedges, and personal belongings. We place a book, handbag, or coat on a table or an empty chair to reserve a place in the library, sunglasses and lotion on a towel to lay claim to a spot on the beach, and a drink on a bar to assert "ownership" of a bar stool (Becker, 1973; Shaffer and Sadowski, 1975). We also use touch to communicate territorial control. For instance, at a game arcade, others are less likely to attempt to use a machine if a person stands near it and touches it than if a person stands off and does not touch it (Werner, Brown, and Damron, 1981).

Physical characteristics and personal effects. We also communicate through the way we look. This includes not only our physical characteristics (such as hair color, skin color, body build, height, the way we groom our bodies) but also the personal effects we choose and display (clothing, jewelry, makeup, choice of beverage, car, the way we decorate our living quarters, and so on). A ring on the fourth finger of the left hand suggests, in our culture, that a person is married. A uniform communicates that the wearer occupies a specific role, such as police officer, airline attendant, or physician. Thus, the uniform sets our expectations for the behavior of the wearer.

Note that some of these aspects of appearance are easily changed. We *choose* our clothing, makeup, grooming styles, and sometimes even hair color. Other aspects of our appearance are not easily changed—such as skin color, height, and body build. Even those aspects of our appearance over which we have little control are used by others to make judgments about us. Black males, for example, sometimes find that their race and gender are viewed as symbols of threat or danger (see the box "Just Walk on By: A Black Man Ponders His Power to Alter Public Space").

Norms define what is considered to be "appropriate dress" in various situations. That's why we tend to have different clothes for different occasions—some for work, some for leisure, some for dress-up nights out. For example, we would think it very odd if a friend attended our backyard cookout in sequined evening dress or a job applicant showed up for an interview in swim trunks and flip-flops. We would probably think such persons socially inept.

Within the range considered situationally appropriate, individuals choose their clothing and other personal effects partly to make a statement about who they are. A woman who wants to be taken seriously as a supervisor at work probably should not wear childish clothing. A manager who

If others attribute meaning to such social characteristics as race and gender, aspects of our appearance serve as symbols for these social categories and communicate information about us.

JUST WALK ON BY: A BLACK MAN PONDERS HIS POWER TO ALTER PUBLIC SPACE

My first victim was a woman — white, well dressed, probably in her early twenties. I came upon her late one evening on a deserted street in Hyde Park, a relatively affluent neighborhood in an otherwise mean, impoverished section of Chicago. As I swung onto the avenue behind her, there seemed to be a discrete, uninflammatory distance between us. Not so. She cast back a worried glance. To her, the youngish black man — a broad six feet two inches with a beard and billowing hair, both hands shoved into the pockets of a bulky military jacket — seemed menacingly close. After a few more quick glimpses, she picked up her pace and was soon running in earnest. Within seconds she disappeared into a cross street.

That was more than a decade ago. I was 22 years old, a graduate student newly arrived at the University of Chicago. It was in the echo of that terrified woman's footfalls that I first began to know the unwieldy inheritance I'd come into — the ability to alter public space in ugly ways. It was clear that she thought herself the quarry of a mugger, a rapist, or worse. Suffering a bout of insomnia, however, I was stalking sleep, not defenseless wayfarers. As a softy who is scarcely able to take a knife to a raw chicken — let alone hold it to a person's throat — I was surprised, embarrassed, and dismayed all at once. Her flight made me feel like an accomplice in tyranny. It also made it clear that I was indistinguishable from the muggers who occasionally seeped into the area from the surrounding ghetto. That first encounter, and those that followed, signified that a vast, unnerving gulf lay between nighttime pedestrians — particularly women — and me. And I soon gathered that being perceived as dangerous is a hazard in itself. I only needed to turn a corner into a dicey situation, or crowd some frightened, armed person in a foyer somewhere, or make an errant move after being pulled over by a policeman. Where fear and weapons meet — and they often do in urban America — there is always the possibility of death. . . .

The fearsomeness mistakenly attributed to me in public places often has a perilous flavor. The most frightening of these confusions occurred in the late 1970s and early 1980s when I worked as a journalist in Chicago. One day, rushing into the office of a magazine I was writing for with a deadline story in hand, I was mistaken for a burglar. The office manager called security and, with an ad hoc posse, pursued me through the labyrinthine halls, nearly to my editor's door. I had no way of proving who I was. I could only move briskly toward the company of someone who knew me. . . .

I began to take precautions to make myself less threatening. I move about with care, particularly late in the evening. I give a wide berth to nervous people on the subway platforms during the wee hours, particularly when I have exchanged business clothes for jeans. If I happen to be entering a building behind some people who appear skittish, I may walk by, letting them clear the lobby before I return, so as not to seem to be following them. I have been calm and extremely congenial on those rare occasions when I've been pulled over by the police.

And, on late-evening constitutions along streets less traveled by, I employ what has proved to be an excellent tension-reducing measure: I whistle melodies from Beethoven and Vivaldi and the more popular classical composers. Even steely New Yorkers hunching toward nighttime destinations seem to relax and occasionally they even join in the tune. Virtually everybody seems to sense that a mugger wouldn't be warbling bright, sunny selections from Vivaldi's *Four Seasons*. It is my equivalent of the cowbell that hikers wear when they know they are in bear country.

Source: Brent Staples, "Just Walk on By: A Black Man Ponders His Power to Alter Public Space," *Ms*, September 1986, pp. 54, 88. Used by permission of the author.

wants to be seen as "one of the guys" probably should not dress too differently from them.

INTENDED AND UNINTENDED SYMBOLS

Communication involves a behavior or an attribute capable of being perceived by someone else — something that can serve as a symbol. Sometimes we *intend* for our behavior or attribute to be interpeted by others; sometimes we do not. Sociologist Erving Goffman (1959) distinguishes between *expressions given* — intended symbols — and *expressions given off* — symbols we transmit unintentionally. Communication occurs whenever some other person perceives and interprets a symbol we transmit, whether we *intended* to transmit that symbol or not.

We usually consider communication to be an intentional process, and it often is. For example, a graduate who majored in accounting may explain to a job interviewer, "In addition to my coursework, I did the accounting for student government during my junior and senior years at college. I think this experience makes me more prepared than many other graduates to enter a job with substantial responsibility." Here, the speaker is sending verbal signals that she hopes will serve as symbols of her suitability as a job candidate. She is also likely to have sent nonverbal messages intended to convey the same meaning — such as dressing in a suit, presenting a neatly prepared résumé, and being punctual for the interview.

But a sender may also deliver messages *without* intending to. The woman in our example almost certainly does *not* intend to send signals indicating that she is extremely nervous during the job interview. Nevertheless, her unsteady voice and trembling hands might communicate her nervousness to the interviewer. Similarly, the woman's wedding band might communicate her maturity and responsibility to the interviewer, even though she hasn't thought about communicating this or may not even be aware that her wedding band has been noticed by the interviewer. In most situations, we

both give and give off expressions — through our appearance and behavior — that are interpreted by others. We communicate both intentionally and unintentionally.

MULTICHANNEL COMMUNICATION

Ordinarily, communication takes place through several communications channels simultaneously. Even on the telephone, both linguistic and paralinguistic cues are available to us, although body movements, facial expressions, spacing, and personal effects are not. In face-to-face conversation, we may use all the channels of communication. Sometimes, the information provided by a single channel can be interpreted in more than one way. For example, intense looking may indicate either love or hostility. A tense body posture may signal respect or hostility. The meaning of such behaviors is usually clarified when we look at the context provided by additional behavior channels. Thus we often impute love to an intense gaze when it is combined with close distance and relaxed posture (Schwarz, Foa, and Foa, 1983). In contrast, intense gaze coupled with loud speech and negative facial expression would probably be interpreted as anger. Thus, we decode most accurately when multiple communication channels convey what appears to be consistent information.

But if we had access to only a single channel of communication, which channel would give us the best (most accurate) assessment of a person's emotion? Research suggests that judgments based on verbal content are the most accurate. One such study presented subjects with passages from the 1976 televised debate between vice-presidential candidates Walter Mondale and Robert Dole. The researchers selected twelve passages for each speaker, half of which seemed to convey positive emotions and half negative. Subjects were presented with only one of several channels of communication available in the standard videotape of the passages: (1) verbal only — a written transcript; (2) video only — with audio removed; or (3) paralinguistic only — the audio track with content filtered out but with paralinguistic features such as pitch, loudness, rate, and so forth, preserved. The subjects' judgments about the positivity or negativity of the emotions being expressed were compared to those of another group of subjects who viewed the standard videotape, which contained both audio and video. The judgments of subjects who read the written transcript — the verbal content — most closely matched the judgments of subjects with complete information (Krauss et al., 1981). The results of this study indicate that when the information provided by various channels is reasonably consistent, the verbal channel contributes most to the *accuracy* of our judgments of positivity and negativity of emotion.

But sometimes the information conveyed through various channels appears *inconsistent*. What do we do when that happens? Albert Mehrabian (1972) designed a study to answer this question. He had actors display contradictory verbal, paralinguistic, and facial cues. In deciding which emotions were the true ones, subjects judging the actors' emotions assigned the most importance to facial cues, less to paralinguistic cues, and the least importance to verbal cues. Although they may disagree on the exact proportion of meaning attributable to verbal and to nonverbal cues, many researchers have found evidence that when observers are faced with inconsistent information, they weigh nonverbal symbols most heavily and tend to give very little weight to verbal symbols (Argyle, Alkema, and Gilmour, 1971; Archer and Akert, 1977; DePaulo, et al., 1978). Perhaps we believe that nonverbal channels are more likely to reveal a person's "true" feelings when we don't trust the verbal channel.

In real life, of course, much depends on the situation, the kind of behavior being judged, and the availability of multiple channels of information. Studies suggest that, when they are available, we make use of multiple channels of information, interpreting each within the context of the others (Zuckerman, Depaulo, and Rosenthal, 1981; Harper, 1985; O'Sullivan et al., 1985).

What We Communicate

The previous section focused on the different types of symbols we use to communicate with others. Now let's turn to *what* we communicate — the various types of meaning we can convey through the use of symbols.

TASK INFORMATION

Some communicative behavior is, of course, task-oriented, or aimed at getting something done. For example, a boss communicates on the job in order to coordinate her actions with those of co-workers to produce a product, such as an automobile or a report. Thus, the boss tells her secretary when a report is needed and specifies the typeface and margins she requires. Or you might communicate with your friends about plans for a party in order to coordinate your actions with theirs so that everyone knows when and where the party will be and so that you don't end up with lots of munchies but no beer. A student calls his parents to tell them that he is working hard, but that this is a particularly difficult semester, in order to prepare them for the disappointing grades he anticipates.

Task information is perhaps the most obvious kind of information we communicate. But we inevitably communicate several kinds of meanings at once. Our communicative behavior reflects the intimacy of our relationships with other persons, reflects and reinforces our relative status in the group, and provides information about ourselves (Patterson, 1988).

EXPRESSIONS OF INTIMACY

Relationships vary in terms of intimacy, or closeness, and we provide symbols to communicate degrees of intimacy and liking to our partners and other, third-party observers. For example, a man might choose particular verbal and nonverbal behaviors to encourage observers of his interaction to perceive him as a loving spouse, a devoted friend, or a disinterested date.

Relationship partners sometimes cooperate to present a particular image of their relationship. A feuding marital couple might agree to present a harmonious image when they are in public. Their nonverbal behaviors, such as hand-holding and mutual gazing, serve to promote the desired image of their relationship. When partners in a close relationship enter a setting where their closeness is unknown to others, they often display "withness cues" (Scheflen and Ashcraft, 1976) or "tie-signs" (Goffman, 1971) to signal that they are a "couple." A jealous partner may initiate higher levels of nonverbal involvement toward his or her partner in order to "stake a claim" to the partner. On the other hand, exaggerated noninvolvement, such as sitting far apart, may be used to signal to others that the relationship is *not* a close one.

We use both verbal and nonverbal symbols to express and promote intimacy.

Intimacy with Words

Some languages, such as French and Spanish, have formal and familiar forms of second-person pronouns. In intimate relationships, the familiar form is used. Similarly, in most languages, forms of address indicate intimacy. We frequently use only first names in interactions with intimates, while titles and last names are more commonly used with strangers or those with whom we have only formal relationships. Imagine your mother's reaction if you were to insist on addressing her as "Mrs." followed by her last name — a more intimate form of address for your own mother is expected. But when you first meet a friend's mother, the formal "Mrs." would be considered appropriate.

Intimacy also affects conversational style. Analyses of telephone conversations have showed that, in comparison to strangers and casual acquaintances, friends use more implicit openings, such as "Hi" or "Hi. It's me." They also introduce more topics into their conversations and are more responsive to their friends (Hornstein, 1985). Other studies suggest that as closeness in-

creases, partners develop communication patterns (part of their internal culture) — including speech rhythms, pitch, and movements — that are increasingly personalized, synchronized, and efficient (Baxter and Wilmot, 1985).

Intimates often develop their own jargon — private symbols, including words and phrases commonly used by others, that have special meanings for them. When these words or phrases are used publicly, intimates may exchange a knowing glance, a wink, or a smile. A person is likely to feel disappointment if her or his partner uses these special words or way of talking with someone else.

Intimacy Without Words

Nonverbal behaviors can also indicate the closeness of relationships. In several studies, observers inferred stronger liking and higher levels of sexual involvement between partners whose level of reciprocated gaze was higher (Kleinke, Meeker, and LaFong, 1974; Thayer and Schiff, 1977). Other studies suggest that postural congruence or matching — in which participants assume postures that are carbon copies or mirror images of one another — reflect greater rapport or the desire to promote a closer relationship (LaFrance and Ickes, 1981).

In close relationships touch signals positive affect, such as support, appreciation, inclusion, sexual involvement, or affection (Jones and Yarbrough, 1985). Support touches are intended to nurture or reassure the other. Appreciation touches, which signal gratitude, are often accompanied by a verbal expression of thanks. Inclusion touches, such as holding hands or putting an arm around a partner, emphasize closeness. Touches signaling sexual interest usually involve holding or caressing the partner on the chest, pelvis, or buttocks. Affection touches are used to express general positive regard toward the partner.

EXPRESSIONS OF STATUS

An individual's status is his or her relative standing vis-à-vis others, and a person's status may differ from one social situation to the next. A college sophomore may have relatively low status compared with seniors but high status relative to freshmen. The same person may have high status among the friends with whom he plays poker on Thursday nights but lower status among those with whom he plays softball on Tuesday afternoons. In social situations, persons with higher status generally exercise greater power and control. Status is reflected and reinforced through communicative behaviors.

Status with Words

Relative status in relationships is clearly communicated by forms of address. People with lower status use formal forms of address for those with higher status. People with higher status often use familiar forms to address those whose status is lower. Two people with equal status tend to employ the same form of address with each other. Both will use either formal ("Dr.," "Mrs.," "Ms.," "Professor") or familiar ("John," "Pat") forms, depending on how well they know each other. When we are unsure about our status relative to someone else, we are faced with a dilemma. A familiar example is the problem of what to call our in-laws — "Mr. and Mrs."? "Mom and Dad"? or (after the arrival of grandchildren) "Grandma and Grandpa"? When we feel uncertain about how to address someone, we sometimes avoid calling him or her anything at all (Little and Gelles, 1975). Other strategies for masking our uncertainty without using a formal title that confers too much status or a familiar address that confers too little include using ambiguous forms of address (such as "Sir," "Miss," "Ma'am," or "Ms.") or inventing an in-between form (such as "Doc" for a physician or professor).

Our choices of vocabularies and pronunciations reflect our relative status and, consequently, influence our relationships. We often adjust our speech to express status differences appropriate to changing situations (Stiles et al., 1984). For example, there are words and phrasings we would use with our children but not with our spouses, and vice versa. A person might tell a child, "Pick up all those magazines you left in the living room, right now!" but the same person would probably address a spouse more politely: "The living room sure is getting messy." In our culture, polite, indirect phrasing is considered more appropriate between equal-status adults.

Similarly, social class and racial, ethnic, and regional differences in vocabulary, pronunciation, and speech style can have a large impact on communication. Recall our discussion in Chapter 3, "Socialization over the Life Course," regarding class differences in communication styles that not only reflect but also perpetuate status differences from one generation to the next.

Paralinguistic behaviors also communicate status. Higher-status speakers talk more frequently, longer, and more loudly and interrupt their partners more in conversations than do lower-status speakers (Brown, 1980; Street and Brady, 1982; Cappella, 1985; Street and Cappella, 1985; Weimann, 1985; Street and Buller, 1988). People with lower status show that they are paying attention by such responses as "Mmmm" at appropriate times. When people of the same status interact, they use these paralinguistic cues more equally (Leffler, Gillespie, and Conaty, 1982). Studies suggest that influence is enhanced by using the paralinguistic behaviors deemed appropriate to one's status in the group (Ridgeway, 1987).

Status Without Words

Status is also communicated through body language (Mazur et al., 1980; Edinger and Patterson, 1983; Givens, 1983). When a person in authority talks to a subordinate, the lower-ranking person listens intently and keeps his or her eyes riveted to the superior. Looking about would indicate disrespect. But when the subordinate is speaking, it is deemed appropriate for the boss to look around or gaze at his or her watch. And people in submissive roles tend to crouch slightly and display self-protective stances (e.g., folding their arms or hugging themselves, crossing their legs, or reaching up and touching their throats). People in dominant roles typically use more expansive gestures, (such as spreading their arms and legs, thereby creating an air of assurance) (Leffler, Gillespie, and Conaty, 1982).

A person can convey his or her higher status by patting a low-status person on the back or shoulder, a behavior not permitted to a person of subordinate rank. And the high-status person takes the lead. If he or she remains standing, then the subordinate is also expected to stand. Only when the high-status person sits can the lower-status person feel free to sit down.

INFORMATION ABOUT OURSELVES: FACEWORK

Some of our communication behavior is designed to deliberately present or enhance an identity or image we have of ourselves or of our relationships. Such actions illustrate that meanings are not fixed entities that set in motion an automatic unfolding of behavior. The activities of others enter as factors in the formation of our own conduct.

The need for the negotiation occurs when interactants do not share definitions of the situation. For example, suppose that Linda, the chairperson of a committee, is making a request of Paul, an older colleague on the committee. If Paul defines the situation as one in which he, an older, experienced committee member, should be advising an inexperienced younger committee member, he and Linda are likely to see each other as being too directive. When this happens, each is likely to ask, "What's going on here?" By getting additional information from each other and making adjustments, Linda and Paul may reach a shared definition of the situation—or they may not. The flow of the interaction will be affected by their ability or inability to arrive at a single script to govern the interaction.

Upon discovering that something is wrong—in this case, each one's thinking that the other is being too directive—Linda and Paul might respond by providing additional information about their own meanings. Linda might say, "Well, as chair of the committee, I think we should . . . ," or Paul might say, "If you had more experience, I think you would see that. . . ." These phrases would at least let each of them know where the other was "coming from."

From here, they might come to agreement by either one's giving up his or her own position in favor of the other's or by reaching a compromise (e.g., the young, inexperienced chair of the committee is making a polite request of the older, experienced, distinguished member of the committee). On the other hand, each might cling to his or her early meanings or adjust them so that they are even more discrepant. For example, Linda might change her definition of the situation to portray herself as the young, promising chair of the committee arguing with an old stick-in-the-mud committee member. Paul's definition might depict himself as the experienced, distinguished committee member being insulted by the uppity young chairperson. Whether Linda's interaction with the older committee member proceeds smoothly or problematically or is terminated altogether depends in part on whether she and Paul can arrive at a mutually acceptable definition of the situation.

In Chapter 1, we first mentioned sociologist Erving Goffman and his ideas about "impression management"—the routine ways in which we try to manage the impressions of ourselves as well as those of others. In everyday life, we often explain our own and other people's behavior through appeals to "face" (Tracy, 1990; Holtgraves, 1992): I was trying to give him a way to *save face*. *Face* is a social phenomenon referring to our concern with personal reputation—the public images we claim for ourselves or attribute to others. The communication strategies we use to enact, support, or challenge these public images are called **facework** (Goffman, 1955). Facework is one of the ways we negotiate with others about the meanings of our actions. The goal of such conduct is to enhance or protect our own face claims and/or to support or challenge others' face claims. According to Goffman (1971), these strategies are either "corrective" or "preventive."

Corrective Facework

Corrective facework consists of practices we employ to restore face *after* it has been attacked or threatened. Sociologist C. Wright Mills noted, in a classic article, that along with learning norms of action for various situations we learn acceptable explanations, which he called "vocabularies of motive" (1940: 909). For example, we often use *accounts* — explanations we offer to make our inappropriate behavior appear more reasonable (Cody and McLaughlin, 1985; Snyder, 1985). Accounts take four forms: excuses, justifications, concessions, and refusals. *Excuses* are statements admitting the inappropriateness of our behavior or its consequence but denying our responsibility for it. For instance, "I know you had to wait a long time because I was late, but I had a flat tire." *Justifications* are statements we provide that admit responsibility for our behavior or its consequence but deny its inappropriateness, reinterpreting it in a more socially acceptable manner: "You would have hit him too if he had said that about your wife."

In a *concession*, we neither deny responsibility nor attempt to justify our conduct. Rather, we simply admit to the failure in question and frequently offer an apology or expression of remorse or offer to make restitution: "I acted foolishly; I'm sorry." On the other hand, *refusals* involve denying that the act in question was actually committed: "I was *not* late! I said I'd be here at 3:30!" Refusals may also include a denial of the other party's right to punish; "Don't you dare scold *me* for being late! How late were *you* last night?" Accounts are discussed further in the box "Facework by Students: Accounts for Absences."

To minimize threats to others' face, we are often studiously inattentive to small lapses in their behavior (Edelman, 1985; Cupach, Metts, and Hazelton, 1986; Knapp, Stafford, and Daly, 1986). For example, we might pretend not to notice the quiet burp emitted by the person seated next to us at the table. We sometimes provide facework to protect the reputations of others. "It's OK, I know you are busy" may give a spouse a (corrective) excuse for her or his failure to pick up the dry cleaning.

Preventive Facework

Whereas corrective facework consists of the practices we engage in *after* our face is damaged or threatened, *preventive facework* consists of the things we do *when we anticipate* damage to face. We use such practices to avoid punishment for a future behavior or to assess the consequences of our actions. For example, asking someone to do something for us reduces our face if we are seen to have acted inappropriately. We can reduce the face threat of making such requests in several ways: (1) by seeking permission to make the request in the first place — "May I ask you a favor?"; (2) by offering an excuse for making the request — "I'm going to *have* to miss our next class because I have a job interview at that time"; or (3) by pleading — "Please, this is very important to me."

We also protect our face by using *disclaimers* intended to convey that, despite our present behavior, we normally abide by the rules: "I normally wouldn't ask to be excused from class, but. . . ." When making what another person might consider a negative statement or criticism, we might use a disclaimer such as, "I know I shouldn't say this, but . . ." or "I'm not prejudiced, but. . . ." When offering advice that may not be well received, we might say, "I know I'm not an expert, but . . ." or "I know it's none of my business, but. . . ." These tactics take away the other person's ability to damage our face by pointing out our weakness: "You're no expert!" or "It's none of your business!"

We may protect the face claims of ourselves and others by preceding a request with a question that suggests to them an excuse for their refusal. For example, "Are you going to be home tonight?" allows the person to answer "No" (without embarrassment to either party) before being placed in the position of refusing a request to pay the person a visit.

Individuals differ in the face concerns they bring to each interaction (O'Keefe and Shepherd, 1987; O'Keefe, 1988). An insecure person may approach the interaction hoping only to avoid embarrassment, while a confident, outgoing person may want to be the focus of attention. And the face wants that individuals pursue may be different in different contexts. For example, sometimes we want to be seen as fun and likable, and other times we want to be seen as firm or even intimidating. This means that communicators need to

FACEWORK BY STUDENTS: ACCOUNTS FOR ABSENCES

Kathleen Kalab (1987) studied the "vocabularies of motive" provided by students when they missed her introductory sociology and social psychology classes. She told her students on the first day of class that they would be expected to give her a written reason for any missed class. Over two semesters, she received 270 notes.

When she analyzed the notes, Kalab found that only about 8 percent contained *justifications*. All of the justifications used by Kalab's students were "appeals to higher loyalties." They suggested that although the student was responsible for missing class—normally a bad thing—doing so was necessary because obligations to relatives and friends had to be placed ahead of the obligation to be in class on a particular date: "The reason I wasn't in your class last Friday and Monday is because my grandmother had a stroke and I had to fly home early." "On [date] I had to attend the funeral of a friend's mother." "Here we go again! I really am sorry to have missed your class [date]. Believe it or not, a friend of mine (not myself) got stranded? at a motel. She called me up Friday morning and like a fool I missed class to pick her up in Russellville. What else could I do?" (Kalab, 1987: 74–75).

Most of the accounts Kalab received were *excuses*. In these notes students admitted to the negative aspect of missing class but attempted to lessen their individual responsibility through the use of five major themes: reference to biological factors, control by another person, oversleeping, other coursework, and accidents. It is not surprising that students made illness their number-one excuse, because illness is commonly recognized as an excuse for not fulfilling various social obligations. It is also an excuse that can be used more than once without being viewed skeptically—and it was used more than once by many of Kalab's students.

Excuses involving control by another person included organizational demands ("The reason for missing your class on Friday, [date] was because I had a cross-country meet to run and we left at 10:30 a.m."); appointments set by others with higher status ("I missed your class on Friday in order to make a doctor's appointment."); and ride providers ("I was absent Friday [date] because my only ride home was leaving at 1:00. I hadn't been home in an awfully long time. Thanks.").

A third, and less common, theme among excuses was oversleeping. Intentional wit and humor were more likely to be used in notes about oversleeping than in those for other excuses. One student wrote, "I'm sorry I missed Friday. My id took over and wouldn't let my superego in until it was too late. Basically I overslept. (I had no intention of missing.) Thank you." Most students who used oversleeping as a reason seemed to recognize it as a rather weak excuse for missing class; very few students used it as an excuse more than once.

Some students' excuses involved missing class in order to do other classwork: "I am sorry that I was not in class on Wednesday [date]. I was studying for a very very important test. Thank you." When using the "other classwork" excuse, students were more serious than when writing about oversleeping. Only one student used this excuse more than once.

The final, and least used, type of excuse Kalab identified in her study involved accidents. Accounts that attribute responsibility to accidents emphasize hazards in the environment. The appeal to accidents often works because we all know that we cannot totally control our environment. Almost half the students' accident notes referred to faulty alarm clocks. The most unique excuse Kalab received was in the accident category:

> I was absent Friday, [date] because the dye I used Thursday night to turn my hair black somehow changed to green when I washed it Friday morning. I'm talking green-bean green! I spent 3 hours and 36 dollars to return my hair to a normal hair color. (Kalab, 1987: 80)

As with oversleeping and other coursework, accident excuses were not used more than once. Kalab notes that accident excuses are not likely to work if they are overused. We honor such excuses precisely because they do not occur often.

A few of the notes Kalab received provided neither excuses nor justifications for missing class. For whatever reason, on these occasions, the students didn't try to explain their negative act in a way designed to protect or restore their face. One note said:

> Yes, I was absent from your class on Friday, [date]. (Bet it was a whole lot quieter!) I have no good excuse. I didn't go home. I blew off *all* my classes Friday. And I'll be honest—I enjoyed every minute of it. Thank you. (Kalab, 1987: 82)

And another simply stated, "I can't remember why I was absent Wed."

decide which aspect of another's identity is governing the other's face claims in a particular situation. In fact, orienting remarks to a contextually inappropriate face of the other may be (or may be seen as) a strategy to attack the other or to enhance one's own face.

Even in a single situation, our face needs may conflict. We want to be connected to, and intimate with, others, but we also want to be independent and autonomous. We might want to be both fair and firm. We want to be honest *and* considerate. Behaviors that support one of the face needs can undermine the other. We sometimes deal with such conflict through a kind of facework called *equivocating* (Bavelas, 1983, 1985; Bavelas and Chovil, 1986; Bavelas et al., 1988). For example, if someone gives us a gift that we don't really like, we might equivocate by responding, "Oh, how thoughtful of you!"

Social situations also sometimes involve tensions between the face needs of interactants. In some situations, to protect our own face, we must challenge someone else's (Craig, Tracy, and Spisak, 1986). For example, to protect her identity as a competent student, a woman who has just received a failing grade on an exam might portray her professor as incompetent by suggesting that he gave inadequate instructions about what the exam would cover, wrote unclear questions on the exam, or misgraded.

Nothing guarantees that our facework, whether corrective or preventive, will soothe the interaction and allow us to avoid or reduce the disruptive consequences of our actions. Instead, the facework itself may become a *second* source of controversy: "You are always late! I'm sick of your excuses!"

We have seen that communication takes place through the exchange of various types of symbols, both verbal and nonverbal, which convey various types of meaning—about tasks, intimacy, status, and self. We have noted that communication involves the negotiation of meanings and have discussed some of the processes through which negotiation takes place. Now let's turn to a discussion of *how* we communicate—the rules of conversation.

How We Communicate: Rules of Conversation

All human encounters involve, in one way or another, the transfer of information. If we were capable of sending and receiving information simultaneously, regardless of the complexity and amount of information presented, we would not need rules governing the flow of information. However, because humans have finite information-processing capacities, human interactions must be governed by some rules of procedure that control the flow of information and signal when speaking and listening roles are to be switched. Besides solving technical problems of sequencing, so that communication can take place more smoothly, these rules of procedure also influence our impressions of who is in control of a situation, who is a competent social actor, who is friendly, and who is shy. Thus, interpersonal power, status, competence, and attraction depend, at least partly, on our ability to control speaking and listening roles (Cappella, 1985).

Both verbal behavior and nonverbal behaviors such as gaze, touch, facial expressions, postural shifts, gestures, and paralinguistic cues often signal immediate or impending changes in the state of conversation (Button and Lee, 1987; Leeds-Hurwitz, 1989; Goodwin and Heritage, 1990; Boden and Zimmerman, 1991; Maynard and Clayman, 1991). The regulation of conversation, such as who should speak when and about what, usually occurs without our awareness. As an analogy, consider how we navigate a crowded sidewalk. Through mutual glances and gestures we communicate with one another about our speed and direction of movement so as to minimize collisions. In effect, these glances and gestures function as routing or crash-avoidance devices. Just as we want to avoid collisions on sidewalks and streets, it is desirable to avoid simultaneous talking in conversations. Typically, we take turns in speaking and listening. We spend relatively little time in mutual silence or simultaneous talking, and usually the transitions from one speaker to another are without perceptible speaker overlap or pause (Trimboli and Walker, 1982, 1984).

How do we manage to avoid verbally bumping into one another in our conversations? The answer lies in the rules and signals with which we regulate conversation.

INITIATING CONVERSATIONS

When and how to start a conversation is governed by several rules. *Initiation rules* encourage us to initiate conversations in some situations and discourage us from doing so in others. For example, whenever we encounter friends or acquaintances we are almost always expected to say "Hi" and are frequently expected to initiate small talk or conversation. We are expected *not* to begin conversations with strangers in the same settings.

Conversations may be initiated with an *attention-getting sequence* such as a greeting, question, knock on the door, or ring of the telephone. Such efforts may be successful or not. In response to an attention-getting attempt, the person being addressed may signal that he or she is paying attention and is ready to interact. In face-to-face interaction, eye contact is a critical signal of availability. For example, a voice from down the hall calls "Sally!" Sally looks toward the voice and sees John, and she returns the greeting, "Hi, John!" John smiles and waves and then turns his gaze back to the bulletin board in front of him. No further interaction takes place. If John smiles and waves and *holds* Sally's gaze, Sally is under an obligation to interact further (Goffman, 1981). When people ignore our attention-getting attempts — violating the rules of conversation — we consider them rude, snobbish, or psychologically absent (absorbed in other thoughts, asleep, intoxicated, and so on).

If the attention-getting sequence is successful, it will probably be followed by a *"how are you"* *sequence* before another topic is introduced. For example:

J: Sally!
S: Hi, John! What's up?
J: Not much. What about with you?
S: Been studying for my physics exam. Are you going to the party on Friday?

Most telephone conversations begin with an attention-getting/answer sequence, followed by an *identification-recognition sequence*, and then by a "how are you" sequence, before another topic is introduced (Schegloff, 1979):

[Ring]
W: Hello.
S: Dr. Wiggins?
W: Yes.
S: Hi. This is Mary Jenkins . . . from your Soc. 51 class. How are you?
W: Fine, thanks, Mary. What can I do for you?
S: Well, um . . . I'm not going to be able to be in class on Friday for the exam.

In face-to-face situations that do not offer us much information about *who* the other person is (such as at a large party where most of the other guests are strangers to us), we may also proceed with an identification-recognition sequence, in part as a search for an opening topic of conversation:

A: Hi, I'm Todd Baker.
B: Hello, I'm Joanne Summers.
A: Are you a friend of Joe's [the party's host]?
B: I guess you could say so. I'm his fiancée. What about you?
A: Oh, I just met Joe. I came to the party with a mutual friend — Paul Andrews.

This sequence offers enough information to continue the conversation if the two participants desire to do so. For example, Todd could ask Joanne about her wedding plans. Joanne could ask how Todd knows Paul Andrews or how Paul Andrews knows Joe. On the other hand, Todd may be hoping for a romantic encounter with someone at the party, and discovering that Joanne is Joe's fiancée may squelch his interest in pursuing the conversation. Similarly, if Joanne doesn't know Paul Andrews, Todd and Joanne's conversation topics are limited, and they may begin to look elsewhere for conversation partners.

In special situations, we dispense with most, if not all, of these initiation sequences. We seldom engage in them with our intimates. In emergencies, we dispense with them even when initiating a conversation with a stranger. For example, Whalen and Zimmerman (1987) have observed that emergency phone calls dispense with greetings in order to get more quickly to the reason for the call:

[Ring]
P: Newton Police.
C: I'd like to report a stolen car.
P: Your name?
C: Jack Jones.
P: Address?

The first response to the attention getter (ring) also verifies for the caller that he has reached the intended party (the police). The caller immediately states his reason for calling. Then the police officer asks questions to obtain the critical information needed to respond to the request for help. A similar modification of face-to-face interaction patterns occurs in emergency situations:

A: Hey! I can use some help here. This woman has fainted.
B: Have you called an ambulance?

Some role relationships allow us to skip initiation sequences. For example, it is acceptable for a waiter to skip the initiation rituals and ask a customer, "Are you ready to order?" Although the customer is otherwise a stranger, his or her strangeness is not absolute. The waiter and customer each are aware of the role of the other, and being in these reciprocal roles makes an initiation ritual unnecessary.

Initiation rules also *discourage* us from initiating conversations in some situations. For example, most of us are hesitant to interrupt when someone is busy, to initiate conversations with strangers, or to talk during class, a movie, or a church service. However, violations of these rules may be excused if prefaced by *intrusion sequences* which offer an acknowledgment or apology for the intrusion:

"Excuse me" or "Sorry to bother you." This may be followed by a signal from the person being addressed which indicates that the speaker can proceed with her or his intended conversation ("That's OK, what is it you want?") or by a signal indicating that the intrusion is not welcome ("I'm busy. What do you want?")

In some encounters with strangers, the rules against initiating conversations are relaxed. Simply sharing a situation with others provides us with some information about them, offering us an excuse for initiating conversation. For example, we may be attending a party, waiting in line for a bus or basketball tickets, or sharing a view of the Grand Canyon. In such situations we probably could comment on the particular situation we are currently sharing without breaching an intrusion rule: "Why don't they stop those guys from breaking into the line?" "Nice camera!" While these comments probably would not be considered offensive, they may or may not lead to an extended conversation, and we would be expected to respect the other's privacy if he or she did not encourage us to pursue the conversation.

KEEPING CONVERSATIONS GOING

We have described how we initiate conversations, but how do we keep them going? Communication is a shared social accomplishment. Through verbal and nonverbal feedback, listeners help us assess how effectively we are communicating. Any subtle vocal or nonverbal response that a listener makes while a speaker is talking is called **back-channel feedback**. This feedback helps us know whether we are keeping our listeners' interest and being understood. Listeners may signal their *attention* to us by simply looking at us, perhaps occasionally nodding their heads. To indicate that they *understand* us, they may use brief vocal insertions such as "Oh," "Yeah," "OK," or "I see"; complete our unfinished sentences; or restate in a few words our preceding thoughts (Kraut, Lewis, and Swezey, 1982; Jefferson, 1984; Heritage, 1984*b*). Smiles and laughs as well as frowns and tears may indicate understanding *if they are appropriate to the speaker's topic.* For example, a listener's laugh following a speakers's joke indicates understanding. However, if it follows a serious comment, it indicates that the listener does not understand or is trying to disrupt the speaker's talking (Jefferson, 1985; Drew, 1987). Listeners also unconsciously display subtle rhythmic body movements — such as swaying, rocking, and blinking — that are precisely synchronized with the speech sounds of the speaker when communication is going well (Kendon, Harris, and Key, 1970).

The timing of feedback is also important, often occurring when the speaker pauses or turns his or her head toward the listener. When listener feedback is mistimed or absent, the speaker may undertake some "repair work" in order to regain the listener's attention and involvement — by inserting "You know," "You see," or "Understand?" prior to or after pauses (Fishman, 1980) or by asking simple yes-no questions such as "OK so far?" or "Are you with me?" (Goodwin, 1987a). If we feel the listener is not paying attention or doesn't understand, we may restart the conversation with such phrases as "What I mean to say . . ." or "My point is. . . ." If these efforts fail to repair the conversation, our speech is likely to deteriorate, becoming more wordy, less efficient, and more general. We may hesitate or even stop talking.

REGULATING TURN TAKING

As speakers, we are interested not only in maintaining our listeners' attention and understanding but also in keeping the floor. We do not want to be interrupted until we have made our points, and we exhibit cues that maintain our turns. One way to do this is to verbally indicate that we intend to make a series of remarks, for example, "First of all" or "To begin with," followed by "Another thing." We may signal our desire to keep speaking by maintaining the same voice pitch and keeping our heads straight, our eyes unchanged, and our hands gesturing. As we near what would normally be the point where someone else would talk, we may talk faster, filling the pauses with sounds such as "uh" and "umm" or deliberately avoid

finishing a sentence by ending each utterance with "and . . ." or "but the umm. . . ." At the same time, our listeners signal their willingness to allow us to continue speaking by using some of the same cues they use to indicate attention and understanding — for example, an "mm-hmm" or a nod of the head (Schegloff, 1987a, b).

However, turns at talking do not always proceed smoothly. Sometimes we are interrupted. As with intrusions in initiating conversations, some interruptions of ongoing talk evoke an apology — an intrusion ritual; others do not. When seeking a point of clarification, a listener may interrupt a speaker by raising a hand and/or saying, "Excuse me. What do you mean?" When attempting to challenge a speaker's information, a listener forgoes the pleasantries of an intrusion ritual; the intruding listener may try to complete the speaker's sentence and then continue on with his or her own sentence, may say something like "Just wait a minute. Do you really believe that? That's absurd," or may laugh when the speaker is obviously being serious. Of course, a speaker can attempt to rebuff an interruption with a raised hand, indicating "Let me finish," or may increase the volume of her or his voice to drown out the interruption.

Some interruptions are more permanent than others. An interruption that takes the floor from the original speaker for a brief time and then returns it to the speaker is called a *side sequence*. A side sequence may be initiated by a listener. For example, a listener might attempt to correct a speaker with a brief phrase: "Classes begin on *Wednesday*, not *Monday*." The length of the side sequence depends on how the speaker responds to the correction. The speaker might accept the correction immediately and proceed without missing a beat, or the speaker could reject the correction, diverting the original conversation to a discussion of the side sequence (Jefferson, 1987; Cheepen, 1988).

A side sequence can be initiated by the speaker as well as the listener. For example, as speakers, we might initiate a side sequence if we are forgetful or uncertain about a piece of information we need to continue talking (Goodwin, 1987a). We may turn to a potentially knowledgeable person and invite that person (with nothing more than a gaze) to share in our search for the information. This has the effect of elevating the status of listener to that of informed speaker. Or when a telephone call interrupts a conversation, the speaker may use an expression such as "Excuse me, please" to initiate the side sequence and another such as "Sorry. Now where were we?" to mark its end and the return to the original conversation.

Having taken a turn at conversation, we can signal that it is the listener's turn to talk. Turn-taking signals involve a number of behavioral cues that are displayed either singly or simultaneously during a conversation. A speaker can indicate a willingness to yield a turn by any of the following signals (Duncan, 1972; Schegloff, 1987a; Sachs, 1990):

1. *Gaze:* The speaker gazes directly at the listener toward the end of an utterance.

2. *Body motion:* The speaker ends the hand gesturing he or she used while talking or relaxes tensed hands. If the speaker asks a question such as "What time is it?" or "Where are you going?" his or her head comes up on "it" or on the *ing* in "going." The speaker's eyes also tend to open wider with the last note of a question, as a signal for the other person to start his or her answer.

3. *Paralingual drawl:* The speaker utters the final syllable or a stressed syllable of a terminal clause in a slow, drawn-out manner.

4. *Intonation:* The speaker raises or lowers his or her voice as evidence of a terminal (ending) clause. An example would be raising the voice on "this" in the question "Do you like this?"

5. *Verbal clues:* The speaker utters a stereotyped expression — "but uh" or "you know" — followed by a phrase: "But uh, I guess that's just the way he is." Questions are also an important turn-yielding signal.

Listeners can signal that they are seeking a turn through cues such as inhaling audibly, gesturing

with their hands, beginning a vocalization while shifting their heads away from us, or expressing especially loud vocal responses indicating interest — "Yes!" Such subtle and taken-for-granted (unconscious) mechanisms make communication easier. They make possible back-and-forth exchange without the need of saying, "Are you finished? Now I will talk."

Because of the absence of nonverbal cues, we might expect more turn-taking problems in telephone conversations. However, research does not support this expectation (Rutter, 1987). In fact, the only clear difference supported by research is that there are *fewer* interruptions on the telephone. Thus, although successful turn taking can be accomplished using nonverbal cues, such cues are not necessary, as interruptions can be avoided through the exclusive use of verbal cues.

TERMINATING CONVERSATIONS

We do not conclude conversations any more arbitrarily than we begin, continue, or interrupt them. Two people do not simply stop talking and abruptly walk away from each other. Just as there are initiation rituals, there are also *termination rituals*. Some rituals are short; others, particularly those that require the negotiation of a conversation closure, take more time (Button, 1987). The length of the termination ritual is influenced by such factors as the status of the participants, the setting, and the willingness of a participant to violate the termination rules.

Termination rituals between persons of equal status usually involve some prepping before the final goodbyes. Such rituals are initiated by one of the participants and may involve many components. For example, a person might close a conversation with an acquaintance by saying, "I'd better be going. Nice talking with you. See you." In this case, the final goodbye was preceded by an initiation of the closing ("I'd better be going") and an appreciation statement ("Nice talking with you").

With friends or intimates, a termination ritual might be more elaborate. For example, a student might say, "Sorry! Gotta run. Okay? Thanks for the help. See you after class. Bye." In this example, not only did the closing include an initiation ("Gotta run"), an appreciation ("Thanks for the help"), and a final goodbye ("Bye"), but it was extended by a request for the friend to approve terminating the conversation ("Okay?") as well as an arrangement for initiating the next conversation ("See you after class"). Some termination rituals might be punctuated with a hug or kiss.

In some situations we terminate conversations with friends or intimates more abruptly. For example, if two friends are accustomed to routinely terminating their conversations at a particular point — during a walk to class or work together, for instance — their termination ritual may be as brief as a nod of the head, "Bye," or "See ya." Other components of the ritual are assumed and therefore not spoken; for example, there is no need to include the explanation for closing and an arrangement for reopening the conversation in the future. On another occasion, the closing may be no more than "Oh, no! I forgot about the pie in the oven!" as the person turns and dashes away. Although the words suggest an explanation for the departure, the loss of eye contact suggests that the person is not asking for anyone's approval to leave (Goodwin, 1987*b*).

A termination attempt may be resisted whether or not it includes an actual request of the other party to approve it. It may be countered with "Oh, just one more thing. . . ." Such resistance is usually hard to overcome, whether it occurs in a face-to-face conversation or on the telephone. There isn't much the participant making the attempt can do other than repeat the termination ritual, emphasizing his or her explanation. The person might suggest another conversation in the near future: "I'll call you back tomorrow." In a face-to-face conversation, he or she can slowly decrease eye contact and move farther away from the other person. But abruptly turning away — or hanging up — without waiting for the other person's goodbye is "against the rules" and therefore requires repair work in the next conversation.

Termination rituals are somewhat different when the parties are of unequal status. For example, a superior may conclude a conversation with a subordinate abruptly, with little fanfare. On the other hand, you know your status is higher when the other person — instead of closing the conversation abruptly — asks if you want to extend the conversation. This occurs, for example, when a salesperson asks, "Can I help you with anything else?"

However, other factors may override the effects of status differences. Television news interviews, for example, usually operate with pre-specified closing times (Clayman, 1989). It would be considered rude for either the interviewer or the interviewee to leave early. However, once the agreed-upon ending time arrives, it is often the higher-status person who exercises the right to terminate the interaction. You have probably noticed that it is not uncommon for the president to leave his press conferences with the press's questions still ringing in his ears.

TALK IN INSTITUTIONAL SETTINGS

The conversational rules we have been discussing apply to mundane (everyday) conversations; thus they apply to a diversity of roles and conversation topics. In social institutions, which involve a narrower range of topics and relatively specialized identities, these conversational rules are often modified to better address the interactional contingencies of the particular setting (Heritage, 1984*a*; Whalen and Zimmerman, 1987; Zimmerman and Boden, 1991). For example, turn taking is governed by different rules within the settings of particular institutions, such as classrooms, courtrooms, emergency rooms, and corporate boardrooms. Institution-specific rules may specify the order of speakers as well as how long each can talk, who can interrupt whom in what manner, and, sometimes, what the topic of conversation is (West and Frankel, 1991). The rules may also specify who can make or enforce these kinds of rules, for example, the judge in a courtroom (Philips, 1990). The incumbents of particular roles such as police officers, teachers, doctors, lawyers, and interviewers typically begin the conversation, ask the questions, sometimes interrupt or select the next speaker, and decide when the conversa-

In social institutions, which involve a narrower range of topics and relatively specialized identities, these conversational rules are often modified to better address the interactional contingencies of the particular setting.

tion will end. These are the people in charge. On the other hand, others such as students, patients, witnesses, and interviewees follow the formers' initiatives. In some instances, the question-answer activities are reversed. For example, in a classroom or at a press conference the teacher or the politician/expert becomes the interviewee, while the students or the press become the interviewers. However, the teacher or politician still initiates the conversation by selecting the questioner and probably sets most of the agenda of the interview.

To the extent that participants in an institutional setting, such as a courtroom, organize their conversations in a way that is distinctive from everyday conversation, they are both *displaying* and *creating* the unique institutional character of that setting (Heritage and Greatbatch, 1991). Each institution has its own unique pattern of modifications. These vary from culture to culture, and they are subject to processes of social change.

THE COOPERATIVE PRINCIPLE

To make their purposes understood, speakers sometimes explicitly state their intent: "I am asking for your help." "I am telling you to stop right now." "I insist that you leave now." "I invite you to come tomorrow." "I apologize for being late." "I promise to get the paper." "I'm warning you that it is not enough." Most languages also provide standard ways of combining words and intonation to convey a speaker's purpose. In English, for example, there are standard ways of using word order, verb forms, and intonation to convey asking ("Is Wendy here?"), telling ("Wendy is here"), and commanding ("Come here, Wendy!").

More often, however, we indicate our intentions much more indirectly. For example, when Carol telephones Tricia and Jonathan answers, she might ask, "Is Tricia there?" Carol expects Jonathan to understand from this that she wants to speak to Tricia; she isn't simply asking for a yes or no answer. If Tricia is home, Carol expects Jonathan to reply, "Yes, I'll get her." If she isn't home, Carol expects something like, "No, may I take a message?" or "No, she'll be back about nine." These answers acknowledge that Carol wants to speak to Tricia, even though she didn't say so directly. Similarly, when you say to your roommate, "I'm hungry," you expect him to know that you are not simply stating a fact but want the two of you to start doing something about it. Depending on the setting, you might mean "Is there anything in the refrigerator that I could eat?" or "Let's stop what we're doing and go get some dinner."

Obviously, people often mean much more than they actually say. How do listeners figure out the more indirect meanings? Philosopher H. Paul Grice (1975, 1978) has argued that we do this, partly, by relying on a **cooperative principle** — an assumption that speakers are trying to be (1) informative (but not overly informative), (2) truthful, (3) relevant, and (4) clear (unambiguous and brief).

Consider this example: Adam is standing by a car on the side of a dusty rural road as Bob comes along on foot. Adam says, "I'm out of gas." Bob replies, "There's a fruit stand around the corner and another one a little farther down the road on the left." How should Adam interpret Bob's reply? Taking Bob's remarks at face value, Adam might think that Bob is entirely unconcerned with his problem and wants him to buy some fruit at the local stand. But if Adam relies on the cooperative principle, his thinking may be along these lines: Bob thinks the fruit stands are my closest sources of help (he is trying to help by giving good information; he knows and is being truthful about where they are). Maybe the fruit stands also sell gas or have a phone I can use to call for help (they must be relevant to my being out of gas). Why did Bob mention two fruit stands? He must think it's possible that the closest stand won't solve the problem (it might be closed), so he gave me more information, just in case. (Adam assumes Bob wouldn't give unnecessary information because the principle of cooperation says speakers should be brief.)

Suppose you point toward a group of ten dancers and say to the friend next to you, "*That* is Sandra's brother." Your friend assumes that, if you are acting cooperatively, you have given her all the information she needs to pick out the unique dancer to whom you are referring. If nine of the dancers are female, your friend will know that Sandra's brother is the sole male dancer. But what if all the dancers are male? She will look for something that sets one dancer apart from the others. ("Really? The *naked* one?")

Cooperation is essential to language use and, more generally, to all communication. Speakers say what they say intending it to be understood a certain way by their listeners. We talk to convince, request, apologize, warn, and promise. To succeed, we have to rely on the cooperative principle (Clark, 1985; Schiffrin, 1990).

Group Differences in Communication

Not everyone uses the same style of communication. We do not all share the same interpretation of particular cues; in other words, not all cues are

significant symbols. Nor do we necessarily interact using the same rules of conversation (e.g., some of us use repair work, which others ignore). Some of these differences occur between individuals; others are differences between groups of people. There are several explanations for the communication differences that distinguish groups (Coupland, Giles, and Weimann, 1991): (1) People use different communication styles (including different languages and jargon) because they come from different cultures or have specialized socialization and training. (2) Different developmental levels of the "same" language may account for different communication styles, such as those seen in conversations between adults and children. (3) People may use different channels of communication because of physical restriction; for example, the sight-, hearing-, or speech-impaired who cannot receive or send information through particular channels and, at the same time, may use cues that the nonimpaired have difficulty interpreting. (4) Biological explanations suggest that genetic differences between categories of persons result in different communication styles. (5) As we have discussed previously, communication differences can be a vehicle for the display of one person's power or status over another. When we encounter someone whose symbols or communication style is different from our own, we often make the judgment that our own style of communication is "the correct one" and other styles are "deviant" — not just different, but bad or *inferior* (Henley and Kramarae, 1991).

Obviously, communication differences, whatever their source, can lead to communication problems between people who have occasion to interact with one another. Our reactions to others whose communication styles are different vary. Sometimes we lower our expectations of the abilities of those using other styles; for example, we may use baby talk when interacting with children, the elderly, the impaired, and even those whose native language is different from our own. Sometimes we attempt to change the communication styles of those whose styles differ from our own; for instance, we may oppose bilingual education. A third way we react to these differences is by avoiding opportunities to interact with dissimilar others; for example, we may adhere to the segregation of ingroup and outgroup members (a topic discussed in Chapter 4, "Social Relationships and Groups"). Of course, segregation can be the *cause* as well as the *effect* of communication differences.

We expect differences when we talk to people who grew up in a different country but not when we talk to people who grew up in "the same culture" and who speak "the same language" as ourselves. So it is perhaps surprising that social psychologists devote a great deal of attention to gender differences in communication.

GENDER DIFFERENCES IN COMMUNICATION

Folklore has long attributed "female intuition" to women. According to this view, women are more adept than men in nonverbal communication. An accumulating body of research supports this popular belief (Hall, 1984). On the whole, psychologists find that women are more visually attentive to other people than are men. And women are better judges than men of the meanings behind voice tones, facial expressions, and body movements — the sorts of cues people cannot or will not put into words.

One explanation for women's superior nonverbal decoding skills and different conversational style is that they are socially oppressed and hence must give greater attention to an accurate reading of the needs and demands of more powerful others. Another speculation is that women in male-dominated societies usually find themselves watching and listening and might therefore develop greater nonverbal ability through sheer practice. Still another is that the ability is genetic, or "prewired," because nonverbal sensitivity on a mother's part might permit her to detect distress in her children or threatening signals from adults, thus enhancing the survival chances of her offspring.

In contrast to these "oppression" and "biological" explanations, another thesis is that gender differences in communication styles emerge from male and female *subcultures* whose norms are learned from, and reinforced by, gender mates from early childhood on (Maltz and Borker, 1982; Maccoby, 1990; Tannen, 1990). According to this explanation, gender differences in communication behavior stem from adherence to the norms of one's own gender group, not so much from status differences that may become salient when men and women interact with one another.

Women's style is seen as reflecting females' greater concern with *intimacy*, or connection with others. This style focuses on minimizing differences and avoiding the appearance of superiority, which would highlight differences among the members of complex networks of friends. Communication, for women, is frequently directed toward establishing connections with others, building relationships, and preserving intimacy.

Men's communication style reflects their greater concern with *status* and independence, with being up rather than down in the hierarchical social order. Thus, men's conversations are negotiations in which they try to achieve and maintain the upper hand if they can and protect themselves from others' attempts to put them down or push them around. This is not to say, of course, that women are entirely unconcerned with status or that men are unconcerned with intimacy. The difference is one of focus and degree — women's primary concern is intimacy, while men's primary concern is status — and this leads to dramatic gender differences in communication styles.

Notice that the difference in the concerns of the two genders reflects two of the main "things we communicate" discussed earlier in the chapter — intimacy and status. Men's greater use of filled pauses (which permit them to keep the floor), faster speech, and interruptions follows from their concern with status: they are competing for conversational floor time and respect. Women's greater use of questions, briefer speech, and more direct gazes reflects their concern with egalitarianism and connection. In this view, men and women come together as citizens of different cultures — thinking that they speak the same language when, in fact, they do not (Hall, 1978).

Perhaps because females are more concerned with interpersonal harmony and/or are more skilled at affecting it, both sexes find interactions with women to be more pleasant and satisfying than interactions with men. Social psychologist Harry Reis (1986) suggests that males and females make different contributions to social interaction. He and his colleagues asked subjects — forty-three male and fifty-three female college seniors — to complete a series of ratings for each interaction of ten minutes or longer that they were involved in during a two-week period.

The researchers found that interactions involving at least one female were rated by the subjects of both sexes as more intimate, more pleasant, and more satisfying. In such interactions, subjects indicated that they and the others involved in the interaction disclosed more. Even when a male interacted with his best male friend, the interaction was rated as less intimate, disclosing, pleasant, and satisfying than interactions between females or between opposite-sex partners. Additionally, among both male and female subjects, the more time they spent interacting with females, the less lonely they reported themselves to be. Reiss's study, however, did not attempt to identify the particular behaviors that made interaction with females more positive.

Gender Differences in Meaning

Because of gender differences in communication skills and approaches to interpersonal interaction, males and females sometimes view the same interaction quite differently. For example, backchannel responses such as "yeah" and "um-hum" have different meanings for men and women. For women, these mean "I'm listening, please continue." For men, they mean "I agree." So, in a male-female conversation, the man may think he is listening but not agreeing, but the woman will think he is not listening. Women frequently ask questions to maintain conversations — to show interest and encourage the speaker to continue. Men are more likely to see questions as requests for information. Women often respond to shared experiences and problems by offering reassurance. Men see the presentation of problems as requests for solutions and respond by giving advice, lecturing, or acting as experts (Aries, 1987). Women who think they are displaying a positive quality — connection — are misjudged by men who see them as lacking independence, which men regard as synonymous with incompetence and insecurity. Men who think they are displaying a positive quality — independence — are misjudged by women who see them as insensitive and uncaring. It is not surprising that communication between men and women is sometimes difficult.

Deborah Tannen, a linguist who has studied gender differences in conversational styles, illustrates how men's and women's different cultural backgrounds can lead to miscommunication:

> When Josh's old high-school chum called him at work and announced he'd be in town on business the following month, Josh invited him to stay for the weekend. That evening he informed Linda that they were going to have a houseguest, and that he and his chum would go out together the first night to shoot the breeze like old times. Linda was upset. . . . Josh had made these plans on his own and informed her of them, rather than discussing them with her before extending the invitation. . . . But when she protests, Josh says, "I can't say to my friend, 'I have to ask my wife for permission'!"
>
> To Josh, checking with his wife means seeking permission, which implies that he is not independent, not free to act on his own. It would make him feel like a child or an underling. To Linda, checking with her husband has nothing to do with permission. She assumes that spouses discuss their plans with each other because their lives are intertwined, so the actions of one have consequences for the other. . . . Linda was hurt because she sensed a failure of closeness in their relationship: He didn't care about her as much as she cared about him. And he was hurt because he felt she was trying to control him and limit his freedom. (1990: 26–27)*

———

* From "Women and Men in Conversation" from *You Just Don't Understand* by Deborah Tannen. Copyright © by Deborah Tannen. Used by permission of William Morrow & Co., Inc.

Miscommunication between the genders is not limited to the interactions of husbands and wives. Antonia Abbey (1982) got her idea for a study about miscommunication between men and women from an encounter she had with strangers. Abbey was with some female friends at a crowded campus bar, sharing a table with two male strangers. While Abbey thought that she and her friends were merely being "friendly," the men appeared to interpret the women's behavior as an indication of sexual interest. She reports that she and her friends finally had to excuse themselves from the table in order to avoid an awkward scene. This made Abbey wonder: Do men often see women's words and actions as more seductive than the women intend?

Abbey designed a study to answer this question. She assigned two males and two females to each of twenty-six four-person groups. When each group arrived for the study, Abbey randomly selected one male and one female to engage in a brief conversation (the actors) while the other male and female observed the conversation from another room (the observers). After the conversation, all four subjects filled out questionnaires indicating their perceptions of the actors' personality traits and chose from among a list of characteristics those that they thought described how each actor was "trying to behave." Although these terms were included with many others, Abbey was particularly interested in how "flirtatious," "seductive," and "promiscuous" the four subjects perceived the two actors to be.

Abbey found that the behavior of the female actor was rated more promiscuous and seductive by both the male actor and the male observer than by either the female actor or the female observer. Overall, the male observers saw the female actors as more interested in and attracted to their partners than did the female observers. The males and females in this study either participated in or observed the same interaction, but both as actors and as observers the males and females perceived it quite differently — mutual understanding was not reached. As Abbey's experience in the bar indicates, this gender difference in "meaning" can lead to problems.

Differences in Conversational "Work" and Control

As we noted earlier in this chapter, the maintenance of a conversation is somewhat problematic and requires the continual, turn-by-turn efforts of the participants. However, this does not mean that there is an equal distribution of work in a conversation. For instance, Pamela Fishman finds that a woman typically carries the greater burden in keeping a conversation moving with a man. Fishman (1978) analyzed fifty-two hours of tapes made in the apartments of three middle-class couples between the ages of twenty-five and thirty-five. The women raised nearly twice as many topics of conversation as the men because many of the women's topics failed to elicit any response. Besides exercising their right to inject new topics, men controlled topics by veto: they would refuse to become full-fledged conversational participants. Both men and women regarded topics introduced by women as tentative, and many of these topics were quickly dropped. In contrast, topics introduced by men were seldom rejected and frequently resulted in a lengthy exchange.

The tapes revealed that the women resorted to attention-getting devices when faced with the men's grunts or long silences. The women asked three times as many questions as did the men. Asking a question is conversational "work"; it is a device used to keep conversation going by eliciting a response from the other party. And more often than the men, the women prefaced their remarks with comments like "D'ya know what?" and "This is interesting"; as talk lagged, the women used the interjection "you know" with considerable frequency. Such phrases function as "go-ahead" signals, indicating that the other party may speak up and that what is said will be heeded.

Deborah Tannen suggests that men see communication as a way to gain status by showing that they know more. Women, on the other hand, see communication as a way to build connections, so they tend to play down their own expertise rather than display it. Because of these differences, men are often more comfortable, and more talkative, in public situations that allow them to "show off." Women are often more comfortable, and more talkative, in private situations that allow them to build rapport. Men are inclined to jockey for position and challenge the authority of others. Women are more likely to avoid confrontation because they feel it is more important to be liked than to be respected. Men see disagreement as more interesting — and more status enhancing — than agreement. Women see disagreement as a threat to intimacy and strive to be more accommodating. Because they are not struggling to compete with others in conversation, women are often seen by men as being powerless or inept.

A number of studies have found that men account for the vast majority of the interruptions in a conversation. One early study found that in cross-sex conversations in public places, over 90 percent of the interruptions were made by men (Zimmerman and West, 1975). A recent study (Smith-Lovin and Brody, 1989) found that, while male and females interrupt at almost identical rates, males are more than twice as likely to interrupt a female as they are to interrupt another male. Females, in contrast, interrupt male and female speakers equally. The men were also found to be more successful at interrupting women.

Some researchers conclude from these findings that women, who do the routine maintenance work in conversations, neither control nor necessarily benefit from the conversational process (West and Zimmerman, 1983; Kollock, Blumstein, and Schwartz, 1985; Pfeiffer, 1985). One explanation for these findings is that widely held beliefs in our society attribute more status, or power, to men than to women and that this difference is reflected in conversational dynamics (Ridgeway and Diekema, 1992). According to this view, differences in communication styles are essential to the maintenance of male dominance (Henley and Kramarae, 1991). A second explana-

tion proposes that these differences are not so much a reflection of or a mechanism for maintaining male dominance but are, instead, another result of the different socialization and resulting cultures of the two genders.

These two explanations are not necessarily mutually exclusive (Smith-Lovin and Robinson, 1992). Both early *socialization* and peer-group interaction may lead boys and girls to develop gender identities that differ substantially in *power*. Although parents don't directly or intentionally socialize children to play or interact differently on the basis of their gender (Maccoby, 1990), they do communicate, subtly, that girls are nicer, less powerful, and less lively than boys. These early experiences shape our views of ourselves and others as males and females. These gender identities are reinforced in same-sex play groups. In adulthood, men's and women's definitions of "male" and "female" differ substantially. When these gender identities are activated, men and women behave differently in carrying out social roles. Thus, according to this view, it is gender-differentiated *identities*, which we hold for ourselves and others, that shape our interactions, including whether we interrupt, encourage someone else to speak, nod attentively, actively disagree, and so on.

Gender Stereotypes and Communication

One conclusion that we might draw from these studies on gender differences in the use of verbal and nonverbal cues is that women should try to adopt the culturally recognized male patterns in order to reap the same rewards. But would they?

When social psychologists began looking for objective cues to identify who would emerge as leader in an initially unstructured group, they found that the emergent leader was often the one centrally located in the group and that group members seated at the ends of the table became leaders more often than those occupying side positions. Psychologist Robert Pellegrini (1971) had subjects rate each person in photographs of five college women seated around a rectangular table, one at the head and two on each side. The woman seated at the head of the table was identified as the most influential, talkative, and leaderlike and as the one who had contributed most to the group. Pellegrini reasoned that we expect the high-status member of a group to be seated at the head of the table in our society, so we automatically attribute status and dominance to the person who occupies that position. The head of the table thus serves as a nonverbal cue to leadership status.

Natalie Porter and Florence Geis (1981) devised a study to determine whether the cues identifying a man as a leader would equally confer leadership on a woman. They decided to use position at the head of the table as the cue they would study, since it would be unlikely that, in photographs of seating position, males and females would seem to be doing this "differently." The research described above showed that the position at the head of the table serves as a leadership cue in same-sex groups. Porter and Geis hypothesized that in *mixed-sex* settings, sex-role stereotypes that define women as nonleaders when a man is available would cause leadership cues to be interpreted differently for males and females.

Using the same procedure that Pellegrini had used, Porter and Geis showed subjects a slide of five individuals seated at a rectangular table, two on each side and one at the head. To make sure that results were not due to a particular stimulus person, the researchers used several slides, with the seating positions of particular individuals varied in each one. Subjects viewed one slide and then rated each group member shown.

As they had predicted, the researchers found that the person at the head of the table was seen as the leader in the all-female, all-male, and mixed-sex groups with a male at the head of the table but not in mixed-sex groups with a female at the head of the table. In fact, a woman at the head of the table in a mixed-sex group was less than half as likely to be seen as the leader as was the person at the head in the other three conditions. This was true among both male and female subjects, including those with feminist as well as those with nonfeminist beliefs. The researchers concluded

that "seeing is not believing" when the objective evidence seen is not consistent with the beliefs encoded in cultural stereotypes. This suggests that women cannot get the same treatment as men simply by displaying the same nonverbal cues.

Men and women are judged differently when they use the same verbal cues as well. Women who attempt to adjust their styles by speaking louder, longer, and more assertively are judged to be acting in an "unfeminine" manner (Tannen, 1990). They may command more attention and respect, but they are likely to be disliked and disparaged as "aggressive" and "unfeminine." A man acting the same way is merely being a masculine male, and he is judged positively as a result. Indeed, women do not have to be particularly aggressive to be criticized.

A study by Harriet Wall and Anita Barry (1985) found that we define success in masculine terms and see these traits as incompatible with femininity. The researchers gave students information about prospective professors — their academic backgrounds, publications, and letters of recommendation — and asked the students to predict how well the candidates would do if hired and what their chances were of winning a distinguished teaching award. Some of the students were given a woman's name and others a man's name for the candidate. Those who believed the materials described a woman candidate were more likely to predict that she would not win the teaching award because, as one student put it, there was "too much business, not enough personality." None of the students who read exactly the same file under a man's name made these negative inferences about personality. In addition, students who believed they were evaluating a woman expected her to be more nurturing and to devote more time to her students outside of class than those who thought they were evaluating a man.

When women use stronger, more direct power cues — cues considered inappropriate to their gender — they often receive negative evaluations (Burgoon and Miller, 1985; Russell, Rush, and Herd, 1988; Heilman et al., 1989; Powell, 1990). This produces a double-bind dilemma for women who aspire to positions of leadership or responsibility. If they use typical female cues, they are ignored — considered "nice mice" who don't possess the necessary leadership qualities. If they use stronger signals, they are viewed as overly emotional, arrogant, and abusive — "dragons" who are trespassing on territory regarded as inappropriate for women. No "right" demeanor can be achieved (Fogarty, Rapaport, and Rapaport, 1971). Consider, for example, the plight of Geraldine Ferraro as the first female candidate for vice president of the United States. The press made much of the fact that in her debate with then Vice President Bush, she had difficulty creating a public image that would be authoritative but not "too masculine" (Epstein, 1988).

Even when journalists set out to praise Ferraro, they often used terms that highlighted the incongruity between her gender and the office she was seeking. Linguist Michael Geis (1987) points out in his book *The Language of Politics* that she was called "spunky" and "feisty" — words, Geis observes, that are used only for small, powerless creatures: for a Pekingese but not a Great Dane, perhaps for Mickey Rooney but not for John Wayne. Our language has built-in gender distinctions that shape our attitudes. It appears that gender is itself a cue that, in some situations, conflicts with or even overrides other communication cues to determine the responses of others (Eagly and Karau, 1991; Eagly, Makhijani, and Klonsky, 1992).

RACE AND CLASS DIFFERENCES IN COMMUNICATION

Race and social class are also sources of communication differences and, as a result, sources of communication problems when members of different races or social classes come together. Although the research literature on racial and social class communication styles is less extensive than that on gender differences in communication, several interesting observations have been made.

In his classic study, anthropologist William Labov (1972) found that African-American males (in this case, young, urban, and mainly lower class) exchanged insults, often in the presence of other peers who served as an audience. This activity was usually competitive in nature, in that each man tried to top the previous insult with one that was more clever, outrageous, or elaborate. The audience members acted as judges in deciding who won the competition of insults. Labov referred to this style of verbal exchange as "ritual insults."

Labov's observations were followed by research aimed at discovering the communication styles of females, whites, and members of the middle class (whatever their gender or race). Researchers observing African-American females found that they adopted the ritual-insult style when interacting with African-American males, and their communication with one another was typified by play songs and cheers that incorporated several aspects of insulting, such as assertive and mocking tones (Goodwin, 1980; Heath, 1983). Studies of white females found that the use of assertive and mocking play songs was not common (Heath, 1983) and that middle-class white females were often intimidated by the more aggressive style of their African-American peers (Schofield, 1982). However, still another study of the interaction among groups of white females found that ritual insulting *was* common among girls who came from working-. or lower-class backgrounds but not among those from the middle class (Eder, 1990). The researcher concluded that social class (not gender or race) was the major determinant of ritual insulting and that communication problems arise when persons from different social classes interact largely because middle-class people interpret working- and lower-class speech styles as both rude and assertive.

In a similar vein, Thomas Kochman (1981) observed differences in the communication styles used by African-Americans and whites in conflict situations. According to Kochman, blacks more frequently use a loud, animated, and confrontational style, while whites more frequently use a quiet, dispassionate, and nonchallenging style. The observations of a second researcher (Donohue, 1985) support those of Kochman: he found that in conflicts between members of the two races, African-Americans tend to be loud while whites are more likely to be extremely solicitous and friendly. Kochman proposes a cultural explanation for the communication differences. He contends that in African-American culture, loudness is viewed as an expression of sincerity and conviction of action — and therefore is positively valued. African-Americans tend to interpret whites' solicitous and friendly style of conflict communication as a mask of hypocrisy and weakness. On the other hand, whites interpret the loudness of African-Americans as overly aggressive and hostile.

Again, however, it is important to note that these studies compare working- and lower-class African-Americans to middle-class whites. Thus, the observed differences in communication styles may reflect *social class* differences rather than *racial* differences. In one study of middle-class college students, males of both races tended to use the quiet, nonchallenging style (there were only a small number of African-American males in the study), and the style differences between the females of the two races were small, although African-American females used the intense, confrontational style somewhat more frequently (Ting-Toomey, 1986).

Several studies suggest that racial differences in the cues that listeners and speakers provide for one another can also cause difficulties in interracial interaction (LaFrance and Mayo, 1976; Erickson, 1979). For example, African-American speakers tend to give fewer and more subtle cues indicating that they expect listener feedback. White speakers tend to look *away* from the listener while talking, whereas African-American speakers look *at* the listener more. White listeners, on the other hand, look at the speaker almost continuously, while African-American listeners look down or away and give fewer and more subtle listening cues (such as nods) than do whites. For example, for white speakers, listening is signaled by gaze, combined with *both* verbal and nonverbal back-channel cues. For African-

American speakers, *either* a vocal ("um-hmm") *or* a nonvocal (head nod) cue signals listening; these cues are rarely given together. White speakers infer from this that the African-American listener is not paying attention or doesn't understand. Consequently, they often repeat points and overexplain, making the African-American listener feel that the speaker thinks she or he is stupid. On the other hand, African-American speakers often feel that a white listener's "staring" indicates hostility.

CULTURAL UNIVERSALS AND DIFFERENCES

As we noted at the beginning of this chapter, the meanings that symbols come to have are arbitrary in the sense that they result from cultural conventions. A symbol can have any meaning that a group of people agree on. This means, of course, that a single symbol may have different meanings for different groups. Our discussion of gender, race, and class differences provides many examples of this. However, there are some commonalities in the use of symbols among various cultures and subcultures. In this section we'll explore both these commonalities and the cultural differences in the use of various kinds of symbols for communication.

Language

Human communities develop languages in order to express thoughts and feelings. All human groups have some features in common, and these are reflected in **linguistic universals** — features common to every language. Every language has nouns and verbs, for example, because all people must refer to objects and actions. Every language has terms for such spatial dimensions as direction (right, left; up, down; front, back), distance, height, and length, because all people use basically the same perceptual capacities to orient themselves to the physical world (Clark and Clark, 1977). Similarly, every language has terms to distinguish between past, present, and future — universally experienced dimensions of time.

Some linguistic universals result from common experiences of social life. These are of particular interest to social psychologists. For example, all cultures have some sort of family structure, although the structures themselves vary. All languages contain terms that allow speakers to distinguish three characteristics of family members — sex, generation, and blood relationship. All languages have precise, simple terms for relatives who spend the most time together, but they usually string together several terms to specify one's exact relationship to relatives who are less central to the family structure. For example, in English, the term "grandmother" designates a female, two generations prior to the referent, and a blood relationship. But the term "cousin" designates only two of the three characteristics — generation and blood relationship but not gender; it takes two words, "female cousin," to completely describe the cousin relationship. All languages have pronouns that facilitate references to self and other — for example, in English, "I/we," "you," and "he/she/they." Other universal language concepts include certain body parts (head, foot, belly, mouth), colors (red, green, black, white), common human actions (eat, sleep, hear, walk), and features of the environment (cloud, earth, rain, moon, fire) (Swadesh, 1971).

All languages have terms for concepts that are central to daily activities. As we have seen, the *common* capacities and experiences of humans lead to the incorporation of certain features in all languages — linguistic universals. But human groups also *differ* in terms of the physical environments they inhabit and the activities they undertake. These differences are also reflected in their languages. The Arabs have some 6,000 different terms for camels. The Hanunoo, a people of the Philippine Islands, have a term for each of ninety-two varieties of rice. Having precise words for frequently needed concepts makes communication easier and more accurate.

When learning to speak a new language, people generally do not pick up all the cultural conventions about how it should be used in different contexts. As a result, they may accidentally send the wrong message. For example, German allows more direct phrasing of requests and complaints than English does (House and Kasper, 1981). Thus, when Germans speak English, they sometimes sound domineering to Americans accustomed to the English convention that considers it impolite to be too direct with status equals. Similarly, research suggests that Israelis are concerned with appearing to be honest and forthright in their communications, while Americans and the British are more concerned with appearing to be polite and considerate (Katriel, 1986). Israeli speakers, in striving to maximize the attributes of honesty and forthrightness, which are valued in their culture, may come across to American and British listeners as rude and inconsiderate.

Body Language

Some gestures have the same or similar meanings in several cultures. An example is the side-to-side head motion meaning "no." However, some behaviors have a specific meaning in one culture but not in another. The French gesture of putting one's fist around the tip of the nose and twisting to signify that a person is drunk is not employed in other cultures. And a gesture may have one meaning in one culture and a different meaning in another culture. Thus, Roman emperors gave the thumbs-up gesture to spare the lives of gladiators in the Colosseum. Today the same gesture is favored by American and Western European airline pilots, truck drivers, and others to mean "all right." But in Sardinia and northern Greece, it is an insulting gesture, paralleling the insulting middle-finger gesture of American society (Ekman, Friesen, and Bear, 1984).

One aspect of body language, however, does seem to have common meanings in different cultures — the *facial expression* of emotion. Paul Ekman (1980) and his associates showed subjects from widely different cultures photographs of individuals' faces that in Western societies are judged to display six basic emotions: happiness, sadness, anger, surprise, disgust, and fear (see photo). The researchers found that college-educated subjects in the United States, Brazil,

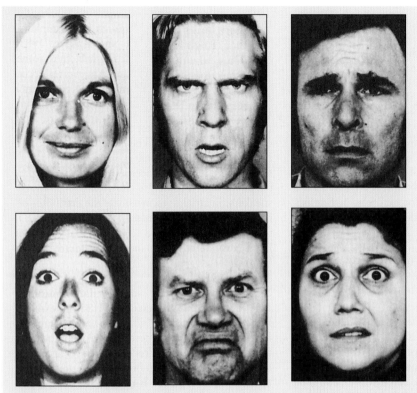

People in many cultures recognize the emotions of happiness, anger, sadness, surprise, disgust, and fear in these photos.

Argentina, Chile, and Japan ascribed the same emotions to the same faces. Moreover, with the exception of their failure to discriminate fear from surprise, even the isolated and preliterate Fore of New Guinea made similar distinctions. (Among the Fore, surprising events are almost always fearful, such as the sudden appearance of a hostile member of another village or the unexpected meeting of a "ghost.")

In a more recent study, Ekman and his colleagues showed photographs depicting the six emotions to college-student observers in ten countries (Ekman et al., 1987). The observers were asked to rate *how intensely* the person in the photo was experiencing the emotion, as well as *which* emotion the person was feeling. Although there were high levels of agreement across cul-

tures about which emotion was being expressed, judgments of intensity showed much lower levels of agreement. The greater variation in intensity than in type of emotion may be a result of cultural differences in "display rules."

Ekman believes this evidence demonstrates that our central nervous systems are genetically prewired for the facial expression of emotion. However, he does not rule out the influence of environment. Learning determines which circumstances will elicit a given emotional expression, and cultures formulate their own display rules to regulate the expression of emotion. For example, in our culture, norms prescribe that even though a guest might feel intense disgust at the thought of eating the specific food served by his hostess, politeness requires that he attempt to mask the expression of this emotion. The guest shouldn't leap back from the table exclaiming, "Oh, yuck, how revolting!" or even sit quietly and wrinkle his nose like the person in the "disgust" photo on page 544. Instead, he should pretend to be delighted by the feast or at least make a polite excuse for not eating the disgusting item ("Oh, that looks delicious, but my doctor has told me I absolutely mustn't eat pickled frog eyes any more") and, at the same time, should make every effort to have his facial expression match his insincere words. Some other cultures might allow freer expression of disgust in this situation.

Interpersonal Spacing

Anthropologist Edward T. Hall (1966) has shown that there are cultural differences in interpersonal spacing. Hall observes that Americans commonly consider Arabs to be pushy and rude. Paradoxically, Arabs also consider Americans to be pushy. This is because interpersonal spacing has different meanings in the two cultures. For example, the visual interaction of Arabs is intense: they stare; Americans do not. Further, Arabs bathe the other person in their breath. To smell another is not only desirable but mandatory; to deny another one's breath is to act ashamed. Whereas Arabs stay inside the olfactory bubble of others, Americans stay outside of it. Hence an American communicates shame to the Arab when, in fact, the American is trying to be polite. These behaviors, Hall explains, derive from the fact that the typical Arab lacks a sense of a private spatial bubble that envelops the body. Rather than viewing a person as extending in space beyond the body, Arabs see the person as existing somewhere down *inside* the body. Thus, they violate the American ego by invading Americans' private space.

In summary, human communication is characterized by both cultural universals and differences. These interest social psychologists because they illustrate the complexity of human experience. On the one hand, we have much in common with others. We inhabit the same earth and are subject to its physical laws. Even some features of social experience are common to all cultures. We all

have parents and other kin, for example; we all feel certain basic emotions, and we must all communicate with others in order to negotiate and align our actions.

On the other hand, members of different cultural groups have different concerns and these are reflected in their communications. Different cultural groups have devised different symbols even for the universal aspects of human experience. Consider, for example, all the different words for mother in the world's languages. Subcultures within a cultural group may assign different meanings to certain symbols and may have jargons all their own. Even a brother and sister growing up in the same family, who have in common not only the larger culture but also the group culture of the family itself, may experience the world very differently from each other — and develop different communication styles and concerns — due to a factor such as gender. Why is this so? It is because our culture assigns meanings to such characteristics as gender, race, social class, and physical beauty, and these meanings affect the way we experience the world — how others react to us and how we come to see ourselves. We'll discuss the process by which this occurs in our next two chapters: Chapter 6, "Social Attitudes and Attributions," and Chapter 7, "The Social Nature of Self."

Summary

1. Communication is the process by which people interact and interpret their interactions. Symbols are objects or actions that stand in, or substitute, for something else. Significant symbols are symbols for which several people share meanings. They are important because they allow us to coordinate our behaviors with those of others.

2. We communicate through several kinds of symbols: language, paralanguage, body language, interpersonal spacing, physical characteristics, and personal effects.

3. We communicate multiple meanings with a single message. Besides conveying task information, our communicative behavior reflects the intimacy of our relationships with other persons, as well as our relative status within the group, provides information about ourselves and our feelings, and is used to manage impressions of ourselves and our relationships. We use facework to support or challenge the public images we claim for ourselves or attribute to others.

4. Our behavior also provides cues to regulate the interaction itself: we signal the initiation of interaction, indicate our willingness to stop or start speaking, and provide feedback to the speaker to indicate our interest and understanding. We often indicate our intentions indirectly, relying on the cooperative principle to decipher a speaker's meaning.

5. Different gender, racial, and social class groups have different norms for regulating conversation. Therefore, when members of these different groups interact, miscommunication may result. Some explanations for gender differences in communication styles relate to women's disadvantaged position in society or their biological role as mothers. The socialization or cultural explanation suggests that males and females interact, as children, in same-gender subgroups whose different norms they learn. Working- and lower-class persons use a loud interaction style in conflict situations which middle-class persons interpret as overly aggressive and hostile. Middle-class persons use a friendly and solicitous conflict style which lower- and working-class persons interpret as hypocritical and weak. African-Americans and whites tend to use different speaking and listening cues — sometimes leading to difficulties in interracial interaction.

6. Common human concerns are reflected in linguistic universals — features that exist in all languages. Language differences also reflect the different concerns of various human groups. Even subgroups of a language group have specialized vocabularies which reflect their particular concerns.

Additional sources:

Photo, p. 673, Stewart Cohen/Index Stock.

Photo, p. 688, David Lissy/eStock Photography/Picture Quest.

Photos, p. 698, Modified and reproduced by special permission of the publisher, Consulting Psychologist Press, Inc., Palo Alto, CA 94303. From *Pictures of Facial Affect* by Paul Ekman and Wallace V. Friesen. Copyright 1976 by Paul Ekman. All rights reserved. Further reproduction is prohibited without the publisher's consent.

Excerpt, pp. 666–667, with permission of *San Francisco Examiner.*

Box, p. 669, with permission of *Time.*

Box, p. 674, with permission of Brent Staples.

Excerpt, p. 691, with permission of William Morrow and Co., Inc.

SELECTION **11-1**

Psychology

Collaboration Option

Comprehension Quiz: Textbook Chapter

Directions: Refer to Selection 11-1 as necessary to complete this quiz.

Options for collaboration: For some of these exercises, your instructor may prefer that you work collaboratively, that is, with other students. These exercises are identified in the margin. *If your instructor directs you to work collaboratively on any of these items,* form groups of three or four classmates to complete the exercise together. Discuss your answers with each other and have one member of the group record the answers. A member of the group may be asked to share the group's answers with the class.

1. Create a test review sheet for one or more of the four main sections of Selection 11-1:

   "Symbols" (pages 666–676)

   "What We Communicate" (pages 676–682)

   "How We Communicate: Rules of Conversation" (pages 682–689)

   "Group Differences in Communication" (pages 689–699)

   Note: Your instructor will give you specific instructions about this assignment.

2. Your instructor will distribute one or more quizzes on the sections in Selection 11-1. You will be allowed to use your review cards and your test review sheet.

Read More about It on the World Wide Web

To learn more about the topic of this selection, visit these websites or use your favorite search engine (such as Yahoo ®). Whenever you go to *any* website, it is a good idea to evaluate it critically. Are you getting good information— information that is accurate, complete, and up-to-date? Who sponsors the website? How easy is it to use the features of the website?

http://www.cyberparent.com/talk/
   This site, called "About Communications," contains numerous suggestions for improving your communication skills.

http://www.collegerecruiter.com/pages/articles/article146.htm
   This site presents five keys to acquiring better communication skills.

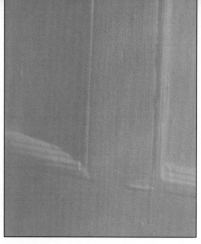

© PhotoDisc

A P P E N D I X

1

An Introduction to Using Computers, the Internet, and the World Wide Web

IN THIS APPENDIX . . .

Appendix 1 provides an introduction to using computers, the Internet, and the World Wide Web. If you are unfamiliar with using computers and the Internet, it will provide you with helpful information that will help you begin to use these valuable tools.

Everyone has heard of the Internet and the World Wide Web, but how significant is their impact? One index of their importance is the time required for a quarter of the world's population to receive information from this source. It took 500 years for 25 percent of the world's population to receive information via the printing press. It took 50 years for a fourth of the world to receive information from television, audio, and video sources. In stark contrast, it required only five years for a quarter of the world's population to receive information via the Internet. This is especially impressive, since the first computer made its historic debut in 1947. (ENIAC, as the first computer was called, weighed 30 tons and filled a 30- by 50-foot room!) The significance of computers and the Internet is evidenced by the fact that most schools now have computers and Internet access. In fact, some public schools in Connecticut, Maine, and New York now provide a laptop computer for each student.

Most colleges and universities have computers available to students in labs or in the library. These are usually hooked up to the Internet, and there is probably a knowledgeable person nearby to help you log on and answer any questions. If you want to set up your own personal computer system with Internet access, you'll need the following equipment:

- Computer
- Modem
- Telephone line
- Internet Service Provider (ISP)

Computers

More and more students these days are choosing to purchase their own personal computer. There are many considerations to keep in mind when buying a computer, but cost is certainly a big one for most students. You'll need to decide how important different features, several of which are explained below, are for you and your needs.

CPU

The central processing unit (CPU) is the brain of the computer, and its speed determines how fast the computer can process information. The two most important features to notice about the CPU are the type of processor, such as the Pentium processor, and its clock speed. The clock speed is measured in megahertz (MHz). (For example, "300 MHz Pentium II" indicates that the processor is running at 300 MHz.) These two features determine, in large part, both the speed and the cost of a computer.

RAM

Random access memory (RAM) functions as a computer's short-term memory, or working storage space. RAM is measured in megabytes (MB = 1.049 million bytes) and is usually expandable. Modern software requires quite a bit of

RAM to operate, especially if you want to use more than one software application at a time. An "insufficient memory" message probably means your computer is running out of RAM and you'll need to close some applications if you want to continue working. The amount of RAM available on new computers is rapidly increasing, and most sold have 96 to 128 MB. If you are thinking of buying an older used computer, consider upgrading its RAM to expand its capabilities.

Hard Disk Drive

The permanent long-term storage area on a computer is the hard disk drive. This is where most of your software applications and documents live. The capacity of modern hard drives is measured in gigabytes (GB = 1.074 billion bytes). Software these days takes up enormous space on hard drives, and if you plan to work with video clips or sound files, you will need an especially large hard disk. You can conserve hard disk space by storing some applications or files on floppy diskettes or zip diskettes, or by compressing files, but many people find this inconvenient. If you are buying a new computer, you probably need at least 3 GB of hard disk storage.

Floppy Drive and CD-ROM Drive

Most computers sold now have a floppy drive for 3 1/2-inch diskettes, although these are becoming obsolete. They are being replaced with a CD-ROM drive that allows you to access data stored on CD-ROMs, and can store the data equivalent of four hundred fifty 3 1/2-inch diskettes. Since CD-ROMs are read-only, you can't store your own data on them; you should consider buying a computer with both floppy and CD-ROM drives.

Modem

A modem is a piece of equipment that changes the information that a computer works with into the kind of information that can be passed over the telephone lines. It is what allows your computer to "talk" to other computers around the world. It can be an external box or an internal card that is placed in the hard drive. Most new computers now come with built-in modems.

To use your modem, you will need a telephone line. You can use your regular telephone line, which will cause a busy signal to callers when you are online, or you can get a "dedicated line," a separate phone line just for internet access. Colleges and universities often have banks of modems accessible through the same number, so when you call the university your call will be directed to the next available modem.

Modems come in different speeds. The speed of a modem determines how quickly you can download or access information from the internet. The most widely used speed is 56K (k = kilobyte = 1,024 bytes); however, modems are continually getting faster, and there is now an option for high-speed connections such as cable modems. If you live on campus, check to see if your dorm room is outfitted with Ethernet port so that you can plug directly into the school's network without having to use a dial-up connection.

Hooking Up to the Internet

Most colleges and universities provide internet access to their students and faculty at an attractive cost, and if you have access to this you should probably use it. If you need to hook up a computer to the Internet on your own, you must go through an Internet Service Provider (ISP). ISPs are companies that run the computers that enable you to get onto the Net; these computers are called servers. It works like this: when you log on to the Net, your modem dials your ISP. When the modem is connected to the ISP, it actually connects to the ISP's modem on the ISP's computer (the computer at the ISP is called the server). The best-known ISPs are national ones like America Online (AOL) and Compuserve. But there are numerous smaller ISPs out there as well.

There are a few considerations to keep in mind in choosing among the many ISPs:

- **Cost.** Do they have a flat fee for unlimited Internet time each month, or will they charge you for each minute you are online? Some services have several different plans you can choose from; the best one for you depends on how much time you spend online each month. Be sure to shop around and find an ISP that offers the best rate plan for you.

- **Traffic.** Some ISPs have high usage, and it can be difficult to get online (particularly with the larger national companies). Find out the "dial up" number (the number your modem calls to link up) of an ISP and call it at different times during the day to see if it's busy.

- **Service.** Some ISPs are courteous and prompt in answering customers' questions and complaints; others have trouble in this area. Ask your friends, acquaintances, and computer science instructors at your school to recommend ISPs that have good service.

Electronic Mail (E-mail)

E-mail is a way of transmitting messages across a phone line to a specified other person's computer. To send or receive e-mail you must have a program called a mail browser (some common ones are Eudora and Microsoft Mail) and an e-mail account through your school or ISP. When you send an e-mail to someone, you type the person's e-mail address in the space provided. E-mail addresses consist of the individual user's name or identification, the @ symbol, and the name of their server and domain: *username@servername.domainname.*

After writing your message in the "body" of the e-mail, you can send it. The message is transmitted across phone lines to the recipient server, which "sorts" the mail and sends it to the individual's e-mail address.

E-mail is generally somewhat informal and not very lengthy. E-mail can be used for many purposes, including sending out memos, keeping up with friends and relatives, telecommuting, and exchanging documents and files.

Here are a few things to keep in mind about using e-mail:

* Try to check your mail every day, especially if you belong to a mailing list. It's amazing how quickly your "mailbox" can fill up with messages.
* Know your *netiquette.* (See below.)
* Don't send anything too confidential or sensitive over e-mail; e-mail is easily accessed by others.
* Proofread your e-mail before you send it.

World Wide Web (WWW)

Since 1992, when the World Wide Web was first launched, it has exploded into mainstream culture. The Web is a goldmine of information for students and faculty, and more is being added every day. As technology becomes more sophisticated, there are an increasing number of websites featuring animation, video, and sound.

Browsers

To get to the World Wide Web, you have to have a computer program called a Web browser. Two well-known and popular Web browsers are Netscape and Microsoft Internet Explorer. You can purchase a browser from a computer store, get one from your ISP, or download one from the Web itself. To download the latest version of Netscape for academic use, go to Netscape's Home Page (http://www.netscape.com). Once you are logged on to the Internet, you simply click to open the browser and you are ready to "surf the Net."

Web Addresses

The Web is made up of millions of websites (or Web pages). Each website has an address, known as the URL (Uniform Resource Locator). A typical URL looks like this: http://www.mcgraw-hill.com. This is the address for the McGraw-Hill website. (McGraw-Hill is the publisher of this textbook.) To get to any website, all you have to do is type in the URL in your Web browser.

You can analyze a website address to figure out who it belongs to and what the individual or organization does. The first part of the address is "http;" it stands for HyperText Transport Protocol, which is the language of the Web. Generally you will see "www," which tells the server that we want to get our information from the World Wide Web. The last two parts of the address are called the domain name. The "domain" indicates what kind of site it is. In McGraw-Hill's case, it is ".com" (pronounced "dot-com"), which stands for "commercial." (A commercial website is one that is owned by a business.) Other domains you will probably come across include: ".edu" = education, ".org" = organization, and ".gov" = government. When you read the address for a website out loud, remember that every "." is pronounced "dot."

Surfing the Web

A key concept to understand in surfing the Web is "links." Links are high-lighted words or images on a Web page that you can click on to go to other pages. (Click means to use the mouse to put the arrow on the screen on what-ever you want, then press down—*click*—the button on the mouse.) Once you find a topic that interests you, it is easy to explore just by clicking on links. Keep in mind that some links will connect you to another page by the same or-ganization; others will take you to an altogether different site.

A person or organization's website usually consists of many pages. The first page you come to when you type in a URL is called the home page. This page usually contains a menu for the entire site and lets you know something about the site's creators and purpose. The home page contains links to other pages within that site, and often to other sites of interest. With most browsers you can go back to a previous link by clicking a button that says "Go Back." You will not get "stuck" someplace you don't want to be, so don't be shy about exploring links.

Websites can be developed by any person or organization on any topic. The amount of information available on the Web today is staggering and continues to grow. You can utilize the Web for general research, as an educational tool, as a shopping mall, to find a long-lost friend, to get a new job, or to answer almost any question you might have. You are limited only by your imagination.

Search Engines

Now that you have a basic idea of the workings of the WWW, how do you go about finding websites that may interest you? A good starting point is to use one of the popular directories on the Web called search engines. A search en-gine allows you to type in keywords for the topic that you are interested in. It then lists any sites that contain the key word. Some of the larger and more pop-ular search engines are:

- Yahoo! http://www.yahoo.com
- Excite http://www.excite.com
- Hot Bot http://www.hotbot.com
- Lycos http://www.lycos.com
- Infoseek http://www.infoseek.com
- WebCrawler http://webcrawler.com
- Alta Vista http://altavista.com
- Google http://google.com

To use a search engine, type in one of the addresses listed above. When the home page for that site comes up, you will notice a "search" box in which you can type a keyword or phrase. The search engine will then bring up as a list of sites all the information that it has available on that topic. Sometimes you will need to narrow your search; for example, if you type "psychology," you will have hundreds or thousands of site listings returned. On the other hand, if you are too specific, such as "women's duck hunting competitions in Texas," you may not have any sites returned. This does not necessarily mean that no sites exist, however.

Bookmarks

If you have your own computer, bookmarks are a handy feature to know about. Once you find a website you will want to return to in the future, you can "bookmark" it. To bookmark a site, go to that site. After it has finished loading, choose "bookmark" from your menu bar and your browser will instantly record the address to that site in your bookmark "list." Anytime you want to return to that site, you simply open the bookmark icon and click on the name of that website. Different ISPs offer different methods for bookmarking sites. America Online, for example, uses a system called "favorite places" that works similarly.

Tips for Using the World Wide Web

Be patient. Accessing a website can take time, depending on how elaborate the site is, how fast your modem can download the information, and what time of day you are online. You can speed things up a bit by turning off the "auto load image" option in your browser. Keep in mind that "hiccups" can occur in the transfer process. Sometimes the server of the website you are trying to reach may be down, there may be a lot of activity on that site, or there may be line noise. Just try again to load the website, or try again later. Because the Web is so dynamic, sites and links change every day. You might find some links on Web pages that go nowhere because the link has moved its pages to a new server or address.

Remember that while the Web is a great source of information, not everything on it is true or worthwhile. It is up to you to evaluate the information you get from the Web

FTP and Telnet

FTP stands for file transfer protocol. FTP sites are software repositories from which you can download shareware software, demos, images, text, sound, and anything else that can be transmitted via the Internet. You can access FTP sites from the Web the same way you would enter any URL (FTP addresses begin with ftp://). Most FTP sites support anonymous FTP, which means that anyone can log on to the site with the user name "anonymous," enter his or her own e-mail address as the password, then download whatever files are of interest. If you download materials from FTP, scan them with antiviral software to be sure they are clean, or you could end up infecting your hard drive with a computer virus.

Telnet enables you to log on to another host computer to run one of its computers or to access information from it. You can Telnet to other hosts from most Web browsers if you have Telnet software configured to work with your browser.

Mailing Lists

Mailing lists (or listservs) are electronic mailing discussion groups that take place through e-mail. They are groups of people who "get together" online to discuss a specific topic. For students, mailing lists can offer a way to participate in lively discussions, stay up-to-date on current research, or hear opinions about burning questions.

There are mailing lists on nearly every topic imaginable. Here's how the system works: You find out about a mailing list dealing with a subject you are interested in discussing with others (e.g., choosing your major). In order to get involved in a discussion group, you have to subscribe to it. To subscribe, you send an e-mail to that mailing list's listserv with the word "subscribe" in the subject line and in the main body of the text. Also include your e-mail address. Usually, the listserv will then register you as a subscriber and send you instructions on how to post to the group. Posting means that you send out a comment to the entire mailing list that you have subscribed to. Every time any member posts to the listserv, all the subscribers get that posting as an e-mail message. Once you have subscribed, you will begin to receive e-mail messages from the mailing list. Be careful, though: some discussion groups have a large following and you may find your mailbox filling up faster than you can read the messages.

Netiquette

"Netiquette" is simply etiquette—or standards of courtesy—for Internet users. Because no one owns or polices the Internet, it is especially important that all users take responsibility for keeping communications civilized. Remember that the written communications of the Internet cannot convey meanings by voice inflection or body language, and it's easy to be misinterpreted.

Here are some helpful netiquette principles to keep in mind:

- Don't assume your correspondents know you are kidding, or being sarcastic, or anything else.
- Don't be too harsh or judgmental with those you disagree with.
- Don't use all capital letters; this may be interpreted as SCREAMING.
- Don't gossip or spread rumors on the Internet. This is a good way to get into trouble.
- Do be kind and thoughtful in your correspondence.
- Do be honest; if you put misinformation onto the Net, it could go to thousands of people.
- Do reply quickly to your correspondents.
- Do make messages and postings brief and to the point.
- Do proofread your messages before you send them.

Flaming

If you frequent the Net, especially discussion groups, you may get "flamed" or see someone else get flamed. Flaming is a hostile response that generally occurs as a result of a disagreement and is meant to humiliate and upset the target. Often it is a direct personal attack. Be warned.

Newsgroups/Usenet

Newsgroups, like mailing lists, are a way of discussing topics over the Internet with other people who share the same interests. However, newsgroups take place on an entirely different "network" called Usenet.

Usenet is composed of thousands of discussion areas called newsgroups. Individual comments that people make to one another on a newsgroup are called articles. You "post an article" when you want to make a comment. The lines of discussion within a newsgroup are called threads. To read the discussions on any newsgroup, you must have a software program called a newsreader.

Generally, your ISP will provide you with a newsreader program as part of the software package. When you open the newsreader, it should download any new newsgroups that have been added. You can look through the entire list and choose which newsgroups interest you. When you find one of interest, you just open it up and begin reading the articles.

Newsgroup addresses are called hierarchies. Listed below are some of the standard hierarchies with an example of each. There are many other categories, some of which are from foreign countries.

- alt—groups generally alternative in nature (e.g., alt.education.distance, alt.alien.visitors)
- bionet—groups discussing biology and biological sciences (e.g., bionet.general, bionet.immunology)
- comp—groups discussing computer or computer science issues (e.g., comp.infosystems)
- misc—groups that don't fit into other categories (e.g., misc.fitness, misc.jobs)
- news—groups about Usenet itself (e.g., news.groups)
- rec—groups discussing hobbies, sports, music, and art (e.g., rec.food, rec.humor)
- sci—groups discussing subjects related to science and scientific research (e.g., sci.med.nursing, sci.psychology)
- soc—groups discussing social issues including politics, social programs, etc. (e.g., soc.culture, soc.college)
- talk—public debating forums on controversial issues (e.g., talk.abortion, talk.religion)

Before you make a posting to a newsgroup, you may want to "lurk" for a while, that is, read the discussion without contributing your own posting. Lurking will give you a sense of the kinds of postings that are appropriate for that newsgroup and what the newsgroup culture is like.

Newsgroups may be frequented by people from all over the world, including some experts in the field. They can be a great source of current information and of community. For example, a person suffering from a relatively rare disorder may not know anyone else with the same problems and concerns on campus or in town, but he or she can participate in a newsgroup specifically for people with that disorder to learn about other peoples' experiences and the latest treatments, and just to commiserate. But, as always, be aware that not everything posted to a newsgroup is necessarily true; you must be a critical thinker.

Emoticons

Emoticons (*emotion icons*) are a fun way to express your feelings in electronic communication. They are a series of keystrokes and symbols that make a sideways picture. Emoticons can communicate to your reader that you are joking, disgusted, flirting, or sad—emotions that are otherwise hard to express in typewritten communication. Here are some examples:

:-) this is the most common emoticon, known as a "smiley"

;-) the smiley, winking

:-p the smiley, sticking out its tongue

(:^) a bald smiley with a pointed nose

:-(a sad smiley

8-) a smiley face with glasses

The Internet offers unlimited possibilities. If you are just getting started, talk with a knowledgeable resource person at your college or a knowledgeable friend. See if your college offers Internet orientation classes through the library or media services. Or you might consider enrolling in an introductory computer course. Computers and the Internet are here to stay, so inform yourself and take advantage of this amazing technology.

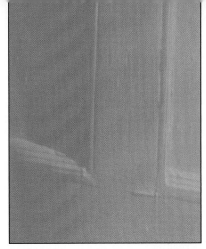

© *PhotoDisc*

Glossary of Key Terms

IN THIS APPENDIX · · ·

Appendix 2 lists key terms from *Opening Doors,* with definitions. This listing will help you review text material and monitor your understanding of the concepts and skills you have studied. The listing is alphabetical; the numbers in parentheses indicate chapters where the key terms are found.

A

annotation: Explanatory notes written in the margins of a textbook to organize and remember information. (Chapter *10*)

appendix: Section at the end of a book which includes supplemental material or specialized information. (*10*)

argument: Point of view or postition the author wants to persuade the reader to believe. (*9*)

average reading: Rate used for textbooks and more complex material in periodicals (200–300 words per minute). (*2*)

B

bar graph: Chart in which the length of parallel rectangular bars is used to indicate relative amounts of the items being compared. (*10*)

bibliography: Textbook feature near the end of the book, giving a list of sources: books, articles, and other works from which the author of the text has drawn information; it may also be called *references, works cited,* or *sources.* Bibliographies sometimes include works the author recommends for further (supplemental) reading. (*10*)

box: Textbook feature consisting of supplementary material separated from the regular text; also called a *sidebar.* (*10*)

C

cause-effect pattern: Writing pattern presenting reasons for (causes of) events or conditions and results (effects) of events or conditions. (*7*)

chapter introduction: Textbook feature opening a chapter, describing the overall purpose and major topics or "setting the scene" with a case study, anecdote, etc. (*10*)

chapter objectives: Textbook features at the beginning of a chapter, telling you what you should know or be able to do after studying the chapter; also called *preview questions, what you'll learn, goals,* etc. (*10*)

chapter outline: Textbook feature at the beginning of a chapter, listing the chapter topics or headings in their order of appearance; also called *chapter contents, preview, overview,* etc. (*10*)

chapter review cards: Study tool and special textbook feature in *Opening Doors;* a way to select, organize, and review the most important information in a chapter; also called *summary cards.* (*1*)

chapter summary: Textbook feature at or near the end of a chapter, in which the author collects and condenses the most essential ideas. (*10*)

comparison-contrast pattern: Writing pattern used to present similarities (comparisons), differences (contrasts), or both. (*7*)

connotation: Additional, nonliteral meaning associated with a word. (*2*)

context clues: Other words in a sentence or paragraph which help the reader deduce the meaning of an unfamiliar word. (*1, 2*)

critical reading: Going beyond basic comprehension to gain additional insights. (*8*)

credibility: Believability of an author's argument. (*9*)

D

definition pattern: Writing pattern presenting the meaning of an important term discussed throughout a passage. (*7*)

denotation: Literal, explicit meaning of a word; its dictionary definition. (*2*)

dictionary pronunciation key: Guide to sounds of letters and combinations of letters in words. A full pronunciation key usually appears near the beginning of a dictionary; an abbreviated key, showing only vowel sounds and the more unusual consonant sounds, usually appears at or near the bottom of each page. (*2*)

distributed practice: Study sessions that are spaced out over time; a more efficient study method than massed practice. (*11*)

E

epigraphs: Quotations that suggest overall themes or concerns of a chapter; this kind of textbook feature is usually found at chapter openings or in the margins. (*10*)

etymology: Origin and history of a word. (*2*)

exhibits: Special textbook features such as student papers, plot summaries, profit-and-loss statements, documents, forms, and printouts. (*10*)

F

fact: Something that can be proved to exist or have happened or is generally assumed to exist or have happened. (*9*)

figurative language: Imagery; words that create unusual comparisons, vivid pictures, and special effects; also called *figures of speech.* (*2*)

flowchart: Diagram that shows steps in procedures or processes by using boxes, circles, and other shapes connected with lines or arrows. (*10*)

G

glossary: Mini-dictionary at end of a textbook, listing important terms and definitions from the entire text. (*10*)

graphic aids: Illustrations that consolidate information and present it more clearly than words alone; graphic aids include figures, cartoons, and photographs. (*10*)

H

hyperbole: Figure of speech using obvious exaggeration for emphasis. (*2*)

I

illustrations: See *graphic aids.* (*10*)

implied main idea: Main point that is not stated directly as one sentence and therefore must be inferred and formulated by the reader. (*5*)

index: Alphabetical listing of topics and names in a textbook, with page numbers, usually appearing at the end of the book. (*10*)

inference: In reading, a logical conclusion based on what an author has stated. (*9*)

intended audience: People an author has in mind as readers; the people he or she is writing for. (*8*)

intended meaning: What an author wants you to understand even when his or her words seem to be saying something different. (*8*)

intermediate goal: Goal you want to accomplish in the next 3 to 5 years. (*1*)

L

learning style: Way in which an individual learns best. (*1*)

line graph: Diagram whose points are connected to show a relationship between two or more variables. (*10*)

list pattern: Series of items in no particular order, since order is unimportant. When set off from the text in some special way, a list is also a useful textbook feature. (*7, 10*)

long-term goal: Goal you want to accomplish during your lifetime. (*1*)

long-term memory: Permanent memory, as contrasted with short-term (temporary) memory. (*11*)

M

mapping: Informal way of organizing main ideas and supporting details by using boxes, circles, lines, arrows, etc. (*10*)

metaphor: Figure of speech implying a comparison between two essentially dissimilar things, usually by saying that one of them *is* the other. (*2*)

mixed pattern: Combination of two or more writing patterns. (*7*)

monitoring comprehension: Evaluating your understanding as you read and correcting the problem whenever you realize that you are not comprehending. (*2*)

monthly assignment calendar: Calendar showing test dates and due dates in all courses for each month of a semester. (*1*)

O

opinion: Belief or judgment that cannot be proved or disproved. (*9*)

organization: Arranging main ideas and supporting details in a meaningful way. Second of three essential study strategies. (*10*)

outlining: Formal way of organizing main ideas and supporting details to show relationships between them. (*10*)

P

paraphrasing: Rewriting someone else's material in your own words. (*6*)

part opening: Textbook feature that introduces a section (part) consisting of several chapters. (*10*)

personification: Figure of speech giving human traits to nonhuman or nonliving things. (*2*)

pie chart: Circle graph in which the sizes of the "slices" represent parts of the whole. (*10*)

point of view: An author's position (attitude, belief, or opinion) on a topic. (*8*)

predicting: Anticipating what is coming next as you read. (*2*)

preface: Introductory section in which authors tell readers about a book. (*10*)

prefix: Word part attached to the beginning of a root that adds its meaning to the root. (*2*)

preparing to read: Previewing a chapter, assessing your prior knowledge, and planning your time. (*3*)

previewing: Examining reading material to determine its subject matter and organization. Previewing is step 1 of the three-step reading process in *Opening Doors.* (*3*)

prior knowledge: What you already know about a topic; background knowledge. (*3*)

purpose: An author's reason for writing. (*8*)

R

rapid reading: Rate used for easy or familiar material (300–500 words per minute). (*2*)

rehearsal: Saying or writing material to transfer it into long-term memory. Third of three essential study strategies. (*3, 10, 11*)

review: See *rehearsal.* (*3, 10*)

review card: Index card with an important question on the front and the answer on the back. (*10*) Also, throughout *Opening Doors,* a technique for reviewing a chapter; *chapter review cards* summarize the most important information in the chapter and therefore are also called *summary cards.*

root: Base word that has a meaning of its own. (*2*)

S

scanning: Information-gathering technique used to locate specific information quickly and precisely. (*2*)

selectivity: Identifying main ideas and important supporting details. First of three essential study strategies. (*10*)

sequence pattern: List of items in a specific, important order. When set off from the text in some special way, a *sequence* is also a useful textbook feature. (*7, 10*)

short-term goal: Goal you want to accomplish in the next 3 to 6 months. (*1*)

short-term memory: Temporary memory. (*11*)

sidebar: See *box.* (*10*)

simile: Figure of speech stating a comparison between two essentially dissimilar things by saying that one of them is *like* the other. (*2*)

skimming: Information-gathering technique that involves moving quickly and selectively through material to find only important material. (*2*)

stated main idea: Sentence in a paragraph that expresses the most important point about the topic. (*4*)

study questions: General term for textbook features such as *activities, exercises, drills,* and *practice sections.* These features may also be called *questions for study and review, review, ask yourself, self-test, check your mastery, mastery test, learning check, check your understanding, topics for discussion, problems,* etc. (*10*)

study reading: Rate used for material that is complex, technical, new, demanding, or very important (50–200 words per minute). (*2*)

study schedule: Weekly schedule with specific times set aside for studying. (*1*)

suffix: Word part attached to the end of a root word. (*2*)

suggested readings: Textbook feature, often at the end of chapters (or parts), listing the author's recommendations for supplemental reading or research, sometimes with annotations (comments); may be called *additional readings, suggestions for further reading, supplementary readings,* etc. (*10*)

summary cards: See *chapter review cards.* (*1*)

summary: Single-paragraph condensation of all the main ideas presented in a longer passage. (*10*)

supplements: Separate aids accompanying a textbook; supplements include *study guides, supplemental readings, student workbooks,* and *computer diskettes.* (*10*)

supporting details: In a paragraph, additional information necessary for understanding the main idea completely. (*6*)

T

table of contents: Textbook feature at the beginning of the book, listing chapter titles and sometimes including headings within chapters as well. (*10*)

table: Material arranged in rows and columns. (*10*)

test review card: Index card with an important question on the front and the answer on the back. (*11*)

test review sheet: Single sheet of paper consolidating and summarizing, on its front and back, the most important information to be covered on a test. (*11*)

textbook feature: Device used by an author to emphasize important material and show how it is organized. (*10*)

"to do" list: Prioritized items to be accomplished in a single day. (*1*)

tone: Manner of writing (choice of words and style) that reflects an author's attitude toward a topic. (*8*)

topic: Word or phrase that tells what an author is writing about. (*4*)

U

underlining and highlighting: Techniques for marking topics, main ideas, and definitions. (*10*)

V

vocabulary aids: Textbook devices that highlight important terms and definitions. Vocabulary aids may be called *key terms, basic terms, terms to know, vocabulary, terms to remember,* etc. (*10*)

W

Webliography: List of websites which feature material related to a topic. (*10*)

word-structure clue: Root, prefix, or suffix that helps you determine a word's meaning. (*2*)

writing patterns: Ways authors organize and present their ideas. (*7*)

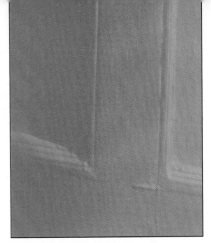

APPENDIX

3

A List of Word Parts

IN THIS APPENDIX . . .

Understanding the meaning of various word parts can help you define many unfamiliar words, especially in context. Most of the word parts listed in this appendix are Greek and Latin; a few are Old English or Slavic. Try to associate each word part (left column) and its meaning (middle column) with the example (right column). Associating the part, definition, and example in this way will help you remember word parts that are new to you.

719

	Word Part	Definition	Example
1.	a	without, not	amoral
2.	ab	from	abstain
3.	acou	hear	acoustic
4.	acro	high	acrobat
5.	alter	another	alternate
6.	ambi	both; around	ambivalent
7.	ambul	walk; go	ambulatory
8.	andr	man (human)	android
9.	annu, anni	year	annual, anniversary
10.	ante	before, forward	antebellum, antecedent
11.	anthrop	humankind	anthropology
12.	anti	against	antifreeze
13.	aqua	water	aquarium
14.	arch	ruler; chief, highest	archbishop, archenemy
15.	astro	star	astronomy
16.	aud	hear	auditory
17.	auto	self	automatic
18.	avi	bird	aviary
19.	belli	war	belligerent
20.	bene	well, good	beneficial
21.	bi	two	bicycle
22.	bio	life	biology
23.	bov	cattle	bovine
24.	by	secondarily	by-product
25.	camera	chamber	bicameral
26.	cani	dog	canine
27.	capit	head	decapitate
28.	card	heart	cardiac
29.	carn	flesh	carnivorous
30.	caust, caut	burn	caustic, cauterize
31.	cav	hollow	cavity
32.	cent	hundred	century
33.	chromo	color	monochromatic
34.	chrono	time	chronology
35.	cide	kill	homicide
36.	contra	against	contraceptive
37.	cosm	universe	microcosm
38.	counter	against	counteract
39.	crat, cracy	rule	democratic
40.	cred, creed	belief	credibility, creed
41.	crypt	secret, hidden	cryptography
42.	cycl	circle	tricycle
43.	deca	ten	decade
44.	dei	god	deity
45.	demo	people	democracy
46.	dent	tooth	dentist
47.	derm	skin	dermatology

	Word Part	Definition	Example
48.	di	two, double	dichotomy
49.	dict	speak	diction
50.	dorm	sleep	dormitory
51.	dyna	power	dynamo
52.	dys	bad, difficult	dysfunctional
53.	enni	year	centennial
54.	epi	upon, outer	epidermis
55.	equ	horse	equine
56.	esque	like, resembling	statuesque
57.	ethn	race, nation	ethnic
58.	eu	good, well	eulogy
59.	ex	out	exit
60.	extra	beyond, over	extravagant
61.	fer	carry, bear	conifer
62.	ferr	iron	ferrous
63.	fid	faith, trust	fidelity
64.	fini	limit	finite
65.	flagr	burn	conflagration
66.	flect, flex	bend	reflect, flexible
67.	fore	before	forewarn
68.	fort	strong	fortress
69.	frater	brother	fraternity
70.	gamy	marriage	monogamy
71.	gastr	stomach	gastric
72.	gene, gen	origin, race, type	genesis, genocide, genre
73.	geo	earth	geography
74.	geronto	old	gerontology
75.	grad, gress	go, step	regress
76.	graph, gram	write, record	telegraph
77.	gyne	woman	gynecology
78.	helio	sun	heliocentric
79.	hemi	half	hemisphere
80.	hemo	blood	hemophilia
81.	hetero	other, different	heterosexual
82.	homo	same	homosexual
83.	hydr	water	hydrant
84.	hyper	over, above	hyperactive
85.	hypo	under, less than	hypodermic
86.	ign	fire	ignite
87.	in, il, im, ir	not	inactive
88.	inter	between	intercept
89.	intra	within	intravenous
90.	itis	inflammation	tonsilitis
91.	ject	throw	eject
92.	junct	join	junction
93.	kilo	thousand	kilometer
94.	later	side	lateral

	Word Part	Definition	Example
95.	leg	law	legal
96.	liber	free	liberate
97.	libr	book	library
98.	lingua	tongue, language	bilingual
99.	lith	stone	lithograph
100.	locu, loqu, log	speak	elocution, colloquial, dialogue
101.	logy	study of	psychology
102.	luc	light, clear	lucid
103.	macro	large	macrocosm
104.	magn	great	magnify
105.	mal	bad, ill	malfunction
106.	mamma	breast	mammal
107.	mania	craving for	kleptomania
108.	manu	hand	manual
109.	matri, mater	mother	maternal
110.	mega	large	megaphone
111.	meter, metr	measure	thermometer, metric
112.	micro	small	microscope
113.	milli	thousand, thousandth	millenium, millimeter
114.	mini	less	minimal
115.	miso	hatred of	misogamy
116.	miss, mit	send	dismiss, transmit
117.	mob, mov, mot	to move	mobile, movable, motion
118.	mono	one	monotone
119.	morph	form	amorphous
120.	mort	death	mortal
121.	multi	many	multitude
122.	nat	born, birth	prenatal
123.	naut	sail	nautical
124.	neo	new	neophyte
125.	nox	harmful	noxious
126.	noct	night	nocturnal
127.	ob, oc, of, op	against	object, occlude, offend, oppress
128.	oct	eight	octopus
129.	ocul	eye	oculist
130.	oid	resembling	humanoid
131.	omni	all	omnipotent
132.	onym	name, word	pseudonym
133.	ortho	correct, straight	orthodontist
134.	osis	condition	psychosis
135.	osteo, ost	bone	osteopath
136.	out	better than	outrun
137.	pac, pax	peace	pacifist
138.	pan	all	panorama
139.	para	beside	parallel, parapsychology
140.	path	feeling, illness	sympathy, pathology
141.	patri, pater	father	paternity

	Word Part	Definition	Example
142.	ped, pod	foot	pedal, tripod
143.	pel	drive	repel
144.	pend	hang	pendulum, pending
145.	penta	five	pentagon
146.	per	through	perspire
147.	peri	around	perimeter
148.	petr	rock	petrified
149.	philo	love	philosophy
150.	phobia	fear of	acrophobia
151.	phono	sound	phonics, phonograph
152.	photo	light	photograph
153.	pneum	air	pneumatic
154.	poly	many	polygon
155.	port	carry	portable
156.	pos	place	position
157.	post	after	postwar
158.	pre	before	prewar
159.	primo	first	primitive, primordial
160.	pro	forward, in favor of	progress, pro-American
161.	pseud	false	pseudoscience
162.	psych	mind	psychic
163.	pugn	fight	pugnacious
164.	punct	point	puncture
165.	purg	cleanse	purge
166.	pyre	fire	pyromania
167.	quad, quart	four	quadruplets, quartet
168.	quint	five	quintet
169.	re	back, again	return, repeat
170.	reg	guide, rule; king	regulate, regal
171.	rupt	break	rupture, disrupt
172.	scend	climb	descend
173.	scope	see; view	telescope
174.	scribe, scrip	write	scribble, prescription
175.	sequ	follow	sequence, sequel
176.	semi	half	semicircle
177.	seni	old	senile
178.	simil	like	similar
179.	sol	sun	solar
180.	soli	alone	solitude
181.	somni	sleep	insomnia
182.	soph	wise	sophomore, sophisticated
183.	spect	see	spectator
184.	spir	breathe	respiratory
185.	strict	tighten	constrict
186.	sub	under	submarine
187.	super, sur	over	supervisor, surpass
188.	surg	rise	surge, resurgent

	Word Part	**Definition**	**Example**
189.	tang, tact	touch	tangible, tactile
190.	tech, tect	skill	technician
191.	tele	far	telepathy
192.	tend, tens	stretch	tendon, tension
193.	terri	earth	territory
194.	tert	third	tertiary
195.	theo	god	theology
196.	therm	heat	thermometer
197.	tomy	cut	vasectomy
198.	tors, tort	twist	distort
199.	toxi	poison	toxic
200.	tract	pull	tractor, extract
201.	tri	three	trio
202.	ultra	beyond, over	ultramodern
203.	unct, ung	oil	unctuous, unguent
204.	uni	one	unity
205.	vacu	empty	vacuum
206.	veni, vent	come	convene, convention
207.	verd	green	verdant
208.	vers, vert	turn	reverse
209.	vid, vis	see	video, vision
210.	vinc	conquer	invincible
211.	vit, viv	life	vitality, vivacious
212.	voc, voke	voice, call	vocal, evoke
213.	voli, volunt	wish	volition, volunteer
214.	volv	roll, to turn	revolve
215.	zoo	animal	zoology

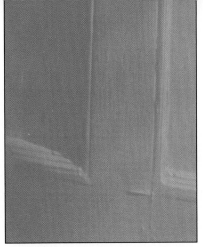

A P P E N D I X

4

World Map and List of World Capitals

IN THIS APPENDIX . . .

Appendix 4 contains a current map of the world. Also included is a list of all 192 countries and the capital of each.

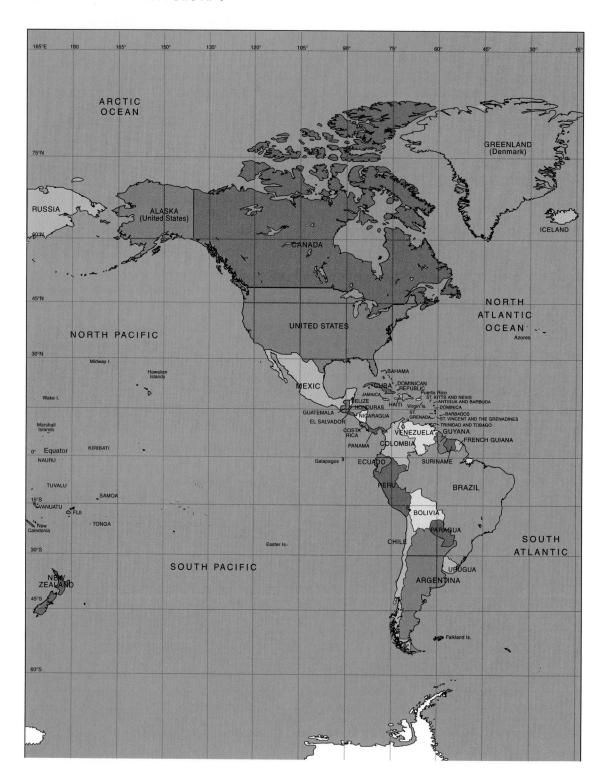

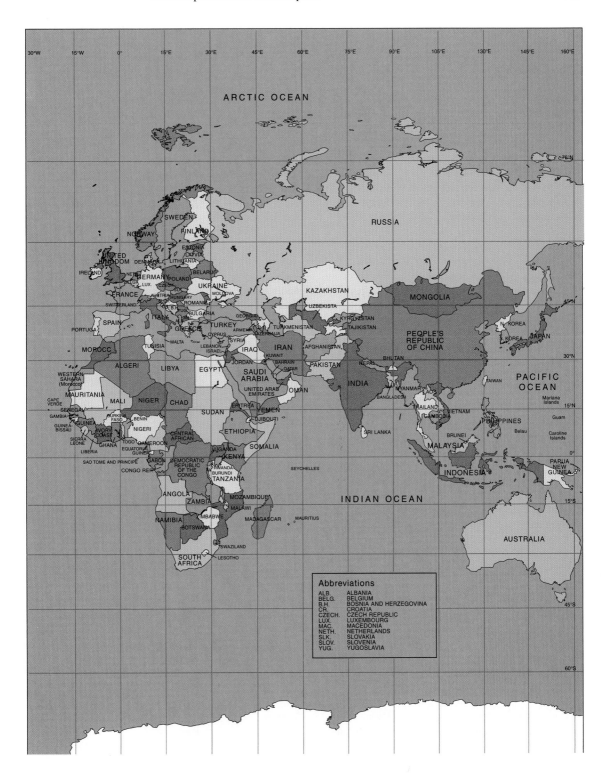

Country	Capital	Country	Capital	Country	Capital
Afghanistan	Kabul	Cuba	Havana	Kiribati	Tarawa
Albania	Tirane	Cyprus	Nicosia	Korea, North	Pyongyang
Algeria	Algiers	Czech Republic	Prague	Korea, South	Seoul
Andorra	Andorra la	Denmark	Copenhagen	Kuwait	Kuwait City
	Vella	Djibouti	Djibouti	Kyrgyzstan	Bishkek
Angola	Luanda	Dominica	Roseau	Laos	Vientiane
Antigua and		Dominican		Latvia	Riga
Barbuda	St. John's	Republic	Santo Domingo	Lebanon	Beirut
Argentina	Buenos Aires	Ecuador	Quito	Lesotho	Maseru
Armenia	Yerevan	Egypt	Cairo	Liberia	Monrovia
Australia	Canberra	El Salvador	San Salvador	Libya	Tripoli
Austria	Vienna	Equatorial		Liechtenstein	Vaduz
Azerbaijan	Baku	Guinea	Malabo	Lithuania	Vilnius
Bahamas	Nassau	Eritrea	Asmera	Luxembourg	Luxembourg
Bahrain	Manama	Estonia	Tallinn	Macedonia	Skopje
Bangladesh	Dhaka	Ethiopia	Addis Ababa	Madagascar	Antananarivo
Barbados	Bridgetown	Fiji	Suva	Malawi	Lilongwe
Belarus	Minsk	Finland	Helsinki	Malaysia	Kuala Lumpur
Belgium	Brussels	France	Paris	Maldives	Male
Belize	Belmopan	Gabon	Libreville	Mali	Bamako
Benin	Porto-Novo	The Gambia	Banjul	Malta	Valleta
Bhutan	Thimphu	Georgia	Tbilisi	Marshall Islands	Majuro
Bolivia	La Paz	Germany	Berlin	Mauritania	Nouakchott
Bosnia and		Ghana	Accra	Mauritius	Port Louis
Herzegovina	Sarajevo	Great Britain	London	Mexico	Mexico City
Botswana	Gaborone	Greece	Athens	Micronesia	Palikir
Brazil	Brasilia	Grenada	St. George's	Moldova	Chisinau
Brunei	Bandar Seri	Guatemala	Guatemala City	Monaco	Monaco
	Begawan	Guinea	Conakry	Mongolia	Ulaanbaatar
Bulgaria	Sofia	Guinea-Bissau	Bissau	Morocco	Rabat
Burkina Faso	Ougadougou	Guyana	Georgetown	Mozambique	Maputo
Burundi	Bujumbura	Haiti	Port-au-Prince	Myanmar	Yangon
Cambodia	Phnom Penh	Honduras	Tegucigalpa	Namibia	Windhoek
Cameroon	Yaounde	Hungary	Budapest	Nauru	Yaren
Canada	Ottawa	Iceland	Reykjavik	Nepal	Kathmandu
Cape Verde	Praia	India	New Delhi	The Netherlands	Amsterdam
Central African		Indonisia	Jakarta	New Zealand	Wellington
Republic	Bangul	Iran	Tehran	Nicaragua	Managua
Chad	N'Djamena	Iraq	Baghdad	Niger	Niamey
Chile	Santiago	Ireland	Dublin	Nigeria	Abuja
China	Beijing	Israel	Tel Aviv	Norway	Oslo
Colombia	Bogota	Italy	Rome	Oman	Muscat
Comoros	Moroni	Jamaica	Kingston	Pakistan	Islamabad
Congo	Brazzaville	Japan	Tokyo	Palau	Koror
Costa Rica	San Jose	Jordan	Amman	Panama	Panama City
Cote d'Ivoire	Abidjan	Kazakhstan	Almaty	Papua New	
Croatia	Zagreb	Kenya	Nairobi	Guinea	Port Moresby

Country	Capital	Country	Capital	Country	Capital
Paraguay	Asuncion	Singapore	Singapore	Tunisia	Tunis
Peru	Lima	Slovakia	Bratislava	Turkey	Ankara
Philippines	Manila	Slovenia	Ljubljana	Turkmenistan	Ashgabat
Poland	Warsaw	Solomon Islands	Honiara	Tuvalu	Funafuti
Portugal	Lisbon	Somalia	Mogadishu	Uganda	Kampala
Qatar	Doha	South Africa	Pretoria	Ukraine	Kiev
Romania	Bucharest	Spain	Madrid	United Arab	
Russia	Moscow	Sri Lanka	Colombo	Emirates	Abu Dhabi
Rwanda	Kigali	Sudan	Khartoum	United States	
Saint Kitts		Suriname	Paramaribo	of America	Washington, D. C.
and Nevis	Basseterre	Swaziland	Mbabane	Uruguay	Montevideo
Saint Lucia	Castries	Sweden	Stockholm	Uzbekistan	Tashkent
Saint Vincent		Switzerland	Bern	Vanuatu	Vila
and the		Syria	Damascus	Vatican City	Vatican City
Grenadines	Kingstown	Taiwan	Taipei	Venezuela	Caracas
San Marino	San Marino	Tajikistan	Dushanbe	Vietnam	Hanoi
Sao Tome		Tanzania	Dar-es-Salaam	Western Samoa	Apia
and Principe	Sao Tome	Thailand	Bangkok	Yemen	Sanaa
Saudi Arabia	Riyadh	Togo	Lome	Yugoslavia	Belgrade
Senegal	Dakar	Tonga	Nuku'alofa	Zaire	Kinshasa
Seychelles	Victoria	Trinidad		Zambia	Lusaka
Sierra Leone	Freetown	and Tobago	Port-of-Spain	Zimbabwe	Harare

Index

Use the space below to record words and definitions in the Vocabulary in Context Quizzes (or from any other part of this book) that were *new* to you. You should also record any words that you *missed*. You may find it helpful to indicate the page on which the word appeared in the book. This simple procedure will help you remember the words and their definitions and, thereby, increase your vocabulary.

Word	Definition	Page

Word	Definition	Page

Many students are required to pass state-mandated reading competency tests or end-of-course (exit) competency tests. The chart below lists competencies that appear on many of these tests along with the chapters in *Opening Doors* in which the skills are presented.

	Chapter	Pages
Vocabulary Skills		
Use Context Clues	2	78–79
Use Word-Structure Clues	2	79–81
Interpret Figurative Language	2	84–88
Understand Connotative Meanings	2	83–84
Basic Comprehension Skills		
Locate Stated Main Ideas	4	195–199
Formulate Implied Main Ideas	5	247–255
Identify Supporting Details	6	297–304
Recognize Patterns of Organization	7	347–364
(Identify Relationships among Ideas)		
Critical Reading and Thinking Skills		
Identify Author's Purpose	8	411–416
Identify Intended Audience	8	411–416
Identify Author's Point of View	8	416–427
Identify Author's Bias	8	416–427
Identify Author's Tone	8	416–427
Understand Author's Intended Meaning	8	421–427
Distinguish Fact from Opinion	9	473–480
Make Logical Inferences	9	480–485
(Draw Conclusions)		
Distinguish Between Deductive and	9	485–487
Inductive Reasoning		
Evaluate an Author's Argument	9	488–498
Identify the Issue		
Determine the Author's Argument		
Identify the Author's Assumptions		
Identify the Types of Support		
Decide If Support Is Relevant		
Determine If Argument Is Objective and Complete		
Evaluate Overall Validity and Credibility		
Identify Propaganda Devices	9	498–503
Study Skills		
Follow Directions	3	141–144
Interpret Graphic Material	10	602–611
Create Outlines and Informal Study Notes	10	591–592
Create Study Maps	10	598–600
Summaries	10	600–601